Jewish Literacy

By Rabbi Joseph Telushkin

The Most Important Things to Know

About the Jewish Religion,

Its People, and Its History

WILLIAM MORROW

An Imprint of HarperCollins*Publishers*

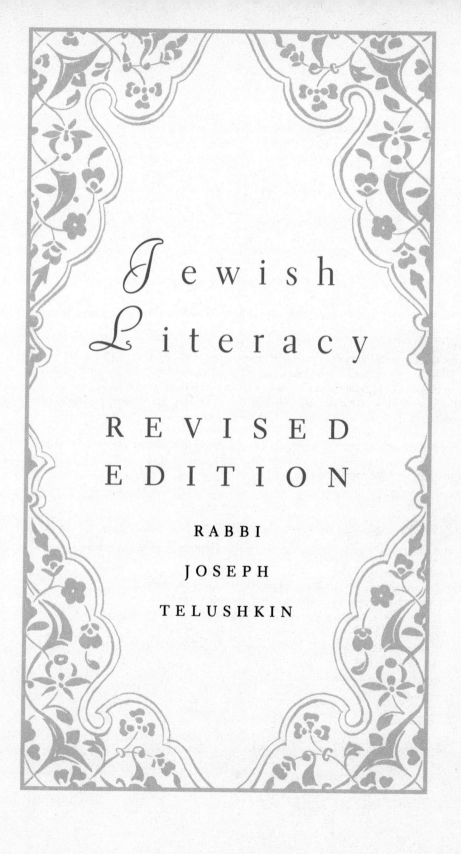

Jewish Literacy

REVISED EDITION

RABBI
JOSEPH
TELUSHKIN

This book was originally published in 1991 by William Morrow and Company, Inc., and reissued in 2001.

JEWISH LITERACY, REVISED EDITION. Copyright © 1991, 2001, 2008 by Rabbi Joseph Telushkin. All rights reserved. Printed in the United States of America. No part of this book may be used or reproduced in any manner whatsoever without written permission except in the case of brief quotations embodied in critical articles and reviews. For information address HarperCollins Publishers, 10 East 53rd Street, New York, NY 10022.

HarperCollins books may be purchased for educational, business, or sales promotional use. For information please write: Special Markets Department, HarperCollins Publishers, 10 East 53rd Street, New York, NY 10022.

FIRST EDITION

The Library of Congress has cataloged the original hardcover edition as follows:

Telushkin, Joseph, 1948–
    Jewish literacy : the most important things to know about the
Jewish religion, its people, and its history / Joseph Telushkin.
        p.   cm.
    ISBN 0-688-08506-7
    1. Judaism—History.   2. Jews—History.   3. Judaism—Customs and
practices.   I. Title.

BM155.2.T44   1991
296—dc20   90-22917
                                                            CIP

ISBN 978-0-06-137498-2 (revised edition)

14   15   WBC/RRD   10   9   8

*D*edication

For my grandfather, Rabbi Nissen Telushkin, of blessed memory, my inspiration to lead a life of Jewish commitment

For my father, Shlomo Telushkin, of blessed memory, my first and favorite teacher

For my mother, Helen Telushkin, my reader and critic

For Dennis Prager, my beloved lifelong friend, co-author, and study partner

And for my wife Dvorah, concerning whom I would rephrase the verse from Proverbs to read, "A woman of valor I have found"

$\mathcal{A}$cknowledgments

At dinner in the winter of 1988, my friend Rabbi Nathan Laufer, vice-president of the Wexner Heritage Foundation, described to me the work being done by Professor E. D. Hirsch, Jr., of the University of Virginia, in identifying the basic units of knowledge an American needed in order to be culturally literate. Nathan suggested that it would be equally valuable to compile a list of terms that every Jew should know. The idea excited me so much that I went straight from the dinner to a bookstore and purchased Hirsch's *Cultural Literacy*. Before the night was over, I had read the book and had immediately started compiling a Jewish literacy list. For the next month, whenever a term, a personality, an historical event, or a biblical value occurred to me I would write it down on a notecard. I even scoured indexes of major Jewish reference works. The next months were spent paring the list down to its most basic components and to a more manageable size. What helped make this period so intellectually stimulating and exciting was that I was joined in this task by Rabbi Herbert Friedman, president of the Wexner Heritage Foundation, Professor Reuven Kimelman of Brandeis University, and Nathan Laufer. The four of us spent whole days going through the various lists we had each compiled, discussing, often arguing, whether a person needed to know a specific term in order to have a proper understanding of Judaism and the Jewish people. While the list I have presented in this book does not precisely match the one our committee eventually compiled— though it is quite close—those days of discussion have helped shape my own views and understanding of Judaism and Jewish history. In addition to Nathan, Herb, and Reuven, I am grateful to Leslie Wexner, founder of the Wexner Heritage Foundation, for providing me the framework within which I could engage in this exploration. Over the past several years I have developed many of the ideas presented in this book in seminars I conducted for the foundation in Houston, Atlanta, Indianapolis, St. Louis, Columbus, Pittsburgh, Detroit, Milwaukee, Minneapolis, and Boca Raton, and I am very grateful to the participants in these seminars.

Several friends and colleagues generously offered to read and critique sections of the manuscript, and others discussed specific entries with me. All of them made suggestions that influenced my writing, and I am therefore happy to have this opportunity to publicly acknowledge their help (while freeing them from responsibility for errors or misinterpretations that may have remained). I wish to thank Rabbi Irwin Kula, Rabbi David Woznica, Daniel Taub, Rabbi Levi Weiman-Kelman, Dr. Dore Gold, Sharon Gillerman, Mona Charen, Rabbi Haim Mayerson, Dr. Mark Strauss, Rabbi Leonid Feldman, Rabbi Joel Wolowelsky, Professor David Shatz, and Beverly Marcus Woznica. I am also deeply grateful to Rabbi Irving "Yitz" Greenberg and Dr. David Elcott of CLAL, the National Jewish Center for Learning and Leadership, for affording me the opportunity these past five years to teach in the extensive network of ongoing adult education seminars CLAL has organized throughout the United States. I owe an intellectual debt as well to Rabbi Greenberg; his understanding of Judaism has deeply affected my own. While writing this book I spent much time at the library of the Jewish Theological Seminary. It is an extraordinary facility and an outstanding Jewish resource, and I am very grateful to its staff. On days I worked at the seminary library I generally had lunch with Rabbi Wolfe Kelman. It was often the highlight of my day. He is no longer with us and I miss him deeply.

Rabbi Michael Berger examined all the biblical and rabbinic sources in the book and, drawing on his vast knowledge of Judaica, challenged me whenever he disagreed with my interpretations. His input enriched the manuscript. David Szonyi, a friend who possesses wide Jewish learning and superb editorial skills, went through the entire manuscript carefully and made thousands of stylistic suggestions. I cannot exaggerate my gratitude to him for improving the book's readability and clarity.

My experience at William Morrow has been joyous. At every stage of the book's writing, my editors gave me advice and, just as important, made me aware of their enthusiasm for the project. I would particularly like to thank Sherry Arden, who acquired the book for Morrow; Jane Meara, who worked with me for many wonderful months; and Elisa Petrini, who stepped in when I thought I was all finished and gently, persistently, and with enormous editorial insight forced me to improve the manuscript one more time. I am very grateful as well for the stylistic and grammatical improvements of Sonia Greenbaum, my copy editor. This is the sixth book on which Richard Pine has served as my agent, and my affection for him as a friend and admiration for him as an agent grows with each project.

There are five other people whose impact on this book has been immense, and it is to them that I have dedicated *Jewish Literacy*.

$\mathcal{I}$ntroduction

AT A TIME WHEN JEWISH LIFE IN THE UNITED STATES IS FLOURISH-ing, Jewish ignorance is too. Tens, if not hundreds, of thousands of teenage and adult Jews are seeking Jewish involvements—even Jewish leadership positions—all the while hoping no one will find out their unhappy little secret: *They are Jewishly illiterate.* The most basic terms in Judaism, the most significant facts in Jewish history and contemporary Jewish life, are either vaguely familiar or unknown to most modern Jews. They can tell you the three components of the trinity, but have an infinitely harder time explaining *mitzvah.* They know what happened to Columbus in 1492, but not what momentous event shattered the whole Jewish world that year (see pages 197–199).

Over the past fifteen years, during which I have lectured in more than three hundred Jewish communities in over thirty states, I have grown increasingly aware of the frustration many Jews feel with their ignorance of basic Jewish terms. My audiences have run the gamut of Jewish life in America: Reform, Conservative, and Orthodox synagogue groups, Hadassah, UJA, Jewish Feder-ations, Jewish Community Centers, and high school and college students. And despite the differences in beliefs among these disparate audiences, on at least one issue their need and desire is virtually identical: to have available a source of basic information about Judaism and Jewish life. People crave this. They are enticed by the knowledge that there is no law in the Ten Com-mandments that commands us not to kill—the biblical verse reads, "You shall not murder"—and by the implications of this semantic difference for Judaism's attitude toward pacifism and capital punishment (see page 42). They are challenged and fascinated to learn that the term *mitzvah* means "commandment," not "good deed," and to find out why the Talmud considers acts motivated by obligation to be on a higher plane than acts performed voluntarily (see page 553).

It is precisely to provide such a resource that I have devoted the last two and a half years to writing this book. But while *Jewish Literacy* is intended to be encyclopedic in scope, I have tried to make it read like a narrative work, not a reference book. Entries, therefore, are presented topically, not alphabetically, so you can easily read through a whole section (for example, Bible, Modern Jewish History, Jewish Ethics) consecutively. For that reason as well, the writing style is anecdotal as much as factual. When you finish reading a chapter, I hope you will not only have understood a term's historical or ritual significance, but will also have a very good idea how the term is used in daily life.

Jewish Literacy lends itself to being used in one of two ways: as a study guide one can read through section by section in order to acquire an overview of Judaism and Jewish history or as a reference book to which one can go to look up a specific term. The book, I hope, will also be of particular help to people studying for conversion to Judaism, and to Jews who have never had a systematic Jewish education. Such people have often lamented to me that they feel ignorant of the Jewish "vocabulary" other Jews seem to possess, and yet they feel embarrassed to expose their ignorance by asking what a term or expression means.

Two technical notes: In the text, when an asterisk precedes a word, it means that the designated word is the subject of its own entry. I have dated events according to the system commonly used by Jewish historians, B.C.E. (Before the Common Era) and C.E. (Common Era), which correspond to B.C. and A.D.

An old Jewish proverb teaches that words that come from the heart enter the heart. If some of the words in this book will touch your heart, and stimulate you to go on expanding your own Jewish literacy, I will feel deeply blessed.

Joseph Telushkin
New York, N.Y.
September 1990

. . .

The warm reception accorded *Jewish Literacy* has been one of, perhaps *the* professional highlight of my life. I have been particularly moved by the fact that the book is widely used, both in introduction to Judaism courses and in classes for people studying to convert to Judaism. At lectures, when people tell me that this was the book that introduced them to Judaism, I feel honored and humbled to have been able to play the role of teacher in so many people's lives.

When Susan Friedland, my editor at HarperCollins, told me of her wish to bring out a new, more attractive version of *Jewish Literacy*, I realized that now, exactly a decade since the book was first issued, was a good opportunity to revise the book. Obviously, the large majority of the entries have remained untouched. No new revelations in the past decade, for example, would cause me to rewrite entries on King Solomon or on the Crusades (numbers 42 and 97, respectively). But new events and more recent information do indeed suggest the need to rewrite and expand some of the old entries while composing a few new ones.

When I wrote about "Righteous Gentiles" who saved Jews during World War II (entry 201), only one such name was very widely known: Raoul Wallenberg. In the past decade, with the extraordinary success of Steven Spielberg's *Schindler's List*, it is only fitting that a book entitled *Jewish Literacy* also tell the story of another remarkable hero, Oskar Schindler. In other instances, I have rewritten entries to reflect the passing of their subjects (see, for example, entry 220 on Rabbi Joseph Soloveitchik, of blessed memory). In a few cases, I have corrected factual errors that readers pointed out to me; in writing, for example, in entry 119 that Jewish conversions to Christianity were widespread in nineteenth-century Europe, I noted that Isaac Disraeli's conversion is what ultimately enabled his son Benjamin to become Britain's prime minister. I thank the reader, whose name I unfortunately have forgotten, who informed me that Isaac Disraeli did indeed arrange for the conversion of his son Benjamin but did not convert himself.

Last, I have added two new entries, my criterion being that these entries reflect events that I believe will influence Jewish life, and be discussed by Jews, for decades: the 1995 assassination of Israeli Prime Minister Yitzchak Rabin, of blessed memory, and, on a happier note, the 2000 nomination of Senator Joseph Lieberman as the Democratic Party's vice-presidential candidate, the first American Jew nominated on a major party's national ticket.

Finally, to all my readers, a very sincere and heartfelt thank-you for the many kind letters and responses you have shared with me.

Joseph Telushkin
New York, N.Y.
February 13, 2001

Since the publication of *Jewish Literacy* in 1991, I have found that the most common sections of the book people question me about are the ones dealing with the Bible and with Jewish ethics. Some years ago, I chose to elaborate on the biblical section in a separate book, *Biblical Literacy*, in which I was able to write at considerably greater length on many of the subjects that were dealt with more briefly in *Jewish Literacy*. And while I have continued to write on issues of Jewish ethics (my most recent book is *A Code of Jewish Ethics*), I thought it appropriate to augment the section in this book on Jewish ethics with some additional entries, including one on the perennially significant subject of forgiveness (including a discussion of the question, when are we required to forgive, and when not?; see entry 286), the not widely known commandment that requires us to reprove others' wrongful behavior (see entry 287), and the commandment that forbids us to stand by when another's blood is being shed (see entry 261). In addition, there are three new entries in the section on Zionism and Israel reflecting events that have occurred over the past few years, including the collapse of the Camp David talks between Israeli Prime Minister Ehud Barak and PLO Chairman Yasir Arafat in 2000, and the ensuing Second Intifada (entry 182), Israel's withdrawal from Gaza in 2005 (entry 183), and the war between Iran-backed Hezbollah and Israel in southern Lebanon in the summer of 2006, and the implications for Israel of Iran's ongoing effort to develop nuclear weapons (entry 184).

Other entries have been amplified. Thus, Holocaust revisionism unhappily continues apace, and new material has been added to this edition detailing the Iranian government's convening of a conference of Holocaust deniers in December 2006 (entry 203). Within the two past years, the Conservative movement issued a series of rulings, the effect of which was to pave the way for the ordaining of gay rabbis (entry 210). And ArtScroll, a large Orthodox publishing house, completed, in 2005, a translation with extensive commentary on the Babylonian Talmud, a publication that enables many more Jews than in the past to study the Talmud on a daily basis (entry 255). These are of course just several of the many changes and updates introduced into this edition of *Jewish Literacy*.

The continuing warm reception accorded this book, the meetings with converts who have told me that *Jewish Literacy* is the book that introduced them to Judaism, the many adult education classes based on it, the many Bar and Bat Mitzvot who are given this book as a gift, and the warm letters of other Jews whose Jewish knowledge and commitment were deepened after reading the book has been, as I have said before, one of, and perhaps the professional highlight of my life.

I wish to thank all those who have written me after reading something in the book that moved them, and those who have written to correct an error they found or to suggest additional material I might have inserted. I would like to thank Rabbi Avi Billet and John Kiernan. I would also like to thank my dear friends Dore Gold, Rabbi Levi Weiman Kelman, Daniel Taub, David Szonyi, and Dr. Jonathan Sarna with whom I consulted about various issues in this revised edition, and who so generously shared with me their expertise.

Joseph Telushkin
New York, N.Y.
May 2007

$\mathcal{C}$ontents

Part 3. EARLY MEDIEVAL PERIOD:
UNDER ISLAM AND CHRISTIANITY

Part 7. **THE HOLOCAUST**

Part 8.   **AMERICAN-JEWISH LIFE**

Part 12. JEWISH ETHICS AND BASIC BELIEFS

Part 13. THE HEBREW CALENDAR AND JEWISH HOLIDAYS

Part 14. LIFE CYCLE

PART ONE

Bible

TANAKH

TORAH

Nevi'im/*Prophets*
Ketuvim/*Writings*

TA-NAKH—RHYMES WITH BACH—IS AN ACRONYM FOR THE THREE categories of books that make up the Hebrew Bible: *Torah, Nevi'im (Prophets)*, and *Ketuvim (Writings)*. Observant Jews do not commonly refer to the Hebrew Bible as the Old Testament—that is a Christian usage.

The first five books of the Hebrew Bible comprise the Torah, and are regarded as Judaism's central document. Along with the stories about the *Patriarchs and *Moses and the Exodus from Egypt, they contain *613 commandments, the backbone of all later Jewish law. In Hebrew the five books are also called *Chumash*, from the Hebrew word *chamesh* (five). According to Jewish tradition, the books were dictated to Moses by God sometime around 1220 B.C.E., shortly after the Exodus from Egypt.

In Hebrew, each book of the Torah is named after its first or second word, while the English names summarize the contents of the book. Thus, the first book of the Torah is called Genesis in English, because its opening chapters tell the story of the creation of the world. In this one instance, the Hebrew name is very similar, since the Torah's opening word, *Brei'sheet*, means "In the beginning." In Hebrew, the Torah's second book is called *Sh'mot*, or Names, because its opening verse reads "*Ay-leh shemot b'nai yisrael*—And these are the names of the children of Israel." In English the book is called Exodus, because it tells the story of the liberation of the Jewish slaves from Egypt. Leon Uris wisely chose to call his novel *Exodus* rather than *Names*.

The Torah's third book, Leviticus (*Va-Yikra* in Hebrew), delineates many of the laws concerning animal sacrifices and other *Temple rituals, which were supervised by the Israelite tribe of *Levites. The fourth book, Numbers (*Ba-Midbar* in Hebrew), is named for the census of Israelites that is carried out early in the book. It also tells the story of *Korakh's rebellion against

Moses' leadership. The final book of the Torah is Deuteronomy (*Devarim* in Hebrew). Virtually the entire book consists of Moses' farewell address to the Israelites as they prepare to cross over to the Promised Land. He knows that he will not be permitted to enter it, but before he dies, he imparts his last thoughts to the nation he has founded.

The second category of biblical books is the *Nevi'im*, twenty-one books that trace Jewish history and the history of monotheism from the time of Moses' death and the Israelites' entrance into Canaan, around 1200 B.C.E., to the period after the Babylonians destroyed the First Temple and the ensuing exile of Jews from Jerusalem to Babylon (586 B.C.E.).

The early books of the *Nevi'im* (Joshua; Judges; I and II Samuel; I and II Kings) are written in a narrative style and remain among the most dramatic and vivid histories that any civilization has produced. These books are sometimes referred to as the "Early Prophets."

The later books, written in poetic form, are what we commonly think of when referring to the prophetic books of the Bible. They primarily consist of condemnations of Israelite betrayals of monotheism's ideals, and of calls for ethical behavior. Here you find nonstop ruminations about evil, suffering, and sin. In English the primary meaning of "prophet" is one who predicts the future; however, the corresponding Hebrew word, *navi*, means "spokesman for God."

The final books of the Tanakh are known as *Ketuvim*, and have little in common. Some are historical; the Books of *Ezra and Nehemiah, for example, tell the story of the Jews' return to Israel following the Babylonian exile, while I and II Chronicles provide an overview of Jewish history. *Ketuvim* also contain *Psalms, 150 poems, some transporting in their beauty, about man's relationship to God.

Another book, Job, grapples with the most fundamental challenge to religion: Why does a God who is good allow so much evil in the world? (see *The Trial of Job* and *Theodicy*). In *Ketuvim* are also found the Five Scrolls, which include perhaps the best-known biblical book aside from the Torah, *Esther.

The Hebrew Bible has been the most influential book in human history; both Judaism and Christianity consider it to be one of their major religious texts. Several of its central ideas—that there is One God over all mankind, and one universal standard of morality; that people are obligated to care for the poor, the widow, the orphan, and the stranger; that people should refrain from work one day a week and dedicate themselves to making that day holy; and that the Jews have been chosen by God to spread His message to the world—have transformed both how men and women have lived, and how they have understood their existence. Even the last of the ideas just enumerated, Jewish chosenness, has powerfully affected non-Jews. Indeed, the idea was so compelling that Christianity appropriated it, contending that the special covenant between God and a people had passed from the Jews (Old Israel) to the Church (New Israel). Islam, in turn, similarly insisted that *Mohammed and his followers had become God's new messengers (see *Chosen People*).

The Bible influences the thought patterns of nonreligious, as well as religious, people. The idea that human beings are responsible for each other, crystallized by *Cain's infamous question: "Am I my brother's keeper?" (Genesis 4:9), has become part of the backbone of Western civilization. Our values in every area of life, even if we have never seen the inside of a synagogue or a church, are suffused with biblical concepts and images. We deride excessive materialists for "worshiping the Golden Calf" (Exodus 32:4), and forgetting that "man does not live by bread alone" (Deuteronomy 8:3). The appeal to a man's conscience can be like "a voice crying in the wilderness" (*Isaiah 40:3). "Pride goes before a fall," Proverbs (16:18) warns us, while the cynical, jaded *Ecclesiastes teaches: "There is nothing new under the sun" (1:9). In daily speech, when we refer to a plague, we are of course harking back to that famous series of *Ten Plagues that struck ancient Egypt.

The Bible is so basic to Jewish life that when I drew up a list of terms that make up basic Jewish literacy, almost twenty percent came from the Bible. And yet, as important as the Bible is, few people today read it. Even religious Jews generally restrict their reading of Tanakh to the Torah, the Psalms, and the Five Scrolls. Yet, without a knowledge of the basic textbook of Judaism, how can any person claim to be Jewishly literate?

SOURCES AND FURTHER READINGS: One of the finest Jewish translations of the Tanakh is that of the Jewish Publication Society. Throughout this book, I generally have relied on the very readable JPS translation, though occasionally I have used other translations, or translated the verses myself. The JPS Torah, by the way, comes to only 334 pages: One can actually sit down and read it like a book. In recent years, several important new translations, with brief commentaries, have appeared: Everett Fox, *The Five Books of Moses*, Richard Friedman, *Commentary on the Torah with a New English Translation*, and Robert Alter, *The Five Books of Moses: A Translation with Commentary*. There are a number of longer, and well-done, Torah commentaries available, including Joseph Hertz, *The Pentateuch and Haftorahs* (Orthodox), Nosson Scherman, *The Chumash: The Stone Edition* (Orthodox), David Lieber, ed., *Etz Hayim: Torah and Commentary* (Conservative), and W. Gunther Plaut, ed., *The Torah: A Modern Commentary* (Reform). Several prominent Bible scholars in the Conservative movement have recently produced a new, rather extensive commentary on the Torah, also published by JPS: *Genesis and Exodus*

(Nahum Sarna), *Leviticus* (Baruch Levine), *Numbers* (Jacob Milgrom), and *Deuteronomy* (Jeffrey Tigay). While the books are all of high quality, I have had occasion to study Milgrom's commentary in depth and found it to be brilliant. The late Nehama Leibowitz, a Torah scholar in Israel who popularized the study of Torah among many people, published six volumes of studies covering all five books of the Torah, entitled *Studies in the Book of. . . .* At the end of each chapter, Leibowitz usually poses questions to prompt further study and discussion. Joan Comay has written a very useful and readable work, *Who's Who in the Bible*, an encyclopedic dictionary of all the people who appear in the Tanakh. A general introduction to and overview of the Bible are contained in my book *Biblical Literacy: The Most Important People, Events, and Ideas of the Hebrew Bible*. A popular guide to the prophets is Hannah Grad Goodman, *The Story of Prophecy*, which actually is a text written for teenagers; I have found it very helpful in understanding what was distinctive in the messages of the various prophets. A very important work is Abraham Joshua Heschel, *The Prophets*. A good one-volume history of the Hebrews during the biblical period is John Bright, *A History of Israel*. The list of common biblical expressions used in English found near the end of this entry is taken from Gabriel Sivan, *The Bible and Civilization*, p. 207.

2

ADAM AND EVE

THE GARDEN OF EDEN

THE TORAH'S OPENING CHAPTER DESCRIBES GOD'S CREATION OF THE world. Genesis' goal is not to give a textbook lesson in science, but to affirm that nature, which many people in the ancient world worshiped as a deity, was created by God. In general, the biblical view of creation is optimistic. Repeatedly, the Torah notes concerning God's creations: "And God saw that it was good" (1:10, 12, 18, 21, 31).

On the sixth day of creation, God creates the first person, Adam, whose name becomes the Hebrew word for human being. As John Milton noted, the first thing God ever specifies as being "not good" is Adam's solitude: "It is not good for man to be alone," He says. "I will make a helpmate for him" (2:18). God puts Adam into a deep sleep, takes a rib (actually, the Hebrew text is not really clear what it was) from his body, and fashions from it the first woman, Eve. The very first of the Torah's *613 commandments is addressed to the couple: "Be fruitful and multiply, fill the earth and master it" (1:28).

Adam and Eve reside in paradise, in a land known as the Garden of Eden. God provides all their needs, imposing but one prohibition on the couple: They are not to eat of the tree of knowledge of good and evil. The shrewd, and strangely talkative, serpent tells Eve that if she eats from the tree she will be as knowledgeable as God Himself: "God knows that as soon as you eat of it, your eyes will be opened and you will be like God" (Genesis 3:5). After a slight hesitation, Eve eats of the tree's fruit—there is no reason, by the way, to suppose that the fruit she eats is an apple—and then persuades Adam to eat from it as well. God is displeased. There was only one command He asked the couple to keep, only one thing in the universe denied to them, yet they were disobedient. His punishment is severe: Adam and Eve are exiled from Eden, they are fated to die, and God will no longer supply their needs. Adam must now earn his living by the sweat of his brow, while Eve is to be subject to her husband's domination, and will bring forth children in pain.

While traditional Jewish commentaries condemn Eve's sin, the late Jewish educator Shlomo Bardin offered a brilliant parable to explain her act of disobedience. "Imagine," Bardin taught, "that a young woman marries a young man whose father is president of a large company. After the marriage, the father makes the son a vice-president and gives him a large salary, but because he has no work experience, the father gives him no responsibilities. Every week, the young man draws a large check, but he has nothing to do. His wife soon realizes that she is not married to a man but to a boy, and that as long as her husband stays in his father's firm, he will always be a boy. So she forces him to quit his job, give up his security, go to another city, and start out on his own. That," Bardin concluded, "is the reason Eve ate from the tree."

In Christian theology this story of disobedience became the Original Sin with which all of mankind was permanently stained. But Jews have never regarded it with the same seriousness. It was an act of defiance, to be sure, and because it transgressed God's command, it was a sin. But the idea that every child is born damned for that sin is alien to Jewish thought.

Despite the harsh sentence, Adam lives more than nine hundred years, and he and Eve's descendants eventually populate the entire world. Genesis' assertion that all mankind descend from this one couple is the basis for the biblical view that human beings—of all races and religions—are brothers and sisters.

3

CAIN AND ABEL (GENESIS 4:1–16)
"Am I My Brother's Keeper?"

PERHAPS NOTHING CONVEYS THE BIBLE'S SOBRIETY ABOUT HUMAN nature more effectively than this tale of the first two brothers in history, one of whom murders the other. The motive for the killing is envy. Both Cain and Abel had brought sacrifices before the Lord, but God was more pleased with Abel's, because he "brought the choicest of his flock," while Cain apparently tried to get by with something less generous. Instead of protesting to God for ignoring his gift, Cain attacks Abel in the field and kills him. Then, when God asks him, "Where is your brother Abel?" he arrogantly responds, "I do not know. Am I my brother's keeper?"

In essence, the entire Bible is written as an affirmative response to this question. "What have you done?" God rails at Cain. "Your brother's blood cries out to me from the earth." The Hebrew word used, *d'mei*, actually is the plural of the Hebrew word for blood, literally meaning "bloods"—"your brother's *bloods* cry out to me from the earth"—which the rabbis understood to mean "his blood and the blood of his unborn descendants" (Mishna *Sanhedrin* 4:5). From this perspective, most killers are mass murderers, since they bear responsibility not only for the victim, but also for his or her unborn descendants, whose lives they have also destroyed.

Given the Torah's repeated insistence on capital punishment for premeditated murderers, why is Cain only condemned to eternal exile—"you shall become a ceaseless wanderer on the earth"? Most probably because of a unique extenuating circumstance: He had not yet witnessed death—the only other human beings at the time were Adam, Eve, and Abel—and so did not understand that his violent actions could kill his brother.

Cain's mother, Eve, soon conceives and gives birth to Seth, thus at least freeing mankind from the sense that they are all descended from the murderer Cain.

At the core of the Cain and Abel story is the insistence that every murder is the murder of one brother by another. Israeli poet Dan Pagis has developed this theme in a short poem about the *Holocaust, "Written in Pencil in the Sealed Freight Car":

> *Here, in this carload, I, Eve, with my*
> *son Abel. If you see my older boy,*
> *Cain, the son of Adam, tell him that I . . .*

SOURCES: The Pagis poem is found in T. Carmi, ed., *The Penguin Book of Hebrew Verse*, p. 575.

4

NOAH'S ARK (GENESIS 6–8)

AS NOTED IN THE PREVIOUS ENTRY, THE TORAH HAS A RATHER SOMBER view of human nature. "The tendency of man's heart is toward evil from his youth," God says in Genesis 8:21 (a similar sentiment is echoed in 6:5). This early assessment of human nature has nothing to do with the previously discussed Christian concept of Original Sin (see *Adam and Eve*). Rather, Genesis is suggesting that evil and selfishness are more natural to man than goodness and altruism. Children are born selfish and have to be educated to altruism. As my friend Dennis Prager once pointed out: "When was the last time you heard a mother yelling at her three-year-old son: 'Johnny, stop being so selfless and giving all your toys away to the other children in the neighborhood' "?

During Noah's time, ten generations after Adam and Eve, the world had become permeated with decadence and horror. The Bible tells us that God is so grieved by His creatures' behavior that He repents ever having given man life. He decides to destroy all humankind, with the exception of Noah's family. As the Torah explains: "Noah was a righteous man: he was blameless in his generation" (6:9).

God informs Noah that He will send a great flood which will drown all the world's creatures. It is clear, however, that the Creator does not want all life to perish. He instructs Noah to construct an enormous ark, and to load into it his family and two (and, in some instances, seven) of every animal in existence. The dimensions of the ark described in Genesis 6:15 suggest that it was about 500 feet long, 80 feet wide, and 50 feet high.

When the flood comes, it is devastating. For forty days and nights it does not stop raining, and the water levels rise higher than the highest mountains. Finally, the rain stops, and the waters begin to recede. Noah and his family emerge from the ark and, through them, the world is re-created.

God vows never to destroy the entire earth again with a flood. As a sign of His promise, He will send a rainbow after a rain, a reminder that the world will not be destroyed.

The ancient world had many stories of a devastating primordial flood that extinguished life in most of the world, suggesting the historical background for the biblical tale. In the most famous Near Eastern parallel, the Babylonian Gilgamesh Epic, the gods also destroy the world through a flood, but not for moral reasons; rather, mankind's noisiness has disturbed their sleep. Only one man, Utnapishtim, is saved because the god Ea intervenes. Utnapishtim is his favorite for personal rather than moral reasons. In Genesis, on the other hand, Noah is God's favorite precisely because he is righteous.

Traditional Jewish teachings tend to be hard, nonetheless, on Noah, and often compare him unfavorably with Abraham (see next entry). When God informs Abraham of His intention to destroy the degenerate cities of *Sodom and Gomorrah, the Patriarch engages the Almighty in a remarkable debate, attempting to persuade Him to cancel His decree. When God tells Noah of His intention to flood the world, Noah does not argue. He builds his ark, knowing the world is about to be destroyed, and apparently never tells anyone why he is doing so.

Noah's reputation suffers in another biblical story, as the first drunk in history. After emerging from the ark, he plants a vineyard, and soon thereafter falls into an intoxicated stupor (9:20–27).

5

THE PATRIARCHS

Abraham, Isaac, and Jacob

THE THREE FOUNDING FATHERS OF JUDAISM ARE ABRAHAM, HIS SON Isaac, and Isaac's son Jacob.

In Genesis God appears to Abraham and commands him: "Go forth from your native land and from your father's house to the land that I will show you. I will make of you a great nation . . ." (12:1–2). The Torah nowhere explains why God chooses Abraham for this mission, though Jewish tradition claims it is because he is the first monotheist since the time of Noah. A Jewish legend teaches that Abraham's father, Terakh, owned an idol shop. One day, while his father was away and Abraham was in charge of the store, he smashed all the idols but the biggest with an ax, and then put the ax in the remaining idol's hand. To his outraged father's question as to what had happened, Abraham explained that the large idol became upset at the other idols and destroyed them.

"You know these idols can't move," Terakh shouted.

"If they can't save themselves," Abraham answered, "then we are superior to them. So why should we worship them?"

Because this rabbinic tale is taught to almost all children in Jewish schools, many Jews mistakenly believe that it is in the Torah itself.

God makes it clear that He expects great things from Abraham and his descendants: "Abraham shall surely become a great and mighty nation, and all the nations of the earth shall be blessed through him. For I have singled him out, that he may instruct his children and his posterity to keep the way of the Lord by doing what is just and right" (Genesis 18:18–19).

Abraham's enduring legacy is ethical monotheism, the belief that there is one God over mankind, and that His primary concern is that people act ethically. On one noted occasion, when God seems to be acting in an ethically arbitrary manner, Abraham challenges Him: "Shall not the judge of all the earth act with justice?" (Genesis 18:25; see *Sodom and Gomorrah*).

The tragedy of Abraham's life is his wife Sarah's infertility. He finally takes her servant, Hagar, as a concubine, and they produce a son, Ishmael. Fourteen years later, Sarah gives birth to Isaac.

Although Abraham's character is well defined, Isaac comes across in the Bible as quite passive, perhaps a traumatized reaction to his father's near sacrifice of him at Mount Moriah (see *The Binding of Isaac*). He is decidedly not an initiator. It is his father's servant, Eliezer, who finds Rebecca and brings her to him as a wife. Later, it is Rebecca, not Isaac, who has the insight to realize that their younger son, Jacob, and not their firstborn, Esau, is better qualified to carry on the family's religious mission. Rebecca prevails, and Jacob leads the next generation.

Jacob's life is largely tragic. His brother Esau wants to kill him (see *The Hands Are the Hands of Esau but the Voice Is the Voice of Jacob*), and he flees to his uncle Laban. There, he falls in love with Laban's youngest daughter, Rachel, but Laban tricks him into first marrying her older sister, Leah. Later, Rachel, whom he deeply loves, dies while giving birth to her second son. A few years later Jacob's other sons sell Rachel's firstborn, *Joseph, into Egyptian slavery (see *Joseph and His Brothers*), and trick their father into believing that he was killed by wild beasts. While self-pity is not a characteristic feature of biblical heroes, it is understandable that when the Egyptian Pharaoh asks Jacob how old he is, he states his age and then adds: "Few and hard have been the years of my life" (Genesis 47:9).

Despite the hardships, Jacob produces twelve sons, from which the entire Jewish people descend, as well as a daughter. Later, after the conquest of Canaan, the land of Israel is subdivided into *twelve tribes, based on the sons of Jacob.

For Jews the Patriarchs are not remote historical figures, but a part of everyday religious life. The *Amidah* prayer, which is recited three times a day, begins: "Blessed are you, Lord our God, and God of our fathers, God of Abraham, God of Isaac, and God of Jacob."

The Patriarchs lived to extremely old ages—Abraham to 175, Isaac to 180, and Jacob to 147. Rabbi Gunther Plaut has noted an unusual mathematical progression in their ages at death.

$$175 = 7 \text{ times } 5 \text{ squared}$$
$$180 = 5 \text{ times } 6 \text{ squared}$$
$$147 = 3 \text{ times } 7 \text{ squared}$$

6

THE MATRIARCHS
Sarah, Rebecca, Rachel, and Leah

WHILE THE BIBLE IS SOMETIMES DISMISSED AS PATRIARCHAL AND SEXist, the four Matriarchs of Judaism, Sarah (wife of Abraham), Rebecca (Isaac's wife), Rachel, and Leah (both married to Jacob), operate on a level of virtual equality with their husbands. For example, when Sarah wishes to expel her servant, Hagar, and Hagar's son, Ishmael, from their house, the Patriarch is very upset and refuses to do so. But God intervenes: "Whatever Sarah tells you, do as she says" (Genesis 21:12). A few chapters later, the Torah makes it clear that Rebecca has far better insight into the character and destiny of her sons, Esau and Jacob, than her husband Isaac does (Genesis 27).

The great tragedy of the first Matriarch, Sarah, is her infertility. When angels inform the ninety-nine-year-old Abraham that his eighty-nine-year-old wife will soon give birth, Sarah overhears and laughs, saying to herself, "Now that I am withered, am I to have enjoyment, with my husband so old?" (Genesis 18:12). A verse later, God says to Abraham, "Why did Sarah laugh, saying, 'Shall I in truth bear a child, old as I am?'" God thus transmits only a part of Sarah's statement; He leaves out the comment about Abraham also being too old to have children. The *Talmud deduces from God's meaningful omission that, for the sake of peace between people, it sometimes is permissible to tell half-truths (*Yevamot* 65b).

Probably as a consequence of Sarah's laughter, her son is named *Yitzchak* (He shall laugh).

Isaac's wife, Rebecca, the second of the Matriarchs, is characterized by her extraordinary kindness. When Abraham's servant, Eliezer, is sent to find Isaac a wife, he asks God for a sign, praying: "When I stand by the spring as the daughters of the townsmen come out to draw water, let the maiden to whom I say, 'Please lower your jar so that I may drink,' and who replies, 'Drink and I will also water your camels' let her be the one whom you have decreed for your servant Isaac" (Genesis 24:14). Four verses later, to Eliezer's great delight, this is *precisely* the response Rebecca gives.

The blessing that Rebecca's family bestows on her when she sets out with Eliezer for Isaac's house, "O sister, May you [through your descendants] grow into thousands of myriads," is still the blessing recited by rabbis to brides at Jewish weddings.

Isaac's and Rebecca's son Jacob becomes the third Patriarch, and his first two wives, Leah and Rachel, the third and fourth Matriarchs. Although Rachel suffers infertility for many years, and later dies during her second son Benjamin's birth, it is Leah's life that still seems the more unhappy. Physically, the Bible describes Rachel as "shapely and beautiful," but notes that her sister "had weak eyes" (Genesis 29:17). While it is not clear what that means, we do know that Jacob had no desire to marry Leah. Rachel was the one woman he loved. During the marriage ceremony, however, Leah's father, Laban, covered her face with a heavy veil, and by the time Jacob realized he was with the wrong sister, he was already wed. (At Jewish weddings today, a procedure called the *ba-deh-kin*, at which the groom personally veils the bride before the ceremony, ensures that the groom's new father-in-law has not slipped in any substitute.) A week later, Jacob takes Rachel as his second wife. The Torah goes out of its way to emphasize how much Leah suffers as the unloved wife. Each time she gives birth, she expresses the wish that Jacob's attitude toward her will now change. When Reuben, the eldest, is born, she declares: "Now my husband will love me" (Genesis 29:32). That hope apparently is not fulfilled, because, after Simon's birth, she declares, "This is because the Lord heard that I was unloved." At the birth of her third son, Levi, she is still hopeful. "This time my husband will become attached to me, for I have borne him three sons." By the time Judah, her fourth son, is born, either she feels fully loved or, more likely, she has given up, saying only, "This time I will praise the Lord." Not surprisingly, Leah's sons later grow to hate Rachel's eldest son, *Joseph.

Rachel dies giving birth to Benjamin on the road to Bethlehem, near Ramah. In Jewish tradition, she becomes the personification of the loving mother. When the *Temple was destroyed by the Babylonians in 586 B.C.E., and the exiled Jews passed her tomb, the prophet *Jeremiah declared:

> *A cry is heard in Ramah,*
> *Wailing, bitter weeping:*
> *Rachel weeping for her children,*

She refuses to be comforted
For her children who are gone (Jeremiah 31:15).

One measure of the Patriarchs' and Matriarchs' enduring significance is reflected in the fact that their names—*Avraham, Yitzchak, Ya'akov, Sarah, Rivkah, Rakhel,* and *Leah*—remain among the most common Hebrew names given to Jewish children.

7

SODOM AND GOMORRAH
(GENESIS 18:16–19:38)

JUST AS TO THE MODERN EAR, BEVERLY HILLS CONNOTES WEALTH, AND Las Vegas gambling, to the Jewish ear the biblical twin cities of Sodom and Gomorrah signify one thing: human wickedness. It therefore comes as a surprise to read the biblical chapters about Sodom and learn that the text specifies only two sins of the inhabitants: extreme inhospitality to guests and homosexual rape (hence, the meaning of sodomy in English).

When visitors come to spend the night at the home of Abraham's nephew, Lot, the Sodomites surround his house and demand that he bring out the visitors "that we may know them." In biblical Hebrew, the verb "to know" also means to have sexual relations—perhaps because human beings are the only creatures who usually look into each other's faces when making love. Shockingly, Lot, the only relatively decent man in Sodom, tries to buy off the Sodomites by offering his virgin daughters to be ravished by them instead. The visitors, who are God's angels, temporarily blind the Sodomites, thereby finally getting their minds off illicit sex.

Despite the text's scarcity of details, the Sodom story is mentioned elsewhere in the Bible. Some biblical prophets mention details of other Sodomite evils that are not specified in Genesis. For example, *Ezekiel speaks of "the sin of your sister Sodom. She . . . had plenty of bread . . . yet she did not aid the poor and the needy" (16:49–50). In both the Bible and

*Talmud, Sodom becomes a byword for selfishness and cruelty. A rabbinic legend tells of an ordinance in Sodom and her sister cities against giving food to travelers. When a soft-hearted girl takes pity on a hungry visitor and gives him bread and water, the outraged citizens tie her up, smear her naked body from head to toe with honey, and expose her near bees until she is stung to death. Another legend relates that the Sodomites would "generously" give bars of gold stamped with their names to a visitor, but then refuse to sell him anything. When the hapless visitor perished of starvation, the inhabitants would gather by the corpse, retrieve their gold bars, and divide up the dead man's clothing.

Despite Sodom and Gomorrah's reputation for cruelty, when God shares with Abraham His intention to destroy the cities, the *Patriarch tries to change His mind. He asks: Since there undoubtedly are some good people in the cities, how can God destroy the innocent with the wicked: "Shall not the judge of all the earth act with justice?" (Genesis 18:25). Abraham also seems to be arguing on behalf of the evil people; otherwise, he would have requested that the good people alone be spared. Instead, he appeals to God to save all the people of the cities, provided some good people be found within them.

This first instance of a human being arguing with God becomes a characteristic feature of the Hebrew Bible, and of Judaism in general. Hundreds of years after Abraham, the Psalmist calls out to God in anger and anguish: "Awake, why do you sleep, O Lord . . . Why do you hide Your face, and forget our suffering and oppression?" (Psalms 44:24–5; see Habakkuk 1:2, and the entire Book of Job for other examples of prophets or righteous men questioning God's ways). The willingness to confront the Almighty stems from the belief that God, like man, has responsibilities, and deserves criticism when He fails to fulfill them. Elie *Wiesel, a Jew who stands in this tradition, has declared: "A Jew can be Jewish with God, or against God, but not without God."

After the Patriarch's initial protest, he entreats God to save the cities if fifty righteous people can be found within them. God agrees, whereupon Abraham starts "bargaining" with God, asking that He spare the cities if He can find forty-five, forty, thirty, twenty, and, finally, only ten righteous people. God accedes to each of Abraham's appeals. Only when it becomes apparent that, with the exception of Lot's family, the entire population of the cities is evil, does God proceed to destroy them.

The angels, who come to Sodom to lead Lot's family out, warn them to flee for their lives and not to look back. In one of the more perplexing verses in the Torah (Genesis 19:26), we learn that "Mrs. Lot" does look back and turns into a pillar of salt. I've never known quite what to make of this verse, though to this day a standard feature of any guided tour of Sodom includes a tall column of salt which tour guides assure visitors is the earthly remains of Mrs. Lot. Several years ago, a friend of mine heard an eighty-five-year-old woman offer a novel insight into Mrs. Lot's fate. "Don't you understand? When you are always looking backwards, you become inorganic."

A number of years ago, some Israeli promoters of tourism suggested transforming the modern city of Sodom into a tourist haven with casinos, nightclubs, and even strip shows. The Chief Rabbinate in Israel is said to have sharply demurred, warning that there was nothing to prevent God from destroying the city a second time. The plan was dropped.

8

THE BINDING OF ISAAC/AKEDAT YITZCHAK

THE CENTRAL EVENT AT THE CORE OF CHRISTIANITY IS GOD'S WILLingness to sacrifice the man Christians believe to be His son for the sake of mankind; one of Judaism's central events is Abraham's willingness to sacrifice his son for the sake of God. At the last moment, God stops Abraham from going through with the sacrifice. People often forget this, because the *Akedat Yitzchak* is commonly spoken of as "the sacrifice of Isaac," rather than "the binding of Isaac." As a result, there is a tendency to forget the story's "punchline": Human sacrifice is precisely what God does not want.

In the text Isaac is born to Abraham when he is one hundred years old and Sarah is ninety. God assures Abraham that "through Isaac, your name shall be perpetuated." But suddenly, without explanation, He commands Abraham to take Isaac to Mount Moriah and offer him as a sacrifice. Strangely, although Abraham challenged God when He confided His intention to destroy Sodom and Gomorrah (see previous entry), Abraham meekly accepts this command.

Early the next morning, he sets out on the three-day journey. At the mountain, Abraham prepares the altar, binds Isaac to it, and raises his knife to slay him. But an angel of the Lord calls out to him, "Abraham, Abraham, do not raise your hand against the boy or do anything to him."

The brief biblical narrative leaves readers with a terrible dilemma. Judaism regards Abraham as the first Jew, and a model of righteousness. Yet every Jew, indeed every person, knows that if he heard of a father setting out to sacrifice his child at God's request, he would want to see the man committed to an insane asylum. How then are modern Jews to relate to Abraham, whose actions seem immoral or insane?

The problem, of course, is more apparent than real. While today we regard child sacrifice as grossly immoral, it is largely because the Bible outlawed it, not because it is self-evident. For thousands of years, human beings have been sacrificed in diverse societies throughout the world, usually to win the favor of the gods and/or to guarantee bountiful crops. Hundreds of years after Abraham, the king of Moab, desperate to forestall an Israelite victory, "took his first-born son, who was to succeed him as king, and offered him up . . . as a burnt offering" (II Kings 3:27).

When God demanded that Abraham sacrifice Isaac, the *Patriarch probably was more distressed than surprised, for he had no way of knowing then that human beings were not to sacrifice their children; certainly, he had heard of his neighbors doing so. What *is* new in "the binding of Isaac" story, therefore, is not God's initial request but his final statement, that He doesn't want human sacrifices. Thus, Abraham is to be *praised* for not withholding from God what was most valuable to him but, as the text makes very clear, *he is not to be emulated.*

Unfortunately, the story entered Western consciousness with "the sacrifice of Isaac" mistranslation. The most famous work ever written on the event is *Fear and Trembling,* by the nineteenth-century Protestant theologian Sören Kierkegaard. Kierkegaard was in love with a young woman, Regina Olsen, in Copenhagen but, fearing that marriage would distract him from his religious vocation, he broke off their engagement. Almost immediately afterward, he went to Berlin and wrote *Fear and Trembling.* It does not take enormous insight to recognize that Kierkegaard understood his own "sacrifice" of Regina in light of the Patriarch's "sacrifice" of Isaac. But Kierkegaard's work, brilliant as it is in explicating the enormous torment Abraham suffered during the interminable three-day journey to Moriah, comes close to ignoring the story's punchline. As Martin *Buber wrote: "[Kierkegaard's analysis] is sublimely to misunderstand God . . . God wants us to come to Him by means of the Reginas He has created, and not by renunciation of them."

God's disavowal of Isaac's sacrifice is, in fact, the first attack on child sacrifice in any literature. Later, the Torah formalized this prohibition among its *613 commandments: "Do not allow any of your offspring to be offered up to Molech" it commands in Leviticus 18:21; and again in Deuteronomy 18:10, "Let no one be found among you who consigns his son or daughter to the fire."

The obvious character missing from the story is Isaac's mother, *Sarah. What did she feel when Abraham took their son off to be sacrificed? Did she even know? Did Abraham leave the house without telling her where he was going? What was her response when father and son returned from their trip, and Isaac told her what Abraham had done? There is a subtle suggestion in the Bible that Sarah was outraged. After Abraham descends from the mountain with Isaac—and we can only imagine Isaac's state of mind at this point—"they departed for Beersheva; and Abraham stayed in Beersheva" (Genesis 22:19). And, only seven verses later: "Sarah died in Kiryat Arba . . . and Abraham came [presumably from Beersheva] to mourn for her" (Genesis 23:2). Is it possible that when Sarah learned what her husband had done, she chose to live apart from him?

The word *akedah* remains significant in Jewish life: It represents Jews' willingness to sacrifice, if necessary, their families and their own lives for God. The medieval Jews, on occasion forced to slaughter their children, wives, and themselves to avoid being forcibly baptized (see *Crusades*), saw themselves as acting in the spirit of Abraham. Unlike him, tragically, they were forced to go through with the sacrifice.

SOURCES AND FURTHER READINGS: The difference between the crucifixion and the *akedah*, noted at the beginning of the entry, is suggested by the Israeli philosopher Yeshayahu Leibowitz. The Buber quote is from "The Question to the Single One" in his *Between Man and Man*, p. 52. The suggestion that Sarah possibly separated from Abraham was made by Rabbi Abraham Chen; cited in Herbert Wiener, 9½ *Mystics*, p. 266. See also Sören Kierkegaard, *Fear and Trembling*.

9

"THE VOICE IS THE VOICE OF JACOB, BUT THE HANDS ARE THE HANDS OF ESAU" (GENESIS 27:22)

ONE OF THE MORALLY PROBLEMATIC EPISODES IN THE TORAH IS JACOB'S deception of his blind father, Isaac. The situation comes about because of Isaac's preference for Jacob's slightly older twin brother, Esau. The reason for Jacob's partiality seems unworthy of a Patriarch. Isaac prefers Esau because he is a hunter who brings him delicious meats (Genesis 25:28). Isaac's wife, Rebecca, prefers the younger son, Jacob.

One day Rebecca hears Isaac tell Esau to go hunt and prepare him some meat, and he will then bestow upon him his "innermost" blessing. It was believed that the son who received the Patriarch's primary blessing would succeed him.

As soon as Esau leaves the house, Rebecca informs Jacob of his father's plan. She then slaughters and prepares a goat, and sends Jacob in to his father's room with it. First, however, she takes the precaution of putting the goat's skin over Jacob's arms so that he will resemble his hairy brother. Isaac is surprised at the speed of his son's return. He asks Jacob if he really is Esau and Jacob answers yes. Still unconvinced, Isaac asks his younger son to come forward, feels his skin, and after touching him, says: "The voice is the voice of Jacob, but the hands are the hands of Esau." Convinced finally that it is Esau standing in front of him, he gives Jacob the "innermost" blessing intended for his brother.

When the blessing is completed, Jacob prudently rushes out, and minutes later in comes Esau carrying a savory meal for his father. Isaac shudders when he realizes that Esau's blessing has been irrevocably bestowed on another. All he can offer the heartsick young man is a far more limited blessing.

Rebecca soon learns that Esau is plotting to murder Jacob, and rushes him away to the farm of his uncle Laban.

The most perplexing aspect of the story is Isaac's insistence that he cannot withdraw the blessing from Jacob and restore it to Esau. The Torah never explains why a blessing given under false pretenses cannot be reassigned to its proper recipient. After all, what would have happened if one of Isaac's servants had procured the blessing instead of Jacob? Isaac's refusal to withdraw the blessing, coupled with the fond good wishes he expresses to Jacob before he flees, leave the impression that at some level he must have recognized Jacob's superior virtues and greater fitness to carry on the family's faith and traditions.

In Jacob's defense, it must also be noted that he had good reason to believe himself entitled to the blessing: Years earlier, Esau had sold him his birthright, the right, in other words, to be regarded as the firstborn son (Genesis 25:29–34).

However, the Torah still seems troubled by Jacob's deception of his father. When Jacob falls in love with his cousin Rachel, and arranges to marry her, his uncle Laban *deceives* him by substituting his older daughter, Leah, under a heavy veil (Genesis 29:20–26; see *Matriarchs*). Many Bible scholars have noted the parallel: Just as Jacob deceived his father, so is he deceived. Still later, Jacob is deceived by ten of his sons, who trick him into thinking that his eleventh son, Joseph, has been killed by a savage beast (Genesis 37:31–35; see *Joseph and His Brothers*).

Though Jewish commentaries find no shortage of justifications for Rebecca and Jacob's behavior, the whole incident is of course distasteful. A friend of mine told me that his eight-year-old son was traumatized when he learned the episode in his day school. "How could Jacob have lied to his daddy?" he asked.

10

JACOB/ISRAEL (GENESIS 32:28–29)

IT IS NOT UNCOMMON IN THE BIBLE, AND IN JEWISH LIFE, FOR PEOPLE to be given new names, even during their adult years. Although for most of his life, Abraham's name was Abram, subsequently the letter *hei* was added, a symbol from God that Abraham "shall be the father of a multitude of nations" (Genesis 17:5). Even now, when a person is very sick, his or her Hebrew name is sometimes changed to make it harder for the Angel of Death to find the person. Sometimes the name *Hayyim*, the Hebrew word for "life," is added to the sick person's name.

No name change, however, has been as significant or peculiar as that of Jacob. After fleeing his uncle Laban's house, Jacob learns that his brother Esau is marching toward him, accompanied by four hundred troops. The Patriarch is very frightened; he cannot forget that when they last saw each other, Esau was plotting to murder him in revenge for Jacob's having deceptively procured from Isaac the blessing intended for Esau (see preceding entry).

That night while sleeping, Jacob is attacked by an angel in the form of a man. Jacob wrestles with the angel, and although this otherworldly spirit wounds him in the thigh, Jacob ultimately succeeds in pinning the angel, refusing to free him until he gives him a blessing. The angel awards Jacob with the additional name of Israel (in Hebrew, *Yisra'el*), "You have wrestled with God and with men and prevailed."

From that point on, the names Jacob and Israel are used interchangeably for the Patriarch. The Jewish people, who descend from Jacob's twelve sons, eventually become known as *B'nai Yisra'el*, the children of Israel.

It is no small matter that Israel, the name for both the Jewish people and the modern Jewish state, implies neither submission to God nor pure faith, but means wrestling with God (and with men). Indeed, one of the characteristic features of the Hebrew Bible and of post-biblical Jewish literature is the readiness of Jews to argue with God (see, for example, *Sodom and Gomorrah*).

JOSEPH AND HIS BROTHERS
(GENESIS 37, 39–50)

THE BIBLICAL DEPICTION OF THE YOUNG JOSEPH MAKES NO EFFORT TO describe a hero. Quite simply, Joseph is a spoiled brat, constantly capitalizing on his most-favored-son status. While his ten older brothers work, he parades about in an elegant coat-of-many-colors. Then, when he does spend time with his siblings, he "tattles" to their father, Jacob, about their various misdeeds.

Joseph also is a dreamer. In his most famous dream, the sun, the moon, and eleven stars bow down to him, a singularly unsubtle symbolism of the lordship that he will exert one day over his family. Small wonder, therefore, that his brothers resent and despise him.

Several elements in the story are perplexing, most notably Jacob's obtuseness in so publicly favoring Joseph, which seems to incite his brothers' hatred. Why does Jacob do so?

Joseph was the older of the two sons of Rachel, the one of his four wives whom Jacob passionately loved. The horror of her death while giving birth to Joseph's younger brother, Benjamin, might well have provoked some resentment on Jacob's part toward that child, leaving only Joseph as the untainted focus of his love. The famous (or, better, infamous) coat-of-many-colors he bestows on Joseph is the kind of garment one normally associates with a young woman. Perhaps Jacob was attempting to create something of a Rachel look-alike. In fact, the *midrash speaks of Joseph curling his hair and painting his eyebrows (Genesis *Rabbah* 84:7). That Joseph might ultimately have come to resent the way Jacob raised him is suggested by his otherwise inexplicable behavior years later in Egypt. During his first twenty-two years there, many as Pharaoh's top aide, he makes no effort to contact Jacob and inform his father that he is alive. Did this favorite son have some resentments of his own against a father who loved deeply, if not wisely (see also *Shabbat* 10b)?

The greatest horror in the Joseph story is of course the vengeance his brothers wreak on him. They sell Joseph into Egyptian slavery, mislead Jacob into thinking that a wild animal ravished him, and then go on with their lives, the "pest" gone, and their father in perpetual misery.

Away from his family and among the gentiles, Joseph finally grows into greatness. This spoiled child becomes a disciplined, highly moral man. His master Potiphar's wife wants to sleep with him, and Joseph refuses. The word for "refused" in Hebrew is *va-ye-ma-ain:* When this Torah portion is chanted in the synagogue, the rabbis put a rare musical note, *shalshelet,* under *va-ye-ma-ain* that lasts for about five seconds. The word, therefore, is sung, "And Joseph re-fu . . . u . . . u . . . sed," from which one might conclude that his refusal was a real struggle. The spurned "Ms. Potiphar" exacts a cruel revenge: She tells her husband that Joseph tried to rape her, and Potiphar has him incarcerated. While the Bible never says so, there is reason to suspect that Potiphar knew his wife was lying. Can one imagine a slave in the American South accused of trying to rape his white mistress, and only being punished with prison? Potiphar might well have doubted his wife's veracity, but concluded that it would be too devastating to his family honor to admit as much.

In prison Joseph emerges as an interpreter of dreams, first those of his fellow prisoners, then of Pharaoh (see next entry). Soon this talent leads to his becoming second only to the king.

A terrible famine in Canaan forces Joseph's brothers to come to Egypt to buy food. They end up at a royal storehouse, where Joseph recognizes them, although they do not recognize him. This is not surprising. He had been a seventeen-year-old youth when they sold him; now he is thirty-nine, and speaks to them in fluent Egyptian through an interpreter.

He tests them to learn whether they have repented for the evil they did to him. The classic test of repentance is to see how a person acts when placed in exactly the same circumstance in which he previously sinned (see *Repentance/Teshuva*). Joseph plants his silver goblet among Benjamin's bags, has his steward arrest all eleven brothers, and then tells them they can return to Palestine as free men, and with food, but that they must leave behind the "thief" Benjamin as a prisoner and slave. The brothers refuse to abandon Benjamin, and Judah asks that he be taken as a slave in his place. That is when Joseph breaks down, secludes himself in a room with his brothers, and cries: "I am Joseph your brother" (45:4).

A full cycle of emotional growth and rapprochement has finally been completed. Four sets of brothers fight in Genesis—*Cain and Abel, *Isaac and

Ishmael, *Jacob and Esau, and Joseph and his brothers—but only in this last case is there a complete reconciliation.

Concerning the first pair, Cain murders Abel.

Abraham expels his son Ishmael from his house, so that he will exert no negative influence on his younger brother, Isaac: The brothers meet only once more, to bury their father.

Esau wants to murder Jacob, but when the two brothers finally meet twenty years later, they fall on each other's neck, kiss, make peace, and bury the hatchet. Apparently, though, each remembers where the hatchet is buried and aside from coming together to bury their father (Genesis 35:29), they never see each other again.

And finally, there are Joseph and his brothers. "I am Joseph," he reveals to them, and soon thereafter, they move from Canaan to Egypt to live with him.

A postscript about this story's repercussions *four thousand years later*: There has never been a pope more beloved by the Jewish community than *John XXIII. His secular name was *Joseph* Roncalli, and in October 1960, about two years after his elevation to the papacy, he requested a meeting with world Jewish leaders. When the leaders entered the room, Pope John's first words to them were, "I am Joseph your brother."

12

SEVEN FAT YEARS, SEVEN LEAN YEARS
(GENESIS 41)

JOSEPH'S RISE FROM SLAVERY TO POWER IN EGYPT COMES ABOUT through a singular ability to interpret dreams. Ironically, it was his own childhood dreams that had gotten him into such troubles with his brothers, particularly two in which he predicted that they would someday bow down and pay homage to him (37:5–11). In Egypt, however, Joseph starts interpreting other people's dreams, and makes some startlingly accurate predictions (40).

One night, Pharaoh has a disquieting dream: "He was standing by the Nile when out of the Nile there came up seven cows, handsome and sturdy, and they grazed in the reed grass. But presently, seven other cows came up from the Nile close behind them, ugly and gaunt, and stood beside the cows on the bank of the Nile; and the ugly gaunt cows ate up the seven handsome sturdy cows" (Genesis 41:1–4). Pharaoh wakes up, but a short while later he falls back asleep, and dreams of seven healthy ears of grain, which are swallowed up by seven thin and scorched ears.

The next morning, he is quite agitated. He relates the dreams to his magicians and wise men, but none can interpret them. He is then told about the dream-interpreting abilities of a young Hebrew slave who currently is in prison. Joseph is summoned, and, after Pharaoh repeats for him the dreams, Joseph says: "Pharaoh's dreams are one and the same; God has told Pharaoh what He is about to do. The seven healthy cows are seven years, and the seven healthy ears are seven years. . . . The seven lean and ugly cows that followed are seven years, as are also the seven empty ears . . . they are seven years of famine. . . . Immediately ahead are seven years of great abundance in all the land of Egypt. After them will come seven years of famine, and all the abundance in the land of Egypt will be forgotten. . . . As for Pharaoh having had the same dream twice, it means that the matter has been determined by God, and that God will soon carry it out" (41:25–32). Joseph tells Pharaoh that during the seven years of rich harvest, he must heavily tax the grain and store what he collects, in preparation for the years of famine.

Pharaoh, impressed both by Joseph's interpretation and by his policy suggestions, appoints him to carry out the economic measures necessary to safeguard Egypt during the years of famine. "Only with respect to the throne shall I be superior to you," he tells Joseph (41:40).

The expression "seven fat years, seven lean years" has entered the Hebrew idiom to symbolize good fortune followed by evil, or wealth followed by poverty. In recent times the "seven fat years" are sometimes applied to 1967–1973, the confident years following Israel's victory in the *Six-Day War, while the post-1973 period—starting with the October *Yom Kippur War—are seen as the lean years.

13

THE TWELVE TRIBES

JUST AS ALL MANKIND DESCEND FROM ADAM AND EVE, JEWS, WITH the exception of converts, all descend from the *Patriarchs. Abraham and Sarah have one son, Isaac, who in turn passes on the monotheistic tradition to one of his sons, Jacob. Jacob has twelve sons from four wives, and the descendants of each of these sons form separate tribes. Six of the sons come from his first wife, Leah: Reuben, Simeon, Levi, Judah, Issachar, and Zebulun; two are from Rachel: Joseph and Benjamin; two are from Zilpah: Gad and Asher; and two are from Bilhah: Dan and Naphtali.

During the centuries of Egyptian slavery (see next entry), the Hebrews apparently maintained their tribal identity. When Joshua leads them into Canaan, he divides the land into separate sections for each tribe. Joseph's descendants are given a double portion, and two tribes are named after his two sons, Ephraim and Menashe. One tribe, Levi, receives no land at all, although the Levites are assigned certain cities in which to live. They are designated as the teachers and spiritual emissaries for the other tribes, all of whom are taxed to support the Levites.

About three centuries later, following the death of King *Solomon, the Jewish state split in two. Ten tribes broke off and formed the kingdom of Israel, and the remaining non-Levite tribe, Judah, formed the kingdom of Judah. In 722 B.C.E., the Assyrians conquered the kingdom of Israel, exiling and scattering its inhabitants. Since then, the Ten Tribes' whereabouts has been unknown. Modern Jews as a result are assumed to descend from either the *Levites (or a subdivision within them called the Priests/*Kohanim), or from the tribe of Judah. See *The Ten Lost Tribes, The Secession of the Northern Tribes,* and *Priest, Levite, Israelite.*

14

MOSES/MOSHE

ALONG WITH GOD, IT IS THE FIGURE OF MOSES (MOSHE) WHO DOMI-
nates the Torah. Acting at God's behest, it is he who leads the Jews out of
slavery, unleashes the *Ten Plagues against Egypt, guides the freed slaves
for forty years in the wilderness, carries down the law from *Mount Sinai,
and prepares the Jews to enter the land of Canaan. Without Moses, there
would be little apart from laws to write about in the last four books of the
Torah.

Moses is born during the Jewish enslavement in Egypt, during a terrible
period when Pharaoh decrees that all male Hebrew infants are to be drowned
at birth. His mother, Yocheved, desperate to prolong his life, floats him in a
basket in the Nile. Hearing the crying child as she walks by, Pharaoh's
daughter pities the crying infant and adopts him (Exodus 2:1–10). It surely is
no coincidence that the Jews' future liberator is raised as an Egyptian prince.
Had Moses grown up in slavery with his fellow Hebrews, he probably would
not have developed the pride, vision, and courage to lead a revolt.

The Torah records only three incidents in Moses' life before God appoints
him a prophet. As a young man, outraged at seeing an Egyptian overseer
beating a Jewish slave, he kills the overseer. The next day, he tries to make
peace between two Hebrews who are fighting, but the aggressor takes
umbrage and says: "Do you mean to kill me as you killed the Egyptian?"
Moses immediately understands that he is in danger, for though his high status undoubtedly would protect him from punishment for the murder of a
mere overseer, the fact that he killed the man for carrying out his duties to
Pharaoh would brand him a rebel against the king. Indeed, Pharaoh orders
Moses killed, and he flees to Midian. At this point, Moses probably wants
nothing more than a peaceful interlude, but immediately he finds himself in
another fight. The seven daughters of the Midianite priest Reuel (also called
Jethro) are being abused by the Midianite male shepherds, and Moses rises to
their defense (Exodus 2:11–22).

The incidents are of course related. In all three, Moses shows a deep, almost obsessive commitment to fighting injustice. Furthermore, his concerns are not parochial. He intervenes when a non-Jew oppresses a Jew, when two Jews fight, and when non-Jews oppress other non-Jews.

Moses marries Tzipporah, one of the Midianite priest's daughters, and becomes the shepherd for his father-in-law's flock. On one occasion, when he has gone with his flock into the wilderness, an angel of the Lord appears to him in the guise of a bush that is burning but is not consumed (see next entry). The symbolism of the miracle is powerful. In a world in which nature itself is worshiped, God shows that He rules over it.

Once He has so effectively elicited Moses' attention, God commands—over Moses' strenuous objections—that he go to Egypt and along with his brother, *Aaron, make one simple if revolutionary demand of Pharaoh: *"Let my people go." Pharaoh resists Moses' petition, until God wreaks the Ten Plagues on Egypt, after which the children of Israel escape.

Months later, in the Sinai Desert, Moses climbs Mount Sinai and comes down with the *Ten Commandments, only to discover the Israelites engaged in an orgy and worshiping a *Golden Calf. The episode is paradigmatic: Only at the very moment God or Moses is doing something for them are they loyal believers. The instant God's or Moses' presence is not manifest, the children of Israel revert to amoral, immoral, and sometimes idolatrous behavior. Like a true parent, Moses rages at the Jews when they sin, but he never turns against them—even when God does. To God's wrathful declaration on one occasion that He will blot out the Jews and make of Moses a new nation, he answers, "Then blot me out too" (Exodus 32:32).

The law that Moses transmits to the Jews in the Torah embraces far more than the Ten Commandments. In addition to many ritual regulations, the Jews are instructed to love God as well as be in awe of Him, to love their neighbors as themselves, and to love the stranger—that is, the non-Jew living among them—as themselves as well.

The saddest event in Moses' life might well be God's prohibiting him from entering the land of Israel. The reason for this ban is explicitly connected to an episode in Numbers in which the Hebrews angrily demand that Moses supply them with water. God commands Moses to assemble the community, "and before their very eyes *order* the [nearby] rock to yield its water." Fed up with the Hebrews' constant whining and complaining, he says to them instead: "Listen, you rebels, shall we get water for you out of this rock?" He then strikes the rock twice with his rod, and water gushes out

(Numbers 20:2–13). It is this episode of disobedience, striking the rock instead of speaking to it, that is generally offered as the explanation for why God punishes Moses and forbids him to enter Israel. The punishment, however, seems so disproportionate to the offense, that the real reason for God's prohibition must go deeper. Most probably, as Dr. Jacob Milgrom, professor of Bible at the University of California, Berkeley, has suggested (elaborating on earlier comments of Rabbi Hananael, Nachmanides, and the Bekhor Shor) that Moses' sin was declaring, "Shall we get water for you out of this rock?" implying that it was he and his brother, Aaron, and not God, who were the authors of the miracle. Rabbi Irwin Kula has suggested that Moses' sin was something else altogether. Numbers 14:5 records that when ten of the twelve spies (see *The Twelve Spies*) returned from Canaan and gloomily predicted that the Hebrews would never be able to conquer the land, the Israelites railed against Moses. In response, he seems to have had a mini-breakdown: "Then Moses and Aaron fell on their faces before all the assembled congregation of the Israelites." The two independent spies, Joshua and Caleb, both of whom rejected the majority report, took over "and exhorted the whole Israelite community" (Numbers 14:7). Later, in Deuteronomy, when Moses delivers his final summing-up to the Israelites, he refers back to this episode: "When the Lord heard your loud complaint, He was angry. He vowed: "Not one of these men, this evil generation, shall see the good land that I swore to give to your fathers, none except Caleb. . . . Because of you, the Lord was incensed with me too, and He said: You shall not enter it either. Joshua . . . who attends you, he shall enter it" (1:34–38).

Despite these two sad episodes, Moses impressed his monotheistic vision upon the Jews with such force that in the succeeding three millennia, Jews have never confused the messenger with the Author of the message. As Princeton philosopher Walter Kaufmann has written: "In Greece, the heroes of the past were held to have been sired by a god or to have been born of a goddess . . . [and] in Egypt, the Pharaoh was considered divine." But despite the extraordinary veneration accorded Moses—"there has not arisen a prophet since like Moses" is the Bible's verdict (Deuteronomy 34:10)—no Jewish thinker ever thought he was anything other than a man. See *And No One Knows His Burial Place to This Day*.

SOURCES AND FURTHER READINGS: The Kaufmann quote is found in his *Religions in Four Dimensions*, p. 43. For an analysis of Moses' three fights against injustice, see Nehama Leibowitz, *Studies in Shemot: The Book of Exodus*, pp. 39–48. Milgrom's explanation of Moses' punishment is found in his *The JPS Torah Commentary, Numbers*, p. 452. See also Martin Buber, *Moses*; Aaron Wildavsky, *The Nursing Father: Moses as a Political Leader*; Michael Walzer, *Exodus and Revolution*; Daniel Jeremy Silver, *Images of Moses*.

BURNING BUSH (EXODUS 3:2–3)

"I Shall Be What I Shall Be/Ehyeh-Asher-Ehyeh" (Exodus 3:14)

DURING HIS YEARS OF EXILE IN MIDIAN, MOSES EARNS HIS LIVING SHEPherding the flock of his father-in-law, Jethro. One day, an angel of the Lord appears to him in a fire blazing forth from a bush. Moses is startled to see the bush all aflame but unconsumed. When he goes to examine this miraculous sight, God calls out from the bush, "Moses, Moses," to which he answers, "Here I am." This is Moses' first encounter with God.

More than a thousand years later, a pagan challenged a rabbi: "Why did God choose a bush from which to appear?" The rabbi responded: "Had He appeared in a carob tree or a sycamore, you would have asked the same question. However, it would be wrong to let you go without a reply, so I will tell you why it was a bush: to teach you that no place is devoid of God's presence, not even a lowly bush" (Exodus *Rabbah* 2:5).

The burning but unconsumed bush recalls nothing so much as the opening chapter of Genesis, in which God's divinity is made manifest by His unique ability to create and control nature. The bush itself has become a widely used symbol to describe the Jews' survival. They are a people who have been literally burned by their enemies, but who have continued to endure.

Having dramatically captured Moses' attention, God tells him that He wishes him to go down to Egypt, confront Pharaoh, and lead the Hebrew slaves out. Moses repeatedly demurs: "Who am I that I should go to Pharaoh and free the Israelites from Egypt?" (3:11). The more Moses refuses, the more God insists. At one point, Moses says to God: "When I come to the

Israelites and say to them, 'The God of your fathers has sent me to you,' and they ask me, 'What is His Name?' what shall I say to them?" God answers: "*Ehyeh-asher-ehyeh.* Thus shall you say to the Israelites, '*Ehyeh* sent me to you.' "

The three-word name God gives Himself is not easy to translate. The most precise rendering is "I shall be what I shall be," although it sometimes is translated as "I am that I am." The 1962 Jewish Publication Society translation of the Torah despaired of coming up with an accurate rendition, and just left the words in their Hebrew original. Although generations of Bible scholars have tried to decipher the name's precise meaning, it really did not seem to matter that much to Moses. Rabbi Gunther Plaut has pointed out that though God gave Moses a new name to take to the Israelites, Moses never again refers to it. Plaut deduces that "the revelation was never meant for the people at all, nor did Moses really inquire for the sake of the people. *Moses had asked for himself, and the answer he receives is also meant for him.*" In some way, God's answer is satisfactory to Moses, if not to us, implying perhaps that when one has a true experience of God, it is very private. In other words, God shall be what God shall be to that person. He cannot adequately be described to others.

SOURCE: W. Gunther Plaut, *The Torah: A Modern Commentary*, pp. 398–409.

16

"LET MY PEOPLE GO/SHE-LAKH ET AMI"
(EXODUS 7:16)

PERHAPS THE MOST FAMOUS POLITICAL DEMAND IN ALL HISTORY IS the one Moses directs at Pharaoh: "Let my people go!" In the three millennia since, this verse has repeatedly been appropriated by oppressed groups. It became a particular favorite of black slaves in the American South. In their most famous folksong, they sang: "Go down Moses, Way down in Egypt-land, And tell old Pharaoh, To let my people go!" Starting in the 1960s, Moses' words served as the international slogan of the protest movement on behalf of Soviet Jewry.

When cited at political rallies, Moses' words are edited: The second part of his statement, "that they may worship Me," is omitted. In the biblical worldview, however, freedom is not a value in and of itself, but only when it is also used to worship God. The late Jewish philosopher Abraham Joshua Heschel complained of the widespread tendency to fracture biblical verses by quoting them in part. The early pre-Zionist builders of the land of Israel, for example, called themselves *BILU, an acronym drawn from a verse in *Isaiah (2:5), "Beit Ya'akov Lekhu Venelkha—Let the House of Jacob go!" This left out, Heschel noted, the prophet's concluding words, "in the light of God." Similarly, the goal of freeing the Hebrew slaves was not just to liberate them from Pharaoh's domination, but to give them the opportunity to worship God. See *Love Your Neighbor as Yourself, I Am the Lord,* and *Let My People Go/Am Yisrael Chai* in the section on Soviet Jewry.

17

THE TEN PLAGUES (EXODUS 7–12)
"And God hardened Pharaoh's heart"

ALTHOUGH THE TEN PLAGUES ARE NOT THE FIRST MIRACLES TO occur in the Bible, they probably are the most significant: They represent the first time God intervenes in history to shape an entire people's destiny. In fact, the Ten Plagues' goal is not to compel Pharaoh to free the Hebrews—the last plague alone would have been sufficient for that; it is to show God's power over the gods of Egypt and to punish the Egyptians for the inhuman slavery they have imposed on the Hebrews.

For years the country drowned male Israelite babies in the Nile. Although most Egyptians did not personally participate in murdering Hebrew infants, the very first of the plagues—the Nile turning to blood—makes it clear that all Egyptians share in the guilt for what their fellow Egyptians have done.

People can no longer deny their country's crime; the river itself gives public witness to the thousands of infants drowned in its waters.

Some of the early plagues cause more nuisance than suffering. A scourge of frogs overruns the entire country, and invades every household. Later plagues inflict economic devastation; a swarm of locusts destroy the crops and wild animals run riot in the fields. The tenth plague is the final revenge for the murder of the Hebrew babies. On one night, the firstborn sons of Egypt perish. At that point, Pharaoh commands that the Israelite slaves immediately be freed.

Exodus reiterates repeatedly that throughout the plagues God hardens Pharaoh's heart, so that he will not let the Hebrews leave. This seems morally problematic: God deprives Pharaoh of free will by hardening his heart, and then punishes him for being hardhearted.

Strangely enough, had God not hardened Pharaoh's heart, it would have deprived the Egyptian monarch of free will. Of course he would have then allowed the Hebrew slaves to go; not out of choice, but out of terror. By hardening Pharaoh's heart, the Egyptian king no longer feared the kind of physical devastation that would terrify and evoke instant obedience from a normal man. There was nothing, however, to stop Pharaoh from intellectually recognizing the injustices he had inflicted on the Hebrew slaves, and letting them go. But moral responses were not Pharaoh's concerns. Only when the firstborn started dying, did he finally realize that he was facing a force immeasurably greater than his own. And perhaps being a firstborn himself, he wanted the Hebrews out in order to save his own life.

Although the Ten Plagues must have been gratifying to the long-suffering slaves, Jewish tradition is somewhat uncomfortable with the devastation they wrought on Egypt. When the plagues are enumerated at the *Passover *Seder, a drop of wine is spilled at the mention of each one, a symbolic statement of a diminution of joy at the suffering of the ancient Egyptians (see next entry).

The Ten Plagues are:

1. The Nile turns to blood (7:14–25)
2. Frogs spread everywhere, including bedrooms and kitchens (7:26–8:11)
3. Lice (8:12–15)
4. Wild animals (8:16–28)
5. Cattle disease (9:1–7)

6. Boils (9:8–12)
7. Hail (9:3–35)
8. Locusts (10:1–20)
9. Three days of darkness so thick that it can be felt (10:21–23)
10. The death of the firstborn (12:29–36)

SOURCES: It was Professor Uri Simon of Bar Ilan University, in Israel, who suggested to me that the first plague might be understood as punishment for the drowning of the Hebrew male babies.

THE SPLITTING OF THE RED SEA
(EXODUS 14)

AFTER THE TENTH PLAGUE—THE DEATH OF THE FIRSTBORN—ONE might assume that Pharaoh would consider himself well-rid of the Hebrew slaves. But within hours of deciding to let them go, he retracts and sends his troops to bring them back. What is remarkable is that his soldiers—who must have been early forerunners of Japanese kamikazes—are willing to go on following his orders.

The Egyptians chase the fleeing Israelites to the Sea of Reeds, commonly known as the Red Sea. The Israelites panic. In back of them are armed troops in chariots, in front, an impassable body of water—hence the expression "to be caught between the devil and the deep blue sea."

But the Ten Plagues have hardly exhausted God's miracles. The Lord sends a mighty east wind that moves the sea's high waters to the sides, leaving a path of dry land in the middle. The Hebrews march down the center, but when the Egyptians follow after them, the walls of water on the sides collapse and drown them.

According to a rabbinic legend, when the angels in heaven started singing God's praises for saving the Hebrews, He turned on them in anger: "My creatures are drowning, and you're singing songs!" This widely known *midrash is probably the basis for the Jewish tradition that one should not overly rejoice at an enemy's downfall and suffering (see also Proverbs 24:17). In Deuteronomy one of the more surprising of the Torah's 613 laws decrees is: "You shall not abhor an Egyptian, for you were a stranger in his land" (23:8). A number of years ago, I saw an article by an Israeli Bible scholar on this command not to hate the Egyptians. He dedicated it to the memory of his son, who was killed by Egyptian troops in the 1973 Yom Kippur War.

AMALEK

IN JEWISH LIFE, THE NATION OF AMALEK IS THE ANCIENT EQUIVALENT of the Nazis: total, merciless enemies of the Jews. The Bible describes the Amalekite attack on the Israelites while they are still wandering in the desert. Rather than confront the Israelites head on, they attack their camp from the rear, where the children and the aged are stationed (Deuteronomy 25:18).

The Amalekites' cruelty and cowardice in going after the most defenseless Israelites provokes God's boundless anger at them. He instructs the Hebrews to wipe out the Amalekites whenever the opportunity presents itself. Hundreds of years later, that is precisely the order the prophet *Samuel issues to King *Saul. Saul defeats the Amalekites in battle, but he does not execute their monarch, King Agag. It is for this act of disobedience that God withdraws the kingship from Saul and replaces him with *David.

It is clear, nonetheless, that the Israelites did not always pursue Amalek, and we even find Amalekites serving in the Israelite army (II Samuel 1:1–13). Still, the biblical belief in the Amalekites' permanent hatred for the Jews is borne out hundreds of years later when *Haman, a descendant of King Agag, organizes a genocidal plot to wipe out all the Jews in one stroke (see *Esther*).

The eternal animosity that the Torah mandates against Amalek is highly unusual, even inexplicable. The Egyptians had caused the Hebrews more suffering than the Amalekites, having enslaved the Israelites for hundreds of years and drowned their boy infants in the Nile. Nonetheless, the Torah ordains: "You shall not abhor an Egyptian, for you were a stranger in his land" (Deuteronomy 23:8). Amalek was somehow seen as worse than Egypt, as the ultimate bullies, soldiers who feared the Israelite troops, and therefore restricted their attacks to the weakest members of the tribe.

MOUNT SINAI AND THE GIVING OF

THE TORAH

ALTHOUGH PEOPLE OFTEN THINK OF THE *TEN PLAGUES AND THE *splitting of the Red Sea as the highlights of the Exodus experience, they were, in actuality, only preliminaries to a higher goal. The Hebrew slaves achieved freedom not as an end in itself, but to serve God. That is why Moses says to Pharaoh, *"Let my people go that they may worship Me" (Exodus 7:16). And that is also why, in the Jewish tradition, the culmination of the Exodus is the giving of the Torah, an event commonly referred to as the revelation at Mount Sinai.

Seven weeks after they leave Egypt, the Israelites reach Sinai. There God, *for the first and only time*, speaks to the entire people, and declares before them the *Ten Commandments. The people are terrified by God's dramatic appearance amid thunder and lightning. They entreat Moses, "You speak to us . . . and we will obey; but let not God speak to us, lest we die." Moses assures the Israelites that God has not brought them from Egypt to Sinai in order to kill them. "For God has come only in order . . . that the fear of Him may be ever with you, so that you do not go astray" (20:16–17). Nonetheless, he agrees that in the future he will relay God's messages to them.

Shortly thereafter, Moses ascends Mount Sinai for forty days and nights. Many Jews are under the impression that Jewish tradition claims that at Sinai, God gives Moses the entire Torah. My friend Dennis Prager has noted that this is logically impossible. At most, God reveals to Moses the Torah's *613 commandments, and the narrative sections that precede his ascending the mountain. It is not reasonable to expect that God also gives to him all of the next three and a half books of the Torah, which tell the story of the Israelites' forty years of wandering in the desert. Is Moses told, for example, the story of the revolt that *Korakh will lead against him many years later (Numbers 16)? According to the rabbis of the Talmud, the Torah itself is given scroll by scroll by God to Moses during the Israelites' sojourn in the desert.

Jewish tradition does hold that the Torah's essence, its laws, are given to Moses at Mount Sinai, and the rabbis of the Talmud sometimes indicate the great antiquity and authoritativeness of a specific Jewish statute by noting that it is "a law given to Moses at Sinai—*halakha le-Moshe mi-Sinai.*"

Given Sinai's significance—the events that happen there dominate the Torah from Exodus 19 through Numbers 10:10—it seems strange that the only geographic detail we are given about the mountain is that it is located in the Sinai Peninsula. Thus, there is no way to deduce precisely where Mount Sinai is located. Rabbi Gunther Plaut has conjectured that this information is omitted deliberately: "Had the locale of the holy mountain been firmly known in later centuries, Jerusalem and its Temple could never have become the center of Jewish life, for they would have been inferior to the sacred mountain."

SOURCE: W. Gunther Plaut, *The Torah: A Modern Commentary*, p. 520.

21

COVENANT/*BRIT*

"We Shall Do and We Shall Hear" (Exodus 24:7)

IN THE DAYS IMMEDIATELY PRECEDING GOD'S REVELATION OF THE TEN Commandments (see next entry), He tells Moses to prepare the Israelites for a ceremony that will formalize their relationship to Him. God also makes it known that the relationship comes with a condition. "*If* you will obey Me faithfully and keep My covenant, you shall be My treasured possession among all the peoples . . . you shall be to Me a kingdom of priests and a holy nation . . ." (19:5–6). Moses relays God's message to the Israelite elders, and the whole nation answers collectively, "All that the Lord has spoken we will do" (19:8).

Moses then leads the Israelites to the foot of *Mount Sinai, where God announces the Ten Commandments. When people today read the First Commandment, "I am the Lord your God who brought you out of the land of Egypt, the house of bondage" (Exodus 20:2), they seldom think of it as the opening statement in a treaty. But that's what it is, the preamble of a treaty between God and the Jewish people, which becomes known as the Sinai Covenant. That explains why this First "Commandment" is not phrased as a command (see next entry), just a statement of what God has done for the Israelites. His accomplishments on their behalf entitles Him to make demands of them.

The basic overview of Israel's covenantal obligations is presented in Exodus 20–23. In brief, these chapters outline laws against idolatry, murder, theft, and the mistreatment of strangers, widows, orphans, and the poor. Additional laws command the observance of the *Sabbath, the Sabbatical year (during which the land must lie fallow), and the feasts of *Passover, *Shavuot, and *Sukkot. Bible scholar Jeremiah Unterman has pointed out that because God's commands cover both ritual and ethical spheres, "any crime committed is against God, whether it be ritual or civil."

The Israelites are warned not to enter into any other covenants with the people of Canaan or with their gods. In return for abiding by God's laws, the covenant guarantees the Israelites' possession of the land of Canaan and, even more remarkably, the removal of sickness, barrenness, and miscarriage from their midst (23:25–26).

Moses relays God's laws to all the people, and they announce in unison: "All that the Lord has commanded we shall do and we shall hear" (24:7). The odd wording of their response is understood by the rabbis as connoting that the Israelites not only agree to obey the laws they already have heard, but also any God-given or rabbinically developed laws they shall hear in the future. An alternative interpretation suggests that they make a commitment to perform the commandments, even before they "hear," i.e., understand, their rationale.

The Hebrew word for covenant is *brit*. The Bible describes two other particularly significant covenants: One guarantees God's commitment to Abraham and his descendants (Genesis 15); the other promises that the kingship will not depart from the House of David (II Samuel 7). In addition, the ceremony of circumcision is known in Hebrew as *brit milah*, the covenant of *circumcision, in line with God's command to Abraham: ". . . you and your offspring throughout the ages shall keep My covenant. Such shall be the covenant between Me and you and your offspring . . . every male among you shall be circumcised . . . and that shall be the sign of the covenant between Me and you" (Genesis 17:9–11). The covenant is understood as a two-way relationship: The Jews are to keep God's laws, and He is to watch over them.

An oft-quoted *midrash* relates that when Israel stood ready to receive the Torah at Sinai, God said to them: "I am giving you my Torah. Bring me good guarantors that you will guard it, and I shall give it to you."

The Israelites ask God to accept the *Patriarchs as their guarantors. But God refuses. They then suggest that the prophets become their guarantors. And again He refuses. Finally, they say: "Behold, our children are our guarantors."

And God responds: "They are certainly good guarantors. For their sake I give the Torah to you" (Song of Songs *Rabbah* 1:24).

SOURCE: Jeremiah Unterman, "Covenant," in Paul Achtemeier, ed., *Harper's Bible Dictionary*, pp. 190–192.

22

THE TEN COMMANDMENTS/ASERET HA-DIBROT

TRY TO NAME ALL TEN.

If you fall short, don't be too discouraged. Even though the Ten Commandments is the cornerstone document of Jewish and Western morality, most people can't name them all. Almost everyone immediately comes up with the prohibitions against murder and stealing, and the admonition to honor one's parents. Fewer remember the ban on adultery. I have found that people are least likely to remember the Ninth Commandment, which forbids perjury.

First then, the actual ten (listed here according to the text in Exodus

20:2–14; a somewhat differently worded version is found in Deuteronomy 5:6–18):

1. I am the Lord your God who brought you out of the land of Egypt, the house of bondage.
2. You shall have no other gods besides Me.
3. You shall not carry the Lord your God's name in vain.
4. Remember the Sabbath day to make it holy.
5. Honor your father and mother.
6. You shall not murder.
7. You shall not commit adultery.
8. You shall not steal.
9. You shall not bear false witness against your neighbor.
10. You shall not covet your neighbor's house; you shall not covet your neighbor's wife, or . . . anything that is your neighbor's.

It is interesting that the First "Commandment" seems to be a statement, not a commandment. That is probably why, in Hebrew, these words are called *Aseret ha-Dibrot*, the Ten Statements, and not *Aseret ha-Mitzvot*, the Ten Commandments. The difference between commandment and statement is more than just a semantic quibble, and has led to considerable controversies among Jewish scholars. *Maimonides, the greatest of Jewish philosophers, contended that the first statement does in fact command belief in God. Later Jewish thinkers, most notably Ibn Crescas and *Abravanel, challenged Maimonides on both empirical and logical grounds. First, the verse says nothing about belief. Second, and more significantly, how can belief be commanded? If you believe in God, it's because you find the doctrine true, not because you are commanded. And if you don't believe in God, then who is commanding you?

Despite Ibn Crescas and Abravanel's compelling logic, most Jewish authorities agree with Maimonides, arguing that belief in God is not only desirable, but is indeed commanded. Nonetheless, in Judaism the central stress has always been on performing commandments, unlike in Christianity where far greater emphasis is placed on faith. As the old joke has it, when the Lutheran minister and his rabbi friend part, the minister says: "Keep the faith." To which the rabbi responds: "Keep the commandments."

Two of the Ten Commandments are commonly mistranslated in English, leading people to ascribe views to the Bible that are actually alien to it. This is particularly true of the Sixth Commandment, which in Hebrew consists of only two words: *Lo tirtzakh*. Most English translations render it as "You shall not kill." Pacifists and opponents of capital punishment commonly cite this verse in support of their position. The only problem is that the Bible rejects pacifism, and prescribes capital punishment, especially for murder. The correct translation of *Lo tirtzakh* is "You shall not murder." Although the Bible abhors unnecessary bloodshed, it does, like every society before and since, distinguish killing from murder—which is nonpermitted killing. That's why we don't speak of "murdering in self-defense," but of "killing in self-defense," an act that the Bible—though not Mahatma Gandhi or Jehovah's Witnesses—heartily endorses. As the rabbis of the Talmud later put it: "If somebody comes to kill you, kill him first" (*Sanhedrin* 72a).

The Third Commandment also has not fared well in English. *Lo tissa et shem Ha-Shem Eloheikha la-shav* is usually translated as "You shall not take the Lord your God's name in vain." Many people think that this means that you have to write God as G-D, or that it is blasphemous to say words such as "god-damn." Even if these assumptions are correct, it's still hard to figure out what makes this offense so heinous that it's included in the document that forbids murdering, stealing, idolatry, and adultery. However, the Hebrew, *Lo tissa*, literally means "You shall not *carry* [God's name in vain]"; in other words, don't use God as your justification in selfish causes. The Third Commandment is the only one concerning which God says, "for the Lord God will not forgive him who carries His name in vain" (Exodus 20:6–7). The reason now seems to be clear. When a person commits an evil act, he discredits himself. But when a religious person commits an evil act in the name of God, he or she discredits God as well. And since God relies on religious people to bring knowledge of Him into the world, He pronounces this sin unpardonable.

The Fourth Commandment, "Remember the *Sabbath day to make it holy," has also suffered from its share of misunderstandings. The sole biblical concern expressed about the Sabbath in the Ten Commandments is that we make the day holy, and refrain from labor. Nonetheless, you'll be hard put to find people who will not tell you that the major goal of the Sabbath is to rest.

The Ten Commandments seem to fall naturally into two divisions: the first four legislating behavior between people and God, the last six between people and others. See also *Ethical Monotheism, Idolatry,* and the *Sabbath*. For further discussion of the Tenth Commandment's prohibition of coveting, see *David and Bathsheba* and *Ahab and Jezebel*.

23

THE GOLDEN CALF (EXODUS 32)

WHEN PEOPLE TELL ME THAT THEY WOULD FIND IT EASIER TO BELIEVE in God were they to see a miracle with their own eyes, I refer them to the thirty-second chapter of Exodus. No generation in history should have had an easier time believing and trusting in God than the Israelites in the desert. These liberated slaves had just witnessed the *Ten Plagues, escaped through the miraculously parted Red Sea, and beheld God's glory at *Mount Sinai. Nonetheless, when Moses tarried on Mount Sinai for forty days, they panicked.

The people surround Moses' brother, Aaron (see next entry), and demand that he fashion them a god. Aaron tells the Israelites to bring him all their jewelry, hoping perhaps that this demand will give them pause. It doesn't. Very quickly, a large mound of jewelry is gathered and molded into a Golden Calf. The people surround it, declaring, "This is your god, O Israel, that brought you out of the land of Egypt" (32:4).

Their statement of faith, "This is your god, O Israel," is very peculiar. The Israelites clearly cannot believe the calf is an active deity. How could the idol they have just fashioned have brought them out of Egypt? Most likely, they want an immediate and tangible messenger to God to replace the missing Moses, and that is the role the calf plays for them.

But I suspect that more is involved here than mere panic at Moses' disappearance. The religious legislation he had imposed on them since the Exodus may have struck many Israelites as too severe and restrictive. The implication of 32:6—"and they rose to make merry"—is that the people engage in an orgy.

God is furious. Like an angry parent wishing to shift responsibility to His spouse, He tells Moses that "the people that *you* brought up out of the land of Egypt have dealt corruptly" (32:7). He wants to destroy Israel and give Moses a better people to lead.

Moses reminds God that He promised the *Patriarchs that He would give

Canaan to their descendants. God relents, and Moses goes back down the mountain, carrying the tablets on which the Ten Commandments (see preceding entry) are inscribed. At the sight of the frenzied scene in the Israelite camp, he, like God, becomes enraged. He throws down and smashes the tablets, burns the Golden Calf and grinds it into powder, and forces the Israelites to drink a concoction of the powder mixed with water. At Moses' direction, the Levites—the only tribe not to have participated in the sin of worshiping the Golden Calf—ungird their swords and kill three thousand sinners.

When Moses confronts his brother, and angrily demands an explanation for his role in the making of the calf, Aaron disclaims responsibility, saying that he simply threw the jewelry into a fire, "and there came out this calf" (32:24). The defense is not a convincing one.

At the end of the episode, Moses again speaks to God and tells Him that if He is still thinking of disowning the Israelites, then "blot me out of the book which You have written" (32:32). God reassures Moses that He will punish only those who actually sinned.

Unfortunately, the incident with the Golden Calf sets the stage for the Israelites' recurrent faithlessness during their forty-year sojourn in the desert. Their attitude seems to be an extreme example of the "What-have-you-done-for-me-lately?" syndrome. At the slightest provocation, they turn on God and Moses, and God finally concludes that a nation raised in slavery is unfit to form a country of free men. As Rabbi Irwin Kula has said: "It was easier to take the people out of Egypt, than to take Egypt out of the people." God declares to Moses that the entire generation of freed slaves must die before the Israelites can enter Canaan (see *The Twelve Spies*).

For me, the episode of the Golden Calf proves that, for most people, faith and doubt exist independently of anything that God does. Although every promise Moses had made in God's name was fulfilled, that was not enough to keep the Israelites faithful for more than forty days. What makes us so sure we would be any different?

24

AARON AND MIRIAM

To this day, most Jews whose last names are Cohen or Katz, and all other Jews who know themselves to be *Kohanim*/Priests (see next entry), trace their descent back to the first Jewish High Priest, Aaron. The priestly functions that the Torah describes him as carrying out might have been his most important responsibility. Yet Aaron also served as spokesman for his brother, Moses, who had a speech defect. He apparently was greatly loved by the Jews in the desert: The Torah hints that the people mourned his death more intensely than that of Moses (compare Numbers 20:29 with Deuteronomy 34:8). Seemingly, Aaron had a much gentler manner than his brother. When the Israelites sinned, Moses raged at them. Aaron, however, did not fight them. When they told him that they wanted a Golden Calf to worship (see preceding entry), he helped them fashion it—although he later denied personal responsibility to his outraged brother. Aaron's acquiescence was so peculiar that one senses the Torah is concealing as much as it is revealing about him. Indeed, some of the most important events in his life remain unexplained. Two of his sons, for example, were struck down by God, but the Bible never tells us exactly what their sin was (besides the mysterious reference to their having offered "strange fire" to God).

In the Jewish tradition, Aaron becomes the exemplar of a peace-loving man. Despite the paucity of biblical material, the best-known legend about him tells that when he heard of two people fighting, he would go to one and say, "So-and-so likes you so much, and is so unhappy that you are angry at him, but he is afraid to approach you." He would then seek out the other party, with the same message. By the time the feuding parties met, they would fall on each other's neck and embrace. In other rabbinic stories, Aaron befriends disreputable people for the purpose of influencing them toward goodness. The very title the Jewish tradition assigned Aaron, *ohev shalom* (a lover of peace), is a mark of great distinction, and for the sake of peace, the rabbis approve of the white lies they attribute to Aaron.

Miriam's greatest claim to fame is watching over her baby brother, *Moses, when his mother sets him afloat in the Nile in a tiny basket. It is she who observes Pharaoh's daughter finding him, and who—although only a young girl—influences the princess to let her mother nurse Moses, and to bring him to Pharaoh's daughter when he is weaned.

Later, after God splits the Red Sea and saves the Israelites from the pursuing Egyptians, it is Miriam who leads the Israelite women in exalted dance.

In a later episode, Miriam is attacked with leprosy for condemning Moses' marriage to a non-Hebrew woman. Moses utters a short five-word prayer— "*El nah refa nah la*—O God, make her well"—and Miriam is cured shortly thereafter. Jewish tradition sees in her sickness the extremely serious punishment God exacts from those who malign others or spread hostile gossip (*lashon ha-ra*).

Although they die before their brother, Aaron and Miriam survive to great ages. Aaron is 123 when he dies, and Miriam even older. Their importance in Jewish life is suggested by the fact that their names are among the most common names given to Jewish children.

SACRIFICES

Priests and Levites/Kohanim *and* Levi'im

ANIMAL SACRIFICES WERE TO ANCIENT JEWS WHAT PRAYER SERVICES are to their modern descendants: the most popular expression of divine worship. About 150 of the Torah's 613 laws deal with sacrifices.

*Maimonides, the greatest medieval Jewish philosopher, believed that animal sacrifices were instituted to wean people from the ancient and horrific practice of human sacrifice. In fact, when God stopped Abraham from sacrificing Isaac (Genesis 22:11–13), the Patriarch immediately sacrificed a ram instead (see *The Binding of Isaac*).

The most famous sacrifice was the one offered on *Passover, and known as the Paschal lamb. It commemorated God's deliverance of the Jews from

Egyptian slavery. A Jew would bring a lamb to the *Temple/*Beit ha-Mikdash* in Jerusalem, and give it to a priest, who would slaughter the animal, sprinkle its blood upon the altar, and burn its entrails and fat. The remainder would be returned to the person who had donated the lamb. The animal was then taken back to the donor's family, which would eat the lamb, along with *matzah, *bitter herbs, and other foods. The festive meal was interspersed with lengthy discussions of the Exodus from Egypt. The roasted shankbone that Jews still place on the *Seder plate on *Passover commemorates this Paschal lamb.

From the time when King *Solomon built the First Temple in Jerusalem about 950 B.C.E., Jewish law stated that sacrifices were to be offered there only. A subgroup within the tribe of Levi, known as *Kohanim* (Priests), were responsible for offering the sacrifices. The tribe of Levi was the only tribe not allocated territory when the Jews entered Canaan. They were assigned forty-eight cities in Israel (Numbers 35:1–8), and were supported through an annual tithe assessed from the other tribes. It was from the tribe of Levi that the country's spiritual leaders and teachers were appointed. The Levites also assisted the *Kohanim* at the Temple.

Some sacrifices were brought every morning and afternoon. To this day, the morning and afternoon religious services (*shakharit* and *minkha*) commemorate these daily Temple offerings. Because the afternoon sacrifice was offered at about 12:30 P.M., Jewish law forbids *minkha* to be prayed before then. Other sacrifices were offered by those wishing to atone for violations of Torah laws through negligence. Still others were gift-offerings to God.

In general, some parts of the sacrificed animal were reserved for the priests to eat; others were given to the person who brought the sacrifice. One kind of sacrifice, however, involved the animal being wholly burned, and came to be known in English as a holocaust.

Only kosher, domesticated animals—cattle, sheep, goats, and birds—could be used for sacrifices. The rabbis explained: "The bull flees from the lion, the sheep from the wolf, the goat from the tiger. Said the Holy One, blessed be He, 'You shall not bring before Me such as pursue, but only such as are pursued'" (*Vayikra Rabbah* 27). By law, the sacrificed animals had to be without blemish (Leviticus 3:6, and 22:17–25).

Besides animals, people brought offerings of their first fruits, wheat, and barley to the Temple.

When the Second Temple was destroyed in 70 C.E., many Jews despaired of ever gaining forgiveness for their sins; there was now no place, after all, where they could offer sacrifices. The great first-century rabbi *Yochanan ben Zakkai revolutionized Jewish thinking with his pronouncement that acts of *loving-kindness now superseded sacrifices as the preferred way of attaining God's forgiveness. In addition to deeds of loving-kindness, the Talmud later taught that "studying of Torah is a greater act than bringing daily sacrifices" (*Megillah* 3b). Indeed, from the Jewish perspective, the Christian emphasis on the atoning sacrifice and atoning blood of Jesus is regarded as a type of throwback to human sacrifice.

*Reform, *Orthodox, and *Conservative Judaism each has distinctive ways of relating to the Temple's sacrifices in their services. Reform Judaism simply has dropped reference to the entire subject from its prayerbook: It views sacrifices as a primitive stage in Jewish religious development, one in which there is no reason to take pride. The Orthodox prayerbook, on the other hand, repeatedly reiterates the hope that the Temple will be rebuilt, and sacrifices offered there again. The Conservative prayerbook has changed all the future references to sacrifices to the past tense: It speaks proudly of the sacrifices that once were brought before God at the Temple, but expresses no desire to have them reinstituted.

Today, of course, sacrifices cannot be offered by religious Jews because there is no Temple in Jerusalem. The reason the Temple cannot be built is that centuries ago Muslims built two mosques on the site of the *Beit ha-Mikdash*. Various extremist Jewish groups periodically have plotted to blow up the mosques of Al-Aksa and the Dome of the Rock, thereby supposedly enabling the Temple to be rebuilt. Instead, such an act might lead to Israel's destruction by provoking an international Muslim *jihad* (holy war) against the Jewish state.

Although few religious Jews would say so publicly, many of them are not heartbroken that these mosques prevent the Temple from being rebuilt. While traditional Jewish theology commits Orthodox Jews to pray for the reinstitution of sacrifices, many are ambivalent about the prospect of again publicly slaughtering and sacrificing animals. In the aftermath of the *Six-Day War, other religious Jews established the Ateret Kohanim Yeshiva in the Old City of Jerusalem. One of the school's primary curricular concerns is the laws of sacrifices, and preparing the *Kohanim* among its students to resume someday their functions at a rebuilt Temple in Jerusalem.

"LOVE YOUR NEIGHBOR AS YOURSELF, I AM THE LORD" (LEVITICUS 19:18)

MOST CHRISTIANS, AND MANY JEWS, BELIEVE THAT THE "GOLDEN RULE" was first formulated by Jesus, not realizing that when the founder of Christianity preached, "Love your neighbor," he was simply quoting the Hebrew Bible.

In the first century B.C.E., more than a thousand years after the Torah was given, a would-be convert asked Hillel, the greatest rabbi of his age, to summarize Judaism briefly (literally, "while standing on one foot"). Hillel responded with a negative—and perhaps more pragmatic—version of the biblical verse: "What is hateful unto you, don't do unto your neighbor. The rest is commentary—now go and study" (*Shabbat* 31a).

Implicit in the command to "Love your neighbor as yourself" is the command that we love ourselves. Psychologists often have noted that people who don't like themselves usually have even greater difficulty liking and being good to others. It is hard to imagine, for example, an abusive parent who has a decent self-image. As for those fortunate people who do like themselves, the *Baal Shem Tov, the eighteenth-century founder of *Hasidism, suggested a guideline on how to carry out this seemingly impossible commandment; he put particular emphasis on the words "as yourself." "Just as we love ourselves despite the faults we know we have, so should we love our neighbors despite the faults we see in them."

The last words in the verse, "I am the Lord," usually are passed over as irrelevant to the commandment. In Jewish thought, however, the rationale for loving our neighbors is precisely because God, who created all of us in His image, demands it. Judaism sees ethics as ultimately dependent on a source above humans, on God. Without God, morality is reduced to a matter of opinion. As Ivan Karamazov mournfully declares in Dostoevski's *The Brothers Karamazov*, "If there is no God, then everything is permitted."

In the Jewish tradition, the verse "Love your neighbor" stands on a higher plane than most other commandments. As Rabbi Akiva taught: " 'Love your neighbor as yourself'—this is the major principle of the Torah" (Palestinian Talmud, *Nedarim* 9:4).

THE TWELVE SPIES (NUMBERS 13–14)

"The Land of Milk and Honey" (Exodus 3:17, 13:5; and Numbers 13:27)

PEOPLE OFTEN WONDER WHY THE ISRAELITES WANDERED THROUGH THE desert for forty years instead of marching directly from Egypt to Canaan. God's initial plan is, indeed, to get them into Canaan inside of a few months. Toward that end, Moses appoints a delegation of twelve Israelites, the respective leaders of each of the *twelve tribes, to go into Canaan and spy out the land. Ten spies return terrified; years of Egyptian slavery have destroyed their self-confidence. They tell their fellow Israelites that the Canaanites are so tall that "we were as grasshoppers in their eyes." Some of their report is positive. They describe Canaan as beautiful and bountiful, with grapes so enormous that a single cluster is borne on a carrying frame held by two men. The whole land is filled with milk and honey. *But,* they warn, it would be suicidal for the Israelites to try to take over the land; the Canaanites would massacre them.

Two spies, Joshua and Caleb, oppose their colleagues' report. They assure the people that there is nothing particularly fearsome about the Canaanites. In any case, God is on their side, and they should go up and possess the land immediately.

Unfortunately, Joshua and Caleb convince no one, including the members of their own tribes. After accepting the majority report, the people turn on Moses in fury: "Did you bring us into the desert to die?"

God's anger at the fearful Israelite mob is as great as their anger at Moses. He decides that the Israelites will wander in the desert until the entire generation that left Egypt dies out. He wants Canaan to be occupied by a new generation, conceived in freedom and devoid of a slave mentality. Of the Israelites who left Egypt with Moses, only two will be allowed to enter Canaan: Joshua, who will become Moses' successor, and Caleb.

Though Jewish tradition has little affection for the ten terrified spies, the term they apply to Canaan (also used by God in Exodus 3:17 and by Moses in Exodus 13:5), "a land of milk and honey," became a popular description of the land of Israel. To this day, Jews commonly sing at Sabbath tables the four-word song "*Eretz zavat khalav u-devash*—"Land of milk and honey." Honey, by the way, is the only product that comes from an unkosher creature (the bee), but is nonetheless kosher.

KORAKH'S REBELLION (NUMBERS 16)

KORAKH'S SHORT-LIVED REVOLT AGAINST MOSES IS THE MOST SERIOUS challenge ever mounted against Moses' leadership. He assembles a distinguished group of disgruntled Israelites both from his own tribe of Levi—Moses' tribe as well—and from the tribe of Reuben. Indeed, what makes Korakh's revolt particularly threatening is the very prominence of the people involved. Korakh himself comes from an Israelite family so important that his own birth is recorded in the Torah (Exodus 6:21).

While we know nothing of Korakh's previous relationship with Moses, the rationale he proposes for rebelling is demagogic and populist. "You have gone too far!" he chides Moses and Aaron in front of a large gathering. "For all the community are holy, all of them, and the Lord is in their midst. Why then do you raise yourself above the Lord's congregation?" (16:3).

Moses is shaken by the accusation of personal aggrandizement, and by the 250 tribal chieftains standing alongside Korakh. At first he says nothing; rather, he falls on his face, presumably in prayer. When he stands up, he tells Korakh and his followers to meet him the following day. God will then declare whom He wishes to lead Israel.

The next day, Korakh, along with Dathan and Abiram, his allies from the tribe of Reuben, gather in front of their tents. The now fully confident Moses announces to the assembled crowd of Israelites: "If these men die as all men die, if their lot be the common fate of all mankind, it was not the Lord who sent me." Moses scarcely finishes speaking, when "the earth opened its mouth and swallowed them up with their households, all Korakh's people and all their possessions. They went down alive into the depths, with all that belonged to them; the earth closed over them and they vanished from the midst of the congregation" (16:29, 32–33).

The Torah's expression "all Korakh's people" apparently refers to his followers, not to his family. Korakh's sons did not join him in the revolt, and therefore were not punished. Few Jews realize that one of the greatest of all Jewish prophets and leaders, *Samuel, was a direct descendant of Korakh (I Chronicles 6:18–22). This is quite remarkable; it is as if Americans were one day to elect a direct descendant of Benedict Arnold or John Wilkes Booth as president.

In Jewish tradition, Korakh remains a symbol of unbridled opportunism. He came from a distinguished family, and saw no reason why Moses and Aaron should be leading Israel instead of him. It was this frustration and uncontrollable envy that most likely explains Korakh's ill-fated rebellion.

BALAAM'S TALKING DONKEY (NUMBERS 22)

"A People That Dwells Alone" (Numbers 23:9)

ALONGSIDE THE SERPENT THAT TEMPTS EVE, THE MOST FAMOUS ANImal in the Bible is the prophet Balaam's talking donkey, which can see an angel of God clearer than the prophet himself can.

Jewish tradition teaches that the non-Hebrew Balaam had the potential to be one of God's greatest prophets. But rather than utilize his gift, Balaam sells his talents to the highest bidder.

King Balak of Moab, petrified at the Israelite advance through the desert, sends generous gifts to persuade Balaam to come to his territory and curse the Israelites. He sets out the next morning. En route, his donkey sees "an angel of the Lord standing in the way, with his drawn sword in his hand." The donkey swerves from the road against a fence, whereupon the outraged Balaam starts beating her. When the donkey tries to right herself, the angel repeatedly moves in front of her until the animal finally gives up and lies down under the prophet. In his fury, Balaam again hits the donkey.

At this point, the most macabre dialogue in the Bible ensues: "Then the Lord opened the donkey's mouth, and she said to Balaam, 'What have I done to you that you have beaten me three times?'"

Balaam, strangely unimpressed by the animal's fluently expressed protest, responded: " 'You have made a mockery of me! If I had a sword with me, I'd kill you.'

"The donkey said to Balaam, 'Look, I am the donkey that you have been riding all along until this day! Have I been in the habit of doing thus to you?'

"And he answered, 'No.' "

God now opens Balaam's eyes, and he sees the angel standing in front of him with drawn sword. The angel scolds Balaam for hitting his donkey, and the prophet—realizing how deeply God opposes his mission to curse the Israelites—tries to pacify him. "If you still disapprove [of what I am about to do], I will turn back." The angel permits him to resume his journey, but with one proviso: "You must say nothing except that which I tell you."

By day's end, King Balak of Moab must have been one disgusted monarch. Instead of damning the Israelites, his hired gun, Balaam, pronounces one blessing after another. Balak rightly feels cheated. "Here I brought you to damn my enemies," he rails at Balaam, "and instead you have blessed them." But to no avail. "No harm is in sight for Jacob," Balaam resumes, "no woe in view for Israel."

One of Balaam's descriptions of the Israelite camp was so beautiful that it became a permanent part of the Jewish liturgy: "*Ma tovu o-ha-lekha, Ya'akov*—How lovely are your tents, O Jacob, Your dwellings, O Israel!" Yet another description he offered of the Jews, "A people that dwells apart, and is not reckoned among the nations," proved as good a summary as any of the paradoxical role the Jews have played in history: active participants in this world yet also servants of another agenda, emissaries of the supernatural God.

But for all of Balaam's eloquent poetry, the most remarkable participant in this whole episode remains his talking donkey. Indeed, Jewish tradition teaches that the animal died right after the incident, so that people would not say, "This is the animal that spoke" and make it an object of worship.

30

"AND NO ONE KNOWS HIS BURIAL PLACE TO THIS DAY" (DEUTERONOMY 34:6)

THE TORAH'S LAST TWELVE VERSES RECORD MOSES' DEATH (DEU-teronomy 34:1–12). He climbs to the top of Mount Pisgah, which overlooks Israel. "This is the land," the Lord tells him, "which I swore to Abraham, Isaac, and Jacob, 'I will give to your offspring.' I have let you see it with your own eyes, but you shall not cross there" (see *Moses*).

The following verse records Moses' death and burial in the land of Moab, where "no one knows his burial place to this day." The best explanation I know for why the gravesite of the greatest Jew who ever lived remains hidden is that of the self-confessed heretic and philosopher of religion, Walter Kaufmann: "[Moses] went away," Kaufmann writes, "to die alone, lest any man should know his grave to worship there or attach any value to his mortal body. Having seen Egypt, he knew . . . how prone men are to such superstitions. Going off to die alone, he might have left his people with the image of a mystery . . . with the thought that he did not die but went up to heaven — with the notion that he was immortal and divine. . . . Instead, he created an enduring image of humanity; he left his people with the thought that, being human and imperfect, he was not allowed to enter the promised land, but that he went up on the mountain to see it before he died. The Jews have been so faithful to his spirit that they have . . . never worshiped him. . . . What the Jews have presented to the world has not been Moses or any individual, but their ideas about God and man. It is a measure of Moses' greatness that one cannot but imagine that he would have approved wholeheartedly. It would have broken his heart if he had thought that his followers would build temples to him, make images of him, or elevate him into heaven. That he has never been deified [like Jesus, Buddha, Confucius, or the Pharaoh of ancient Egypt] is one of the most significant facts about the ideas of God and man in the Old Testament."

Even in death, Moses, "the servant of the Lord," and of the Jews, continues to serve God and the Jewish people.

SOURCE: Walter Kaufmann, *Religions in Four Dimensions*, p. 44.

31

JOSHUA AND THE WALLS OF JERICHO
(JOSHUA 6)

THE CAPTURE OF JERICHO WAS THE FIRST AND MOST FAMOUS ISRAELITE victory in Canaan. The peculiar nature of the conquest was memorialized long ago in a famous black ballad: "Joshua fought the battle of Jericho, and the walls came tumbling down." As simple as the song's refrain makes the battle sound, it really doesn't exaggerate the Bible's account of the event.

In accord with God's express command to Joshua, the Israelite troops launch their attack on Jericho with a psychological onslaught against the walled city. For six successive days, they march around the city once each day. On the seventh day, they encircle it seven times, led by priests blowing rams' horns (see *Shofar*). At that point, the Israelites "raised a mighty shout and the wall collapsed. The people rushed into the city, every man straight in front of him, and they captured the city" (Joshua 6:20).

The instant collapse of Jericho's walls was not a gratuitous wonder thrown in by God to impress the future readers of Joshua. Without this miracle, the Israelites would have had no chance to capture the town, since they lacked the battering rams and scaling ladders necessary to overcome a walled city.

After Jericho was captured, the Israelite troops razed the city, and Joshua pronounced a curse upon anyone who would rebuild it: "He shall lay its foundation at the cost of [the life of] his first-born, and set up its gates at the cost of his youngest" (6:26). Strangely enough, this somber malediction is one of the few prophecies that the Bible records as having been literally fulfilled. Although Jericho remained unoccupied for four centuries, a ninth-century B.C.E. Israelite, Hiel, ignored Joshua's admonition and, as the Bible records, "he laid its foundations at the cost of [the life of] Abiram, his first-born, and set its gates in place at the cost of Segub his youngest, in accordance with the words that the Lord had spoken through Joshua son of Nun" (I Kings 16:34). Whether or not Hiel's two sons died in building accidents we will never know, but with the fulfillment of Joshua's curse, Jericho again became habitable; and we even find the prophets Elijah and Elisha spending time there (II Kings 2:4 and 2:18–22).

The Book of Joshua does not make for pleasant reading. It is filled with bloody, ruthless battles as the ancient Hebrews strive to win their land from the Canaanites. Yet the issues facing Joshua are remarkably similar to the issues facing Israel and the Jewish people today: how to secure and maintain a homeland in the face of violent hostility from one's neighbors.

32

THE LAND OF CANAAN —

THE SEVEN NATIONS OF CANAAN

THE BIBLE'S DEPICTION OF THE EARLY HEBREWS IS ANYTHING BUT flattering. Their most notable failing is recurrent lapses into *idolatry, influenced, in large measure, by the Canaanite nations among whom they live. This is the backdrop for *the most morally problematic command in the Torah*—to wipe out the Canaanite nations who refuse to leave Israel: "You shall utterly destroy them . . . as the Lord your God commanded you, lest they lead you into doing all the abhorrent things that they have done for their gods and you stand guilty before the Lord your God" (Deuteronomy 20:17–18). The Torah explicitly warns the Hebrews against copying the Canaanites' sexual perversities and rituals involving child sacrifice, and threatens that the land will "vomit them out" if they do any of these things.

Joshua (see preceding entry), *Moses' successor, undertakes to subjugate and destroy these surrounding and hostile groups.

To place the Bible's aggressive and cruel mode of warfare in context, one must remember that three thousand years ago, this is how wars were fought. "Ancient documents from Mesopotamia to Egypt," a recent book notes, "abound in joyous references to annihilating neighbors—frequently the very same peoples the Bible mentions. For example, in the Amarna letters, the Amorites were said to be troublesome foes of the house of Egypt's Pharaoh and deserved annihilation. . . . Officials writing these letters [to Pharaoh] promised to bind all the Amorites: 'a chain of bronze exceedingly heavy shall shackle their feet . . . and [we shall] not leave one among them.'"

As important, the main reason these injunctions so disturb us is because *the Bible itself* has sensitized us to high standards of respect for human life. As the late Princeton philosopher Walter Kaufmann wrote, "The reproach of callousness and insufficient social conscience can hardly be raised. Our social conscience comes largely from the religion of Moses." In large measure, it is only because of other verses in the Bible commanding us to love our neighbors and to love the stranger that the verses commanding total war trouble us. "[But] to find the spirit of the religion of the Old Testament in *Joshua*," Kaufmann noted, "is like finding the distinctive genius of America in the men who slaughtered the Indians."

The Bible's troubling ethics of warfare can perhaps best be explained in terms of monotheism's struggle to survive. Monotheism started out as a minority movement with a different theology and ethical system than the rest of the world. It expanded and developed because it had one small corner in the world where it could grow unmolested. Had the Hebrews continued to reside amid the pagan and child-sacrificing Canaanite culture, monotheism itself almost certainly would have died. That most likely explains the troubling ethics of warfare preached in the Bible.

In the middle of the Second World War, in 1942, an antireligious group arose in Palestine that became known as the "Canaanites." Although its founders were Jewish, they argued that Jews should drop their Jewish identity in favor of a Hebrew/"Canaanite" one. During their short history, the "Canaanites" exerted influence on Hebrew literature and art, but far less so on politics. They were particularly intent on eliminating Hebrew words that reflected a Diaspora influence, while they reintroduced into modern Hebrew archaic terms stemming from biblical times. In Israel today, to refer to someone as a

"Canaanite" is to identify the person as a radical assimilationist and self-hating Jew.

SOURCES: The comment about the cruel mode of ancient warfare is found in Eunice Riedel, Thomas Tracy, and Barbara Moskowitz, *The Book of the Bible*, p. 40. Walter Kaufmann, *The Faith of a Heretic*, pp. 260–261 and p. 193. The Israeli Bible scholar Yehezkel Kaufmann argues that the wars against the Canaanite nations "had important social and religious consequences. Israel did not assimilate into the indigenous population. . . . It provided Israel's new religious idea with an environment in which to grow free of the influence of a popular pagan culture" (*The Religion of Israel*, p. 254).

DEBORAH THE PROPHETESS

(JUDGES 4–5)

MOST OF THE GREAT WOMEN IN THE BIBLE EITHER ARE MARRIED TO A great man or related to one. Sarah is primarily known as Abraham's wife, and Miriam as Moses' sister. Even *Esther, who saves the Jewish people from Haman's attempted genocide, is guided by her adviser and cousin, Mordechai. A rare exception to this tradition is the prophetess and judge Deborah, perhaps the Bible's greatest woman figure.

Deborah stands exclusively on her own merits. The only thing we know about her personal life is the name of her husband, Lapidot. "She led Israel at that time," is how the Bible records it. "She used to sit under the palm tree of Deborah . . . and the Israelites would come to her for judgment" (4:4).

During Deborah's time, a century or so after the Israelite entry into Canaan, the valley in which she and her tribe lived was controlled by King Jabin of Hazor. Deborah summoned the warrior Barak and instructed him in God's name to take ten thousand troops and confront Jabin's general, Sisera, and his army's nine hundred iron chariots, on Mount Tabor.

Barak's response to Deborah shows the high esteem in which this ancient prophetess was held: "If you will go with me, I will go; if not I will not go."

"Very well, I will go with you," Deborah consents, but she can't resist gibing at Barak about the sexism of their society. "However, there will be no glory for you in the course you are taking, for then the Lord will deliver Sisera into the hands of a woman" (4:8–9).

The battle takes place during the rainy season, and Sisera's chariots quickly bog down in the mud. The Israelites overwhelm Hazor's army, and inflict heavy casualties. Sisera, fleeing on foot, escapes to the Kenite camp, where Yael, the clan leader's wife, invites him to stay. He falls asleep in her tent, whereupon Yael lifts a mallet and drives a tent peg through his head.

The famed "Song of Deborah," in chapter 5, exults in the breaking of the Canaanite stranglehold over much of the country: "So may all Your enemies perish, O Lord," is Deborah's parting shot, though the true Jewish victory went even deeper than the destruction of Sisera and his chariots. According to the Talmud, Rabbi *Akiva, one of the greatest figures in Jewish history, was a direct descendant of Sisera. That a descendant of this great enemy of the Jews became a great Jewish rabbi and scholar represented the Jews' ultimate victory over their ancient Canaanite opponent.

34

SAMSON AND DELILAH (JUDGES 13–16)

SAMSON'S NAME HAS BECOME A BYWORD FOR INCREDIBLE STRENGTH, just as the name of Delilah, the woman he loved, is a byword for betrayal. Samson's parents had long been childless when an angel of the Lord reveals to his mother that she will give birth to a son. She is instructed to raise the boy as a Nazirite to God; he is never to imbibe liquor or cut his hair. "He shall be the first to deliver Israel from the Philistines," are the angel's parting words. The Philistines had then been ruling over the Israelites for some forty years.

Although Jewish tradition regards Samson as both a judge and a prophet, he is unlike every other judge and prophet. While the judges lead the whole Jewish community, Samson always acts alone; whereas the prophets deliver messages from God, Samson leaves behind no prophetic words. There is, however, one divinely endowed skill unique to Samson, "a physical prowess that so transcended the ordinary that it was obviously divine in origin" (Adin Steinsaltz, *Biblical Images*, p. 112). On one occasion, he slays a lion with his bare hands; on another, he kills a thousand pursuing Philistine troops with an ass's jawbone.

In the end, this Jewish Hercules is destroyed not because of superior Philistine might, but because of his lust and obsession for non-Israelite women. His first wife is a Philistine (the Bible suggests that this was God's will, Judges 14:4); after her death he sleeps with Philistine harlots, and finally he falls in love with Delilah.

The Philistine leadership appeal to Delilah's materialism: "Coax him and find out what makes him so strong, and how we can overpower him, tie him up, and make him helpless; and we will each give you eleven hundred shekels of silver" (16:5).

Delilah accepts, and immediately starts nagging Samson to reveal the source of his strength. Her appeal sounds almost contemporary: "How can you say you love me when you don't confide in me?" (16:15). For a good while, Samson resists Delilah's entreaties. Finally, though, "he was wearied to death, and . . . confided everything to her. . . . 'No razor has ever touched my head, for I have been a Nazirite to God since I was in my mother's womb. If my hair were cut, my strength would leave me and I should become as weak as an ordinary man' " (16:16–17).

Delilah wastes no time communicating the good news to the Philistine lords. After she collects her silver, she lulls Samson to sleep on her lap. She summons a soldier to cut his hair, then sadistically calls out: "Samson, the Philistines are upon you!" Samson jumps up, ready for battle, only to realize that his strength has departed. The Philistine troops gouge out his eyes, and turn Samson into a mill slave in prison.

Weeks later, the Philistines decide to publicly celebrate the capture and humiliation of their greatest enemy. They haven't noticed, however, that Samson's hair has started to grow back. Three thousand men and women come together in a stadium, and Samson is brought from prison and ordered to dance for them. When he finishes, he is left standing between the pillars of the stadium, and the program resumes. Samson prays: "O Lord God! Please remember me, and give me strength just this once, O God, to take revenge on the Philistines, if only for one of my two eyes." With a final cry of "Let me die with the Philistines!" he pulls down both columns: He kills more people in death than he did during his lifetime.

Was Delilah in the stadium, rejoicing in her ex-lover's humiliation, when the building collapsed? The Bible doesn't say. With her betrayal of Samson, she disappears from the story.

In recent years, the expression "Samson complex" has been applied on occasion to Israel, specifically to the assumption that if it were being destroyed in a war, it would unleash its atomic weapons on its attacking neighbors, in line with Samson's cry, "Let me die with the Philistines!"

SAMUEL (I SAMUEL 1–16; 28:3–19)

"We Must Have a King Over Us That We May Be Like All the Other Nations" (I Samuel 8:19–20)

LIKE SO MANY OTHER GREAT BIBLICAL FIGURES, SAMUEL IS THE OFF-spring of a once-barren woman. His mother, Hannah, is desperate to have a child, and goes to pray at the temple in Shiloh. "If You will grant Your maid-servant a male child," she silently vows to God, "I will dedicate him to the Lord for all the days of his life" (1:11). Eli, the head priest, sees Hannah's lips moving, but because he hears no words he concludes that she is drunk and sharply rebukes her. When he finally realizes the depth of her pain, Eli blesses her, adding his prayer that the Lord should fulfill whatever request she has made.

In keeping with his mother's vow, Samuel spends most of his childhood being trained by Eli to be a man of God.

He later leads the Israelites, as a prophet and a judge, during a particularly unhappy period. The *twelve tribes of Israel are militarily dominated by the Philistines, while spiritually, paganism and idolatry are as widely practiced as monotheism. During his years as judge, Samuel brings about a return to God, and inspires at least one mighty victory against the Philistines.

Unfortunately, Samuel's sons are not "cut from the same cloth," and when he starts to grow older, the representatives of the tribes approach him with a request that breaks his heart: "Appoint a king for us, to govern us like all other nations" (8:5). The people's rationale for wanting a monarch—to be governed *like all other nations*—indicates to him how superficial their return to God has been.

Samuel prophetically warns the Israelites of the exploitation they will suffer if they are ruled by a king: "He will take your sons and appoint [some] to his chariots . . . and some to plow his ground and reap his harvest. . . . He will take your daughters to be perfumers and cooks and bakers. He will take the best of your fields and vineyards . . . a tenth of your grain . . . the best of your cattle . . . a tenth of your flocks, and you shall be his slaves" (8:10–18).

But the people are not to be deterred. "We must have a king over us that we may be like all the other nations," they repeat. "Let our king rule over us and go out at our head and fight our battles" (8:19–20). At God's behest, Samuel conducts a lottery, which selects *Saul, of the tribe of Benjamin, as king. Samuel anoints the young man and the people call out, *"Ye-khi ha-melekh*—Long live the king!" (10:24).

Later, however, Saul disobeys an explicit command of God (see next entry). God instructs Samuel to tell him that "because you have rejected the word of the Lord, He has also rejected you as king over Israel" (15:26). God then commands Samuel to find *David and anoint him as the new king. The prophet is afraid Saul will hear what he is planning to do and kill him, so God advises Samuel to announce that he is going off to offer a sacrifice. This would seem to be a clear-cut biblical and divine mandate for telling a lie, or at least a half-truth—Samuel does, in fact, offer a sacrifice, though that is not the point of his trip—when one's life is at stake (16:2).

Samuel anoints David, though it takes many years until he actually rules as king. In the meantime, Samuel disappears from the Bible, except for one stunning reappearance.

Years later, the still-ruling King Saul is under attack by a vastly superior Philistine army. He seeks out a necromancer, and demands that she summon the spirit of the deceased Samuel so that he can question him as to what he should do. The prophet indeed reappears, though he offers no consolation to the terrified monarch. "Why have you disturbed me by bringing me up? . . . Tomorrow, you and your sons shall be with me; the Lord will give the army of Israel also into the hands of the Philistines" (28:15–19). Samuel's unprecedented postmortem appearance remains the clearest proof of the Bible's belief in an *afterlife.

36

SAUL (I SAMUEL 9–31)

SAUL EVOLVES FROM A SHY AND LIKABLE YOUNG MAN INTO A DARING warrior and king, then ends his life pathetic, vengeful, and paranoid.

Saul was the first king of Israel: Had he obeyed God's word, the kingdom presumably would have remained in his family instead of being transferred to *David and his descendants. But Saul has a flaw that is fatal in a leader—a desperate need to be liked. He is instructed by the prophet Samuel (see preceding entry) to launch an all-out war against Israel's historic enemy, *Amalek, to destroy their property, and to wipe them out. Instead, when the battle ends, Saul rewards his soldiers with the booty—"I was afraid of the people [or troops]," is his defense for violating God's command, "and I yielded to them" (15:24)—and spares Amalek's murderous king Agag, most likely out of respect for a fellow monarch.

Samuel, outraged at Saul's flouting of God's command, informs him, in God's name, that the kingdom will be taken from him: He then summons Agag. "As your sword has bereaved women," he tells the Amalekite king, "so shall your mother be bereaved among women." Samuel then kills Agag himself (15:33).

From this point on, the king too "tender-hearted" to kill Agag becomes merciless. Fearful that the kingship will pass to David, he murders eighty-five men in the city of Nob when he learns that they had given David a night's lodging. The poor citizens of Nob weren't even aware of the tension between David and the king. Jewish tradition contrasts Saul's behavior toward the murderer Agag and his killing of the innocent men of Nob with the comment: "He who is merciful when he should be cruel, will in the end be cruel when he should be merciful" (*Ecclesiastes Rabbah* 7:16).

The last days of Saul's rule make King Lear's life look almost pleasant. Obsessed with the threat to his kingdom from David, he hurls a spear at his own son, Jonathan, for remaining friendly with David (see *David and Jonathan*), and accuses his closest advisers of conspiring against him (22:8).

He goes into his final battle against the Philistines robbed of all hope. The night before, Samuel had prophesied to him that he and his sons would die the next day. But Saul does not flee. Apparently, death has come to seem preferable to life. In the end, Saul is wounded and, fearing that the Philistines will capture and humiliate him, he falls on his sword and dies, along with three of his sons.

DAVID AND GOLIATH (I SAMUEL 17)

OF THE FORTY-TWO KINGS AND QUEENS WHO RULED OVER JUDAH AND Israel, David was the most important. To this day, *three thousand years* after he lived, Jews still sing in Hebrew of "David, king of Israel, who lives and flourishes." It was he who established Jerusalem as the capital of the Jewish people, and the religious center of Jewish life. Jewish tradition dictates that the Messiah will descend directly from David.

Because the Bible details David's life more fully than that of almost any other figure, I will tell about his life through its five best-known encounters and relationships.

During David's youth, the usual unhappy situation is prevailing in Israel— the Israelites are being subjected to Philistine domination and bullying. On one particular occasion, their armies face each other across a narrow ravine. Neither side wishes to charge first because its soldiers will become easy targets when they struggle up the opposite slope.

The Philistine commander suggests that the stalemate be ended by staging a battle between each camp's top warrior. He promptly sends out the nine-and-a-half-foot-tall Goliath (at least that's how tall he appears to the Israelites), carrying a javelin, sword, and spear. "Choose one of your men and let him come down against me," Goliath calls out. "If he bests me in combat and kills me, we will become your slaves, but if I best him and kill him, you will be our slaves and serve us." Day after day, no "kamikaze" volunteers can be found in the Israelite camp to fight Goliath.

At the time, David, the youngest of eight brothers, is working as a shepherd. He is too young even to be in the army. But when his father sends him to the Israelite camp with food for his three oldest brothers, he is shocked at how demoralized the troops have become because of Goliath's taunts.

The young shepherd speaks to many soldiers, and tries to stir them up. King *Saul hears of his efforts and summons him to a meeting. David tells the king that he will take on the Philistine giant himself.

Saul offers him his own armor and sword, but David shrugs them off; they are too heavy. Instead, he confronts Goliath with a stick, a sling, and five smooth stones. "Am I a dog that you come to me with sticks?" the infuriated Goliath rages.

In response, David lifts his sling, and lets fly a stone. It strikes Goliath in the forehead, killing him instantly. Seeing their greatest hero struck down by an unarmored boy, the Philistine troops flee in panic. David lops off the giant's head, and presents it to the king.

Saul's gratitude is short-lived, however. When he hears the new song being sung by Israelite women,

> Saul has slain his thousands
> David, his tens of
> thousands,

he stops seeing David as his loyal warrior, and starts to see him rather as a potential threat.

SOURCE: Joan Comay, *The World's Greatest Story*, pp. 106–108.

DAVID AND JONATHAN
(I SAMUEL 18–II SAMUEL 1)

THERE ARE TWO MODELS OF FRIENDSHIP IN THE BIBLE, ONE FEMALE, *Ruth and Naomi, the other male, David and Jonathan.

In a certain sense, David and Jonathan's friendship is the more remarkable, for unlike Ruth and Naomi, the two men have competitive interests. Jonathan is the oldest son of King *Saul, and heir apparent to the throne. David, Saul's leading soldier, is the "people's choice" to be the future king.

Yet their potential competition does not stand in the way of their friendship. When Jonathan recognizes David's greater gifts of leadership, it only incites in him the desire to be the top aide in his friend's future kingdom: "You are going to be king over Israel and I shall be second to you" (I Samuel 23:17).

Jonathan pays a heavy price for this friendship; it alienates him from his father, Saul, who is convinced that David represents a threat to his throne. King Saul is doing everything in his power to kill David, only to be constantly thwarted by Jonathan, who warns his friend of his father's schemes. Saul denounces his son. "I know that you side with [David] . . . to your shame, and to the shame of your mother's nakedness" (I Samuel 20:30). On one occasion, he even throws a spear at Jonathan.

Nonetheless, Jonathan continues to honor his father, and even accompanies him on his final, suicide mission against a vastly superior Philistine force. Perhaps a part of Jonathan feared that, despite his friendship with David, there would be no room for him in David's administration; heirs apparent are not easily converted into chiefs of staff. All this, of course, is pure conjecture, since we can never know what goes through Jonathan's mind during this final battle, in which he dies along with his father and two younger brothers.

The messenger who rushes to David with news of the royal family's death, and who brags that he personally delivered the death blow to Saul, undoubtedly anticipates a generous reward. Instead, an enraged David slays him after crying out, "How did you dare to lift your hand and kill the Lord's anointed?" (II Samuel 1:14). He then delivers a tender farewell to his dear friend. "I grieve for you, my brother Jonathan. You were most dear to me. Your love was wonderful to me, more than the love of women" (II Samuel 1:26).

This passage, along with several others describing David and Jonathan's affection for each other, have often been cited to suggest that the two men were lovers. As Frederick Buechner observed: "It's sad, putting it rather mildly, that we live at a time when in many quarters two men can't embrace or weep together or speak of loving one another without arousing the suspicion that they are also lovers" (*Peculiar Treasures*, p. 76).

DAVID AND BATHSHEBA (II SAMUEL 11)

THE MORAL LOW POINT IN DAVID'S LIFE OCCURS WHEN HE STEPS onto the roof of his palace and spots a beautiful woman bathing across the way. This shocking public display is presumably due to the king's palace being one of the highest buildings in Jerusalem, and to the woman not realizing that she could be observed.

Even after he learns that the woman, Bathsheba, is married to an officer in his army, David summons her to his palace and sleeps with her. In quick order, David thereby violates two of the *Ten Commandments, the prohibitions against coveting and adultery, while setting the stage for a violation of the even more serious commandment against homicide. For shortly thereafter, Bathsheba informs the king that she is pregnant. David immediately understands the terrible predicament into which he has placed himself. He presumably fears that if his troops learn how he has behaved with one of their wives while they are off battling for him, they might mutiny.

The quick-thinking monarch summons Bathsheba's husband, Uriah, back from the front, asks him a few inconsequential questions, and then tells him to go home and rest. Surely, David reasons, if they have one night together, no one will be suspicious when Bathsheba has an early delivery months later. But Uriah has an unusually noble character; he will not go home and enjoy himself with his wife while his fellow soldiers are locked in battle. The next day, David plies Uriah with liquor, and sends him home again, only to learn later that Uriah spent the night at the palace.

Very quickly, what started as a violation of the seemingly minor injunction against coveting has placed David in a catastrophic circumstance, propelling him to greater and greater evils. He sends Uriah back to the front with a secret letter for his top general, Joab. "Place Uriah in the front lines where the fighting is fiercest, then fall back so that he may be killed." We can only imagine the strange conjectures that must have run through Joab's mind when he read David's letter, with Uriah perhaps still standing in front of him.

Joab quickly stages the battle that brings about Uriah's death, and sends the happy news back to the king. David's own morality has been so compromised by his need to see Uriah dead that he isn't even upset to learn that other soldiers have also died in this unnecessary battle. As long as Uriah is dead, he feels safe.

When Bathsheba's period of mourning ends, David has her brought to his palace and marries her. But this, of course, is not the end of the story. "The Lord was displeased with what David had done, and the Lord sent Nathan to David" (11:27–12:1; see next entry).

Despite their relationship's inauspicious beginning, Bathsheba later becomes the mother of David's most famous son, and successor, *Solomon.

40

DAVID AND NATHAN

"Atta ha-Ish/You Are the Man!" (II Samuel 12)

THE PROPHET NATHAN'S PRETEXT FOR SEEING DAVID IS TO SEEK HIS advice on a minor, albeit disturbing, crime. "There were two men in the same city," he begins, "one rich and one poor. The rich man had very large flocks and herds, but the poor man had only one little . . . lamb that he had bought.

He tended it, and it grew up together with him and his children, it used to share his morsel of bread, drink from his cup, and nestle in his bosom. . . . One day, a traveler came to the rich man, but he was loath to take anything from his own flocks and herds . . . and prepare a meal for the guest . . . so he took the poor man's lamb and prepared it for the man who had come to him."

David flies into a rage. "As the Lord lives," he tells Nathan, "the man who did this deserves to die."

"*Atta ha-Ish*," Nathan responds. "You are the man!" The prophet then enumerates the numerous things God has done on David's behalf, who has responded to this goodness by killing Uriah and taking his wife.

Until this encounter, David had undoubtedly found some way to rationalize his own behavior with Bathsheba. As Freud reputedly said, "When it comes to self-justification, we are all geniuses." But in the face of Nathan's withering condemnation, he immediately recognizes and acknowledges the evil he has done. "I stand guilty before the Lord," he tells Nathan.

What marks this whole unhappy episode off as special is not David's crime. Acts like his were routinely carried out by monarchs in both the ancient and not-so-ancient world. What is special about biblical religion is that a prophet is able to denounce the king in the name of a higher law without risking his own life, and that the king acknowledges his sin and repents. Furthermore, it is the prophets, not the kings, who write the historical accounts that present the kings as they really were, moral blemishes included.

41

DAVID AND ABSALOM (II SAMUEL 13−19)

"O Absalom, My Son, My Son!" (II Samuel 19:1)

AS SUCCESSFUL AS DAVID IS AS A MONARCH, SO IS HE UNSUCCESSFUL as a father. His oldest son, Amnon, is a rapist. His third son, Absalom, is very handsome, and very spoiled. The Bible lavishes uncharacteristic attention on Absalom's dazzling looks: "No one in all Israel was so admired for his beauty as Absalom; from the sole of his foot to the crown of his head he was without blemish" (14:25).

Absalom does, however, have a spiritual blemish; he is a power-hungry demagogue. When people come to David for judgment, he accosts them and assures them that, if he were king, he would support their cause. It is no wonder that Absalom soon steals "the hearts of the people of Israel" (15:6).

Absalom also steals the heart of David's top adviser, Ahitophel, and organizes a full-scale revolt. He has himself anointed as king in the city of Hebron, then marches on Jerusalem with a large force of soldiers. Caught totally unawares, David is forced to flee.

Ahitophel offers Absalom excellent advice, to pursue David immediately before he can reorganize. Another adviser, Hushai, who is still working secretly for David, persuades Absalom to wait until he personally can lead a large-scale attack against his father. Hushai's advice appeals to Absalom's ego, and the crucial delay gives David time to regroup.

Soon David counterattacks, and as he prepares for the final battle, he issues strict orders that Absalom is not to be killed. But in fleeing the battle, Absalom's long hair becomes entangled in the branches of a tree. David's leading general, Joab, finds him and, outraged at Absalom's treachery, kills him.

For David the victory over Absalom proves more bitter than sweet. He cannot stop weeping, and calling out, "My son Absalom! O my son, my son Absalom! If only I had died instead of you! O Absalom, my son, my son!" (19:1).

Like many other fathers before and since, David loved more deeply than wisely.

42

SOLOMON (I KINGS 1–11)

JEWISH TRADITION CONSIDERS SOLOMON, KING DAVID'S SON, THE wisest of men. Hearing reports of his brilliance, The Queen of Sheba in Ethiopia travels to Israel to test him with her hardest questions. Solomon answers them all. "There was nothing that the king did not know," is the

Bible's comment on the encounter (10:3). Elsewhere, the Bible reports that Solomon composed three thousand proverbs and over a thousand songs, and that kings from all over the world dispatched messengers to hear him speak (5:12, 14). Jewish tradition ascribes to Solomon authorship of three biblical books: the Song of Songs, Proverbs, and *Ecclesiastes.

One incident in particular establishes Solomon's reputation for brilliance. Two prostitutes come before him for judgment. The first says that several days earlier, both had given birth to sons. The preceding night, however, the other woman's child had died, and the woman had switched the dead baby with hers. In the morning, when she got up to nurse her child, she immediately realized that the dead baby in her arms was not the one she had borne. The second woman insists that the live child is hers, and that no switch occurred.

Solomon commands that a sword be brought to him. "Cut the live child in two," he says, "and give half to one, and half to the other."

"Please . . ." one of the women cries out in horror, "give her the live child, only don't kill him." The other woman remains stoic. "Cut it in two," she says.

"Give the child to the first woman," Solomon rules. "She is its mother."

"When all Israel heard the decision that the king had rendered, they stood in awe of the king; for they saw that he possessed divine wisdom to execute justice" (3:16–28).

Solomon commences his reign with a tremendous advantage; his father's battles have bequeathed to him the largest and securest kingdom in Jewish history. As a result, he has the time to focus on intellectual pursuits, and on building projects. It is Solomon who builds the first *Beit ha-Mikdash* (Great Temple; see next entry), which survives until 586 B.C.E.

Unfortunately, as brilliant as he is in some areas, is Solomon unwise in others. To raise the funds needed to build the Temple, he imposes exceptionally high taxes, then drafts ten thousand Israelites a month for forced labor in Lebanon to pay for the raw materials he has purchased there. This combination of high taxes and forced labor—particularly among a people whose bitterest memories were of slavery in Egypt—causes considerable resentment, especially when the "emergency taxes" continue to be levied even after the Temple is built.

Solomon was also the most polygamous Jew in history. The Bible claims that he had seven hundred wives and three hundred concubines. Many, if not most, of his wives were foreign women of noble birth, whom he married in order to secure good diplomatic relations with their native lands.

Unfortunately, however, instead of influencing his non-Jewish wives to become monotheists, they compromise his own religiosity. Of the very king responsible for building the magnificent *Beit ha-Mikdash*, the Bible observes: "He was not as wholeheartedly devoted to the Lord . . . as his father David had been." Solomon apparently even built idolatrous temples so that his non-Jewish wives would have places to worship (11:3–10).

In outrage, God declares that He will take away the kingship from Solomon's descendants, leaving them only the tribe of Judah to rule over—and *that* only for the sake of his father David (see *Secession of the Ten Northern Tribes*).

What then is the final verdict on Solomon? On this issue, there is a discrepancy between the Bible and Jewish tradition. Though the Bible's depiction of Solomon starts out positively, in the end he is harshly condemned. In Jewish tradition, however, the image of the early, wise Solomon endures. Indeed, Solomon—*Shlomo* in Hebrew—remains a popular name among religious Jews, expressing the parents' hope that their child will be as wise as his ancient namesake.

43

THE TEMPLE/*BEIT HA-MIKDASH*

THE CROWNING ACHIEVEMENT OF KING SOLOMON'S REIGN (SEE PRE-ceding entry) was the erection of a magnificent Temple (*Beit ha-Mikdash*) in Jerusalem. His father, King *David, had wanted to build a great Temple for God a generation earlier, as a permanent resting place for the Ark containing the *Ten Commandments. A divine edict, however, had forbidden him from doing so. "You will not build a house for My name," God said to him, "for you are a man of battles and have shed blood" (I Chronicles 28:3).

The Bible's description of Solomon's Temple suggests that it was 180 feet long, 90 feet wide, and 50 feet high. He spares no expense in the building's creation. He orders vast quantities of cedar from King Hiram of Tyre (I Kings 5:20–25), has huge blocks of the choicest stone quarried, and commands that the building's foundation be laid with hewn stone. To complete the massive project, he imposes forced labor on all his subjects, drafting people for work shifts lasting a month at a time. Some 3,300 officials are appointed to oversee the Temple's erection (5:27–30). Solomon assumes such heavy debts in building the Temple that he is forced to pay off King Hiram with twenty towns in the Galilee (I Kings 9:11).

When the Temple is completed, Solomon inaugurates it with prayer and sacrifice, and even invites non-Jews to come and pray there. He urges God to pay particular heed to their prayers: "Thus all the peoples of the earth will know Your name and revere You, as does Your people Israel; and they will recognize that Your name is attached to this House that I have built" (I Kings 8:43).

Until the Temple was destroyed by the Babylonians some four hundred years later, in 586 B.C.E., *sacrifice was the predominant mode of divine service there. Seventy years later, a second Temple was built on the same site, and sacrifices again resumed. During the first century B.C.E., *Herod greatly enlarged and expanded this Temple. The *Second Temple was destroyed by the Romans in 70 C.E., after the failure of the *Great Revolt.

As glorious and elaborate as the Temple was, its most important room contained almost no furniture at all. Known as the Holy of Holies (*Kodesh Kodashim*), it housed the two tablets of the Ten Commandments. Unfortunately, the tablets disappeared when the Babylonians destroyed the Temple, and during the Second Temple era, the Holy of Holies was a small, entirely bare room. Only once a year, on *Yom Kippur, the High Priest would enter this room and pray to God on Israel's behalf. A remarkable monologue by a Hasidic rabbi in the Yiddish play *The Dybbuk* conveys a sense of what the Jewish throngs worshiping at the Temple must have experienced during this ceremony:

"God's world is great and holy. The holiest land in the world is the land of Israel. In the land of Israel the holiest city is Jerusalem. In Jerusalem the holiest place was the Temple, and in the Temple the holiest spot was the Holy of Holies. . . . There are seventy peoples in the world. The holiest among these is the people of Israel. The holiest of the people of Israel is the tribe of Levi. In the tribe of Levi the holiest are the priests. Among the priests, the holiest was the High Priest. . . . There are 354 days in the [lunar] year. Among these, the holidays are holy. Higher than these is the holiness of the Sabbath.

Among Sabbaths, the holiest is the Day of Atonement, the Sabbath of Sabbaths. . . . There are seventy languages in the world. The holiest is Hebrew.
Holier than all else in this language is the holy Torah, and in the Torah the
holiest part is the Ten Commandments. In the Ten Commandments the holiest of all words is the name of God. . . . And once during the year, at a certain
hour, these four supreme sanctities of the world were joined with one
another. That was on the Day of Atonement, when the High Priest would
enter the Holy of Holies and there utter the name of God. And because this
hour was beyond measure holy and awesome, it was the time of utmost peril
not only for the High Priest but for the whole of Israel. For if in this hour
there had, God forbid, entered the mind of the High Priest a false or sinful
thought, the entire world would have been destroyed."

To this day, Orthodox Jews pray three times a day for the Temple's restoration. During the centuries the Muslims controlled Palestine, two mosques
were built on the site of the Jewish Temple. (This was no coincidence; it has
been a common Islamic practice to build mosques on the sites of other people's holy places.) Since any attempt to level these mosques would lead to an
international Muslim holy war (*jihad*) against Israel, the Temple cannot be
rebuilt in the foreseeable future.

SOURCES: James Harpur, ed., *Great Events of Bible Times*, pp. 86–89. The scene
from *The Dybbuk*, is found in Joseph Landis, *The Great Jewish Plays*, pp. 51–52.

44

SECESSION OF THE TEN NORTHERN

TRIBES, ABOUT 930 B.C.E. (1 KINGS 12)

REHOBOAM, KING *SOLOMON'S SON AND SUCCESSOR, HAS THREE BAD
traits; he is greedy, arrogant, and a fool. This devastating combination causes
the Jewish kingdom to split in two.

When King Solomon dies, the people approach Rehoboam to plead that
he cut back the heavy taxes and forced labor that his father has imposed.

Rehoboam tells them to return in three days, then turns to his aides for advice. The older advisers tell him to respond with kind words and moderation, so that the people will forever be his loyal subjects. But the young advisers have personalities as charming as their master's. They tell him to ruthlessly reject every demand.

When the people return three days later, the king says to them: "My father made your yoke heavy, but I will add to your yoke, my father flogged you with whips, but I will flog you with scorpions" (a particularly painful whip; 12:14).

Rehoboam's subjects are not intimidated. "We have no portion in [the House of] David," they answer, and return home. They immediately choose Jeroboam as their new king. Only the tribe of Judah, and the tiny neighboring tribe of Benjamin, remain loyal to the House of David.

Rehoboam's first instinct is to attack the Ten Tribes and compel them to return to his kingdom. But realizing that the odds are against him, he backs off. From then on, the country is divided into two states: Judah (or Judea), and Israel (or the Ten Tribes). Each state maintains its own royal house. The Ten Tribes of Israel survive until 722 B.C.E., when they are defeated and then destroyed by Assyria; the tiny state of Judah lasts until Babylon destroys it in 586 B.C.E.

Much of this tragedy might have been averted had the wise King Solomon transmitted some of his wisdom to his singularly unwise son. See *Nebuchadnezzar, The Babylonian Exile*, and the next entry.

45

AHAB AND JEZEBEL (I KINGS 16:29–22:40)

"Have You Murdered and Also Inherited?" (I Kings 21:19)

IN THE CASE OF KING AHAB AND HIS NON-JEWISH QUEEN, JEZEBEL, WE see again, as in the case of *David and Bathsheba, how violation of the Tenth Commandment, "You shall not covet," can lead to far more serious sins.

Ahab, king of the ten northern tribes, covets a vineyard adjoining the royal lands. The owner, a man named Navot, refuses to sell him the plot. The land has been in his family since the Israelites entered Palestine, and he has no desire to dispose of so precious a family possession.

Ahab falls into a depression until Jezebel, daughter of the Phoenician king of Sidon, and a woman totally unrestrained by biblical morality, tells him: "Be cheerful! I will get the vineyard of Navot . . . for you." She arranges for two false witnesses to testify that they heard Navot publicly revile both God and king. Not only is this a capital crime, but the property of people convicted of treason also is confiscated by the king.

What started with an act of coveting has now led to violation of the commandments against bearing false witness, stealing, and murder. Within days, Navot is executed, and the king joyfully goes to possess his new field. But the Lord has already informed the prophet *Elijah of the royal couple's evil doings. "Go down and confront King Ahab . . . in Navot's vineyard," God instructs Elijah. "Say to him. 'Thus said the Lord, Have you murdered and also inherited?' "

Elijah waits for Ahab at the field, delivers God's message, and prophesies the downfall of Ahab and the royal family. He concludes with a prophecy that dogs shall devour the body of Jezebel in Navot's stolen vineyard.

Although Ahab's reign is very successful in both the economic and military spheres, the only detail that matters to the Bible is that "there was never anyone like Ahab, who committed himself to doing what was displeasing to the Lord, at the instigation of his wife, Jezebel." Indeed, the couple become the biblical prototype of an evil king and queen.

In addition to instigating the murder of Navot, Jezebel suppresses the worship of God and imports hundreds of idolatrous priests into Israel (see next entry). Her influence is pervasive and long-lived: Two of her sons, Ahaziah and Jehoram, become kings of Israel, while her daughter Athaliah becomes queen of Judah (II Kings 8:18).

Jezebel's downfall—along with the rest of her family—comes in a coup d'état by the religious reformer Jehu. Once she realizes that Jehu's revolt has succeeded, Jezebel meets her death with characteristic audacity. Standing inside a building located on Navot's vineyard, she paints her eyes, arranges her hair, then taunts Jehu from the window, "Is all well . . . murderer?" The rebel leader sends in troops to throw her out the window, and she dies immediately. When the soldiers come back some hours later to bury her, all they find are her skull, feet, and hands. "It is just as the Lord spoke through his servant Elijah . . . ," Jehu observes, "the dogs shall devour the flesh of Jezebel in the field of [Navot of] Jezreel" (II Kings 9:36).

46

THE PROPHET ELIJAH/*ELIYAHU HA-NAVI* (I KINGS 17–19, 21; KINGS 2)

THE CHARACTER NAMED ELIJAH IN THE BIBLE BEARS ALMOST NO RELA-tionship to the Elijah of Jewish folklore. The "legendary" Elijah is the man who visits every *Passover *Seder, where children watch to see if the wine has diminished in the special Elijah cup (*kos Eliyahu*) that has been prepared for him. He attends every *circumcision, where a special Elijah chair (*kissei Eliyahu*) is set aside for him.

Talmudic and medieval lore detail many episodes in which Elijah makes earthly visits to saints, scholars, and Jews in distress. One of the last biblical prophets, Malachi, announces that it is Elijah who will perform the final mir-acle before the coming of the *Messiah: "And he shall reconcile the hearts of fathers to sons and the hearts of sons to fathers" (Malachi 3:24). Centuries after Malachi, when the rabbis of the Talmud could not resolve certain dis-putes, they would suspend discussion until "Elijah comes and resolves it."

From these disparate, but warm-hearted, roles one probably would guess that the Elijah of flesh-and-blood, the prophet who appears in both books of Kings, was a kindly, lovable, and diplomatic sort. But one would be dead wrong. There is no biblical prophet more furious, impassioned, and uncom-promising. Hiking through the hills of Israel, dressed in his loincloth and carrying a stick, Elijah declares war on idolatry and on the Phoenician queen Jezebel (wife of King Ahab; see preceding entry) for introducing the idol Baal into the Jewish state. During an extended drought, he challenges the 450 priests of Baal employed by Jezebel to meet him in a competition. Each side is to prepare a slaughtered bull, lay it on an altar, and then invoke its god by name. The Israelites will witness whose god sends down fire to consume the sacrifice. The priests of Baal try first, praying, performing wild dances, and finally, desperate to elicit a reaction, gashing themselves with knives until their blood streams down. But nothing happens.

It is then that Elijah, standing alone, entreats God to prove His power. He does so in a great fire. The large crowd of Israelites watching are awe-struck, and spontaneously declare over and over: "*Adonai hu ha-Elohim*" ("The Lord, He [alone] is God" [I Kings 18:39]), words which three thousand years later are still used to conclude the *Yom Kippur service. Afterward, Elijah rouses the crowd to kill the 450 priests of Baal.

On another occasion, when Queen Jezebel arranges the judicial murder of Navot followed by the expropriation of his vineyard for her husband Ahab (see preceding entry), Elijah waits for the king to enter the plot, then damns him: "Have you murdered and also inherited?" (I Kings 21:19).

Of all possible biblical figures, why is this outraged prophet singled out to become the beloved grandfather figure and miracle-maker of Jewish legends? There are at least three reasons, it would appear, two grounded in the text, the third admittedly speculative. First, the Bible suggests that Elijah does not die. He is walking with his disciple, Elisha, when he suddenly ascends heavenward in a chariot of fire (II Kings 2:11; Enoch is the only other biblical character whose nondeath is implied — see Genesis 5:22–24). This intimation of immortality is itself sufficient to account for Elijah's postmortem return visits to earth.

Second, there is no prophet more qualified to perform miracles than Elijah. Two of his wondrous acts, multiplying food and bringing the dead back to life, seem to be the basis for miracles attributed to Jesus more than eight hundred years later.

But the most satisfying explanation I have heard, suggested by my father, Shlomo Telushkin, of blessed memory, links Elijah's presence at both the *Seder and *circumcisions to the very fact of his anger. In the immediate aftermath of Elijah's defeat of the priests of Baal, he flees from the enraged Jezebel into the desert, where he spends forty days in solitude. During this time, Elijah cries out angrily to God that "the Israelites have forsaken your covenant and . . . I alone am left" (I Kings 19:14) — presumably meaning that he is the only Jew and only monotheist left on earth. God does not permit Elijah to wallow in self-righteousness: He gives him new tasks and sends him on his way. But perhaps here, in Elijah's exaggerated condemnation of every other Jew, is the kernel of the reason for his many reappearances. He who sees himself as the last Jew is fated to bear constant witness to the eternity of Israel, to be present when every male Jewish child enters the covenant, and when every Jewish family celebrates the Seder (to this day, circumcision and the Seder remain the most commonly observed Jewish rituals). Elijah stands in a long line of despairing Jews who have erroneously prophesied the end of the Jewish people. See *The Vanishing American Jew*.

47

THE TEN LOST TRIBES, 722 B.C.E.

SEVERAL ATTEMPTS HAVE BEEN MADE TO WIPE OUT THE JEWISH PEOPLE; thankfully, all have failed. One of the closest to succeeding occurred in 722 B.C.E., when Assyria defeated the kingdom of Israel and resolved to destroy the rebellious state once and for all. The Assyrians exiled most of Israel's inhabitants—some escaped to safety in the surviving Jewish kingdom of Judah—and brought in new settlers from Babylon and Syria. In lieu of Israel, they called the new province Samaria. Ever since, no Jews have been able to trace their ancestry accurately or definitively to any tribe except for Judah and Levi (see *Priest, Levite, Israelite*).

Because we lack precise information on the Ten Tribes' fate (II Kings 17:6 describes only the places to which they were initially exiled), a large body of legends has grown up speculating on what became of them. As a rule, any nation that has acted sympathetically to the Jews (for example, England after it issued the *Balfour Declaration), or practiced any ritual that corresponds to some ritual in the Torah (as do some American Indian tribes), has been rumored to be descended from the Ten Lost Tribes. To this day, some rabbinic authorities claim that the Jews of Ethiopia are descended from the tribe of Dan. In the early 2000s, a group in northern India, calling themselves B'nai Menashe, and claiming to descend from the ancient tribe of Menashe, started making *aliya* to Israel. Because of uncertainty about their claim to be Jewish, the Israeli rabbinate insisted on their undergoing formal conversion to Judaism.

In the darkest periods of the Middle Ages, when almost all Jews lived under Christian or Muslim oppression, tales spread of a mighty kingdom beyond the legendary river Sambatyon, inhabited by the Ten Tribes, which would someday come and rescue its suffering brothers.

In actuality, it appears that most of the Ten Tribes' descendants assimilated into the societies in which they were exiled. And unlike the *Marranos, many of whom maintained a secret tradition affirming their Jewishness, the assimilation of the Ten Tribes appears to have been total and irrevocable.

48

NEBUCHADNEZZAR, KING OF BABYLON
(604–562 B.C.E.)

IN THE NON-JEWISH WORLD, NEBUCHADNEZZAR IS KNOWN FOR THE "hanging gardens of Babylon," the terraced roof gardens on top of his palace, which the Greeks listed as one of the seven wonders of the world. In the Jewish world, his reputation is less wondrous. He is the biblical paradigm of a sadist. After he suppresses a Jewish revolt in 586 B.C.E., Nebuchadnezzar blinds King Zedekiah, but only after first murdering his sons before his eyes, so that he can be haunted by that image for the rest of his life (II Kings 25:7).

After that, Nebuchadnezzar, furious at this second Judean revolt against him in twelve years, orders the destruction of the *Beit ha-Mikdash, the Great Temple in Jerusalem.

The Book of Daniel depicts Nebuchadnezzar as later undergoing one of the least impressive repentances in history. The king erects an enormous gold statue, and orders all his officials to worship it. Word soon reaches him that three Jewish officials, Shadrach, Meshach, and Abednego, have refused to bow down to the statue. Nebuchadnezzar warns them of the consequences of not doing so, but to no avail. In typical, sweet manner, Nebuchadnezzar has his furnace stoked to seven times its normal heat, and orders soldiers to tie up the three men and throw them inside. As the trio are thrown in, a tongue of fire leaps out of the fiery furnace, killing the soldiers carrying them. That doesn't faze Nebuchadnezzar, but what impresses him is that he now sees four men in the furnace, "walking about unbound and unharmed, and the fourth looks like a divine being." He immediately releases the three men, gives them job promotions, and decrees that anyone who "blasphemes the God of Shadrach, Meshach and Abednego shall be torn limb from limb . . . for there is no other God who is able to save in this way. . . ." (Daniel 3:25, 29).

THE BABYLONIAN EXILE, 586 B.C.E.

THE BABYLONIAN EXILE IS THE SECOND EXPULSION FROM THEIR LAND
(see *The Ten Lost Tribes*) of a people who have lived far more of their history
in exile than in their homeland.

When Nebuchadnezzar (see preceding entry) destroys Judah and the
Temple in 586 B.C.E., he resolves to put a permanent end to the troublesome
Jewish state. He takes the country's most prominent citizens to his own
homeland in captivity, leaving only the poorest Jews behind.

In Babylon the Jews keenly feel the pain of their exile. Perhaps the most
poignant of the 150 *psalms is the one composed during those years of captivity:

> By the rivers of Babylon,
> Where we sat down,
> And wept,
> When we remembered Zion . . .
> Our tormentors [for their own amusement] asked
> "Sing us one of the songs of Zion."
> How can we sing a song of the Lord on alien soil?
> If I forget you, O Jerusalem,
> let my right hand wither . . . (Psalms 137:1–5)

Every year on the *ninth of Av, Jews fast and read aloud the scroll of
Lamentations, which commemorates the destruction of Judah and the First
Temple.

In a letter to the Babylonian Jewish community, the prophet *Jeremiah
urges them to "seek the welfare of the city to which I [God] have exiled you,
pray to the Lord on its behalf, for in its prosperity you shall prosper" (Jeremiah 29:7).

Jeremiah's cautious words of advice—he probably feared that the Jews would engage in revolutionary activity in Babylonia as they had done in Jerusalem (see *Jeremiah*)—seem to have been heeded. Ancient records show that Jews worked as craftsmen and builders in royal buildings in Babylon, and that the government gave the Jews considerable authority to run their own religious affairs. Less than seventy years later, when King *Cyrus of Persia defeated Babylon and invited its exiled Jews to return home, the large majority demurred. Like many of their Diaspora descendants some 2,500 years later, they were content sending charitable contributions to Jews living in Israel, rather than settling there themselves.

ISAIAH

"Nation Shall Not Lift Up Sword Against Nation, Neither Shall They Learn War Anymore" (2:4)

"A Light Unto the Nations" (Based on 49:6)

THE WORDS THAT ADORN THE WALL ACROSS THE STREET FROM THE United Nations in New York are taken from the prophet Isaiah: "Nation shall not lift up sword against nation, neither shall they learn war anymore" (2:4). For many years the quote was posted without attribution, apparently out of fear that the Communist and Muslim delegations to the U.N. would be angered by having a verse from the Hebrew Bible in so prominent a place.

Isaiah's ancient call for world peace is based on his faith that the nations of the world ultimately will choose monotheism and Torah over polytheism and warfare: *"Ki mi-Tzion tey-tzey Torah*—For out of Zion shall go forth the Torah," he declares, "and the word of God from Jerusalem" (2:3).

Isaiah does not only have great plans for the Jewish world; he exhorts the Jews to play an active role in history and become an *or la-Goyim,* ("light unto the nations"). These words, with their implication of a Jewish mission to the world, continue to influence all Jews who believe that their people have been chosen to make God and His ethical standards known to the world (see *Chosen People*).

In the first chapter of Isaiah, the prophet insists that justice is God's supreme demand. He ridicules the religious hypocrisy of those who punctiliously observe Judaism's rituals but ignore its ethics: "What need have I of all your sacrifices? says the Lord . . . I have no delight in lambs and he-goats" (1:11). Rather, "Cease to do evil. Learn to do good. Devote yourselves to justice. Aid the wronged. Uphold the rights of the orphan; Defend the cause of the widow" (1:16–17).

In chapter 11, Isaiah prophesies a future messianic age in which "the wolf shall dwell with the lamb, [and] the leopard lie down with the kid" (11:6). In recent years, Woody Allen has appended that utopian vision to read: "And the wolf and the lamb shall lie down together, but the lamb won't get any sleep."

Isaiah's characteristic stress on justice was so well known in the Western world that President Franklin Delano Roosevelt nicknamed the Jewish Supreme Court Justice Louis *Brandeis, "Isaiah."

While Isaiah lived in the eighth century B.C.E., most Bible scholars assume that chapters 40–66 (or at least 40–55) were written some two centuries later, after the destruction of the Temple in 586 B.C.E. The author of these later chapters is commonly referred to by Bible scholars as the Second Isaiah.

51

JEREMIAH

NEXT TO *JOB, JEREMIAH IS PROBABLY THE MOST UNHAPPY CHARACTER in the Bible. A word based on his name, jeremiad, has entered the English language to describe mournful complaints and lamentations.

Jeremiah lived around 600 B.C.E., in the last days of the First Temple. In his role as prophet, he repeatedly warns King Zedekiah and his fellow Jews not to revolt against Babylon: Their situation will be improved only by a total cessation of evil and idolatrous behavior.

Both the king and the people ignore the prophet's pleas. Because the Temple is in Jerusalem, they are certain that God Himself will guarantee the city's security. A few years later, when Judah and the Temple are destroyed (see *Nebuchadnezzar* and *The Babylonian Exile*), one might think that Jeremiah would at least have the gratification of being able to say, "I told you so." But he is heartbroken. The biblical prophet is not a dispassionate oracle, indifferent to the fate of the people about whom he prophesies. If anything, he feels an additional measure of guilt for not having delivered his message in a way that would have motivated people to heed it.

The roots of Jeremiah's unhappiness run even deeper: He is the only character in the Hebrew Bible denied a family. Early in his career, God instructs him not to marry or have children because of the terrible fate that would await them: "For thus said the Lord concerning any sons and daughters that may be born in this place. . . . They shall die gruesome deaths. They shall not be lamented or buried. . . . They shall be consumed by the sword and by famine, and their corpses shall be food for the birds of the sky and the beasts of the earth. . . . For I have withdrawn My favor from that people, declares the Lord" (16:3–5).

It is the fate of any true prophet to be at war with his times. When the Jews are affluent, but spiritually debased, Jeremiah denounces them. When the people simplemindedly decide to join a revolt against a vastly superior army, Jeremiah mocks them. But when the Jews lose everything, and are overtaken by despair, the normally morose Jeremiah turns into a prophet of hope. As the Jews prepare to march into exile, certain they will never again see their homeland, Jeremiah expends his last funds buying land in Israel. He tells the departing exiles to set up markers to remind them how to get back to Israel. Although no other exiled nation had ever returned to its homeland, Jeremiah promises the Jews that they will be back. In a "Zionist" prophecy that is still sung, *2,600 years later*, at every religious Jewish wedding, he declares: "*Od yeshama*—Again there shall be heard in this place . . . in the [desolate] towns of Judah and the [deserted] streets of Jerusalem . . . the sound of mirth and gladness, the voice of bridegroom and bride" (33:10–11).

During the revolt against King Nebuchadnezzar, Jeremiah predicts that the Babylonians will triumph over the Jews, not because of military superiority alone, but because God has sent them to punish Judah. To many Jews of his time (and to many modern ones as well) Jeremiah's insistence that national suffering comes as punishment for national wrongdoing is offensive. Indeed, would anyone have the audacity to say such a thing about the Holocaust? Nonetheless, in its time, this controversial idea saved the Jewish people from extinction.

In the ancient world, it was common to assume that the gods of the victor were superior to the gods of the loser. That is why citizens of a nation that lost a war so often accepted the victor's gods. But precisely because the Jews believed that God, not Nebuchadnezzar, was behind their defeat, they were not tempted by the Babylonian gods. It was easy for them to remain Jews in Babylon, because they believed that the same God Who exiled them there would ultimately return them to Israel—if they but mended their immoral ways.

As clear-cut as Jeremiah's task seems in retrospect, he pays an unbearably heavy price for his opposition to his fellow Jews' revolt. Many, if not most, of his contemporaries consider him a traitor. He is flogged at the Temple (20:1–2), left in a muddy pit to die (38:6), and has to flee from a group of priests and false prophets who try to kill him (26:8–11). In no other prophet do we find such unalloyed pain and depression:

> Cursed be the day I was born . . .
> Cursed be the man
> Who brought my father the news,
> And said, "A boy is born to you . . ."
> Why did I ever issue from the womb,
> To see misery and woe
> To spend all my days in shame (20:14–15, 18).

Yet after Jeremiah dies, the Jews regard him as a hero. They preserve his message, including his devastating critiques of their behavior. They accept his insistence that God's presence is universal, and He can be worshiped in exile. Even in the darkest days of exile, their spirits are lifted by his optimism that someday they will return to Israel. Most important, they learn from his emphasis on the centrality of ethics, capsulized in two verses in chapter 9:

> Thus says the Lord:
> Let not the wise man glory in his wisdom
> Let not the strong man glory in his strength
> Let not the rich man glory in his riches
> But only in this should one glory
> In his earnest devotion to Me.
> For I, the Lord, act with kindness
> Justice and equity in the world
> For in these I delight, declares the Lord (9:22–23).

During my many years of study of this remarkable prophet, I have come across five quotations that apply to him with particular force.

1. Nietzsche—"Some men are born posthumously." When Jeremiah died, he undoubtedly saw himself as a failure. Yet more than 2,500 years later, he still influences Jewish life.
2. Sören Kierkegaard—"The tyrant dies and his rule is over, the martyr dies and his rule begins."
3. Napoleon—"Ten men who speak make more noise than ten thousand who are silent."
4. Rabbi Tarfon—"It is not your obligation to complete the work [of perfecting the world], but you are not free to desist from it either."
5. A Yiddish proverb—"Truth never dies, but it lives a wretched life."

EZEKIEL

The Valley of the Dry Bones (37:1–14)

AS STARK A PESSIMIST AS HIS CONTEMPORARY JEREMIAH (SEE PREVIOUS entry), the prophet Ezekiel bequeaths to Israel one of its most enduring images of hope.

As a young man, Ezekiel serves as a priest in the Temple. In 598 B.C.E., when the Babylonians first occupy Jerusalem, he is exiled to Babylon along with several thousand other prominent Jews, and becomes the first prophet to live outside the land. From his exile, Ezekiel prophesies that Jerusalem will be destroyed, as indeed it is in 586 B.C.E. After the destruction, he prophesies that the Jews will return to their homeland. He has numerous fantastic visions detailing Israel's future: On one occasion, a celestial architect gives him a personal tour of the new Temple that will be rebuilt on the site of the destroyed one.

His most famous vision, however, is a metaphor for the revival of the seemingly "dead" Jewish people. According to Ezekiel, God sets him down in a valley filled with lifeless bones—they have been in the hot sun so long that the flesh has been stripped from them—and asks: "O mortal, can these bones live again?"

"Only You know," Ezekiel replies, whereupon God orders him to prophesy to the bones: "O dry bones, hear the word of the Lord. . . . I will cause breath to enter into you and you shall live again."

Even as Ezekiel pronounces the Lord's words, the bones stir, and begin coming together. Flesh grows over them, and soon the bones form into bodies, but there is still no breath in them. And God instructs Ezekiel: "Say to the breath, thus said the Lord God: 'Come, O breath, from the four winds, and breathe into these slain, that they may live again.' "

The breath enters into the corpses, and they stand on their feet, a vast multitude. And God tells Ezekiel, "O mortal, these bones are the whole House of Israel. They say, 'Our bones are dried up, our hope is gone; we are doomed.' " And God instructs Ezekiel to prophesy to the House of Israel: "Thus said the Lord God: I am going to open your graves and lift you out of the graves, O My people, and bring you to the land of Israel. . . . I will put My breath into you and you shall live again, and I will set you upon your own soil."

Many Jews have seen in the creation of the State of Israel only three years after the Holocaust the seeming fulfillment of Ezekiel's rather bizarre, 2,600-year-old vision. Throughout Jewish history, this prophecy also has been cited as proof that God will someday resurrect the dead.

Nonetheless, it is Ezekiel's image of a dried-up, exiled, and hopeless Jewish people coming back to life in their homeland that makes him as much a prophet of the twentieth century C.E. as of the sixth century B.C.E.

53

AMOS

*"Let Justice Well Up Like Water, Righteousness Like
a Mighty Stream" (5:24)*

THE EARLY PROPHETS, MEN SUCH AS *NATHAN AND *ELIJAH, HAVE THEIR prophecies recorded as parts of larger books—Judges, I and II Samuel, and I and II Kings—that form the general history of the ancient Israelites. There is no book, therefore, named for Nathan or Elijah. Two biblical books are named for *Samuel, but he is dead before the second book begins, and is not even the main character in most of the first book.

The Book of Amos inaugurates a new stage in Jewish religious development. Amos is the first of what are known as the later, or literary, prophets, men whose writings are preserved in books called by their names. The previously discussed *Isaiah, *Jeremiah, and *Ezekiel also are literary prophets. The Book of Amos consists of prophecies he delivers to the Jews of Israel between 775 and 750 B.C.E.

Amos comes from Tekoah, a small town twelve miles from Jerusalem. He lives during a successful and secure era for the kingdoms of Judah and Israel. Israel's historic enemy, Syria, has been crushed in war, and the victor, Assyria, is ruled by a series of weak kings who leave the Mediterranean area undisturbed. The kingdom of Israel prospers under this policy of benign neglect. As trade expands significantly, a new, wealthy class of Israelites emerge. We read reports of people living in winter and summer homes, sleeping on fine beds inlaid with carved ivory, and anointing themselves with the choicest of oils (3:15, 6:4–6). Unfortunately, the poorer classes do not share in the wealth; if anything they sink into even greater poverty.

All this would be troublesome enough if the newly prosperous Israelites fulfilled the Torah's commands to help the poor, but they don't. Though Deuteronomy 15:7–8 had legislated that Jews must lend their impoverished neighbors "sufficient for [their] needs," Amos declares that people in debt are being sold as slaves, even when the debt is as small as the price of a pair of shoes (2:6). Though Exodus 22:25–6 had ruled that a creditor who took a debtor's night garment as collateral had to return it every evening—a practice so cumbersome that it was clearly intended to discourage the taking of pledges from the poor—Amos describes wealthy Jews reclining at the Temple's altar on "garments taken in pledge" (2:8). He is particularly upset that these rich oppressors of the poor are somehow very scrupulous about observing the rituals at the Temple. He elaborates on the multitude of sacrifices wealthy people are bringing there (tithes, thank offerings, and free-will offerings), all the while deluding themselves that they are fulfilling God's primary demand from them.

Amos's fury is equally directed at the Temple's priests, who assure their wealthy patrons that as long as they bring sacrifices—which also enrich the priests—they will find favor in God's eyes.

Amos's rage is matched by his courage. He personally appears one holiday morning at the chief temple of the kingdom of Israel in Beth-El, and in the presence of rich donors and priests, proclaims in God's name:

> I loathe, I spurn your festivals,
> I am not appeased by your solemn assemblies
> If you offer Me burnt offerings or your meal offerings
> I will not accept them
> I will pay no heed to your gifts of fatlings (5:21–22).

According to Amos, only one thing will appease and please God: "Let justice well up like water, righteousness like a mighty stream" (5:24). Unless this happens, God personally will ensure the destruction of the kingdom of Israel (7:9).

Amos further warns the Jews not to expect favored treatment from God just because they are the *Chosen People. Indeed, the very fact of chosenness imposes additional obligations on them, not rights. "You alone have I singled out of all the families of the earth. That is why I call you to account for all your iniquities" (3:2).

Amos's obsession with righteousness is surely his dominant motif. But from the perspective of Judaism's history, his most important contribution is recording his prophecies in writing. Most likely he does so as an "insurance policy," to guarantee that his message not die with him. In this he certainly succeeds. Though we have no way of knowing the efficacy of Amos's message in his own time, the fact is, we continue to read and be affected by his verses some 2,800 years after they were written.

POSTSCRIPT:

Were the ancient Jews a particularly loathsome people? They certainly seem so from the writings of Amos and the other prophets.

The Jews are depicted very critically by the prophets—Israel Zangwill once said, only half-humorously, that they were among the world's first anti-semites. Indeed, medieval Christian theologians often cited the prophets to prove the eternally evil character of the Jews.

But this is naive; it is as if a scholar five hundred years from now were to write a history of the world during the 1960s based exclusively on *Pravda's* panegyrics to communism and *The New York Times's* exposés of corruption in the United States, and conclude that Russia was a much better place to live than America.

We know quite a bit about the Jews' neighbors. Although they left behind no comparable tradition of moral self-criticism, we know that the sins they committed, including mass murder, the exiling of other nations, and ripping open the bellies of pregnant women (see Amos 1–2), were much more serious than the sins Amos attributes to the Jews. Israel is reproved at length not because it is worse, but because it is held accountable to a higher standard (3:2).

As serious as are the sins committed by the ancient Israelites, one thing must be said to the Israelites' credit: They canonized their critics. They took writings that other people would have burned and turned them into holy books to be studied by Jews throughout their history.

This is something that no other nation or religion did. The New Testament and Koran do not have a large body of statements denouncing evil behavior by early Christians and Muslims. Thus, we must conclude that either the early Christians and Muslims were overwhelmingly righteous, or that they did not have a tradition of self-criticism.

SOURCES AND FURTHER READING: Shalom Spiegel, "Amos vs. Amaziah," in Judah Goldin, ed., *The Jewish Expression*, pp. 38–65.

54

JONAH AND THE WHALE

THE ONE "FACT" EVERYONE KNOWS ABOUT THE PROPHET JONAH, THAT he is swallowed by a whale, is probably wrong. The only detail the Bible tells us about the creature that swallows Jonah is that it is a "big fish."

The dubious distinction of living inside a fish's belly for three days is one of two unusual details we learn about Jonah. He also is the only prophet to reject a command of God. Though *Moses and *Jeremiah plead with God to release them from their prophetic mission, Jonah goes further. When God instructs him to go to the non-Jewish city of Nineveh, the capital of Assyria, and warn the inhabitants of their city's impending destruction, he immediately boards a boat and heads in the opposite direction.

Why he does so is made clear only in the book's final chapter. Jonah hates Nineveh—Assyria is, after all, the country that destroyed the Ten Tribes of Israel in 722 B.C.E. He wants the city punished, not offered the opportunity to repent.

Yet Jonah's solution, fleeing God, is of course impossible. God sends a sudden, raging storm, so unexpected that the pagan sailors aboard Jonah's ship are convinced that one of their gods has brought it upon them as a punishment. While the sailors entreat their gods to save them, Jonah goes into the hold of the ship and falls into a deep sleep. Having alienated himself from God, Jonah seems to have given up on life itself. Eventually, the sailors draw lots to determine who is responsible for their predicament. After the lottery repeatedly falls on Jonah, they demand an accounting. "I am a Hebrew," he responds and explains that it is his God who is behind the storm, and that their only hope for saving the ship is to throw him overboard. They do so, albeit reluctantly, and the sea promptly calms.

The "big fish" then swallows Jonah and spits him out uninjured on dry land three days later. The prophet proceeds to Nineveh, and announces: "Forty days more, and Nineveh will be destroyed." At that point, a miracle only slightly less remarkable than Jonah's survival in the fish's belly occurs: The people actually listen to his message. The king himself "rose from his throne, took off his robe, put on sackcloth, [and] sat in ashes." He issues a command: "Let everyone turn back from his evil ways and from the injustice of which he is guilty" (3:6–8). A national transformation takes place, so that "God saw what they did, how they were turning back from their evil ways. And God renounced the punishment He had planned to bring upon them, and did not carry it out" (3:10).

The power of Nineveh's repentance so impressed the rabbis that they chose this short book to be a central reading in the synagogue on *Yom Kippur, the Day of Repentance. They were particularly struck by the fact that the sole criterion the Bible used for assessing Nineveh's repentance was moral. As the *Mishna teaches: "It doesn't say that God saw them put on sackcloth and fasting [and then forgave them]. Rather, that God saw what they did, how they were turning back from their evil ways" (*Mishna Ta'anit* 2:1). If the Book of Jonah had appeared in the New Testament or the Koran, the undoubted proof of the Ninevites' repentance would have been their conversion to Christianity or Islam. The Hebrew Bible makes a considerably more restrained appeal to the non-Jewish world: just that people refrain from evil behavior, and do good. And that, not the "fish story," is the most important thing to remember about Jonah.

55

MICAH

"He Has Told You, O Man, What Is Good, and What the Lord Requires of You: Only to Do Justice and to Love Goodness, and to Walk Modestly with Your God" (6:8)

THE PROPHET MICAH INITIATES AN UNUSUAL AND ADMIRABLE TRADItion in Jewish life: the willingness to "reduce" Judaism to its ethical essence. In the most direct language possible, Micah summarizes the "bottom-line" requirement that God makes of the Jews: "To do justice and to love goodness, and to walk modestly with your God" (6:8).

Micah's message is so simply stated that people sometimes think it is banal. "So what's the big insight?" I once heard someone say. "Doesn't every-body agree that God's primary demand of human beings is to act ethically?"

But is that true? Think of the messages being put forth by most Jewish, Christian, and Muslim religious leaders today; they rarely cite Micah's guide-line for assessing people's obedience to God. Ask any Jew—religiously obser-vant or not—whether another Jew is religious, and the question is invariably answered by noting the person's observance of Jewish rituals, not of Jewish ethics. As if God regarded ethical observance as a voluntary, extra-credit activity (see *Rabbi Israel Salanter*).

Although Micah is the first great teacher to put this central emphasis on ethics, two of the greatest rabbis of the Talmud restated his insight hundreds of years later. When a would-be convert asked *Hillel to provide him a one-sentence definition of Judaism's essence, the sage answered in ethical terms: "What is hateful unto you, don't do unto your neighbor. The rest is com-mentary—now go and study." More than a century after that, Rabbi *Akiva taught: " 'Love your neighbor as yourself,' this is the major principle of the Torah" (see *Love Your Neighbor as Yourself*).

Micah, one of the literary prophets (that is, those who wrote down their messages), lived in Judah in the second half of the eighth century B.C.E. He was the first prophet to predict that Judah would be destroyed because of her religious and political leaders' evil behavior: "Assuredly, because of you, Zion shall be plowed as a field, and Jerusalem shall become heaps of ruins, and the Temple Mount a shrine in the woods" (3:12).

Not surprisingly, this gloomy sense of the future awaiting the Jewish peo-ple accounts for the book's sometimes desperate tone. Micah urges the peo-ple to transform themselves very quickly; time is running out. The last half of the book also contains prophecies of hope, most notably Micah's parallel ver-sion of *Isaiah's best-known prophecy, "Nation shall not lift up sword against nation" (4:3). It is uncertain who said these words first, though most Bible scholars assume it was Isaiah.

Micah's fame in Jewish life today, however, rests primarily on his com-pelling and challenging one-sentence summation of what the Lord requires of man.

56

PSALMS/*TEHILLIM*

"The Lord Is My Shepherd, I Shall Not Want"
(Psalms 23:1)

"If I Forget Thee, O Jerusalem, Let My Right Hand Wither"
(Psalms 137:5)

THE 150 PSALMS ARE THE MOST FAMOUS RELIGIOUS POEMS EVER written. They have become so much a part of Western culture that many Jews are unaware that they come from the Hebrew Bible. A man I know took his son to the funeral of a Protestant friend, and on the way home, the boy remarked wistfully: "I wish we Jews had beautiful prayers like 'The Lord is my shepherd, I shall not want.' " That line, of course, is the opening of the most famous psalm, the twenty-third.

While Jewish tradition attributes authorship of the Book of Psalms to King David (in the tenth century B.C.E.)., some of the psalms clearly postdate David's reign. Psalm 137, for example, is a lament sung by Jews exiled from Israel to Babylon in 586 B.C.E.: "By the rivers of Babylon, where we sat down and wept, when we remembered Zion" (137:1). The psalm's fifth verse subsequently became a credo of Jewish nationalism, and a reminder to all Jews of their eternal ties to the land of Israel: "If I forget you, O Jerusalem, let my right hand wither, and let my tongue cleave to the roof of my mouth."

The 150 psalms vary greatly in length. Psalm 117 is only two verses, while Psalm 119 is an acrostic in which each of the twenty-two letters of the Hebrew alphabet initiates eight verses, for a total of 176 verses.

The Book of Psalms is the backbone of the Hebrew prayerbook. Psalm 145, for example, comprises almost all the *Ashrei* prayer, which is so familiar to religious Jews that they can often recite the entire psalm by heart. Familiarity, however, can sometimes breed ignorance. Professor Reuven Kimelman told me that he often stumps his religious friends by asking them to summarize the *Ashrei*'s contents. Few of them can do so. They are so used to saying the psalm's words that they rarely analyze its two main themes: the happiness of those who believe in God and praise Him, and God's openness to all those who need His help.

Religious Jews regard the recitation of psalms as one of the most effective ways of beseeching God's mercy, and therefore recite them on behalf of ill people, or when the Jewish community is imperiled. At the *Western Wall, the *Kotel*, in Jerusalem, the two books available for visitors are a prayerbook and Psalms.

57

THE TRIAL OF JOB

THOUGH JOB WAS DEEPLY RELIGIOUS AND A SAINT, I DON'T THINK A SIN-gle Jewish child has ever been named for him. That's because he led the most pained life of any character in the Bible.

There are a few odd elements in the biblical book that bears his name: The angel Satan makes his only appearance in the Hebrew Bible, and God is cast in the morally dubious role of wreaking havoc on Job's life, just to show off to Satan.

The story starts in the heavenly court, where a discussion is taking place about Job, an unusually generous and pious man. Satan mocks Job's piety, claiming that it is no great wonder he is so religious, since God has bestowed every possible blessing on his head. "But lay Your hand upon all that he has, and he will curse You to Your face" (1:11).

God accepts the challenge; do anything you want to Job and his family, He tells Satan, and you will see that he will remain loyal to Me. In short order, Satan destroys Job's wealth, kills his ten sons and daughters, and afflicts him with unspeakably painful boils. Job's wife pleads with him to curse God; that way perhaps God will kill him and put him out of his misery. But Job refuses: "Should we accept only good from God and not accept evil?" (2:10). Elsewhere he declares: "The Lord gives and the Lord takes away. Blessed be the name of the Lord" (1:21).

Three of Job's friends hear of his sufferings, and come to console him. They remain with him seven days (a basis for the Jewish practice of sitting *shiva, seven days of mourning, following the death of an immediate family member). Job's friends urge him to repent of the sins that have provoked God to punish him. But Job insists that he has committed no sins proportionate to the evil that has befallen him. The friends are offended at Job's intransigence. "Does punishment come to the innocent?" they ask. But Job does not give in to their scolding, he will not condemn himself falsely. That God has sent these sufferings upon him, he is willing to acknowledge; that they are punishment for sins, he is not.

Throughout the book, Job repeatedly demands that God tell him why this evil has befallen him.

After thirty-seven tense chapters, God finally speaks:

> "Get prepared like a man,
> I will ask you and you tell me.
> Where were you when I established the world?
> Tell me, if you know so much . . .
> Did you ever command forth a morning? . . .
> Have death's gates been revealed to you? . . .
> Have you examined earth's expanse?
> Tell me, if you know.
> Can you . . . guide the bear with her cubs? . . .
> Does the hawk soar by your wisdom?
> Does the eagle mount at your command,
> And make his nest on high? . . ."
> God answered Job and said:
> "Will the contender with God yield?
> He who arraigns God, must respond."
> Job answered God and said:
> "Lo, I am small, how can I answer you?
> My hand I clap to my mouth.
> I have spoken once, I will not reply . . .
> I talked of things I did not know,
> Wonders beyond my ken. . . ." (38:3–4, 12, 17–18, 32; 39:26–27; 40:1–5)

As Dennis Prager and I wrote in *The Nine Questions People Ask About Judaism*, "God is God, and who are we to assume that we can understand everything that happens in this world? Who established the world, we or

God? Admittedly, this may not be the answer we hoped for, but *what answer would we desire?* If God is God and man is man, is there any other possible answer than the one given to Job?" (pp. 36–37).

Because the Book of Job deals with the single greatest challenge to religion, why God allows evil in the universe, its questions have preoccupied almost all sensitive religious figures. Jews living in the aftermath of the Holocaust often turn to this book for guidance. It is hard to say, though, if the situation of post-Holocaust Jews parallels Job's. While God never tells Job why he suffers, the mere fact that Job finally hears God's voice assures him that God exists, and thus there must be a reason for everything that has happened. God's revelations to the world since the Holocaust have been less unambiguous, so that people are left not only with Job's question, "Why?" but with the more agonizing question of God's existence.

It is perhaps because of the less than flattering light in which the Book of Job casts God that one of the leading rabbis in the Talmud claimed that Job never lived, and that the entire book is an allegory about the problem of God and evil. See *Theodicy.*

SOURCE AND FURTHER READING: Nahum Glatzer, ed., *The Dimensions of Job*, an anthology of wide-ranging reflections on the themes raised in Job.

RUTH AND NAOMI

"Your People Shall Be My People, and Your God
My God" (Ruth 1:16)

IN FOUR SIMPLE HEBREW WORDS, RUTH, A MOABITE WOMAN WHO wishes to convert to Judaism, describes the essence of what it means to be a Jew. "*Ameikh ami, ve'Elo-hai-ikh Elo-hai—*Your people shall be my people, and your God my God." Three thousand years after she spoke these words, this inseparable fusion of peoplehood and religion continues to distinguish Judaism from other faiths.

At first blush, one might think Ruth a peculiar candidate to become a biblical hero. She was a Moabite, and Moab was a longtime enemy of Israel. She was married to a Jew, but didn't become one until after her husband's death.

When Ruth's husband died in Moab, her mother-in-law, Naomi, decided to return to Israel, where she had originally lived. Ruth accompanied her on the journey, repeatedly rejecting Naomi's fervent appeals that she stay in her native land with her native gods, and remarry. "Wherever you go, I will go," she tells her mother-in-law. "Wherever you lodge, I will lodge. . . . Where you die, I will die" (1:16–17). The friendship of the two women becomes as much a biblical model of friendship as that of *David and Jonathan.

A short time later, after they arrive in Israel, Naomi instigates Ruth's marriage to Boaz, Naomi's cousin. Three generations later, the descendant of that marriage is David (4:17), destined to be the king of Israel and the ancestor of the *Messiah.

The Book of Ruth has long served as an important antidote for any Jew prone to exaggeratedly nationalistic leanings. How chauvinist can one become in a religion that traces its Messiah to a non-Jewish convert to Judaism?

59

ECCLESIASTES/KOHELET

"Vanity of Vanities, All Is Vanity"

(Ecclesiastes 1:2)

EVERY YEAR ON *SUKKOT, WHEN THE SHORT BOOK OF ECCLESIASTES (*Kohelet*) was read in the synagogue, my deeply religious father would lament its inclusion in the liturgy. "It's a very un-Jewish book," he insisted, an odd complaint, I thought, to voice against a book in the Bible. With the passage of time, however, I have increasingly come to agree with my father's assessment. Ecclesiastes is so relentlessly pessimistic that many rabbis did indeed oppose its inclusion in the Bible. In the end, they included it for two reasons: because of their belief that it was written by King Solomon, and because of its concluding verse—which defies the rhetoric of the rest of the book—"The sum of the matter when all is said and done: Fear God and observe His commandments, for that is the whole duty of man" (12:13).

Ecclesiastes is, indeed, one of three books attributed by Jewish tradition to the tenth-century-B.C.E. king *Solomon. The rabbis believed he wrote the exuberantly romantic Song of Songs as a young man, the wise and reflective Proverbs in his middle years, and the gloomy Ecclesiastes in his old age. Today, few scholars accept the attribution of the book's authorship to Solomon. For one thing, Ecclesiastes uses words that were unknown in Solomon's time. For example, *pardes* (see 2:5), a Persian word meaning both "grove" and "paradise," first became known to the Jews probably no earlier than the sixth century B.C.E. Finding it included in a work supposedly written four centuries earlier is as jarring as it would be to find the word "Lexus" in a sonnet attributed to Shakespeare.

Ecclesiastes's central message is largely summed up in the book's second verse: *"Hevel havalim . . . hakol havel*—Vanity of vanities . . . all is vanity" (1:2). The new Jewish Publication Society translation of the Bible has rendered the verse more accurately, though less elegantly, as "Utter futility! . . . All is futile!" The book's author, who calls himself Kohelet, writes that he was the king of Israel and the son of King David (hence the attribution to Solomon), that he had accumulated great wisdom, but saw that his life was just as pointless as if he had accumulated none at all. The British-Jewish writer Leonard Woolf once expressed a strikingly similar sentiment: "Looking back at the age of eighty-eight, I see clearly that I achieved practically nothing. The world today and the history of the human anthill during the last fifty-seven years would be exactly the same if I had played Ping-Pong instead of sitting on committees and writing books and memoranda." With similar optimism, Kohelet concludes: "There is nothing better for a man than to eat and drink, and enjoy pleasure" (2:24).

Ecclesiastes's emotional exhaustion is familiar, and one that we all periodically experience; the feeling that our lives and efforts are pointless, and that none of our achievements will make a real difference. If I argue that Ecclesiastes's pessimism is atypical of the Bible, how does traditional Jewish thought address this demoralizing sense of futility? As a rule, by acknowledging that human beings can achieve only limited goals, yet simultaneously insisting that they achieve those limited goals. As the second-century sage Rabbi Tarfon put it: "It is not your obligation to complete the work [of perfecting the world], but you are not free to desist from it either" (*Ethics of the Fathers* 2:16). The twentieth-century secular writer Albert Camus expressed the same wish more concretely, "Perhaps we cannot prevent this world from being a world in which children are tortured. But we can reduce the number of tortured children."

One of the most famous sections of Ecclesiastes is its third chapter, which became widely popularized during the 1960s in a song by the Byrds:

> To everything there is a season
> And a time to every purpose under heaven.
> A time to be born and a time to die.
> A time to plant and a time to pluck up that which is planted.
> A time to kill and a time to heal.
> A time to break down and a time to build up.
> A time to weep and a time to laugh . . .
> A time to keep silent, and a time to speak.
> A time to love and a time to hate.
> A time for war and a time for peace (3:1–8)

Ecclesiastes has particular scorn for people who devote their lives to accumulating money. "A lover of money never has his fill of money" (5:9), he says in one place, elsewhere noting: "As a man came out of his mother's womb, so must he depart at last, naked as he came. He can take nothing of his wealth to carry with him. So what is the good of his toiling for the wind?" (5:14–15).

One of the book's particularly disturbing features is its wholesale rejection of an afterlife and a belief in reward and punishment. Ecclesiastes insists that God does not treat good people differently from evil ones. "For the same fate is in store for all: for the righteous and for the wicked, for the good and pure and for the impure, for him who sacrifices and for him who does not. . . . That is the sad thing about all that goes on under the sun; that the same fate is in store for all" (9:2–3). To reinforce the point, Ecclesiastes notes that there is no action, reasoning, or learning once one dies (9:10).

I sometimes wonder if, by attributing the book to Solomon, the rabbis were exacting a gentle revenge on the ancient Jewish monarch. For while Jewish tradition regards him as the wisest man who ever lived, the Bible makes it very clear that in his final years Solomon became a bit of a fool, and an arrogant one at that (see *Solomon*). Thus, in attributing Ecclesiastes to Solomon's last years, perhaps the rabbis were delivering a "hidden," if ironic, assessment of their true feelings about the value of this work.

60

ESTHER

MORDECHAI

HAMAN

*"There Is a Certain People . . . Whose Laws Are Different from
Any Other People and It Is Not in Your Majesty's Interest to
Tolerate Them" (Esther 3:8)*

ESTHER MIGHT WELL BE THE ODDEST HEROINE IN THE BIBLE: A JEWISH
girl who wins a beauty contest, marries the gentile king of Persia, and ultimately uses her position to save the Jews from a brilliantly conceived program
of extermination.

Aside from the Torah, Esther is the Bible's best-known book among modern Jews. Its story, read in the synagogue every *Purim, relates how Esther is
drafted into King Ahasuerus's beauty contest, all the while—at her cousin
Mordechai's behest—keeping her religious origins a secret. A short time later,
after Esther has won the contest and married the king, Mordechai infuriates
Ahasuerus's most powerful adviser, Haman, by refusing to bow low before
him. Haman considers it beneath his dignity to wreak vengeance upon Mordechai alone. Instead, he concocts a plan to wipe out all the Jews at once.
Using arguments that have remained part of the arsenal of antisemites ever
since, he tells Ahasuerus: "There is a certain people, scattered and dispersed
among the other peoples in all the provinces of your realm, whose laws are different from those of any other people and who do not obey the king's laws, and
it is not in your majesty's interests to tolerate them" (3:8).

The king acquiesces to Haman's plan, both of them unaware that Ahasuerus's beloved queen is Jewish.

When news of Haman's plot surfaces, Mordechai urges Esther to intervene with the king. Her first instinct is to refuse. To go to the king without
being summoned, she informs her cousin, is a capital crime. Mordechai per-
sists: "Do not imagine that you, of all the Jews, will escape with your life by

being in the king's palace. . . . And who knows, perhaps you have attained [this] royal position for just such a crisis?" (4:13–14).

Esther goes to Ahasuerus and succeeds in turning him against his evil adviser. Haman is hanged, the Jews are saved, and Esther presumably lives happily ever after.

One of the more significant, though infrequently mentioned, lessons of Esther is that the Jewish community should be very cautious before it despairs of any Jew. Esther's very name seems to betray a highly assimilated background, sounding suspiciously like the Babylonian goddess Ishtar (similar to a Jewish woman today bearing the name Christine). And one might well think an intermarried beauty queen who conceals her religious identity an unlikely candidate to risk her life on behalf of her people. But Esther does so and, as reflected by the number of Jewish women who bear her name, remains one of Jewish history's greatest heroines.

Even more than Pharaoh, Haman becomes for Jews the symbol of the Jewhater, the would-be Hitler of his day. That is why the retaliation carried out against him is of the eminently satisfying *"eye for an eye" variety. He is hanged from the very gallows he set up for Mordechai, who is in turn rewarded with Haman's former job.

For all the happiness at the book's end, the character of Haman unfortunately is far from unique in the Jewish experience. As one bitter Yiddish proverb summarizes the unhappier episodes of Jewish history, "So many Hamans, and only one *Purim."

61

DANIEL IN THE LION'S DEN

The Writing on the Wall

THE BIBLICAL BOOK OF DANIEL TELLS THE STORY OF A YOUNG JEW who, in the years following the Babylonian exile (586 B.C.E.), rises to a position of great power under the Persian king Darius.

Daniel serves as one of the king's three highest officials. The two officers who serve with him, along with many lower government officials, resent the power Darius has entrusted to Daniel and plot to destroy him. They entreat the king to issue a thirty-day ordinance forbidding everyone in the kingdom from addressing any petitions to anyone, including God, other than the king. Violators are to be thrown into the lion's den.

When the law goes into effect, Daniel ignores it, and continues to pray morning and night in his house. His enemies burst in, catch him in prayer, and turn him over to the king. Darius loves Daniel, and has no desire to carry out the edict. But his hands are tied: Persian law forbids a king from canceling an ordinance, even one he has issued himself.

That evening Daniel is thrown into the lion's den, and a rock is placed over the den's opening so that he cannot flee. The king is so upset about Daniel's punishment that he cannot sleep, and early in the morning he comes out to investigate. "As he approached the den, he cried to Daniel in a mournful voice . . . 'Daniel, servant of the living God, was the God whom you served so regularly able to deliver you from the lions?' " Daniel responds: "My God sent his angel, who shut the mouths of the lions so that they did not injure me" (6:19–23).

Darius is vastly relieved and issues an ordinance that all the people in his kingdom are to revere the God of Daniel.

The Talmud retells this story—with minor variations—as happening to Rabbi Tanhum. After the lions left him unmolested, "an unbeliever remarked: 'The reason the lions did not eat him is that they are not hungry.' Whereupon they threw the unbeliever to the lions, and he was eaten" (*Sanhedrin* 39a).

An earlier episode in the Book of Daniel is set at a feast in the palace of Babylonian King Belshazzar, son of *Nebuchadnezzar, the monarch who destroyed the First Temple. The king brings out the gold and silver vessels that his father stole from the *Temple in Jerusalem, and serves drinks in them to his officers and their concubines. The feast suddenly is interrupted by a giant, unattached human finger that writes letters in an unknown alphabet on the wall. The petrified king Belshazzar summons his magicians and soothsayers to explain the mysterious writing, but they are unable to do so. In an episode that recalls the Joseph story of the *seven fat years and seven lean years, the queen suggests that Belshazzar summon Daniel, who has a reputation for being very wise. Daniel deciphers the strange writing, which reads: *Mene Mene Tekel Upharsin.* He interprets this: *Mene*—God has numbered your kingdom and brought it to an end. *Tekel*—you have been "weighed" and judged and found wanting. *Upharsin*—your kingdom will be divided between the Medes and Persians. That night, Belshazzar is slain (chapter 5).

I once read of an alcoholic comedian who decided to stop drinking when he read "the handwriting on the floor."

62

CYRUS THE GREAT, KING OF PERSIA

ALONG WITH *NOAH, THE PERSIAN KING CYRUS IS THE BIBLE'S MOST important non-Jewish hero. The prophet *Isaiah, in an unparalleled burst of admiration for a non-Jewish monarch, calls Cyrus both the "anointed" and the "shepherd" of God (Isaiah 45:1; 44:28). Unlike the Babylonians, who exiled the nations they defeated, Cyrus encourages those under his rule to stay in their lands and develop their cultures. When he defeats Babylon in 539 B.C.E, he offers the Jews living there the opportunity to return to their Judean homeland and rebuild the *Temple. Although most elect to remain in Babylon (see *The Babylonian Exile*), about forty thousand take up his offer and reestablish a Jewish state under Persian rule.

In the Bible Cyrus is portrayed less as an independent Persian king than as an emissary of the God of Israel. His edict allowing the Jews to return to Palestine begins: "The Lord God . . . has given me all the kingdoms of the earth and has charged me with building Him a house in Jerusalem, which is in Judah . . . (Ezra 1:2).

Not surprisingly, Cyrus remains for Jews the prototype of a moral, philo-semitic leader. In 1917, when Lord Arthur Balfour issued the *Balfour Declaration, announcing England's support for the creation of a Jewish homeland in Palestine, Jews saw him as a modern Cyrus.

EZRA AND NEHEMIAH

*The Rebuilding of the Jewish Community in Israel,
Fifth Century B.C.E.*

THOUGH THE NAMES EZRA AND NEHEMIAH ARE ALWAYS LINKED, IT IS uncertain if the two men ever met. They remain, however, the two most influential figures in the Jewish return to Israel after the *Babylonian exile.

In Jewish tradition, Ezra is considered the more significant of the two. The Book of Ezra opens before Ezra's birth, with King Cyrus's edict (see preceding entry) permitting the Jews to return to Israel and rebuild the Temple. About a century later, Ezra is commissioned by the then Persian king to go and direct Jewish affairs in Judea. The king gives him extraordinary power "to regulate Judaism and Jerusalem according to the law of your God" (Ezra 7:14): Ezra even has the authority to punish those who violate the Torah's laws (7:26).

Upon his arrival—most probably in either 458 or 428 B.C.E.—Ezra encounters what Jews generally think of as a contemporary problem: inter-marriage. Large numbers of Jewish men, particularly from the upper classes, have taken non-Jewish wives (9:2).

Ezra's response is drastic and unequivocal: Working in conjunction with local Jewish leaders, he carries out the immediate dissolution of all mixed marriages, and the expulsion of the non-Jewish wives and children.

He then convenes an enormous gathering in Jerusalem, to which men and women come from all over the country. Starting at daybreak, he reads aloud from a Torah scroll until noon. This procedure continues for several days, at the conclusion of which all the Jews who are present pledge not to inter-marry, not to do business on the Sabbath, and to give charity to support the Temple in Jerusalem (Nehemiah 10:31ff).

Jewish tradition regards Ezra as having saved the Jewish people from extinction. The Talmud declares: "Ezra would have been worthy of receiving the Torah for Israel had not Moses preceded him" (*Sanhedrin* 21b). His pub-lic reading of the Torah democratized the holy document, making it as much a possession of the commonest Jewish laborers as of the priests. As harsh as Ezra's measures against intermarriage were, had they not been carried out there might be no Jews today; they probably would simply have assimilated into the religions and lifestyles of their neighbors.

Unlike Ezra, Nehemiah is less a religious leader than a political one. Living in Persia several generations after the return to Palestine, he still feels so connected to the Jewish community there that when he hears reports that it is faltering, he "sat and wept, and was in mourning for days, fasting and praying to the God of Heaven" (Nehemiah 1:4).

Nehemiah was the personal cupbearer of King Artaxerxes. This honored, though potentially dangerous, position involved tasting drinks prepared for the king to ensure they were not poisoned. A short time after hearing the disturbing news from Jerusalem, Nehemiah was serving Artaxerxes wine when the monarch startled him by asking: "How is it that you look bad, though you are not ill?" Summoning his courage, Nehemiah answered, "How should I not look sad when the city . . . of my ancestors lies in ruins and its gates have been consumed by fire?" (Nehemiah 2:2–3). Artaxerxes was touched by Nehemiah's pain, and sent him on an official mission to fortify Jerusalem. Despite the vicious opposition Nehemiah encountered from non-Jewish opponents of the project, he oversaw the building of a wall around the city, which restored physical security to the Jewish community there. Like Ezra, he also campaigned vigorously against intermarriage.

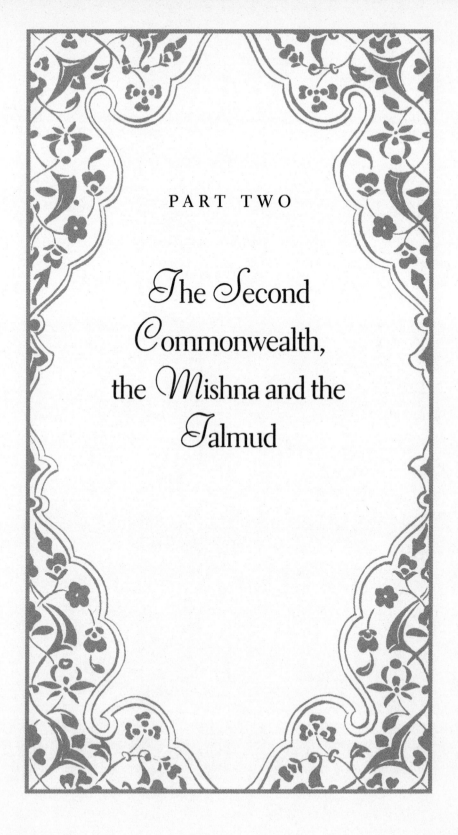

PART TWO

The Second
Commonwealth,
the Mishna and the
Talmud

64

ANTIOCHUS EPIPHANES, KING OF SYRIA, AND THE SELEUCID EMPIRE (175–163 B.C.E.)

THE SYRIAN KING ANTIOCHUS WAS BOTH CRUEL AND ARROGANT, A NOT uncommon combination in tyrants. The title he chose for himself, *Epiphanes*, Greek for "god-manifest," is itself the clearest indication of the high regard in which he held himself.

One of the unfortunate provinces under Antiochus's rule was Judea. He became convinced—possibly at the instigation of Hellenized Jews—that the Jewish religion was at the root of the widespread opposition to his policy of Hellenization, and so undertook a systematic effort to outlaw Judaism (the first, but unfortunately, not the last such effort in Jewish history).

The Syrian monarch struck first at Judaism's most basic laws and symbols. On pain of death, he outlawed *circumcision, *Sabbath observance, and even possession of a Bible. On one occasion, he arrested two mothers who secretly had circumcised their sons, and publicly paraded them through the streets of Jerusalem, their children at their breasts. All four were then thrown down to their deaths from the city's walls. Later, he ordered his soldiers to sacrifice pigs at the *Temple, then compelled Jews to do the same. A statue of the Roman god Jupiter was set up in the Temple's Holy of Holies. What is amazing is not that the Jews ultimately rebelled against these policies, but that many assimilated Jews initially went along with them.

Had Antiochus's effort to wipe out Judaism succeeded, he would have transformed not only Jewish but also world history. The Jews of the second century B.C.E. were the only monotheists in the world: Had Judaism been eradicated, Christianity and Islam probably would never have come into existence.

Antiochus's fanatical oppression happily sparked a successful revolt, led by Mattathias and the Maccabees (see the next entry). After that, Antiochus

Epiphanes (or Anthony God-Manifest in modern English) faded from Jewish history. He died four years later, in 163 B.C.E., after sacking a temple in Persia, apparently the victim of venereal disease. Antiochus undoubtedly would be shocked to learn that virtually the only people still familiar with his name are the descendants of the religious Jews he once oppressed. They devote eight days every *Hanukka to commemorating their ancestors' revolt against his attempt to destroy Judaism. See *Hannah and Her Seven Sons.*

SOURCES AND FURTHER READINGS: I and II Maccabees.

MACCABEES

HASMONEANS

MATTATHIAS

JUDAH MACCABEE

ONE OF THE SADDER IRONIES OF JEWISH HISTORY IS THAT THE Maccabees led a successful revolt against King Antiochus's antisemitic oppression (see preceding entry) only to turn into oppressors of the Jews themselves.

The revolt against Antiochus started in 167 B.C.E. in the city of Modi'in, seventeen miles northwest of Jerusalem. Antiochus, having desecrated the *Temple in Jerusalem, now sent his soldiers from town to town in Judea, ordering local Jewish leaders to offer sacrifices of swine. In Modi'in a government official insisted that the elderly priest Mattathias (in Hebrew, *Matityahu*) bring the sacrifice, but he refused. Another Jew immediately stepped forward to fulfill the royal command. Mattathias jumped up, killed both the man and the government official, tore down the altar, and turned to the crowd and shouted: "Follow me . . . everyone of you who is zealous for the law and strives to maintain the covenant" (I Maccabees 2:27). Many in the large crowd of Jews did follow him, and the Maccabean revolt began.

Aided by his five sons, Mattathias undertook a guerrilla war against the Syrian troops. Within his own community, he also had to combat some strange ideas. According to 1 Maccabees (2:32–38), in the early stages of the revolt, a large group of pious Jewish soldiers refused to defend themselves on the *Sabbath; they believed that fighting, even in self-defense, desecrated the holy day. The fighters quickly were annihilated by Antiochus's troops. Mattathias rejected the martyrs' reasoning, and ruled with admirable common sense: "If we all do as our brothers have done . . . then [the Syrians] will soon wipe us off the face of the earth." On that day Maccabees records, the Jewish revolutionaries "decided that, if anyone came to fight against them on the Sabbath, they would fight back, rather than all die as their brothers . . . had done" (I Maccabees 2:40–41; see *Where Life Is at Stake/Pikuakh Nefesh*). (Although Mattathias's decision is often cited as a precedent for permitting Jewish soldiers to fight on the Sabbath, I have always found the passivity of the Jewish martyrs inexplicable. As my father put it: "More than eight hundred years earlier, King David had fought many wars. If his opponents knew that he and his troops wouldn't fight on the Sabbath, wouldn't they have always attacked them then?")

Within a year of launching the revolt, Mattathias died, after leaving instructions that his third son, Judah, should assume the military command. Judah's fighting style was so aggressive that he was nicknamed Maccabeus, "the Hammer." The name was fitting. He "hammered away" continuously at every Syrian outpost, and two years later the Syrians sued for peace. The Jews were ceded control of Jerusalem, and in return the Syrians were allowed to maintain a stronghold, the Acra, opposite the city's walls.

Upon entering Jerusalem, Judah and his troops found the *Temple in ruins. They rent their clothes, and after observing several days of mourning, began to repair and rebuild it. In December 164 B.C.E. (the twenty-fifth of *Kislev*, according to the Jewish calendar), three years to the day since the Syrians had begun sacrificing pigs at the Temple, the Jewish rebels rededicated their holiest building. During the next eight days, crowds of Jews swarmed to the Temple to celebrate (in lieu of the *Sukkot holiday which the Jews had been unable to observe that year), and to bring sacrifices in God's honor. The holiday of *Hanukka commemorates these eight days during which the Temple was rededicated.

Distraught by the Maccabean victory, some of the local Jewish Hellenizers joined forces with Syrian soldiers and continued to harass Judah. In 160, the Syrians returned en masse, killed Judah, and defeated the Jews. Two years later, Judah's brother Jonathan emerged from a desert hiding place, and initi-ated another rebellion. He succeeded in winning a measure of Jewish auton-omy, but after a few years, the Syrians returned again and murdered him. His brother Simon now took over the battle. In 142, the Maccabees finally achieved an enduring victory, and Jews reckoned sovereignty from this year: "And the people of Israel began to write in their agreements and contracts, 'In the first year of Simon, the great high priest, general and leader of the Jews' " (I Maccabees 13:42).

Unfortunately, the Maccabees were more noble in opposition than in power. They had grown so accustomed to fighting that they seemed inca-pable of working with anyone who disagreed with them about anything. Simon's grandson, King Alexander Yannai, executed eight hundred of his *Pharisee opponents, after first forcing them to witness the murders of their wives and children. While the slaughter was going on, Yannai was present, hosting a Greek-style drinking party. (For Jews the episode was doubly tragic; it was as if the descendants of the *Marranos had later become the leaders of the *Spanish Inquisition.)

The Maccabees' terrible moral and religious decline explains why there is almost no mention of them in the Talmud. Today, in fact, when Jews think of the miracle of Hanukka, they are less apt to think of the Maccabean rebellion than of the small cruse of oil that burned for eight days when the Temple was rededicated.

The term "Hasmoneans" is used interchangeably in Jewish sources for Maccabees. It is the term by which *Josephus called the Maccabees, but is nowhere found in the Book of Maccabees itself.

In 63 B.C.E., during a civil war that erupted between two Hasmonean brothers, the Romans came to adjudicate and ended up occupying Jerusalem. The tragedy was now complete. The original Maccabees had freed the Jews from foreign rule; their corrupt descendants now returned the Jews to subjugation under an alien (and pagan) power. The Maccabees had themselves become the kind of Jews that their great-grandfather, Mattathias, had once killed as traitors. Their fate inspires one to a paraphrase of David's lament over *Saul and Jonathan, "How [the descendants of] the mighty have fallen" (II Samuel 1:25). See *Rome Takes Over Jerusalem*.

SOURCES AND FURTHER READINGS: Elias Bickerman, *From Ezra to the Last of the Maccabees*; Elias Bickerman, "The Maccabean Uprising: An Interpretation," in Judah Goldin, ed., *The Jewish Expression*, pp. 66–86.

66

HANNAH AND HER SEVEN SONS

PERHAPS THE SADDEST OF ALL JEWISH STORIES IS THE ONE ABOUT HANnah, whose seven sons sacrificed their lives rather than bow to an idol.

The whole family had been captured by Antiochus's troops and were brought before the Syrian tyrant. He ordered the oldest boy to worship an idol. The boy refused, citing the biblical verse: "I the Lord am your God" (Exodus 20:2), and the king had him summarily executed.

The second son followed in his brother's path, and his refusal to worship the idol was supported by yet another scriptural verse: "You shall have no other god besides Me" (Exodus 20:3). The third, fourth, fifth, and sixth sons acted the same way; each, in turn, was killed.

Finally, Antiochus came to the seventh son, a young boy. "Worship the idol," the emperor commanded. The boy refused. Either from pity for the child because of his youth or, more probably, to show his subjects that he could compel obedience, Antiochus whispered a compromise to the child. He would drop his ring on the floor; all the boy had to do to live was pick it up and bring it to him. Antiochus told the boy that the witnesses present would assume that he had bowed down to the king, but, in actuality, the boy would have performed no act of idolatry.

He refused. "Woe to you," he told Antiochus. "If you are so worried about your honor, how much more must I worry about the honor of God." Antiochus ordered that the child be killed.

Before the boy was taken away, his mother asked that she be permitted a moment with him, to "kiss him a little." She leaned over and said to him, "My son, go and say to Abraham your father, 'You erected one altar [on which you prepared to sacrifice Isaac—see *The Binding of Isaac*], I have erected seven altars.'" The mother then went up on the roof, hurled herself down, and died.

In Jewish tradition, Hannah and her seven sons are models of Jews who died *al kiddush ha-Shem*—to sanctify God's name.

SOURCES: There are several versions of the Hannah story. I have followed the account appearing in the Babylonian Talmud, *Gittin* 57b. Another version appears in II Maccabees, ch. 7, in which the emperor demands that the boys eat swine. Normally, a Jew is permitted to eat pig if his life is at stake, but in a time of persecution—when an attempt is being made to destroy Judaism—every Jew is commanded to sacrifice his life for even the most minor commandment. See *Where Life Is at Stake/Pikuakh Nefesh.*

ROME TAKES OVER JERUSALEM,
63 B.C.E.

IT IS ONE OF THE LESS PROUD FACTS OF JEWISH HISTORY THAT ROME occupied Jerusalem in 63 B.C.E. not by invasion, but by invitation.

When Queen Shlomtzion Alexandra died in 67 B.C.E., the kingship logically should have passed to her eldest son, Hyrcanus II. His younger brother, Aristobulus, however, commanded support from the army and ousted him. The supporters of each brother soon were engaged in a full-scale civil war. At the time this conflict was going on, Rome was in the process of annexing Judea's neighbor, Syria. The two brothers decided to submit their dispute to Pompey, the Roman general in Syria, who ruled in favor of Hyrcanus, apparently believing him to be the more pliable of the two. No match for the Roman Army, Aristobulus surrendered to Pompey. Hyrcanus's ability to rule depended now entirely on Roman support; thus, he invited the Roman Army to occupy Jerusalem.

Pompey encountered resistance only at the Temple Mount. After a three-month siege, the Romans succeeded in entering the *Temple after killing several thousand of its priests and defenders. Pompey further horrified Jewish sensibilities by walking straight into the Temple's Holy of Holies, a room which, according to Jewish law, was to be entered only once a year, on *Yom Kippur and then only by the High Priest.

Pompey's occupation marked the end of the Jewish state's independence. He wasted no time in converting the Jewish kingdom into a Roman tributary. Hyrcanus's major responsibility was to collect the tribute for his Roman masters.

The Jews of the first century B.C.E. must have reflected often and sadly on the fact that this had all come about because *Jews* had called in Rome to settle an internal Jewish dispute. As if to discourage excessive Jewish breast-beating over Hyrcanus and Aristobulus's self-destructive act, historian Menachem Stern suggests the following meager consolation: "Once Rome had decided to annex Syria, its intervention in Judah became inevitable. The fraternal war that broke out . . . only accelerated the intervention."

SOURCES AND FURTHER READINGS: M. Stern, "The Period of the Second Temple," in H. H. Ben-Sasson, ed., A *History of the Jewish People*, pp. 222–223; Uriel Rappaport, in the *Encyclopedia Judaica*, vol. 8, pp. 1145–1146.

HILLEL

*The Golden Rule: What Is Hateful Unto You,
Do Not Do Unto Your Neighbor."*

The Prosbul

HILLEL IS JUDAISM'S MODEL HUMAN BEING. THE VIRTUES JEWISH sources ascribe to him are curiously similar to those ascribed to that model American, Abraham Lincoln. Both possess a love of learning and of people, and overcome a background of horrific poverty. For Hillel two of those traits are captured in the story with which he enters Jewish consciousness:

"Every day [Hillel] used to work and earn one *tropaik*, half of which he gave to the doorkeeper at the House of Learning, the other half he spent for his food and that of his family. One day he found nothing to earn and the guard at the House of Learning would not permit him to enter. He climbed to the building's roof and went over to the skylight to hear the word of the living God from the mouths of [the great scholars] Sh'mayah and Avtalyon. It was Friday evening, in the winter, and snow fell upon him from heaven. When the dawn rose, Sh'mayah said to Avtalyon: 'Brother Avtalyon, on every day this house is light and today it is dark, is it perhaps a cloudy day?' They looked up and saw a man's figure in the window. They went up and found him covered by four feet of snow. They removed him, bathed and anointed him [acts not normally permitted on the Sabbath], and placed him opposite the fire, and they said: 'This man deserves that the Sabbath be violated on his behalf' " (Yoma 35b). Within a few years, Hillel was Sh'mayah and Avtalyon's successor, and acknowledged as the greatest scholar of his generation.

However, Hillel's greatest legacy was neither his assiduous commitment to study nor his warm personality, but his forceful intellect, which directed Judaism toward the goal of *tikkun olam, the ethical bettering (literally, perfecting) of the world. In the most famous tale told about Hillel, a non-Jew approaches and asks Hillel to convert him to Judaism on the condition that he can define Judaism's essence while standing on one foot. "What is hateful unto you do not do unto your neighbor," Hillel responds. "The rest is commentary—now go and study" (Shabbat 31a).

His most significant piece of judicial crafting concerned loans and debt collection. Apparently with the goal of preventing the creation of a permanent underclass of debtors, the Torah had legislated that personal debts were to be canceled every seventh year (Deuteronomy 15:1–2). Unfortunately, this utopian legislation hurt the very class it was intended to help. People were loath to make loans to the poor, particularly near the end of the recurring seven-year cycles.

Concerned that the utopian Torah law was destroying the Torah ethic of helping the poor, Hillel found a way around the law. The biblical legislation only canceled personal debts, not debts due a court, in the seventh year. Even before Hillel's time, people would avoid having personal debts canceled in the seventh year by transferring them to a court, which became their appointed agent. For example, if A borrowed money from B, he would owe the money to the court, which would collect the debt and pay it to B. Because transferring the debt to the court could be a cumbersome process, Hillel instituted a procedure called prosbul, by which the lender only had to note before the court that he was going to collect his debt. By virtue of this prescribed declaration, the debt simply was transferred automatically from the lender to the court.

In effect, the prosbul maintained the Torah ethic of helping the poor, while vitiating the Torah law. Of course, one can argue that there was no need for Hillel to circumvent the Torah. Instead, he should have insisted that people make loans to the poor whether they would be paid back or not. But Hillel wished to assist the poor, not to preach ineffectual sermons. In later times, the Talmud explained that Hillel instituted the *prosbul mipnei tikkun olam* (for the betterment of the world), because he saw that people refrained from making loans to one another.

Hillel's willingness to base Jewish law on *tikkun olam*, not just on tradition, established a precedent that enabled later rabbis to meet many new ethical challenges. For example, a basic Jewish legal principle is that *adam mu'ad le'olam* (a man is always liable for any damage he causes). Nonetheless, in the case of a "Good Samaritan," *Maimonides, the great twelfth-century codifier of Jewish law, ruled: "If one chases after the pursuer in order to rescue the pursued, and he breaks objects belonging . . . to anyone else, he is exempt. This rule is not [a matter of] strict [biblical] law, but is an enactment made in order that one should not refrain from rescuing another or lose time through being too careful when chasing a pursuer." The Talmud itself acknowledged that, according to strict justice, the "Good Samaritan" should be liable for damages, "but if you will not rule thus, no man will save his neighbor from a pursuer" (*Sanhedrin* 74a).

Hillel is credited with a large number of insightful proverbs, many of which are found in *Pirkei Avot* (*Ethics of the Fathers*). "One who is shy will not learn," was one of his teachings (2:5), by which he meant that a person too shy to ask questions never will achieve proper understanding. He also held that "an ignoramus cannot be a saintly person" (2:5), because righteousness requires that one do the right thing, not just have the right intentions, and this demands study and knowledge. His most famous declaration in the *Ethics of the Fathers* is "If I am not for myself, who will be for me, and if I am only for myself, what am I? And if not now, when?" (1:14).

In Jewish life, Hillel is also remembered as the perennial opponent of Rabbi Shammai; the Talmud records numerous disputes between the two men, and later between their disciples. Although each school had a large number of followers, Jewish law almost always rules in accordance with Hillel. One of the most unusual tales in the Talmud explains how this came about: "A heavenly voice declared: The words of both schools [Hillel and Shammai] are the words of the living God, but the law follows the rulings of the School of Hillel, because the Hillelites were gentle and modest, and studied both their own opinions and the opinions of the other school, and humbly mentioned the words of the other school before their own" (*Eruvin* 13b). Given that many, if not most, of Hillel's and Shammai's disputes were on matters of *ritual*, it is fascinating that the decision in favor of Hillel was made on *moral* grounds—"because the Hillelites were gentle and modest . . . and humbly mentioned the words of the other school before their own." This omnipresent emphasis on the ethical, even when matters of ritual are at stake, is perhaps the most enduring part of Hillel's two-thousand-year-old legacy.

SOURCES AND FURTHER READINGS: Nahum Glatzer, *Hillel the Elder: The Emergence of Classical Judaism*; Aaron Blumenthal, *If I Am Only for Myself: The Story of Hillel.*

SANHEDRIN

THE SANHEDRIN—THE NAME FOR THE JEWISH HIGH COURTS OF ancient Judea—were located in every city. The highest court, or Great Sanhedrin, the ancient Jewish equivalent of the United States Supreme Court, had seventy-one members and met in the Temple in Jerusalem (the odd number of members guaranteed that there would be no tie votes). The Sanhedrin was the highest legal and religious authority in Jewish life. Its most important mission was to interpret biblical laws, as the Supreme Court's mandate is to interpret the Constitution. Unlike the Supreme Court, however, it was also empowered to enact new laws when necessary. The justices met daily from morning until midafternoon.

The local courts, or Lesser Sanhedrin, consisted of twenty-three justices. They were situated throughout Judea, and presided over civil and criminal cases.

In criminal cases, the judicial system practiced by the Sanhedrin differed greatly from the American adversary system. When a capital case came before it, the Sanhedrin's head would appoint different judges, some to investigate evidence pointing to the defendant's guilt, others to probe evidence pointing to his innocence. The examining judges then reported the results of their inquiries to their colleagues. Unlike contemporary prosecutors or defense attorneys, the Sanhedrin's judges had no vested interest in developing a good record of convictions, or in enabling guilty defendants to be acquitted. A peculiar provision of the Sanhedrin regulated that if its members voted unanimously to convict a defendant in a capital case, the person was not executed; the very unanimity of the vote made the rabbis fearful that no judge had actively sought exonerating evidence. Otherwise, thirty-seven or more justices were sufficient to sustain a conviction. On days when the judges voted in a capital case, they were forbidden to eat food or drink liquor. When the vote was taken, the youngest, most recently appointed justices voted first, so that they would not be intimidated by the votes of their more mature colleagues.

Two talmudic texts (*Sanhedrin* 17a and 36b) cite the necessary qualifications for Sanhedrin appointees: They had to be well versed in Torah and in the general sciences, including both mathematics and medicine. Although Jewish law forbade witchcraft, Sanhedrin judges had to be familiar with its ceremonies, so that they would be qualified to judge a case involving witches. They also had to be fluent in many languages, to avoid relying on interpreters. Aged men and eunuchs were not appointed to the court, because it was feared they would be lacking in tenderness. The same was true for men who were childless; the rabbis believed that the experience of raising children makes a person more sympathetic and humble. *Maimonides later codified seven additional qualifications for being appointed a judge in a Jewish court: "wisdom, humility, fear of God, hatred of ill-gotten gain, love of truth, love of one's fellow man, and a good reputation."

After the Second Temple's destruction in 70 C.E., the Sanhedrin was reconvened in Yavneh. After the failure of the *Bar-Kokhba revolt, it met in various Galilean cities. The Sanhedrin seems to have disbanded under Roman persecution about 425 C.E.

When Israel was founded in 1948, the state's first minister of religion, Rabbi Judah Leib Maimon, urged that a modern Sanhedrin be reconstituted to deal with new dilemmas facing Jewish life. Most of the country's religious leadership rejected his proposal, feeling it would be presumptuous for modern Jews to arrogate to themselves the stature of the great rabbis of the Talmud. When the secular prime minister David *Ben-Gurion sarcastically asked Maimon where, in any case, he would find seventy-one judges who fulfilled the Torah criterion of hating ill-gotten gains (Exodus 18:21), the sharp-tongued Maimon responded, "Give me enough money, and I'll find you seventy-one judges who hate ill-gotten gains." See *Napoleon's Sanhedrin*.

SOURCES: The regulations regarding the qualifications for becoming a member of the Sanhedrin can be found in Maimonides's code of Jewish law, the *Mishneh Torah*,

"Laws of the Sanhedrin," ch. 2. The statement regarding the seven qualifications for being a Jewish judge is found in 2:7. See also Gedaliah Alon, *The Jews in Their Land in the Talmudic Age*, pp. 185–252; Sidney Hoenig, *The Great Sanhedrin*; Hugo Mantel, *Studies in the History of the Sanhedrin*.

70

HEROD, KING OF JUDEA (37–4 B.C.E.)

I SOMETIMES THINK OF HEROD AS THE PUNISHMENT GOD INFLICTED on the Jews for violating a basic principle of Judaism, never to convert non-Jews forcibly. That is precisely what the Hasmonean king John Hyrcanus did in 125 B.C.E. after he defeated Idumea, a small state south of Jerusalem. He compelled the conquered Idumeans to embrace Judaism, the only known instance in Jewish history of non-Jews being forcibly converted. Among those the king brought to Judaism were Herod's grandparents.

Through extraordinary sycophancy, intrigue, and ruthlessness, Herod succeeded in having the Roman Senate appoint him king of Judea. Perhaps the most vile human being ever to serve as a Jewish king, he inaugurated his regime by murdering forty-five members of the Jewish high court, the Sanhedrin (see preceding entry). Herod did not fall, however, into that category of people who are cruel only to outsiders, and nice to their own family. He murdered his first wife, the *Hasmonean princess Mariamne, and their two sons. Later, he executed Antipater, a son from a different marriage, impelling the Roman emperor Augustus to observe: "It is better to be Herod's pig than his son." For good measure, he also murdered his mother-in-law, brother-in-law, and the High Priest. Hardly surprising that when a false rumor spread the good "news" that he had died, a popular uprising erupted against his regime. In characteristically brutal fashion, Herod had forty-two of its leaders burned to death.

When he wasn't murdering people, Herod was a singularly productive king. He beautified and massively expanded the Second *Temple, a project that occupied ten thousand laborers and a thousand priests for nine years. The Royal Portico (at the southern end of the Temple's platform) alone had

162 columns, the tallest a hundred feet high. Given that we don't know of a single strain of religiosity in Herod's soul, he apparently hoped this project would win him some affection among his subjects.

Herod also rebuilt the walls of Jerusalem, created the new port city of Caesarea, which became the Roman capital of Palestine, and constructed fortresses, theaters, stadiums, and harbors throughout Palestine. Ironically, it was this lackey of Rome who rebuilt *Masada, which a century later served as the final outpost of the Jewish revolt against Rome (see *The Great Revolt*).

When Herod died in 4 B.C.E., the emperor Augustus divided his kingdom among three of Herod's surviving sons. Archelaus, who was awarded Judea, failed so totally that Augustus subsequently banished him. From then on, Rome ruled Judea directly, through procurators. Another of Herod's sons, Herod Antipas, who ruled over the Galilee, seems to have inherited his father's sweetness of character. To please Salome, the New Testament relates, Herod Antipas had John the Baptist murdered, and his head presented to her on a platter (Mark 6:21–28).

71

JESUS

THE CRUCIFIXION

PONTIUS PILATE

THE NEW TESTAMENT

THE NEW TESTAMENT DEPICTION OF JESUS SUGGESTS THAT HE WAS largely a law-abiding and highly nationalistic Jew, and a man with strong ethical concerns. Like many of Judaism's great rabbis, he saw love of neighbor as religion's central demand. Though many Christians are under the impression that he opposed Judaism's emphasis on law, in actuality he criticized anyone who advocated dropping it. "Do not imagine that I have come to abolish the Law [the Torah] or the Prophets," he declared to his early disciples. "I tell you solemnly, till heaven and earth disappear, not one dot, not one little stroke, shall disappear from the Law until its purpose is achieved." The law's "purpose," of course, is the universal recognition of God, a goal which neither Christianity nor Judaism believes was realized in Jesus' time, or since. Jesus concluded his message with a severe warning: "Therefore, the man who infringes even the least of these commandments and teaches others to do the same will be considered the least in the kingdom of heaven" (Matthew 5:17–19).

On at least one specific legal issue, Jesus identified with the stricter rather than the more lenient rabbis. The prevailing School of *Hillel taught that divorce was permitted for any reason, while the School of Shammai only permitted it in cases of sexual misconduct (*Mishna Gittin* 9:10)—the position later attributed to Jesus in the New Testament (Matthew 5:31–32). The subsequent Catholic ban on all divorce seems to represent an even stricter legal standard than the one Jesus established.

A perennially interesting, though probably unanswerable, question is how Jesus regarded himself. Did he see himself as the *Messiah? Probably, although one must remember that in the first centuries of the Common Era the word "Messiah" had a different meaning than it has today. Contemporary believers usually think of the Messiah as a wholly spiritual figure. Then, it meant a military leader who would free the Jews from foreign (i.e., Roman) rule, bring them back from the four corners of the earth, and usher in an age of universal peace. A century after Jesus, many Jews accepted the military general, *Bar-Kokhba, as the Messiah, although even his greatest supporter, Rabbi *Akiva, made no claims regarding his spiritual greatness. Indeed, it was precisely because of the military association with the word "Messiah" that the occupying Roman authorities must have seen Jesus as dangerous and decided to crucify him. That the Romans hung over Jesus' body a sign proclaiming his crime, KING OF THE JEWS, again underscores the apparently militant and political direction of his activities.

Jesus' nationalism, which occasionally spilled over into an unpleasant chauvinism, is illustrated by a story in Matthew: "Jesus . . . withdrew to the region of Tyre and Sidon. Then out came a Canaanite woman from that district and started shouting, 'Sir, Son of David, take pity on me. My daughter is tormented by a devil.' But he answered her not a word. And his disciples went and pleaded with him. 'Give her what she wants,' they said, 'because she is shouting after us.' He said in reply, 'I was sent only to the lost sheep of the House of Israel.' But the woman had come up and was kneeling at his feet.

'Lord,' she said, 'help me.' He replied, 'It is not fair to take the children's food and throw it to the house-dogs.' She retorted, 'Ah, yes, sir; but even house-dogs can eat the scraps that fall from their master's table.' Then Jesus answered her, "Woman, you have great faith. Let your wish be granted' " (Matthew 15:21–28).

Concerning Jesus' executioner, Pontius Pilate, we have a considerable body of data that contradicts the largely sympathetic portrayal of him in the New Testament. Even among the long line of cruel procurators who ruled Judea, Pilate stood out as a notoriously vicious man. He eventually was replaced after murdering a group of Samaritans: The Romans realized that keeping him in power would only provoke continual rebellions. The gentle, kind-hearted Pilate of the New Testament—who in his "heart of hearts" really did not want to harm Jesus—is fictional. Like most fictions, the story was created with a purpose. When the New Testament was written, Christianity was banned by Roman law. The Romans, well aware that they had executed Christianity's founder—indeed the reference to Jesus' crucifixion by the Roman historian Tacitus is among the earliest allusions to him outside the New Testament—had no reason to rescind their anti-Christian legislation. Christianity's only hope for gaining legitimacy was to "prove" to Rome that its crucifixion of Jesus had been a terrible error, and had only come about because the Jews forced Pilate to do it. Thus, the New Testament depicts Pilate as wishing to spare Jesus from punishment, only to be stymied by a large Jewish mob yelling, "Crucify him." The account ignores one simple fact. Pilate's power in Judea was absolute. Had he wanted to absolve Jesus, he would have done so: He certainly would not have allowed a mob of Jews, whom he detested, to force him into killing someone whom he admired.

Crucifixion itself, a Roman form of execution, was forbidden by Jewish law because it was torture. Some 50,000 to 100,000 Jews were themselves crucified by the Romans in the first century. How ironic, therefore, that Jews have historically been associated with the cross as the ones who brought about Jesus' crucifixion (see *Christ-killer*).

Is there a Jewish consensus on how *Jews* are to regard Jesus? Perhaps not, but in recent decades many Jewish scholars have tended to view him as one of several first- and second-century Jews who claimed to be the Messiah, and who attempted to rid Judea of its Roman oppressors. However, almost no Jewish scholars believe that Jesus intended to start a new religion. Were Jesus to return today, most Jews believe, he undoubtedly would feel more at home in a synagogue than a church. An increasing number of Jewish scholars believe that Christianity's real founder was another first-century Jew, Paul (see next entry).

Most statements attributed to Jesus in the New Testament conform to Jewish teachings. This is, of course, not surprising, since Jesus generally practiced *Pharisaic (rabbinic) Judaism. However, at least three innovative teachings ascribed to Jesus diametrically oppose Jewish teachings.

1. *Jesus forgives all sins:* "The Son of man has the authority on earth to forgive sins" (Matthew 9:6). Judaism believes that God Himself only forgives those sins committed against Him. As the *Mishna teaches: "*Yom Kippur [the Day of Atonement] atones for sins against God, not for sins against man, unless the injured party has been appeased" (*Yoma* 8:9). The belief that Jesus can forgive *all* sins is fraught with moral peril. Some fifteen hundred years after he lived, Protestant reformer Martin *Luther, writing in the spirit of Jesus' statement, taught: "Be a sinner and sin vigorously; but even more vigorously believe and delight in Christ who is victor over sin, death and the world. . . . It is sufficient that we recognize through the wealth of God's glory the lamb who bears the sins of the world; from this sin does not sever us, even if thousands, thousands of times in one day we should fornicate or murder" (letter to Philip Melanchthon, August 1, 1521). Humorist Jules Feiffer has bitingly satirized positions such as Luther's: "Christ died for our sins. Dare we make his martyrdom meaningless by not committing them?"

2. *Jesus' attitude toward evil people:* "Offer the wicked man no resistance. On the contrary, if anyone hits you on the right cheek, offer him the other as well" (Matthew 5:38–39), and "Love your enemies and pray for your persecutors" (Matthew 5:44). The Torah commands that one offer the wicked man powerful resistance: "You shall burn the evil out from your midst" (Deuteronomy 17:7). Elsewhere, the Torah approvingly records *Moses' killing of a brutal Egyptian overseer who was beating a Jewish slave.

America's survival in the Second World War came about only because almost all American Christians rejected Jesus' advice to "resist not evil." One of the few religious groups to incorporate this principle into their everyday life, the Jehovah's Witnesses, were used in Nazi concentration camps as barbers. The SS was confident that they would do nothing to harm them or other Nazi mass murderers. Judaism, likewise, does not demand that one love one's enemies. Jews are not commanded, for example, to love Nazis, as the statement in Matthew demands.

3. *Jesus' claim that people can come to God only through him:* "No one knows the Father except the Son, and anyone to whom the Son chooses to

reveal Him" (Matthew 11:27). The implication of this statement—and the continuing belief of many fundamentalist Protestants—is that only one who believes in Jesus can come to God. Judaism holds that anyone can come to God; as the Psalmist teaches: "God is near to all who call unto Him" (Psalms 145:18).

SOURCES AND FURTHER READINGS: Dennis Prager and Joseph Telushkin, *The Nine Questions People Ask About Judaism*, pp. 78–91. The Martin Luther quote is cited in Walter Kaufmann, *Religions in Four Dimensions*, p. 156. The use of Jehovah's Witnesses as barbers in Nazi concentration camps is cited in Evelyn Le Chene, *Mauthausen*, p. 130. My understanding of Jesus has been largely shaped by Hyam Maccoby, *Revolution in Judaea*.

PAUL

ACCORDING TO HIS OWN AUTOBIOGRAPHICAL ACCOUNT, PAUL OF TARsus grew up as a religious Jew named Saul. In his youth, he writes, he was a Pharisee (see next entry) and a follower of Rabbi Gamliel; he claims that he even persecuted Jesus' followers for their false beliefs.

On a trip to Damascus, Paul had a mind-altering experience, a vision of Jesus as god. This vision transformed not only his own life, but the history of the world as well. Before Paul's vision, Jesus' followers saw themselves as Jews and observed the Torah. The characteristic that set them apart from other Jews was their belief that Jesus was the *Messiah, and that he would one day return to redeem the Jewish people.

Paul radically redefined this small Jewish sect into a new religion that sharply broke with Judaism. According to him, what mattered to God was not observance of the Torah, but faith in Jesus. Those surviving Christians who had known Jesus personally—Paul had not—strenuously resisted this teaching. The New Testament Book of Acts 10:14 records that Peter, whom the Catholic Church regards as its first pope, scrupulously observed *kashrut. According to Acts 2:46 and 3:1, Jesus' disciples regularly prayed at the Temple. Jesus' brother, James, dispatched emissaries to teach that everyone born

Jewish was required to be circumcised (Acts 15:1; see also Galatians 2:12):
He also ordered Paul to observe Jewish law (Acts 21:24). Paul rejected James's
command. "We conclude," he taught instead, "that a man is put right with
God *only through faith* and not by doing what the Law commands" (Romans
3:28; my emphasis).

Paul's, not James's, teaching prevailed in Christianity. Consequently,
Catholics came to assess people's righteousness in God's eyes primarily by virtue
of their faith in Jesus as well as their performance of the sacraments. Protestantism's founder, Martin *Luther, differed from the Church only in teaching
that *faith* alone (without sacraments) is sufficient. In *On Christian Liberty*, a
pamphlet he issued in 1520, Luther wrote: "Above all things, bear in mind what
I have said, that faith alone without works, justifies, sets free and saves."

Paul vigorously fought the Jewish belief that observing the Torah's ritual
and ethical laws made one righteous in God's eyes. If that were true, he reasoned, people could achieve righteousness through their own efforts: It
would mean that there was no purpose to the crucifixion, and "Christ would
have died in vain" (Galatians 2:21).

Paul believed, as did the Jews, that God had given mankind the Torah.
However, unlike the Jews, he maintained that people could only be saved if
they followed the Torah's laws perfectly. Since it is impossible to do so, and
since God will damn people for any violations whatsoever, the Torah's many
laws must be seen as a curse, not a blessing. To be saved, mankind must be
redeemed from the Law, a redemption which can only come through belief
in Jesus (see Galatians 3:10, 21–22; and Romans 3:28).

Judaism rejected virtually every element in Paul's reasoning process.
While it advocated complete observance of the Torah, it also recognized that
people inevitably would sin (Ecclesiastes 7:20). Well before Jesus and Paul, it
had worked out an extensive process for repentance (known in Hebrew as
*teshuva). Unfortunately, Paul's claim that God damns people for violating
any Torah law has helped lead many people in the Western world to believe
that the God of the Hebrew Bible is a harsh, vengeful figure.

As long as the small sect of Christians differed from their fellow Jews only
with regard to certain beliefs about Jesus, they remained part of the Jewish
community. But once Paul dropped the Torah, and dropped any legal
requirements for converting to Judaism, Christianity ceased being a sect and
became a separate religion. From the perspective of Christianity, this made
Paul into a great hero, Saint Paul. Most Jews find it hard to regard him with
equal adulation.

SOURCES AND FURTHER READINGS: Two contrasting Jewish views of Paul—the first hostile, the second far more sympathetic—are found in Hyam Maccoby, *The Mythmaker: Paul and the Invention of Christianity*, and Richard Rubenstein, *My Brother Paul*. See also Alan Segal, *Paul the Convert*; E. P. Sanders, *Paul and Palestinian Judaism*; Dennis Prager and Joseph Telushkin, *The Nine Questions People Ask About Judaism*, pp. 78–91.

73

PHARISEES

SADDUCEES

ESSENES

DEAD SEA SECT

MANY JEWS THINK THAT THE CURRENT DIVISION OF THEIR COMMUnity into different denominations is a new phenomenon, that before modernity all Jews thought and acted alike. In actuality, the Jewish sects that existed during the *Second Temple period had differences as profound as those that separate Reform, Conservative, and Orthodox Judaism today.

Pharisees.   The most important thing to know about the Pharisees is that they are the ancestors of all contemporary Jews. The other sects that existed contemporaneously with them died out shortly after the Second Temple's destruction. Once they disappeared, the Pharisees no longer were called by that name; their religious practices became normative Judaism. *Unfortunately*, at the very time all Jews were increasingly identifying as Pharisees, the word began to acquire a new, highly pejorative meaning. The New Testament repeatedly depicted the Pharisees as small-minded religious hypocrites. Eventually, the word "pharisee" came to be synonymous in English with "hypocrite"—a distortion as obnoxious to Jews as the expression "to jew," meaning "to bargain down or to cheat." In actuality, the greatest teachers of talmudic Judaism, men like *Hillel, Rabbi *Yochanan ben Zakkai, and Rabbi *Akiva, were Pharisees.

The Pharisees' understanding of Judaism was characterized by their belief in the *Oral Law. They believed that when God gave the Torah to *Moses, He also gave him an oral tradition that specified precisely how its laws were to be carried out. For example, although the Torah demands "an eye for an eye," the Pharisees maintained that God never intended that physical retribution be exacted. Rather, a person who blinded another was required to pay the victim the value of the lost eye (for the reasoning behind this ruling, see *An Eye for an Eye*). The Pharisees believed that the Oral Law also empowered them to introduce necessary changes into Jewish law, and to apply the law to unanticipated circumstances.

In a famous legend (*Aggadata*) in the Talmud, the rabbis describe Moses being summoned forward some thirteen hundred years to sit in on a lecture by Rabbi Akiva. Moses understands nothing of what Akiva is expounding and is growing increasingly depressed. Then Akiva announces a specific ruling and his disciples say to him, "From where do you know it?" He answers, "It is a law given unto Moses at Sinai." At that point, the Talmud says, Moses is comforted (*Menakhot* 29b). Akiva, of course, was not lying when he said, "It is a law given unto Moses at Sinai." He saw himself as issuing a ruling based on principles that Moses had established.

In defiance of their Sadducean opponents, the Pharisees also believed in an *afterlife in which God rewards the righteous and punishes the wicked. They also believed in the coming of a *Messiah, who would usher in an age of universal peace and return the Jewish people from the four corners of the earth to Israel. Finally, they believed in the somewhat paradoxical notion that human beings have full freedom of moral choice even though God knows every detail of the future.

Sadducees. The Pharisees' opponents, the Sadducees, generally belonged to the wealthier classes: Many were priests who served at the Temple. While the Sadducees had some orally transmitted traditions of their own explaining how to carry out the Torah's law, they rejected the Oral Law of the Pharisees, and came close to being biblical literalists. For example, they interpreted literally *"an eye for an eye." They rejected the notion of an afterlife because it did not appear in the Torah.

Their major religious focus apparently was the Temple rituals and sacrifices. The Pharisees complained about what they felt was the Sadducees' obsessive interest in these matters: "the [ritual] uncleanness of the knife [used in a murder at the Temple] was to them worse than the murder itself"

(*Tosefta Yoma* 1:10). Unfortunately, no Sadducean writings survive, so all that we know about them comes from their Pharisaic opponents.

The Sadducees went out of existence after the *destruction of the Temple in the year 70. Their religious life was apparently so centered around the Temple that its destruction robbed them of their *raison d'être*. Some scholars speculate that the religious practices of the medieval *Karaites (a Jewish sect that also rejected the Oral Law) were based in part on Sadducean teachings.

Essenes. In drawing historical parallels it is sometimes hard not to be reductionist; nonetheless, the third sect, the Essenes, come across as an ascetic and disciplined group of ancient hippies. Believing that city life was corrupting, they moved to sparsely populated parts of Palestine, particularly to the desert near the Dead Sea. Most Essene communities were celibate; thus, their survival depended on constantly winning new converts. More than anything else, their celibacy is probably what accounted for the group's short life-span.

Unlike the Sadducees, the Essenes wanted nothing to do with the Temple; they apparently felt it had been corrupted by the Sadducean priests. The Essene communities practiced very strict laws of purity and impurity; immersion in a ritual bath seems to have been one of their most important ceremonies.

The Essenes were not tolerant of dissent, and members who violated the group's regulations were excommunicated. Reputedly, this punishment was sometimes in effect a death sentence for those proscribed individuals who continued to believe that the only ritually permitted food was that prepared in the community. Once that food source was cut off, they starved.

Essene regulations resembled those of a monastic order. Members ate their meals together in strict silence, except for prayers at beginning and end. They had no private dwellings, but lived together and pooled their income.

Dead Sea Sect. Among the sects living in the desert was another that came to be known as the Dead Sea Sect. Its existence, and its writings, were unknown until 1947, when a Bedouin shepherd discovered scrolls they had left behind in the cave of Qumran. The scrolls of this sect suggest that they were an extremist offshoot of the Essenes.

SOURCES AND FURTHER READINGS: Josephus, *The Jewish War*, has an account of each sect's main beliefs. See also Lee Levine, ed., *Jewish Sects, Parties and Ideologies in the Second Temple*.

74

THE GREAT REVOLT (66–70 C.E.)
Zealots

THE JEWS' GREAT REVOLT AGAINST ROME IN 66 C.E. LED TO ONE OF the greatest catastrophes in Jewish life and, in retrospect, might well have been a terrible mistake.

No one could argue with the Jews for wanting to throw off Roman rule. Since the Romans had first occupied Israel in 63 B.C.E., their rule had grown more and more onerous. From almost the beginning of the Common Era, Judea was ruled by Roman procurators, whose chief responsibility was to collect and deliver an annual tax to the empire. Whatever the procurators raised beyond the quota assigned, they could keep. Not surprisingly, they often imposed confiscatory taxes. Equally infuriating to the Judeans, Rome took over the appointment of the High Priest (a turn of events that the ancient Jews appreciated as much as modern Catholics would have appreciated Mussolini appointing the popes). As a result, the High Priests, who represented the Jews before God on their most sacred occasions, increasingly came from the ranks of Jews who collaborated with Rome.

At the beginning of the Common Era, a new group arose among the Jews: the Zealots (in Hebrew, *Ka-na-im*). These anti-Roman rebels were active for more than six decades, and later instigated the Great Revolt. Their most basic belief was that all means were justified to attain political and religious liberty.

The Jews' anti-Roman feelings were seriously exacerbated during the reign of the half-crazed emperor Caligula, who in the year 39 declared himself to be a deity and ordered his statue to be set up at every temple in the Roman Empire. The Jews, alone in the empire, refused the command; they would not defile God's Temple with a statue of pagan Rome's newest deity.

Caligula threatened to destroy the Temple, so a delegation of Jews was sent to pacify him. To no avail. Caligula raged at them, "So you are the enemies of the gods, the only people who refuse to recognize my divinity." Only the emperor's sudden, violent death saved the Jews from wholesale massacre.

Caligula's action radicalized even the more moderate Jews. What assurance did they have, after all, that another Roman ruler would not arise and try to defile the Temple or destroy Judaism altogether? In addition, Caligula's sudden demise might also have been interpreted as confirming the Zealots' belief that God would fight alongside the Jews if only they would have the courage to confront Rome.

In the decades after Caligula's death, Jews found their religion subject to periodic gross indignities, Roman soldiers exposing themselves in the Temple on one occasion, and burning a Torah scroll on another.

Ultimately, the combination of financial exploitation, Rome's unbridled contempt for Judaism, and the unabashed favoritism that the Romans extended to gentiles living in Israel brought about the revolt.

In the year 66, Florus, the last Roman procurator, stole vast quantities of silver from the Temple. The outraged Jewish masses rioted and wiped out the small Roman garrison stationed in Jerusalem. Cestius Gallus, the Roman ruler in neighboring Syria, sent in a larger force of soldiers. But the Jewish insurgents routed them as well.

This was a heartening victory that had a terrible consequence: Many Jews suddenly became convinced that they could defeat Rome, and the Zealots' ranks grew geometrically. Never again, however, did the Jews achieve so decisive a victory.

When the Romans returned, they had 60,000 heavily armed and highly professional troops. They launched their first attack against the Jewish state's most radicalized area, the Galilee in the north. The Romans vanquished the Galilee, and an estimated 100,000 Jews were killed or sold into slavery.

Throughout the Roman conquest of this territory, the Jewish leadership in Jerusalem did almost nothing to help their beleaguered brothers. They apparently had concluded—too late, unfortunately—that the revolt could not be won, and wanted to hold down Jewish deaths as much as possible.

The highly embittered refugees who succeeded in escaping the Galilean massacres fled to the last major Jewish stronghold—Jerusalem. There, they killed anyone in the Jewish leadership who was not as radical as they. Thus, all the more moderate Jewish leaders who headed the Jewish government at the revolt's beginning in 66 were dead by 68—and not one died at the hands of a Roman. All were killed by fellow Jews.

The scene was now set for the revolt's final catastrophe. Outside Jerusalem,

Roman troops prepared to besiege the city; inside the city, the Jews were engaged in a suicidal civil war. In later generations, the rabbis hyperbolically declared that the revolt's failure, and the Temple's destruction, was due not to Roman military superiority but to causeless hatred (*sinat khinam*) among the Jews (*Yoma* 9b). While the Romans would have won the war in any case, the Jewish civil war both hastened their victory and immensely increased the casualties. One horrendous example: In expectation of a Roman siege, Jerusalem's Jews had stockpiled a supply of dry food that could have fed the city for many years. But one of the warring Zealot factions burned the entire supply, apparently hoping that destroying this "security blanket" would compel everyone to participate in the revolt. The starvation resulting from this mad act caused suffering as great as any the Romans inflicted.

We do know that some great figures of ancient Israel opposed the revolt, most notably Rabbi Yochanan ben Zakkai (see next entry). Since the Zealot leaders ordered the execution of anyone advocating surrender to Rome, Rabbi Yochanan arranged for his disciples to smuggle him out of Jerusalem, disguised as a corpse. Once safe, he personally surrendered to the Roman general Vespasian, who granted him concessions that allowed Jewish communal life to continue (see next entry).

During the summer of 70, the Romans breached the walls of Jerusalem, and initiated an orgy of violence and destruction. Shortly thereafter, they destroyed the Second Temple. This was the final and most devastating Roman blow against Judea (see *Destruction of the Second Temple*, 70 C.E.).

It is estimated that as many as one million Jews died in the Great Revolt against Rome. When people today speak of the almost two-thousand-year span of Jewish homelessness and exile, they are dating it from the failure of the revolt and the destruction of the Temple. Indeed, the Great Revolt of 66–70, followed some sixty years later by the *Bar-Kokhba revolt, were the greatest calamities in Jewish history prior to the Holocaust. In addition to the more than one million Jews killed, these failed rebellions led to the total loss of Jewish political authority in Israel until 1948. This loss in itself exacerbated the magnitude of later Jewish catastrophes, since it precluded Israel from being used as a refuge for the large numbers of Jews fleeing persecutions elsewhere.

SOURCE: Solomon Zeitlin, *The Rise and Fall of the Judean State*, vol. 3. It is Zeitlin's thesis, which I believe he argues quite plausibly, that the provisional government knew the revolt was hopeless, and therefore did nothing to help the Galilee.

75

RABBI YOCHANAN BEN ZAKKAI
"Give Me Yavneh and Its Sages"

WHILE ALMOST ALL CONTEMPORARY JEWS REGARD RABBI YOCHANAN ben Zakkai as a hero, many Jews of his own day saw him as a traitor, and some, such as the Jews who fought at *Masada, would have gladly killed him.

Rabbi Yochanan lived in Jerusalem in the year 70, when the city was under Roman siege (see preceding entry). To prevent any inhabitants from surrendering to the Romans, the Jewish rebel leaders forbade people, on pain of death, from leaving Jerusalem. Rabbi Yochanan was determined to find a way out of the besieged city; he realized that Rome would soon overpower the rebel forces and destroy Jerusalem—perhaps even the Temple—thereby threatening Judaism's very survival. He sent for his nephew, Abba Sikra, one of the revolt's leaders, and said: "Find some way for me to leave the city. Perhaps I will be able to save something."

"Abba Sikra replied: 'Pretend to be sick and let people come to visit you. Get something with a bad odor and let the smell become overpowering, and people will then say you have died. Then let [two of] your disciples carry you out, and no one else.'

"He carried out this procedure. Rabbi Eliezer carried him by the head and Rabbi Joshua by the feet and Abba Sikra walked in front. When they reached the city gate, the guards asked, 'What is this?' They replied: 'A dead man. Do you not know that a corpse may not be kept overnight in Jerusalem?' [The guards] wanted to pierce him through to make certain he was a corpse. Abba Sikra said to them, 'The Romans will [hear about it and] say, 'They pierced their own master . . .'

"[The guards] opened the gate and the group left. Rabbi Yochanan was carried to a cemetery outside the city, the others left him there and returned. He went to the camp of [the Roman general] Vespasian."

Delighted at the surrender of so prominent a Jewish leader—one who in addition prophesied that someday he would be Caesar—Vespasian said to Rabbi Yochanan: "You can make one request and I will grant it."

"Give me Yavneh and its sages," he asked of Vespasian; in other words, permit him to establish a seminary in the outlying town of Yavneh. Vespasian granted the request.

This tale is one of several that illustrate Rabbi Yochanan's strong doubts about the wisdom of the rebellion against Rome. He was a man of extraordinary common sense, and from the rebellion's very outset he understood that it was not winnable. It must have frustrated him terribly to see masses of Jews swept along in messianic frenzy, naively certain that God would intervene to compensate for Rome's overwhelming military superiority. Rabbi Yochanan allowed no such mystical thinking to intrude on life-and-death decisions. He once advised: "If you should happen to be holding a sapling in your hand when they tell you that the Messiah has arrived, first plant the sapling, and then go out and greet the Messiah."

When the catastrophic defeat occurred, and both Jerusalem and the *Temple were destroyed, many Jews fell into the deepest depression, certain that God had deserted them (see *Jeremiah*). Not Rabbi Yochanan. He was too busy establishing a new center of Jewish life in Yavneh. When a disciple expressed despair that the Temple's destruction made it impossible to bring sacrifices and atone for sins, Rabbi Yochanan consoled him: "My son, be not grieved. We have another atonement as effective as this . . . *acts of loving-kindness, as God says [in the Bible], 'For I desire mercy, not sacrifice' " (Hosea 6:6).

Rabbi Yochanan's academy of Jewish learning in Yavneh soon became a worthy successor to the *Sanhedrin in Jerusalem. More than any other figure, he must be credited with establishing a model of a Judaism that could survive without a Temple, without sacrifices, and even without a state.

SOURCES: The story of Rabbi Yochanan's surrender to Vespasian is told in the Talmud, *Gittin* 56a–b; I have generally followed the translation of Judah Nadich, *Jewish Legends of the Second Commonwealth*, pp. 273–275. Rabbi Yochanan's statement that acts of loving-kindness have replaced sacrifices is found in *Avot d'Rabbi Nathan*, ch. 4, Judah Goldin's translation. See also Gedaliah Alon, *The Jews in Their Land in the Talmudic Age*, pp. 86–118.

DESTRUCTION OF THE SECOND TEMPLE,
70 C.E.

IN TERMS OF SHEER HUMAN SUFFERING, THE DESTRUCTION OF THE Second Temple was hardly the worst thing that befell the Jews during the *Great Revolt. In terms of the Jewish psyche, however, it was. To this day, when Jews speak of the tragedy of the failed revolt against Rome, they usually mention first the *Churban Bayit Sheni* (Destruction of the Second Temple).

The Temple's destruction seems to have come about quite quickly. On the *ninth of *Av* (which is still observed as a Jewish fast day), in the summer of the year 70, Roman soldiers threw torches at the Temple, starting an enormous conflagration. By the time it was extinguished, all that survived of Judaism's holiest place was one outer wall, on the western side of the Temple's courtyard. This has been known ever since as the *Western Wall (*Kotel ha-Ma'aravi*); it remains to this day the holiest site in Jewish life.

The Temple's fall, more than any other loss, signaled to the Jews the final failure of the revolt. The Talmud speaks of Jews who went into a permanent state of depression, who "became ascetics, binding themselves neither to eat meat nor to drink wine. Rabbi Joshua got into a conversation with them and said to them: 'My sons, why do you not eat meat nor drink wine?' They replied: 'Shall we eat meat which used to be brought as an offering on the altar, now that the altar is no more? Shall we drink wine which used to be poured as a libation on the altar, but now no longer?' He said to them: 'If that is so, we should not eat bread either, because the meal offerings have ceased.' They said: '[That is correct, and] we will manage with fruit.' 'We should not eat fruit either, [he said] because there is no longer an offering of firstfruits.' The ascetics responded that they would manage with other fruits. Rabbi Joshua said, 'But we should not drink water because there is no longer any ceremony of the water libation.'" To this they had no answer, whereupon the pragmatic Rabbi Joshua advised them: "My sons, come and listen to me. Not to mourn at all is impossible, because the blow has fallen. To mourn overmuch is also impossible, because we do not impose on the community a hardship which the majority cannot endure." He therefore suggested three ways Jews should mourn for the Temple's destruction. "A man may stucco his house, but he should leave a little bare. . . . A man can prepare a full-course banquet, but he should leave out an item or two. . . . A woman can put on all her ornaments, but leave off one or two" (*Bava Batra* 60b). Not many Jews—particularly, I sometimes think, Jewish caterers—realize that these regulations are still considered binding.

Orthodox Jews still pray three times a day for the restoration of the Temple and the sacrifices.

FLAVIUS JOSEPHUS (37 C.E.–C. 100)

THOUGH FLAVIUS JOSEPHUS LIVED ALMOST TWO THOUSAND YEARS AGO, Jews still passionately debate whether he was a loyal Jew or a traitor. Even his greatest detractors, however, concede that Josephus's writings are the most important historical source on the *Great Revolt against Rome.

As a young man, Josephus visited Rome and was impressed by her massive military power. It is thus odd that when the Jews launched the revolt against Rome in 66 C.E., he was appointed as general of the Galilee. He later admitted that he had always regarded the revolt as hopeless.

The Galilee was quickly defeated by the Romans, with the Jewish fighters suffering massive casualties. When the city of Jotopata fell, Josephus fled with forty men to a cave. Finding themselves besieged by Roman troops, and unwilling to surrender, they resolved to kill each other. Josephus later wrote that he manipulated the ensuing lottery so that he would be among the last two to survive. He then persuaded the other surviving soldier to go with him and surrender.

Josephus charmed the Roman general, Vespasian, who appointed him to record the war's progress. Vespasian's clear affection for the Jewish general was apparently influenced by Josephus's confident prediction that Vespasian would be the next Roman emperor. In the late stages of the war, when the Jews inside the besieged city of Jerusalem refused to surrender, Josephus took up a position outside the city's gates. In a loud voice, he called to the people inside to give up the fight, even quoting the words of the prophet *Jeremiah, who, six hundred years earlier, had urged the Jews to abandon their hopeless revolt against Babylon. Josephus's appeal made little impact. The great nineteenth-century Jewish historian Heinrich Graetz posed the question: Both Jeremiah and Josephus advocated surrender. Why is it that subsequent generations of Jews regarded Jeremiah as a hero and Josephus as a traitor? The difference between the two, he answered, is that Jeremiah advocated surrender while speaking from within Jerusalem, while Josephus advocated it from the camp of the Romans. Graetz's insight is poignant but somewhat polemical. Had Josephus advocated surrender from inside Jerusalem, he undoubtedly would have been killed immediately.

After the war, Josephus went to Rome, where he wrote his account of the revolt, *The Jewish Wars*, the only extended account by a contemporary writer of the uprising. Because he was living under Roman protection, Josephus provided a sympathetic account of Rome's behavior during the war. In order to mitigate Rome's anger at the Jews, he blamed the *Zealots for the revolt, arguing that this small group of Jewish revolutionaries "dragged" the entire Jewish populace into insurrection. Josephus identified himself as a *Pharisee, and wrote of them very sympathetically.

In his later years, Josephus also produced a comprehensive work of Jewish history, *The Antiquities*, as well as a sharp, polemical response to an Egyptian antisemite, *Against Apion*.

Josephus's importance to the Christian world derives from a Slavonic edition of his works, in which he reputedly wrote of Jesus, "And there arose a man, if you could indeed call him a man." If this passage truly was written by Josephus, it would be the only relatively contemporaneous passage outside of the New Testament (aside from Tacitus's notation of Jesus' crucifixion) that speaks of Jesus. But virtually all scholars today believe that the paragraph about Jesus was inserted later by a Christian writer, and is definitely a forgery.

SOURCES AND FURTHER READINGS: Gaalyahu Cornfeld, ed., *Josephus, The Jewish War*, a very readable and aesthetically pleasing edition of Josephus's important book. William Whiston, trans., *The Works of Josephus: Complete and Unabridged*.

MASADA, 73 C.E.

MASADA TODAY IS ONE OF THE JEWISH PEOPLE'S GREATEST SYMBOLS. Israeli soldiers take an oath there: "Masada shall not fall again." Next to Jerusalem, it is the most popular destination of Jewish tourists visiting Israel. As a rabbi, I have even had occasion to conduct five *Bar and Bat Mitzvah services there. It is strange that a place known only because 960 Jews committed suicide there in the first century C.E. should become a modern symbol of Jewish survival.

What is even stranger is that the Masada episode is not mentioned in the Talmud. Why did the rabbis choose to ignore the courageous stance and tragic fate of the last fighters in the Jewish rebellion against Rome?

After Rome destroyed Jerusalem and the Second Temple in 70, the *Great Revolt ended—except for the surviving Zealots, who fled Jerusalem to the fortress of Masada, near the Dead Sea. There, they held out for three years. Anyone who has climbed the famous "snake path" to Masada can understand why the surrounding Roman troops had to content themselves with a siege. Masada is situated on top of an enormous, isolated rock: Anyone climbing it to attack the fortress would be an easy target. Yet the Jews, encamped in the fortress, could never feel secure; every morning, they awoke to see the Roman Tenth Legion hard at work, constructing battering rams and other weapons. If the 960 defenders of Masada hoped that the Romans eventually would consider this last Jewish beachhead too insignificant to bother conquering, they were to be disappointed. The Romans were well aware that the *Zealots at Masada were the group that had started the *Great Revolt; in fact, the Zealots had been in revolt against the Romans since the year 6. More than anything else, the length and bitterness of their uprising probably account for Rome's unwillingness to let Masada and its small group of defiant Jews alone.

Once it became apparent that the Tenth Legion's battering rams and catapults would soon succeed in breaching Masada's walls, Elazar ben Yair, the

Zealots' leader, decided that all the Jewish defenders should commit suicide. Because Jewish law strictly forbids suicide, this decision sounds more shocking today than it probably did to his compatriots. There was nothing of Jonestown in the suicide pact carried out at Masada. The alternative facing the fortress's defenders were hardly more attractive than death. Once the Romans defeated them, the men could expect to be sold off as slaves, the women as slaves and prostitutes.

Ironically, the little information we have about the final hours of Masada comes from a man whom the Jews there considered a traitor and happily would have killed: Flavius Josephus (see previous entry). When he wrote the history of the Jewish revolt against Rome, he included an extensive, largely sympathetic section on Masada's fall. According to Josephus, two women and five children managed to hide themselves during the mass suicide, and it was from one of these women that he heard an account of Elazar ben Yair's final speech. Josephus probably added some rhetorical flourishes of his own, but Elazar's speech clearly was a masterful oration: "Since we long ago resolved," Elazar began, "never to be servants to the Romans, nor to any other than to God Himself, Who alone is the true and just Lord of mankind, the time is now come that obliges us to make that resolution true in practice. . . . We were the very first that revolted [against Rome], and we are the last that fight against them; and I cannot but esteem it as a favor that God has granted us, that it is still in our power to die bravely, and in a state of freedom." Even at this late juncture, Elazar could not accept that the main reason the revolt had failed was because Rome's army was vastly superior. Instead, he dwelt on his belief that the Lord had turned against the Jewish people. Finally, he came to an inescapable conclusion: "Let our wives die before they are abused, and our children before they have tasted of slavery, and after we have slain them, let us bestow that glorious benefit upon one another mutually." Elazar ordered that all the Jews' possessions except food be destroyed, for "[the food] will be a testimonial when we are dead that we were not subdued for want of necessities; but that, according to our original resolution, we have preferred death before slavery."

After this oration, the men killed their wives and children, and then each other.

I suspect there are two reasons the Talmud omits the story of Masada. First, many rabbis still felt a lingering anger toward the extremist Zealots who died at Masada. We know that Rabbi *Yochanan ben Zakkai had to flee Jerusalem secretly to avoid being killed by the sort of people who died there. Furthermore, at a time when the rabbis were desperately attempting to reconstruct a Judaism that could survive without a *Temple and without a sovereign state, they hardly were interested in glorifying the mass suicide of Jews who believed that life without sovereignty was not worth living.

The story of Masada survived in the writings of Josephus. But not many Jews read Josephus, and for well over fifteen hundred years, it was a more or less forgotten episode in Jewish history. Then, in the 1920s, the Hebrew writer Isaac Lamdan wrote "Masada," a poetic history of the anguished Jewish fight against a world full of enemies. According to Professor David Roskies, Lamdan's poem, "more than any other text, later inspired the uprising in the *Warsaw Ghetto." In recent years, Masada became widely known through the excavations of the late Israeli archaeologist Yigael Yadin. In addition to finding two *mikvaot* (ritual baths; see *Mikveh*) and a synagogue used by Masada's defenders, he uncovered twenty-five skeletons of men, women, and children. In 1969, they were buried at Masada with full military honors.

The term "Masada complex" is sometimes applied critically to advocates of right-wing policies in the Israeli government. Political scientist Susan Hattis Rolef has defined this "complex" as "the conviction . . . that it is preferable to fight to the end rather than to surrender and acquiesce to the loss of independent statehood."

SOURCES AND FURTHER READINGS: Yigael Yadin, *Masada*. The quote about the "Masada complex" is found in Susan Hattis Rolef, ed., *Political Dictionary of the State of Israel*, p. 214. See also David Roskies, *The Literature of Destruction*, p. 358.

79

RABBI AKIVA (?–C. 135 C.E.)

RABBI AKIVA IS A LARGER-THAN-LIFE FIGURE, ARGUABLY THE TALMUD'S greatest scholar, and certainly its greatest martyr.

Unlike many of Judaism's leading sages, he was not descended from a prominent rabbinical family, but was the son or the grandson of a convert to

Judaism. As a young man, he worked as a shepherd and received no education at all. Nonetheless, Rachel, the daughter of his very wealthy employer, Kalba Savua, recognized something special in his spirit and agreed to marry him on condition that he start learning Torah. Such a prospect seemed discouraging to the forty-year-old Akiva, until one day he came across a stone that had been hollowed out by falling drops of water. He reasoned: "If water, which is soft, can hollow out a stone, which is hard, how much more will the words of the Torah, which are hard, cut through and make an impression on my heart, which is soft."

He and Rachel married over the objections of Kalba Savua, who immediately disowned his daughter. But despite the horrendous poverty into which the couple were thrust, she continued to encourage Akiva in his studies.

Within a few years, it was not just Rachel who recognized the special qualities of Akiva's mind. The formerly illiterate shepherd was rapidly elevated by the rabbis to higher and higher positions until finally he was recognized as the leading scholar of his age.

Akiva was courageous as well as bright. When the Roman government made the study of Torah a capital offense, he continued teaching. A colleague, Pappos ben Judah, was shocked at his seemingly foolhardy courage. "Akiva," he challenged him, "are you not afraid of the wicked government?" Akiva responded with a parable. "To what is the matter like? To a fox who was walking along the banks of a stream, and saw some fishes gathering together to move from one place to another. He said to them, 'From what are you fleeing?' They answered: 'From nets which men are bringing against us.' He said to them: 'Let it be your pleasure to come up on the dry land, and let us, I and you, dwell together, even as my fathers dwelt with your fathers.' They replied: 'Are you the animal who they say is the shrewdest of animals? You are not clever, but a fool! For if we are afraid in this place which is our life-element, how much more so in a place which is our death-element!' So also is it with us: If now, while we sit and study Torah, in which it is written, 'For this is your life and the length of your days' [Deuteronomy 30:20] we are in such a plight, how much more so if we neglect it?' " (*Brakhot* 61b).

Akiva's anti-Roman actions, however, went far beyond teaching Torah. When Simon Bar-Kokhba (see next entry) organized a rebellion against Rome in 132 C.E., Akiva became one of his most ardent followers. In an error of tragic proportions, he became convinced that Bar-Kokhba was the *Messiah, and urged thousands of his disciples to follow him in what proved to be an ill-fated rebellion. One of Akiva's contemporaries, Rabbi Yochanan ben

Torta, ridiculed him for conferring the messianic title on Bar-Kokhba. "Akiva," he said, "grass will grow out of your cheekbones and the Messiah will still not have arrived."

After the Romans put down the revolt, they sentenced Rabbi Akiva to death. He was led off to his execution early one morning, at the hour at which the prayer *Sh'ma Yisrael—"Hear, O Israel, the Lord our God, the Lord is One"—is recited. Even as he was being burned, Akiva continued reciting the words of the Sh'ma, with a smile on his lips. The Roman general in charge of the execution was shocked at his insensitivity to pain and asked him if he was a sorcerer. "No," Akiva replied, "but all my life, when I said the words, 'You shall love the Lord your God with all your heart, with all your soul, and with all your might,' I was saddened, for I thought, when shall I be able to fulfill this command? I have loved God with all my heart, and with all my might [which means, with all one's means], but to love him with all my soul [i.e., my life itself] I did not know if I could carry it out. Now that I am giving my life, and the hour for reciting the Sh'ma has come, and my resolution remains firm, should I not smile?' As he spoke, his soul departed" (Palestinian Talmud Brakhot 9:5; see also Brakhot 61b).

The quintessential martyr, Akiva died *al kiddush ha-Shem—to sanctify God's name. During the more than eighteen hundred years since, Jews have studied his life as a model both of how to live and how to die.

SOURCE AND FURTHER READING: Louis Finkelstein, Akiba: Scholar, Saint and Martyr.

BAR-KOKHBA REBELLION (132–135 C.E.)

AS A RULE, PEOPLE REGARD BOLD ACTIONS THEY ADMIRE AS COURA-geous, and those of which they disapprove as foolhardy. In 1980, Israeli General Yehoshafat Harkabi shocked Israeli public opinion by arguing that one of the great Jewish national heroes, Simeon Bar-Kokhba, the leader of a second-century revolt against Rome, should be placed into the category of the fool-hardy rather than the courageous. Harkabi, himself a former head of Israeli military intelligence, argued that Bar-Kokhba initiated a revolt that was unnecessary and, more important, unwinnable.

The reasons for the outbreak of the Bar-Kokhba revolt are obscure. Some talmudic texts claim that the Romans had embarked on a campaign to eradicate Judaism; they had made *circumcision and the study of the Torah capital offenses. The same sources note that the age's greatest spiritual leader, Rabbi Akiva (see preceding entry), enlisted in Bar-Kokhba's struggle and greatly promoted it by announcing that Bar-Kokhba was the *Messiah. Other talmudic sources, however, express considerable skepticism about Bar-Kokhba's character, and about the messianic claims made on his behalf.

If, in fact, the Romans *were* trying to eradicate Judaism, it is understandable that the Jews would have revolted no matter how hopeless the odds. But Harkabi cites a significant, seldom noted detail which suggests that the Romans were not warring against Judaism. The Galilee, in Israel's north, did not participate in the Bar-Kokhba revolt, and after it was crushed, Galilean Jews were allowed to go on practicing their religion as usual. Indeed, because of the destruction the Romans inflicted on Judea, where the revolt occurred, the Galilee became the new center of Jewish life. Less than a century later, the *Mishna was composed there. Thus, Judaism's very survival might not have been imperiled during Bar-Kokhba's time. The revolt might have been the outgrowth rather of the ongoing Jewish desire for independence from Roman rule.

Bar-Kokhba himself must have been a charismatic figure; tens of thousands of Jews flocked to join his army. In the revolt's early stages, his troops inflicted heavy casualties on the Roman forces, and even took control of Jerusalem. This was a particularly important victory because the Roman emperor Hadrian was trying to turn Jerusalem into a pagan, Roman city (a detail that challenges Harkabi's thesis that the revolt was unnecessary).

The winning of Jerusalem was unfortunately temporary and, as Harkabi notes, "In war, the main thing is to win the last battle, not the first." This, the Jews could not do. Eventually, the Romans sent Julius Severus at the head of a mighty army. The Roman historian Dio Cassius provided a detailed description of the Roman general's strategy: "He was reluctant to fight the enemy face-to-face after seeing their great numbers and desperate anger. Instead, his practice was to have his numerous soldiers and officers capture them singly or enclose and besiege them in their fortified places, thus depriving them of food supplies. In this way he was able, by degrees and with little risk, to frustrate, immobilize, and destroy them. Very few [Jews] were saved. Fifty of the Jews' strongest fortresses were destroyed by the Romans, and nine hundred and eighty-five of their most important settlements razed. Five hundred and eighty thousand Jews were slaughtered in battles and skirmishes and countless numbers died of starvation, fire, and the sword. Nearly the entire land of Judea lay waste."

The Jewish soldiers did inflict heavy casualties on the Romans, so many that when the emperor Hadrian sent notice of his victory to the Roman Senate, he refrained from using the customary opening, "I and my troops are well." Nonetheless, the Jews were defeated in battle after battle, until they were pushed back to their last fortress, at Betar, southwest of Jerusalem. According to Jewish tradition, it fell on the *ninth of Av, the anniversary of the day on which both Temples were destroyed.

By the time the Romans finished putting down the rebellion, 50 percent of Judea's population was dead. After the collapse of the Bar-Kokhba revolt in 135, the Jews found themselves outnumbered by non-Jews in their own country. The Judeans who survived the war did not fare well at all. Tens of thousands of Jewish men and women were sold into slavery, while other women were forced to become prostitutes. Jews also were forbidden to visit Jerusalem.

In the opinion of many Jewish historians, the failure of the Bar-Kokhba rebellion, along with that of the *Great Revolt, were the greatest catastrophes to befall the Jewish people prior to the Holocaust.

SOURCES AND FURTHER READINGS: Yehoshafat Harkabi, *The Bar-Kokhba Syndrome*; Gedaliah Alon, *The Jews in Their Land in the Talmudic Age*, pp. 592–637; Samuel Abramsky, "Bar Kokhba," in the *Encyclopedia Judaica*, vol. 4, pp. 227–239; H. H. Ben-Sasson, ed., A *History of the Jewish People*, pp. 330–335.

81

BERURIAH

OVER FIFTEEN HUNDRED RABBIS ARE MENTIONED IN THE TALMUD, ALL men. There is one woman, however, whose learning equaled theirs: Beruriah, the wife of the second-century rabbi Meir. In recent years she has become a heroine to religious Jewish feminists, her rising status reflected in the naming of a prominent women's seminary in Jerusalem after her.

Although the talmudic stories about Beruriah emphasize her sharp intellect, they also capture more complex dimensions of her personality. In some stories she is sweet; in others, angry, and in some tragic. The happiest anecdote is told in tractate *Brakhot* (10a). When hoodlums harassed her husband, Meir, he prayed to God that they should die. Beruriah reproached him for his violent words. "Do you justify yourself because of the Psalmist's plea, 'Let sins cease from the land?' But sinners don't have to die for sins to cease; it is sufficient that they stop sinning." Whereupon, Rabbi Meir prayed that the hoodlums repent of their evil behavior, and they did.

In another episode, it is Beruriah, not Meir, who is the angry one. Apparently, she had been offended by a popular rabbinic adage, "Don't speak much to women." When Rabbi Yossi the Galilean asked her, "By which route shall we travel to Lod?" she mocked him: "You foolish Galilean. Don't the sages teach, 'Don't speak much to women.' You should have said, 'To Lod, how?' " (*Eruvin* 53b).

The most famous tale about Beruriah deals with the paramount tragedy of both her and Meir's life. One Shabbat afternoon, their two sons died— whether they were murdered or were victims of an accident or epidemic, the Talmud does not say. When Rabbi Meir returned home from synagogue, he asked after the boys, but Beruriah put him off, so that instead he recited **havdala*, the prayer concluding the Sabbath. She then posed a question to him: "Some time ago, I was given a treasure to guard, and now the owner wants it back. Must I return it?"

"Of course," Meir said, no doubt perplexed by the query. Whereupon,

Beruriah led him into the bedroom and showed him the two bodies. "These are the treasures, and God has taken them back" (*Yalkut* Proverbs 964).

If these were the sole tales about Beruriah, she would have entered Jewish consciousness as a talented person, and as a scholarly inspiration for Jewish women. But the notion of Beruriah as a role model apparently troubled some fiercely conservative Jews, who didn't like the idea of women delving into advanced religious texts. A story began to circulate—it doesn't appear in the Talmud, only in a very important medieval talmudic commentary—that depicted both Beruriah and Rabbi Meir in a very bad light. According to the tale, Beruriah mocked a rabbinic adage, "Women are lightheaded [easily manipulated]." Vexed by her contempt for a rabbinic saying, Meir set out to prove that it was true. He persuaded one of his students to try to seduce her. When the student succeeded, Beruriah, deeply shamed that she had let passion carry her into adultery, hanged herself, while Rabbi Meir went off in disgrace. The lesson was obvious: This learned woman of easy virtue was not to be emulated. Fortunately, in modern religious life, the story has generally been ignored or repudiated, and Beruriah's good name restored.

SOURCE: The story of Beruriah's supposed act of adultery is recorded in Rashi's commentary on Talmud *Avodah Zara* 18b.

82

ORAL LAW/*TORAH SHE-BE-AL-PEH*
WRITTEN LAW/*TORAH SHE-BIKHTAV*

THE WRITTEN LAW IS ANOTHER NAME FOR THE *TORAH. THE ORAL Law is a legal commentary on the Torah, explaining how its commandments are to be carried out. Common sense suggests that some sort of oral tradition was always needed to accompany the Written Law, because the Torah alone, even with its 613 *commandments, is an insufficient guide to Jewish life. For example, the fourth of the *Ten Commandments, ordains, "Remember the *Sabbath day to make it holy" (Exodus 20:8). From the Sabbath's inclusion in the Ten Commandments, it is clear that the Torah regards it as an important holiday. Yet when one looks for the specific biblical laws regulating how to observe the day, one finds only injunctions against lighting a fire, going away from one's dwelling, cutting down a tree, plowing and harvesting. Would merely refraining from these few activities fulfill the biblical command to make the Sabbath holy? Indeed, the Sabbath rituals that are most commonly associated with holiness—lighting of candles, reciting the *kiddush, and the reading of the *weekly Torah portion—are found not in the Torah, but in the Oral Law.

The Torah also is silent on many important subjects. We take it for granted that the large majority of couples want their wedding ceremony to be religious, but the Torah itself has nothing to say concerning a marriage ceremony. To be sure, the Torah presumes that people will get married—"Therefore shall a man leave his mother and father and cleave to his wife and they shall be one flesh" (Genesis 2:24)—but nowhere in the Torah is a marriage ceremony recorded. Only in the Oral Law do we find details on how to perform a Jewish wedding.

Without an oral tradition, some of the Torah's laws would be incomprehensible. In the *Sh'ma's first paragraph, the Bible instructs: "And these words which I command you this day shall be upon your heart. And you shall teach them diligently to your children, and you shall talk of them when you sit in your house, when you walk on the road, when you lie down and when you rise up. And you shall bind them for a sign upon your hand, and they shall be for frontlets between your eyes" (see Deuteronomy 6:4–8).

"Bind them for a sign upon your hand," the last verse instructs. Bind what? The Torah doesn't say. "And they shall be for frontlets between your eyes." What are frontlets? The Hebrew word for frontlets, *totafot*, is used three times in the Torah—always in this context (Exodus 13:16; Deuteronomy 6:8, 11:18)—and is as obscure as is the English. Only in the Oral Law do we learn that what a Jewish male should bind upon his hand and between his eyes are *tefillin* (phylacteries).

Finally, an Oral Law was needed to mitigate certain categorical Torah laws that would have caused grave problems if carried out literally. The Written Law, for example, demands an *"eye for an eye" (Exodus 21:24). Did this imply that if one person accidentally blinded another, he should be blinded in return? That seems to be the Torah's wish. But the Oral Law explains that the verse must be understood as requiring monetary compensation: the *value* of an eye is what must be paid.

For these three reasons—the frequent lack of details in Torah legislation, the incomprehensibility of some terms in the Torah, and the objections to following some Torah laws literally—an Oral Law was always necessary.

Strangely enough, the Oral Law today is a written law, codified in the Mishna and Talmud (see next entry). Orthodox Judaism believes that most of the oral traditions recorded in these books date back to God's revelation to Moses on Mount *Sinai. When God gave Moses the Torah, Orthodoxy teaches, He simultaneously provided him all the details found in the Oral Law. It is believed that Moses subsequently transmitted that Oral Law to his successor, Joshua, who transmitted it to his successor, in a chain that is still being carried on (*Ethics of the Fathers 1:1).

Given this chain of authority, one might wonder why the Mishna and Talmud are filled with debates between rabbis; shouldn't they have all been recipients of the same, unambiguous tradition? Orthodox teachers respond that the debates came about either because students forgot some of the details transmitted by their teachers, or because the Oral Law lacks specific teachings on the issue being discussed.

While *Conservative and *Reform Judaism also believe that some kind of Oral Law was always necessary to make the Torah comprehensible and workable, they reject the belief that most of the Talmud dates back to Moses' time. They are more apt to see the Talmud and the Oral Law as an evolving system, in which successive generations of rabbis discussed and debated how to incorporate the Torah into their lives. Thus, they feel more free than the Orthodox to ignore, modify, or change the Oral Law.

The differing views of Orthodox and Conservative Judaism on both the antiquity and binding nature of the Oral Law are one of the major, perhaps *the* major, issues separating them.

SOURCES AND FURTHER READINGS: George Foote Moore, *Judaism in the First Centuries of the Christian Era*, vol. 1, pp. 3–124, 235–280; Ephraim E. Urbach, *The Sages: Their Concepts and Beliefs*, pp. 286–314; Hyam Maccoby, *Early Rabbinic Writings*. A traditional Orthodox view of the relationship between the Oral and the Written Law is found in H. Chaim Schimmel, *The Oral Law*.

83

BABYLONIAN TALMUD, PALESTINIAN TALMUD, MISHNA

Rabbi Judah the Prince

Tanna'im, Amora'im

THE JEWISH COMMUNITY OF PALESTINE SUFFERED HORRENDOUS losses during the *Great Revolt and the *Bar-Kokhba rebellion. Well over a million Jews were killed in the two ill-fated uprisings, and the leading *yeshivot, along with thousands of their rabbinical scholars and students, were devastated.

This decline in the number of knowledgeable Jews seems to have been a decisive factor in Rabbi Judah the Prince's decision around the year 200 C.E. to record in writing the Oral Law (see preceding entry). For centuries, Judaism's leading rabbis had resisted writing down the Oral Law. Teaching the law orally, the rabbis knew, compelled students to maintain close relationships with teachers, and they considered teachers, not books, to be the best conveyors of the Jewish tradition. But with the deaths of so many teachers in the failed revolts, Rabbi Judah apparently feared that the Oral Law would be forgotten unless it were written down.

In the Mishna, the name for the sixty-three tractates in which Rabbi Judah set down the Oral Law, Jewish law is systematically codified, unlike in the Torah. For example, if a person wanted to find every law in the Torah about the Sabbath, he would have to locate scattered references in Exodus, Leviticus, and Numbers. Indeed, in order to know everything the Torah said on a given subject, one either had to read through all of it or know its contents by heart. Rabbi Judah avoided this problem by arranging the Mishna topically. All laws pertaining to the Sabbath were put into one tractate called *Shabbat* (Hebrew for "Sabbath"). The laws contained in *Shabbat*'s twenty-four chapters are far more extensive than those contained in the Torah, for the Mishna summarizes the Oral Law's extensive Sabbath legislation. The tractate *Shabbat* is part of a larger "order" called *Mo'ed* (Hebrew for "holiday"), which is one of six orders that comprise the Mishna. Some of the other tractates in *Mo'ed* specify the Oral Laws of **Passover* (*Pesachim*); **Purim* (*Megillah*); **Rosh ha-Shana*; **Yom Kippur* (*Yoma*); and **Sukkot*.

The first of the six orders is called *Zera'im* (*Seeds*), and deals with the agricultural rules of ancient Palestine, particularly with the details of the produce that were to be presented as offerings at the **Temple* in Jerusalem. The most famous tractate in *Zera'im*, however, **Brakhot* (*Blessings*) has little to do with agriculture. It records laws concerning different blessings and when they are to be recited.

Another order, called *Nezikin* (*Damages*), contains ten tractates summarizing Jewish civil and criminal law.

Another order, *Nashim* (*Women*), deals with issues between the sexes, including both laws of marriage, *Kiddushin*, and of divorce, *Gittin*.

A fifth order, *Kodashim*, outlines the laws of sacrifices and ritual slaughter. The sixth order, *Taharot*, contains the laws of purity and impurity.

Although parts of the Mishna read as dry legal recitations, Rabbi Judah frequently enlivened the text by presenting minority views, which it was also hoped might serve to guide scholars in later generations (*Mishna Eduyot* 1:6). In one famous instance, the legal code turned almost poetic, as Rabbi Judah cited the lengthy warning the rabbinic judges delivered to witnesses testifying in capital cases:

"How are witnesses inspired with awe in capital cases?" the Mishna begins. "They are brought in and admonished as follows: In case you may want to offer testimony that is only conjecture or hearsay or secondhand evidence, even from a person you consider trustworthy; or in the event you do not know that we shall test you by cross-examination and inquiry, then know that capital cases are not like monetary cases. In monetary cases, a man can make monetary restitution and be forgiven, but in capital cases both the blood of the man put to death and the blood of his [potential] descendants are on the witness's head until the end of time. For thus we find in the case of **Cain*, who killed his brother, that it is written: 'The *bloods* of your brother cry unto Me' (Genesis 4:10)—that is, his blood and the blood of his potential descendants. . . . Therefore was the first man, Adam, created alone, to teach us that whoever destroys a single life, the Bible considers it as if he destroyed an entire world. And whoever saves a single life, the Bible considers it as if he saved an entire world. Furthermore, only one man, **Adam*, was created for the sake of peace among men, so that no one should say to his fellow, 'My father was greater than yours. . . . Also, man [was created singly] to show the greatness of the Holy One, Blessed be He, for if a man strikes many coins from one mold, they all resemble one another, but the King of Kings, the Holy One, Blessed be He, made each man in the image of Adam, and yet not one of them resembles his fellow. Therefore every single person is obligated to say, 'The world was created for my sake' " (*Mishna Sanhedrin* 4:5). (One commentary notes, "How grave the responsibility, therefore, of corrupting myself by giving false evidence, and thus bringing [upon myself] the moral guilt of [murdering] a whole world.")

One of the Mishna's sixty-three tractates contains no laws at all. It is called *Pirkei Avot* (usually translated as *Ethics of the Fathers*), and it is the "Bartlett's" of the rabbis, in which their most famous sayings and proverbs are recorded.

During the centuries following Rabbi Judah's editing of the Mishna, it was studied exhaustively by generation after generation of rabbis. Eventually, some of these rabbis wrote down their discussions and commentaries on the Mishna's laws in a series of books known as the Talmud. The rabbis of Palestine edited their discussions of the Mishna about the year 400: Their work became known as the *Palestinian Talmud* (in Hebrew, *Talmud Yerushalmi*, which literally means "Jerusalem Talmud").

More than a century later, some of the leading Babylonian rabbis compiled another editing of the discussions on the Mishna. By then, these deliberations had been going on some three hundred years. The Babylon edition was far more extensive than its Palestinian counterpart, so that the Babylonian Talmud (*Talmud Bavli*) became the most authoritative compilation of the Oral Law. When people speak of studying "the Talmud," they almost invariably mean the *Bavli* rather than the *Yerushalmi*.

The Talmud's discussions are recorded in a consistent format. A law from the Mishna is cited, which is followed by rabbinic deliberations on its meaning. The Mishna and the rabbinic discussions (known as the *Gemara*) comprise the Talmud, although in Jewish life the terms *Gemara* and Talmud usually are used interchangeably.

The rabbis whose views are cited in the Mishna are known as *Tanna'im* (Aramaic for "teachers"), while the rabbis quoted in the *Gemara* are known as *Amora'im* ("explainers" or "interpreters"). Because the *Tanna'im* lived earlier than the *Amora'im*, and thus were in closer proximity to Moses and the revelation at Sinai, their teachings are considered more authoritative than those of the *Amora'im*. For the same reason, Jewish tradition generally regards the teachings of the *Amora'im*, insofar as they are expounding the Oral Law, as more authoritative than contemporary rabbinic teachings.

In addition to extensive legal discussions (in Hebrew, **halakha*—see next entry), the rabbis incorporated into the Talmud guidance on ethical matters, medical advice, historical information, and folklore, which together are known as **aggadata* (see next entry).

As a rule, the *Gemara*'s text starts with a close reading of the Mishna. For example, Mishna *Bava Mezia* 7:1 teaches the following: "If a man hired laborers and ordered them to work early in the morning and late at night, he cannot compel them to work early and late if it is not the custom to do so in that place." On this, the *Gemara* (*Bava Mezia* 83a) comments: "Is it not obvious [that an employer cannot demand that they change from the local custom]? The case in question is where the employer gave them a higher wage than was normal. In that case, it might be argued that he could then say to them, 'The reason I gave you a higher wage than is normal is so that you will work early in the morning and late at night.' So the law tells us that the laborers can reply: 'The reason that you gave us a higher wage than is normal is for better work [not longer hours].' "

Among religious Jews, talmudic scholars are regarded with the same awe and respect with which secular society regards Nobel laureates. Yet throughout Jewish history, study of the Mishna and Talmud was hardly restricted to an intellectual elite. An old book saved from the millions burned by the Nazis, and now housed at the YIVO library in New York, bears the stamp THE SOCIETY OF WOODCHOPPERS FOR THE STUDY OF MISHNA IN BERDITCHEV. That the men who chopped wood in Berditchev, an arduous job that required no literacy, met regularly to study Jewish law demonstrates the ongoing pervasiveness of study of the Oral Law in the Jewish community.

SOURCES AND FURTHER READINGS: The text of the admonition to the witnesses generally follows the text of the Soncino translation of the Talmud. The commentary is also from the Soncino commentary, *Sanhedrin*, p. 234, n. 6. The text from *Bava Mezia* 83a is cited in Louis Jacobs, *Jewish Law*, pp. 57–61. See also Jacob Neusner, *Judaism: The Evidence of the Mishnah*; Hyam Maccoby, *Early Rabbinic Writings*; Adin Steinsaltz, *The Essential Talmud*; Ephraim E. Urbach, *The Sages: Their Concepts and Beliefs*, two volumes, translated by Israel Abrahams. H. Danby, *The Mishnah*, is a translation of the entire Mishna; the Soncino Press of England has published a translation of the entire Babylonian Talmud, edited by Isidore Epstein. A new, very readable translation of the entire Talmud, by ArtScroll, a publisher in Brooklyn, New York, has recently been completed and, with its help, an increasing number of people are now studying the Talmud daily.

84

HALAKHA
AGGADATA
MIDRASH

THE TALMUD (SEE PREVIOUS ENTRY) IS THE MOST COMPREHENSIVE
compilation of the *Oral Law. Throughout its many volumes, one finds the
rabbis engaged in two types of discussions, *halakha* (purely legal matters),
and *aggadata* (ethical and folkloristic speculations).

The opening Mishna in the tractate *Bava Mezia* is a classic *halakhic* discussion:

"Two men are holding a cloak [and come before a judge]. This one says: 'I
found it,' and the other one says, 'I found it.' If this one says, 'It is all mine,'
and the other one says, 'It is all mine,' then this one must swear that he does
not own less than a half, and the other must swear that he does not own less
than a half and they divide it [dividing means that each gets half of the value
of the cloak].

"If this one says: 'It is all mine,' and the other one says, 'It is half mine'
[because he believes that they discovered it simultaneously]—then the one
who says, 'It is all mine' must swear that he does not own less than three quarters, and the one who says, 'Half of it is mine' must swear that he does not
own less than a quarter, and this one takes three quarters and this one takes
one quarter."

The Talmud's discussion of this Mishna is very extensive, and directly and
indirectly raises numerous legal nuances. For one thing, since each party
concedes that he only found the cloak but never purchased it, what about the
man to whom the cloak originally belonged—shouldn't it be returned to
him? We must assume, therefore, that the cloak either had been abandoned
or that efforts to find the owner had proven futile. (There are extensive laws
in the Talmud dealing with restoring lost objects to their owners, based on
the biblical laws recorded in Deuteronomy 22:1–3.)

Secondly, it is no coincidence that the Mishna portrays both parties coming into court *holding* the cloak. As a rule, Jewish law accepts the principle that "possession is nine tenths of the law." In noting that both litigants are holding the garment, the text underscores that each has a tangible claim. If, in fact, only one party held the cloak, the cloak would be presumed to belong to him unless the second litigant could produce evidence that the first person had taken it from him.

Third, why the need for an oath at all? Why not just divide the cloak? The purpose of the oath is to induce fear in the liar, to discourage him from persevering in his dishonesty. Without an oath, a person might be more prone to lie, feeling that no harm is involved, since he is not depriving the real finder of something that had cost him money, but only of something he had found. Rabbi Louis Jacobs summarizes the principle behind the oath: "While a man may be willing to tell an untruth in order to obtain something that is not his, he will be reluctant to swear in court that he is telling the truth when he is not really doing so." In Jewish law, perjury is a particularly serious sin, and outlawed by the ninth of the *Ten Commandments.

Fourth, why do the rabbis impose so strange an oath? Since each litigant claims "it is all mine," why not have each one swear that the entire cloak belongs to him? What is the sense in saying "I swear that I own not less than a half." There is a moral consideration behind the strange wording. Were each party to swear to owning the entire garment, the court knowingly would be administering a false oath: *Two* people would be swearing to full ownership of *one* garment. Yet were each party to swear that he owns only half of the garment, he would be discrediting his earlier claim that he owns it all. That is why each party swears, "I own not less than a half." This is the only oath that might possibly be truthful, for the two litigants might have picked up the garment simultaneously.

As for the Mishna's second part—in which one party claims ownership of the whole garment, and the other ownership of half—why the strange wording of the oath, and why give one litigant three quarters of the garment's value and the other only one quarter? The Talmud reasons: Since the person who claims that he owns only a half admits that the other half of the garment belongs to the first litigant, the dispute facing the court is restricted to the remaining half. That half, the court in turn divides in half, so that one party gets three quarters and the other a quarter.

This lengthy discussion about halves reminds me of an old Jewish joke about a man who complains to his friend, "A horrible thing. My daughter is getting married tomorrow and I promised a five-thousand-ruble dowry. Now, half the dowry is missing."

"Don't worry," his friend consoles him. "Everybody knows that people usually pay only half the promised dowry."

"That's the half that's missing."

Aggadata refers to all of the Talmud's nonlegal discussions, including such varied matters as medical advice, historical anecdotes, moral exhortations, and folklore. One particularly well-known bit of *aggadata* is found in the talmudic tractate *Bava Mezia* 59b. The *aggadata* follows a *halakhic* discussion in which the rabbis debated whether an oven that had become impure could be purified. While almost all the sages felt it couldn't be, Rabbi Eliezer, a lone voice but a great scholar, disagreed:

"On that day, Rabbi Eliezer put forward all the arguments in the world, but the Sages did not accept them.

"Finally, he said to them, 'If the *halakha* is according to me, let that carob-tree prove it.'

"He pointed to a nearby carob-tree, which then moved from its place a hundred cubits, and some say, four hundred cubits. They said to him, 'One cannot bring a proof from the moving of a carob-tree.'

"Said Rabbi Eliezer, 'If the *halakha* is according to me, may that stream of water prove it.'

"The stream of water then turned and flowed in the opposite direction.

"They said to him, 'One cannot bring a proof from the behavior of a stream of water.'

"Said Rabbi Eliezer, 'If the *halakha* is according to me, may the walls of the House of Study prove it.'

"The walls of the House of Study began to bend inward. Rabbi Joshua then rose up and rebuked the walls of the House of Study, 'If the students of the Wise argue with one another in *halakha*," he said, "what right have you to interfere?'

"In honor of Rabbi Joshua, the walls ceased to bend inward; but in honor of Rabbi Eliezer, they did not straighten up, and they remain bent to this day.

"Then, said Rabbi Eliezer to the Sages, 'If the *halakha* is according to me, may a proof come from Heaven.'

"Then a heavenly voice went forth and said, 'What have you to do with Rabbi Eliezer? The *halakha* is according to him in every place.'

"Then Rabbi Joshua rose up on his feet, and said, 'It is not in the heavens' (Deuteronomy 30:12).

"What did he mean by quoting this? Said Rabbi Jeremiah, 'He meant that since the Torah has been given already on Mount Sinai, we do not pay attention to a heavenly voice, for You have written in Your Torah, 'Decide according to the majority' (Exodus 23:2).

"Rabbi Nathan met the prophet Elijah. He asked him, 'What was the Holy One, Blessed be He, doing in that hour?'

"Said Elijah, 'He was laughing and saying, "My children have defeated me, my children have defeated me." ' "

The British-Jewish scholar and writer Hyam Maccoby has commented: "This extraordinary story strikes the keynote of the Talmud. God is a good father who wants His children to grow up and achieve independence. He has given them His Torah, but now wants them to develop it. . . ."

A third category of rabbinic literature is *midrash*, of which there are two types. *Midrash aggada* derive the sermonic implications from the biblical text; *Midrash halakha* derive laws from it. When people use the word *midrash*, they usually mean those of the sermonic kind. Because the rabbis believed that every word in the Torah is from God, no words were regarded as superfluous. When they came upon a word or expression that seemed superfluous, they sought to understand what new idea or nuance the Bible wished to convey by using it. Thus, we find the following discussion on a verse from Genesis concerning *Noah.

"This is the story of Noah. Noah was a righteous and blameless man in his generation" (Genesis 6:9).

What words seem superfluous? "In his generation." So why, the rabbis ask, did the Torah include them?

Characteristically, more than one view is offered. Rabbi Yochanan said: "In *his* [particularly awful] generation [Noah was a righteous and blameless man] but not in other generations." Resh Lakish maintained: "[If even] in his generation—how much more so in other generations" (*Sanhedrin* 108a).

Aside from the ingenuity of these explanations, this *midrash* also demonstrates that a reader understands a text in light of his own experiences. Take Resh Lakish's point: If even in *his* generation Noah was righteous, how much more so would he have been had he lived in another society? Elsewhere, the Talmud informs us that Resh Lakish became religious only as an adult. Earlier on, he had been a thief, a gladiator, or a circus attendant. Resh Lakish knew firsthand how much harder it is to be a good person when you come out of a seedy or immoral environment. In his eyes, if Noah could emerge from so immoral a society as a righteous man, how much greater would he have been had he been raised among moral people.

Midrash continues to be created. For example, Genesis 19:26 records that when Lot and his family were fleeing the destruction that God wrought on *Sodom and Gomorrah, they were told not to look back. "But Lot's wife looked back, and she thereupon turned into a pillar of salt."

What possible relevance could this verse have to our lives? A friend of mine was teaching this chapter at a home for the aged, and the residents were debating the verse's meaning. An eighty-five-year-old woman broke into the discussion: "Don't you understand what it means? When you are always looking backwards, you become inorganic."

Finally, in modern Jewish life, the word *halakha* refers to any issue of Jewish law. If a person wants to know the Jewish law on a specific issue, he will ask a rabbi, "What is the *halakha* in this case?" The word also is used for the Talmud's legal sections, the codes of Jewish law (for example, the *Shulkhan Arukh) or any of Judaism's legal writings (e.g., *Responsa).

Aggadata, as noted, describes the non-*halakhic* sections of the Talmud, and the word *aggada* in modern Hebrew refers to any legendary or folkloristic writing.

Midrash most commonly refers to the famous compilation of *Midrash Rabbah,* a compilation of the rabbis' comments on each of the five volumes of the Torah. But to this day, you can hear a Jew who has some novel interpretation of a Torah passage say, "I want to give you a *drash* [from *midrash*] on this week's Torah portion."

SOURCES AND FURTHER READINGS: The discussion of the Mishna concerning the two litigants and the cloak is based on Louis Jacobs, *Jewish Law,* pp. 33–36. The *aggadata* about Rabbi Eliezer is particularly well translated in Hyam Maccoby, *The Day God Laughed,* pp. 141–142. A brief but beautiful selection from the *midrash* is found in Nahum Glatzer, ed., *A Midrash Reader.* See also Ephraim Urbach, *The Sages: Their Concepts and Beliefs* (two volumes); Louis Ginzberg, *The Legends of the Jews* (seven volumes); C. G. Montefiore and H. Loewe, *A Rabbinic Anthology;* Glatzer, *The Judaic Tradition;* Judah Nadich, *Jewish Legends of the Second Commonwealth;* Louis Jacobs, *Jewish Law.*

PART THREE

Early Medieval Period

UNDER ISLAM AND CHRISTIANITY

85

MOHAMMED (C. 571–632)

IN HIS EARLY YEARS, MOHAMMED HAD GENUINE AFFECTION FOR JEWS and Judaism; he willingly conceded that his knowledge of God came from the Jews. Later, in the Koran, he cited Moses' name on more than one hundred occasions, and claimed that the Arabs were descendants of the *Patriarch Abraham, through his son Ishmael. In the early years of his new religion, Mohammed even prayed in the direction of Jerusalem and observed the Jewish fast of *Yom Kippur.

Unfortunately, this deep affection turned to violent fury when the Jews refused to reciprocate Mohammed's goodwill by acknowledging him as a prophet of God. As was the case with Christianity, the Jews believed that what was true in Mohammed's message was not new, and what was new was not true. Further, Mohammed's knowledge of the Hebrew Bible was spotty. In Sura (chapter) 28:38, he has Pharaoh (from Exodus) ask Haman (of the Book of Esther) to erect the Tower of Babel, an episode in the beginning of Genesis. In addition, the Jews—and for that matter, Christians—were presumably not impressed by Mohammed's instruction to beat disobedient wives (4:34).

Unfortunately for the Jews, Mohammed's angry response to their rejection of him was recorded in the Koran, the holy book of Islam. In it Mohammed attacked the Jews and Judaism in several ways. For one thing, he made Abraham a Muslim rather than a Jew: "Abraham was neither Jew nor Christian. [He] surrendered himself to Allah. . . . Surely the men who are nearest to Allah are those who follow . . . this Prophet" (3:67–68). Mohammed accused the Jews of deliberately omitting prophecies about him from their Bible (9:32). Most remarkably, he accused the Jews of not being true monotheists, because he claimed they worshiped the prophet *Ezra as a god (9:30). This accusation is particularly shocking to modern Jews, most of whom would be hard put to identify who Ezra was.

Unfortunately, the angry words Mohammed hurled at his Jewish opponents have often been assumed by Muslims to be divinely based and applicable to

all Jews at all times. In 2:61, for example, Mohammed said: "And humiliation and wretchedness were stamped upon them and they were visited with
wrath from God." In the years before he concluded a peace treaty with Israel,
Egyptian President Anwar *Sadat was fond of quoting this verse to describe
the kind of treatment Muslims would impose on Jews when Egypt defeated
Israel.

Although Mohammed was furious with the Jews, his ultimate argument
was with Judaism. As a rule, any Jew who converted to Islam was fully
accepted into Muslim society.

SOURCES AND FURTHER READINGS: S. D. Goitein, *Jews and Arabs: Their
Contacts Through the Ages*; Bernard Lewis, *The Jews of Islam*; Dennis Prager and
Joseph Telushkin, *Why the Jews? The Reason for Antisemitism*, pp. 95–100.

86

PACT OF UMAR
Dhimmis

THERE IS A POPULAR MYTH IN THE WEST THAT JEWS LIVED AS EQUAL
citizens in the Muslim world until the rise of Zionism provoked anti-Jewish
feelings among the Arabs. In truth, throughout almost all of their more than
thousand-year sojourn in the orbit of Islam, Jews—and Christians too—lived
as second-class, and often humiliated, citizens.

Their status was still superior to that accorded nonmonotheists. In areas
conquered by Muslim troops, such people were offered the choice of conversion to Islam or death. Jews and Christians, or *dhimmis* as they are referred to
in Islam, were permitted to practice their religion. Their lives were regulated
by the Pact of Umar, a document assumed to date from around 720. It mandated that *dhimmis* acknowledge their subservience to Muslims in many
ways. As was the case with blacks in the days of the segregationist "Jim Crow"
laws in the South, Jews and Christians were obligated to "rise from [their]
seats when [Muslims] wish to sit." Both Jews and Christians were prohibited

from converting anyone to their religions, and were forbidden from trying to prevent any of their adherents from converting to Islam. *Dhimmis* even had to vow not to raise their voices when following their dead at funerals. A particularly cruel restriction forbade them to ride on horses or mules; this was considered incompatible with their low status. They were permitted to ride only donkeys, and were forbidden to use saddles.

Unfortunately, the Pact of Umar marked only the beginning of anti-*dhimmi* legislation. During the next centuries, and in diverse Muslim societies, Jews and Christians were periodically subjected to humiliating laws. They were sometimes ordered to wear ridiculous outfits, both to make them immediately identifiable and to look silly. In 807, for example, the Abbassid caliph Haroun al-Raschid of Baghdad legislated that Jews were required to wear a tall, conical cap and a yellow belt. (This decree is probably the original model for the *yellow badge imposed on Jews in medieval Europe.) In eleventh-century Baghdad, Jewish women had to wear one black and one red shoe, and to have a small brass bell attached to their neck or shoe.

Fortunately, there were golden ages when such regulations were not enforced and Jews could reach high positions (see *The Golden Age of Spanish Jewry*), and in the Middle Ages, Jews in the Arab world were generally more secure than Jews in Europe. Nonetheless, in eleventh-century Egypt, the Fatimid caliph Hakim ordered Christians to wear a cross with arms two feet long, while Jews had to wear five-pound balls around their necks, in "commemoration" of the calf's head their ancestors had once worshiped (see *The Golden Calf*). Until their departure from Yemen in 1948, all Jews, men and women alike, were compelled to dress like beggars, in accordance with their lowly status as *dhimmis*.

In nineteenth-century Palestine, before the Arab-Zionist conflict, Jews had to walk to the left of Muslims because Islam identifies the left side with Satan. When meeting a Muslim on a narrow sidewalk, a Jew was required by law to step into the road and let him pass. Synagogues had to be located in hidden, remote areas, and Jews could pray only in muted voices. In his book *Stirring Times*, James Finn, the British consul in Palestine in the 1850s, described how "Arab merchants would dump their unsold wares on their Jewish neighbors and bill them, safe in the knowledge that the Jews so feared them that they would not dare return the item or deny their purchase."

As for the twentieth century, Albert Memmi, the noted French-Jewish novelist who grew up in North Africa, summarized the Arab-Jewish condition as follows: "Roughly speaking and in the best of cases, the Jew is protected like a dog which is part of a man's property, but if he raises his head or acts like a man, then he must be beaten so that he will always remember his status." In June 1941, more than six hundred Jews were killed in a full-scale *pogrom in Iraq.

The *dhimmis'* inferior status explains why many Jews from the Arab world supported the idea of a Jewish state as vigorously as did their European brothers. Indeed, in large measure because of their bitter historical experience, the Jews in Israel who come from the Arab world tend to be disproportionately represented among the groups least willing to trust and make compromises with the Arab world.

SOURCES: Bat Ye'or, *The Dhimmi: Jews and Christians Under Islam*; Bernard Lewis, *The Jews of Islam*; Norman Stillman, *The Jews of Arab Lands: A History and Source Book*. The terrible discrimination under which Yemenite Jewry lived is described in S. D. Goitein, *Jews and Arabs*, pp. 74–78. The low status of Jews in nineteenth-century Palestine is detailed in David Landes, "Palestine Before the Zionists," *Commentary*, February 1976, pp. 47–56. The Albert Memmi quote is from his *Jews and Arabs*, p. 33. See also Dennis Prager and Joseph Telushkin, *Why the Jews? The Reason for Anti-semitism*, pp. 100–107. A general overview of Islamic antisemitism is found in Jane Gerber, "Anti-Semitism and the Muslim World," in David Berger, ed., *History and Hate*, pp. 73–93.

87

SA'ADIAH GAON (882–942)

The Gaonim

IN THE CENTURIES FOLLOWING THE *GREAT REVOLT AND THE *BAR-Kokhba rebellion, Babylon (modern-day Iraq) replaced Palestine as the major center of Jewish religious creativity. It was at Babylon's great *yeshivot, located in the cities of Sura, Nehardea, and Pumbedita, that the standard edition of the Talmud (known to this day as the *Babylonian Talmud*) took shape. From the eighth century, the heads of the Babylonian yeshivot were known as *gaonim* (singular, *gaon*, a word that in modern Hebrew means "genius"). The *gaonim*, spiritual leaders for all Babylonian Jewry, answered religious questions posed to them from throughout the Jewish world, and supervised the installation of the *Resh Galuta*/Exilarch (see next entry), Babylonian Jewry's political leader.

During five centuries of *gaonim*, we know of only one who was not a native of Babylon: the Egyptian Jew Sa'adiah ben Joseph. That the foreign-born Sa'adiah was appointed to head the Sura yeshiva reflects the extraordinary regard in which he was held. In addition to being the greatest Jewish scholar of his age, Sa'adiah was a fiery leader who did not back off from confrontations. When Exilarch David ben Zakkai insisted that Sa'adiah support a legal and financial ruling he had issued, one which the *gaon* regarded as self-serving and erroneous, he refused. The exilarch continued to pressure Sa'adiah, and eventually he and the *gaon* excommunicated each other. For the Jewish community, this made for a very serious rift. It would be as if the president of the United States and the Chief Justice of the Supreme Court each declared the other unfit for office. Sa'adiah appointed another exilarch, and the exilarch appointed another *gaon*. As the battle raged, the charges traded by the two sides grew increasingly acrimonious and ludicrous. At one point, Sa'adiah's opponents accused him of bribing government officials on the Sabbath—a preposterous charge. After many years, Baghdad's wealthiest Jew, a banker named Bishr ben Aaron, finally arranged peace between Sa'adiah and the exilarch.

Today, however, Sa'adiah is known for his writings, not his political fights. He is most renowned for his *Book of Beliefs and Opinions (Sefer Emunot ve-Deiot)*, the first systematic philosophical explanation of Judaism. That this tenth-century book is still in print (the English edition is published by Yale University Press) almost eleven hundred years after it was written indicates its extraordinary significance. Sa'adiah also translated the Bible into Arabic, and prepared a uniform prayerbook for the Jews living in the Arab world.

Sa'adiah also wrote extensive critiques of the *Karaites, a Jewish sect that preached biblical fundamentalism, and that attracted many followers of mainstream Judaism. Sa'adiah endeavored to show that the movement's literal understanding of the Torah's words often made nonsense of the Torah's message. So many Karaite scholars responded to his attacks that, *nine hundred years later*, a nineteenth-century Karaite scholar published *Karaite Literary Opponents of Sa'adiah Gaon*, a compilation of no fewer than forty-nine countercritiques of the man Karaites regarded as their foremost Jewish opponent.

A fitting tribute to Sa'adiah was rendered more than two centuries after his death by Moses *Maimonides. In his *Epistle to Yemen* the great Jewish sage wrote: "Were it not for Sa'adiah, the Torah might have disappeared from the midst of Israel."

SOURCES AND FURTHER READINGS: Alexander Marx, *Essays in Jewish Biography*, pp. 3–38; Sa'adiah Gaon, *The Book of Beliefs and Opinions*, translated by Samuel Rosenblatt; Henry Malter, *Life and Works of Sa'adiah Gaon*.

88

RESH GALUTA/EXILARCH

RESH GALUTA LITERALLY MEANS "HEAD OF THE GALUT" (DIASPORA), the official title for the lay leaders of the Babylonian Jewish community. Most Jews are surprised to learn that this position existed until the twelfth century C.E. According to Jewish tradition, the men who held the position, known in English as "exilarch," were direct descendants of King David. The exilarchs' major responsibility was to represent the Jewish community before governmental authorities.

As a rule, the exilarchs worked in close partnership with Babylon's two leading rabbis who headed the *yeshivot at Sura and Pumbedita. The religious leaders and the *Resh Galuta* were interdependent; the exilarch appointed the heads of the yeshivot, who in turn had to approve the appointment of a new exilarch. This approval was not just a formality. Although the exilarch was an inherited office, it was not automatically bestowed on the oldest son; the rabbis and leading Jewish businessmen had the right to choose the son they deemed most appropriate. In one famous eighth-century case, the facts of which are widely disputed, the oldest candidate, Anan, was passed over because the rabbis regarded him as a heretic. Incensed, he broke with the Jewish community and founded the Karaite sect (see next entry).

The twelfth-century Jewish traveler Benjamin of Tudela visited Baghdad in 1168 and was deeply impressed by the extraordinary respect accorded the exilarch David ben Hisdai. Benjamin reports that en route to his weekly meeting at the caliph's palace, the exilarch's carriage was preceded by horsemen who called out along the way, "Make way for the son of David." Jews, and even Muslims, rose to their feet in the exilarch's presence.

At varying times, the exilarchs were assigned very broad powers, including the right to tax the Jewish community and to fine and imprison offenders. The twelfth-century rabbi Petahiah of Regensburg wrote of an exilarch who maintained his own prison.

In time, many of the exilarch's religious powers were transferred to the rabbinic leadership, while the state assumed their political powers. As a result, the role of exilarch died out in the Middle Ages.

Nowadays, one sometimes hears it said of Jews aspiring to leadership roles in the American Jewish community that they want to become the new *Resh Galuta.*

KARAITES

THE KARAITES BROKE AWAY FROM THE JEWISH COMMUNITY OF eighth-century Baghdad to form a separate sect. The movement rejected the *Oral Law, and insisted that the Torah be interpreted literally. As a result, the Karaites soon practiced strikingly different rituals from the rest of Jewry. For example, they understood Exodus 35:3 as forbidding the use of any kind of fire on the *Sabbath and thus spent the day in darkness. The resulting sense of gloominess was further exacerbated by a Karaite prohibition on leaving one's house throughout the Sabbath except to attend synagogue.

Due to an argument over the meaning of Leviticus 23:15–16, the Karaites observed the holiday of *Shavuot (which commemorates the giving of the Torah) on a different day than did the rest of Jewry, and did not observe *Hanukka at all because the holiday was not mentioned in the Bible.

Widely accepted Jewish observances, such as the donning of *tefillin* (phylacteries) and the prohibition of eating milk and meat together, were rejected on the grounds that they were not specifically legislated in the Torah, only in the Oral Law. Even when Jews and Karaites agreed, such as on the right of an unhappily married couple to divorce, problems arose. The Karaite religious officials issued divorce decrees that were differently worded and formulated from those of the rest of Jewry, so that the rabbis eventually declared Karaite divorces invalid.

A popular medieval story claimed that the sect arose out of a political fight within the Baghdad Jewish community. A Jewish exilarch (see preceding entry) who was childless had two nephews, Anan and Hananiah. When the exilarch died, Anan, the older child, normally should have succeeded him. However, the Jewish communal leaders mistrusted his character and religiosity, and awarded the office to Hananiah. The outraged Anan founded an illegal breakaway group, and was soon imprisoned and sentenced to death. A fellow inmate told Anan that his only hope for survival was to convince the caliph that he was not a rebel against Judaism (if he was, the Jews had the right to demand his death) but the leader of an altogether different religion. Anan succeeded in doing so, and thus Karaism was born.

Whether this story accurately depicts the movement's origins, or was invented in order to discredit Karaism, is impossible to ascertain. The Karaites, who label the story as fiction, claim that their sect represents the true religion of the Bible, and that it was the *Talmud and the Oral Law that introduced ill-needed changes into Judaism. Indeed, Karaism might well have derived from remnants of early Jewish sects such as the *Sadducees, that had challenged the validity of the Oral Law since the Second Temple era.

During their first centuries, the Karaites had considerable success in winning adherents to their cause. The tenth-century scholar *Sa'adiah Gaon devoted a great deal of energy to refuting their interpretations of Torah and Jewish law. He might not have succeeded in convincing many Karaites, but his writings did help stem the tide of Jews going over to the Karaite camp. Since Sa'adiah's time, the Karaite community was never again very large, although it has never gone out of existence—no small accomplishment for a sect that is now some twelve centuries old. At varying times, the Karaites established centers in Israel, Spain, the Byzantine Empire, and Egypt. In the late Middle Ages, there were significant Karaite outposts in Lithuania and the Crimea. In nineteenth-century Russia, the Karaites were officially designated as a new religion and were thus spared the czar's antisemitic legislation. This change of classification literally saved thousands of Karaite lives a century later when Germany invaded the Soviet Union. In one of the most bizarre episodes of the *Holocaust, the German authorities asked three Jewish scholars (Zelig Kalmanovitch, Meir Balaban, and Yitzchak Schipper) whether the Karaites were biologically Jewish. To save the Karaites' lives, the three scholars lied, saying the Karaites were not of Jewish origin.

In recent years, Jewish scholar Daniel Lasker has offered a provocative theory on why the Karaites never became a mass movement; after all, Christianity and Reform Judaism too had rejected the Oral Law, but had much greater success than did the Karaites in gaining adherents. "An apparent reason for [Christianity and Reform Judaism's] attractiveness," Lasker answers, "was their renunciation of Jewish law as a means of salvation. If Anan had similarly encouraged a release from talmudic legislation without replacing it with his own, more stringent, code, he might have won more followers." Later Karaite teachers *did* modify some of the more stringent regulations, but by then, Lasker concludes, "the fate of the contest had already been decided."

Today there are approximately ten thousand Karaites, most of whom live in Israel. They are ruled by their own rabbinical courts. See *Pharisees and Sadducees* and *Oral Law*.

SOURCES AND FURTHER READINGS: Daniel J. Lasker, "Rabbanism and Karaism: The Contest for Supremacy," in Raphael Jospe and Stanley Wagner, eds., *Great Schisms in Jewish History*, pp. 47–72. The quotes cited in this entry are found on p. 72, n. 50, and p. 65. An account of the Nazi query to Jewish scholars about the Karaites' origins is found in the *Encyclopedia Judaica*, vol. 10, p. 776; Leon Nemoy, trans. and ed., *Karaite Anthology*.

90

CAIRO GENIZA

IN THE JEWISH TRADITION, SACRED WORKS, SUCH AS TORAH SCROLLS, prayerbooks, and the Talmud, are regarded as too hallowed to be thrown out. When they become unusable, they are generally buried in the ground—indeed, in 1988, several Torah scrolls that had been partially burned by vandals were publicly interred in a New York cemetery. Alternatively, they may be stored above ground, as was done in the medieval Ezra synagogue in Cairo. A large attic called a *geniza* (storing or hiding place) was set aside to store holy papers and books. With the passage of time, medieval Egyptian Jews, confident that the room's contents would be left unmolested, began storing other important documents there. The Cairo Geniza soon contained personal letters, business correspondence, historical documents, and an extraordinary variety of religious writings.

For hundreds of years, the material lay undisturbed and uninspected. There was a superstition among the Jews of Cairo that disaster would befall anyone who touched the sacred papers (similar perhaps to the belief that a curse would befall anyone opening Tutankhamen's tomb). But more than superstition dissuaded would-be probers from inspecting the Geniza. The room was hardly accessible; it had no doors or windows and could be reached only by a ladder leading up to a large hole on the attic's side.

The Geniza finally was opened in 1896. Shortly thereafter, its contents were examined by the great Jewish scholar Solomon *Schechter. Under his direction, some 100,000 pages of the Geniza material were transferred to Cambridge University in England, where Schechter taught for many years. A permanent scholar is still employed, *a century later*, to oversee studies of the collection.

In the years since they were discovered, the Geniza's 250,000 documents have been recognized as one of the great treasures of Judaica. Perhaps the most famous find was of most of the Hebrew original of the *Apocryphal Book of Ecclesiasticus, which was previously known only in its Greek translation. More significant, however, was the uncovering of numerous documents on the history of Jews in Egypt and Israel from the time of Mohammed until the First *Crusade. Nothing had previously been known about this period. Much material on the history of the *Karaites was also uncovered. One great scholar, Shlomo Dov Goitein, spent fifty years studying the Geniza's holdings, on the basis of which he published five volumes, entitled *A Mediterranean Society*. Goitein depicts with extraordinary detail the day-to-day religious, intellectual, and social lives of medieval Arabic Jewry.

SOURCES AND FURTHER READINGS: S. D. Goitein, *A Mediterranean Society: The Jewish Communities of the Arab World as Portrayed in the Documents of the Cairo Geniza* (five volumes); Geoffrey Khan, "Twenty Years of Genizah Research," in the *Encyclopedia Judaica Year Book 1983–1985*, pp. 163–171.

THE GOLDEN AGE OF SPANISH JEWRY

The tenth to twelfth centuries are known as the Golden Age of Spanish Jewry, and are often regarded as the closest parallel in Jewish history to the contemporary golden age of American-Jewish life. During these three centuries, many Jews were invited to hold high government positions, and Jewish religious and cultural life flourished.

Throughout the Golden Age, most of Spain was ruled by a series of remarkably tolerant Muslim leaders (this was before Spain was reconquered by the Christian world. Muslim rule started in 711 and lasted in parts of Spain until 1492.) Hasdai ibn Shaprut, the outstanding Jewish personality of the tenth century, epitomized the success Jews could achieve during this time. He served as personal physician and diplomatic adviser to two caliphs, represented the government on numerous diplomatic missions, and was widely regarded as one of the most influential people in Spain. Hasdai was a deeply committed Jew, and was very willing to use his power and influence to support Jewish scholars and Jewish schools.

He is particularly remembered for a moving correspondence that he carried on with King Joseph, one of the last of the Jewish leaders of Khazaria (see next entry). In Hasdai's letter to the world's only Jewish monarch, he expressed his deep wish that he and his fellow Jews could also have political independence. King Joseph was impressed by the eloquence and intelligence of Hasdai's letter, and invited him to come serve in his government. Whether he would have done so is a moot point; within a few years Russia had conquered Khazaria, and the Jewish kingdom was destroyed.

Several great Jewish poets and philosophers flourished in the Golden Age, the most renowned of whom was the poet and philosopher Judah Halevi (see next entry). A half-century before Halevi lived the poet and philosopher Solomon ibn Gabirol, whose writings deeply influenced the medieval Christian world as well as the Jewish. In addition to his philosophical and poetic talents, Ibn Gabirol possessed keen psychological antennae: "Would you know who is your friend and who is your enemy?" he asked in *Pearls of Wisdom*. "Note what is in your own heart." Elsewhere in this same work, he wrote: "My friend is he who will tell me my faults in private." Another Jewish thinker during the Golden Age was Bakhya ibn Pakuda, whose systematic presentation of Jewish moral theology, *Duties of the Heart* (*Khovot ha-Levavot*), is still studied in *yeshivot throughout the world. Reflecting the unusually good relations then existing between Jews and their neighbors, Bakhya mentioned in his introduction Sufi Muslims from whom he had learned, and even referred to them as *hasidim* (pious men). One does not find many similar expressions of warmth for non-Jewish teachers in other medieval Jewish writings. The outstanding figure of the Golden Age's last period was Abraham ibn Ezra, a Bible scholar whose commentary on the Torah is still studied by religious Jews.

Even the Golden Age, however, had its share of dross. In 1066, there was an antisemitic outburst against Joseph ibn Nagdela, the rather haughty vizier to the king of Granada. Rumors were spread by Joseph's enemies that he was plotting to betray the kingdom to its enemies, and take over the kingship. The palace in which he dwelt was attacked. Joseph hid in a charcoal cellar, and tried to blacken himself in disguise. To no avail. He was murdered and fastened to a cross. The Granadans then launched an enormous *pogrom; by the time it was over, close to four thousand Jews were dead. Nevertheless, in the rest of Spain, Jewish life flourished for almost another century.

Unfortunately, when the Golden Age of Spanish Jewry did end, it was with a bang, not a whimper. In the twelfth century, the Muslim *Almohades, who had come to power in North Africa, gained control of Spain. Suddenly, the prosperous and successful Jewish community found itself confronted with three unpalatable alternatives: conversion to Islam, exile, or death. There were subsequent improvements in the condition of Spanish Jewry, but the process that would culminate with the *expulsion of Spanish Jews in 1492 had already begun.

SOURCES AND FURTHER READINGS: Max Margolis and Alexander Marx, *A History of the Jewish People*, pp. 308–333. Unfortunately, as regards Hasdai ibn Shaprut, there is reason to believe that power went to his head. Another surviving example of his correspondence is far less edifying than the letter he wrote to the king of the Khazars. Menahem ibn Seruq was a poet who had worked at one time for Hasdai, and indeed had written the original draft of the Khazar letter. The two men had a falling out, and Ibn Seruq subsequently wrote a letter to Hasdai in which he complained: "They beat me before your eyes, divesting me of my robe on the holy day of rest and plucking my hair on the holy Sabbath.... And on the festival day ... you ordered my home to be destroyed." Hasdai's response was curt and arrogant: "If you did wrong . . . I have already meted out punishment to you; and if you have done no wrong I have already led you to eternal life." Ibn Seruq refused to back off: "Now when you said, 'If you did wrong and if you have done no wrong.' Is it proper to judge on an 'if'? . . . You are made of the same stuff as I," he courageously chided the leader of Spanish Jewry, "and He who made me is your Maker. . . . And though justice be delayed now, I await the day of judgment . . . [when] the mighty cannot resort to force." The exchange between Ibn Seruq and Hasdai ibn Shaprut is cited in H. H. Ben-Sasson, ed., A *History of the Jewish People*, pp. 452–453.

92

JUDAH HALEVI (C. 1080–C. 1142)
The Kuzari

THE COUNTRY OF KHAZARIA WAS LOCATED BETWEEN RUSSIA AND Turkey, and populated by people of Turkish stock. A Khazar tradition relates that about the year 740, the religiously unaffiliated king Bulan hit upon a novel method for choosing a religion. He invited Jewish, Christian, and Muslim representatives to argue before him the merits of their separate faiths. In the end, Bulan chose Judaism: Although he did not insist that his subjects follow his example, many did.

Whether the royal family of Khazaria's conversion to Judaism came about exactly in the manner described in this tale, we probably will never know. What we do know, however, is that a Jewish kingdom of Khazaria existed as an independent state for more than two centuries. Unfortunately, communications in the medieval world were infrequent and slow: By the time world Jewry learned about Khazaria, the country was enjoying its last days of independence. In 969, it was conquered by Russia.

Approximately 150 years later, Judah Halevi, the greatest Jewish poet of the Middle Ages, wrote a philosophic masterpiece set in Khazaria, *The Kuzari: A Book of Argument in Defense of a Despised Religion*. In this philosophical novel, he imaginatively reconstructs the arguments that the different religious spokesmen might have made before King Bulan. Early on, for example, the king probes the religious views of the Christian and Muslim representatives, both of whom clearly state that, with the exception of their own religion, they regard Judaism as the highest faith. To Halevi, it is obvious why the religious spokesmen would make such a statement. Christianity and Islam acknowledge God's revelation to Moses, and thus believe that the Torah is true, only that it has been superseded by a subsequent revelation. However, neither religion believes in the equal truth of the other's revelational claims.

So impressed is King Bulan by the positive statements he hears about Judaism that he decides to summon a rabbi to the encounter. The remainder of *The Kuzari* consists of the king's dialogue with this individual.

The rabbi argues that the truth of Judaism is a historical fact: Judaism began with a divine revelation before hundreds of thousands of people. Had the Jews in the desert not heard God's voice at Sinai, they would never have accepted the statements in the Torah recording that they had. Therefore, except for converts, Jews trace their religious roots back to people who personally experienced God's presence at Sinai.

An unappealing feature of *The Kuzari* is Halevi's belief in the Jews' inherent spiritual superiority. Only Jews, he believes, can be prophets. But though Halevi's thinking has a definite racial bias, it would be unfair simply to dismiss him as a racist. After all, the whole thrust of *The Kuzari* is the effort to persuade a non-Jewish king to become a Jew. When the king challenges the Jewish spokesman's chauvinism—"Thy words are poor after having been so pleasant"—and points to the Jews' low status and great sufferings throughout the world, the rabbi answers that Jewish suffering is voluntary and therefore no disgrace. If Jews would only consent to convert to Christianity or Islam, they could immediately stop all persecution. But few choose to do so.

The Kuzari is passionate about the Jews' need to return to their homeland. Just as Halevi saw the people Israel as uniquely spiritual, so he saw a unique spirituality in the land of Israel, and believed that Jews could only achieve their full religious vitality in the Holy Land (a major reason Halevi remains one of the most popular Jewish philosophers among religious Israelis). At the book's conclusion, the Jewish spokesman informs the king that he is planning to emigrate immediately to Israel.

In Halevi's case, fact followed fiction. Late in life, he left Spain and made the arduous journey to Israel. In many ways, he had been preparing to go there for much of his life. "My heart is in the East," he had written in his most famous poem, "but I am in the ends of the West." Unfortunately, almost as soon as Halevi arrived in Jerusalem, an Arab horseman killed him.

SOURCES AND FURTHER READINGS: Judah Halevi, *The Kuzari*, translated by Hartwig Hirschfeld, with an introduction by H. Slonimsky; Meyer Waxman, *A History of Jewish Literature*, vol. 1, pp. 227–231, 333–339; Jacob S. Minkin, "Judah Halevi," in Simon Noveck, ed., *Great Jewish Personalities in Ancient and Medieval Times*, pp. 181–201.

The problem of racism in Halevi's thinking has been addressed by Dr. Norman Lamm, president of Yeshiva University: "Only a deliberate misreading of the *Kuzari* . . . can mistake it for a precursor of modern racialism. . . . At the end of the book, the king converts to Judaism—surely an astonishing conclusion to a tract supposedly elaborating an exclusive doctrine of Jewish racialism" (*The Condition of Jewish Belief*, p. 128). See also D. M. Dunlop, *The History of the Jewish Khazars*.

ALMOHADES

THE ALMOHADES WERE A FANATICAL AND POWERFUL GROUP OF MUS-lims who offered Jews and Christians the choice of conversion to Islam or death, although sometimes they were "humane" enough to offer exile as a third option. Their sudden appearance in Morocco and Spain in the twelfth century inaugurated a horrendous decline for Jews living in the orbit of Islam.

Before the Almohades's ascendancy, all Muslims regarded Jews and Christians as "people of the Book" (that is, the Bible): Both religions were tolerated because they were monotheistic. As long as "the people of the Book" willingly accepted the public and private humiliations of living as *dhimmis*, Islam guaranteed them the right to live.

The Almohades, however, formulated a religious rationale for revoking this tolerance. Their leaders claimed to have uncovered an ancient teaching of *Mohammed, according to which the Muslim tolerance of Jews was to end after five hundred years. If at that time the Jewish Messiah had not arrived, the Jews were to give up their religion and become Muslims.

In 1146, Abd al-Mu'min, the builder of the Almohade empire in North Africa and Spain, offered the Jews of Fez, Morocco's capital, the choice of Islam or the sword: Shortly thereafter, nearly every Jew in Fez was murdered. The few Jews who did convert were kept under constant surveillance, and those caught keeping Jewish rituals were executed.

In response to Almohade threats, tens of thousands of Jews fled Spain and
Morocco for more tolerant environments. The most famous victim of the
Almohade persecutions was Moses Maimonides (see next entry), who fled
with his family from Spain to Morocco to Egypt. Shlomo Dov Goitein, the
great historian of Jewish life under Islam, sums up the Jewish century under
the Almohades in one sentence: "All the horrors of the Spanish Inquisition
were anticipated under Almohade rule."

SOURCES: Salo Baron, *A Social and Religious History of the Jews*, vol. 3, p. 124; S. D.
Goitein, *Jews and Arabs: Their Contact Through the Ages*, p. 80.

94

MAIMONIDES/RAMBAM (1135–1204)

IF ONE DID NOT KNOW THAT MAIMONIDES WAS THE NAME OF A MAN,
Abraham Joshua Heschel wrote, one would assume it was the name of a university. The writings and achievements of this twelfth-century Jewish sage
seem to cover an impossibly large number of activities. Maimonides was the
first person to write a systematic code of all Jewish law, the *Mishneh Torah*;
he produced one of the great philosophic statements of Judaism, *The Guide
to the Perplexed*; published a commentary on the entire *Mishna; served as
physician at the court of the sultan of Egypt; wrote numerous books on medicine; and, in his "spare time," served as leader of Cairo's Jewish community.
It is hardly surprising that when Shmuel ibn Tibbon, the Hebrew translator
of *The Guide to the Perplexed* (which had been written in Arabic), wrote Maimonides that he wished to visit him to discuss some difficult points in the
translation, Maimonides discouraged him from coming:

> I dwell at Fostat, and the sultan resides at Cairo [about a mile-and-a-half
> away]. . . . My duties to the sultan are very heavy. I am obliged to visit him every
> day, early in the morning, and when he or any of his children or any of the
> inmates of his harem are indisposed, I dare not quit Cairo, but must stay during
> the greater part of the day in the palace. It also frequently happens that one of
> the two royal officers fall sick, and I must attend to their healing. Hence, as a

rule, I leave for Cairo very early in the day, and even if nothing unusual happens, I do not return to Fostat until the afternoon. Then I am almost dying with hunger . . . I find the antechamber filled with people, both Jews and gentiles, nobles and common people, judges and bailiffs, friends and foes—a mixed multitude who await the time of my return.

I dismount from my animal, wash my hands, go forth to my patients and entreat them to bear with me while I partake of some slight refreshment, the only meal I take in the twenty-four hours. Then I go forth to attend to my patients, and write prescriptions and directions for their various ailments. Patients go in and out until nightfall, and sometimes even, I solemnly assure you, until two hours or more in the night. I converse with and prescribe for them while lying down from sheer fatigue; and when night falls I am so exhausted that I can scarcely speak.

In consequence of this, no Israelite can have any private interview with me, except on the Sabbath. On that day the whole congregation, or at least the majority of the members, come to me after the morning service, when I instruct them as to their proceedings during the whole week; we study together a little until noon, when they depart. Some of them return, and read with me after the afternoon service until evening prayers. In this manner I spend that day.

Maimonides's full name was Moses ben Maimon; in Hebrew he is known by the acronym of *Rabbi Moses ben Maimon, Rambam.* He was born in Spain shortly before the fanatical Muslim Almohades (see preceding entry) came to power there. To avoid persecution by the Muslim sect—which was wont to offer Jews and Christians the choice of conversion to Islam or death—Maimonides fled with his family, first to Morocco, later to Israel, and finally to Egypt. He apparently hoped to continue his studies for several years more, but when his brother David, a jewelry merchant, perished in the Indian Ocean with much of the family's fortune, he had to begin earning money. He probably started practicing medicine at this time.

Maimonides's major contribution to Jewish life remains the *Mishneh Torah,* his code of Jewish law. His intention was to compose a book that would guide Jews on how to behave in all situations just by reading the Torah and his code, without having to expend large amounts of time searching through the *Talmud. Needless to say, this provocative rationale did not endear Maimonides to many traditional Jews, who feared that people would rely on his code and no longer study the Talmud. Despite sometimes intense opposition, the *Mishneh Torah* became a standard guide to Jewish practice: It later served as the model for the *Shulkhan Arukh,* the sixteenth-century code of Jewish law that is still regarded as authoritative by Orthodox Jews.

Philosophically, Maimonides was a religious rationalist. His damning attacks on people who held ideas he regarded as primitive—those, for example, who understood literally such biblical expressions as "the finger of God"—so infuriated his opponents that they proscribed parts of his code and all of *The Guide to the Perplexed*. Other, more liberal, spirits forbade study of the *Guide* to anyone not of mature years. An old joke has it that these rabbis feared that a Jew would start reading a section in the *Guide* in which Maimonides summarizes a rationalist attack on religion, and fall asleep before reading Maimonides's counterattack—thereby spending the night as a heretic.

How Maimonides's opponents reacted to his works was no joke, however. Three leading rabbis in France denounced his books to the Dominicans, who headed the French Inquisition. The Inquisitors were only too happy to intervene and burn the books. Eight years later, when the Dominicans started *burning the Talmud, one of the rabbis involved, Jonah Gerondi, concluded that God was punishing him and French Jewry for their unjust condemnation of Maimonides. He resolved to travel to Maimonides's grave in Tiberias, in Israel, to request forgiveness.

Throughout most of the Jewish world, Maimonides remained a hero, of course. When he died, Egyptian Jews observed three full days of mourning, and applied to his death the biblical verse "The ark of the Lord has been taken" (I Samuel 4:11).

To this day, Maimonides and the French-Jewish sage *Rashi are the most widely studied Jewish scholars. Contemporary yeshiva students generally focus on the *Mishneh Torah*, and his *Book of Commandments (Sefer ha-Mitzvot)* a compilation of the Torah's *613 commandments. Maimonides also formulated a credo of Judaism expressed in thirteen articles of faith, a popular reworking of which (the *Yigdal* prayer) appears in most Jewish prayerbooks. Among other things, this credo affirms belief in the oneness of God, the divine origins of the Torah, and the afterlife. Its twelfth statement of faith—"I believe with a full heart in the coming of the Messiah, and even though he may tarry I will still wait for him"—was among the last words said by some Jews being marched into Nazi gas chambers.

Maimonides was one of the few Jewish thinkers whose teachings also influenced the non-Jewish world; much of his philosophical writings in the *Guide* were about God and other theological issues of general, not exclusively Jewish, interest. Thomas Aquinas refers in his writings to "Rabbi Moses," and shows considerable familiarity with the *Guide*. In 1985, on the 850th anniversary of Maimonides's birth, Pakistan and Cuba—which do not recognize Israel—were among the co-sponsors of a UNESCO conference in Paris on Maimonides. Vitali Naumkin, a Soviet scholar, observed on this occasion: "Maimonides is perhaps the only philosopher in the Middle Ages, perhaps even now, who symbolizes a confluence of four cultures: Greco-Roman, Arab, Jewish, and Western." More remarkably, Abderrahmane Badawi, a Muslim professor from Kuwait University, declared: "I regard him first and foremost as an Arab thinker." This sentiment was echoed by Saudi Arabian professor Huseyin Atay, who claimed that "if you didn't know he was Jewish, you might easily make the mistake of saying that a Muslim was writing." That is, if you didn't read any of his Jewish writings. Maimonides scholar Shlomo Pines delivered perhaps the most accurate assessment at the conference: "Maimonides is the most influential Jewish thinker of the Middle Ages, and quite possibly of all time" (*Time* magazine, December 23, 1985). As a popular Jewish expression of the Middle Ages declares: "From *Moses [of the Torah] to Moses [Maimonides] there was none like Moses."

SOURCES AND FURTHER READINGS: Isadore Twersky, ed., *A Maimonides Reader*; Salo Baron, "Moses Maimonides," in Simon Noveck, ed., *Great Jewish Personalities in Ancient and Medieval Times*, pp. 204–231; Jacob S. Minkin, *The World of Moses Maimonides*; Abraham Joshua Heschel, *Maimonides*; David Yellin and Israel Abrahams, *Maimonides*; Leon Stitskin, trans. and ed., *Letters of Maimonides*; Abraham Halkin, trans., *Crisis and Leadership: Epistles of Maimonides*—discussions by Dr. David Hartman follow the text.

95

BAN ON POLYGAMY

The Takkanot *(Decrees) of Rabbi Gershom*

THE TENTH-CENTURY RABBI GERSHOM OF GERMANY IS CREDITED WITH a number of legal decrees that dramatically raised the status of women in Jewish law, and updated Jewish morality in other areas. The three most famous laws attributed to him were bans against polygamy, divorcing a woman against her will, and reading other people's mail.

The ban on multiple wives is the best known of these decrees, even though polygamy had not been widely practiced among Jews for at least a millennium. Of the more than fifteen hundred rabbis mentioned in the Talmud, we know of none who had more than one wife. Nevertheless, plural marriage was never outlawed and was still practiced occasionally.

Rabbi Gershom regarded polygamy as a *khillul ha-Shem (desecration of God's name) because Jews were seen as having a lower morality than their monogamous Christian neighbors. Rabbi Gershom might also have been influenced by the curious fact that although Torah *law* permitted polygamy, Torah *narrative* opposed it. Virtually every polygamous relationship described in the Bible is miserably unhappy. For example, although *Sarah herself encouraged *Abraham to take Hagar as a concubine, the two women ended up hating each other. Two generations later, *Jacob married the sisters *Leah and *Rachel: The unhappiness resulting from this polygamous marriage spilled over into the next generation, as Leah's sons hated Rachel's firstborn son, *Joseph. Much later, the Bible described disapprovingly the numerous wives taken by King *Solomon, because they introduced idolatry into Israel. Thus, although the Bible permits polygamy, its clear preference seems to be "one man, one wife." "Therefore," the Torah teaches in Genesis, "shall a man leave his father and mother and cleave to his wife, and they shall be one flesh" (2:24). Indeed, the most obvious evidence of the Torah's preference for monogamy is that the first human beings God created were *Adam and Eve, not Adam, Eve, and Joan.

Unlike their European brothers, the Jews living within the orbit of Islam, where plural wives were a status symbol, felt no self-consciousness about polygamy, and did not accept Rabbi Gershom's ban. In 1948, when Israel was created, some Jews who emigrated there from the Arab world, particularly from Yemen, came with more than one wife. The government permitted those marriages already in existence to stay in force, while forbidding any new polygamous marriages. Today, therefore, the ban on polygamy is universally accepted in the Jewish state and throughout the Diaspora.

Rabbi Gershom's decree that prohibited divorcing a woman against her will corrected a long-standing injustice in the Jewish legal code. Under biblical and talmudic law, a man could divorce his wife against her will for virtually any reason. The rabbis tried to inhibit men from doing so by demanding a hefty alimony payment (see *Ketuba* and *Get*), but this was not always a sufficient deterrent. Since the time of Rabbi Gershom, divorce has to be mutually accepted by both parties.

The decree banning the reading of other people's mail was particularly important at a time when letters were not sent through an impersonal government office, but entrusted to messengers. Although the decree might seem self-evident, Rabbi Gershom had good reason to think it was necessary. Even today, many people do not regard mail as private property in quite the same way they regard other personal possessions. They are apt to have fewer scruples about reading other people's mail without permission than about borrowing other people's cars without permission. From the perspective of Jewish law, both acts are strictly forbidden. When I lived in Israel, I occasionally would see written on an envelope flap *"Takkanat Rabbenu Gershom* [The Decree of Rabbi Gershom]," a reminder to would-be snoops of this tenth-century ban on reading mail addressed to someone else.

There is a special poignancy to a fourth decree of Rabbi Gershom. This one forbids reminding Jewish apostates who have returned to the Jewish community of the sin they had committed. Rabbi Gershom himself had a son who was forcibly converted to Christianity and died before he could repent. Nonetheless, he carried out the laws of mourning for him.

The comprehensive nature and humanitarian concerns of Rabbi Gershom's decrees earned him a title, which is almost invariably appended to his name in Hebrew, *"Rabbenu Gershom Me'or ha-Golah* [Rabbi Gershom, who brought light to the Jews in exile]."

SOURCE AND FURTHER READING: Louis Finkelstein, *Jewish Self-Government in the Middle Ages,* pp. 20–35.

96

RASHI (1040–1105)
RABBENU TAM (1100–1171)
THE *RISHONIM*

ALTHOUGH *MAIMONIDES IS REGARDED AS MEDIEVAL JUDAISM'S greatest philosopher and intellect, Rashi is its greatest teacher. Since his death almost nine hundred years ago, Jews who study either the *Torah or the *Talmud, Judaism's two most important works, invariably do so with the help of his commentary. Of the many Talmud editions that have been printed since the sixteenth century, almost none has come out without this French sage's glosses. In fact, had Rashi not written a Talmud commentary that explained its difficult Aramaic words and guided students through its intricate and often confusing forms of logic, the Talmud might have become a largely forgotten work.

This greatest of Jewish teachers was born in Troyes, France, in 1040. His full name was Rabbi Shlomo ben Isaac, of which Rashi is the acronym. Throughout his lifetime, only one hundred or so Jews lived in Troyes. That such a great scholar came from so small a town seems quite remarkable, since modern Jews who live in small Jewish communities usually lament that it is impossible to give their children an adequate Jewish education.

As a young man, Rashi spent several years in the *yeshiva in Mainz that had been established by Rabbi Gershom (see preceding entry). When he was about twenty-five, he returned to Troyes and opened his own Jewish school. However, Rashi refused to draw a salary for his work, earning his living instead from several vineyards that he owned. His professional labors were occasionally time-consuming, and in one letter we find him apologizing for the shortness of his response, explaining that he and his family were busy with the grape harvest. In general, however, the vineyards seemed to leave Rashi ample time to work on his commentaries. The last years of his life were marred by the antisemitic *Crusades that swept over France and Germany. Although Troyes itself was untouched by the Crusaders, tremendous devastation was wreaked elsewhere in Europe. Thousands of Jews were murdered by the Crusaders, thousands more badly injured, and additional thousands impoverished. In addition, there were many Jews who converted to Christianity to save their lives, and who later wished to return to Judaism. Rashi advocated an accepting, tolerant attitude toward them: "Let us beware of alienating those who have returned to us. . . . They became Christians only through fear of death; and as soon as the danger disappeared they hastened to return to their faith."

Perhaps the most noted feature of his commentaries is their succinctness and clarity. He repeatedly revised his commentaries, striving to make them more precise and brief. On one occasion, he allegedly reproved his grandson, Rabbi Samuel, for a lengthy comment on a talmudic passage: "If you had done all the Talmud like this it would have been as heavy as a chariot."

To this day, Rashi's literary style influences Hebrew writing. The great Hebrew poet Hayyim Nahman Bialik spoke of Rashi as an inspiration, as did Shmuel Yosef Agnon, in his 1966 speech accepting the Nobel Prize for Literature.

In his Torah commentary, Rashi explains terms both on the basis of *peshat* (literal meaning) and *derash* (homiletical or sermonic meaning—see *Midrash*). Often the two are combined in one comment. For example, Genesis 25:21 reads: "Isaac pleaded with the Lord on behalf of his wife, because she was barren; and the Lord responded to his plea, and his wife Rebecca conceived." Rashi first notes that the meaning of *vaye'tar* (pleaded) is "to pray much and earnestly. Many biblical quotations support this meaning of the word." He then seizes on a peculiar expression in the Hebrew text, noting that *le-nokhach ishto*, although commonly translated as " '[pleaded] for his wife,' literally means 'opposite his wife,' which is the basis for the talmudic suggestion that 'Isaac prayed in one corner and Rebecca in another.' " Not only has Rashi explained to the reader the literal meaning of the Torah's words, he also has conveyed a visual representation of the room in which Isaac and Rebecca prayed. We can well imagine that later on many Jewish couples, plagued by infertility, took up praying positions in opposite corners of the room, in line with Rashi's explanation.

Rashi's predilection for citing talmudic and midrashic legends in his Torah commentary led a later Bible commentator, Abraham ibn Ezra, to attack him sharply: "In [Rashi's] work, there is not one rational explanation out of a thousand." This is, of course, a grotesque exaggeration, although it is true that in his later years, Rashi confided to his grandson, Rabbi Samuel, that if he had had more time he would have rewritten his commentary to correspond more closely to the text's literal meaning.

Rashi's opening commentary on the first verse in the Torah, "In the beginning, God created the heavens and the earth" (Genesis 1:1), almost sounds as if it were written with the contemporary Arab-Israeli conflict in mind: "Strictly speaking," he notes, "the Torah should have commenced with the verse, 'This month shall be to you the beginning of months' [Exodus 12:2], which is the very first commandment given to [the Jews]. Why, then, did the Torah begin with the account of the creation? In order to illustrate that God the Creator owns the whole world. So, if the peoples of the world shall say to Israel: 'You are robbers in conquering the territory of the seven Canaanite nations,' Israel can answer them: 'All of the earth belongs to God—He created it, so He can give it to whomsoever He will.' "

His commentary on Genesis 6:9—"*Noah was a righteous man; he was blameless in his age"—conveys both sides of the well-known rabbinic dispute on Noah's character: "Some of the sages interpret the verse in Noah's favor, by observing that if he had managed to be righteous in such a wicked milieu, how much more righteous he would have been had he lived in an age of righteous people! Others, however, interpret the phrase to his discredit by noting that it implies that Noah was righteous only by the standard of his own generation, but that had he lived in Abraham's generation, he would have been considered a nobody."

Rashi's Torah commentary achieved such wide acceptance that it became mandatory for Jews to review the weekly *Torah portion with his commentary. In 1475, Rashi's commentary became the first book printed in Hebrew—even before the Torah itself was. As Dr. Philip Birnbaum has written: "[Torah] with Rashi has meant the average Jewish education everywhere throughout many generations." During the past nine centuries, an additional hundred commentaries have been written—just on Rashi's commentary on the Torah.

If anything, his Talmud commentary filled an even greater need than that on the Torah. The Torah's vocabulary is quite simple. But the Talmud, with its combination of Aramaic, Hebrew and, occasionally, Greek terms, is a far more daunting work. To this day, students of the Talmud are encouraged to read Rashi's commentary as they are reading the text, before trying to deduce the text's meaning on their own.

In every printed edition of the Talmud, opposite Rashi's commentary, is another commentary known as Tosafot. The Tosafot commentary is a creation put together over two centuries, dominated by five of Rashi's descendants—two sons-in-law and three grandsons. One of the grandsons, Rabbi Jacob Tam (known as Rabbenu Tam), became the leader of the French-Jewish community several decades after Rashi's death. As well as being a first-rate scholar, he was a self-assured and decisive leader. On one occasion, Rabbenu Tam authorized the excommunication of any Jew who questioned the legality of a Jewish *get (divorce decree) on the basis of a technicality. Rabbenu Tam was concerned that Jewish women would remarry after a divorce, then suddenly find their divorces challenged and themselves accused of adultery.

His most famous dispute was with his revered grandfather, Rashi, and concerned the order in which the Torah texts inserted into the *tefillin (phylacteries) should be placed. Although the Jewish community has followed Rashi's interpretation, respect for Rabbenu Tam remains so great that some religious Jews don two pairs of *tefillin* each morning, first those of Rashi, then those of Rabbenu Tam (indeed, they are known as Rabbenu Tam *tefillin*).

The term *Rishonim* (First Ones) applies to all Jewish scholars who lived before Rabbi Joseph *Karo, the author of the sixteenth-century code of Jewish law known as the *Shulkhan Arukh*. Because of the *Rishonim's* prominence and closer proximity to the time of *Moses and the Revelation, their writings are usually regarded as more authoritative than those of the post-*Shulkhan Arukh* scholars, known as *Akharonim* (Later Ones). Among the most prominent *Rishonim* are Rashi, Rabbenu Tam, the authors of the Tosafot, *Maimonides, Nachmanides, and lbn Ezra.

SOURCES AND FURTHER READINGS: The selections from Rashi's commentary are drawn from Chaim Pearl, *Rashi: Commentaries on the Pentateuch*. Pearl has published a brief biography, *Rashi*. See also Philip Birnbaum, *Encyclopedia of Jewish Concepts*, pp. 571–572.

97

CRUSADES

WHEN I WAS EIGHT YEARS OLD AND MY FAMILY WAS SPENDING SEV-
eral days at my grandparents' house, I took with me a one-volume history of the
world, written for children. Having just read the section on the Middle Ages, I
piped up in the middle of a holiday meal, "Weren't the Crusaders wonderful
people, risking their lives for God?" There was an eerie silence at the table,
much as if I had proposed substituting pork chops for my grandmother's gefilte
fish. I came to understand later that the word "Crusades" reverberates very differently in the ears of Christians and Jews. For some, perhaps many, Christians
the Crusades represent a high point of religious idealism: They admire the Crusaders for forsaking their careers and homes, and sometimes sacrificing their
lives, to capture Jerusalem from the Muslims. For most Jews, the word "Crusades" has two very different associations: murder and forced baptism.

In 1095, when Pope Urban II called for the Crusades to regain Palestine
from the "infidels," tens of thousands of Christians set out for the Holy Land.
Those Jews unfortunate enough to live in the cities through which the Crusaders passed were generally offered the choice of conversion or death; a few
lucky communities were permitted to pay a large bribe to be left unmolested.
In May 1096, Crusaders besieged the Jewish community of Worms, Germany. The local bishop offered to save the Jews from their attackers if they
converted to Christianity. Almost all of the Jews refused, and eight hundred
were murdered.

Approximately twelve thousand Jews were killed in the early months of the
First Crusades—often, it must be noted, against the will of local bishops.
These Jews are regarded by Judaism as having died *al * kiddush ha-Shem*, in
order to sanctify God's name. The weekly Sabbath morning service still contains a petition to the *Av ha-Rakhamin* (Merciful Father) to remember them,
and to avenge their blood. This *Av ha-Rakhamim* prayer, probably composed
during the Crusades of 1096, speaks of "the holy communities who offered
their lives for the sanctification of God's name. They were beloved and pleasant in their lives, and not parted [from Judaism] in their deaths."

In 1099, when the Crusaders captured Jerusalem, they gathered all the city's Jews into a synagogue and burned them alive. Afterward, they banned all non-Christians from living in Jerusalem.

Some Jews saved themselves by converting to Christianity: After the Crusaders left, many of them tried to return to Judaism. In those cities where secular rulers were in control, they were permitted to do so; in jurisdictions where the Church was dominant, however, they were forced to remain Christians. More than a century later, in September 1201, Pope Innocent III formalized this prohibition in a papal bull: ". . . he who is led to Christianity by violence, by fear and by torture, and who received the sacrament of baptism to avoid harm receives indeed the stamp of Christianity . . . [and] must be duly constrained to abide by the faith [he] had accepted by force."

For the Jews, the Crusades signaled a terrible decline in their fortunes in Europe. For centuries afterward, they found themselves subjected to violent attacks, libelous accusations, and expulsions. See *Kiddush ha-Shem*, *Blood Libel*, and the next five entries.

SOURCES AND FURTHER READINGS: An extensive overview of the Jewish experience during the time of the Crusades is found in Leon Poliakov, *The History of Anti-Semitism: From the Time of Christ to the Court Jews*; the quote from Pope Innocent III is cited on p. 47. See also Robert Chazan, *European Jewry and the First Crusade*.

98

FOURTH LATERAN COUNCIL

YELLOW BADGE

JESUS WAS A JEW, HIS APOSTLES WERE JEWS, HIS MESSAGE WAS TO THE Jews, and the Jews, the only people who knew him, rejected the claims Christianity made on his behalf. Not surprisingly, the Jews' very presence became a considerable irritant to some Christians, particularly to the deeply antisemitic Pope Innocent III.

At the Fourth Lateran Council, convened by Innocent in 1215, the Church decreed that Jews living in Christian lands were at all times to wear a distinctive badge on their clothing. This badge, generally a solid yellow circle sewed on to an upper garment, was periodically reimposed on European Jews for hundreds of years. It became the model for the *yellow star that the Nazis forced Jews to wear during the Second World War. Historians Max Wurmbrand and Cecil Roth have written that "the result of the introduction of the badge was to mark the Jews apart from other men as a different and inferior race, liable at all times to insult or attack."

Another decision at the Fourth Lateran Council, accepting the doctrine of transubstantiation as official Church dogma, seemingly had no relevance for the Jews. The doctrine simply meant that the wine and wafer used in the Catholic Mass were assumed to be miraculously transubstantiated into the actual blood and body of Jesus. But within thirty years, this dogma led to the annihilation of the entire Jewish community of Berlitz, Germany, which was charged with kidnapping a wafer and torturing it. The Berlitz massacre unfortunately was not a unique event. "In Prague, in 1389," a historical study of antisemitism notes, "the Jewish community was collectively accused of attacking a monk carrying a wafer. Large mobs of Christians surrounded the Jewish neighborhood and offered the Jews the choice of baptism or death. Refusing to be baptized, three thousand Jews were murdered. In Berlin, in 1510, twenty-six Jews were burned and two beheaded for reportedly 'desecrating the host.' "

The decisions made at the Fourth Lateran Council helped fulfill the vision for the Jews Pope Innocent III had earlier articulated in a letter to Count Nevers: "Jews, like the fratricide *Cain, are doomed to wander about the earth as fugitives and vagabonds, and their faces must be covered with shame."

SOURCES: Max Wurmbrand and Cecil Roth, *The Jewish People*, pp. 140–142. The passage on Jewish suffering occasioned by charges of host desecration is from Dennis Prager and Joseph Telushkin, *Why the Jews? The Reason for Antisemitism*, p. 86–87.

99

BURNING OF THE TALMUD

THE TWO LITERARY PILLARS OF JUDAISM ARE THE BIBLE AND THE *Talmud. While the Bible has become a central document in Christianity, the Talmud has remained of interest almost exclusively to Jews. In the medieval world, some Christian leaders concluded that if the Talmud were destroyed, and Jews were left only with the Bible, they would be more amenable to converting to Christianity. On fifteen occasions, Catholic officials, sometimes even popes, declared the Talmud a forbidden work and ordered it burned. The most famous such burning occurred in 1240 after the Talmud was put on trial in Paris and convicted of blasphemy.

Ironically, it appears that Jewish zealots helped provoke this terrible event. Three French rabbis, outraged by supposed heresies in *Maimonides's *The Guide to the Perplexed,* approached the Dominicans and asked that the book be burned. The Dominicans, who directed the French Inquisition, obliged, and took advantage of the unexpected request to start looking into other Jewish texts as well.

Several years later, Nicholas Donin, a Jewish apostate, submitted a memorandum to Pope Gregory IX leveling thirty-five accusations against the Talmud, among them that it allegedly expressed hatred for Christianity and blasphemed against Jesus and Mary. King Louis IX of France ordered the Talmud to be put on trial. At the trial, Rabbi Yechiel of Paris, head of the rabbinic defense team, declared before Queen Blanche: "We are prepared to die for the Talmud. . . . Our bodies are in your power, but not our souls."

The predetermined verdict, of course, was guilty. Two years later, on June 17, 1242—in response to an order issued by an inquisitorial committee—twenty-four wagonloads of handwritten volumes of the Talmud were cremated.

Despite the fourteen subsequent instances in which the Talmud was

burned, it remains today alive and well, and still constitutes the core curriculum at most rabbinical schools.

SOURCES AND FURTHER READINGS: Hyam Maccoby, *Judaism on Trial*, pp.
19–38; Jacob Marcus, ed., *The Jew in the Medieval World*, pp. 145–150; Yvonne Glik-
son, "Burning of Talmud," in the *Encyclopedia Judaica*, vol. 15, pp. 767–771.

100

JEWISH-CHRISTIAN DISPUTATIONS
MOSES NACHMANIDES AND THE DEBATE
IN BARCELONA, SPAIN, 1263

JEWS HAVE LONG HAD A REPUTATION FOR BEING A VERBAL, SOMETIMES
argumentative people. The great Yiddish writer Isaac Peretz characterized
them as "a people who can't sleep and don't let anybody else sleep." The least
favorite arguments in which the Jews have ever engaged, however, were with
Christian opponents in Western Europe during the Middle Ages.

The debates were generally ordered by monarchs acting at the behest of
Catholic priests. The Church's goal in arranging the disputations was clear:
If their priests could defeat the Jewish representatives, masses of Jews would
recognize the truth of Christianity and convert. To make it harder on the Jewish participants, the Church hierarchy imposed sharp limitations on the
arguments they could use. They were forbidden, for example, to say anything
that could be regarded as offensive to Christianity, with the priests generally
the judges of what was offensive. Not surprisingly, the Jews regarded the
debates as a no-win situation; if they were bested by the priests, they would be
expected to convert. If they came out ahead, however, they might well find
themselves, and their fellow Jews, subjected to physical attacks.

The most famous of all Jewish-Christian disputations was between the
apostate Jew Pablo Christiani and Moses Nachmanides, one of the greatest
Jewish scholars of the Middle Ages. Several priests worked as counselors in
conjunction with Pablo Christiani throughout the encounter. The debate

was held in the presence of the Spanish king James of Aragon, and Nachmanides secured rare permission from the monarch to speak without fear of censorship or retribution. He addressed three questions:

1. Has the *Messiah come as the Christians say, or has he yet to come as the Jews say?
2. Is the Messiah divine as the Christians say, or human as the Jews say?
3. Do the Jews practice the true law or do the Christians?

To the first question, Nachmanides answered that Jews do not believe that Jesus was the Messiah because he did not fulfill the messianic prophecies delineated in the Hebrew Bible. Most important, he did not usher in an age of universal peace as *Isaiah had prophesied: "Nation shall not lift up sword against nation, neither shall they learn war anymore" (2:4). Not only have Isaiah's words not been fulfilled, Nachmanides said, but worse, Jesus' followers often have been great spillers of blood.

Nachmanides argued that the central issue separating Christianity and Judaism was *not* the issue of Jesus' messiahship, but whether or not Jesus was divine. There was no basis in Judaism, Nachmanides said, for believing in the divinity of the Messiah or, indeed, of any man. To Nachmanides, it seemed most strange "that the Creator of heaven and earth resorted to the womb of a certain Jewess and grew there for nine months and was born as an infant, and afterwards grew up and was betrayed into the hands of his enemies who sentenced him to death and executed him, and that afterwards . . . he came to life and returned to his original place. The mind of a Jew, or any other person, cannot tolerate this." Nachmanides told the Spanish monarch, "You have listened all your life to priests who have filled your brain and the marrow of your bones with this doctrine, and it has settled with you because of that accustomed habit." Had King James heard these ideas propounded for the first time when he was already an adult, Nachmanides implied, he never would have accepted them.

Nachmanides's opponents tried to have his "blasphemies" silenced, but he refused to back down. He was engaging in no gratuitous insults, he insisted, and his priestly opponents could hardly be impartial judges as to what arguments should or should not be permitted.

With regard to the third question, whether or not Jewish law was still binding, Nachmanides answered that nothing had changed in the character of the world or of mankind to make the Torah's commandments superfluous.

All of King James's good intentions notwithstanding, when the debates ended, Nachmanides found it prudent to leave Spain and emigrate to Palestine.

The two other famous Jewish-Christian debates were far sorrier episodes. The first, held in Paris in 1240, ended with the burning of the Talmud (see preceding entry). A much longer debate in Tortosa, Spain, in 1413–1414, was held under "siege" conditions. Jewish rights were already being attacked in Spain, and the rabbinic participants in the twenty-one-month debate feared for their lives whenever their arguments angered their Christian opponents. At the end of the debate, new ordinances were issued in Spain lowering the Jews to the status of pariahs.

It is probably fair to say that Christianity—or any religion for that matter—was not at its most sublime when it had political power. The Jewish/Christian disputations are as good a proof of that as any.

SOURCES: An extraordinarily fine book on the subject of Jewish-Christian debates is *Judaism on Trial: Jewish-Christian Disputations in the Middle Ages,* by the English-Jewish scholar Haym Maccoby. Maccoby analyzes the major debates and translates them as well. See also H. H. Ben-Sasson, "Jewish-Christian Disputations and Polemics," in his *Trial and Achievement: Currents in Jewish History,* pp. 257–285.

101

EXPULSION OF JEWS FROM ENGLAND, 1290

WHILE MANY JEWS ARE FAMILIAR WITH THE *EXPULSION OF SPANISH Jewry in 1492, few know that Jews have been expelled at one time or another from almost every European society in which they have lived. They were expelled from France in 1306 and 1394; Hungary between 1349 and 1360; Austria in 1421; numerous localities in Germany between the fourteenth and sixteenth centuries; Lithuania in 1445 and 1495; Spain in 1492; Portugal in 1497; and Bohemia and Moravia in 1744–1745. Between the fifteenth century and 1772, Jews were not permitted in Russia: When they were finally admitted, they were restricted to an area known as the Pale of Settlement.

Between 1948 and 1967, almost all the Jews of Aden, Algeria, Egypt, Iraq, Syria, and Yemen, though not officially expelled, fled these countries, fearing for their lives.

However, the first countrywide expulsion occurred in England in 1290. The motives seem to have been a combination of economic tension and religious hatred. Many noblemen, heavily indebted to Jewish moneylenders, wished to rid themselves of their creditors. The British monarch, King Edward I, supported the idea of expulsion; he, too, coveted the Jews' property, and upon their expulsion he and other members of the royal family confiscated much of it.

The local populace was more apt to support the expulsion on religious grounds. The people had been conditioned to hate Jews by centuries of antisemitic calumnies, and by accusations of ritual murder—the *blood libel itself originated in England. Only thirty-five years before the expulsion, nineteen Jews were hanged without trial in the city of Lincoln, falsely charged with crucifying a young boy named Hugh.

The order of expulsion was issued on July 18, 1290. The Hebrew date was the ninth of Av (see *Tisha Be-Av), the saddest day in the Jewish calendar, a fast day that commemorates the destruction of the two Temples.

The Jews were not permitted back into England for almost four centuries, until the rule of Oliver Cromwell in the 1650s. Even during their years of exile, however, antisemitism did not abate. In Chaucer's Canterbury Tales, written a century after the Jewish expulsion, the author accused the Jews of ritual murder, and two centuries later, Shakespeare depicted a Jew as a moneylender who collected his debt in human flesh (see Shylock).

Strangely enough, as deeply antisemitic as England was during the Middle Ages, there seemed to thrive in the country a strong, if small, current of philosemitism. At the very time Zionism was spreading among nineteenth-century Jewry, there evolved in England a Christian Zionist movement that influenced the later issuance of the *Balfour Declaration in 1917.

SOURCE: Dennis Prager and Joseph Telushkin, Why the Jews? The Reason for Antisemitism, pp. 81–83.

102

SPANISH INQUISITION (1481–1808)
Marranos

THE SPANISH INQUISITION WAS A PERVERSE ATTEMPT TO SAVE people's souls by torturing their bodies. Since only Christians of pure faith could go to heaven, the Inquisitors reasoned, and all others would be sentenced to the eternal torments of hell, it made sense to temporarily torture people of impure faith until they accepted Jesus, and thereby save their souls from the never-ending tortures of the next world.

Contrary to a popular misconception, the Inquisition was not directed against Jews, but against all supposed heretics, particularly former Jews who had converted to Christianity. Since these Jews had generally converted under duress, either to save their lives or their livelihoods, the Church had good reason to mistrust their sincerity. Inquisition officials, aided by informers, continually and carefully scrutinized these new Christians. If any of their actions indicated that they might be secretly practicing Judaism — perhaps they were observed never to eat pork or cook on the Sabbath — these "new Christians" were summoned before the Inquisition. The Inquisitors, all of whom were priests, asked the accused if they were secret Jews. If they confessed immediately, and supplied the Inquisition with names of other secret Jews, they got off lightly: a religious ceremony at which they made a public confession, and suffered various humiliations. If they were convicted of being secret Jews and only then confessed, they were guaranteed a less painful execution: They were strangled before being burned at the stake.

Those people who refused to confess even after being convicted, or who were courageous enough to acknowledge that they were still Jews, were repeatedly tortured to force them to concede the truth of Christianity. During the centuries in which the Inquisition had power, thousands of secret Jews were put on the rack, had water forced down their throats after their noses were pinched shut, or subjected to other tortures. All these actions were carried out by priests who claimed to be motivated only by love of the people they were torturing.

Those Jews whom the Inquisitors couldn't win back to Christianity were burned at a public ceremony known as an *auto-da-fé*. Among the Inquisition's thousands of victims a Jew named Balthazar Lopez stands out for the ironic sense of humor he displayed till the last moments of his life. In June 1654, Lopez was sentenced along with nine other secret Jews to be burned at the stake. His confessor persuaded him at the last moment to avoid the worst tortures by verbally declaring that Christianity was true. Lopez did so, whereupon another priest told him to rejoice, as his repentance meant that he would now enter Paradise. As the hangman prepared to strangle him, the same priest asked Lopez if he was truly repentant. "Father," he said, "do you think that this is a time to joke?"

The Inquisition went after dead heretics with equal fervor. On one day in the late 1480s, the bones of one hundred dead people who had lived as secret Jews were exhumed and publicly burned.

The Spanish Jews who converted to Christianity but who lived as secret Jews became known as Marranos, a contemptuous term meaning "swine." Marranos kept their identities hidden from all except immediate family members and other people whom they knew to be Marranos. Sometimes they would descend into their cellars to carry out Jewish rituals in secret; the cellar was where they usually conducted the *Passover *Seder. Marranos almost always kept their young children ignorant of their Jewish identity, telling them about it only when they reached an age at which their discretion could be trusted. Many Marranos subsequently escaped from Spain, and headed toward more tolerant European societies, especially Holland.

Over the centuries, almost all of the Marranos who did not leave Spain and who were not caught by the Inquisition, assimilated into Spanish society. Historians have long noted the strange anomaly of staunch Spanish Catholics bearing such names as Levine. For centuries, some Marrano families, particularly in Portugal where the Inquisition was established later than in Spain, maintained secret traditions faintly echoing their Jewish origins. In the twentieth century, a group was discovered in Portugal which did not eat pork on Saturday, though they had no idea how this custom had originated. In recent years, an increasing number of people of Spanish descent who were raised as Catholics (many of them in the southwestern United States) have come to rabbis and told of Jewish practices long carried out in their families (such as lighting candles on Friday night). Some of these people have subsequently converted to Judaism.

SOURCES: Cecil Roth, *The Spanish Inquisition;* the story of Balthazar Lopez is found on pp. 129–130. See also Max Margolis and Alexander Marx, *A History of the Jewish People,* pp. 460–469.

103

DON ISAAC ABRAVANEL (1437–1508)

DON ISAAC ABRAVANEL WAS PERHAPS THE HIGHEST-RANKING JEW IN A foreign government since the time of *Joseph and the Pharaoh of Egypt. Abravanel was the finance minister for King Ferdinand and Queen Isabella of Spain. Whereas Joseph started as a slave in Egypt, then rose to a position of status and power, for Abravanel the power and glory came first. In his later years, when the Jews were expelled from Spain (see next entry), he accompanied them into exile. Ferdinand and Isabella were upset by Abravanel's decision; they urged him to embrace Christianity and exempt himself from the expulsion decree. More loyal to the God of Israel than to the monarchs of Spain, Abravanel refused to do so.

As great as Abravanel's diplomatic talents were his scholarly achievements. His commentaries on the Bible, written during the years he held high government office, are still studied by Jews. The commentaries are written in a more modern tone than those of many of his contemporaries. When dealing with the biblical institution of monarchy (I Samuel 8) Abravanel notes similarities and differences with the prevailing social structure in Europe. While he often argues against christological interpretations of verses, he willingly accepts on occasion interpretations of Christian exegetes: "Indeed," he writes in his commentary to 1 Kings 8, "I regard their words on this matter to be more acceptable than those of the rabbis to which I have referred." His commentaries also include comprehensive introductions to the prophetic books in which he draws comparisons between the style and method of the various prophets.

According to one account, which some dismiss as legendary, when Ferdinand and Isabella issued the order of expulsion against the Jews of Spain, Abravanel approached them to offer an enormous bribe to cancel the decree. While the discussion was still going on, Tomás de Torquemada, head of the Spanish Inquisition (see preceding entry), came in, flung his cross on the floor, and cried out to Ferdinand: "Will you betray our Lord Jesus for thirty thousand dinars as Judas did for thirty pieces of silver?"

Recognizing that his cause was hopeless, Abravanel escaped to Italy, where he continued to write Bible commentaries and works of philosophy in which he tried to console the demoralized, exiled Jews.

SOURCES AND FURTHER READINGS: Ben Zion Netanyahu, *Don Isaac Abravanel*; Jacob S. Minkin, *Abravanel and the Expulsion of the Jews from Spain*; Menachem Kellner, *Dogma in Medieval Jewish Thought: From Maimonides to Abravanel*, pp. 179–195.

104

THE SPANISH EXPULSION, 1492

"IN THE SAME MONTH IN WHICH THEIR MAJESTIES [FERDINAND AND Isabella] issued the edict that all Jews should be driven out of the kingdom and its territories, in the same month they gave me the order to undertake with sufficient men my expedition of discovery to the Indies." So begins Christopher Columbus's diary. The expulsion that Columbus refers to was so cataclysmic an event that ever since, the date 1492 has been almost as important in Jewish history as in American history. On July 30 of that year, the entire Jewish community, some 200,000 people, were expelled from Spain.

Tens of thousands of refugees died while trying to reach safety. In some instances, Spanish ship captains charged Jewish passengers exorbitant sums, then dumped them overboard in the middle of the ocean. In the last days before the expulsion, rumors spread throughout Spain that the fleeing refugees had swallowed gold and diamonds, and many Jews were knifed to death by brigands hoping to find treasures in their stomachs.

The Jews' expulsion had been the pet project of the Spanish *Inquisition, headed by Father Tomás de Torquemada. Torquemada believed that as long as the Jews remained in Spain, they would influence the tens of thousands of recent Jewish converts to Christianity to continue practicing Judaism. Ferdinand and Isabella rejected Torquemada's demand that the Jews be expelled until January 1492, when the Spanish Army defeated Muslim forces in Granada, thereby restoring the whole of Spain to Christian rule. With their most important project, the country's unification, accomplished, the king and queen concluded that the Jews were expendable. On March 30, they issued the expulsion decree, the order to take effect in precisely four months. The short time span was a great boon to the rest of Spain, as the Jews were forced to liquidate their homes and businesses at absurdly low prices. Throughout those frantic months, Dominican priests actively encouraged Jews to convert to Christianity and thereby gain salvation both in this world and the next.

The most fortunate of the expelled Jews succeeded in escaping to Turkey. Sultan Bajazet welcomed them warmly. "How can you call Ferdinand of Aragon a wise king," he was fond of asking, "the same Ferdinand who impoverished his own land and enriched ours?" Among the most unfortunate refugees were those who fled to neighboring Portugal. In 1496, King Manuel of Portugal concluded an agreement to marry Isabella, the daughter of Spain's monarchs. As a condition of the marriage, the Spanish royal family insisted that Portugal expel her Jews. King Manuel agreed, although he was reluctant to lose his affluent and accomplished Jewish community.

In the end, only eight Portuguese Jews were actually expelled; tens of thousands of others were forcibly converted to Christianity on pain of death. The chief rabbi, Simon Maimi, was one of those who refused to convert. He was kept buried in earth up to his neck for seven days until he died. In the final analysis, all of these events took place because of the relentless will of one man, Tomás de Torquemada.

The Spanish Jews who ended up in Turkey, North Africa, Italy, and elsewhere throughout Europe and the Arab world, were known as *Sephardim— *Sefarad* being the Hebrew name for Spain. After the expulsion, the Sephardim imposed an informal ban forbidding Jews from ever again living in Spain. Specifically because their earlier sojourn in that country had been so happy, the Jews regarded the expulsion as a terrible betrayal, and have remembered it ever since with particular bitterness. Of the dozens of expulsions directed against Jews throughout their history, the one from Spain remains the most infamous. In the 1930s, Jewish scholar Abraham Joshua Heschel isolated one consoling feature in Spanish Jewry's terrible sufferings: "The Jews [of Spain] . . . had held imposing positions [before their expulsion]. The conquest of the New World was accomplished without their collaboration. Had they remained on the Iberian peninsula, they most probably would have taken part in the enterprises of the conquistadores. When the latter arrived in Haiti, they found over one million inhabitants. Twenty years later one thousand remained. The desperate Jews of 1492 could not know what a favor had been done for them." See *The Golden Age of Spanish Jewry, The Spanish Inquisition/Marranos,* and *Abravanel.*

SOURCES AND FURTHER READINGS: Max Margolis and Alexander Marx, *A History of the Jewish People,* pp. 470–476. The Heschel quote is from his German book *Don Jizchak Abravanel,* and is cited in Hillel Goldberg, *Between Berlin and Slabodka,* p. 203, n. 53. Jacob Marcus, *The Jew in the Medieval World,* pp. 51–55.

PART FOUR

Late Medieval
Period

105

GHETTO

GHETTO IS THE NAME OF THE OVERCROWDED NEIGHBORHOODS INTO which medieval Jews were forcibly confined. The word "ghetto" itself apparently was derived from the Italian *getto*, which means cannon factory. The earliest ghetto, in Venice, was located next to a cannon factory, and the name was soon applied to the Jewish area alongside it.

In Italy, where the institution originated, the ghettos were under the rule of the popes. The virulently antisemitic Pope Paul IV formalized the institution in a papal bull, *Cum nimis absurdum* (1555), in which he argued that it was absurd for Christians to act lovingly to the very people who had been condemned by God for their sins. He therefore legislated that Jews residing in areas under papal rule be segregated into ghettos. Although Jews would be permitted to leave the ghetto to go to work, they would be forbidden to be outside it at night. The ghetto gates were to be closed each evening, and on Christian holidays as well. Each ghetto was to be allowed but one synagogue. The Jews were to wear a distinctive yellow hat when they were outside the ghetto, so that Christians could immediately recognize them. Subsequent to Paul IV's bull, ghettos spread very quickly throughout Italy, and from there to the rest of Europe. In some areas, government authorities purposely situated brothels inside the ghetto or alongside it.

The Vatican had almost absolute authority over the Italian ghettos. In one notorious case, in 1858, an Italian maid confessed to a priest that, six years earlier, she had secretly baptized a deathly sick Jewish infant under her care, and the boy had subsequently recovered. The priest consulted higher Church authorities; several days later, papal police went into the ghetto of Bologna and took the boy, Edgar Mortara, away from his parents. Despite their pleas, and protests by international Jewish and non-Jewish leaders, the seven-year-old child was never returned to his family and grew up to be a priest.

When papal authority ended in Italy in 1870, so did the institution of the ghetto. The Nazis, however, revived it some seventy years later, to incarcerate those Jews who fell under their rule. The most famous was the *Warsaw Ghetto, which contained at one point some 500,000 Jews.

Today, the word "ghetto" is generally used to describe neighborhoods in which heavy concentrations of Jews dwell *voluntarily*. One might hear someone speak for example of Borough Park (an Orthodox Jewish neighborhood in Brooklyn) as "a real Jewish ghetto," without intending any negative connotation. Ghetto, therefore, generally carries no pejorative association when used among Jews today. The word's more unhappy connotations, however, still exist when applied to areas in which many poor people live, such as the black ghettos of Brownsville or Watts.

SOURCE: Max Wurmbrand and Cecil Roth, *The Jewish People*, pp. 260–269.

KABBALAH

KABBALAH IS THE NAME APPLIED TO THE WHOLE RANGE OF JEWISH MYSTIcal activity. While codes of Jewish law focus on *what* it is God wants from man, kabbalah tries to penetrate deeper, to God's essence itself.

There are elements of kabbalah in the Bible, for example, in the opening chapter of *Ezekiel, where the prophet describes his experience of the divine: "... the heavens opened and I saw visions of God.... I looked and lo, a stormy wind came sweeping out of the north—a huge cloud and flashing fire, surrounded by a radiance; and in the center of the fire, a gleam as of amber" (1:1,4). The prophet then describes a divine chariot and the throne of God.

The rabbis of the *Talmud regarded the mystical study of God as important yet dangerous. A famous talmudic story tells of four rabbis, Azzai, Ben Zoma, Elisha ben Abuyah, and *Akiva who would meet together and engage in mystical studies. Azzai, the Talmud records, "looked and went mad [and] Ben Zoma died." Elisha ben Abuyah became a heretic and left Judaism. Rabbi Akiva alone "entered in peace and left in peace" (see *Tosefta Hagigah*, chapter 2). It was this episode, the later experiences of individuals who became mentally unbalanced while engaging in mystical activities, and the disaster of the false Messiah *Shabbetai Zevi that caused seventeenth-century rabbis to legislate that kabbalah should be studied only by married men over forty who were also scholars of Torah and Talmud. The medieval rabbis wanted the study of kabbalah limited to people of mature years and character.

The most famous work of kabbalah, the *Zohar, was revealed to the Jewish world in the thirteenth century by Moses De Leon, who claimed that the book contained the mystical writings of the second-century rabbi Shimon bar Yochai. Almost all modern Jewish academic scholars believe that De Leon himself authored the Zohar, although many Orthodox kabbalists continue to accept De Leon's attribution of it to Shimon bar Yochai. Indeed, Orthodox mystics are apt to see Bar Yochai not so much as the Zohar's author as the recorder of mystical traditions dating back to the time of *Moses. The intensity with which Orthodox kabbalists hold this conviction was revealed to me once when I was arguing a point of Jewish law with an elderly religious scholar. He referred to a certain matter as being in the Torah, and when I asked him where, he said: "It's in the Zohar. Is that not the same as if it was in the Torah itself?"

The Zohar is written in Aramaic (the language of the Talmud) in the form of a commentary on the five books of the Torah. Whereas most commentaries interpret the Torah as a narrative and legal work, mystics are as likely to interpret it "as a system of symbols which reveal the secret laws of the universe and even the secrets of God" (Deborah Kerdeman and Lawrence Kushner, The Invisible Chariot, p. 90). To cite one example, Leviticus 26 records "a carrot and a stick" that God offers the Jewish people. If they follow his decrees, He will reward them. But if they spurn them, God will "set His face" against the people: "I will discipline you sevenfold for your sins. . . ." and "I will scatter you among the nations" (26:28, 33). At the chapter's conclusion, God says: "Yet, even then, when they are in the land of their enemies, I will not reject them or spurn them so as to destroy them, breaking My covenant with them, for I am the Lord, their God" (26:44).

On this series of admonitions, the Zohar comments: "Come and see the pure love of the Blessed Holy One for Israel. A parable: There was a king who had a single son who kept misbehaving. One day he offended the king. The king said, 'I have punished you so many times and you have not [changed]. Now look, what should I do with you? If I banish you from the land and expel you from the kingdom, perhaps wild beasts or wolves or robbers will attack you and you will be no more. What can I do? The only solution is that I and you together leave the land.' So . . . the Blessed Holy One said as follows: 'Israel, what should I do with you? I have already punished you and you have not heeded Me. I have brought fearsome warriors and flaming forces to strike at you and you have not obeyed. If I expel you from the land alone, I fear that packs of wolves and bears will attack you and you will be no more. But what can I do with you? The only solution is that I and you together leave the land and both of us go into exile. As it is written, 'I will discipline you,' forcing you into exile; but if you think that I will abandon you, Myself too [shall go] along with you.' "

There are many strands of teaching in the kabbalah. Medieval kabbalists, for example, were wont to speak of God as the *En Sof* (That Which Is Without Limit). The *En Sof* is inaccessible and unknowable to man. But God reveals Himself to mankind through a series of ten emanations, *sefirot*, a configuration of forces that issue from the *En Sof*. The first of these *sefirot* is *keter* (crown) and refers to God's will to create. Another *sefira*, *binah* (understanding), represents the unfolding in God's mind of the details of creation, while *hesed* (loving-kindness) refers to the uncontrolled flow of divine goodness. Most of the *sefirot* are regarded as legitimate objects for human meditation; they represent a way in which human beings can make contact with God. Through contemplation and virtuous deeds, human beings can also bring down the divine grace to this world.

The greatest scholar and historian of kabbalah in the past century was the late Professor Gershom Scholem of Hebrew University in Jerusalem. Scholem, himself a nonobservant Jew, was fond of explaining how he became attracted to so esoteric a discipline: "My decision to study Jewish mysticism came the day I visited the home of a famous German rabbi, a person with a reputation for scholarship in the kabbalah. . . . Seeing on his shelf some mystical texts with intriguing titles, I had, with all the enthusiasm of youth, asked the rabbi about them. 'This junk,' the rabbi had laughed at me. 'I should waste time reading nonsense like this?' It was then . . . that I decided here was a field in which I could make an impression. If this man can become an authority without reading the text, then what might I become if I actually read the books?"

As a rule, *mekubbalim* (people who actively study and practice kabbalah) are skeptical of men like Scholem, who studied kabbalah as a university discipline and not from a personal conviction of its truth. One *mekubbal*, Rabbi Abraham Chen, declared on one occasion before a seminar of Scholem's students: "A scholar of mysticism is like an accountant: He may know where all the treasure is, but he is not free to use it." A precisely opposite view on the value of kabbalah was taken by the late Professor Saul Lieberman, a confirmed rationalist and the great Talmud scholar of the Jewish Theological Seminary. In an introduction to a lecture Scholem delivered at the seminary, Lieberman said that several years earlier, some students asked to have a course here in which they could study kabbalistic texts. He had told them that it was not possible, but if they wished they could have a course on the history of kabbalah. For at a university, Lieberman said, "it is forbidden to have a course in nonsense. But the history of nonsense, that is scholarship."

Lieberman's caustic comment aside, kabbalah has long been one of the important areas of Jewish thought. Ideas that many contemporary Jews might think of as un-Jewish sometimes are found in the kabbalah, most notably, the belief in reincarnation (*gilgul neshamot*). Between 1500 and 1800, Scholem has written, "kabbalah was widely considered to be *the* true Jewish theology," and almost no one attacked it. With the Jewish entrance into the modern world, however—a world in which rational thinking was more highly esteemed than the mystical—kabbalah tended to be downgraded or ignored. In recent years, there has been an enormous upsurge of interest in kabbalah, and today it is commonly studied among *Hasidic Jews, and among many non-Orthodox Jews who are part of the counterculture, and for those, including many non-Jews, looking into an alternative path of spirituality.

SOURCES AND FURTHER READINGS: The most accessible introduction to kabbalah is Herbert Wiener, 9½ Mystics; Scholem's account of how he became involved in kabbalah, and Rabbi Chen's critique of students of kabbalah as accountants, are found in that book on pp. 60 and 278. The major overview of the whole field of kabbalah is Gershom Scholem, *Major Trends in Jewish Mysticism*. See also Deborah Kerdeman and Lawrence Kushner, *The Invisible Chariot: An Introduction to Kabbalah and Jewish Spirituality*, and Louis Jacobs, *A Jewish Theology*, pp. 28–29. Daniel Matt, *Zohar*, contains selections from the standard kabbalistic text; the excerpt cited from Leviticus 26 is found on pp. 159–160. In recent years, Daniel Matt has started bringing out a major multivolume translation and commentary on the Zohar, called *The Zohar: Pritzker Edition*.

107

THE CODE OF JEWISH LAW —
SHULKHAN ARUKH
JOSEPH KARO (1488–1575)
MOSES ISSERLES, THE RAMA
(C. 1525–1572)

THE LEGAL CODE KNOWN AS THE *SHULKHAN ARUKH*, COMPILED BY the great Sephardic rabbi Joseph Karo in the mid-1500s, is still the standard legal code of Judaism. When rabbis, particularly if they are Orthodox, are asked to rule on a question of Jewish law, the first volume they consult generally is the *Shulkhan Arukh*. A major reason for its universal acceptance is that it was the first code to list the differing customs and laws of both *Sephardic and *Ashkenazic Jewry. (*Maimonides's earlier *Mishneh Torah*, for example, contained only the legal rulings of Sephardic Jewry, which differed in certain areas from European Jewry's practices.) This unique feature was not intended by Joseph Karo, but came about through a happy coincidence. At the very time that Karo was compiling his code, a similar undertaking was being planned by Rabbi Moses Isserles of Poland. Isserles, known in Jewish life as the *Rama*, was thrown into some despair when he first heard about Karo's work, for he knew Karo to be a greater scholar than himself. Nonetheless, he soon realized that both Karo's legal code and his own would not by themselves meet the needs of all Jews. Thus, the *Shulkhan Arukh* was published with Karo's rulings listed first, and Isserles's dissents and addenda included in italics.

The *Shulkhan Arukh* is divided into four volumes:

1. *Orakh Hayyim*—laws of prayer and of holidays
2. *Yoreh Deah*—diverse laws, including those governing charity (*tzedaka), Torah study (see *Talmud Torah*), and the Jewish dietary laws (see *Kosher*)

3. *Even ha-Ezer*—laws concerning Jewish marriage and divorce
4. *Khoshen Mishpat*—Jewish civil law

To this day, rabbinic ordination (**semikha*) usually is given to a student only after he has been examined on the *Shulkhan Arukh*, particularly on those sections that deal with *kashrut* (dietary laws). More than rote knowledge of the *Shulkhan Arukh*'s rulings, however, is expected. A popular Jewish folktale tells of a young student who came to a prominent rabbi to be tested for ordination. The rabbi's first question was, "Name the five volumes of the *Shulkhan Arukh*."

The student, thinking that the rabbi had made a slip of the tongue, named the four volumes, but the rabbi asked him to name the fifth.

"There is no fifth volume," the student said.

"There is indeed," the rabbi said. "Common sense is the fifth volume, and if you don't have it, all your rulings will be of no use, even if you know the other four volumes by heart."

The *Shulkhan Arukh*'s exhaustive presentation of the details of Jewish law is suggested by the following, taken from the section listing the laws of Torah study, in which Karo gives directives to both teachers and pupils:

"The rabbi should not be angry with his pupils if they do not understand but he should repeat the matter over and over again until they grasp the proper depth of the law. The pupil should not say that he understands when he does not but should ask over and over again. And if the rabbi is angry with him he should say, 'Rabbi, it is the Torah and I want to know it, but my mind is inadequate' " (*Yoreh Deah* 246:10).

SOURCES AND FURTHER READINGS: Isadore Twersky, "The *Shulkhan Arukh*: Enduring Code of Jewish Law," in Judah Goldin, ed., *The Jewish Expression*, pp. 322–343. A selection of brief passages from the *Shulkhan Arukh* in English translation with commentary is found in Louis Jacobs, *Jewish Law*, pp. 146–171.

108

MARTIN LUTHER AND THE PROTESTANT REFORMATION

MARTIN LUTHER (1483–1546) IS THE MOST EXTREME EXAMPLE IN HIS-tory of a Jew-lover who turned into a Jew-hater when the Jews refused to convert to his ideology (see also *Mohammed*).

Luther is, of course, primarily known as a Catholic monk who revolted against the Vatican and founded the breakaway faith that became the Lutheran Church. During his revolt's early years, Luther was sure he would accomplish what the Catholic Church had failed to do: bring large numbers of Jews to Christianity. Toward that end, in 1523 he wrote a pamphlet, *That Jesus Christ Was Born a Jew*, in which he denounced the *blood libel as a slander, and blamed the Church for alienating the Jews: "And if I had been a Jew and had seen such idiots and blockheads ruling and teaching the Christian religion, I would rather have been a pig than a Christian." Luther argued passionately for the elimination of anti-Jewish legislation, to enable the Jews to compete fairly in the marketplace.

Yet, less than twenty years later, this same man was to pen the most anti-semitic writings produced in Germany until the time of Hitler. Incensed that the Jews had not followed his brand of Christianity, Luther outlined eight actions to be taken against them:

Burn all synagogues.

Destroy all Jewish homes.

Confiscate all Jewish holy books.

Forbid rabbis to teach, on pain of death.

Forbid Jews to travel.

Confiscate Jewish property.

Force Jews to do physical labor.

[And, in case the preceding restrictions proved insufficient] Expel all the Jews.

On one occasion, this earlier exponent of Christian love said: "I would threaten to cut their tongues out from their throats, if they refuse to acknowledge the truth that God is a trinity and not a plain unity."

Unfortunately, these antisemitic ravings were not peripheral jottings of Luther's; instead, they became well known throughout Germany. Four hundred years later, Hitler proudly claimed Luther as an ally: "He saw the Jew as we are only beginning to see him today." When the Nazis carried out the infamous *Kristallnacht pogrom on November 9–10, 1938, they announced that the action was taken in honor of Luther's birthday (November 10). At the Nuremberg trials, Nazi propagandist Julius Streicher defended himself with the claim that he had not said anything worse about the Jews than had Martin Luther.

For all of Luther's anti-Jewish animosity, the Reformation that he inaugurated was a positive development for the Jews. Before him, Europeans had been united in one Christian Church, and the Jews were the only major group outside it. With the breakdown of Christian unity, many different religious groups developed within Europe. This helped produce greater tolerance, since the multiplicity of groups residing near each other eventually recognized the need for pluralism. It is quite likely that the rise of Protestantism helped set the stage for democracy. It is one of history's ironies that a process inaugurated by a vehement antisemite ultimately proved beneficial to the Jews.

SOURCES: Luther's eight proposals against the Jews were published in *Concerning the Jews and Their Lies*, sections of which can be found in Jacob Marcus, ed., *The Jew in the Medieval World*, pp. 167–169. Hitler's claim of Luther as an ally is found in Friedrich Heer, *God's First Love*, p. 286. Julius Streicher's defense at Nuremberg is cited in A. Roy Eckhardt, *Your People, My People*, p. 24.

109

ASHKENAZIM AND SEPHARDIM

Yiddish and Ladino

THE JEWISH COMMUNITY IS COMMONLY DIVIDED INTO ASHKENAZIC and Sephardic Jews. This division seems odd, since *Ashkenaz* is the Hebrew word for Germany, and *Sefarad* means "Spain." In practice, however, most Jews whose families come from Europe are regarded as Ashkenazim, and those whose families come from either Spain or the Arab world are called Sephardim. However, if one meets a Jew whose last name is Ashkenazi, he almost certainly is a Sephardi. Many generations ago, a European ancestor of his undoubtedly went to live among Sephardic Jews, where he was referred to as the "Ashkenazi," a name that stuck even when his descendants assumed a Sephardic identity.

Throughout the medieval period, the Sephardim from Spain regarded themselves as an elite among the Jews. Unlike most of their brethren elsewhere in Europe, Spanish Jews often had high levels of secular education and, not infrequently, great wealth. Even after their *expulsion from Spain in 1492, Spanish Jews maintained a strong sense of group pride. They were apt to sign correspondence with the Hebrew initials *shin tet*, which probably stood for *sephardi tahor* (pure Sephardi), indicating that there was no Ashkenazic blood in the signatory's veins. Some historians claim that the letters stood rather for *sofo tov* (one who had a good end) and meant only that the writer had fled Spain as a Jew and had never converted to Christianity. Whatever the case may be, the Sephardim who fled Spain and settled elsewhere in Europe discriminated against non-Sephardic Jews. At the Sephardic synagogues in eighteenth-century Amsterdam and London, Ashkenazic Jews could not sit with the rest of the congregation; they had to stand behind wooden barriers. In 1766 in London, the Sephardic community ruled that if a Sephardi married an Ashkenazi woman and died, no Sephardic charity funds could be used to assist the widow. With the passage of time, these harsh attitudes generally abated.

The Jews living in the Arab world also became known as Sephardim, most likely because their liturgical and ritual practices followed Sephardic as opposed to Ashkenazic custom. Today when people speak about the Sephardic Jews living in Israel, they are usually referring to the Jews who have come there from the Arab world, Morocco, Iraq, Yemen, etc. Unlike the Spanish Sephardim, these Jews have often been among the less affluent inhabitants of Israel. In the United States, however, Jews from the Arab world have frequently achieved great financial success. The best known Sephardic community in the New York area is the seventy thousand or more Syrian Jews of Brooklyn and New Jersey, most of whose ancestors came from Aleppo shortly after the turn of the century. They are a highly cohesive community and have among the lowest intermarriage rates of any Jewish community in the United States, along with very high rates of children who attend Jewish day schools. There are now also large communities of Sephardic Jews from Iran living in Los Angeles and New York. They too are a highly cohesive and financially successful community.

Among the Ashkenazim, as among the Sephardim, there tended to be a hierarchy. German Jews generally regarded themselves as being on a higher intellectual plane than their East European brethren. Those who came to the United States contributed generously to help settle the Polish and Russian Jews who came after them, but they did look down upon them. When German Jews established the *B'nai B'rith organization in 1843, they initially barred Jews born in Eastern Europe from membership.

The East European Jews had their own set of prejudices toward their German-Jewish brethren. At an early Zionist congress, Chaim *Weizmann, a Russian Jew par excellence, had a fight with some German-Jewish delegates and later observed: "You know what the problem is with German Jews? They have all the charm of Germans, and all the modesty of Jews." German Jews were nicknamed Yekkes, a word of uncertain provenance. The nickname is still used among Jews to designate Jews of German origin, though it is frequently applied to anyone who has the character traits stereotypically associated with Yekkes: precise, prompt, punctiliously honest, and somewhat cold.

When the Jews lived in Spain, they spoke Spanish, albeit with some distinctive Jewish influences. After their expulsion, they continued to speak a form of Judeo-Spanish that became known as Ladino. Relatively few people today speak Ladino, although in recent years many of its classic works of literature have been translated into Hebrew and English.

In Europe many Jews spoke Yiddish, a Jewish language based largely on

German and Hebrew. The word for Jew in Yiddish is *Yid*, which is why people who are speaking Yiddish will sometimes say they are speaking "Jewish." This usage, however, is incorrect; the language's correct name is Yiddish.

As a rule, Jews only spoke Yiddish in societies where they did not have equal rights: The Jews of Poland and Russia, for example, spoke Yiddish, while the overwhelming majority of Jews in nineteenth-century France and Germany spoke French and German. When Jews migrated to countries where they had equal rights, they usually spoke Yiddish for the first generation. In the 1920s, Yiddish newspapers published in New York sold over 200,000 copies daily.

Yiddish is an unusually colorful language, and in the United States many of its more evocative words have entered the vocabulary of non-Jews. When Jeane Kirkpatrick, former U.S. ambassador to the United Nations, was asked if she would run for the American presidency in 1988, she answered: "I don't mind the campaigning, or the *shlepping* [dragging or running] around. For me, the difficulty of running is the asking—and the risking." Actress Candice Bergen confessed in a magazine article that she was not a "China *maven*" (expert). *Kibitz* is a Yiddish word, as are the two words for a ne'er-do-well, *shlemiel* and *shlemazal*. Jewish folkore has it that a *shlemazal* is the one who invariably spills his glass of tea, and the *shlemiel* is the one on whom it inevitably falls. Other Yiddish words in common American usage include *mensch (a fine person), meshugga (crazy), bagel, and yenta (an overly talkative person).

The only Jewish communities among whom Yiddish is still the primary language are certain *Hasidic sects. It would be premature, however, to predict the language's demise. Isaac Bashevis Singer, the Yiddish writer who won the Nobel Prize in 1978, noted that people had been predicting the end of Yiddish since his arrival in the United States in 1935; nonetheless, the language goes limping along, blissfully unaware that it is supposed to be dead.

SOURCES AND FURTHER READINGS: H. J. Zimmels, *Ashkenazim and Sephardim: Their Relations, Differences, and Problems as Reflected in the Rabbinical Responsa*. On p. 62, Zimmels cites the harsh anti-Ashkenazi regulations adopted by the seventeenth-century Sephardim of Amsterdam and London. See also Moshe Lazar, ed., *The Sephardic Tradition*, and Herbert Dobrinsky, *A Treasury of Sephardic Laws and Customs*.

110

CHMIELNITZKI MASSACRES (1648–1649)

ALTHOUGH FEW PEOPLE TODAY KNOW ABOUT IT, THERE WAS A NAZILIKE
war against the Jews three centuries before the *Holocaust.

The Chmielnitzki massacres of 1648–1649 were led by Bogdan Chmielnitzki, a Ukrainian Cossack who led a successful revolt against Polish rule
over his country. Because many Jews worked for Polish noblemen who
owned land in the Ukraine, Chmielnitzki's ire was also directed against the
Jews. Like Hitler, Chmielnitzki hated *all* Jews indiscriminately. It is estimated that his Cossack troops murdered well over 100,000 Jews at a time
when world Jewry probably numbered no more than a million and a half.

The following contemporaneous description vividly portrays the atrocities
that occurred in a typical Chmielnitzki massacre. If you have a weak stomach, don't read it. I myself have grave reservations about including such a
horrifying passage, but I fear that this tragic episode in Jewish history is in
danger of being forgotten.

"Some of them [the Jews] had their skins flayed off them and their flesh
was flung to the dogs. The hands and feet of others were cut off and they were
flung onto the roadway where carts ran over them and they were trodden
underfoot by horse. . . . And many were buried alive. Children were slaughtered in their mother's bosoms and many children were torn apart like fish.
They ripped up the bellies of pregnant women, took out the unborn children, and flung them in their faces. They tore open the bellies of some of
them and placed a living cat within the belly and left them alive thus, first
cutting off their hands so that they should not be able to take the living cat
out of the belly . . . and there was never an unnatural death in the world that
they did not inflict upon them."

It is hard to believe that human beings created in God's image could be
capable of such sadism. It is equally hard to believe that Bogdan Chmielnitzki is still regarded in the Ukraine as a great national hero. Russian nation-
alists, too, hail Chmielnitzki as a "great patriot" for bringing about the
Ukraine's unification with Russia. When I visited the Soviet Union in 1973,

my Intourist guide explained to me that a major street in Moscow is named after Chmielnitzki because "he was a great soldier and hero." She was surprised that I knew who Chmielnitzki was, and even more surprised that my assessment of him was considerably less enthusiastic.

Many Jews who were not murdered during the massacres were sold as slaves, usually to Constantinople's slave markets. For many years, Jewish communities throughout Europe raised money to redeem these slaves and free them (see *Redeeming Captives/Pidyon Shvuyim*).

It would seem that the horror and depression occasioned by the Chmielnitzki massacres were important factors in influencing many Jews to follow the false Messiah Shabbetai Zevi (see next entry) less than two decades later.

SOURCES: The description of a Chmielnitzki massacre is from a Hebrew document, N. Hanover, *Yeven Mezulah*, pp. 31–32. Probably the best novel written about this awful period in Jewish life—and one of the best Jewish historical novels ever written— is Isaac Bashevis Singer's *The Slave*.

111

SHABBETAI ZEVI (1626–1676)

In 1665, perhaps half or more of world Jewry believed that Shabbetai Zevi, a Turkish Jew, was the Messiah, who would soon liberate Palestine from Turkish rule and restore it as an independent Jewish state. There are records of English Jews making bets and giving ten-to-one odds that the messianic restoration would come within two years. In Germany, upper-class Jews packed large barrels with food and clothing in preparation for the long journey to Palestine.

In lieu of a return to Zion, there was a catastrophe. Instead of Shabbetai confronting the Turkish sultan with his demand for Palestine, the monarch conveyed to Shabbetai a threat: either he convert to Islam or be tortured to death. Shortly thereafter, Shabbetai entered the sultan's palace, donned a turban, and took the Muslim name Mehemet Effendi.

The shock to the Jewish community was overwhelming. Once again, the

Jews had suffered a great failure with a "messiah." *Jesus had become the father of Christianity, *Bar-Kokhba had led the Jews into a disastrous revolt, and now Shabbetai had become a Muslim.

The mass support that Shabbetai inspired is somewhat surprising because he had long given evidence of being highly peculiar. On one notable occasion he conducted a symbolic marriage ceremony between himself and a Torah scroll; on another, he pronounced the ineffable name of God, an act that Jewish tradition permitted only to the High Priest on *Yom Kippur, and then, only in the *Temple in Jerusalem. In addition, Shabbetai had married twice, but both marriages were not consummated and ended in divorce.

Nonetheless, masses of Jews, along with a substantial number of rabbinic scholars, were swept along in the messianic frenzy. Part of the credit must go to Shabbetai's brilliant publicist, Nathan of Gaza. Nathan dispatched persuasively written communiqués throughout the Jewish world predicting the imminent return of the *Ten Lost Tribes, the overthrow of the Turkish sultan, and Shabbetai's triumphant reign thereafter as Messiah. Widespread, and often naive, religious piety made the message irresistible to large numbers of Jews. In Europe, Nathan's letter was greeted with particular enthusiasm, coming as it did on the heels of the horrendous Chmielnitzki *pogroms during which more than one hundred thousand Jews had been murdered (see preceding entry). In fact, it was the pogroms' very horror that apparently persuaded so many Jews that the messianic age must be imminent.

Even after Shabbetai's conversion to Islam, Nathan continued to insist that he was the Messiah but that his messianic task mandated that he "descend" into the lower world of Islam to redeem its impure sparks. Thousands of Jews who had staked their reputations on Shabbetai being the messianic redeemer accepted Nathan's far-fetched explanation.

In Turkey a Jewish group called the Doenmeh converted to Islam while continuing to believe that Shabbetai was the Messiah. So powerfully did they cling to this belief that they survived as a distinct and separate Islamic sect until after World War I.

In Eastern Europe, decades after Shabbetai's death, a scoundrel by the name of Jacob Frank claimed to be his successor. He organized a movement that asserted that Jewish laws were voided in the new messianic age. Frank even organized wife-swapping orgies, which quickly led to his ostracism and persecution by the organized Jewish community. In 1759, the Frankists converted en masse to Catholicism, whereupon they charged their former coreligionists with murdering Christians and drinking their blood.

Most Jews, of course, stopped believing that Shabbetai was the Messiah when they heard about his conversion to Islam. The agony following their earlier ecstatic anticipation must have been particularly painful, coming so soon after the Chmielnitzki pogroms.

Did any good at all come from this sorry episode? Gershom Scholem, the great scholar of *kabbalah and the author of a thousand-page biography of Shabbetai, argues that, for a few months in 1665–1666, world Jewry was united in believing that it was about to be redeemed and restored to Palestine. The brief taste of what freedom might be like made it impossible for many Jews—even after Shabbetai was revealed as a false Messiah—to go on passively accepting their powerless status quo. Scholem sees Zionism and the Jewish struggle for equal rights as in some measure resulting from the social and religious upheaval produced by "Sabbatianism."

As for the "Messiah" himself, was he a malevolent fraud or a madman? Some contemporary analyses speculate that Shabbetai was severely manic-depressive. Three centuries after his death it is impossible to assess the accuracy of this diagnosis, but it does seem to conform to the biographical and anecdotal accounts we have of his life, in which periods of exultation alternate with periods of withdrawal and deep depression. It is possible that Shabbetai anticipated his meeting with the sultan in just such a mood of exultation, expecting that he would be handed Palestine. Unfortunately, the sultan's threat very quickly dropped him from manic heights to terror and depression. He lived only ten more years after his conversion, dying in exile in Albania.

SOURCES AND FURTHER READINGS: Gershom Scholem, *Sabbatai Sevi: The Mystical Messiah 1626–1676*; Scholem, "Redemption Through Sin," in his *The Messianic Idea in Judaism*, pp. 78–141; Hayim Greenberg, "Shabbetai Zevi—The Messiah as Apostate," in his *The Inner Eye: Selected Essays*, Shlomo Katz, ed., vol. 2, pp. 84–98.

112

EXCOMMUNICATION OF SPINOZA, 1656
Kherem

THE NOTED JEWISH HISTORIAN ARTHUR HERTZBERG USED TO DESCRIBE Baruch (Benedict) Spinoza (1632–1677) as the first modern Jew because he was the first to leave the Jewish community without becoming a Christian.

Spinoza was a pantheist: He believed that God was within nature, not a separate Being with an independent will. "In Spinoza's system," Jewish philosopher Louis Jacobs has written, "God and Nature are treated as different names for the same thing. God is not 'outside' or apart from Nature. He did not *create* Nature but is Nature." This doctrine set Spinoza at loggerheads with both Judaism and Christianity. It was absurd in his view to credit God with attributes such as will or intellect; that was like demanding that Sirius bark, just because people refer to it as the Dog Star. Spinoza tried to posit a system of ethics based on reason, not supernatural revelation.

Spinoza's excommunication by the rabbis of Amsterdam when he was in his mid-twenties was caused by his denial of angels, the immortality of the soul, and God's authorship of the Torah. Communal leaders warned Spinoza to desist from such heresies, and when the warnings went unheeded, they issued this ban: "Cursed shall be he when he goes out and cursed when he comes in. May the Lord not forgive his sins. May the Lord's anger and wrath rage against this man, and cast upon him all the curses that are written in the Torah. May the Lord wipe his name out from under the Heavens; and may the Lord destroy him and cast him out from all the tribes of Israel. . . ." Spinoza's excommunication, known in Hebrew as a *kherem*, was total. No Jew was to conduct business with him, speak with him, or stand within four paces of him. Subsequent to the *kherem*, there is no evidence that Spinoza ever again spoke to a Jew.

In his later writings, Spinoza was an early forerunner of biblical criticism. In his anonymously published *Theological-Political Tractate*, he argued that the Torah could not have been written by one person, and not all of it dated to Moses' time. He posited that the Torah was set down some eight hundred years after Moses, by Ezra. He treated the Torah not as the revealed word of God, but as a human document. In line with his philosophy, Spinoza believed that the miracles described in the Bible were impossible because they run contrary to natural laws.

Liberal Jews have long decried the *kherem* against Spinoza because it is religiously intolerant. During the 1950s, Israeli Prime Minister David *Ben-Gurion suggested that the *kherem* be withdrawn retroactively. The rabbis of Amsterdam did not act on Ben-Gurion's motion.

During the past century, bans of excommunication have been issued very rarely in Jewish life, which is fortunate, since their effect can be devastating. A few years before Spinoza, another Dutch Jew, Uriel da Costa (1585–1640), also ran afoul of Amsterdam's religious authorities and likewise was excommunicated. Unlike Spinoza, da Costa was emotionally traumatized by the rejection of his fellow Jews and recanted the views that had caused his excommunication. The degrading punishment that he was forced to undergo before being readmitted to the Jewish community included a public whipping in front of both men and women. Almost immediately afterward, da Costa committed suicide.

Bans of excommunication are almost never issued today, except occasionally against men who refuse to give their wives a Jewish divorce (see *Get*).

SOURCES AND FURTHER READINGS: On Spinoza's pantheism and his statement about Sirius barking, see Paul Johnson, *A History of the Jews*, pp. 289–294; Yirmiyahu Yovel, *Spinoza and Other Heretics: The Marrano of Reason*; Louis Jacobs, *A Jewish Theology*, pp. 63–64. A recent work on Spinoza is Rebecca Goldstein, *Betraying Spinoza: The Renegade Jew Who Gave Us Modernity*.

113

COURT JEWS
Shtadlanim

WHATEVER LIMITED RIGHTS JEWS HAD IN MEDIEVAL EUROPE GENERALLY came not through force of law, but through force of personality. The right of settlement, for example, usually came when a non-Jewish leader invited Jews to settle in his community. Jews, thus, were understandably nervous when a friendly gentile ruler died; his successor might well decide to expel them, expropriate their property, or tax them more heavily.

Jews who represented their co-religionists to the outside world were known as *shtadlanim*, a term dating back to the eleventh century. The *shtadlanim* often were court Jews (the title bestowed on Jews who served as agents to local rulers). There were numerous court Jews, particularly in Germany, which was divided into many small principalities.

The court Jews' main responsibility was to extend and negotiate loans, and to arrange for the purchase of army supplies. In good times, court Jews, who were usually the wealthiest members of the Jewish community, held a position of power and influence. In bad times, however, the court Jews themselves were often the first victims of antisemitic sovereigns. The most famous court Jew was the eighteenth-century Joseph Süss Oppenheimer (1698–1738), the finance minister to the duke of Württemberg. He acquired so much influence that he was a power in his own right. When the duke suddenly died, however, Oppenheimer's enemies immediately had him seized and sentenced to death. A Pastor Rieger told him he could save his life if he converted to Christianity. Although not an observant Jew, Oppenheimer refused: "I am a Jew and will remain a Jew. I would not become a Christian even if I could become an emperor. Changing one's religion is a matter for consideration by a free man; it is an evil thing for a prisoner." He died with the words of the *Sh'ma* on his lips.

Because court Jews and *shtadlanim* pleaded for their fellow Jews on the basis of personal favors and bribes, not on the basis of rights, the word *shtadlan* has today a negative, and rather pathetic, connotation. When some Jews favor holding a public demonstration on a certain issue, and others advocate quiet diplomacy, the activists are apt to accuse the would-be diplomats of being *shtadlanim*, the Jewish equivalent of Uncle Toms.

SOURCE AND FURTHER READING: S. Stern, *The Court Jew.*

HASIDIM AND MITNAGDIM

ISRAEL BA'AL SHEM TOV (1700–1760)

ALTHOUGH CONTEMPORARY JEWS OFTEN USE THE WORD "HASID" AS A synonym for ultra-Orthodox, Hasidism, a religious movement that arose in eighteenth-century Eastern Europe, was originally regarded as revolutionary and religiously liberal. Its opponents, known as Mitnagdim, were themselves Orthodox Jews. More than anything else, the stories that each group told about its rabbinic leaders exemplify the differences among them. The Mitnagdim were proud of the fact that their leader, the Vilna Gaon (see following entry), had delivered an advanced discourse on the *Talmud when he was less than seven years old, and that he studied Jewish texts eighteen hours a day.

The founder of Hasidism, Israel Ba'al Shem Tov, was the hero of very different sorts of tales. The Hasidim told of how he spent his teenage years working in a job with low status, as assistant in a Jewish elementary school, a *cheder*. He would round up the students from their homes each morning and lead them to school singing songs. Later, after he married, he and his wife went to live in the far-off Carpathian Mountains. There, the Ba'al Shem Tov worked as a laborer, digging clay and lime, which his wife then sold in town. The couple later kept an inn.

During these years, the Ba'al Shem Tov spent much time in the nearby forest in meditation and solitude. His Hasidic followers subsequently likened this period to the years of isolation and meditation that *Moses spent in Midian, tending the flocks of his father-in-law.

Around 1736, the Ba'al Shem Tov revealed himself as a healer and a leader. His last name, which literally means "Master of the Good Name," was one that was frequently applied in Jewish life to miracle workers and healers. In 1740, he moved to Meziboz, a town near the borders of both Poland and the Ukraine, and not far from Lithuania. Disciples started coming to him from the surrounding countries, but the talks delivered by the Ba'al Shem Tov differed dramatically from lectures offered at a *yeshiva; they focused far more on an individual's personal relationship with God and with his fellow-man than on the intricacies of Jewish law. The stories Hasidim later told about the Ba'al Shem Tov—usually referred to by his acronym, the Besht—invariably depict him with a pipe in hand, telling seemingly secular tales with deep religious meanings. He died in 1760, leaving behind Dov Baer of Mezrich as his successor. Shortly before his death, the Besht told the people standing near his bed: "I grieve not at my death, for I can see a door opening while the other is closing."

Many of the dominant themes in the Besht's teachings became the central emphases in the Hasidic movement that his followers developed. There were statements of the Besht, not entirely innovative, which placed great stress on aspects of Judaism that the Mitnagdim generally ignored or downplayed: the heart, for example. The Besht was particularly fond of a talmudic statement, "God desires the heart" (Sanhedrin 106b), which he interpreted as meaning that for God, a pure religious spirit mattered more than knowledge of the Talmud. It is told of the Besht that one *Yom Kippur a poor Jewish boy, an illiterate shepherd, entered the synagogue where he was praying. The boy was deeply moved by the service, but frustrated that he could not read the prayers. He started to whistle, the one thing he knew he could do beautifully; he wanted to offer his whistling as a gift to God. The congregation was horrified at the desecration of their service. Some people yelled at the boy, and others wanted to throw him out. The Ba'al Shem Tov immediately stopped them. "Until now," he said, "I could feel our prayers being blocked as they tried to reach the heavenly court. This young shepherd's whistling was so pure, however, that it broke through the blockage and brought all of our prayers straight up to God."

Another ancient Jewish doctrine that was given particular emphasis by the Ba'al Shem Tov was based on a verse in *Isaiah: "The whole world is full of His glory" (6:13), If the whole world is full of God's glory, the Besht reasoned, then the Mitnagdim and the ascetics were wrong in thinking that one had to turn one's back on the pleasures of the world. "Don't deny that a girl is beautiful," the *Besht* would say. "Just be sure that your recognition of her beauty brings you back to its source—God." If one could do that, then even physical pleasures could bring about spiritual growth.

Because the world was full of God, the *Besht* believed that a person always should be joyful. Indeed, the greatest act of creativity comes about in an atmosphere of joy: "No child is born except through pleasure and joy," the *Besht* declared. "By the same token, if one wishes his prayers to bear fruit, he must offer them with pleasure and joy." This doctrine was a strong challenge to many ideas current among Jews in the *Besht*'s time. Many religious Jews, particularly among the *kabbalists, preached asceticism, and advocated that Jews fast every Monday and Thursday. The Ba'al Shem Tov warned people against such practices, fearing that they would lead to melancholy, not joy.

To outsiders, unaccustomed to the *Besht*'s teachings, Hasidic prayer services sometimes seemed undignified, even chaotic. In fulfillment of the *Psalmist's ecstatic declaration, "All my bones shall say, Lord, who is like You?" (Psalms 35:10), worshipers were capable of performing handstands. Characteristically, the *Besht* defended such practices at Hasidic services with a story. A deaf man passed by a hall where a wedding reception was being celebrated. When he looked through the window, he saw people engaged in exultant and tumultuous dancing. But because he could not hear the music, he assumed they were mad.

The *Besht* also taught that the *Tzaddik* (the religious leader of the Hasidim) should serve as a model of how to lead a religious life. However, he did not emphasize the doctrine of the *Tzaddik* nearly as much as some of his successors, particularly Dov Baer of Mezrich, who made it central to Hasidism. Dov Baer, the leader of the Hasidim after the Baal Shem Tov's death, taught that God revealed Himself through the *Tzaddik*'s most trivial actions; one of Dov Baer's followers said, "I didn't go to him to learn Torah, but to see him unbuckle his shoes." Dov Baer taught that the ideal *Tzaddik* had a closer relationship to God than the average Jew, and could bestow blessings on people. In return, it was understood that the Hasidim must bring their *Tzaddik* gifts.

The belief in the power and greatness of the *Tzaddik* became one of Hasidism's strongest—and most controversial—ideas. Hasidism's opponents charged that the *Tzaddikim* (plural) often enriched themselves at the expense of their followers. In the generation after Dov Baer, numerous new Hasidic groups were formed, each with its own *Tzaddik*, referred to as a *rebbe*. These *rebbes* became a kind of Jewish royalty. When one died, he was succeeded by either his son or son-in-law. Those Hasidic groups that established eminent family dynasties became successful. Many Hasidic groups, however, went into decline when their *rebbe* died and left behind less capable successors.

The best known group of Hasidim in the United States are the *Lubavitcher, who are headquartered in Brooklyn. Their *rebbe*, until his death in 1994, was Menachem Mendel Schneersohn, the seventh leader since the movement was founded in the late 1700s. But though Lubavitch is the one Hasidic group non-Orthodox Jews are most apt to meet—because of the movement's various outreach programs—there are dozens of other Hasidic dynasties in the United States (many of them located in Brooklyn) and in Israel.

In their early years, the Hasidim were actively persecuted by the Mitnagdim, who feared they would become another heretical sect, similar to that of *Shabbetai Zevi. But in its formative stages, Hasidism wisely put its primary emphasis on personal religious growth rather than on national salvation, and it downplayed the *messianic element. This was not enough, however, to appease the Mitnagdim. Other Hasidic traits, such as their laissez-faire attitude toward the appropriate hours for prayer, bitterly provoked their opponents. The Hasidim answered that they couldn't legislate precise hours for reciting each of the three daily prayer services; they prayed with such intensity (*kavannah*) that they couldn't do so while looking at a watch.

The Israeli historian Jacob Katz has documented how other practices provocatively separated the Hasidim from their neighbors. For example, Hasidim advocated using a sharper knife when slaughtering animals than the one used by the Mitnagdim's slaughterers. Such stringency had a socially divisive effect: The Hasidim no longer could eat at the Mitnagdim's homes. The Hasidim also adopted a different prayerbook, so that their synagogue service differed somewhat from that of other Jews and had to be conducted separately. Their most brilliant act of "public relations" was labeling themselves Hasidim, the Hebrew word for both "pious" and "saintly," while calling their adversaries Mitnagdim, Hebrew for "opponents." These terms made the Hasidim seem like the more dynamic and positive of the two groups.

With the passage of time, the Hasidim and Mitnagdim recognized that their differences were increasingly inconsequential, particularly after both groups found themselves facing a common enemy: the nineteenth-century *Haskala*, or Jewish Enlightenment. Jewish parents who once feared that their Hasidic or Mitnagdish child might go over to the other camp, were now far more afraid that their child might become altogether irreligious.

An additional factor that lessened the Hasidic-Mitnagdish split was nineteenth- and twentieth-century Hasidism's increasing emphasis on Talmud study. As the movement expanded, it put less emphasis on meditation and communing with God, and more on traditional Jewish learning. As a result, Hasidim today are no longer regarded as revolutionaries; in fact, they are often the conservative stalwarts of *Orthodox Judaism, easily recognized by the eighteenth- and nineteenth-century black coats and hats worn by most of their male adherents.

Nonetheless, the Hasidic approach to Judaism significantly differs from that of the Mitnagdim. Hasidism generally places a much greater stress on *simcha shel mitzvah*—the joy of performing a commandment.

SOURCES AND FURTHER READINGS: Gershom Scholem, *Major Trends in Jewish Mysticism*, pp. 325–350; Jacob Katz, *Tradition and Crisis: Jewish Society at the End of the Middle Ages*, pp. 231–244. Jerome Mintz and Dan Ben Amos, *In Praise of the Baal Shem Tov: The Earliest Collection of Legends About the Founder of Hasidism*; Jacob Minkin, *The Romance of Hasidism*; Martin Buber, *Tales of the Hasidim* (two volumes), and *The Way of Man According to the Teachings of Hasidism*. Immanuel Etkes, *The Besht: Magician, Mystic and Leader*.

115

VILNA GAON (1720–1797)

HIS ACTUAL NAME WAS RABBI ELIJAH OF VILNA. THE TERM GAON, suggesting a genius, was the appellation given to him early on, so that the name by which he is known, the Vilna Gaon, translates as the "genius of Vilna."

The Vilna Gaon is to religious Jews what Albert *Einstein is to other Jews: *the* standard of genius. Just as people might remark of a child with a less than towering intellect, "He's no Einstein," religious Jews will say, "He's no Vilna Gaon."

While popular folk wisdom suggests that Einstein, as a child, was himself "no Einstein," the historical data indicate that the Gaon's brilliance was apparent from an almost impossibly early age. At six, he was already studying

Bible and Talmud on his own, since teachers were having trouble keeping up with him. Less than a year later, he delivered a discourse on the Talmud at Vilna's main synagogue. Afterward, the Chief Rabbi of Vilna interviewed him, suspecting that the child had been primed like an actor for the lecture. He quickly concluded that the young boy understood all the intricacies of the talk he had delivered.

Despite the Gaon's mastery of almost all Jewish religious literature by his teens, he continued learning eighteen hours a day until his death at age seventy-seven. A popular Jewish legend relates that one of his disciples was asked why his master continued studying so assiduously, long after he knew almost every important Jewish text by heart. The disciple responded: "If the Vilna Gaon studies Torah eighteen hours a day, the other rabbis in Poland will study ten. If the other rabbis in Poland study ten hours a day, then in the more enlightened climate of Germany the rabbis will study six. If the rabbis in Germany study six, then the rabbis in England will study two. And if the rabbis in England study two hours a day, then the Jews of England will at least keep the Sabbath. *But*, if the Vilna Gaon studies only ten hours a day, then the other rabbis in Poland will study only six, and the rabbis in Germany only two, and the rabbis in England only a half-hour. And if the rabbis in England study Torah only a half-hour a day, what will become of the Sabbath observance of English Jewry?"

While the Gaon's writings were not published during his lifetime, this austere Orthodox scholar anticipated many modern literary methods in his textual analyses. He had no compunctions about declaring even a talmudic passage erroneous if it was inconsistent with other passages — and his encyclopedic memory enabled him to uncover many such passages. The Gaon himself was fond of saying, "There is no personal regard where truth is involved."

An ascetic by nature, the Gaon accepted no official position in the Jewish community, preferring to study on his own and be free from the pressures of public office. Nonetheless, he was accepted as the undisputed spiritual leader of Lithuanian and Russian Jewry.

Later in his life, when he did aggressively enter the public arena, the results were catastrophic. The Gaon became convinced that the new Hasidic movement (see preceding entry), initiated in the mid-1700s by Israel Ba'al Shem Tov, was a threat to Judaism. He had heard reports of the ecstatic praying at Hasidic prayer services, often accompanied by an indifference to the appropriate times for prayer. The Gaon also was distressed by the veneration the Hasidim accorded their rabbinic leaders, men whom the Gaon generally regarded as ignoramuses. Furthermore, he understood the Hasidic emphasis on God's presence everywhere, and in everything, to be a form of pantheism (see *Excommunication of Spinoza). The Gaon became convinced that a false messianic movement was afoot.

In 1781, and again in 1796, he issued a *kherem (a ban of excommunication) against the Hasidim, forbidding Jews to conduct business with or marry them. "If I were able," he declared, "I would do unto them as Elijah the prophet did to the priests of Baal." Since Elijah led the Jews in killing 450 priests of the idol Baal (I Kings 18:40), this may be the most malevolent statement ever publicly uttered by a major Jewish leader: It makes the contemporary Orthodox-Reform conflict (see Denominational Conflicts) seem almost cordial.

In 1797, when the Gaon died, rumors flew in Vilna that the local Hasidim had danced upon hearing the news. The Gaon's followers determined to exact a terrible revenge. One of them informed the Russian authorities that Shneur Zalman of Liady, the founding rebbe of the *Lubavitcher Hasidim, was working with Turkish authorities against the Russian government. This seemingly absurd charge gained a patina of credibility because the rebbe was sending money to his followers in Palestine, which then was under Turkish rule. Taken off in chains, the rebbe was sentenced to death; he was finally released after fifty-three days in prison. The nineteenth of Kislev (which usually falls in December), the day of his release, remains to this day a major festival among Lubavitcher Hasidim.

Yet the Gaon's brilliance was so preeminent that, despite his anti-Hasidic animosity, he still is widely respected among Hasidim.

A Hebrew proverb teaches, "What the mind cannot accomplish, time will." Religious Jews today regard both Israel Ba'al Shem Tov, the founder of Hasidism, and the Gaon as great men, although in his own time the Gaon saw the Ba'al Shem Tov and Hasidim as mortal enemies of God and Judaism.

A CHARACTERISTIC TEACHING

On unethical religious Jews—The Torah is to the soul of man what rain is to the soil; rain makes any seed placed into the soil grow, producing nourishing as well as poisonous plants. The Torah also helps him who is striving for self-perfection, while it increases the impurity of those that remain uncultivated (Commentary on Proverbs 24:31 and 25:4).

SOURCES AND FURTHER READINGS: Louis Ginzberg, "The Gaon, Rabbi Elijah Wilna," in *Students, Scholars and Saints*, pp. 125–144. The statement about doing to the Hasidim what Elijah did to the priests of Baal is found in H. H. Ben-Sasson, *A History of the Jewish People*, p. 774; Meyer Waxman, "Vilna Gaon," in Simon Noveck, ed., *Great Jewish Personalities in Ancient and Medieval Times*, pp. 309–327. Immanuel Etkes, *The Gaon of Vilna: The Man and His Image*.

MOSES MENDELSSOHN (1729–1786)

Enlightenment/Haskala

ALTHOUGH MOSES MENDELSSOHN, THE MOST IMPORTANT GERMAN Jew of the eighteenth century, was a religious man, four of his six children converted to Christianity; one of them, Abraham, even claimed that his dead father would not have disapproved. Jewish scholars to this day dispute whether this Jewish philosopher's inability to inculcate loyalty to Judaism in his own family was the fault of his philosophy or the result of secular and political pressures that Jews experienced in Germany in the late 1700s.

Mendelssohn was reared in a Germany that was passionately antisemitic. When he visited Dessau, the city of his birth, he was required to pay a head tax, a special payment imposed on all cattle and Jews entering the town. Mendelssohn lived most of his life in Berlin, but had to wait many years until he was legally designated a "privileged Jew," one who had a permanent right to live there. Even those Jews who procured this status could normally bequeath the privilege of living in Berlin only to their eldest sons. In the eighteenth century, German Jews could not even marry when they fell in love, unless they procured governmental permission. This permission was often awarded reluctantly, for German rulers had no desire to see their Jewish population increase.

But all was not bleak. During Mendelssohn's lifetime—and in large measure because of his erudition, charm, and intelligence—there arose a distinguished group of Germans who started clamoring for better treatment of the Jews. Foremost among them was the great German writer Gotthold Lessing, who had befriended Mendelssohn at a chess game. In one of Lessing's most famous plays, *Nathan the Wise*, the hero is modeled on Mendelssohn. An earlier play, *The Jews*, also depicted a heroic Jewish character.

German antisemites regarded Lessing's positive depiction of Jews as outrageous: They reacted as nineteenth-century southern whites might have responded to a playwright who cast a black man as a scholar and a saint. Johann Michaelis, a prominent German theologian, declared that *The Jews* was moving, but that no Jew of the type Lessing wrote about existed. The anguished Mendelssohn responded with poignant insight: "Is it not enough that we must suffer the cruel hatred of the Christian world in countless ways? Must calumny and slander be added and our character be defamed in order to justify the injustices committed against us?"

Most of Mendelssohn's writings deal with matters of general philosophy, rather than with particularly Jewish issues. In 1767, an essay he wrote, attempting to prove that metaphysical truths could be as easily proven as scientific ones, won an award from the Prussian Academy. More remarkably, one of the other philosophers in the competition whom he bested was Immanuel Kant.

Mendelssohn became the Jew the Germans liked to love, the one they could point to and say, "If only all Jews were like him." The Germans even were willing to forgive Mendelssohn his scrupulous observance of Jewish law because he seemed so quintessentially German. At a time when he himself suffered from government-backed antisemitism, he criticized King Frederick for writing poetry in French, not German.

Mendelssohn always remained a proud Jew, and the education and privileges he secured for himself he wished to win for all his co-religionists. He wanted nothing less than to transform both the Jewish and the German worlds, so that the Jews would acquire a worldly education (most of Mendelssohn's Jewish contemporaries communicated in Yiddish and spoke a broken German), and the German Christians would recognize the country's Jews as their equals.

His translation of the Bible into German, which he published along with a Hebrew commentary, comprised his major effort to upgrade Jewish education. A major goal of Mendelssohn's project was to encourage German Jews to learn to write and speak fluent German. He succeeded: Tens of thousands of

Jews learned German by studying Mendelssohn's translation. Although some Jewish religious leaders greeted his Bible translation enthusiastically at first, within a short time, many rabbis condemned it. Rather than disseminating knowledge of the Bible, they realized, the new translation was teaching the German language, and through it German culture, to the masses. Ever since, Mendelssohn has been regarded with suspicion in Orthodox circles.

At the same time that he was "Germanizing" the Jews, Mendelssohn was urging Christian Germans to open up professional opportunities to them. "They tie our hands," he protested, "then reproach us that we do not use them."

Unfortunately, in his attempt to make Judaism seem more attractive both to Germans and to secularly educated Jews, Mendelssohn put forth a philosophy of Judaism that often undermined commitment to it. He believed that one did not have to be Jewish to accept Judaism's most important truths: the unity of God, *Divine Providence, and the immortal soul. Mendelssohn regarded these ideas as the legacy of all mankind.

The vast corpus of Jewish laws, on the other hand, were to be regarded as the commandments that Jews, and Jews alone, were obligated to keep. While such laws bound the Jews together as a people, Mendelssohn apparently did not believe that they contained universal truths or lessons. "The paradox," Dr. Alfred Jospe has written, "was that he, the rationalist and man of enlightenment, the thinker for whom no belief was valid if it was contrary to reason, declared that all those concepts and ideas which were rational were not Judaism, and that Judaism consisted solely of elements which were not rational, which reason could neither prove nor understand, which had to be accepted on faith, and which God, therefore, had to disclose to Jews in a mysterious and nonrational act of revelation." This philosophical flaw in his thinking perhaps helps account for so many of his followers' subsequent defections from Judaism.

The movement developed by Mendelssohn's disciples became known as *Haskala* (Enlightenment). The *maskilim* (enlightened ones) urged the Jews to drop what they regarded as a medieval mind-set, and enter the modern world. They wrote in Hebrew rather than *Yiddish, which they dismissed as a German jargon. The *maskilim* tried to bring about a Jewish cultural renaissance, which would draw on the best to be found both within Judaism and the secular world. In the end, however, they generally judged Judaism by the standards of the secular world, and often found it provincial; the legal discussions in the *Talmud—which made up the primary curriculum at most *yeshivot—concerning subjects such as goring oxes struck them as picayune and irrelevant to contemporary Jewish life.

Decades later, the *Haskala* spread from Western Europe to the Jews of Russia and Poland. Orthodox Judaism fought the Enlightenment, regarding it as the first step on the road to assimilation. Indeed, they often pointed to the conversion to Christianity by four of Mendelssohn's children as proof that the mix of the secular with the Jewish would lead to Judaism's demise.

The Orthodox leadership were wrong in their unqualified rejection of Mendelssohn and the *Haskala*. But the philosophical and cultural solutions propounded by Mendelssohn and the *Haskala* also did not make for a successful synthesis of the Jewish and secular worlds. Neither Enlightenment thinkers nor their opponents have yet succeeded in fully answering the question that has obsessed Jewry ever since Jews were admitted into the Western world: Can modernity and the Jewish tradition be made fully congruent?

SOURCES AND FURTHER READINGS: Alfred Jospe, "Moses Mendelssohn," in Simon Noveck, ed., *Great Jewish Personalities in Modern Times*, pp. 11–36. Michael Meyer, *The Origins of the Modern Jew: Jewish Identity and European Culture in Germany, 1749–1824*, pp. 11–114. Arthur Hertzberg, "Modernity and Judaism," in Stanley Wagner and Allen Breck, eds., *Great Confrontations in Jewish History*, pp. 123–135. The standard biography of Mendelssohn is Alexander Altmann, *Moses Mendelssohn: A Biographical Study*.

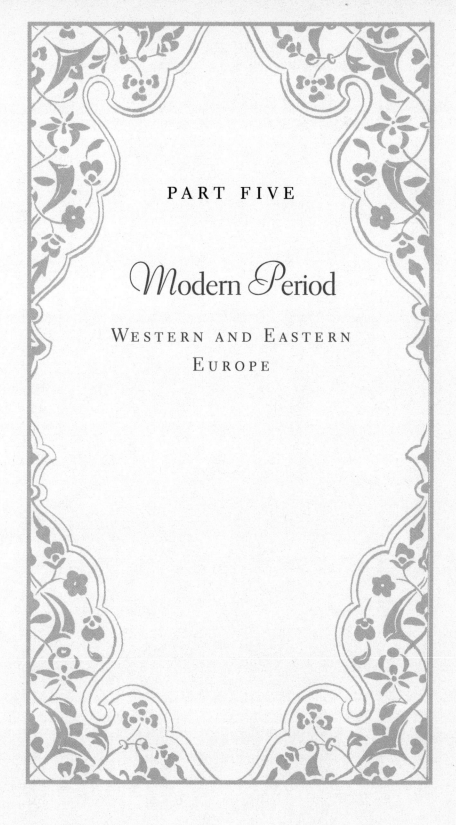

PART FIVE

Modern Period

WESTERN AND EASTERN EUROPE

EMANCIPATION

"To the Jews as individuals, all rights.
To the Jews as a people, no rights"

ASK JEWS TO NAME THE ONLY COUNTRY IN WHICH THEY HAD EQUAL rights in 1780, and you rarely will receive a correct reply. People usually guess France, Germany, Holland, or England. The answer is the United States, but since only about two thousand Jews were living in America at the time of the Revolution, American Jewry's emancipation did not become significant for Jewish life until the next century.

France was the first European country to give the Jews equal rights: It did so in 1791, in the aftermath of the French Revolution. During the debate in the French National Assembly over emancipation, even the measure's proponents insisted that Jews be granted their rights conditionally. As one delegate, Clermont-Tonnerre, expressed it: "To the Jews as individuals, all rights. To the Jews as a people, no rights." In the aftermath of emancipation, it was understood that French Jews were to cease feeling ties with Jews of other lands.

Within several decades of the French National Assembly's action, the new *Reform movement in Judaism responded to Clermont-Tonnerre's challenge by dropping peoplehood as a component of Judaism. A century later, the American Reform movement restored peoplehood to its integral place in Jewish life. Today, two centuries after Clermont-Tonnerre's challenge to the newly emancipated Jews to drop every aspect of Jewishness that was not exclusively religious, peoplehood is the primary element in many, if not most Jews' Jewish identity.

SOURCES AND FURTHER READINGS: Jacob Katz, *Out of the Ghetto: The Social Background of Jewish Emancipation, 1770–1870*; Howard M. Sachar, *The Course of Modern Jewish History*, pp. 53–71.

NAPOLEON'S SANHEDRIN

THE *SANHEDRIN WAS THE NAME OF THE JEWISH HIGH COURT OF ancient Israel. It had authority in both religious and political matters, and thus was the main symbol of Jewish religious sovereignty.

In 1806, the French emperor Napoleon Bonaparte decided to revive this ancient Jewish institution. His intention was hardly to restore Jewish autonomy; on the contrary, Napoleon's goal was to establish the French Jews' exclusive loyalty to France. Calling the institution the Sanhedrin, however, was a brilliant tactical device. It made French Jews, and many other Jews throughout Europe, feel that Napoleon was restoring to them some of their ancient glory.

The Sanhedrin, which was composed of seventy-one delegates, was convened in Paris in February 1807. Napoleon posed a series of questions to it, with the hope that the answers would establish that Jewish law mandated no obligations from Jews that were inconsistent with their being loyal Frenchmen. The first question was: Are Jews permitted to have more than one wife? In line with Rabbi *Gershom's tenth-century decree, the answer was a clear no. Several other questions focused on Judaism's attitude toward non-Jews (for example, do Jews regard Frenchmen as brothers or strangers?), and toward the French government (do Jews born in France consider France their country, and would they be willing to defend it and obey its laws?). Once again, the Sanhedrin had no difficulty providing Napoleon with the answers he desired. French Jews were Frenchmen first, they answered, and Judaism was solely a religious affiliation. French Jews loved their fellow citizens, and would gladly fight on France's behalf. In response to another question, they noted that Jewish law categorically forbade any deceptiveness in business dealings with non-Jews, and outlawed usurious rates of interest.

The only question to which the Sanhedrin could not respond precisely as Napoleon wanted was: Can Jews and Christians marry? The delegates noted that while secular French law permitted intermarriage, Jewish law does not sanction it.

In many ways, this last response has proved prophetic. Today, almost two hundred years later, committed Jews living in democratic countries, even many who participate fully in almost all other aspects of their host society, oppose intermarriage.

Napoleon's Sanhedrin was never convened again. As a result, it played no important role in Jewish life. Today, it is remembered mainly as a curiosity of nineteenth-century Jewish history.

SOURCES AND FURTHER READINGS: Howard M. Sachar, *The Course of Modern Jewish History*, pp. 58–65; Simon Schwarzfuchs, *Napoleon, the Jews and the Sanhedrin*.

119

BAPTISM AND APOSTASY

AN OLD JEWISH STORY TELLS OF A MAN WHO WANTS TO JOIN A COUNTRY club but can't get in because he is Jewish. He converts and applies for membership.

"What's your name?" the admissions committee asks him.

The man gives one of those pompous constructions like "Hutchinson River Parkway III."

"And your profession?"

"I own a seat on the New York Stock Exchange, and I have an estate where I raise horses."

He looks like a shoo-in for membership.

"One last question, sir. Your religion?"

"My religion? Why, I am a *goy.*"

Historically, most Jews who have converted to Christianity have not done so because of a conviction that Christianity was truer than Judaism. In the Middle Ages, Jews who converted generally did so under duress; their lives were at risk if they did not (see *Crusades*). In the past two centuries, most Jews have converted not so much to become Christians as to become *goyim,* non-Jews, part of the majority; in short, to avoid the enormous social and professional disadvantages suffered by Jews. For example, in nineteenth-century Germany, one Heinrich Marx converted so that he would be permitted to practice law: In 1824, he converted his children, including his son Karl, so that they too could avoid being victimized by antisemitism. At about the same time, Isaac Disraeli converted his son Benjamin to the Church of England, an act that eventually enabled Benjamin to become the prime minister of England. As one famous Jewish apostate to Christianity, Heinrich Heine, put it: "Baptism is the Jew's entrance ticket to European culture."

The Jewish apostates in nineteenth-century Europe had quite varied reactions to their former co-religionists. Men like Heine and Disraeli remained sympathetic to the Jews; the latter even became actively involved in English Jewry's struggle for equal rights. But Karl Marx, the grandson of two Orthodox rabbis, turned into a virulent Jew-hater (see *Leon Trotsky*).

In Western Europe many thousands of Jews converted to Christianity in the first half of the nineteenth century. In large measure, these conversions resulted from the triumph of Enlightenment thinking. The Enlightenment influenced many Jews to become less religious: For many "enlightened" Jews, it made increasingly less sense to suffer for a religion in which they no longer believed. David Friedlander, one of Moses *Mendelssohn's leading disciples and a man deeply influenced by the Enlightenment, requested permission from Berlin Pastor William Teller to convert along with other prominent Jews, on the condition that they not be required to accept the divinity of Jesus and other Christian dogmas. The request was refused. A century later, Theodor *Herzl, in his pre-Zionist days, toyed with the idea of initiating the conversion of prominent Jews to Catholicism, thereby inaugurating mass conversions, and an end to antisemitism. Here, too, the motivation for conversion had nothing to do with belief in Christianity.

One of the distinctive features of American-Jewish life is that conversions to Christianity are uncommon, and are apt to be prompted by religious rather than social considerations. In America, unlike in Europe, Judaism has status: indeed, the United States is the first country to define itself as Judeo-Christian, and is also is the first society in which more non-Jews convert to Judaism than Jews convert to Christianity.

SOURCE AND FURTHER READING: Michael Meyer, *The Origins of the Modern Jew: Jewish Identity and European Culture in Germany, 1749–1824*.

120

REFORM JUDAISM

REFORM JUDAISM AROSE IN GERMANY IN THE EARLY 1800S BOTH AS A reaction against what some Jews regarded as Orthodox rigidity and backwardness, and as a response to Germany's new, more liberal political climate—a climate that seemed to be open to Jews who were willing to drop traditions that isolated them from their German neighbors. Of the three pillars of Judaism—God, Torah, and peoplehood—Reform radically altered the last two.

Most significantly, it dropped the belief that the Jews are a people. Rather, argued the movement's leading thinkers, Judaism is only a religion: Jews have no special feelings of kinship with other Jews, particularly not for those living in other lands. In 1840, Abraham Geiger, soon to be Germany's leading Reform rabbi, opposed efforts to help the Damascus Jews falsely accused in a blood libel (see *Damascus Blood Libel*), on the grounds that "for me it is more important that Jews be able to work in Prussia as pharmacists or lawyers than that the entire Jewish population of Asia and Africa be saved, although as a human being I sympathize with them." (In his later years, Rabbi Geiger expressed concern for Rumanian Jews suffering from anti-semitic attacks.)

With regard to the Torah, or Jewish law, Reform's earliest changes largely consisted of reforming the synagogue service. In light of the movement's opposition to peoplehood and Jewish nationalism, prayers for a return to Palestine were dropped. In addition, some prayers were recited in German, and the rabbi gave a sermon in that language as well. Strangely enough, the German sermon vexed the Orthodox leadership no end; some Orthodox rabbis even tried to influence the German government to ban such sermons because they supposedly constituted a forbidden religious innovation. The Orthodox lost that battle: Not long thereafter, many of their own rabbis were giving talks in German.

In order to elevate the aesthetic experience of prayer, the Reform services often were accompanied by an organist. Since traditional Jewish law opposes the playing of instruments on the *Sabbath, this innovation also inflamed traditional Jews.

As Reform Judaism developed, it increasingly *dropped* rather than *reformed* Jewish laws. Within a few decades of the movement's founding, few Reform Jews were keeping *kosher. Some of the movement's more radical rabbis even advocated the abolition of *circumcision—though he never publicly opposed it, Rabbi Geiger referred to it in a letter as a "barbaric bloody rite"—and the Reform congregation of Berlin shifted the Sabbath service to Sunday so as to enable Jews to observe their day of rest on the same day as their Christian neighbors. While the most radical elements never became dominant in European Reform Judaism, they deeply influenced nineteenth-century Reform Judaism in the United States (see *Pittsburgh Platform, 1885*).

The prayer service was greatly abridged, and those parts which were not cut, were soon recited mainly in German. In the preface to a new Reform prayerbook in Berlin, the following explanation was offered: "Holy is the language in which God once gave the Law to our fathers [in itself a remarkably traditional statement] . . . but seven times more holy unto us is the language in which our philanthropic and just king . . . proclaims his law to us."

The real reason for praying in German was that fewer and fewer Jews knew Hebrew. The Reform acquiescence to this sorry fact, however, only further inflamed the Orthodox. As Rabbi Akiva Eger wrote: "This prevalent ignorance . . . implies contempt for our holy language, inasmuch as [the Reformers] do not teach it to their children. They teach them French, Latin, and other languages, but not the sacred tongue. We are then worse than all nations, for each of them cultivates its language while we neglect ours." Of course, one of the reasons for Reform's indifference to Hebrew was that its leaders saw little reason to perpetuate a language that united Jews throughout the world.

As for belief in God, Reform adhered to traditional Jewish monotheism: It coined the term "ethical monotheism" to convey the belief that the world is ruled by one God, Whose primary demand of human beings is ethical behavior. This doctrine remains one of Reform Judaism's great teachings, and is fully consistent with the Torah's golden rule (see *"Love Your Neighbor as Yourself, I Am the Lord"*), and the teachings of the prophet *Micah and Rabbi *Hillel. The virtually *exclusive* stress on Judaism's ethical teachings, however, resulted to some degree from Reform's implicit, and sometimes explicit, rejection of the *Talmud (which puts great emphasis on ritual matters) in favor of the biblical prophets, who focused predominantly on issues of ethics and monotheism. As the radical Reform rabbi Samuel Holdheim declared: "The Talmud speaks with the ideology of its own time, and for that time it was right. I speak from the higher ideology of my time, and for this age I am right."

The contemporary Reform theologian Jakob Petuchowski has compared nineteenth-century Reform Judaism to a train station leading some alienated Jews back into the fold while simultaneously taking others on the road from Judaism to Christianity. In this century, the Reform movement has reaccepted many aspects of Judaism that their forebears rejected, most notably the idea of peoplehood and the need for a greater amount of religious ritual (see entry on *Reform Judaism* in the section on American-Jewish Life).

While many Jews agreed that nineteenth-century Judaism required some reformation, particularly one that emphasized ethics more than rituals (see *Musar*), many of the early Reform leaders dropped so much Jewish content that they often seemed intent on creating a new religion rather than restoring Judaism to its original form.

SOURCES AND FURTHER READINGS: Michael Meyer, *Response to Modernity: A History of the Reform Movement in Judaism*; W. Gunther Plaut, *The Rise of Reform Judaism*; Meyer Waxman, *A History of Jewish Literature*, vol. 3, pp. 351–370. See also Jakob J. Petuchowski, *Prayerbook Reform in Europe*, and Gerald Blidstein, "Early Reform and its Approach," *Tradition* 11:3, Fall 1970, pp. 80–89. Geiger's statement expressing his lack of concern for the suffering Jews of Damascus is cited in H. H. Ben-Sasson, ed., *A History of the Jewish People*, p. 848.

121

SAMSON RAPHAEL HIRSCH (1808–1888)

Neo-Orthodoxy

THE MOVEMENT OF NEO-ORTHODOXY, ASSOCIATED WITH GERMAN RABBI Samson Raphael Hirsch, was largely a response to Reform Judaism's innovations in Jewish life (see preceding entry). On the one hand, Hirsch was unyielding in his Orthodoxy on matters of Jewish law; he believed that it was Jews, not Judaism, who were in need of reform. On the other hand, he was willing to break with his Eastern European rabbinic colleagues on those issues he considered nonessential. For example, Hirsch advocated that Jews attend university—he himself matriculated in the University of Bonn for one year—although almost every Orthodox rabbi of stature in Russia and Poland forbade secular studies; they regarded them as the first step toward nonreligiosity. Hirsch also delivered sermons in German, though it would have been unthinkable for his Eastern European rabbinic counterparts to give public orations in Polish or Russian.

In his philosophical writings, some of Hirsch's ideas were similar to those of his Reform opponents. He taught that the "mission of Israel" was to spread "pure humanity" among the nations, a concept not terribly dissimilar from Reform's notion of "ethical monotheism" (see preceding entry). Like the Reformers, Hirsch saw a positive function for Jews in exile: to spread the knowledge of God among their neighbors. In part as a consequence of this belief, Hirsch had little interest in seeing Jews return to Palestine to build their own homeland. After his death his followers were generally antagonistic to Zionism.

Yet for all his talk of "pure humanity" and Jewish mission, Hirsch was no religious liberal. He adamantly opposed cooperation or association between representatives of Orthodox and Reform Judaism.

Hirsch was regarded in the Orthodox world as a new kind of rabbi, particularly because he was able to present Judaism's most ancient teachings in a modern idiom. No other Orthodox rabbi of the time wrote in German. His first book, *The Nineteen Letters of Ben Uzziel*, written when he was twenty-eight, made the case for an unapologetic Orthodox religious lifestyle. Throughout his life he remained a spirited, if somewhat verbose, writer.

Hirsch's followers in the United States, who number in the thousands, have translated his voluminous writings into English, including a six-volume Torah commentary and the two-volume *Horeb*, an explanation of the Torah's 613 laws. Hirsch called his new approach to Judaism, *Torah im derekh eretz* (Torah with modern culture). Indeed, his Orthodox followers in Germany—unlike their counterparts in Eastern Europe—generally practiced secular professions while adhering scrupulously to Jewish law. For Hirsch, the ideal Jew was the *Jissroelmensch* (Israel-man), an enlightened Jew who observed the precepts.

Although Hirsch had a following throughout Germany, his most ardent supporters were in Frankfurt, where for thirty-seven years he served as rabbi. His synagogue functioned along Hirschian lines after his death in 1888, until the Nazis destroyed the community a half-century later.

When thousands of German Jews escaped to the United States in the mid-1930s, many of Hirsch's followers settled in Manhattan's Washington Heights.

Even today, more than a century after Hirsch's death, the area still remains a center of his Orthodox teachings and practices.

SOURCES AND FURTHER READINGS: Meyer Waxman, *A History of Jewish Literature*, vol. 3, pp. 399–406; Noah Rosenbloom, *Tradition in an Age of Reform*.

THE DAMASCUS BLOOD LIBEL, 1840

THE DAMASCUS BLOOD LIBEL WAS AN IMPORTANT TURNING POINT IN Jewish history. For the first time, Jews all over the world united to fight antisemitism.

The facts of the case are simple and tragic. After the disappearance of a Capuchin monk, Brother Thomas, in Damascus, Syria, in 1840, the local French consul, Ratti-Menton, told police authorities that the Jews probably had murdered him in a religious ritual (see *Blood Libel*). Several Jews were arrested and, under torture, one confessed. Syrian authorities also seized more than sixty Jewish children to coerce their parents into confessing where Brother Thomas's blood was hidden. Prodded by French officials, Syria's ruler, Mohammed Ali, was preparing to try the arrested men when Jewish leaders throughout the world started reacting. Most prominent among them was Sir Moses Montefiore, the English-Jewish philanthropist, who personally traveled to Ali's headquarters in Egypt to express the indignation of both the Jewish community and the British government. Joining Montefiore was the French-Jewish leader Adolphe Cremieux, who courageously opposed his own government, which was promoting the blood libel. In the United States, Jews urged President Martin Van Buren to issue a statement of protest. There was no need to use pressure; the president, on his own initiative, had sent a letter even before being approached by the Jewish community.

International Jewish pressure forced both France, Mohammed Ali's major supporter, and Ali himself to back off from their blood libel charges. After several months, the surviving Jewish victims—seven of whom remained permanently disabled from having been tortured (two had died)—were released.

Unfortunately, once the blood libel was introduced into the Arab world, it did not die out. In the 1970s, King Faisal of Saudi Arabia repeatedly told newspaper interviewers and visiting world leaders that Judaism required its adherents to kill non-Jews and drink their blood. In the early 2000s—and among the most disturbing examples of contemporary antisemitism—cartoons of Jews drinking Arab blood appeared in newspapers throughout the Arab world, along with articles supposedly "documenting" this Jewish practice.

By the way, the murderer of Brother Thomas was never found. I always thought it would be ironic if it turned out to be Ratti-Menton, the French consul who turned the authorities against the Jews.

SOURCES: Myrtle Franklin and Michael Bor, *Sir Moses Montefiore, 1784–1885*, pp. 41–57. H. H. Ben-Sasson, ed., *A History of the Jewish People*, pp. 847–849 (the section is written by S. Ettinger).

123

RABBI ISRAEL SALANTER (1810–1883)

The Musar *Movement*

"YOU DON'T HAVE TO BE AN ANGEL," ALBERT SCHWEITZER ONCE SAID, "in order to be a saint." The nineteenth-century rabbi Israel Salanter came remarkably close to being both. Although an erudite scholar, Salanter's primary concern in his own life and teachings was ethics. Two of the most famous tales told about him speak of his ethical scrupulousness on that most ritually demanding of holidays, Yom Kippur.

One year, on Yom Kippur eve, Salanter did not show up in synagogue for services. The congregation was extremely worried; they could only imagine that their rabbi had suddenly taken sick or been in an accident. In any case, they would not start the service without him.

During the wait, a young woman in the congregation became agitated. She had left her infant child at home asleep in its crib; she was certain she would only be away a short while. Now, because of the delay, she slipped out to make sure that the infant was all right. When she reached her house, she found her child being rocked in the arms of Rabbi Salanter. He had heard the baby crying while walking to the synagogue and, realizing that the mother must have gone off to services, had gone into the house to calm him. "To appreciate this act of Salanter," the scholar Louis Ginzberg has written, "it must be remembered what the service at the synagogue on the eve of the Day of Atonement meant to a man like him, who was in the habit of withdrawing from the world for forty days preceding Yom Kippur, and spending his time in prayer and devotion."

On a different Yom Kippur, Rabbi Salanter became involved in a serious controversy with many of his rabbinical colleagues. In 1848, there was a cholera epidemic in Vilna. Several doctors warned Salanter that if people fasted on Yom Kippur, they would weaken their resistance and become more susceptible to the life-threatening disease. The day before the holiday, Salanter posted notices throughout Vilna telling Jews that they had permission to eat on the fast day that year, and urging everyone to pray less so they could spend more time helping the sick. The following morning, he learned that few people had taken advantage of his lenient ruling; even though their health might be endangered, few Jews could bring themselves to eat on this most solemn of holidays. In the late morning, according to one account, Rabbi Salanter mounted the Podium of Vilna's main synagogue, recited the blessing over wine and food, and ate and drank in the presence of his congregation. Once they saw their sainted rabbi eating, the rest of the congregation followed suit. Although some rabbis later criticized him for this "desecration" of the holiday, Salanter always maintained that he was proud that God had granted him this opportunity to save many lives (see *Where Life Is at Stake/Pikuakh Nefesh*).

Salanter's saintliness thus did not express itself solely in "sweet" acts; when the occasion demanded, he could be confrontational. One well-known Salanter encounter occurred during the reign of Czar Nicholas I, when Jewish communities were forced to provide the Russian Army with young Jewish boys for twenty-five-year terms of service. Local community councils passed regulations to ensure that as long as there was a family from which no sons had been taken, no other family would be forced to offer up a second son. Once, when visiting a city, Rabbi Salanter met a poor widow who was sobbing bitterly. She told him that she had just learned that her second son was to be drafted because a wealthy member of the community had intervened illegally with the authorities to make sure that none of his sons would be taken. The community leadership had acquiesced to the wealthy man's pressure, and chose instead to offer up the widow's second son to the draft.

That afternoon Salanter went to the local synagogue, and when one man rose to lead the prayer service, the rabbi cried out: "It is forbidden for you to lead us in prayer, for you are a heretic; you don't believe in God or in the Torah." Another man rose and Salanter shouted the same thing at him. It happened a third time. Finally, the congregants asked Rabbi Salanter to explain his behavior. "The fact that you pray," he answered, "does not prove that you are believers. You pray only because your fathers prayed. If you really believed that the Torah was the voice of God commanding you, how would you dare ignore Torah laws which forbid oppressing a widow, and favoring prominent people in judgment? That you are willing to ignore such laws shows that you do not really believe in God and His Torah."

Salanter had a consuming passion to restore ethics to their central position in Judaism (see *Micah* and *Hillel*). Toward this end, he initiated the *Musar* movement (*musar* is Hebrew for "morality"), which emphasized the study of Judaism's ethical writings. The most popular text among the *Musar* devotees was the eighteenth-century *Mesilat Yesharim* (*Path of the Upright*), by Moshe Chaim Luzzatto. When a man once told Rabbi Salanter that he had only fifteen minutes a day for study, and wanted to know if he should devote those fifteen minutes to studying Talmud or *Musar*, Salanter advised him to study *Musar*, but added, "The first thing you will realize is that you should structure your day so that you have more than fifteen minutes a day available for study."

Since its founding, the *Musar* movement has remained a small but influential force within the Orthodox Jewish world, affecting the curriculum of almost all major yeshivot. Its most famous, and most extreme, offshoot is the Navaradok school of *Musar*, founded by Rabbi Joseph Horowitz of Navaradok, a disciple of Rabbi Salanter. Reb Yaizel, as Rabbi Horowitz was called, believed that if his students were ever to have the strength to propagate their distinctive vision of Judaism, they needed first to learn to become indifferent to how other people reacted to them. To help inure his students to ridicule, he put them through strange tests, for example, telling them to ask for eggs in hardware stores so that people would laugh at them. In that way, Reb Yaizel believed, they would accustom themselves not to care about taunts and so gain courage to advocate their views of Judaism to an often hostile world.

CHARACTERISTIC TEACHINGS OF THE *MUSAR* MOVEMENT

"Normally, we worry about our own material well-being and our neighbor's souls; let us rather worry about our neighbor's material well-being and our own souls" (Rabbi Israel Salanter).

"A rabbi they don't want to drive out of town is no rabbi, and a rabbi who lets himself be driven out is no man" (Rabbi Israel Salanter).

"It is related that a king once gave his servants buckets and instructed them to draw water from the well. When they began, they noticed that the buckets had many holes and that the water leaked out by the time the buckets were drawn to the top of the well. They stopped. When the king later asked them if they had done as he had told them, they replied that they had stopped because of the holes. 'You should have continued,' the king said. 'I didn't ask you to draw water because I wanted the water, but because I wanted the buckets cleaned.' So it is with Torah. The substance of what one has studied may later be forgotten, but the process of studying is itself purifying" (Rabbi Nathaniel Bushwick).

SOURCES AND FURTHER READINGS: Louis Ginzberg, *Students, Scholars and Saints*, pp. 145–194; Rabbi J. J. Weinberg, "The 'Musar' Movement and Lithuanian Jewry," in Leo Jung, ed., *Men of the Spirit*, pp. 213–283. The episode concerning Rabbi Salanter and the decrees of Czar Nicholas I is cited from Dennis Prager and Joseph Telushkin, *The Nine Questions People Ask About Judaism*, pp. 70–71. Mendel Glenn, *Israel Salanter: Religious-Ethical Thinker*; Hillel Goldberg, *Israel Salanter: Text, Structure, Idea*. Yiddish writer Chaim Grade wrote several fictional works about the Navaradok school of *Musar*, including *The Yeshiva* (two volumes), and "My Quarrel with Hersh Rasseyner," a short story in Irving Howe and Eliezer Greenberg, eds., *A Treasury of Yiddish Stories*. There are varying accounts concerning Rabbi Salanter's behavior during the cholera epidemic, ranging from the account reported here in which he himself publicly ate, to other reports that he simply made food available in a room and instructed all those who felt weak to eat.

THE ROTHSCHILDS

THE ROTHSCHILDS ARE TO JEWISH LIFE WHAT THE ROCKEFELLERS ARE to Americans: *the* symbols of wealth. Although the Rothschilds, like the Rockefellers, are no longer the richest family among their people, their name still symbolizes Jewish wealth and power. The growth of the family's fortune has even been recorded in a Hollywood movie and a Broadway play.

The family patriarch, Meyer Amschel Rothschild, born in 1743, controlled a banking firm in Frankfurt, Germany. He eventually sent his sons, Nathan, James, Salomon, and Karl, to establish banks in four great cities of Europe: London, Paris, Vienna, and Naples. A fifth son, Amschel, remained with him in Frankfurt.

Even as their individual banking empires expanded, the brothers remained very close. Their mutual cooperation eventually made them into the greatest banking power in Europe. Government leaders routinely turned to the Rothschilds for financial help, and the family, in turn, often used its power to better the condition of all Jews. At the Congress of Vienna in 1814–1815, the Rothschilds lobbied aggressively, and sometimes successfully, for Jewish emancipation.

In their early days, the Rothschilds were Orthodox Jews. With the passage of time, the family's religiosity declined, although most branches remained fiercely loyal to the Jewish people. In the late nineteenth century, Baron Edmond de Rothschild of Paris singlehandedly supported many Jewish settlements in Palestine. He gave his charity anonymously, but his identity was an open secret: The Jews of Palestine referred to him as *"Ha-nadvan ha-yadu'a"* (the known benefactor). In England, a few decades later—at a time when much of English Jewry's upper class opposed Zionism—a Rothschild served as head of the Zionist Federation. It was to this "Lord Rothschild" that perhaps the most important letter in twentieth-century Jewish history, the *Balfour Declaration, was addressed on November 2, 1917.

Some decades earlier, Lionel Rothschild, a grandson of Meyer Amschel of

Frankfurt, had played a pivotal role in British Jewry's march toward equal rights. In 1847, he became the first Jew elected to the House of Commons. However, Lionel Rothschild was not permitted to take his seat because he refused to take the oath of office "on the true faith of a Christian." Election after election, his London constituency returned him to Parliament, and each time he was forbidden to take his seat. Finally, in 1858, after a prolonged and bitter fight, the law was amended to permit the oath to be administered on a Hebrew Bible, and without the Christian wording. Oddly, once Lionel Rothschild entered the House of Commons, he never spoke up in a single debate.

From the nineteenth century on, the Rothschilds figured heavily in Jewish folklore. In England, it was quipped, when the heads of Jewish charitable projects piously intoned, "The Lord will provide," they meant Lord Rothschild. One story has it that a Rothschild stopped off at an inn in a small Russian *shtetl, where he was served two eggs for breakfast. At the meal's end, he was handed a bill for twenty-five rubles, an enormous sum.

"This is absurd," Rothschild thundered angrily. "Are eggs so rare here?"

"No," the innkeeper said. "But Rothschilds are."

European Jews were proud of the Rothschilds. In an age when Jews were not yet fully emancipated, the family dealt as equals with kings and heads of state. Although many other nouveau-riche Jews converted to Christianity, no Rothschild ever did. To this day, the Rothschilds remain the aristocrats of Jewish life.

SOURCES AND FURTHER READINGS: Cecil Roth, *Essays and Portraits in Anglo-Jewish History*, pp. 277–281; Frederic Morton, *The Rothschilds: A Family Portrait*.

125

MARTIN BUBER (1878–1965)
I and Thou

Since the telling of tales was central to the way Martin Buber taught his philosophy of life, it is perhaps fitting to begin this entry with an incident that happened to Buber himself, one that he claimed determined the direction of his life. While still a young man, Buber was at home editing a scholarly manuscript when the doorbell rang. The visitor whom he admitted seemed a bit distraught and anxious to speak, but as Buber was anxious to get back to his work, he hurried him along. He answered the man's questions politely but, as Buber later expressed it, "I did not answer the questions which were not asked." He found out that just a few days after their brief encounter the young man died, an apparent suicide. From then on, Buber concluded that encounters with people must take precedence over scholarship and mystical speculation.

Buber's lifelong obsession with the human encounter forms the basis for his best-known work, *I and Thou*. In it, he distinguishes two types of relationships that people have with each other and with the world: I-Thou and I-It.

The I-Thou relationship is one in which a person responds with his whole being. In studying the Bible, for example, such an approach opens the reader up to the very specific and personal meaning that the biblical text has for him. For example, after *Adam and Eve sin in the Garden of Eden, they become ashamed and try to hide from God. God calls out to Adam: "*Ayehka*—Where are you?" (Genesis 3:9). On a purely rational level, God's question makes no sense; by virtue of being God, He already knows where Adam is. Buber resolved this conundrum, however, by citing Rabbi Shneur Zalman of Liady, the founder of the *Lubavitch movement. " '*Ayekha*—Where are you?' " Shneur Zalman said, "is the question God directs to every man in every generation who is trying to hide from Him. Where are you?"

In Buber's view the I-Thou relationship always applies to a person's relationship to God, and is always potentially possible in an individual's encounter with another human being.

The popular misconception that Buber denigrated the I-It relationship is undoubtedly caused in part by the pejorative connotation of the word "It." Actually, Buber viewed the I-It relationship as essential if the world is to function. The term simply describes a relationship that does not have a significant emotional encounter at its core. When a person steps into a taxi he wants the driver to take him to his destination; he does not desire, and the driver does not expect, a deep interpersonal encounter. In certain relationships, such as a physician operating on a patient, an I-Thou relationship would even be detrimental, if not dangerous.

Nonetheless, I-Thou relationships represented for Buber the peaks of human existence. Much of his literary output was devoted to showing how the I-Thou relationship formed the cornerstone of early *Hasidism. What particularly fascinated him were Hasidic folktales, which he believed could illuminate the human condition more concretely than a philosophical system. For example, one can speculate whether human beings must try to find meaning and inspiration in their own lives or rely on a rabbi or teacher to provide them. Buber conveyed his thinking on the issue by relating a story Rabbi Bunam used to tell about Rabbi Isaac, son of Yekl of Cracow:

> After many years of great poverty which had never shaken his faith in God, he dreamed someone bade him look for a treasure in Prague, under the bridge which leads to the king's palace. When the dream recurred a third time, Rabbi Isaac prepared for the journey and set out for Prague. But the bridge was guarded day and night and he did not dare to start digging. Nevertheless, he went to the bridge every morning and kept walking around it until evening. Finally the captain of the guards, who had been watching him, asked in a kindly way whether he was looking for something or waiting for somebody. Rabbi Isaac told him of the dream which had brought him here from a faraway country. The captain laughed: "And so to please the dream, you poor fellow wore out your shoes to come here! As for having faith in dreams, if I had it, I should have had to get going when a dream once told me to go to Cracow and dig for treasure under the stove in a room of a Jew—Isaac, son of Yekl, that was the name! Isaac, son of Yekl! I can just imagine what it would be like, how I should have to try every house over there, where one half of the Jews are named Isaac and the other half Yekl." And he laughed again. Rabbi Isaac bowed, traveled home, and dug up the treasure from under the stove. . . .

Buber's emphasis on the soul's spontaneous response to various life situations put him at odds with Jewish Orthodoxy. Orthodoxy is based on a *halakhic* (legal) system, which legislates precise modes of behavior for virtually any situation in which a person finds himself. Buber found little room in his life or philosophy for responses that were not spontaneous or personal. There is no one way to hallow God, he argued. Some do it by eating, others by fasting, some by learning Torah, others by praying. The Orthodox, of course, responded that one person can do all four, eating luxuriously and reciting the blessings on the *Sabbath, fasting on *Yom Kippur and other fast days, learning Torah, and praying three times a day.

Buber felt, however, that the *halakhic* system stifled spontaneity and forced its practitioners to imitate other holy men's actions. He loved to tell the story of the Hasidic son who was criticized for acting differently from his father. The son denied the accusation. "I do as my father did. He obeyed God in his way, and I obey Him in my way." Because every person can find his own distinctive way to God, there is no reason, Buber argued, to model one's behavior on that of someone else. As Rabbi Zusha used to say: "When I die and come before the heavenly court, if they ask me, 'Zusha, why were you not Abraham?' I'll say that I didn't have Abraham's intellectual abilities. If they say, 'Why were you not Moses?' I'll say I didn't have Moses' leadership abilities. For every such question, I'll have an answer. But if they say, 'Zusha, why were you not Zusha?' for that, I'll have no answer."

Buber's *I and Thou* and his two-volume *Tales of the Hasidim* deeply influenced many Christian as well as Jewish thinkers: Indeed, some argue that Buber had more influence on Christian thought than on Jewish thought. The universal impact of his philosophy of life was reflected in Herman Hesse's nomination of Buber for a Nobel Prize for Literature for his writings on Hasidism.

Buber also was an active Zionist. He emigrated from Nazi Germany to Palestine in 1938, and was appointed to the faculty of Hebrew University in Jerusalem. His politics were on the left of the Israeli political spectrum, and for many years he advocated a binational Jewish-Arab state.

It is one of the ironies of history that the personally nonritually observant Buber was responsible for making the punctiliously observant Hasidism known to Western man, and to large numbers of Jews in particular.

SOURCES AND FURTHER READINGS: Martin Buber, *Tales of the Hasidim* (two volumes), and *The Way of Man According to the Teachings of Hasidism*; Maurice Friedman, "Martin Buber," in Simon Noveck, ed., *Great Jewish Thinkers of the Twentieth Century*, pp. 183–209; Friedman has also written a three-volume study, *Martin Buber's Life and Work*. Malcolm Diamond, *Martin Buber, Jewish Existentialist*. Buber's encounter with the young man who committed suicide is told in Herbert Weiner, 9½ Mystics, p. 133.

126

FRANZ ROSENZWEIG (1886–1929)

FRANZ ROSENZWEIG'S ENDURING IMPACT ON THE JEWISH WORLD IS due at least as much to the drama and heroism of his life as to his philosophical writings.

Rosenzweig grew up in an assimilated Jewish family in Germany. Though he had a religious disposition, the superficiality of his family's Jewish knowledge and observance led him to conclude that Judaism had nothing to offer him. While still a young man, he decided to seek answers to his spiritual quest in Christianity. A sense of honor and loyalty, however, motivated him to convert in the manner of the earliest Christians—after first living, if only briefly, as a Jew. On the *Yom Kippur before his anticipated baptism, he attended services at a small Orthodox synagogue in Berlin. Rosenzweig never put on paper exactly what transpired that day, but when the holiday ended, he put aside all thought of becoming a Christian. Instead, he spent the rest of his life learning and teaching Judaism.

During World War I, Rosenzweig was drafted into the German Army and spent part of the war in Poland. He utilized this opportunity to meet with Jews in Warsaw, and was repeatedly struck by the piety and vitality of this highly traditional community. Throughout the war, he sent home postcards and letters filled with theological reflections; they subsequently became the basis of his most famous book, *The Star of Redemption*.

A few years after returning to Germany, Rosenzweig founded the Frankfurt Lehrhaus, an innovative Jewish Free University, where college-age students and adults could register for courses on Judaism, Jewish history, and Hebrew. The atmosphere at the Lehrhaus was both less formal and more emotionally intense than at a university. There was no pretense of pure academic objectivity; the school's goal was to promote Jewish literacy and to encourage Jewish involvement. The Lehrhaus, however, did not push any one philosophical or denominational view of Judaism. In the United States, Rosenzweig's program has served as the model for many Jewish adult education programs. Rosenzweig recruited many of the great figures of German-Jewish life to teach in his school, including Martin Buber (see preceding entry), Gershom Scholem, Leo Strauss, and Erich Fromm.

Rosenzweig and Buber subsequently collaborated on a new translation of the Bible into German. There was no shortage of German-language Bibles, but none had captured the cadence of the original Hebrew. More often than not, the existing translations employed a stilted, somewhat pompous German, and so failed to convey the immediacy of the Hebrew text, which was meant to be read aloud. At first, the project's daunting scale caused Rosenzweig to resist Buber's prodding. But then Buber overcame Rosenzweig's reluctance by offering him a few examples of how different a dynamically worded translation could be.

An example of the revolutionary Buber-Rosenzweig translation is their rendering of Genesis 2:4–8: "On the day that HE, God, made earth and heaven, every bush of the field was not yet on the earth, every plant was not yet sprung up, for HE, God, had not caused it to rain over the earth, and there was no man, Adam, to attend to the soil, Adama: out of the earth rose a vapor and moistened all the face of the soil, and HE, God, formed man, dust from the soil, and blew into his nostrils breath of life, and man became a living being."

In 1966, when *Commentary* magazine sponsored a symposium of many prominent American rabbis on "The State of Jewish Belief," Milton Himmelfarb, who wrote the introduction to the symposium, noted that Rosenzweig was by far the most often cited influence on the Reform and Conservative participants. A major reason for this may be his openness to the entire Jewish tradition, which he achieved by not identifying exclusively with any one denomination or approach. A characteristic story relates that when Rosenzweig once was asked whether he put on *tefillin* (phylacteries), he answered, "Not yet." Although he did not feel spiritually ready at the time to incorporate into his life that particular *mitzvah*, he did not assume that this unreadiness would be permanent; he could envision a day when wearing *tefillin* would be a natural expression of his religiosity. Rosenzweig's "not yet" approach still has the capacity to unite Jews across denominational lines, since all Jews must answer "not yet" if asked: "Do you fully observe all of Judaism's ritual and ethical laws?"

Rosenzweig died at age forty-two, after suffering an excruciating illness for the last seven years of his life. A progressive paralysis spread from his limbs throughout his entire body, including his vocal cords. Within a short time, he could no longer speak or write. His spirit, however, was indomitable. A special typewriter was constructed for him and, with his arm hanging in a sling alongside it, he would indicate to his wife the letters he wished typed. Throughout most of his illness, his creative work continued; in fact, his collaboration with Buber on the Bible translation was undertaken only when he was already ill.

During the first years of his ailment, Rosenzweig managed to maintain good cheer. To his mother he wrote: "The words *pain* and *suffering* which you use, seem quite odd to me. A condition into which one has slithered gradually, and consequently become used to, is not suffering, but simply a condition . . . that leaves room for joy and suffering like any other. . . . What must appear suffering when seen from the outside is actually only a sum of great difficulties that have to be overcome." Given that this letter itself had to be composed in the convoluted manner described above, his tone seems remarkably composed.

Rosenzweig's subtle intellect remained intact even as his body approached total deterioration. A few months before his death, he wrote: "I can say with Hamlet, 'I have of late lost my mirth. . . . ' I have only now come to the point where I would welcome the end. Of course this isn't quite true either, as self-analytical generalities never are. I'm still able to enjoy things; it's only that my capacity for suffering has increased more rapidly than my capacity for enjoying."

Rosenzweig's final words were poignant—and exceedingly tantalizing. Using the typewriter-alphabet method, he communicated to his wife: "And now it comes, the point of all points, which the Lord has truly revealed to me in my sleep, the point of all points for which there—" and then he died, the sentence left incomplete.

It was Kierkegaard who said, "The tyrant dies and his rule is over; the martyr dies and his rule begins." So, too, is it apparently with that martyr to a terrible illness, Franz Rosenzweig.

SOURCES AND FURTHER READINGS: Nahum Glatzer, "Franz Rosenzweig," in Simon Noveck, ed., *Great Jewish Thinkers of the Twentieth Century*, pp. 159–182. There are extensive selections from Rosenzweig's writings in Glatzer, *Franz Rosenzweig: His Life and Thought*. See also Franz Rosenzweig, *The Star of Redemption*, translated by William Hallo; unfortunately, the book is very difficult to understand.

127

SHTETL

CHEDER

THOUGH JEWS ARE UNIFORMLY THOUGHT OF AS CITY PEOPLE, MANY, IF not most, American Jews trace their ancestry to the small villages and towns of Eastern Europe, known in Yiddish as *shtetlakh* (singular, *shtetl*).

Most Jews and many non-Jews are familiar with the *shtetl* through the romanticized depiction of Anatevka in the musical *Fiddler on the Roof.* While it has become common for Jews to speak of *shtetl* life nostalgically, the reality was that most Jews who lived in the *shtetlakh* were very poor and fled to America by the millions in the late nineteenth and early twentieth centuries.

As poverty-ridden as the *shtetlakh* were, however, their communal life was characterized by the extraordinary sense of responsibility that inhabitants felt for each other. My grandfather, Nissen Telushkin, the rabbi in the small Russian *shtetl* of Dukor, told me that each year before *Passover he would go to every house in the village to collect charity for those in need (see Ma'ot Chittim). Either one gave charity or one received it, but no one was allowed to be indifferent to the poor.

An often much less appealing feature of Jewish life, both in the *shtetlakh* and in the larger cities, was the institution known as the *cheder* (Jewish elementary school). In Hebrew the word *cheder* means "room," an appropriate name, since the schools often consisted of only one room, sometimes located in the teacher's house. Learning was largely by rote: Students would read a verse in Hebrew from the Torah, and then immediately recite its translation in Yiddish.

Unfortunately, the job of teaching young children conferred little status or money. As a result, teachers were not usually of the highest quality, and discipline was very harsh. In one autobiographical work, the great twentieth-century Hebrew poet Hayyim Nachman Bialik gave an unremittingly negative depiction of *cheder* life: He recalled that the teachers "knew only how to hurt, each one in his own way. The *rebbe* used to hit with a whip, with his fist, with his elbow, with his wife's rolling pin, or with anything else that would cause pain, but his assistant, whenever my answer to his question was wrong, would advance toward me, with the fingers of his palm extended and bend before my face and seize me by my throat. He would look to me then like a leopard or a tiger or some other such wild beast and I would be in mortal dread. I was afraid he would gouge out my eyes with his dirty fingernails and the fear would paralyze my mind so that I forgot everything I had learned the previous day." While Bialik's experience no doubt was extreme, I have often heard only slightly less horrifying stories from elderly Jews who attended *cheder* in their youth. There were, of course, wonderful *teachers*— Bialik himself had one a few years later—but this was largely a question of luck. Far too many teachers were not good at all. The low quality of Jewish education received in the *cheder* was one of the factors that accounted for large numbers of Jews abandoning Jewish observance when they arrived in America.

Today, in certain ultra-Orthodox circles, one still hears parents speaking of their school-age children as going to *cheder*; here, it is a synonym for elementary school.

SOURCES AND FURTHER READINGS: The quote from Bialik is cited in M. Z. Frank, "Hayyim Nachman Bialik," in Simon Noveck, ed., *Great Jewish Personalities in Modern Times*, pp. 175–176. See also Mark Zborowski, *Life Is with People: The Jewish Little-Towns of Eastern Europe*. An excellent anthology and overview of Jewish life in Eastern Europe is found in Lucy Dawidowicz, *The Golden Tradition: Jewish Life and Thought in Eastern Europe*.

128

POGROM

Organized Riots Accompanied by Murder and Pillage of the Jewish Community

POGROM IS ONE OF FOUR WORDS THAT ANTISEMITISM HAS GIVEN TO the contemporary vocabulary—the others are *genocide*, the attempt to kill an entire people; *Holocaust*, the Nazi murder of six million Jews between 1939 and 1945; and *ghetto*, the name given to the enclosed areas in many European cities where Jews were forced to live until the twentieth century, and during the Holocaust.

While technically, the word "pogrom" refers to three waves of attacks against the Jews of Russia (in 1881–1884, 1903–1906, and 1918–1920), today the term is used to refer to any murderous antisemitic attack.

The Russian pogroms radically affected Jewish life. American Jews, many of whose ancestors come from Russia, are very likely living here because of the pogroms. In 1881, when the pogroms began, more than half of world Jewry lived under Russian rule. However, the violent attacks quickly prompted waves of Jews to flee the country, with most going to the United States. Twenty years later, during a second wave of pogroms, the number of Jewish immigrants in 1905–1906 alone exceeded 200,000.

The pogroms also caused a major upsurge in Jewish support for Zionism. The First Aliyah (wave of immigration to Palestine) came in response to the 1881 Russian pogroms, and the Second Aliyah in reaction to the ones that began in 1903. In 1989–1990, rumors of impending pogroms caused an immediate and enormous upsurge in Soviet-Jewish emigration to Israel.

In addition to the killings and looting, the most disquieting feature of the pogroms was the support they received from the Russian government. In the aftermath of six hundred pogroms that took place between 1903 and 1906, it was revealed that the pamphlets calling for the attacks had been printed on the press of the czar's secret police. My grandfather Nissen Telushkin, the rabbi of the small *shtetl* of Dukor, told me that Russian Jews used to wish for a corrupt police chief because he could be bribed to stop a pogrom. It was the "idealistic" police chief whom the Jews dreaded because when the order to make a pogrom was issued he could not be bribed.

What was a pogrom like? Shocking eyewitness testimony was given by Sholem Schwartzbard. I offer it hesitantly. The description is so sickening that images from it have on occasion haunted my nights. Schwartzbard himself was a survivor of the pogroms of 1918–1920, which occurred during the brief interval when the Ukraine was an independent republic under the rule of Simon Petlura. After the Soviets defeated the Ukrainian forces, Petlura escaped to Paris, where Schwartzbard assassinated him in 1926. After a three-week trial, in which Schwartzbard offered evidence of what Petlura, his troops, and the Ukrainian masses had done to the Jews, a French court acquitted him. This excerpt reveals the nature of a pogrom:

> At the end of August [1919], when I was in Kiev, Petlura's advance guard entered. They murdered all the Jews they met on their way. In the center of Bolshaya Vasilkovskaya Street, I saw the corpse of a young man stretched out on the pavement and, her head on his dead body, a woman lamenting for her one and only son. Hoodlums shouted obscenities, mocking her despair. One sermonized: "This is good. We'll show you, damned Jews, we'll slaughter you all."
>
> [Elsewhere] they forced unfortunates to eat their excrement. They shoveled earth over them and buried them alive. Nor did they spare the dead. . . . In Tripole on the Dnieper, Petlura's birthplace, after the fifth pogrom, forty-seven corpses of the old, the sick, and the children were left lying in the street, and no living soul remained after them. Dogs began to pick at the bodies, and pigs to nibble. Finally, a Gentile who used to work for Jews, out of pity dug a grave and buried them. The Haidamacks [Ukrainian soldiers] learned of it and for that they murdered him. . . .

All of the events described above occurred in the twentieth century.

SOURCE: Schwartzbard's account of the pogrom is printed in "Memoirs of an Assassin," in Lucy Dawidowicz, ed., *The Golden Tradition: Jewish Life and Thought in Eastern Europe*, pp. 448–457.

129

KISHINEV POGROM

THE KISHINEV POGROM THAT OCCURRED ON EASTER, APRIL 6 AND 7, 1903, horrified both the entire Jewish world and large numbers of civilized non-Jews. Outrage at the attack was an important factor in the formation of the American Jewish Committee, which was created largely to fight anti-semitism. The pogrom also prompted Hayyim Nachman Bialik, the great twentieth-century Hebrew poet, to write two of his most powerful creations, "The City of Slaughter," and "On the Slaughter," in which he furiously attacked the mobs' cruelty:

> Behold on tree, on stone, on fence, on mural clay,
> The spattered blood and dried brains of the dead.

Bialik also castigated God for His apparent indifference to Jewish suffering. "And if there is justice, let it appear immediately. . . ."

His strongest attacks, however, were directed against the Jews themselves for not fighting back. Though they were "sons of the *Maccabees," the oppressed Russian Jews had been reduced, in Bialik's view, to a less than human state:

> It was the flight of mice they fled,
> The scurrying of roaches was their flight,
> They died like dogs, and they were dead.

Jewish outrage at the horror, reinforced by Bialik's widely read polemics, led to the formation of self-defense units throughout Russia, and to increasing worldwide Jewish support for Zionism. The Kishinev Pogrom also converted the young Russian-Jewish poet Vladimir *Jabotinsky to the Zionist cause, and prompted the large migration to Palestine that became known as the Second Aliyah. Kishinev and hundreds of other pogroms throughout

Russia resulted in hundreds of thousands of Russian Jews emigrating to the United States.

One final detail about the Kishinev Pogrom: The total number of Jews killed in Kishinev was *forty-nine*. The world was apparently quite a different place in 1903, for the forty-nine victims prompted infinitely more concern and anger than did the thousands of Jews murdered by the Nazis each day during much of the *Holocaust.

130

SHOLOM ALEICHEM (1859–1916)

Pen Name of Yiddish Writer Sholom Rabinowitz

SHOLOM ALEICHEM WAS THE MARK TWAIN OF THE JEWISH PEOPLE. The parallel between these contemporary writers was noted even during their lifetimes. Reputedly, when the two met, Sholom Aleichem said: "They call me the Jewish Mark Twain." To which Twain responded: "They call me the American Sholom Aleichem."

Sholom Aleichem's most enduring creation was Tevye the Dairyman, a character whose life became widely known among all Yiddish-speaking Jews through a series of short stories. Tevye has become known to Jews and non-Jews alike through the musical (and later the movie) *Fiddler on the Roof*. Set in late nineteenth- and early-twentieth-century Russia, *Fiddler* was one of the most successful musicals in the history of Broadway.

Tevye had seven daughters, and a good part of his life was consumed by ambitious plans to arrange "good" marriages for each of them. To no avail. Tevye's daughters had independent personalities. Like their father, they were strong-willed and had every intention of arranging their own love lives. The eldest girl chose a very fine, but poor, tailor. The second one fell in love with a young Jewish revolutionary, and accompanied him when the czarist government sentenced him to a far-off exile. The third converted to Christianity to marry a non-Jew: The brokenhearted Tevye felt he had no choice but to disown her for abandoning her religion and people. The fourth daughter fell in love with the son of a wealthy and prominent widow, who did not want her boy to marry into a family as simple as Tevye's. The widow forced the relationship to end. In perhaps the most poignant and painful scene Sholom Aleichem ever wrote, he described Tevye finding his daughter's body in a river after she had drowned herself.

When summarized, the stories sound almost unremittingly bleak. Yet Tevye's spirit was so playful that one finds oneself laughing even at the moment tears well up. As the Yiddish literary critic Shmuel Niger wrote: "Although [Tevye] is beset by one disaster after another we don't insult him with our small feelings of pity because we see that his troubles do not oppress or discourage him, but merely deepen his humanity."

Most of the Tevye stories feature the protagonist's ongoing monologues with God. A deeply religious man, Tevye was constantly flinging up biblical verses at the Creator, and then offering his own commentaries on them: "Blessed are they that dwell in Thy house"—'Right! I take it, O Lord, that Thy house is somewhat more spacious than my house.'" Or, "The Lord is good to all"—'And suppose He forgets somebody now and again: Good Lord, hasn't He enough on His mind?'"

Tevye's creator, Sholom Aleichem, was empathetic with human weaknesses; rather than railing against them, he was prompted to deliver some of his most hilarious observations. Consider, for example, one of his characters' brilliant advice on how to avoid provoking jealousy from one's neighbors: "A man must always be considerate of the feelings of his neighbors. . . . So, for instance, if I went to the fair . . . and did well, sold everything at a good profit, and returned with pocketfuls of money, my heart bursting with joy, I never failed to tell my neighbors that I had lost every kopeck and was a ruined man. Thus I was happy, and my neighbors were happy. But if, on the contrary, I had really been cleaned out at the fair and brought home with me a bitter heart and a bellyful of green gall, I made sure to tell my neighbors that never since God made fairs, had there been a better one. You get my point? For thus I was miserable and my neighbors were miserable with me."

For Sholom Aleichem, the line between pathos and humor often was thin. In a short tale, "A Pity for the Living," he writes of a small boy whose mother tells him to grate some onions. Before she leaves the room, she warns him to keep his eyes closed lest he start crying. "And if I catch you crying, I'll smack you."

The boy sits and ponders his mother's words with rising indignation. "It's so unjust," he thinks, "to threaten me like that." Then he starts thinking about other injustices, such as the time he saw the maid kick a cat for allegedly eating some food she had prepared. Later, the maid found the "consumed" food. When the boy told her to apologize to the cat, she yelled at him. Or, he remembers, the Saturday when, dressed in his best pants, he saw two peasant boys throwing stones at a bird's nest. When he went over to them and told them to stop, they beat him up and ripped his pants. When he arrived home, and before he could explain what had happened, his father hit him again for getting into a fight on the Sabbath and ruining his pants. He then thinks of a much bigger injustice: There was a crippled girl who lived in his courtyard, whom he used to carry around the street on his back, and laugh and play with. One day, *pogromists (see preceding two entries) came and threw the girl out the window of her home, killing her. When he recalls the girl lying lifeless on the street, the little boy starts crying. At that point, his mother reenters the room, observes his tears, and smacks him: "I told you to keep your eyes closed when you grate onions."

Sholom Aleichem's soul seems to have been as gentle as those of the fictional characters he created. He left a request in his will that on his *yahrzeit (the anniversary of his death), his family get together and read some of his more humorous stories.

SOURCES AND FURTHER READINGS: Louis Falstein, "Sholom Aleichem," in Simon Noveck, ed., *Great Jewish Personalities in Modern Times*, pp. 207–226; Shmuel Niger, "The Humor of Sholom Aleichem," in Irving Howe and Eliezer Greenberg, eds., *Voices from the Yiddish*, pp. 41–50; Irving Howe and Ruth Wisse, eds., *The Best of Sholom Aleichem*.

131

SIGMUND FREUD (1856–1939)

KARL MARX, ALBERT *EINSTEIN, AND SIGMUND FREUD ARE OFTEN cited as the three Jews who most deeply affected the Western world in the nineteenth and twentieth centuries. However, it stretches the meaning of the word "Jew" to include Marx in this listing. He was converted to Christianity by his father at age six, and was a vicious antisemite throughout his life. Einstein, on the other hand, had so positive a Jewish identity that when Chaim *Weiz-mann, Israel's first president, died, he was offered the country's presidency. He did not accept, but he responded with a gracious letter, explaining how moved he was by the proposal.

Sigmund Freud's Jewish identity was much more positive than Marx's, and more complicated than Einstein's. Freud was an avowed atheist, and found little in Judaism's rituals to attract him. Yet as much as he rejected Judaism's core beliefs, he was proud to belong to a people who had maintained its convictions in the face of persecution and unremitting hostility. Freud believed that this Jewish strength and stubbornness had given him some of the fortitude he needed to maintain his psychoanalytic theories in the face of an almost uniformly hostile medical establishment. "Because I was a Jew," Freud declared before the Viennese *B'nai B'rith lodge of which he was a member, "I found myself free from many prejudices which restricted others in the use of their intellect; and as a Jew I was prepared to join the opposition and to do without agreement with the 'compact majority.'"

Freud occasionally wrote on issues of specific Jewish interest. His work on humor, *Jokes and Their Relation to the Unconscious*, contains more material on Jewish humor than on that of any other group. He was particularly impressed by the degree to which Jews were willing to joke about their shortcomings: "I do not know," he wrote, "whether there are many other instances of a people making fun to such a degree of its own character." He particularly relished the healthy sense of ego manifest in Jewish chutzpa. One of his favorite jokes told of a Jewish beggar who "approached a wealthy baron with a request for some assistance for his journey to [the resort of] Ostend. The doctors, he said, had recommended sea-bathing to restore his health. 'Very well,' said the rich man, 'I'll give you something toward it. But must you go precisely to Ostend, which is the most expensive of all sea-bathing resorts?' 'Herr Baron,' was the reproachful reply, 'I consider nothing too expensive for my health.'"

Freud's last book, *Moses and Monotheism*, dealt almost exclusively with a Jewish theme, though it gained him few friends in the Jewish community. With a palpable preference for theory over facts, Freud posited that *Moses was not a Hebrew, but an Egyptian who led a revolt of Hebrews against Pharaoh and was later murdered by the Jews he had helped. Freud speculated that the Jewish murderers subsequently experienced such feelings of guilt and remorse over their crime that they became, in the words of Ernest van den Haag, "zealous and obedient sons to the 'father' they had slain."

Throughout the book, one senses that Freud regarded himself as something of a Moses, revealing the "Torah" of psychoanalysis to an often hostile world.

Freud did, however, offer a provocative explanation for antisemitism in *Moses and Monotheism:* that Jews were hated not as *Christ-killers but as Christ-givers. The Christian world, he believed, always resented the far-reaching moral demands that Jesus made of them. They vented their frustration and anger on the Jews, who by making these demands—both through their religion and through the character of Jesus—had become the Western world's bad conscience.

Throughout his life Freud was, if not obsessed, then deeply interested in trying to understand the ferocity of Jew-hatred. "With regard to anti-semitism," he wrote, "I don't really want to search for explanations; I feel a strong inclination to surrender my affects in this matter and find myself confirmed in my wholly nonscientific belief that mankind on the average and taken by and large are a wretched lot." In one of the most moving passages in *The Interpretation of Dreams,* Freud related hearing his father speak of anti-semitism in Vienna: "I may have been ten or twelve years old, when my father began to take me with him on his walks and reveal to me in his talks his views upon things in the world we live in. Thus it was, on one such occasion that he told me a story to show me how much better things were now than they had been in his day. 'When I was a young man,' he said, 'I went for a walk one Sunday in the streets of [Vienna]. . . . I was well dressed, and had a new fur cap on my head. A Christian came up to me and with a single blow knocked off my cap into the mud and shouted: 'Jew! Get off the pavement.' 'And what did you do?' I asked. 'I went into the roadway and picked up my cap,' was his quiet reply.' " Learning that his father was the protagonist in so demoralizing a story was quite a trauma for the young boy.

Freud lived almost his entire life in Vienna. But a year before he died, the Nazis occupied Austria. The Gestapo raided his house three times, and brought his daughter Anna to their headquarters for questioning. Austrian Jews were living in such terror that Anna took Veronal with her so that she could commit suicide if she was tortured. With the help of prominent non-Jews throughout the world, Freud won permission for himself and his daughter to emigrate to England. Before allowing the pair to leave, the Gestapo demanded that Freud sign a statement certifying that he had been well treated. With typical mordant wit, he wrote: "I am happy to give the Gestapo my best recommendation."

"The irony was apparently lost on the Gestapo," historian George Berkley has written. "[They] accepted [the note] and let the Freuds go." During World War II, Freud's four elderly sisters, who remained behind in Austria, were murdered by the Nazis.

Throughout Freud's life, Jews were among the most enthusiastic proponents of his psychoanalytical theories. In the movement's early days, Freud particularly prized the involvement of C. G. Jung, the only non-Jew in his inner circle. "It was only by his appearance on the scene," Freud wrote in a letter, "that psychoanalysis escaped the danger of becoming a Jewish national affair." Indeed, Freud was long fearful that antisemites would dismiss psychoanalysis as a Jewish science, which is, of course, what the Nazis later did. To this day, psychiatry has continued to exert a particular fascination for Jews, and there is probably no other branch of medicine in which Jews are as heavily represented as in psychiatry.

FREUD'S ASSESSMENT OF THE ADMIRATION
IN WHICH JEWS HELD HIM

"The Jewish societies in Vienna and the University of Jerusalem (of which I am a trustee), in short the Jews altogether, have celebrated me like a natural hero, although my service to the Jewish cause is confined to the single point that I have never denied my Jewishness."

SOURCES AND FURTHER READINGS: Robert Wistrich, "The Jewishness of Sigmund Freud," in his *Between Redemption and Perdition: Modern Antisemitism and Jewish Identity*, pp. 71–85. Marthe Robert, *From Oedipus to Moses: Freud's Jewish Identity*; George Berkley, *Vienna and Its Jews*, pp. 260–261; Dennis Klein, *The Jewish Origins of the Psychoanalytic Movement*; Ernest van den Haag, *The Jewish Mystique*, p. 84; Van den Haag also cites data showing that while Jews are overrepresented in medicine by 231 percent proportionate to their percentage of the population, their overrepresentation in psychiatry is 478 percent. Freud's statement on antisemitism is found in Ernst L. Freud, ed., *The Letters of Sigmund Freud and Arnold Zweig*, translated by Elaine and William Robson-Scott, p. 3.

132

LEON TROTSKY (1880–1940)

LEON TROTSKY WAS ONE OF THE KEY LEADERS OF THE 1917 COMMU-
nist revolution in Russia, and later head of the Red Army. Born Lev Bron-
stein, he was a Jew, though only by birth.

During the two-year civil war that followed the 1917 revolution, anti-
Communist Ukrainian troops murdered fifty thousand Ukrainian Jews. The
soldiers' antisemitic passions were raised by their leader, General Simon
Petlura (see *Pogrom*), who constantly reminded them that the Bolshevik
armies were led by "the Jew Trotsky." Yet when Moscow's chief rabbi Mazeh
appealed to him as a Jew to use the Red Army to stop the pogroms, Trotsky
denied his Jewishness. "You are mistaken," was Trotsky's characteristic response when his Jewish origins were mentioned. "I am a social-democrat.
That's all." At the conclusion of his meeting with Trotsky, Rabbi Mazeh is
reported to have said: "The Trotskys make the revolutions, and the Bronsteins
pay the price." Historian Paul Johnson has noted that, more than any other
figure, Trotsky "was responsible for the popular identification [of the Communist revolution] with the Jews."

Jews, of course, *have* paid a heavy price for their association in the popular
mind with communism. While antisemites have had an easy time documenting the large percentage of Jews in Communist movements, what they
fail to mention is that Jewish Communists have generally been as hostile to
Jewish interests as the antisemites themselves. Karl Marx, the founder of
Communist theory, was born to a Jewish family in 1818, but was converted
by his parents to Christianity when he was six. His first major essay, *On the
Jewish Question*, is filled with a hatred of Jews and Judaism so extreme that it
sounds Nazilike: "What is the secular cult of the Jew? *Haggling*. What is his
secular god? *Money*. Well then! Emancipation from *haggling* and *money*,
from practical real Judaism would be the self-emancipation of our time. . . .
Money is the jealous God of Israel, beside which no other God may stand."
Hitler later claimed that some of his own antisemitic realizations were
shaped by reading this essay.

Marx set the tone for the hostility of many later Jewish Communists toward Jews and Judaism. While Trotsky's antisemitism never approached that of Marx, he actively opposed Jewish interests. During his years of power and leadership in Russia, the overwhelming majority of synagogues were shut down—the Russian Orthodox Church was attacked as well—the study of Hebrew was banned and the Russian Zionist movement, which had 300,000 members, was destroyed. Movement leaders were sent to prison camps, from which few emerged alive.

Given Trotsky's prominent role in helping to cripple Jewish life in Russia, it must have been particularly galling that his own Jewish origin was a—perhaps *the*—major reason Stalin, and not he himself, succeeded Lenin. Winston Churchill acutely depicted the frustration this must have provoked in Trotsky: "He was still a Jew. Nothing could get over that. Hard fortune when you have deserted your family, repudiated your race, spat upon the religion of your father . . . to be balked of so great a prize for so narrow-minded a reason."

Years later, after he was expelled from Russia and exiled to Mexico, Trotsky denounced Stalin's antisemitism. Ironically, American-Jewish Communists then assailed him for claiming that antisemitism existed in a society they "knew" was devoid of Jew-hatred.

To this day, Trotsky is regarded as the greatest intellectual among the early Bolshevik leaders. Yet, assessing his intellect solely from his writings on Jewish issues, one finds little that is impressive. To cite two examples: In 1904, he ridiculed Zionism and predicted its imminent disappearance. In July 1940, almost a year after the outbreak of World War II, he was still attacking Zionism, saying it was incapable of helping Jews. Instead, he asserted: "Never was it so clear as it is today, that the salvation of the Jewish people is bound up inseparably with the overthrow of the capitalist system." Even moderately knowledgeable Jews were already aware that they had never encountered as much tolerance and relatively little antisemitism as they had in capitalist societies. Trotsky was too doctrinaire a Communist to acknowledge a fact that challenged his theories.

Only a month after making this prophecy, Trotsky was murdered in his Mexican exile by an assassin sent by Stalin.

SOURCES AND FURTHER READINGS: Robert Wistrich, *Revolutionary Jews from Marx to Trotsky*, pp. 189–207; Joseph Nevada, *Trotsky and the Jews*; Paul Johnson, *A History of the Jews*, pp. 448–454; Hayim Greenberg, *The Inner Eye*, vol. II, pp. 229–243; Dennis Prager and Joseph Telushkin, *Why the Jews? The Reason for Antisemitism*, pp. 45–46, 123–126.

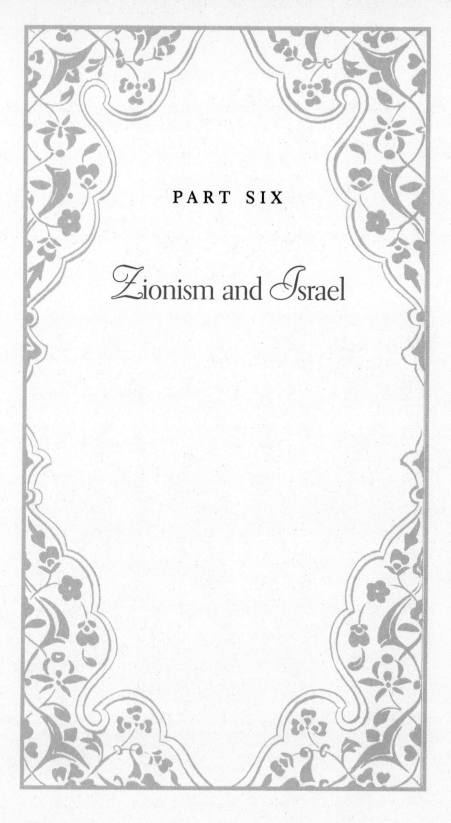

PART SIX

Zionism and Israel

133

"IF I FORGET THEE, O JERUSALEM"
(PSALMS 137:5)

DURING THE ALMOST TWO THOUSAND YEARS THAT THE JEWISH PEOPLE were exiled from Israel, the land always remained at the very center of Jewish consciousness. When Jews throughout the world made their annual prayer for rain on *Shmini Atzeret, it was during the season when rain was needed in Israel, not when it was needed in their native countries. The nineteenth-century British prime minister Benjamin Disraeli was so struck by the unusual devotion of Jews to the Holy Land, he ventured a prophecy: "A people that celebrates the wine harvest even when it does not reap grapes any more, will regain its vineyards." Three times a day, religious Jews prayed—and still do—that God restore the Jewish people to its homeland. The most widely observed of all Jewish rituals, the *Passover *Seder, concludes with the call "Next year in Jerusalem." The haunting 137th psalm, composed during the first Jewish exile in Babylonia in the sixth century B.C.E., contains a well-known admonition:

> If I forget thee, O Jerusalem,
> Let my right hand wither,
> Let my tongue cleave to the roof of its mouth . . .

Throughout the centuries, small numbers of Jews continued to live in Israel, even under the most adverse circumstances. In the second century, the Romans forbade Jews to enter Jerusalem, and tried to turn the Jewish holy city into a pagan center, which they called Aelia Capitolina (formed by combining the name of the reigning emperor, Aelius Hadrianus, with that of the Roman god Jupiter Capitolinus). During the long centuries of Muslim rule over Palestine, Islamic leaders went back and forth in their treatment of the Jews, acting sometimes as brutal oppressors, and at other times as mild oppressors. When the Christian *Crusaders captured Jerusalem, they murdered every Jew living there.

Yet Jews never ceased coming to live, and sometimes to die, in Israel. From the Middle Ages on, world Jewry was so supportive of Jewish settlement in the Holy Land that communities throughout the world sent charitable contributions—later known as the *khalukah*—to their co-religionists there. In some respects, the *khalukah* was a forerunner of the *United Jewish Appeal. Palestinian Jews needed this charity because the land was so poor that few of its inhabitants could support themselves.

Even during the centuries when the Jews comprised only a small minority of the population, no other people ever claimed the land as their country. Palestine was simply regarded in the Arab world as southern Syria, and the Arabs living there were considered Syrians.

The rise of Zionism in the late 1800s was a new political movement in Jewish life; in its focus on Israel as the Jewish homeland, however, the movement was basing itself on an idea as old as Judaism itself. Jewish history began with God's revelation to *Abraham. At that first encounter with the Patriarch, God did not speak about monotheism; the first words He proclaimed to Abraham were about the land of Israel: "Go . . . to the land that I will show you" (Genesis 12:1).

From then on, Jews felt an extraordinary attachment to Israel. During a terrible famine, when *Jacob was forced to go to Egypt with his sons, he made *Joseph promise that he would be buried in Israel (it was still known then as Canaan).

Hundreds of years later, when the Babylonians exiled the Jews from their homeland (see *The Babylonian Exile*), the prophet *Jeremiah used his remaining funds to buy a parcel of land in Israel. Even as he left for what appeared to be permanent exile, he wanted a deed that could be passed to later Jews, showing that they owned land in Israel.

The consciousness of living in exile was common to Jews throughout the world. It explains why Zionism, a small political movement at its inception, could grow within a half-century to be the largest and most unifying movement in Jewish life. Polls conducted in the United States have repeatedly shown that more than 80 percent of America's Jews would regard the destruction of Israel as one of the greatest tragedies that could happen to them. Those Jews who oppose Israel's existence are seen by the rest as hostile or peripheral to Jewish life (see *Neturei Karta* and *Self-hating Jews*).

When the State of Israel was declared in 1948, the Jews became the first people in history to have regained their homeland after having been exiled from it.

SOURCES AND FURTHER READINGS: Arthur Hertzberg, *The Zionist Idea*; Walter Laqueur, *A History of Zionism*; Howard M. Sachar, *A History of Israel* (two volumes); Yigal Losin, *Pillar of Fire: The Rebirth of Israel—A Visual History*.

BILU

THE YEAR THE *POGROMS BEGAN IN RUSSIA, 1881, IS THE YEAR Russian Jews started emigrating in large numbers to the United States. A smaller number of them, however, turned their eyes toward Zion; in 1882, several thousand Russian Jews emigrated to Palestine. Prior to this, most Jews who made *aliyah to Israel did so for religious reasons; it was considered meritorious, for example, to die in the Holy Land. *Living* in Palestine, however, was considerably harder. It was an impoverished land, many—if not most—of whose Jewish inhabitants depended on worldwide Jewish charitable contributions.

In 1882 also, a new Jewish organization was founded that had a very different scenario in mind for Jewish life in Israel. The group was called BILU, an acronym based on a verse from *Isaiah (2:5), "*Beit Ya'akov Lekhu Venelkha/Let the house of Jacob go!" BILU's founders believed that the time had come for Jews not only to live in Israel, but to make their living there as well.

The Bilu'im were influenced by Marx as well as the Bible, and hoped to establish farming cooperatives in Palestine. For the fourteen ex-university students who comprised the first group of Bilu'im, farming represented a complete change of lifestyle. (Because Jews had been forbidden to own land in Russia, the country had almost no Jewish farmers.) Arriving in Palestine with enormous "funds" of good will and energy, but with little money and experience, the Bilu'im found life very difficult. Two Palestinian Jews who had already raised money to buy land gave the group a tract to set up a farm in the settlement of Rishon Le-Zion. Within a few months, the Bilu'im faced starvation, and most had to leave.

A few years later, the eight members of the group who had remained in Palestine were offered land in G'dera. Here they struggled against both difficult farming conditions—meals eventually consisted only of radishes and potatoes—and Arab marauders. "They violated our boundaries," one of the Bilu'im recorded in his diaries, "and dispossessed us of whole tracts of our land—and we were helpless." Ironically, the G'dera outpost was eventually saved through the philanthropic efforts of one of the arch-capitalists of the Jewish world, Baron Edmund de *Rothschild of France. The dispirited, and by now demoralized, Bilu'im soon left the settlement. Some went to other parts of Palestine, others returned to Europe.

Although the BILU movement failed completely, its vision of Jewish cooperative farms was carried out very successfully a few decades later by the *kibbutz and moshav movements. Ever since, the BILU dream of Jews living and supporting themselves in their own homeland has been regarded as one of the important forerunners of the international Zionist movement which Theodore *Herzl organized fifteen years later.

SOURCE AND FURTHER READING: Howard M. Sachar, A *History of Israel*, pp. 26–32.

135

DREYFUS TRIAL

IN 1894, ALFRED DREYFUS, A CAPTAIN IN THE FRENCH ARMY, WAS accused of spying for Germany. Before the case was finally resolved twelve years later, a French government fell, the power of the deeply antisemitic Catholic Church in France was curbed, and the French Army was profoundly jolted. But until that happened, the Jews as usual suffered vicious antisemitic attacks.

Disinterested investigators quickly discovered that the charges against Dreyfus were false. There was indeed a high-level French spy working for the

Germans, but the evidence clearly pointed to a Colonel Esterhazy as the guilty party. Nonetheless, the French Army, in cooperation with the right-wing government's leaders, conspired to quash all evidence pointing to Dreyfus's innocence. Unfortunately, although France had been the first European country to grant the Jews equal rights, there remained a deep tradition of Jew-hatred in the country, a tradition fed by both the right and left wings. Right-wing French diplomats had helped bring about the *Damascus Blood Libel in 1840, while left-wing French socialists insisted on identifying all Jews of all classes with the wealth of the *Rothschilds. During the Dreyfus Affair—in France it was known simply as "L'Affaire"—the left, although it routinely opposed the government, the military, and the Church, refused to involve itself on the unfortunate captain's behalf. France's leading socialists published a manifesto urging non-participation in the Dreyfus case, lest "Jewish capitalists . . . use the rehabilitation of a single Jew to wash out 'all the sins of Israel.'" Years later, some of France's socialists did adopt a pro-Dreyfus stance.

But just as the villains in the Dreyfus case were non-Jews, so too were the heroes. The greatest was the novelist Emile Zola, who shocked all France with a stunning denunciation in a newspaper article entitled, "J'accuse." "May all my works perish," Zola wrote, "if Dreyfus is not innocent . . . I [do] not want my country to remain in lies and injustice. One day, France will thank me for having helped to save its honor." Zola's impassioned statement so roused public opinion that the government had no choice but to release Dreyfus or to order Zola's arrest. Unfortunately, it took the latter course: Zola was convicted of libel and had to flee to England so as to avoid a prison sentence.

As irregularities at the original Dreyfus trial became increasingly evident, the government was finally forced to order a new trial; it arranged, however, to have Dreyfus convicted again. Finally, however, he was exonerated and returned as a free man from his prison cell on Devil's Island. He was reinstated in the army and remained in France until his death in 1935.

Ironically, the victim of this antisemitic outrage was himself not a committed Jew. One of Dreyfus's supporters commented that had another Jew been the victim, it is unlikely that Dreyfus would have involved himself in the case.

An important outcome of the Dreyfus case in Jewish history is that it impelled Theodor Herzl (see next entry) to become a Zionist.

SOURCES: Norman Kleeblatt, ed., *The Dreyfus Affair*; Jean-Denis Bredin, *The Affair: The Case of Alfred Dreyfus*, translated by Jeffrey Mehlman.

136

THEODOR HERZL (1860–1904)
The Jewish State

HUMAN HISTORY HAS GIVEN AMPLE EVIDENCE OF THE POWER OF individuals to do evil. Theodor Herzl's short life—he died when he was only forty-four—gives irrefutable evidence of an individual's power to do massive good. Though the notion of a Jewish return to Palestine had been gathering strength throughout the second half of the nineteenth century, it was Herzl who turned Zionism into an international movement. He electrified the Jewish world with his oft-repeated declaration, "*Im tirtzu, ain zo agadah*—If you will it, it is no legend."

The masses of Eastern European Jews who became Herzl's most fervent supporters often compared him to *Moses. One striking similarity between the two men was that both had been raised in environments very different from that of the people whom they were trying to save. Moses had been reared in the court of Pharaoh, Herzl in the Western, and nonghettoized, environments of Budapest and Vienna. Contrary to a popular myth, Herzl was not raised in a totally assimilated Jewish home. He attended services with his parents quite regularly at the liberal synagogue in Budapest, and throughout his life adhered to the traditional practice of asking his parents for a blessing before he undertook major projects.

Nonetheless, in his early years, Judaism and the Jewish people were peripheral issues in Herzl's life. By the early 1890s—he was then a little over thirty—Herzl had achieved a reputation throughout Europe as a brilliant journalist. His strength lay in writing *feuilletons*, brief, witty essays that captured a mood or scene. During those years, the only Jewish issue that seemed to concern him was antisemitism. At one point, he even advocated having Europe's most prominent Jews publicly convert to Catholicism, in the belief that this would inaugurate a mass conversion of the rest of Jewry. An end to the Jewish people, Herzl reasoned, would also end antisemitism. He quickly realized, however, that this "euthanasia" of Judaism was neither practical nor moral.

The Dreyfus trial (see preceding entry) turned Herzl toward the Zionist solution. Before being exiled to life imprisonment on Devil's Island, Alfred Dreyfus was publicly humiliated at a ceremony in Paris. His sword was broken, and his military medals ripped off his uniform. What particularly struck Herzl, who was present at the ceremony, were the cries of the frenzied French mobs. In addition to calling for Dreyfus's death, they repeatedly shouted: "Death to the Jews!"

As long as Jews lived in non-Jewish societies, Herzl concluded, they would be collectively blamed and hated for the wrongful actions of any one of them. If "Death to the Jews!" was the reaction in liberal France—the first European country to grant the Jews equal rights—it meant that they were not safe anywhere except in a land of their own.

Herzl became obsessed with the vision of a renewed Jewish state. His first instinct was to solicit the support of some of the world's wealthiest Jews, the *Rothschilds and Baron de Hirsch of France—to no avail. In a burst of creativity, he wrote a sixty-three-page pamphlet, *Der Judenstaat (The Jewish State)*, in which he outlined a program for creating a Jewish state, and explained why doing so was entirely feasible. "Let me repeat once more," he wrote on the book's final page, "the Jews who wish for a state will have it."

Between Dreyfus's humiliation and Herzl's death elapsed but ten years. In that decade, however, Herzl laid the foundations for all the major structures of the Zionist movement. In 1897, he convened the First Zionist Congress (see next entry) in Basel, Switzerland. Each year, the congresses grew in size. More and more Jews came to see Zionism not as a Jewish fantasy, but as the one political movement that could solve the Jewish problem.

During Herzl's first years of Zionist activity, he expended most of his efforts on procuring the support of Turkey's sultan—Turkey then controlled Palestine—and of the sultan's major supporter in Europe, the German kaiser. After several years of raised hopes, then fruitless negotiations, his efforts shifted toward England, which proved to be far-sighted. In 1917, thirteen years after Herzl's death, England wrested control of Palestine from Turkey and issued the *Balfour Declaration, an announcement of British support for a Jewish homeland in Palestine.

Herzl and his family paid a heavy personal price for his Zionist involvement. When his wife, Julie Naschauer, married him in 1889 she had not bargained for a liaison with an obsessed man who had far more time for his vision than for his family. In addition, there appears to have been a touch of mental illness on Julie's side of the family. The fate of Herzl's children was tragic. His older daughter, Pauline, died of drug addiction, and his son, Hans, committed suicide on the day of her funeral. The younger daughter, Trude, spent much of her life in and out of hospitals before dying in the Nazi concentration camp of *Theresienstadt. Because Herzl's only grandson (Trude's child) committed suicide in 1946, there are today no heirs of Herzl.

What he did leave behind was a movement that grew into a state. Before he died, Herzl specified in his will that he wished to be buried next to his father in Vienna, until such time as the Jewish people would bring his remains to Palestine for burial. In 1949, his wish was carried out: Today, his burial place on Jerusalem's Mount Herzl is a major tourist attraction.

Herzl's extraordinary decade of intense Jewish activism made his one of the most significant Jewish lives lived in the last two centuries.

SOURCES AND FURTHER READINGS: Amos Elon, *Herzl*; Ernst Pawel, *The Labyrinth of Exile: A Life of Theodore Herzl*; Theodor Herzl, *The Jewish State*: In the Dover edition of Herzl's book, there is an excellent forty-page biography of him by Alex Bein.

137

FIRST ZIONIST CONGRESS, 1897

BASEL, SWITZERLAND, HAS NEVER HAD A JEWISH POPULATION OF MORE than a few thousand. Nonetheless, as the site of the First Zionist Congress in 1897, it is one of the most famous cities in modern Jewish history.

In organizing the congress, Theodor Herzl (see preceding entry) hoped to make an international statement about the growing vitality of the Zionist movement. He originally wished to convene the congress in Germany, then the major center of Jewish life in Western Europe. The leading figures of German Jewry, however, wanted no part of Herzl or of his movement. They feared that Zionism, with its emphatic insistence that Jews throughout the world were one people, would call into question the loyalty of German Jews to Germany. They exerted pressure to ensure that Herzl could not rent the facilities to convene his congress. In Basel, a Swiss city just across the German border, he found a friendlier reception.

Some 204 delegates from nineteen countries attended the first congress. What until now had been unstructured, grass-roots movements, coalesced into a unified, if still small, political force. Herzl was later to declare that at Basel he founded the Jewish state. "If I were to say this today," he confided to his diary, "I would be greeted with laughter. In five years, perhaps, and certainly in fifty, everyone will see it." Exactly fifty years later, in 1947, the United Nations voted to partition Palestine into an Arab and a Jewish state (see *U.N. Vote for Partition*).

The tone of the congress was decidedly formal; Herzl entered the assembly in full morning dress with a top hat. This formality was intentional. Even during Zionism's bleakest days, Herzl's appearance and public utterances were intended to convey that he headed a dynamic and powerful world organization. "We are here to lay the foundation stone of the house which is to shelter the Jewish nation," is how he publicly summarized the congress's aim.

The proceedings electrified the delegates, and the wider Jewish world. The Second Zionist Congress, held a year later, drew 394 delegates. Among them was Chaim *Weizmann, a Russian-born chemist, who came closest to assuming Herzl's mantle after his death in 1904. A major fight erupted at the sixth congress, when Herzl urged the delegates to consider the British offer of Uganda (see next entry) as a temporary alternative to Palestine.

At first, the Zionist congresses were held annually; after the fifth congress, however, they convened less frequently. The last one to be held outside Israel met in Basel in 1946. Since Israel's creation in 1948, the congresses have continued to meet periodically—but now always in Jerusalem.

138

UGANDA

HAD THEODOR HERZL HAD HIS WAY, THE JEWISH HOMELAND TODAY might be Uganda, not Israel.

By 1903, six years after the First Zionist Congress, Herzl had grown discouraged at the possibility of gaining Jewish control over Palestine in the near future. At the same time, the outbreak of pogroms in Russia, particularly the savage massacre of Jews in Kishinev (see *Kishinev Pogrom*), made finding a Jewish haven very urgent.

Britain stepped into the picture, offering Herzl land in the largely undeveloped area of Uganda (today, it would be considered an area of Kenya). While Herzl hardly saw Uganda as an ideal or permanent solution, his compassion for oppressed Jews made him ready to accept it as an immediate refuge. Uganda, he hoped, would be a way station on the path to Palestine.

Herzl raised the British offer at the 1903 Zionist congress, but to his chagrin many delegates, particularly those representing Russia's persecuted Jews, rejected the proposal. He was shocked by the intensity of the opposition, and hurt by the personal attacks leveled against him. A young Eastern European Jew, outraged at what he regarded as Herzl's betrayal of Zionism, shot Max Nordau, his closest ally. Fortunately, Nordau survived the attack.

Despite the opposition, and after many hours of acrimonious debate, a majority of delegates voted to send an expedition to Uganda to examine its viability as a refuge. Herzl's concluding speech—the last he delivered to a Zionist congress—emphasized that Uganda would be only a temporary expedient. Raising his right hand, Herzl closed his remarks in Hebrew, with words drawn from Psalm 137: *"If I forget thee, O Jerusalem, let my right hand wither."*

Nonetheless, despite Herzl's loyalty to Palestine, many Jews throughout the world feared that what would start out as a "temporary expedient" might become permanent. Unfortunately, the battle over Uganda further exhausted the already sickly Herzl; less than a year later he was dead from a heart ailment.

In retrospect, both sides in the Uganda controversy showed an impressive level of idealism. The Western European Zionists, most of whom supported the proposal, had no personal interest in relinquishing the dream of Palestine; they considered the possibility of Uganda solely because of Russian Jewry's dire situation. The Eastern European delegates, the ones most desperately in need of a Jewish homeland, refused to compromise on the issue of Palestine. Indeed, among those who voted against the Uganda proposal were the delegates from Kishinev.

SOURCE AND FURTHER READING: Amos Elon, *Herzl*, pp. 374–394.

139

RABBI ABRAHAM ISAAC KOOK — RAV KOOK
(1865–1935)

IN MODERN JEWISH HISTORY, THERE HAVE BEEN FEW ORTHODOX RABbis as deeply loved by non-Orthodox Jews as Rabbi Abraham Isaac Kook. He also was the preeminent hero of religious Zionists. Rav Kook, as he was known, became a passionate Zionist during the movement's early days, at a time when most Orthodox leaders were denouncing Zionism as a Jewish heresy. In their view, the revival of a Jewish state had to be brought about by God, not men. Kook insisted, rather, that Jews were forbidden to sit back passively and rely on God alone to shape their destiny; they had to play an active role as well. He emigrated from Russia to Palestine in 1909, and became Chief Rabbi of Jaffa; in 1921, he was appointed Chief Rabbi of Palestine.

Unlike most members of the insular Orthodox world of early twentieth-century Palestine, Rav Kook felt an enormous kinship with all Jews involved in the building and settling of Israel, even though most Zionist pioneers were religiously nonobservant. Some Orthodox Jews attacked Rav Kook for the close personal relations he maintained with non-religious Jews, but he was undaunted by this criticism. When the Great *Temple was built in Jerusalem, he was fond of noting, the construction workers would go in and out of the

Holy of Holies while working on it. Only when the Temple was complete was entry to the Holy of Holies restricted to the High Priest. So, too, at a time when the Jews were building a new Jewish state, *all* Jews had an important part to play in its creation. Still, Kook worked hard at trying to influence the largely secular *kibbutzim to become *kosher (observe the Jewish dietary laws), and to adopt other Jewish traditions.

Unlike many of his Orthodox rabbinic colleagues, Rav Kook saw value in secular education. He understood that the exclusively religious curriculum studied by *yeshiva students was inadequate for developing a Jewish community capable of maintaining its own sovereign state. He also established his own yeshiva to propagate his particular religious-nationalistic, and pro-Zionist, understanding of Judaism.

Today, more than seventy years after his death, Israeli Jews fight over Rav Kook's legacy. Many, perhaps most, of his disciples are found on the Israeli right. Rav Kook's mystical belief in the sanctity of the land of Israel, they argue, means that he would have opposed giving back any of *Judea or Samaria (the *West Bank), even for peace with the Arab world. Gush Emunim, for many years the leading organization of Israeli hawks, has been largely headed by men who regard themselves as followers of Rav Kook. However, other religious Zionists see Kook's primary significance in his calls for greater tolerance between religious and nonreligious Jews, and in his repeated declarations of his love for all humanity.

"According to the Talmud," he used to say, "the Second Temple was destroyed because of causeless hatred within the Jewish community. Perhaps it will be rebuilt through causeless love." Unfortunately, when one considers the intensely bitter controversies that have typified Israeli political and religious life since the state's creation, it seems as if the compassionate, tolerant teachings of Rav Kook have had insufficient impact on the country's political and religious culture.

SOURCES AND FURTHER READINGS: Jacob Agus, *High Priest of Rebirth: The Life, Times, and Thought of Abraham Isaac Kuk*; Abraham Isaac Kook, *Selected Letters*, translated and annotated by Tzvi Feldman.

140

ELIEZER BEN-YEHUDA (1858–1922) AND THE REVIVAL OF HEBREW

ELIEZER BEN-YEHUDA WAS THE CHIEF FIGURE IN ONE OF THE LEAST-known miracles of the twentieth century—the revival of Hebrew as a spoken language.

Today, it is taken for granted that Hebrew is Israel's official language. In the late 1800s, however, no one used Hebrew as a language of daily inter-course. East European Jews generally spoke Yiddish, some Sephardic Jews spoke Ladino, and most Jews spoke their country's language. Of course, Jews prayed in Hebrew, as Catholics recited the Mass in Latin. But nobody *con-versed* in Hebrew. Occasionally, a learned Jew, visiting a far-away land and finding no common language with the local Jews, might deliver himself of a few thoughts in Hebrew. But that was the extent of it. Hebrew, therefore, was like Latin and many other languages: Once widely spoken, it had apparently died out. Indeed, prior to Hebrew's revival, there was no instance of a "dead language" being resurrected.

Eliezer Ben-Yehuda was *meshugga le-davar* (a Hebrew expression mean-ing crazy about one thing) over the revival of Hebrew. When he and his wife arrived in Palestine, they took a vow; only Hebrew would be spoken in their home. This was no small undertaking at a time when the Hebrew language lacked words for many of the most elementary items. Hebrew was rich in names for God, in philosophic terms, and in words designating the different sacrifices at the *Temple. It was far poorer, however, in words for "soldier," "newspaper," "toothbrush," and "fire hydrant." Yet, Ben-Yehuda insisted in 1880, "in order to have our own land and political life . . . we must have a Hebrew language in which we can conduct the business of life."

The major undertaking of his life was the publication of a modern dic-tionary of the Hebrew language. In compiling it, he created hundreds of new words. Ben-Yehuda was well qualified to do so. Though irreligious as an adult, he had a yeshiva background and, from his youth on, had spent years studying Hebrew texts. He also was a largely self-taught but very talented linguist. Nonetheless, the task he undertook would have daunted almost anyone else. When he started the project, there was not even a real word for "dictionary" in Hebrew; the expression generally used was *sefer millim,* literally a "book of words." Ben-Yehuda undertook to rectify the situation. Typically, he took as his base the Hebrew word *millah* (word), and created from it *millon* (dictionary), one of his first contributions to modern Hebrew. There was no Hebrew word for soldier, just the archaic expression *ish-tsavah* (a man of the army). Ben-Yehuda came up with the word *khayal,* and even gave it a feminine form, *khayellet,* a term which proved very useful a half-century later when the Israeli Army started inducting women as well as men. There was no word for newspaper when Ben-Yehuda started out, so he took the Hebrew word for time, *et,* and came up with *itton.*

"If you would be remembered," it has been said, "do one thing superbly well." Eliezer Ben-Yehuda was involved in other projects in his life—he was one of the earliest proponents of Zionism—but among committed Jews today he is known for one thing—bringing about the revival of the Hebrew language.

SOURCES AND FURTHER READINGS: Robert St. John, *The Tongue of the Prophets.*

141

ALIYAH

Chalutz, Chalutzim

UNLIKE THE ENGLISH WORD "IMMIGRATE," ALIYAH (THE HEBREW FOR "to go live in Israel") is not neutral. Aliyah literally means "to go up," implying therefore the moral and spiritual superiority of living in Israel. According to ancient Jewish law, if a married man or woman wants to make aliyah and his or her spouse refuses, the partner desiring to live in Israel can compel a divorce (*Mishna Ketubot* 13:11).

Moving away from Israel likewise inspires a far more loaded term in Hebrew than the English word "emigrate": *yerida, which means "to descend."

The modern State of Israel was largely populated through involuntary aliyot (plural of aliyah). The mass migrations of German Jews in the 1930s, of Holocaust survivors in the late 1940s, of refugees from the Arab world in the late 1940s and 1950s, of Russian Jews since the 1970s, of Ethiopian Jews since the 1980s, were largely forced migrations—of Jews fleeing persecution and/or terrible poverty, and usually having nowhere else to go. In fact, there has never been a large-scale voluntary aliyah of Jews from a non-antisemitic society.

The institutions of the Jewish state, however, were largely created by the much smaller, voluntary aliyot, largely of young Eastern European Jews who arrived in Palestine during the first quarter of the twentieth century. While these Jews also fled antisemitism, their aliyah was voluntary in the sense that they had the option of migrating elsewhere; indeed, the overwhelming majority of their brethren who left Eastern Europe chose to live either in the United States or in Western Europe.

A popular term for the Jewish settlers who migrated to the rural parts of Palestine was chalutzim (singular, chalutz), which means "pioneers." These chalutzim had less in common with their fellow Jews in the United States—who generally lived in Jewish ghettos in large American cities—than with the cowboys who settled the American West. The chalutzim established *kibbutzim and moshavim in places where few other Jews lived. Through extraordinarily hard physical labor, they often created farmland from areas that had previously been malaria-ridden swamps—while under constant Arab attacks. To this day in Israel, the word chalutz remains a great compliment, and refers to any person who undertakes risks in order to develop a new field.

SOURCE AND FURTHER READING: For an overview of Jewish migration to the land of Israel, see the collection of articles in the Encyclopedia Judaica, vol. 9, pp. 508–567.

142

KIBBUTZ/KIBBUTZIM
MOSHAV/MOSHAVIM

THE KIBBUTZIM (COMMUNAL FARMING SETTLEMENTS) ARE PERHAPS THE
most widely known feature of Israeli life. It therefore surprises many people
to learn that today, only about 2 percent of Israelis live on kibbutzim.
Nonetheless, the importance of kibbutzim in Israel's development is very disproportionate to their relatively small population.

The first kibbutz, Degania, was established by Jewish settlers in 1910,
thirty-eight years before Israel itself came into existence. (The first child born
on Degania was the future military hero Moshe *Dayan.) The Jewish immigrants to Palestine generally knew little, if anything, about farming. In Russia,
the point of origin for many early Zionist settlers, Jews were not even permitted to own land. It was a fierce tenet of Zionist ideology, however, that Jews
would never achieve sovereignty until they learned how to work the land.
Because a large percentage of the arriving settlers were socialists, they did not
want to establish privately owned farms. They wanted, rather, to own their
land in unison with others, to work it together, and to live communally.

Each of the more than three hundred kibbutzim established since Degania
has followed the same economic pattern. The land, farming equipment, and
homes are all owned by the kibbutz. In other words, the kibbutz is a communistic society, though as far as I know it is the only communistic society actually run according to the ideal of "from each according to his ability to each
according to his need." The kibbutzim also differ from other Communist societies in that their residents all live there voluntarily. Members (kibbutzniks)
who choose to leave are given a financial settlement by the kibbutz—based on
their years of residence—to help them start life anew.

Over the years, kibbutzim have undergone some major social transforma-
tions. During the first decades of the kibbutz movement, children were raised
in communal houses. For the children this was in some sense like being in
camp year-round. They visited with their parents for several hours every day,

then returned to their bunks. For many years, however, the members have voted to have children sleep in their parents' cottages.

Meals on the kibbutz are eaten communally in large dining halls, although members can choose to eat at home. Kibbutz members do the cooking and serving. They might be assigned to this work for several months or years, then be reassigned to agricultural or other work.

In recent years, as kibbutzim have expanded, every kibbutz has established industries in addition to farming. Throughout Israel one finds, for example, stores selling furniture produced on different kibbutzim. Not infrequently, kibbutzim hire outside laborers to work in their fields and factories, a practice that comes perilously close to the kind of capitalist activity that kibbutz ideology supposedly abhors.

The socialist-Zionist pioneers who created the kibbutzim generally were secular: Many were antireligious. Consequently, some twenty years after Degania's creation, religious Jews started building their own kibbutzim. Today, there are three federations of kibbutzim in Israel:

Ha-kibbutz ha-Artzi—The most secular of the kibbutz federations, it consists of eighty-five kibbutzim, and was founded by the left-wing *Ha-Shomer ha-Tza'ir* movement. At many of the movement's kibbutzim, children still live in separate children's houses. The movement opposes, on principle, the settlement and establishment of kibbutzim in *Judea and Samaria.

Ha-kibbutz ha-Dati—The religious kibbutz movement, it comprises sixteen kibbutzim and its ideology is based on the notion of *Torah va'avodah* (Torah together with labor). These kibbutzim generally represent the more religiously liberal wing of Israeli Orthodoxy; they have a positive attitude toward secular studies, and work in cooperation with nonreligious kibbutzim.

Takam—The largest of the kibbutz federations, it has 165 member kibbutzim; it is affiliated with the Israeli *Labor party; and includes several kibbutzim established by the Reform and Conservative movements.

Kibbutzim long supplied an extraordinarily high percentage of Israel's leadership. Two of the country's most famous prime ministers, David *Ben-Gurion and Golda *Meir, were kibbutz members, and a substantial percentage of the Labor party's *Knesset members have been kibbutzniks. During the first decades of Israel's existence, the kibbutzim contributed an estimated 25 percent of the army's officers.

Over the years, many members—and more frequently, their children and grandchildren—have chosen to leave the kibbutz. The communal environment, departing members often claim, can be quite confining. For example, democratically elected committees determine what work each member is assigned. One man I know worked as a newspaper editor outside of the kibbutz, and contributed his salary to the collective; it was the only work he was happy doing. Nonetheless, after several years, the kibbutz assigned him to a job back on the kibbutz. The prospect so depressed him that he left.

Younger members who wish to study at a university have to convince the rest of their fellow kibbutzniks that their years away, and their course of study, will ultimately benefit the kibbutz. Unless a majority votes to permit the young people to attend university, they will not be given the funds to do so, which effectively means they cannot achieve their desire without leaving the kibbutz.

It is perhaps not surprising that very few of the million Russians who emigrated to Israel starting in the 1970s have chosen to live on kibbutzim. Although the kibbutzim are fully democratic, their economic structure is too reminiscent of the Communist society from which the Russians have come.

Moshavim also are farming settlements, and are similar to kibbutzim in that the farmlands and equipment are owned jointly. On some moshavim the farmers even work the land together, dividing equally expenses and profits. But the work arena is the sole sphere of communal endeavor. People own their own homes, live full time with their own families, and dispose of their income as they wish.

SOURCES AND FURTHER READINGS: Melford Spiro, *Children of the Kibbutz* and *Gender Culture: Kibbutz Women Revisited;* Hugh Nissenson, *Notes from the Frontier;* Murray Weingarten, *Life in a Kibbutz;* Bruno Bettelheim, *The Children of the Dream.*

143

THE BALFOUR DECLARATION
(NOVEMBER 2, 1917)
The British Mandate

THE ISSUING OF THE BALFOUR DECLARATION IN 1917 MAY WELL HAVE been in its time the happiest event in Jewish life since the beginning of the Common Era. In this document, England, on the verge of capturing Palestine from Turkey, committed herself to supporting a Jewish national homeland in Palestine. While an important motivation for declaring this support was to garner worldwide Jewish support for British war efforts (particularly from American Jews) there also was a long-standing pro-Zionist tradition among many British non-Jews, the most prominent of whom was Foreign Secretary Lord Arthur Balfour.

The Balfour Declaration first was approved by the British cabinet, and then written in the form of a letter to Lord *Rothschild, president of the British Zionist Federation: "His Majesty's Government," the letter's central paragraph states, "view with favour the establishment in Palestine of a national home for the Jewish people, and will use their best endeavours to facilitate the achievement of this object. . . ."

Unquestionably, much of England's political leadership subsequently regretted the declaration's unequivocal support for Zionism, and desperately tried to undo it. Later, in 1939, in a stunning reversal, the *White Paper declared that "His Majesty's Government now declare unequivocally that it is not part of their policy that Palestine should become a Jewish state."

Nonetheless, it was too late to rewrite history; the Balfour Declaration had already been accepted by the League of Nations in 1922 as part of the rationale for the British Mandate over Palestine. That mandate continued until Britain withdrew from Palestine in 1948 (see *U.N. Vote for Partition*).

Lord Arthur Balfour remains to this day a hero among Jews. In the aftermath of the declaration, a fair number of Jewish children were named

Balfour, and there are Balfour Streets in Israel's major cities. Lord Balfour's motives for issuing the declaration definitely seem to have sprung more from idealism than *realpolitik*. "The treatment of the [Jewish] race has been a disgrace to Christendom," he declared on one occasion, and he saw his support for a Jewish state as an act of amends. Lady Dugdale, Balfour's niece, reported that "near the end of his days, he said to me [that] . . . he felt what he had been able to do for the Jews had been the thing he looked back upon as the most worth doing." No small words from a man who had been England's prime minister as well as foreign secretary. In 1939, his nephew, Robert Arthur Litton, third earl of Balfour, offered the family estate and home in Whittingham as a training school for Jewish refugee children from Germany. See the next entry on *Chaim Weizmann*.

SOURCES AND FURTHER READINGS: Leonard Stein, *The Balfour Declaration*; Ronald Sanders, *The High Walls of Jerusalem: A History of the Balfour Declaration and the Birth of the British Mandate for Palestine*; Isaiah Friedman, *The Question of Palestine, 1914–1918*.

CHAIM WEIZMANN (1874–1952)

THERE IS A POPULAR JEWISH LEGEND THAT CHAIM WEIZMANN DEVELoped TNT for the British Army during World War I, and that the grateful British rewarded him by conquering Palestine and issuing the Balfour Declaration (see preceding entry). Like many legends, the story is built on a grain of truth, with the emphasis on "grain."

Weizmann was a Russian-born Jew who fell under Theodor Herzl's influence early in life. He did not become a "professional" Zionist, however, and earned his living as a chemist. At age thirty, he was appointed to the University of Manchester faculty. Early during his stay in England, in 1906, Weizmann met the then prime minister Arthur Balfour and lobbied him on behalf of the Zionist cause. Balfour was friendly but had nothing concrete to offer Weizmann.

Some ten years later, during World War I, Weizmann did produce, at the British Admiralty's request, large quantities of the volatile, flammable liquid acetone (an important ingredient of the cordite used in ammunition), which greatly aided the British war effort. By this time, Balfour, a former British prime minister who was now serving as foreign secretary, had come to believe strongly in the idea of restoring the Jews to Palestine. Weizmann was the most prominent Jewish leader in the negotiations that led to the issuance of the Balfour Declaration (see preceding entry).

From then on, Weizmann remained one of the—and often *the*—leading figures in the Zionist movement. Not surprisingly, he also maintained a passionate affection for England. Even when England later drew back from her Zionist commitment, Weizmann advocated a policy of moderation toward her. David *Ben-Gurion, and much of the Zionist world, criticized Weizmann for being an Anglophile. It was true. In 1944, when the underground *Lekhi group assassinated Lord Moyne, a high British official, Weizmann said that Moyne's death hurt him as deeply as that of his own son in the British Air Force.

In the months immediately preceding the declaration of Israel's statehood, Weizmann traveled to Washington and met with President Harry *Truman, whose commitment to Zionism seemed to be wavering. "The old doctor," as Truman affectionately called Weizmann, deeply impressed the American president, and kept him securely aligned with the pro-Zionist camp. When statehood was declared, the United States became the first country to recognize Israel. "Now the old doctor will believe me," Truman told his aides.

Upon Israel's creation, Ben-Gurion became the country's first prime minister, and Weizmann was offered the presidency. He accepted the post, not fully aware that Ben-Gurion had arranged for the position to be without any real power and to be almost purely ceremonial. It was deeply frustrating to the perpetually active Weizmann to find his sphere of activities so restricted. "My handkerchief," he is said to have lamented to a friend, "is now the only thing I can stick my nose into." Weizmann was, in actuality, very active in the creation and development of the Weizmann Institute, Israel's leading scientific center.

When Weizmann died in 1952, he was mourned as perhaps the greatest Zionist figure after Herzl.

SOURCES AND FURTHER READINGS: Norman Rose, *Chaim Weizmann, A Biography*; Jehuda Reinharz, *Chaim Weizmann: The Making of a Zionist Leader*; Chaim Weizmann, *Trial and Error* (an autobiography).

HAGANAH

IRGUN — BOMBING OF THE KING

DAVID HOTEL

LEKHI

PALMACH

In the 1930s, the British government drew back from the pro-Zionist commitment of the *Balfour Declaration, and in 1939 even barred Palestine as a place of refuge for the overwhelming majority of Jews trying to flee the Nazis (see *The British White Paper*). Although Jewish resentment against Britain was great, when World War II broke out, almost all Jews rallied behind Britain to fight the greater foe, Nazism. As David *Ben-Gurion, the leading figure in Palestine's Jewish community, put it at the time: "[We shall] war against Hitler as though there were no White Paper, and we shall war against the White Paper as though there were no Hitler." The Irgun, a militant group—originally founded by followers of Ze'ev *Jabotinsky to retaliate against Arab terrorism, and which later dedicated itself to forcing the British out of Palestine—likewise ceased anti-British activities; its commander, David Raziel, was killed in Iraq in 1941 while on a special mission for the British.

One Jewish group, Lekhi (Freedom Fighters for Israel), founded by the Hebrew poet Abraham Stern, opposed calling off the war against England. Stern believed that Britain's preoccupation with fighting the Nazis made it more vulnerable in the Middle East. He hoped, therefore, to push the British out of Palestine, and open the country up to Jews fleeing Hitler. Toward that end, Lekhi sponsored anti-British terrorism throughout the war. Its most famous action was the assassination of Lord Moyne—one of the highest-ranking British officials outside of England—in Cairo in November 1944. Moyne was targeted for death largely because of his high governmental position. His two assassins were quickly tried and executed.

Lekhi's violence was not directed only at gentiles. When the organization ran low on funds in 1942, Lekhi members held up a Jewish bank in Tel Aviv and killed two Jewish employees who didn't want to turn over the bank's funds. Abraham Stern, also known as Ya'ir, seemed to have an unhealthy obsession with violence. "Like a rabbi," he wrote in one poem, "who carries his prayerbook in a velvet bag to the synagogue/ so carry I my sacred gun to the temple . . ." One of the three heads of Lekhi after the British killed Stern was Yitzhak Shamir, who later became Israel's prime minister.

In January 1944, as Allied victory over the Nazis became increasingly certain, the Irgun, under the leadership of Menachem *Begin, renewed its battle to chase England out of Palestine. The Irgun opposed terrorism against civilians, generally restricting its attacks to British army officers. Begin was particularly outraged by British insensitivity to Jewish dignity. When the British started flogging captured Irgun members, Begin ordered that British soldiers be kidnapped and flogged. The British floggings quickly stopped. The British also executed captured Irgun members, even those charged with offenses less serious than murder. During 1947, Britain's last full year of rule in Palestine, seven Jews were hanged. At one point, as the British prepared to hang three Irgun members, the Irgun captured two British sergeants and announced that they would be hanged in retaliation. Despite extraordinary pressure on Britain to commute the death sentences, the government went ahead with the hangings—and the Irgun hanged the two British soldiers. Ironically, one of the soldiers hanged by the Irgun had a Jewish mother. Hanging the two sergeants not only infuriated the British—a British-Jewish friend told me that the day of the hangings he was beaten up in school, then was blamed by the principal for provoking the beating—it demoralized them as well, and so played an important role in Britain's subsequent decision to give up the mandate.

The Irgun's most famous terrorist act was the bombing in 1946 of the King David Hotel in Jerusalem, a wing of which served as British army headquarters in Palestine. Irgun members planted explosives in the hotel inside large milk cans, then phoned in a warning to evacuate the building. British officials assumed the warning was phony and disregarded it. Minutes later, the bombs detonated. Not only was the whole wing of the hotel demolished, over ninety people were killed.

The Haganah was originally founded in 1920 to protect Jewish lives and property from Arab attacks. Unlike the Irgun, it had a much less confrontational policy toward the British and opposed the use of terror. Throughout its history, the Haganah's primary preoccupation was creating a strong Jewish army. In the 1930s, Haganah troops, among them Moshe *Dayan, received valuable instruction in fighting off Arab assaults from a British officer, Orde Wingate. The British were so upset by Wingate's pro-Jewish leanings that they shipped him out of Palestine.

During World War II, British-trained Haganah members were parachuted over Nazi-occupied Europe in a mission aimed at rescuing Allied prisoners of war and organizing Jewish resistance. The most famous of these "infiltrators" was Hannah Senesh, who was one of seven Haganah parachutists executed by the Nazis. Thousands of Haganah members joined the British Army and later served in the Palestine Jewish Brigade. After the war, much of the Haganah's activities was devoted to developing a Jewish army and to smuggling "illegal" Jewish immigrants into Palestine (see *The British White Paper* and *DP Camps*). It is estimated that by the end of 1947, the Haganah had brought in ninety thousand of these "illegals." Within the Haganah, the elite fighting force was known as the Palmach. The Palmach largely represented the most politically left-wing elements of the Israeli labor movement, and contained many of Israel's finest soldiers as well.

At varying points, the Haganah cooperated with the Irgun and Lekhi in anti-British activities; at other times, it furiously turned against them, arguing that terror—even when directed only against British soldiers, not civilians—contravened the ideals of Zionism. On the night of October 31–November 1, 1945, however, a joint Haganah-Irgun-Lekhi action blew up railway lines and bridges in 153 places. Once the State of Israel was declared in 1948, the Haganah went out of existence and became the backbone of *Tzahal*, the Israeli Army.

SOURCES AND FURTHER READINGS: Menachem Begin, *The Revolt*; Gerold Frank, *The Deed* (on Lekhi and the killing of Lord Moyne); Yigal Allon, *The Making of Israel's Army*; M. P. Waters (Moshe Pearlman), *Haganah: Jewish Self-Defense in Palestine*.

146

DAVID BEN-GURION (1886–1973)

DAVID BEN-GURION IS THE GEORGE WASHINGTON OF ISRAEL, THE country's founding father and first prime minister. He held that position for almost all of Israel's first fifteen years of existence.

Ben-Gurion was a man of unshakable convictions and extraordinary stubbornness, traits that were probably his greatest strengths as well as weaknesses. In the early months of 1948, many of Ben-Gurion's closest advisers urged him to delay the declaration of statehood; they feared the new country would not survive the Arab invasion that would surely follow. Ben-Gurion persevered in his determination to bring Israel into existence as soon as possible, and declared the state on May 14, 1948, the fifth of *Iyyar* in the Hebrew calendar. He was convinced that the newly formed Israeli Army could withstand the Arab attacks, and he was right. A heavy price was paid in the *War of Independence — 1 percent of Israel's population was killed — but Ben-Gurion was convinced it was a price worth paying, and there are few Jews today who would disagree with him.

Ben-Gurion's feelings concerning the underground Irgun movement (see preceding entry), and its leader Menachem *Begin, were equally intense and forthright. Ben-Gurion opposed the political terrorism practiced by the Irgun, and felt that the organization had fascist tendencies. On occasion, he even urged Jews to turn Irgun members in to the British mandatory authorities. Later, just after the state was declared, he became convinced that Begin was plotting a coup against him, and he ordered the Israeli Army to fire on the *Altalena*, an Irgun-owned ship that was bringing in weapons and volunteers for Israel's army.

Ben-Gurion was capable of ferocity toward friends as well as foes. For many of the last years of his life, he was not on speaking terms with Israeli Prime Ministers Levi Eshkol and Golda Meir, both of whom had previously been among his closest associates. He profoundly disagreed with them on a sensitive political issue, and could not forgive their "treachery" in rejecting his point of view.

Ben-Gurion was born David Green in Poland, and emigrated to Palestine in 1906. The country was then under Turkish rule, and Ben-Gurion subsequently went to Istanbul to study law. During the First World War, the Turks exiled him and many other European-born Jews from Palestine, and he spent the war years in the United States. There, he met his future wife, Paula, with whom he returned to Palestine after the British took control of the country (see *Balfour Declaration*).

Ben-Gurion soon emerged as a leader of the socialist Labor party, which dominated Israeli politics from well before the state's declaration to Menachem Begin's electoral victory in 1977.

Though personally not religiously observant, Ben-Gurion was deeply influenced by the Bible, particularly by the writings of the prophets. During his years as prime minister, he actively participated in Bible study sessions, which met at his home. He once caused a governmental crisis by publicly questioning the accuracy of the verse in Exodus that claimed that 600,000 adult Jewish males accompanied Moses on his departure from Egypt: Ben-Gurion insisted that the number of Jews who wandered in the desert must have been much smaller. Members of the Israeli religious party Mizrachi, which formed part of Ben-Gurion's coalition, threatened to bolt from the government if he did not cease attacking the Bible's credibility.

Ben-Gurion was something of a renaissance man. In his later years, he studied Greek so that he could read Plato and Aristotle in the original. Long before yoga became fashionable in the Western world, Ben-Gurion practiced it, and pictures circulated of him standing on his head.

Ben-Gurion's accomplishments were enormous. He served as minister of defense as well as prime minister during Israel's *War of Independence. He forged the Israeli Army, *Tzahal, into a unified fighting force, after first disbanding the prestate military groups that were struggling to maintain themselves as separate forces in the army (see *Altalena*). During his tenure in office, the Jewish population of Israel tripled (from a little over 600,000 to almost 2,000,000), through a wide-scale program of immigration which he supervised. And he pushed repeatedly and quite successfully for the development of Israel's wilderness area, the Negev.

More than most heads of state, Ben-Gurion symbolized Israel to the world. He seemed to represent a new sort of Jew, passionately Jewish, but not religious, and willing to fight back hard and successfully against his enemies. "What matters," he was fond of saying, "is not what the gentiles say, but what the Jews do." He himself remained a doer almost till the end of his life. When he resigned as prime minister, he went to live on a pioneering *kibbutz in the Negev Desert. Even after his resignation, Ben-Gurion's grip over the Israeli imagination remained so great that during the crisis-ridden weeks just before the 1967 *Six-Day War, many Israelis—including Menachem Begin, the man he had once tried to kill—urged him to become prime minister again. Ben-Gurion then was over eighty, and tired; he refused.

After the Six-Day War, Ben-Gurion was jubilant, but he also urged Israel's leadership not to annex the newly captured territories. Annexation, he felt, would make peace with the Arabs permanently impossible. Though in his earlier years Ben-Gurion had hoped to see the borders of Israel expanded, *Knesset member Michael Bar-Zohar heard him say shortly after the Six-Day War: "For a real peace, we should give up all the occupied territories except for Jerusalem and the Golan Heights." He died quietly on his kibbutz on December 1, 1973, shortly after the *Yom Kippur War.

When John Wesley, the eighteenth-century founder of the Methodist Church, died, it was said of him that all he left behind was a knife, a fork, two spoons, and the Methodist Church. Of Ben-Gurion it may be said that he left behind him a Jewish state.

SOURCES AND FURTHER READINGS: Shabtai Teveth, *Ben-Gurion: The Burning Ground, 1886–1948*; Dan Kurzman, *Ben-Gurion: Prophet of Fire*. Ben-Gurion's statement to Michael Bar-Zohar about the territories captured in the Six-Day War was printed in *The Jerusalem Post International Edition*, May 26, 1990, p. 9.

147

VLADIMIR JABOTINSKY (1880–1940)

The Revisionists

VLADIMIR JABOTINSKY WAS THE MOST CHARISMATIC ZIONIST LEADER IN the generation after Herzl. To this day, he also remains the most controversial; no other Zionist leader has had such loving admirers, none such bitter enemies. To Jabotinsky's followers, he was the *one* Zionist leader with the vision and diplomatic abilities to win the Jews a state. To his detractors, he was head of the "fascist" wing of the Zionist movement; on occasion, Ben-Gurion (see preceding entry) stooped so low as to call him Vladimir Hitler.

Jabotinsky himself grew up as much a Russian as a Jew. When a young man, he wrote poetry of such high quality that Maxim Gorky predicted a great future for him as a Russian poet. The *pogroms of 1903, however, convinced Jabotinsky that helping his people protect themselves was more important than writing beautiful verses. He helped organize resistance to the antisemitic violence, then spent the rest of his life trying to create a Jewish state.

Jabotinsky represented what became known as the "maximalist" wing of the Zionist movement. He wanted Britain immediately to fulfill its original mandate promise—a Jewish state in all of Palestine. When he testified in 1937 before the British-appointed Peel Commission, which was investigating the possibility of partitioning Palestine into separate Arab and Jewish states, he explained why he could not compromise on this issue: "Whenever I hear the Zionist . . . accused of asking for too much. . . . I really cannot understand it. . . . I should understand it if the answer were, 'It is impossible,' but when the answer is, 'It is too much,' I cannot understand it. I would remind you of the commotion which was produced in that famous institution when Oliver Twist came and asked for 'more.' He said 'more' because he did not know how to express it; what Oliver Twist really meant was this: 'Will you just give me that normal portion which is necessary for a boy of my age to be able to live?' I assure you that you face here today, in the Jewish people with its demands, an Oliver Twist who has, unfortunately, no concessions to make. What can be the concessions? We have got to save millions, many *millions*. . . ."

The Peel Commission had to decide, Jabotinsky said, between "the claims of appetite and the claims of starvation." The Arabs had many states in which they could settle; the Jews had only one.

Ironically, although the British considered Jabotinsky and his followers as their greatest opponents among the Jews, he had long regarded himself as a passionate Anglophile. When World War I erupted, most Zionist leaders advocated neutrality; they feared alienating one of England's enemies, Turkey, which still controlled Palestine. Jabotinsky rightly foresaw that no matter how the war ended, the Ottoman Empire would be disbanded. He therefore advocated Jewish support for England, and organized a Jewish legion to fight on Britain's behalf.

In 1920, after the war, he headed Jewish defense against Arab attacks in

Jerusalem. The British "rewarded" Jabotinsky's earlier support by arresting him for carrying illegal arms, and sentencing him to fifteen years in prison. There was so great a public outcry that he was released from prison only a year later.

In the 1930s, Jabotinsky broke with the mainline Zionist leadership, who he believed were too moderate in the demands they were making of England. Jabotinsky found this moderation particularly objectionable because conditions for Jews in Europe were rapidly deteriorating. Although he never actually predicted the Holocaust, he regarded the situation in Europe as desperate, and wanted to initiate the immediate migration to Palestine of a minimum of 150,000 European Jews annually. Jabotinsky, whose followers were known as Revisionists, called his breakaway Zionist group the New Zionist Organization, and the group soon had almost as many supporters—particularly among European Jews—as the other Zionist organizations combined.

When World War II began, Jabotinsky was broken-hearted. His belief that European Jewry was facing a catastrophe proved even more true than he could ever have guessed. Once again Jabotinsky agitated, as he had twenty-five years earlier, for the establishment of a Jewish army. He came to the United States to help organize this effort, and died in New York in the summer of 1940. After the creation of Israel, Jabotinsky's followers coalesced into the Herut (later *Likud) party, under the leadership of Menachem *Begin. In 1977, Begin was elected prime minister of Israel.

In his will, Jabotinsky asked to be buried in whatever country he died until the head of an independent Jewish state requested that his remains be brought to Israel. For the first fifteen years after the creation of the state, Prime Minister David Ben-Gurion stubbornly refused to invite Jabotinsky's followers to reinter him in Israel. When Levi Eshkol became prime minister in 1963, he issued the request, and Jabotinsky's remains were brought to Israel.

Ben-Gurion's hatred for Jabotinsky was very deep, in large measure fed by the latter's opposition to the socialist doctrines that Ben-Gurion held so dear. Jabotinsky regarded the need to create a Jewish homeland as so preeminent that he opposed workers' strikes—he advocated binding arbitration instead—until the Palestinian Jewish community was on a totally sound economic footing.

Ben-Gurion also opposed Jabotinsky's willingness to negotiate with anyone who might help the Zionist cause, including Fascist leaders like Italy's Mussolini, whom he, along with other Zionist leaders, considered beyond the pale. As a result of these policy differences, Ben-Gurion concluded that Jabotinsky himself was a fascist, a charge that was of course not true. While politically right wing and a pragmatist, he was, nonetheless, ardently prodemocracy.

Jabotinsky was a master orator and stylist. He was fluent in about a dozen languages. An early primer he wrote on learning Hebrew became one of the most popular vehicles for teaching the language. One Hebrew term that was very critical to Jabotinsky's worldview was *hadar*—pride, dignity. Jabotinsky believed that Jews must live with *hadar* if they were ever to win respect for themselves and their cause. An autobiographical essay he wrote, "Memoirs by my Typewriter," reveals the stubborn yet charming spirit of the man:

"Once an Odessa contemporary said, 'Such and such happened just in that year when you were expelled from gymnasium [high school].' I was much amused there was such a myth; one is quite pleased with a bit of a myth about oneself even if it is only among a half dozen colleagues who join you for coffee in the same cafe. I did not deny it then, but a word in print, as everyone knows, must be the truth, the whole truth, and nothing but the truth. The myth is an undeserved honor. There was no reason for me to be expelled from the gymnasium. I was not engaged in any revolution. The extent of my liberalism was that I forgot to get a haircut. Though I hated school like poison, I was not expelled. It was much worse. I ran away on my own—two months before the end of the term, of the seventh, the next to last class. Running away from a Russian gymnasium, which had been so difficult [for a Jew] to get into, was a great foolishness, especially a year and two months before completing it. And until today I thank the Lord that I did so, not listening to the advice of friends and uncles and aunts. Because I believe that life is logical. If one completes a Russian gymnasium in the normal way, then one must go to a Russian university; and then one becomes a lawyer. Then, when a war comes, one already has a wealthy practice and one cannot leave for England and become a soldier. So one remains in Russia until a Bolshevik upheaval erupts and then, considering my deeply reactionary world outlook, one would lie six feet underground without a gravestone. But I am continuing another career, one which started with a foolishness. I am thinking of writing a scientific tractate on the importance of not being afraid to commit foolishnesses. It is one of the most successful ways of living like a human being."

SOURCES AND FURTHER READINGS: Jabotinsky's testimony before the Peel Commission is reprinted in Arthur Hertzberg, ed., *The Zionist Idea*, pp. 559–570. "Memoirs by my Typewriter" is found in Lucy Dawidowicz, *The Golden Tradition: Jewish Life and Thought in Eastern Europe*, pp. 394–401. Joseph Schechtman, *The Life and Times of Vladimir Jabotinsky* (two volumes, entitled *Rebel and Statesman* and *Fighter and Prophet*); Shmuel Katz, *Lone Wolf: A Biography of Vladimir Jabotinsky* (two volumes).

JOSEF TRUMPELDOR (1880–1920)

JOSEF TRUMPELDOR IS THE NATHAN HALE OF JEWISH HISTORY: A MAN known more for his final, heroic words than for anything else.

Trumpeldor had an atypical background for a Zionist hero. An officer in the czar's army, he was decorated for heroism during the Russo-Japanese War (1904)—a remarkable accomplishment for a Jew in the deeply anti-semitic Russian Army. Unfortunately, he also lost his left arm in combat. In 1912, Trumpeldor came to Palestine. During World War I, he helped organize the Jewish Legion, which fought against Turkey on behalf of Britain. After the war, he helped organize Jewish self-defense against Arab attacks. On March 1, 1920, he was a part of a group of Jewish settlers and volunteers who were attacked at Tel-Hai, a settlement in northern Israel. Trumpeldor was shot in the stomach; he quickly understood that the wound was fatal. *"Tov lamut be'ad artzaynu*—It is good to die for our country," were reputed to have been his last words to his compatriots. This phrase quickly became a popular motto among Zionist settlers, and among Jews worldwide.

HEBRON MASSACRE, 1929

THE CITY OF HEBRON IN *JUDEA (ALTERNATIVELY, THE *WEST BANK) is one of the oldest continually inhabited cities in the world. The Torah describes Abraham's purchase of a burial plot in Hebron for his wife, Sarah (Genesis 23:3–20), more than fifteen hundred years before the Common Era. Later, Abraham also was buried there, as were Isaac, Jacob, Rebecca, and Leah. The cave in which the Patriarchs and Matriarchs are believed to have been interred—known in Hebrew as the *Ma'arat ha-Machpela*—has long been one of Judaism's holiest sites. Along with Jerusalem, Safed, and Tiberias, Hebron is regarded as one of Israel's four holy cities.

In 1929, during anti-Jewish riots organized by the Mufti, the religious leader of the Muslims in Palestine, a particularly vicious *pogrom was carried out against Hebron's Jews. The city's Jewish quarter and its *yeshiva were invaded. Of the seven hundred Jews then living in Hebron, sixty-seven were murdered and sixty wounded. Many, it should be noted, were saved by Arab neighbors who hid them. Nonetheless, after the massacre, the Jews left Hebron.

For all that Arab religious and political leaders of the time repeatedly claimed that they only hated Zionists, not Jews, many of the people murdered in the Hebron massacre were ultra-Orthodox Jews; most of them were non-Zionists and some were even anti-Zionists.

Two years after the pogrom, thirty-five families resettled in the city. Five years later, they were evacuated by the British in the face of the Arab's renewed anti-Jewish attacks.

During the Israeli *War of Independence in 1948, Hebron was captured by Jordan. Nineteen years later, in the *Six-Day War of 1967, Israel captured the West Bank. Large numbers of Jews came to visit the caves of the Patriarchs; for almost a year, however, no Jews moved back into the city. The government was not anxious to encourage Jewish settlement in the Arab-populated West Bank, and few wanted to be the only Jewish residents in an Arab city. In 1968, however, Israeli Rabbi Moshe Levinger, masquerading as a Swiss tourist, made reservations for himself and nine other families at an Arab hotel for *Passover. Even before the holiday ended, the group barricaded themselves inside the hotel and announced that they would not leave until they were given permission by the Israeli government to move into Hebron. The government acceded to the demand, and the Jewish neighborhood of Hebron has since grown into one of the largest Jewish settlements on the West Bank. Unfortunately, it was in Hebron, on February 25, 1994, that a Jewish doctor and political extremist, Baruch Goldstein, shot to death twenty-nine Muslim worshipers at a prayer service at the Cave of the Patriarchs.

For Jews the Hebron massacre continues to symbolize Arab opposition not only to Zionism, but to any Jewish presence in the land of Israel.

SOURCES: Outside the Jewish world, the Hebron pogrom apparently did not provoke an outpouring of sympathy. In England the well-known leftist political ideologue Beatrice Webb—whose husband, Sidney, was serving as the British colonial secretary in charge of Palestine—told Chaim Weizmann: "I can't understand why the Jews make such a fuss over a few dozen of their people killed in Palestine. As many are killed every week in London in traffic accidents, and no one pays any attention" (see Howard M. Sachar, A *History of Israel*, p. 174). On the Jewish return to Hebron in 1968, see Sachar, A *History of Israel*, vol. 2, p. 174.

THE BRITISH WHITE PAPER

(MAY 17, 1939)

FOR JEWS THE WHITE PAPER REPRESENTS TWO THINGS: THE BETRAYAL by England of its commitment to Zionism (see *Balfour Declaration*), and a clear message to Hitler that Britain really did not care what he did to the Jews.

The White Paper limited Jewish immigration into Palestine to an absolute total of 75,000 people over a period of five years. At that point, further Jewish immigration would be permitted "only if the Arabs are prepared to acquiesce in it." The document also stated that "His Majesty's Government now declares unequivocally that it is not part of their policy that Palestine should become a Jewish state."

Throughout World War II, and despite all the revelations of the death camps, the British government refused to change its immigration policy. More than anything else, it was the cruelty of the White Paper, combined with the far greater cruelty of Hitler, that converted almost all identifying Jews into active supporters of Zionism. As the Zionist leader Chaim *Weizmann mournfully observed: "There are now two sorts of countries in the world, those that want to expel the Jews and those that don't want to admit them."

The British commitment to enforcing the White Paper was fierce. In one particularly pathetic instance, a boat called the *Struma*, containing 769 Jews fleeing from Romania, broke down outside Istanbul. The Turkish government refused to allow the refugees to disembark, and Jewish leaders begged the British to allow the refugees into Palestine. The British refused. Finally, after two months, the Turkish government had the unseaworthy vessel towed out of the harbor. The ship sank almost immediately, and these Jews who had successfully fled Hitler—428 men, 269 women, and 70 children—drowned. There were two survivors.

At the outset of the war in 1939, David *Ben-Gurion, speaking for the majority of Jews, declared: "[We shall] war against Hitler as though there were no White Paper, and [we shall] war against the White Paper as though there were no Hitler." The Jewish community desperately tried to smuggle "illegal" immigrants into Palestine. One group of Jews, *Lekhi, (in English, the FFI—Freedom Fighters for Israel), argued that there was really not much to choose between the Nazis and the British; the Nazis were murdering Jews, and the British were preventing them from being saved. Lekhi thus advocated taking advantage of Britain's preoccupation with the war in Europe to try to expel the British from Palestine, and then open up the country's gates. Even had Lekhi succeeded, it is unclear what the result would have been, since England's expulsion from Palestine might well have brought about Palestine's capture by the Nazis.

Martin Gilbert, Winston Churchill's official biographer, told me that when Churchill became England's prime minister, he intended to rescind the White Paper. But in his expanded World War II cabinet of over forty members, he found only one other supporter for this proposed action.

The legacy of the White Paper's limitation on Jewish migration into Palestine was so odious that the Israeli *Knesset's first legislative act was the *Law of Return, which granted any Jew, from anywhere in the world, the right to emigrate to Israel and claim immediate citizenship.

SOURCES: The Ben-Gurion quote is from Shabtai Teveth, *Ben-Gurion: The Burning Ground*, p. 718. As regards the fate of the *Struma*, see Howard M. Sachar, *A History of Israel*, p. 237.

DP CAMPS

THE *EXODUS*

WHEN WORLD WAR II ENDED, THE OVERWHELMING MAJORITY OF NAZI
soldiers returned to their homes. Those Jews whom the Nazis had not succeeded in murdering, however, had been deprived of homes to which they
could return. They usually found themselves living in special camps for displaced persons (DPs).

Almost all Jews inside the camps had one goal, to leave Europe. A bitter
joke told of a Jew who received a visa to emigrate to Australia. He left his
German DP camp and went to the airport.

An official asked him: "Where are you going?"

"To live in Australia."

"But that's so far away."

"From where?"

Although many Holocaust survivors did emigrate to Australia, the United
States, Canada, and elsewhere, Palestine was where most Jews wanted to go.
It was the only place on earth they could now think of as home. Unfortunately, the British were still enforcing very tight restrictions on Jewish immigration to Palestine (see preceding entry). They announced that only a few
thousand concentration camp survivors would be admitted annually. The
Jewish underground organizations succeeded in "illegally" smuggling thousands of homeless Jews into Palestine. Those whom the British caught, however, were sent off to a new DP camp on the British-controlled island of
Cyprus, tantalizingly near to Palestine. Over 26,000 Holocaust survivors were
soon living in Cyprus in badly overcrowded quarters.

In early 1947, Zionist organizations bought an American ship, the *Chesa-
peake Bay*. It was packed with 4,500 displaced persons, and sent off from a
French port toward Palestine. The Jews renamed the ship *Exodus—1947*. As
the *Exodus* traveled through the Mediterranean, it soon found itself escorted
by six British destroyers: One might have thought that British intelligence

had suddenly uncovered a ship carrying Hitler and the rest of the Third Reich's leadership. Twelve miles outside of Palestine, the destroyers closed in; British troops tried to board the boat, but the Jews fought them off. Ultimately, the British withdrew their troops and opened fire. Three Jews were killed, and a hundred wounded. While the battle raged, the *Exodus*'s crew radioed details of the fight to the *Haganah in Tel Aviv, which rebroadcast the reports throughout the world. Only when the British threatened to sink the *Exodus*, along with its 4,500 passengers, did the crew surrender the ship.

At that point, the British foreign minister, Ernest Bevin, decided to make an example of the ship's passengers. They would not be allowed into Palestine, not even into the Cyprus internment camps. Rather, the 4,500 Holocaust survivors would be returned to Europe.

The Jews were taken back on British transport ships, converted into floating prisons. When they arrived in France, the Jews refused to disembark. Journalist Ruth Gruber described the mad scene at the French port: "Squeezed between a green toilet shed and some steel plates were hundreds and hundreds of half-naked people who looked as though they had been thrown together into a dog pound. . . . Trapped and lost, they were shouting at us in all languages, shattering each other's words. . . . Old women and men sat weeping unashamed, realizing what lay ahead."

France finally ordered the ship to depart, and Bevin—nicknamed by the Jews Bergen-Bevin, after the Nazi concentration camp Bergen-Belsen—sent the ship back to Germany. There, club-wielding British troops forcibly carried the Jews off the boat.

For the British, the defeat they inflicted on the *Exodus* and its passengers proved to be a pyrrhic victory. The details of the ship's tragic journey, transmitted daily and in great detail around the world, aroused tremendous international sympathy and support for Zionism. There were 250,000 Jewish refugees in Europe, the world now knew, who had but one place they wished to go, Palestine; and as long as Britain held the mandate they would not be allowed in.

A year after the *Exodus*, the State of Israel came into being. Eleven years later, Leon Uris published his novel *Exodus*, a fictionalized account of the ship's fate and of Israel's founding. Whether fictionalized or not, the story of the *Exodus* still had enormous power to move people. The book became a runaway best seller, and a highly popular movie. I once interviewed former Israeli Foreign Minister Abba Eban, who told me that during his tenure as Israeli ambassador to the United States, nothing aroused as much pro-Israel sentiment in America as Uris's *Exodus*.

SOURCES AND FURTHER READINGS: The account of the DP camps and of the fate of the *Exodus* is based, in large measure, on Howard M. Sachar, *A History of Israel*, vol. 1, pp. 279–283. See also Abram Sachar, *The Redemption of the Unwanted: From the Liberation of the Death Camps to the Founding of Israel*.

UNITED NATIONS VOTE FOR PARTITION
(NOVEMBER 29, 1947)

BY THE 1970S IT WOULD HAVE BEEN DIFFICULT FOR ANYONE TO IMAGine that the United Nations had once been pro-Zionist (see *U.N. Resolution on Zionism*). Yet it was the U.N. that voted Israel into existence in November 1947. At the time, the world body was much smaller—it had only fifty-six members. Although the Arab states unanimously opposed partitioning Palestine into Jewish and Arab states, the large majority of U.N. members supported the idea.

In the United States, President Harry *Truman prevailed over State Department opposition to a Jewish state, and guaranteed American support for the resolution. And although the Soviet Union had long been hostile to Zionism, its leader, Josef Stalin, was attracted to the possibility of forcing Britain out of the Middle East. Some of the most pro-Zionist speeches in U.N. history were delivered by the Soviet deputy foreign minister, Andrei Gromyko.

Great Britain abstained during the vote for partition, although all the Commonwealth nations, with the exception of India, backed the proposal.

The partition motion required a two-thirds majority to pass. In the last days before the vote, the necessary votes seemed to be lacking. Pro-Zionist forces stalled the discussion during the session of Wednesday, November 27. On the next day, the American holiday of Thanksgiving, the U.N. was closed and precious hours were thereby secured to lobby the still undecided nations. By the time the vote was cast on Friday, the resolution passed 33 to 13, with 10 abstentions. Except for Cuba and Greece, every state that voted against partition was either Muslim or Asian. Greece's opposition was rooted in fear for the safety of more than 100,000 Greeks living in Egypt.

Ironically, had the Arab states accepted partition, the Jewish state would have been barely viable. All that the U.N. offered the Jews was a tiny homeland, comprising 5,500 square miles, in which 538,000 Jews would live alongside 397,000 Arabs (the Arab Palestinian state was to have 4,500 square miles, in which 804,000 Arabs and only 10,000 Jews would live). During the *War of Independence, which began when six Arab armies invaded Israel on May 14, 1948, the day she was created, Israel significantly enlarged her borders.

Despite hesitations about the state's small size, Jews greeted the partition vote with undiluted joy. In Palestine they danced in the street throughout the night. Isaac Herzog, the chief rabbi, declared: "After a darkness of two thousand years the dawn of redemption has broken." One of Jerusalem's prominent streets is named *Rekhov Kaf-tet b'November*—November 29 Street—after the U.N. vote.

QUOTE ABOUT THE PARTITION VOTE

"Timing was absolutely crucial to Israel's birth and survival. Stalin had the Russian-Jewish actor Solomon Mikhoels murdered in January, 1948, and this seems to have marked the beginning of an intensely antisemitic phase in his policy. The switch to anti-Zionism abroad took longer to develop but it came decisively in the autumn of 1948. By this time, however, Israel was securely in existence. American policy was also changing, as the growing pressures of the Cold War . . . forced Truman to listen more attentively to Pentagon and State Department advice. If British evacuation had been postponed another year, the United States would have been far less anxious to see Israel created and Russia would almost certainly have been hostile. . . . Israel slipped into existence through a fortuitous window in history which briefly opened for a few months in 1947–48. That too was luck; or providence" (Paul Johnson, *A History of the Jews*, p. 526).

SOURCES AND FURTHER READINGS: Howard M. Sachar, *A History of Israel*, pp. 292–295; Walter Laqueur, *A History of Zionism*, pp. 578–582.

PROCLAMATION OF ISRAEL'S INDEPENDENCE, MAY 14, 1948/ THE FIFTH OF *IYYAR*

MEDINAT YISRAEL/THE STATE OF ISRAEL

ON MAY 14, 1948, BRITISH RULE OVER PALESTINE ENDED. AT 8:00 A.M., the Union Jack was lowered in Jerusalem. Hours later, the armies of six Arab nations launched an invasion of the Jewish state. At 4:00 P.M., David *Ben-Gurion read over the radio the new nation's Proclamation of Independence. In Jerusalem the citizens of the new state could not hear the broadcast; their besieged city was without electricity.

The proclamation was a forthright statement of the new country's Jewish identity: "The Land of Israel was the birthplace of the Jewish people . . . ," it began. "Here they wrote and gave the Bible to the world."

The proclamation went on to recount the Jews' fierce loyalty to the land of Israel during two thousand years of exile, and spoke of the herculean efforts by Jewish settlers during the preceding century; "They brought the blessings of progress to all inhabitants of the country."

The *raison d'être* of Israel, to provide a homeland for all Jews, was underscored in yet another paragraph: "The State of Israel will be open to the immigration of Jews from all the countries of their dispersion."

In another passage that rarely is cited, the proclamation announced that the state's values "will be based on the precepts of liberty, justice and peace taught by the Hebrew prophets." Non-Jewish citizens were promised full freedom of conscience, and offered a guarantee that the sanctity and inviolability of all sacred places would be maintained.

God was not mentioned in the proclamation, which struck many as odd, since the major Jewish contribution to mankind was the notion of one God. Some of Israel's secular leaders had informed *Ben-Gurion that they would not sign a document mentioning God, while the religious leaders would not sign a document ignoring Him. A compromise was achieved through use of an ambiguous phrase. The final paragraph of the Proclamation speaks of ". . . trust in the Rock of Israel," a term the religious delegates understood as referring to God, and which the secular delegates understood as referring to God-knows-what.

The proclamation officially named the new country the State of Israel, *Medinat Yisrael*. Prior to the proclamation, it was uncertain what the state's name would be. Some people suggested "Judea," the name of the Jewish state ruled by the descendants of the House of David. The State of Israel in the Bible, however, was a renegade nation that was dispersed and destroyed in 722 B.C.E. Nonetheless, because *Eretz Yisrael* (the Land of Israel) had been for so long the name Jews applied to the country the rest of the world called Palestine, the name "Israel" was chosen.

HATIKVAH

NAFTALI HERTZ IMBER, A HEBREW POET WHO DIED IN 1909, IS KNOWN today only for one of his poems: *Hatikvah* (*The Hope*). The poem, which was put to music in Palestine in the early 1880s, was later sung at Zionist congresses and subsequently became Israel's national anthem. Today it comes closer than any other poem to being the national song of the entire Jewish people. The poem's recurring stanza expresses the Jewish people's enduring desire to return to Zion:

> *Our hope is not yet lost*
> *The hope of two thousand years*
> *To be a free people in our own land*
> *The land of Zion and Jerusalem.*

SOURCE: Eliyahu Ha-Cohen, "How *Hatikvah* Became the National Anthem of Israel," in Ivan Tillem, ed., *The 1987–1988 Jewish Almanac*, pp. 319–321.

HARRY TRUMAN

(U.S. PRESIDENT, 1945–1953)

WHEN PRESIDENT FRANKLIN D. ROOSEVELT DIED ON APRIL 12, 1945, most American Jews had no idea if his successor, Harry Truman, would be "good for the Jews." They certainly had no inkling that Truman would soon be regarded as the best friend the Jews had ever had in the White House.

Harry Truman's popularity among American Jews stems from his pivotal role in helping bring about Israel's establishment. During the 1947 U.N. debate on partition, he lobbied aggressively for a Jewish state (see *U.N. Vote on Partition*). When Israel's independence was declared on May 14, 1948, he extended the new state immediate diplomatic recognition. Nowadays, critics of Truman's policy contend that his pro-Zionist actions were motivated less by idealism than by his desire to secure the Jewish vote in the roughly contested 1948 presidential election. Whatever his motives were—and there is good reason to believe that Truman strongly identified with the Jewish cause—he bucked heavy anti-Zionist pressure from the Pentagon and the State Department. Both feared an intensely hostile Arab reaction to America's pro-Israel policy.

In the months before Israel's creation, Truman himself came under such heavy Zionist pressure that at one point he resolved no longer to meet with the movement's representatives. A short while later, Chaim *Weizmann, the future president of Israel, arrived in the United States, and found himself subject to the presidential ban. Zionist leaders contacted Eddie Jacobson, a Jewish businessman and one of Truman's closest friends, and had him fly up to Washington to see the president. In an interview with Merle Miller many years later, Truman provided an extraordinary recollection of this meeting: "[After Jacobson told Truman on the telephone that he was in Washington, the president said to him]: " 'Eddie, I'm always glad to see old friends, but there's one thing you've got to promise me. I don't want you to say a *word* about what's going on over there in the Middle East. Do you promise? And he did.' " Nonetheless, when Jacobson arrived in his office, "great tears were running down his cheeks, and I took one look at him, and I said, 'Eddie, you son of a bitch, you promised me you wouldn't say a word about what's going on over there.' And he said, 'Mr. President, I haven't said a word, but every time I think of the homeless Jews, homeless for thousands of years, and I think about Dr. Weizmann, I start crying. I can't help it. He's an old man, and he's spent his whole life working for a homeland for the Jews, and now he's sick, and he's in New York and wants to see you. And every time I think about it I can't help crying.'

" 'I said, "Eddie, that's enough. That's the last word." '

" 'And so we talked about this and that, but every once in a while a big tear would roll down his cheek. . . . I said, "Eddie, you son of a bitch, I ought to have you thrown right out of here for breaking your promise; you knew damn well I couldn't stand seeing you cry." ' "

As soon as Jacobson left, Truman arranged to see Weizmann, and reiterated his support for Israel's creation and for her control of the Negev.

Moments after Israel declared independence, Truman ensured that the United States was the first country to recognize the new state. The following year, Israel's chief rabbi came to see the president and told him: "God put you in your mother's womb so that you could be the instrument to bring about the rebirth of Israel after two thousand years."

Eleven years later, when Truman related this story to Merle Miller, tears started flowing down his cheeks.

As far as Israel's survival was concerned, Truman's record was not unblemished. Despite the diplomatic recognition he extended Israel, he enforced a U.S. arms embargo to the warring parties. This had a much worse effect on Israel, which had very few arms, than on the heavily armed Arabs. Strangely, it was the Soviet Union, headed by the ferocious anti-semite Josef Stalin, that allowed Israel to buy arms through Czechoslovakia, a Soviet satellite.

Nonetheless, Truman must be regarded as instrumental in Israel's coming into existence. Ironically, while Franklin D. Roosevelt, Truman's predecessor, was a personal hero to most American Jews, he was apparently somewhat indifferent to the mass murder of the Jews by the Nazis and a bit hostile toward Zionism. David Niles, a Roosevelt adviser, said: "There are serious doubts in my mind that Israel would have come into being if Roosevelt had lived."

SOURCES AND FURTHER READINGS: Merle Miller, *Plain Speaking: An Oral Biography of Harry S. Truman*, pp. 230–236. The Niles quote about Roosevelt is found in Howard M. Sachar, *A History of Israel*, p. 255. See also Michael J. Cohen, *Truman and Israel*.

DEIR YASSIN

SINCE APRIL 9, 1948, THE ARAB WORLD HAS CLAIMED THAT JEWISH troops carried out a massacre of Arab men, women, and children in the Arab village of Deir Yassin, near Jerusalem. While all parties concede that between 116 and 250 Arab soldiers and civilians were killed by Jewish soldiers, there is an unresolved debate in the Jewish community over what really happened at Deir Yassin.

Menachem *Begin, head of the *Irgun, whose troops carried out the military action at the village along with soldiers of *Lekhi, repeatedly noted that Deir Yassin was actively used by Arab troops as a base for attacks against the Jews; that is why it became a military objective in the first place. When Jewish troops surrounded the town on April 9, loudspeakers warned the Arab inhabitants of an impending attack and told them to flee. "By giving this humane warning," Begin wrote, "our fighters threw away the element of complete surprise and thus increased their own risk in the ensuing battle." More than two hundred residents of Deir Yassin listened to the warning, and left unharmed. Only later did Irgun and Lekhi troops mount a heavily fortified attack. Begin always claimed that all the Arabs killed at Deir Yassin died during this offensive.

His opponents, most significantly *Ben-Gurion and the *Labor party, claimed that many Arabs, including women and children, were killed in an orgy of violence after the Arabs were defeated. Begin has long denounced this as slander.

The Deir Yassin attack unquestionably accelerated the Arab exodus from the Jewish parts of Palestine. After April 9, 1948, hundreds of thousands of Arabs became convinced that their lives were at risk if they stayed in the Jewish areas of the country. Historian Howard Sachar, who believes that the

Irgun carried out a massacre at the Arab village, points out that the reason the events at Deir Yassin spread like wildfire among the Palestinians was because they "knew well how their own guerrillas had stripped and mutilated Jewish civilians; *photographs of the slaughter were peddled openly by Arab street vendors*" (emphasis mine).

Since 1948, Deir Yassin has remained a mainstay of the Arab world's anti-Israel propaganda. Yet even if one accepts the worst-case scenario of what transpired there, as horrifying as it is, it would be no worse than the fate the Arab leadership repeatedly stated it intended to inflict on all the Jews of Israel (see next entry). Their announced intent to drown all of Palestine's Jews in the Mediterranean Sea is a matter of record.

A Jewish publication has noted that the reason Deir Yassin is raised so often by Arab anti-Israel propagandists is that "they have little else to raise. This is in contrast to the nearly endless list of premeditated Arab bombings and [hijackings and terrorist] attacks on tourists, hikers, schoolchildren and other civilians."

SOURCES: Menachem Begin, *The Revolt*, pp. 162–165; Howard M. Sachar, *A History of Israel*, p. 333. The final quote is from Leonard Davis, Eric Rozenman, and Jeff Rubin, *Myths and Facts 1989*, pp. 108–110.

157

WAR OF INDEPENDENCE (1948–1949)

ON MAY 14, 1948, THE DAY THE STATE OF ISRAEL WAS DECLARED, she was invaded by armies from six Arab countries: Egypt, Syria, Jordan, Lebanon, Iraq, and Saudi Arabia. Azzam Pasha, secretary general of the Arab League, was so certain that the Arabs would destroy the new country that he felt no need to temper his rhetoric with a dash of diplomacy: "This will be a war of extermination," he predicted, just three years after the Holocaust. The spiritual leader of Palestine's Muslims, Haj Amin al Husseini, delivered a similarly edifying message to his followers: "I declare a Holy War, my Muslim brothers! Murder the Jews! Murder them all!"

The Jews had good reason to fear that the Arabs might achieve this goal. Only a few days earlier, the American secretary of state, General George Marshall, a man of wide military experience, summoned Ben-Gurion's colleague Moshe Shertok (Sharett) to warn him that Israeli independence must not be declared; the likelihood that the Arabs would wipe out the Jews was simply too great.

*Ben-Gurion ignored the warning. Within days of the invasion, it was clear that the larger number of troops and superior armaments on the Arab side was not going to produce a quick victory for the Arabs. In battle after battle, even when the Arabs had significant advantages, the Israelis engaged them head on and, more often than not, won. "*Ein breira* [(we have) no alternative]," is how the Israelis explained their readiness to fight, even in the most adverse circumstances. The Jews truly had no alternative; the Arabs did not want concessions from them, they wanted to exterminate them.

Perhaps the major handicap facing Israel was a nearly worldwide boycott of armament sales to her. In a historical quirk, Soviet dictator Josef Stalin allowed Israel to purchase arms through his satellite, Czechoslovakia. In the United States, many Jews organized illegal arms shipments to Israel. Large crates supposedly containing vegetables or furniture were filled with rifles instead. Hank Greenspun, a Las Vegas newspaper publisher, was one of several American Jews who served prison sentences for defying the American boycott. In the early 1960s, American President John F. Kennedy pardoned Greenspun, thereby restoring all his civil rights and enabling him to run for governor of Nevada. A man I know rented a mineshaft in the Denver area. He had no intention of working it, he just needed a legal excuse to purchase explosives. These, too, were promptly shipped to Israel.

From the war's inception, Israel urged the Arab states to accept a cease-fire. The Arabs agreed to do so only after it became clear that they were not going to win, and that Israel was starting to capture territory from them.

The war itself was fought in three stages, with temporary cease-fires arranged by the U.N. separating each stage. When the final cease-fire was declared in January 1949, Jerusalem was cut in two. The newer neighborhoods of the city were under Jewish control, while the Old City, including the *Western Wall—Judaism's holiest site—was under Jordanian rule. In the armistice accord, the Jordanians agreed to allow Jews access to their holy sites. The provision was never honored, however, and Jews only regained access to their holy places when Israel captured the Old City in the 1967 *Six-Day War.

When the War of Independence ended, Israel was also in control of the southern area of the country, known as the Negev, and of the northern area, the Galilee: She now had a somewhat larger state than had been promised under the *U.N. partition agreement. Indeed, in the seven wars Israel has fought with her Arab neighbors, her borders have never been diminished.

The human cost to the country, however, was appalling. Six thousand Israelis, almost 1 percent of the population, were killed in the War of Independence.

SOURCES AND FURTHER READINGS: Larry Collins and Dominique Lapierre, *O Jerusalem*; Dan Kurzman, *Genesis 1948: The First Arab-Israeli War*; Chaim Herzog, *The Arab-Israeli Wars*, pp. 15–108; Bernard Postal and Henry Levy, *And the Hills Shouted for Joy: The Day Israel Was Born*; Leonard Slater, *The Pledge*.

THE ALTALENA

IN 1948, A JEWISH-OWNED SHIP, LOADED WITH BADLY NEEDED ARMA-ments and volunteers coming to fight in Israel's War of Independence (see preceding entry), was fired upon and sunk. Twelve people were killed. Most shockingly, the attack was not carried out by any of the surrounding Arab nations, but by the army of Israel.

The sinking of the *Altalena* remains one of the most controversial episodes in Zionist history; the morality of the attack has long been debated in Israel. Why, in fact, did Israeli Prime Minister David *Ben-Gurion order the ship's sinking, and later declare: "Blessed be the gun that set the ship on fire"?

Ben-Gurion claimed that the *Irgun, whose international supporters had gathered the arms on the ship, was planning to use those arms to launch a coup d'état, and take over the Israeli government.

Menachem *Begin, head of the Irgun—and himself a future prime minister—was on the ship when the Israeli troops opened fire. As the boat started sinking, his supporters dragged him off into a lifeboat. That night, facing arrest from Ben-Gurion's government, Begin went on the Irgun's under-ground radio station to urge his followers not to answer Ben-Gurion's attack with violence. Begin realized that the civil war that would have ensued would have brought about the state's destruction. He denied then, as he has since, any intention of a coup d'état against the government of Israel. He has always maintained that all he wanted was to keep 20 percent of the arms to give to Irgun troops fighting in the Jerusalem area.

The attack on the *Altalena* must be understood within the context of Ben-Gurion's effort to establish a single, consolidated army for the new Jewish state. After the *Altalena* incident, the separate battalions of Irgun members were disbanded. At about the same time that Ben-Gurion forced the right-wing Irgun to disband and submit to army discipline, he imposed the same demand on the left-wing *Palmach. And oddly enough, just as the Irgun charged Ben-Gurion with murdering Jewish volunteers on the *Altalena*, so did Ben-Gurion claim to an American writer that the Palmach had murdered Colonel Mickey Marcus, an American officer he had brought over to help lead the Israeli Army. As is unfortunately common when you study history, the more you know the uglier it becomes.

SOURCES: H. H. Ben-Sasson, ed., A *History of the Jewish People*, pp. 1060–1061. Ben-Gurion's belief that the Palmach killed Mickey Marcus—the greatest American-Jewish hero in Israel's history—is reported in Dan Kurzman, *Ben-Gurion: Prophet of Fire*, p. 291. At the time Marcus was killed, it was announced that he had been acci-dentally shot by a sentry. But after studying the events, Ben-Gurion concluded: "The Palmach deliberately killed [Marcus] . . . It couldn't have been an accident. It isn't log-ical. It was the Palmach." The Palmach, Ben-Gurion noted, had been infuriated just a few days earlier when he named Marcus head of the Jerusalem front; they wanted no "outsider" telling them how to fight.

The Altalena incident has remained so controversial that when the *Encyclopedia Judaica*, one of the most important works of modern Jewish scholarship, was published, it had no entry on the subject; indeed, the word *Altalena* does not even appear in the encyclopedia's extraordinarily detailed index.

159

INGATHERING OF THE EXILES/*KIBBUTZ GALUYOT*

"Operation Magic Carpet"

ON THE DAY THAT ISRAEL WAS CREATED IN 1948, ITS JEWISH INHABI-tants numbered a little over 600,000. Within three years, that population had almost doubled, in what was perhaps the quickest demographic growth of any nation in history. The explosion in numbers was due to two enormous migrations: of Holocaust survivors and Jews from the Arab world.

When World War II ended, many Jewish survivors of Hitler's concentration camps found themselves put into *DP (Displaced Persons) camps. Those sur-vivors who wanted to go to Palestine quickly learned that the British allowed very few Jews in. Jews caught fleeing to Palestine were sent back to Europe or to British DP camps on the nearby island of Cyprus. Shortly after Israeli state-hood was declared, fifty-two refugee camps were closed in Europe, as were the Cypriot DP camps: Within a few years, more than 200,000 Holocaust sur-vivors were brought to Israel.

At the same time, the creation of Israel accelerated the deterioration of Jewish life in the Arab world. Arab Jews, fearing for their lives, fled Egypt, Iraq, Syria, and Yemen en masse, leaving behind small remnants of formerly large communities. In almost every instance, Arab governments confiscated the property of the fleeing Jews, many of whom were rich. As a result, most arrived in Israel penniless. Israel itself was a very poor country in 1948, and little money was available to help integrate the new immigrants. Many, but not exclusively, Arab Jews were housed in hastily created *ma'abarot* (transit camps). To this day, the recollection of the primitive *ma'abarot* arouses deep feelings of resentment among the *Sephardic Jews from the Arab world.

One of the more happily integrated Arab-Jewish communities in Israel came from Yemen. Yemenite Jewry had lived for many centuries in one of the poorest countries in the Arab world. In addition, the antisemitic restrictions imposed on them had been in strict accord with fundamentalist Islamic teachings. They were forbidden to wear bright garments, to bear weapons, or to use saddles. They were also compelled to clean the sewers of San'a, Yemen's capital city. Arab schoolchildren routinely threw stones at Jews, and when the leaders of the Jewish community tried to have this frightening and dangerous activity outlawed, Muslim religious leaders insisted that it was a religiously mandated custom that could not be forbidden. Yemen itself was so primitive that few inhabitants had ever seen an appliance, tool, or vehicle operated by electricity. When airplanes started arriving in Yemen to take the Jews to Israel, the deeply pious Jews were reminded of the verse in the Torah "You have seen . . . how I bore you on eagle's wings and brought you to Me" (Exodus 19:4). The rescue of the Yemenite community seemed so miraculous that it became known as "Operation Magic Carpet."

Unfortunately, when discussions are held today about the status of Palestinian refugees, the larger number of Jewish refugees forced out of the Arab countries are invariably ignored. Few people even think of them as refugees, because, unlike the Arab world, Israel made massive, if not always fully successful, efforts to end their refugee status and to integrate them.

The return of Jews to Israel from all the countries of their dispersion is known in Hebrew as *kibbutz galuyot*, the ingathering of the exiles.

SOURCES AND FURTHER READINGS: Howard M. Sachar, *Aliyah: The Peoples of Israel*; Joseph Schechtman, *On Wings of Eagles*; S. Barer, *The Magic Carpet*.

160

KNESSET

Labor Party, Likud, Religious Parties

THE KNESSET, ISRAEL'S PARLIAMENT, HAS 120 MEMBERS. IN AMERICAN terms, it can be best understood as a combination of the United States Senate and House of Representatives, and a body in which the head of state sits as well. Unlike the United States, no member of the Israeli parliament is elected by popular vote or represents a specific geographical district. In Israeli elections, voters select parties. If a party gets 20 percent of the votes, then it is entitled to 20 percent of the seats in the Knesset. It is the party, therefore — not the voters — that determines which people will represent it in the Knesset. This electoral method results in Knesset members almost never voting in defiance of their party's instructions.

The Israeli voting system encourages a much larger number of parties than that of the United States, since a party need capture only 2 percent of the popular vote to earn a seat in the Knesset.

As many as twenty parties have on occasion sat in the Knesset. For the first twenty-nine years of Israel's existence, the most important party was Labor. Even in its heyday, Labor was never able to win an absolute parliamentary majority — sixty-one seats; it always ruled in coalition governments. During Israel's early years, the personalities who symbolized the country to the outside world generally came from Labor — Prime Minister David *Ben-Gurion, Prime Minister Golda *Meir, General Moshe *Dayan, and Foreign Minister Abba Eban.

Labor's economic orientation is socialist; it has, however, always allowed for private ownership of businesses. The party's foreign policy consistently aligned Israel with the Western, rather than the Communist, bloc.

Though ideologically secular, Labor routinely sought out the religious parties to serve in its coalition governments. On the most significant current issue in Israeli political life, the future of the *West Bank and the Gaza Strip, most Labor party members advocate "territory for peace," by which they mean returning substantial parts of the lands conquered in 1967 to the Arabs in the context of a peace settlement, and retaining only major parts of Jerusalem and other small areas deemed necessary for Israeli security.

The Labor party's dominance of Israeli political life ended in 1977 when Menachem *Begin and the Likud party came to power. Though procapitalist, the issue that has long mattered most to Likud is retention of Judea and Samaria (the West Bank), or at least large parts of it. In foreign-policy terms, it is, therefore, to the right of Labor.

Likud's capture of power in 1977, however, was due only in part to its stance on the West Bank. Its electoral victory had far more to do with capturing the loyalty of many Sephardic voters — Jews from the Arab world — who currently constitute more than 50 percent of the Israeli electorate. With considerable justification, the *Sephardim had long felt that Labor was overwhelmingly the party of the *Ashkenazim (European Jews), and one in which they were unlikely to be given positions of authority. Many Sephardim also believed that the Israelis who supported Labor were often the sort who looked down upon them as a lower-class and "primitive" group, and who had little regard for their traditional Jewish orientation.

Begin, a sentimental Jew of East European origins, projected to the Sephardim that he saw all Jews as part of one Jewish community, in which the Sephardim and Ashkenazim were two equal branches of the same family. He also portrayed himself as someone who had been kept out of the Labor circle of power, as they also had been. Over the years, Begin became a heroic figure to many Sephardic Jews. I remember being in a taxicab in Jerusalem in the early 1980s, passing the prime minister's residence. "Do you see that building?" the driver said to his son, who was seated next to him. "A king lives there. The king of Israel."

Begin's elevation to power in 1977 was also connected to the *Yom Kippur War, which had been fought less than four years earlier. Although Israel had rallied back after Egypt's and Syria's successful surprise attacks, and had won the war, Labor party leaders never recovered from the widely held perception that they had been "caught napping." In the aftermath of the Yom Kippur War, many Israelis were able to imagine for the first time a country ruled by a party other than Labor.

In addition, many religious voters were attracted by the Likud's right-wing orientation, which seemed more nearly aligned to their own generally traditional worldviews. For that reason, although Likud came to power with only forty-three seats—just over a third of the Knesset—Begin found little difficulty in enticing the religious parties into his coalition. He even invited the ultra-Orthodox Agudat Yisrael into the government, although the party was non-Zionist.

Since 1977, Likud has often been in power, and for several years it shared power with Labor in a "national unity government," one in which each party's head, Likud's Yitzhak Shamir and Labor's Shimon Peres, served as prime minister for two years. However, in 2005, when Prime Minister Ariel Sharon came under attack from large segments of Likud for authorizing the withdrawal of Israel from Gaza, he left Likud to form a new party, Kadima (Hebrew for "forward"). The number two position in the party was given to Shimon Peres, the former Labor prime minister. Both Sharon and Peres brought along with them some widely respected members of their former parties. In its platform, Kadima argued that though Israel had a national and historical right to all of the land of Israel, it recognized that implementing this right would make it impossible for Israel to be both a Jewish state (because such a large percentage of its population would be Arab) and a democracy. Therefore, Kadima favored making territorial concessions to the Palestinians, and agreed to the creation of a Palestinian state, although it insisted that Jerusalem and the large settlement blocks in the West Bank must remain under Israeli rule. National elections were scheduled for March 2006. On January 4, two months before the elections, Prime Minister Sharon suffered a physically and mentally disabling stroke. Ehud Olmert, also formerly of the Likud Party, was chosen to head Kadima, and Peres retained the number two position. In the March elections, Kadima emerged as the largest party with twenty-nine seats, and Olmert became prime minister. That summer, only a few months after Olmert's election, Hezbollah initiated attacks on Israel, and in the ensuing war (see pages 376–380), Israel did not succeed in achieving its stated objectives, to bring back the two soldiers kidnapped by Hezbollah, and to disarm the terrorist group and drive it out of Southern Lebanon. Olmert and his government came under strong criticism for their conduct of the war (a government-sponsored investigation criticized him by name), and for various instances of scandalous behavior by government officials, and there appeared throughout Israel a general sense of pessimism, cynicism, and the fear that during a period of great national crisis (during which Iran, a sworn enemy of Israel, was growing near to developing a nuclear bomb), the country suffered a serious lack of leadership.

The religious parties generally win over twenty seats in the Knesset election, which lends them enormous power, since Likud or Labor, or whatever party wishes to rule, almost always needs their "swing votes" to form a majority government. During Israel's first decades, the largest religious party was Mizrachi (now Mafdal), an ardently pro-Zionist party. Mizrachi's participation in every coalition government ensured that there would be adequate funding for Israeli religious schools, and that authority over marriage and divorce would remain in the hands of the rabbinate.

Until the 1984 election, the other major religious party was Agudat Yisrael, which is generally perceived as the party of ultra-Orthodox Jews. The party itself is wishy-washy on the issue of Zionism. Although it has had representatives in every Knesset, it has always had difficulty coming to terms with a Jewish state ruled by non-religious Jews, and not governed by Jewish law. In the late 1960s, for example, it opposed Golda *Meir as a candidate for prime minister because Jewish tradition opposes women ruling over men. In the 2006 election, the party ran under the name, Torah and Shabbat Judaism, and received six seats in the Knesset.

Since 1984, Agudat Yisrael's power has diminished in the face of a Sephardic ultra-Orthodox party, Shas. Just as secular Sephardim often claimed that Labor looked down upon them, ultra-Orthodox Sephardim voiced the same complaint about Agudat Yisrael. Agudat Yisrael's leading figures, all rabbis, were wont to conduct their meetings in Yiddish, a language unknown to most Sephardim. Shas quickly became a powerful vehicle for Sephardim to express their religious and ethnic pride: The party has won as many as seventeen seats in the Knesset. Unlike Agudat Yisrael, it has also succeeded in attracting some non-Orthodox voters, Sephardim who wish to vote for a Sephardic party.

Shas tends to have a more positive attitude toward Zionism than Agudat Yisrael. Yet, its Knesset representatives periodically have expressed worldviews that make non-fundamentalist Jews shudder. When a terrible bus accident killed twenty-three Israeli schoolchildren from Petakh Tikvah, Shas's Knesset leader speculated that the accident might have been God's divine judgment against secularist agitation for opening the city's movie theaters on the Sabbath. Another Shas representative in the Knesset conjectured that the many Israeli soldiers killed in the *Lebanese War of 1982 might have died as divine retribution for the alleged promiscuity of Israel's female soldiers.

Israel has other parties as well. In the 2006 election, a right-wing political party (Yisrael Beiteinu [Israel, Our Home]) headed by the Russian-born Avigdor Lieberman received eleven Knesset seats. The party is pushing for Israel to annex Jewish areas in Judea and Samaria, while transferring the governance of certain Arab cities in Israel, such as Umm Al-Fahm, to the Palestinian Authority, thereby effectively reducing Israel's Arab population. As the party platform declares: "Israel is our home; Palestine is theirs." Occasionally, non-ideological parties representing special interest groups gain an unexpected following. Such was the case with Gil, a pensioner's party, that received seven seats in the most recent elections.

In any given Knesset, there are ten or more Arab members, most of whom represent Arab political parties.

Because of the many parties pushing radically different agendas, Knesset debates tend to be much more acrimonious than those in the American Congress. On one noted occasion, January 7, 1952, when Prime Minister

Ben-Gurion advocated that Israel accept reparations from Germany for the Holocaust (see *German Reparations*), Menachem Begin made a thinly veiled threat of violence against any member who voted to accept such "blood money." He was subsequently denied his Knesset seat for fifteen months.

The Knesset is elected for a four-year period but can dissolve itself with a no-confidence vote, which results in an earlier election date being set. In the mid-1990s, Israel introduced a major change in its election laws, the direct election of the prime minister. While Knesset elections continued under the old system, Israelis now voted directly for the prime minister. Under this new election system, Likud leader Benjamin Netanyahu narrowly defeated the Labor leader Shimon Peres in 1996, only to be decisively defeated three years later by Labor leader Ehud Barak. In turn, Barak was overwhelmingly defeated by the Likud's Ariel Sharon in February 2001. Although the direct election of the prime minister was intended to bring greater stability to the Israeli political process, its effect has been increased instability, as voters supported one of the major party candidates for prime minister and were more apt to cast ballots for one of the many small parties to represent them in the Knesset. In consequence, in 2003 the law changed back to the old system, in which the leader of the party winning the largest number of seats in the Knesset becomes prime minister.

SOURCES AND FURTHER READINGS: Susan Hattis Rolef, ed., *Political Dictionary of the State of Israel*, pp. 180–185; Moshe Rosetti, *The Knesset: Its Origins, Forms and Procedures*; Asher Zidon, *The Knesset*.

ISRAEL DEFENSE FORCES/TZAHAL

Reserve Duty/Mi-lew-im

THE ISRAELI ARMY—MAN FOR MAN—GENERALLY IS REGARDED AS ONE of the best armies in the world. In Israel itself it is known almost exclusively by its initials, *TzaHaL—Tzva Haganah Le-Yisrael*—Israel Defense Forces, or IDF. The name very much describes the army's self-image; it is intended to fight only in defense of the Jewish state and the Jewish people.

Tzahal came into being with the creation of Israel in 1948. Prior to the state's establishment, there were four separate and often uncoordinated Jewish fighting forces: the *Haganah, *Palmach (made up of troops from *Ha-Shomer ha-Tza'ir*), *Irgun, and *Lekhi. Shortly after the declaration of statehood, Israeli Prime Minister David *Ben-Gurion disbanded all the separate forces and combined them into one unified army. Though Ben-Gurion himself was not religiously observant, he agreed to maintain *kashrut* at all army facilities, so that units would not have to be divided on the basis of religious commitment. To this day, there are signs in Israeli mess halls reading: KEEP KOSHER—THIS IS AN ORDER.

Tzahal's fighting reputation was established in the 1948 *War of Independence. At that time, six Arab armies simultaneously invaded Israel. Though outnumbered and vastly outarmed, the Israelis succeeded in overcoming their Arab adversaries and forcing them to accept a cease-fire. Unfortunately, the armistice agreements that both parties signed ended the fighting only temporarily. During Israel's first forty years of existence, *Tzahal* fought the Arabs five more times, in the Suez War of 1956, the *Six-Day War of 1967, the War of Attrition with Egypt in 1968–1970, the *Yom Kippur War of 1973, and the *Lebanese War of 1982. This conflict became the most controversial in the country's history: Many Israelis felt that it was more an aggressive than a defensive war. In 2006, a less conventional, but frightening and highly damaging, war was fought with Iranian-armed Hezbollah troops in Lebanon (see pages 376–380).

Tzahal has assumed responsibility for defense against Arab terrorism as well. It was an elite *Tzahal* unit that coordinated the rescue of more than one hundred Jewish hostages held by Palestinian and German terrorists at *Entebbe, Uganda, in 1976.

An oft-commented-upon feature of *Tzahal* is its widespread use of female soldiers. Though women were occasionally used as fighters in the War of Independence, they have not been permitted in fighting units since 1949, largely out of fear for their fate were they to be captured. Israeli women are drafted into *Tzahal* for two years at the age of eighteen. Exemptions are granted to married women, and to those requesting deferment on religious grounds; about one third of the women make such a request. The religious exemption is not because of Jewish opposition to all warfare; indeed, there is no significant pacifist tradition in Judaism. It is rather that many religious parents fear that a girl who leaves her home to live on an army base will soon be practicing a much looser form of sexual morality. Religious girls who don't wish to join the army but who do wish to volunteer their services to the country may opt to join *Sherut Leumi*, a program of national service which involves working in such areas as special education, hospitals, nursing homes, and with at-risk teens.

Israeli males are drafted for three years of service at the age of eighteen. Exemptions are granted for reasons of health and to *yeshiva students.

Unlike the armies of surrounding Arab countries, *Tzahal* is largely based on its reserve forces. Only some 105,000–125,000 soldiers are on duty at any given time (it is estimated that Syria's standing army is about 480,000). With forty-eight hours of warning time, however, *Tzahal* can complete its reserve call-up and become an army of over 600,000 troops. As a result of the army's dependence on its reserve troops, service in *Tzahal* continues for twenty or more years beyond the first three-year term. While the ages differ for the various branches of service, soldiers can be summoned for reserve duty up to the ages of forty to forty-five, and may be called up for active duty immediately in times of crisis. It is the constant training and retraining of its reserve army that helps explain Israel's stunning military achievements. However, in the aftermath of the 2006 war against Hezbollah, it was revealed that many reservists had not received adequate training in recent years, and were often not supplied with necessary equipment.

Reserve duty has often wreaked considerable havoc on the country's economy. There have been times when more than 5 percent of the work force has been in the army. A heavy personal price is paid as well; there are children's books published in Israel to help children cope with the shock and trauma of "daddy's" annual, and sometimes one-month or longer, disappearances.

Several Israeli friends have also told me that reserve duty can sometimes have a beneficial effect on their marriages, insofar as it allows for a mandated and short annual separation. On the other hand, when I conveyed that thought to an Israeli friend with three small children, he snapped: "Why don't you ask their wives?" No one denies that one of the extraordinary benefits of real peace between Israel and her neighbors will be the end of reserve duty.

Tzahal is so central a force in Israel that its leading officers are well-known figures in Israeli life. While most Americans would be hard put to name three American generals or admirals—who, for example, are the current heads of the air force, the navy, and the marines?—most Israelis know the names and accomplishments of many of the army's leading figures.

SOURCES AND FURTHER READINGS: Susan Hatis Rolef, ed., *Political Dictionary of the State of Israel*, pp. 151–155; Ze'ev Chafets, *Heroes and Hustlers, Hard Hats and Holy Men*, pp. 209–211; Aaron Wolf, *A Purity of Arms: An American in the Israeli Army*; Chaim Herzog, *The Arab-Israeli Wars*; Ze'ev Schiff, *A History of the Israeli Army*; Edward Luttwak and Dan Horowitz, *The Israeli Army*.

162

MOSHE DAYAN (1915–1981)

IN A POPULAR 1960S JOKE, PRESIDENT RICHARD NIXON TOLD ISRAELI Prime Minister Golda *Meir that he would trade her any three American generals she wanted in return for General Moshe Dayan. "Okay," Golda agreed. "Give me General Motors, General Electric, and General Dynamic."

If indeed *Tzahal*, the Israeli Army (see preceding entry), was often regarded in the 1960s and 1970s as one of the finest armies in the world, its shining jewel was Moshe Dayan. Though he never headed Israel's government, Dayan—with the trademark black eyepatch over his left eye—symbolized the country to the world. Few people knew, though, that he did not lose his eye fighting for Israel, but rather on behalf of Britain, during World War II.

During Israel's 1948 *War of Independence, Dayan commanded the defense of the Jordan Valley, and then of Jerusalem. He headed Israel's army during the invasion of Sinai in 1956. In May 1967, with Dayan retired from the army and Israeli Prime Minister Levi Eshkol also serving as minister of defense, Egypt and Syria formed a military alliance and announced their intention to drive the Jews into the sea. As Arab threats escalated, Israeli public opinion clamored for Eshkol to give up the Defense portfolio and appoint Dayan—the man Israelis most trusted to lead their army—instead. Within days of Dayan's appointment, Israel launched a preemptive strike against her enemies and destroyed the air forces of Egypt, Syria, and Jordan in one day. Though the dimensions of the surprise attack had been prepared before Dayan's elevation to the Defense Ministry post, he received much of the credit both at home and abroad for Israel's remarkable victory. After the war, Dayan announced that Jerusalem was waiting only for a telephone call from Arab leaders to start peace negotiations.

Unfortunately, Dayan's reputation took a hard pounding during the *Yom Kippur War six years later. Still serving as minister of defense, Dayan did not believe that the Egyptian Army was capable of mounting a serious attack against Israel. Although his military judgment had almost always been astute, in this instance he erred badly. Israel eventually won the war, but it also lost 2,700 soldiers—many in the first few days of fighting—and much of the public that had once clamored for him now clamored against him. For several months after the war's end, Dayan found himself hounded on Israeli streets by family members of the dead soldiers who shouted "Murderer" at him.

After Menachem *Begin's election as prime minister in 1977, Dayan's fortunes turned for the better. Although Dayan had long been affiliated with the Labor party, Begin appointed him minister for foreign affairs, and he, alongside Begin, played a major role in negotiating the Camp David accords. Henry Kissinger was to write of him: "War was Dayan's profession, peace was his obsession. . . . History will record him as a principal architect of the peace treaty with Egypt."

For much of his life, Dayan represented to the world the quintessential Israeli. Indeed, he was the first child born on the first Israeli *kibbutz, Degania. He was also an enthusiastic participant in one of Israel's national pastimes: archaeology. Dayan dug up numerous artifacts from both the First and Second Temple periods. In his later years, he would autograph some of the pottery he collected, and sell the pieces for high prices. Dayan was also known as a womanizer, a fact that his daughter Yael Dayan dwelled on in her bittersweet memoir, *My Father, His Daughter*.

Despite some personal failings, Dayan symbolized for Jews the world over the new type of Jew being forged in Israel—tough, unemotional, and totally self-sufficient.

SOURCES AND FURTHER READINGS: Yael Dayan, *My Father, His Daughter*; Shabtai Teveth, *Moshe Dayan*; Moshe Dayan, *Breakthrough: A Personal Account of the Egyptian-Israel Peace Negotiations*.

163

THE SIX-DAY WAR, 1967
The "Green Line"

MAY 1967, THE MONTH BEFORE THE SIX-DAY WAR, WAS AMONG THE saddest, most frightening months in Jewish history; June 1967, among the happiest. The Six-Day War, fought June 5–10, was a conflict Israel desperately wanted to avoid. But by the time it ended, the Jewish state was almost four times as large as it had previously been, and it was in possession of Judaism's holiest sites.

Israel struck the first blow on June 5, 1967, but the stage had been set earlier by Gamal Abdel Nasser, Egypt's president. In May, Nasser—believing perhaps that the Arab states had finally achieved military superiority over Israel—entered into a process of brinksmanship with the Jewish state, repeatedly announcing his intention to exterminate the "Zionist entity." On May 22, in contravention of international agreements, he declared the Straits of Tiran closed to all Israeli ships and to any foreign ships carrying strategic materials to the Jewish state. Under international law, such an attempt at economic strangulation constituted a *casus belli*, legal grounds to go to war, but Israel did not do so. Unfortunately, this restraint apparently fed Nasser's belief that Israel knew herself to be weaker than the Arabs.

At the end of May, Foreign Minister Abba Eban was dispatched to Europe and the United States to enlist international support for Israel's cause. French President Charles de Gaulle is reputed to have complimented Eban on his eloquent French, but Eban left empty-handed except for the advice "Do not make war! In any event, do not be the first to fire."

Meanwhile, the Arab world's rhetoric grew increasingly ferocious. On May 27, Nasser declared: "Our basic objective will be the destruction of Israel." Four days later, Iraq's president Abdel Rahman Aref announced: "Our goal is clear—to wipe Israel off the map."

Earlier, Egypt and Syria had concluded an agreement to combine their armies in the coming war against Israel. Subsequently, Nasser flew to Jordan and signed a military agreement with King Hussein to join in the battle.

World Jewry felt ever more despondent. The three largest countries bordering Israel were now militarily joined in an alliance to destroy her, while other Arab regimes publicly broadcast their readiness to send troops to join in the war. The Iraqi Army was already preparing to move troops into Jordan. It seemed as if another Holocaust might be in the making.

In Israel itself, the mood was somber. In addition to the grave security threat, the call-up of almost all Israeli males between eighteen and fifty-five was strangling the economy. The country's morale was not helped when Israel's elderly prime minister, Levi Eshkol, began stuttering during an address to the nation (it later emerged that he had trouble pronouncing an odd word that a speechwriter had included in his speech). During this desperate period, large numbers of Israelis agitated for military hero Moshe Dayan (see preceding entry) to be appointed minister of defense. Eshkol, who had been holding this post himself, finally acquiesced.

Two days later, Israel launched an extraordinary preemptive strike. In one day, the Israeli Air Force destroyed the entire Egyptian Air Force as well as the overwhelming majority of Syria's planes. Israel asked U.N. intermediaries to plead with Jordan's King Hussein not to join the war. But Hussein was convinced that the Arabs would win, and he didn't want to miss out on the spoils. From positions in the Jordanian-controlled West Bank, Jordanian artillery opened fire on Jerusalem, Tel Aviv, and several Israeli airfields. Hussein publicly appealed on Radio Amman to "kill the Jews" wherever they could be found, with one's hands, one's nails, anything. His air force, too, was destroyed.

The rapid loss of the Egyptian Air Force shocked and humiliated Nasser. Shortly thereafter, he telephoned King Hussein, unaware that Israeli intelligence was listening in on their conversation. "Shall we say that the United States is fighting on Israel's side?" he asked Hussein. "Shall we say the United States and England or only the United States?"

"The United States and England," Hussein replied. Three hours later, Radio Cairo announced that Israel's success was due to American and British military support. Soon thereafter, almost the entire Arab world broke diplomatic relations with America. Hussein refrained from doing so, and a week later apologized for the lie he had helped originate. It is not known whether Hussein would have done so had Israel not released the contents of his conversation with Nasser.

The war proceeded well for Israel on all three fronts. Israeli troops quickly occupied the entire Sinai Peninsula. In two days of brutal fighting, June 6 and 7, her soldiers took control of Jordan's West Bank, which had been annexed by Jordan in 1948. For Jews this victory was the emotional highlight of the war; it meant that the Old City of Jerusalem and the Western Wall of the Temple (see next entry) were again in Jewish hands. Yet Israel also suffered heavy losses in the battle for Jerusalem because she refused to use artillery in the Old City, out of a desire to preserve the holy sites of all the religions represented there.

In many ways, Israel's hardest battle was fought on the Golan Heights, then held by Syria. Here Israeli soldiers literally had an uphill struggle. For nineteen years, Syrian soldiers on the Golan Heights had fired down on Israeli *kibbutzim and settlements. By June 10, however, the heights had been secured for Israel.

The war itself, though it lasted only six days, claimed the lives of 679 Israelis, a painfully high price for a country as small as Israel.

Despite the heavy casualties, the country—and the whole Jewish world— were euphoric on June 10. Two weeks earlier, Israel had faced destruction. Now it was universally acknowledged as the greatest military power in the Middle East.

The pre-1967 borders were referred to as the "Green Line" because the armistice maps drawn up after the *War of Independence had colored Israel's borders in that color. The lands conquered from Jordan were known as the *West Bank (of the Jordan River), and are often called by their biblical names, Judea and Samaria.

When the war ended, Israel found that the Arab population within her borders had grown from 15 percent to over 40 percent. At the time, most Israelis were not terribly concerned about this enormous demographic shift; they assumed that the Arabs would give up their obsessive dream of destroying Israel, and sue for peace in return for the lost lands. In the war's immediate aftermath, the Israeli government was willing to make substantial territorial concessions for peace. But the massive nature of Israel's victory only hardened Arab hatred for the Jewish state. Two months after the war, the entire leadership of the Arab world met in Khartoum, Sudan, and issued three no's: "No peace with Israel, no negotiations with Israel, no recognition of Israel." Thus, Israel's massive victory, rather than hastening peace, intensified the Israeli-Arab conflict.

However, the Six-Day War dramatically affected American- and Soviet-Jewish life. The Israeli Army's great valor and heroic victory increased the pride of almost all Jews. In the weeks before, during, and after the war, American Jews contributed enormous sums of money to Israel; the *United Jewish Appeal (UJA) campaign for 1967 was three times the size of the 1966 campaign. In the war's aftermath, American Jews began visiting Israel and moving there in unprecedented numbers.

A new generation of Jews, many of them raised in affluent American suburbs with low levels of Jewish commitment, suddenly became involved in UJA activities, and more eager to know more about their Jewish identity and religion.

For Soviet Jews the effect was even more profound. Zionism had long been declared illegal by the Communist regime. Prior to the Six-Day War, many young Soviet Jews barely realized that a Jewish state existed. Yet, although the Soviet Union was an avowed enemy of Israel and the major arms supplier to her Arab adversaries, its media could not conceal the magnitude of the Israeli victory.

In the aftermath of the Six-Day War, *Exodus*, Leon Uris's novel about the creation of the State of Israel, became a kind of bible for the Soviet-Jewish underground. Since it was a criminal offense to own the book, Soviet Jews secretly passed around illegal typewritten translations of the novel. A Russian-Jewish friend of mine, Rabbi Leonid Feldman, told me how he was given the book in a park one night and instructed to return it to the same place twelve hours later, whether he had finished the book or not. He stayed up all night reading Uris's novel, and almost immediately decided that he wanted to live in the Jewish state. Throughout Russia, small bands of Jews started studying Hebrew, and by 1969, Soviet Jews started agitating for permission to migrate to Israel.

In my own life I can say with certainty that the Six-Day War and the years immediately following it were the happiest times I have ever known in which to be a Jew.

SOURCES AND FURTHER READINGS: Chaim Herzog, *The Arab-Israeli Wars*, pp. 143–191; S.L.A. Marshall, *Swift Sword*; Abraham Rabinovich, *The Battle for Jerusalem, June 5–7, 1967*; J. Robert Moskin, *Among Lions: The Battle for Jerusalem*. An extraordinary book, Avraham Shapiro, ed., *The Seventh Day*, records the reflections of soldiers who fought in the war and their attempts to maintain humane values even during battle. Nadav Safran, *From War to War: The Arab-Israeli Confrontation, 1948–1967*. Michael Oren, *Six Days of War: June 1967 and the Making of the Modern Middle East*.

164

WESTERN WALL/KOTEL HA-MA'ARAVI

WHEN ROME DESTROYED THE SECOND *TEMPLE IN 70 C.E., ONLY one outer wall remained standing. The Romans probably would have destroyed that wall as well, but it must have seemed too insignificant to them; it was not even part of the Temple itself, just an outer wall surrounding the Temple Mount. For the Jews, however, this remnant of what was the most sacred building in the Jewish world quickly became the holiest spot in Jewish life. Throughout the centuries, Jews from throughout the world made the difficult pilgrimage to Palestine, and immediately headed for the *Kotel ha-Ma'aravi* (the Western Wall) to thank God. The prayers offered at the *Kotel* were so heartfelt that gentiles began calling the site the "Wailing Wall." This undignified name never won a wide following among traditional Jews; the term "Wailing Wall" is not used in Hebrew.

The Western Wall was subjected to far worse than semantic indignities. During the more than one thousand years Jerusalem was under Muslim rule, the Arabs often used the Wall as a garbage dump, so as to humiliate the Jews who visited it.

For nineteen years, from 1948 to 1967, the *Kotel* was under Jordanian rule. Although the Jordanians had signed an armistice agreement in 1949 guaranteeing Jews the right to visit the Wall, not one Israeli Jew was ever permitted to do so. One of the first to reach the *Kotel* in the 1967 Six-Day War (see preceding entry) was Israeli Defense Minister Moshe *Dayan, who helped revive a traditional Jewish custom by inserting a written petition into its cracks. It was later revealed that Dayan's prayer was that a lasting peace "descend upon the House of Israel."

The custom of inserting written prayers into the *Kotel*'s cracks is so widespread that some American-Jewish newspapers carry advertisements for services that insert such prayers on behalf of sick Jews.

The mystical qualities associated with the *Kotel* are underscored in a popular Israeli song, a refrain of which runs: "There are people with hearts of stone, and stones with hearts of people." A rabbi in Jerusalem once told me that the Hebrew expression "The walls have ears" was originally said about the Western Wall.

Unfortunately, even a symbol as unifying as the *Kotel* can become a source of controversy in Jewish life. Ultra-Orthodox Jews have long opposed organized women's prayer services at the Wall; prayer services, they maintain, may only be conducted by males (see *Minyan*). On occasion they have violently dispersed such services, throwing chairs and other "missiles" at the praying women. Under intense public pressure, however, the right of women to pray collectively at the *Kotel* is gradually being won, though currently women's prayer groups are required to use a designated area near Robinson's arch for organized services.

In addition to the large crowds that come to pray at the *Kotel* on Friday evenings, it is also a common gathering place on all Jewish holidays, particularly on the fast of *Tisha Be-Av, which commemorates the destruction of both Temples. Today the Wall is a national symbol, and the opening or closing ceremonies of many Jewish events are conducted there.

PLO — PALESTINE LIBERATION ORGANIZATION

Munich Massacre, 1972

Oslo Accords, 1993

MOST AMERICANS ARE SURPRISED TO LEARN THAT YASIR ARAFAT WAS not the founder of the Palestine Liberation Organization. That "distinction" belongs to Ahmed Shukeiry, the organization's founding chairman. When asked on one occasion what would happen to the Jews if an Arab invasion succeeded in defeating Israel, Shukeiry responded: "Those [Israelis] who survive will remain in Palestine. I estimate that none of them will survive." Most

Americans also believe that the PLO was founded after the *Six-Day War, with the goal of winning back the territories conquered by Israel. In fact, the organization was founded in January 1964, before Israel had captured the West Bank, and its goal was the elimination of the Jewish state and its replacement by an Arab state called Palestine.

Arafat took control of the PLO after the Six-Day War, with the same goal in mind. Toward that end, he taught his followers that all Israelis and Jews are enemies, and any means are justified in fighting them. Over the years, PLO troops occupied an Israeli elementary school and shot schoolchildren to death, and pushed a paralyzed American Jew in a wheelchair off a boat so that he drowned. In 1973, Arafat personally ordered the murder of the American ambassador to Sudan, whom his followers previously had kidnapped. The PLO regarded Americans as enemies because their government supported Israel's right to exist and sent her aid. The airplane hijackings undertaken by Palestinian terrorists in the late 1960s brought about the security provisions now in effect at all airports.

Perhaps the most infamous act carried out under Arafat's direction was the kidnapping and murder of eleven Israeli athletes at the 1972 Munich Olympics. The Olympics' head, Avery Brundage, long rumored to be an antisemite, justified the rumors by refusing to postpone or cancel Olympic events while the Jewish athletes were being held by the kidnappers. In response, Israel sent out a hit squad, which ultimately killed almost every terrorist involved in planning and carrying out the Munich massacre.

But if almost all Jews perceived the PLO to be a deadly enemy of Israel and of Jewry, a growing number of Arab, Third World, and Communist countries agitated for the PLO receiving international diplomatic recognition. During the tenure of former Nazi army officer Kurt Waldheim as secretary general of the U.N. General Assembly, Yasir Arafat was invited to address the international organization.

Besides Israel, the United States was for a long time the country that was most resistant to according diplomatic recognition to the PLO. In 1975, Secretary of State Henry Kissinger announced the criteria that had to be fulfilled for America to enter into negotiations with the PLO: acknowledgment of Israel's right to exist, and acceptance of U.N. Resolutions 242 and 338 (see next entry). Later, the U.S. Congress added renunciation of terrorism. Several years later, Andrew Young, the U.S. ambassador to the U.N., privately met with the PLO's U.N. representative—in violation of official American policy—and was forced to resign.

In the fall of 1988, Arafat made an ambiguously worded statement in which he seemed to accept the American demands, and Secretary of State George Shultz announced that the United States was initiating political talks with the PLO. Several years later Israel did so as well, and unofficial talks between Israeli and PLO representatives led to the signing of the Oslo Accords in September 1993. In letters exchanged prior to the signing of the accords, Yasir Arafat, on behalf of the PLO, recognized the right of Israel to exist and renounced the use of violence, while Prime Minister Yitzchak Rabin, on behalf of Israel, recognized the PLO as the representative of the Palestinian people.

The Oslo Accords set out interim arrangements for a five-year period, in which Israel granted self-rule to the Palestinians, first in the Gaza Strip and in and around the city of Jericho and subsequently in other areas of the West Bank. The most difficult "final status" issues, among them Jerusalem, the Jewish settlements on the West Bank, security arrangements, and Palestinian refugees, were to be resolved by the end of this period. However, even after several extensions no agreement was reached. In addition, Palestinian schools continued to teach hatred of Israel and Israelis in their textbooks, in violation of the Oslo Accords. Sadly as well, the one hope many Israelis placed in the Oslo Accords, that they would lead to an end of terror attacks inside Israel, did not come about either. See entry on Camp David, 2000 (p. 370).

SOURCES AND FURTHER READINGS: Neil Livingstone and David Halevy, *Inside the PLO*; Harris Schoenberg, *A Mandate for Terror: The United Nations and the PLO*. Since Arafat's death in 2004, the PLO has been led by Abu Mazen, who heads the Palestinian Authority as well.

UNITED NATIONS RESOLUTIONS
242 AND 338

SINCE ITS PASSAGE ON NOVEMBER 22, 1967, SECURITY COUNCIL Resolution 242 has been regarded by the international diplomatic community as the basis for a lasting peace between Israel and her neighbors. Feelings about "242" in Israel tend to be more mixed, particularly because of the resolution's insistence on "withdrawal of Israeli armed forces from territories occupied in the recent [*Six-Day War] conflict."

Arthur Goldberg, a deeply committed Jew, was the U.S. ambassador to the U.N. at the time the resolution was passed. Goldberg subsequently insisted that the resolution never intended to bring about a complete Israeli withdrawal from every inch of land occupied in 1967. Goldberg noted that the resolution spoke of Israeli withdrawal "from territories," and not from "all the territories." Lord Caradon, the former British representative to the U.N. and a diplomat much less friendly to Israel than Goldberg, confirmed the American ambassador's view. "It would have been wrong," Caradon explained to the Beirut *Daily Star* on June 12, 1974, "to demand that Israel return to its positions of June 4, 1967, because those positions were undesirable and artificial. After all, they were just the places where the soldiers of each side happened to be on the day the fighting stopped in 1948. They were just armistice lines. That's why we didn't demand that the Israelis return to them, and I think we were right not to. . . ."

Nonetheless, Resolution 242 clearly calls for a substantial Israeli withdrawal from the areas captured in 1967. And, in fact, when Menachem Begin signed a peace treaty with Egypt in 1978, he agreed to withdraw from all areas conquered from Egypt, with no territorial modifications whatsoever (see *Camp David*).

The resolution has another clause, insisting on the right of every state in the region to "live in peace within secure and recognized boundaries free from threats or acts of force." Unfortunately, this clause has long been rejected by almost all of the Arab states, although in 1988 Yasir Arafat of the PLO announced that he accepted it (see preceding entry).

Resolution 242 also speaks of the need for "a just settlement of the refugee problem." The neutral word "refugee," was used rather than "Palestinian refugees" to underscore the two refugee problems in the Israeli conflict: Palestinian-Arab and Jewish. More than 700,000 Jews have fled the Arab world since Israel's creation in 1948, in comparison with the estimated 550,000 Arabs who fled the territory that became Israel. Neither Jewish nor Arab refugees have ever received financial compensation for their confiscated property.

Resolution 338, issued in the final days of the *Yom Kippur War—October 22, 1973—simply calls for a cease-fire, an implementation of Resolution 242, and a "just and durable peace in the Middle East."

Although "338" is far less ambitious in scope than "242," the two resolutions are always mentioned in tandem in international documents.

SOURCE AND FURTHER READING: Leonard Davis, Eric Rozenman, and Jeff Rubin, *Myths and Facts 1989*, pp. 45–51; the resolutions themselves can be found on pp. 294–295.

167

GOLDA MEIR (1898–1978)

FOR ALL PRACTICAL PURPOSES, GOLDA MEIR, THE FIRST FEMALE HEAD of a Jewish state since the time of the Bible, had no last name. Throughout the Jewish world, everyone knew her as just "Golda."

A woman of extraordinary common sense, she had a knack for penetrating to the fatal flaw in an opponent's argument. In the early years of the state, several rapes had been committed in Israel, and at a cabinet meeting a member suggested that no women be allowed out alone at night until the rapists were caught. "I don't understand," Golda protested. "Men are committing the rapes. Men should not be allowed out at night."

Golda lived her life in the three major twentieth-century centers of

Jewish life. Born in Russia, she grew to adulthood in the United States, and spent the rest of her life in Israel. Her earliest childhood memory was of her father nailing boards over the front door to protect his family from an impending *pogrom. Seventy years later, when Pope Paul VI criticized Israel's "fierceness" at a private audience, she said: "Your Holiness, do you know what my earliest memory is? A pogrom in Kiev. When we were merciful and when we had no homeland and when we were weak, we were led to the gas chambers."

While still a young girl, her family moved from Russia to Milwaukee, Wisconsin. She became a schoolteacher—and an active recruit to Zionism. In her early twenties, she married, moved to Palestine, and joined a *kibbutz. She soon became a leader in a wide variety of *Labor party activities, and a close associate of *Ben-Gurion, who later claimed, "Golda's the only man in my cabinet." In 1948, just before Israel was declared, Ben-Gurion dispatched her on a secret and dangerous meeting with King Abdullah of Jordan, in an unsuccessful effort to persuade the monarch not to join the Arab war against the soon-to-be established Jewish state.

After Israel's creation, Golda was posted as the country's first ambassador to the Soviet Union. Her appearance that *Rosh ha-Shana at the main synagogue in Moscow brought out a massive welcoming demonstration of tens of thousands of Russian Jews. Unfortunately, the KGB were also present, with cameras, and more than a few of the people who came to greet her served long terms in Soviet prison camps.

Later Golda served as Israel's foreign minister, and initiated a policy of active help for, and cooperation with, the newly established nations in Africa. Upon Levi Eshkol's death in 1969, she became prime minister. Though perceived by many on the political left as a hard-liner—she was unalterably opposed to a Palestinian state, and denied the existence of a Palestinian people—Golda passionately hoped to resolve peacefully the Arab-Israeli conflict. In the late 1960s, while Israel was fighting a slow and very costly war of attrition with Egypt, she was asked when there would be peace with Egypt. "I have given instructions," she answered, "that I be informed every time one of our soldiers is killed, even if it is in the middle of the night. When President Nasser leaves instructions that he be awakened in the middle of the night if an Egyptian soldier is killed, there will be peace."

Her final years were tormented by a sense of guilt for not having mobilized Israel's reserve army in the days before the *Yom Kippur War. Though she herself felt that a war seemed imminent, she accepted the confident assurances of her military advisers that there was no reason for concern. When the combined Egyptian-Syrian surprise attack was launched, hundreds of overwhelmed Israeli troops were quickly killed: More than 2,700 soldiers died in the ensuing weeks. "I shall live with that terrible knowledge for the rest of my life," she wrote in her autobiography.

Perhaps most characteristic of Golda's spirit is her well-known statement: "The only thing I cannot forgive the Arabs for is that they forced our sons to kill their sons."

SOURCES AND FURTHER READINGS: The best source of information about Golda Meir's life is her exceptionally interesting autobiography, *My Life*. There is also a brief overview of her life by *New York Times* correspondent Israel Shenker, published in Arthur Gelb, A. M. Rosenthal, and Marvin Siegel, *Great Lives of the Twentieth Century*, pp. 456–464.

168

YOM KIPPUR WAR, 1973

EVEN THOUGH ISRAEL EVENTUALLY WON THE YOM KIPPUR WAR, IT remains one of the great calamities in the country's history. The war started on October 6, 1973, on *Yom Kippur, the holiest day in the Jewish calendar. Egypt and Syria simultaneously invaded the territories Israel captured in the 1967 *Six-Day War; Egypt attacked in the Suez, and Syria in the Golan Heights. The size of their attacking armies equaled the combined forces of NATO in Europe.

Because of the religious holiday, many Israeli soldiers had been given leave to go home. The seventy thousand Egyptian troops who crossed the Suez Canal found themselves opposed by fewer than five hundred Israeli soldiers. The Egyptians soon overran them. In the Golan too, the Syrians made rapid advances.

In retrospect, attacking the Jewish state on its holiest day was a tactical miscalculation. Precisely because it was Yom Kippur and so many Jews were either in synagogue or at home, it was relatively easy for the Israeli Army to contact and mobilize all active soldiers, as well as those on reserve duty.

Within a week, Israel had driven Egypt and Syria's forces back to where they had been before the war. Yet the price the war exacted was horrifying. By the time it ended, 2,700 Israeli soldiers were dead, four times as many as had died in the *Six-Day War.

The Yom Kippur War changed few Israeli minds on how to deal with the country's Arab neighbors. At the war's end, "doves" argued that had Israel shown more willingness to compromise on the territories captured in the Six-Day War, the Yom Kippur War might have been averted. "Hawks" insisted that the war demonstrated the necessity of retaining the territories: Without the buffer these areas provided, the Arab invaders in 1973 might have penetrated Israel's interior and killed thousands of civilians.

Prime Minister Golda Meir (see preceding entry), Defense Minister Moshe *Dayan, and the Israeli Army came under heavy attack in the war's aftermath for not having anticipated the Arab invasion. There was some justification for the criticism. Dayan, and much of the army leadership, apparently had totally miscalculated Egypt's military intentions. Dayan believed that Egypt would not attack unless it had superior air power, and that Syria would not go to war without Egypt. While the second calculation was correct, the first was not.

In addition, there were diplomatic constraints limiting Israel's response. A few hours before the war erupted, when it was clear to Israeli intelligence that an invasion was imminent, Chief of Staff David Elazar requested permission to launch a preemptive attack against Syria and Egypt. Although she knew the request to be militarily sound, Golda Meir refused it: She knew that any preemptive strike by Israel would be severely opposed by the United States. Israel was too dependent on American support to risk incurring U.S. wrath.

A month after the war, a government commission, headed by Israeli Supreme Court Justice Dr. Simon Agranat, was convened to assess the government's and the army's behavior. The commission exonerated Golda Meir and Dayan, and assessed heavy blame on several of the leading generals in the army. Shortly after the report was released, Golda Meir resigned as prime minister.

Despite the heavy loss of life, the Yom Kippur War had one beneficial result: It convinced Egyptian President Anwar *Sadat that the Arabs would never defeat Israel in a war. Egypt and Syria had started the Yom Kippur War with a tremendous advantage, and still had not been able to withstand the Israeli counterattack. Paradoxically, the war also made Sadat more amenable to peace because he felt that the heavy casualties suffered by the Israeli Army had redeemed Arab honor for the humiliating loss of 1967 (see *Six-Day War*). Four years after the Yom Kippur War, Sadat made his famous trip to Jerusalem, and subsequently concluded a peace treaty with Israel at *Camp David.

The war seems to have been an important factor in the Israeli electorate's repudiation of the Labor party in 1977. Labor had ruled Israel since its creation in 1948. After the Yom Kippur War and the revelations of the Agranat Commission, many Israelis, for the first time since the state's creation, could imagine an Israel not ruled by Labor. Less than four years later, the *Likud party came to power.

In the war's early days, Israel suffered tremendous loss of armaments, and the only country capable of resupplying her and willing to help was the United States. In her autobiography, Golda Meir wrote that although it drove her liberal Jewish friends in the United States crazy whenever she said it, much of the credit for Israel's victory must be given to President Richard Nixon, who authorized a massive arms shipment to Israel.

Even with America's help, the war badly damaged Israel's economy. It is estimated that the three-week battle cost Israel an entire year's gross national product. After the Yom Kippur War, Israel became increasingly dependent on American financial aid.

The war also caused Israel to become more isolated in the international arena. Most African nations, acting under Arab pressure, broke off diplomatic relations with Israel. Only two years after the war, the Arabs were able to push through the *United Nations a resolution condemning "Zionism as racism." In the aftermath of the Yom Kippur War, the Arab world also started using oil as a "bargaining chip" to turn the Western world against Israel.

Most significantly, the Yom Kippur War shook, perhaps permanently, the self-confidence of Israeli society.

SOURCE AND FURTHER READING: Chaim Herzog, *The War of Atonement.*

169

WEST BANK VERSUS JUDEA AND SAMARIA

Gush Emunim

THE LARGEST BLOCK OF LAND THAT ISRAEL CAPTURED DURING THE
*Six-Day War was the Sinai Desert, which alone was almost triple the size of
Israel. Emotionally speaking, however, the area that mattered far more to
most Jews was the much smaller West Bank of the Jordan River, captured
from Jordan. From the time of the Bible to 1948, the West Bank, which
includes the Old City of Jerusalem (containing the *Western Wall) and
Hebron (where the biblical *Patriarchs and *Matriarchs are buried), had
always been part of the land of Israel. While the media refer to this area as the
"West Bank," many Israelis, particularly those on the political right, call these
territories by their biblical names, Judea (*Yehuda*—see Ezra 5:1), and Samaria
(*Shomron*—see I Kings 16:29).

An Israeli who refers to these lands as the "West Bank" usually implies that
he would accept their being returned to the Arabs as part of a peace settlement. An Israeli who calls them "Judea and Samaria" is often making the
opposite statement: He or she views them as an inextricable part of the land
of Israel. However, by the early 2000s even Israelis on the right, though perhaps not the far right, were acknowledging that Israel would eventually cede
large parts of this area if an agreement was reached to establish a Palestinian
state.

The status of Judea and Samaria call to mind the old Jewish joke about the
Plotnick diamond. A very beautiful young woman sits down at a wedding
reception with her much older husband. The woman sitting next to her stares
at the gorgeous diamond ring the young woman is wearing. "Why that is the
most beautiful diamond I have ever seen," she says.

"This is a famous diamond," the young woman responds. "It's known as
the Plotnick diamond. There's even a curse associated with it."

"How romantic," the other woman comments. "What is the curse?"

"Mr. Plotnick."

Judea and Samaria are indeed a jewel. But they come with between two and two and a half million Palestinian Arabs who have no desire to live under Jewish rule. What to do with Judea and Samaria clearly is the most nettlesome problem facing Israel. Were Israel to annex the West Bank, her population immediately would become 40 percent Arab. Because the Arabs have a much higher birthrate than the Jews, within a few decades the Arabs might well comprise a majority of Israel's population and Israel would no longer be a Jewish state—that is, unless Israel annexes Judea and Samaria but does not give the Arab inhabitants political rights. In that case, the Jewish state would survive, but not as a democracy. In short, by annexing Judea and Samaria, Israel will either remain a Jewish state but not a democracy, or remain a democracy but not a Jewish state.

One Israeli group that profoundly disagrees with this analysis is the Gush Emunim (Bloc of Believers), founded in February 1974 in the aftermath of the deeply demoralizing Yom Kippur War (see preceding entry). A religious group—as its name implies—Gush Emunim deems it a religious obligation for Israel to incorporate Judea and Samaria permanently into her borders. Many Gush members have settled in small Jewish enclaves on the West Bank: They are convinced that a massive Jewish civilian presence throughout the area will be the most effective guarantee against these lands being returned to the Arabs.

It was from Gush Emunim's ranks that a Jewish terrorist underground was formed in the early 1980s to avenge Arab attacks against Jews. Unfortunately, the underground's activities were not limited to Arabs who actually attacked Jews. In one infamous instance, the terrorists were stopped at the last minute from planting bombs on buses operating in Arab neighborhoods. After the Jewish underground members were arrested, Gush Emunim's leaders decried their terrorist deeds, yet they subsequently agitated for their release from prison.

Gush Emunim's spiritual godfather is the late Rabbi Zvi Yehuda Kook, the son of Chief Rabbi Abraham Isaac *Kook. Zvi Yehuda Kook regarded the building up of Israel's security as perhaps the preeminent commandment of his generation. For that reason, he believed that the Israeli Army and even its weapons were "holy." For him, the very land of Israel was so sacred that no part of it could ever be given over to non-Jewish rule. "I tell you explicitly," he wrote of Judea and Samaria, "that the Torah forbids us to surrender even one inch of our liberated land." A disciple of Rabbi Kook, Rabbi Shlomo Aviner, subsequently expanded on Kook's command: "Let me draw you an analogy. It's as if a man goes into his neighbor's house without permission and stays there for many years. When the original owner returns, the invader claims: 'It's my house, I've been living here for years!' All of these years he has been nothing but a thief. Now he should make himself scarce and pay rent on top of it. Some people might say that there's a difference between living in a place for thirty years and living in a place for two thousand years. Let us ask them: Is there a statue of limitations that gives a thief the right to his plunder?"

Many, perhaps most, members of Gush Emunim are not bothered by the prospect of annexing Judea and Samaria without giving its Arab inhabitants full rights. They argue that Israel is not obligated to extend political rights to people who openly declare their opposition to the state's very existence—which, indeed, is the position of most Arabs living on the West Bank. Other members do advocate extending democratic rights to Arabs on the West Bank, and believe that a large migration to Israel of Diaspora Jews will guarantee that the state remains Jewish. The issue became somewhat muted in the late 1990s when Israel granted Palestinians self-rule over most of the West Bank.

UNITED NATIONS RESOLUTION ON
ZIONISM, 1975

FOUNDED IN 1945, THE UNITED NATIONS PLAYED A MAJOR ROLE IN bringing about the creation of Israel (see *U.N. Vote for Partition*). By the 1970s, however, the U.N. had become a center of anti-Israel activity. Its votes were generally determined by the twenty Arab states, the USSR and Soviet bloc, and a collection of Third World dictatorships. The "lockstep" voting of these three blocs virtually guaranteed passage of any resolutions introduced by any one of them.

The one issue that particularly united the Arab and Communist blocs was hatred of Israel and of Zionism, the Jewish national movement that had brought the state into being. Beginning in the early 1970s, Arab delegates regularly tried to have Zionism denounced as "racist" in the official resolutions of all international conferences. The results were often ludicrous. At the International Women's Year Conference in Mexico City in June 1975, the final resolution denounced Zionism, but not sexism, as an enemy of all women. A condemnation of sexism would have been perceived as an attack on the Arab-Muslim world, in which women's rights are greatly abridged.

On November 10, 1975, Resolution 3379 denouncing Zionism as "a form of racism" passed the U.N. General Assembly by 72 to 35, with 32 abstentions. Although the resolution had no tangible significance—General Assembly resolutions are recommendations and have no binding effect—its symbolic significance was considerable. In the bluntest terms, Jews were told that, though they might regard themselves as a people, they had no right to a homeland. On the day the resolution was adopted, the United States ambassador to the United Nations, Daniel Patrick Moynihan, denounced it as "an obscene act." Israeli Ambassador Chaim Herzog tore up the resolution and declared: "Hitler would have felt at home . . . listening to the proceedings in this forum."

The resolution's passage provided great encouragement to antisemites, who could now disguise their Jew-hatred under the label anti-Zionist. In England, antisemitic university groups tried to expel Jewish student groups from British campuses on the grounds that they were pro-Zionist, and hence racist.

Few of Israel's enemies tried to explain how a state could be racist when citizens of every race lived there and enjoyed equal rights. In recent years, while disturbing reports of blacks being used as slaves in the Arab world have circulated in the West, Israel has been evacuating and taking in the long-suffering *black* Jews of Ethiopia (see *Ethiopian Jewry*).

The virulent hatred expressed toward Israel at the United Nations has long alienated the once strong Jewish support for the international organization. In *Jews and American Politics*, Stephen Isaacs writes of a 1970 fund-raising effort for the upcoming presidential campaign of Senator George McGovern. A meeting was arranged between McGovern and some of America's wealthiest Jews. When asked his position on the Middle East, McGovern repeatedly advocated that a settlement be worked out through the offices of the United Nations. Business mogul Meshulam Riklis expressed the sentiment shared by most of those present. "Let me ask you a question, Senator," he challenged McGovern. "What did you expect this group would ask you?

Why are you so poorly prepared on a question of this importance?" Since the early 1970s, Jews have understood that when someone speaks out aggressively on behalf of the United Nations, they are usually ignorant of, indifferent, or hostile to Jewish interests.

In December 1991, with the collapse of the Soviet Union, the General Assembly of the United Nations officially revoked the resolution condemning Zionism as racism.

SOURCES AND FURTHER READINGS: Itamar Rabinovich and Jehuda Reinharz, eds., *Israel in the Middle East*, pp. 309–312; Stephen Isaacs, *Jews and American Politics*, pp. 1–6; Sidney Lukofsky, "U.N. Resolution on Zionism," in Morris Fine and Milton Himmelfarb, eds., *American Jewish Year Book 1977*.

ENTEBBE (JULY 4, 1976)

WHAT HAPPENED IN ENTEBBE, UGANDA, ON JULY 4, 1976, WAS ONE of the happiest events in modern Jewish history: A group of Jews destined to be murdered was saved from its attackers.

The crisis at Entebbe had been precipitated on June 27, when terrorists of the Popular Front for the Liberation of Palestine hijacked an Air France plane to Uganda. The choice of country was no accident; Uganda's dictator, Idi Amin, was one of the few world leaders willing to go on record as an admirer of Adolf Hitler's treatment of the Jews. The hijackers seemed intentionally to evoke the association with German Nazism. The hijacking was carried out by a combined force of Arab and German terrorists. Jewish and Israeli passengers were quickly separated from non-Jews in a manner reminiscent of the Nazis. Once they had their hostages in hand, the terrorists announced that they would murder the Jews unless Israel and other countries released fifty-three Palestinian "freedom fighters."

Israel entered into negotiations with the PLO, even as Israeli antiterrorist units examined all possible military options for freeing the captives. Fortunately, Israel had detailed photographs of the Entebbe airport that had been taken several years earlier when a friendlier government was in power, and Israel had helped train the Ugandan Air Force. Israeli agents grilled the non-Jewish passengers who had been released, and learned many details about the terrorist operation, most important of all being the precise location of the hostages and the guards. On the afternoon of July 3, less than a day before the hostages were due to be murdered, Defense Minister Shimon Peres ordered the rescue mission on its way.

The lead Israeli plane flew at a sufficiently low altitude to evade Uganda radar, then landed in a remote part of the airport. Three other planes followed. A Mercedes-Benz was lowered out of the first plane, with a hefty Israeli soldier inside made up to resemble Amin. The Israeli imitation of the usual Amin entourage confused the Ugandan and terrorist troops for several seconds. The Israelis burst into the terminal where the hostages were held, and within fifteen seconds killed the terrorists guarding them. Less than an hour after the first Israeli plane arrived, the hostages were flown out of the country. Unfortunately, one elderly Jewish woman, Dora Bloch, had been taken earlier to a Ugandan hospital. After the Israelis left, Amin had her murdered. Three other hostages were killed during the operation.

The commander of the Israeli force, Captain Yonatan Netanyahu, was the only Israeli soldier killed during the mission. He has since become one of the heroic figures of modern Jewish life, and a large selection of his letters were published posthumously in a deeply moving book.

On July 4, 1946—thirty years to the day before Entebbe—forty-two Jewish survivors of the Holocaust who had returned to their hometown village of Kielce, Poland, were murdered in a brutal pogrom by their Christian neighbors. On July 4, 1976, over a hundred Jews who were about to be murdered were saved by the Israeli Army. More than anything else, Entebbe continues to symbolize for Jews the importance of there being a Jewish state. When they didn't have a nation of their own, Jews could be killed with impunity. With a state, for the first time in two thousand years, Jews who were threatened had a fighting chance.

SOURCES AND FURTHER READINGS: Yehuda Ofer, *Operation Thunder*; William Stevenson, *Ninety Minutes at Entebbe*; Yonatan Netanyahu, *Self-Portrait of a Hero: The Letters of Jonathan Netanyahu*.

172

MENACHEM BEGIN ELECTED PRIME MINISTER, 1977

THOUGH ISRAEL HAS BEEN A DEMOCRACY SINCE ITS CREATION IN 1948, it did not have a change of government during its first twenty-nine years. The ruling party, *Labor, invariably shared power with many of the smaller parties. But it always excluded the Communists and, almost always, the right-wing Herut party from coalitions.

In 1977, for the first time, the Labor party lost control of the *Knesset, the Israeli parliament. The victor was the right-wing *Likud party (a merger of Herut and the General Zionists), headed by Menachem Begin. Likud's victory signaled a change in Israeli political life on many levels. A large segment of Begin's support came from *Sephardim—Jews from the Arab world—who had long felt that their needs were ignored by the Labor establishment. By and large, religious Jews also were pleased with Begin's win, for he was the first moderately religious Jew to become an Israeli head of state. Other Israelis were less inclined to support Labor after the heavy losses suffered in the *Yom Kippur War.

Most significantly, Begin's victory signaled a move to the right by the Israeli electorate. Unlike the United States, where right-left designations usually refer to socioeconomic policies and in the past to attitudes toward communism, the right-left split in Israel refers overwhelmingly to one issue—the lands won by Israel during the *Six-Day War. For Begin the land won from Jordan was not the *West Bank, but *Judea and Samaria—parts of ancient Israel—and it was forbidden for any Israeli government to give them away. The Israeli left has long favored exchanging the territories for peace.

Before his election as prime minister, Menachem Begin's main claim to fame had been his leadership of the *Irgun, the underground group that violently fought against the British occupation of Palestine in the 1940s. After Israeli independence was achieved in 1948, Begin served continuously in the Israeli Knesset. Although most observers assumed he would never come to power, Begin never lost hope: He continued to lead his party in election after election.

Israeli journalist Ze'ev Chafets has observed that Begin "spent a lifetime believing in a series of highly improbable ideas—and [watched] them come true, one by one." When Begin became a Zionist in the 1920s, almost no one thought that there would be a Jewish state within a few decades. Begin never doubted it. Begin likewise believed in the prophecy of his mentor, Vladimir *Jabotinsky, that European Jewry was heading for an unprecedented disaster. This belief, of course, also came true during the Holocaust. When Begin arrived in Israel in the early 1940s, most Zionists believed that violence against the British was counterproductive, and that only diplomacy would end the British occupation of Palestine. Begin insisted that it was the Irgun's violent fight against the British, and not diplomacy, which would precipitate Britain's withdrawal from Palestine. Throughout the first nineteen years of the state's existence, Begin held to the increasingly "eccentric" idea that someday the Old City of Jerusalem and all of Judea and Samaria would be returned to Jewish rule. Which, of course, happened during the Six-Day War. And, despite eight electoral losses, Begin believed that he would someday be Israel's prime minister.

Many liberal Jews hoped that Likud's electoral victory was an aberration, and that Labor would be returned to power in the next election. Following Likud's 1977 win, however, it and Labor for many years shared approximately equal political strength. During much of the 1980s, the two ruled together in "national unity governments." This in effect, checkmated the maneuvering ability of both parties. There were enough Israelis on the political right to block the return of all the territories on the West Bank, and enough on the left to prevent the government from annexing the area.

During Israel's first years of statehood, Prime Minister David *Ben-Gurion's power was such that he could push through almost any policy that he wanted. Since the Likud's accession to power in 1977, it is clear that no Israeli party or politician has such power—and it is unlikely that such a leader will emerge in the foreseeable future.

SOURCE AND FURTHER READING: Ze'ev Chafets, *Heroes and Hustlers, Hard Hats and Holy Men*, pp. 65–87; in addition to the chapter on Begin, Chafets's book gives the best overview of any book I know of day-to-day life in Israel in the 1980s.

173

ANWAR SADAT'S VISIT TO JERUSALEM
CAMP DAVID, 1978

HAD ANYONE PREDICTED IN 1975 THAT EGYPTIAN PRESIDENT ANWAR Sadat would fly into Israel two years later and proclaim Israel's right to exist before the *Knesset, he would have been dismissed as a madman. Egypt, after all, had been Israel's arch-enemy from literally the day the state was created (see *War of Independence*). In less than thirty years, Egypt had fought four major wars with Israel—in 1948, 1956, 1967, and 1973—and an unofficial but very costly War of Attrition in 1968–1970.

There also was nothing in Sadat's background to suggest any tendencies toward moderation. As a young man, he had been pro-Nazi—indeed, during World War II he spied for the Germans—and well into the 1970s his public declarations were repeatedly characterized by crude antisemitism. In a particularly notorious speech before Egyptian army officers on April 25, 1972, Sadat declared; "The most splendid thing our prophet *Mohammed, God's peace and blessing on him, did, was to evict [the Jews] from the entire Arabian peninsula. . . . I pledge to you that we will celebrate on the next anniversary, God willing and in this place with God's help, not only the liberation of our land but also the defeat of the Israeli conceit and arrogance so that they must once again return to the condition decreed [for Jews] in our holy book: 'humiliation and wretchedness.' . . . We will not renounce this [teaching]."

But Sadat *did* renounce Mohammed's antisemitic teaching. Why? It appears that he felt that the heavy casualties Egyptian troops had inflicted on Israel in the *Yom Kippur War had assuaged Arab dignity for the humiliating loss suffered in the 1967 *Six-Day War. "We have recovered our pride and self-confidence after the October, 1973 battle," was how Sadat put it in his autobiography, *In Search of Identity*.

Sadat also was realistic enough to recognize that Israeli military power was so substantial that the only hope for regaining Egyptian territory was through peaceful negotiations. Strangely enough, Sadat did not launch his peace initiative during the many years the more "dovish" *Labor party was in power. He waited until the "hawks"—the *Likud party of Menachem *Begin—came to power. Sadat probably concluded that only the Israeli right wing had the clout to get the *Knesset to approve the territorial concessions he wanted in exchange for a formal peace treaty. Had Labor tried to get such a treaty approved, Begin might well have sabotaged it.

An important fact that is rarely noted probably also influenced Sadat's decision to journey to Jerusalem: In June 1977, the Israeli government literally saved Sadat's life. Israeli General Yitzchak Chofi, director of the Mossad (Israel's CIA), uncovered evidence of a plan to assassinate Sadat directed by Libyan dictator Muammar Qaddafi. Chofi transmitted this information to Begin, who arranged—through the good offices of King Hassan of Morocco—a meeting between Chofi and Lieutenant General Kamal Hassan Ali, the director of Egypt's military intelligence. Chofi supplied Ali with detailed information on the assassins' names and their whereabouts in Cairo. Egyptian authorities immediately arrested the men and found extensive incriminating documents on them. There is no doubt, as historian Howard Sachar has noted, that Sadat was "genuinely grateful."

A few months later, Sadat announced in Egypt that he was willing to go to the Israeli Knesset itself to talk to the Israelis about peace and the return of the territories. Many people thought he was grandstanding, but when Prime Minister Begin extended him an official invitation, Sadat immediately accepted. He arrived in Israel on November 19, 1977. Israeli troops stood ready at Ben-Gurion Airport, lest the whole initiative prove to be false and the plane doors open to reveal armed Egyptian troops prepared to gun down the assembled Israeli leadership. Among the Israeli leaders who greeted Sadat at the airport was Israel's former prime minister, Golda *Meir. She had but one question for the Egyptian president: "What took you so long?"

In his speech to the Knesset, Sadat essentially offered peace in exchange for land. But it wasn't only the Egyptian territories lost in the Six-Day War that Sadat wished to see restored. If there was to be a real peace, he said, the Israelis must withdraw to their pre-1967 borders and grant the Palestinians a homeland.

In September 1978, U.S. President Jimmy Carter hosted both Begin and Sadat at Camp David, outside Washington, D.C. During thirteen torturous days of negotiations, Begin agreed to return all Egyptian land conquered in 1967. In the final accords, the perennially thorny issue of the Old City of Jerusalem was sidestepped, and Begin agreed to negotiate the issue of Palestinian autonomy on the West Bank. In return, Sadat announced full recognition of Israel, including an exchange of ambassadors and full trade relations. A year later, Sadat and Begin shared the Nobel Peace Prize.

In the aftermath of Sadat's peace initiative to Israel, virtually the entire Arab world broke off diplomatic relations with Egypt. An enraged Qaddafi renewed his call for Sadat's murder. Four years later, on October 6, 1981, during a military parade celebrating the anniversary of the Yom Kippur War, Sadat was assassinated by Muslim extremists who were opposed to his recognition of Israel and committed to a fundamentalist Muslim Egypt.

Since Sadat's death, under the rule of Hosni Mubarak, the Israeli-Egyptian peace has held firm—though unquestionably it has been a "cold peace." There is still little trade between the two countries, and few diplomatic exchanges. Nonetheless, the peace survived, even during Israel's 1982 war in Lebanon, and during Israel's war with Hezbollah in Lebanon in 2006. Apparently, the notion that a "cold peace" is preferable to a "hot war" has been accepted by Egypt's leaders.

SOURCES AND FURTHER READINGS: Howard M. Sachar, A *History of Israel*, vol. 2, pp. 41–81; the story of the Mossad's saving of Sadat's life is found on pp. 46–47. Moshe Dayan, *Breakthrough: A Personal Account of the Egyptian-Israel Peace Negotiations*.

174

PEACE NOW/*SHALOM AKHSHAV*

PEACE NOW IS TO THE ISRAELI LEFT WHAT *GUSH EMUNIM IS TO THE Israeli right, a permanent pressure group not affiliated with any one political party. The organization was founded in 1978 by 350 reserve army officers. Fearing that Prime Minister Menachem *Begin's negotiations with Egyptian President Anwar Sadat might fail because of Begin's refusal to make territorial compromises, they wrote him a public letter: "A government that prefers . . . the Land of Israel above peace would cause us grave difficulties of conscience. . . . A government that prefers settlements across the *Green

Line [i.e., the *West Bank] to the ending of the historic conflict . . . would raise questions for us about the justice of our cause." The letter's signatories included their army ranks after their names to forestall criticism that they were left-wing pacifists. The organization they founded became known as Peace Now (*Shalom Akhshav* in Hebrew).

That September, as Begin prepared to negotiate with Sadat and U.S. President Jimmy Carter at Camp David, 100,000 Israelis gathered at a Peace Now demonstration in Tel Aviv to urge Begin to conclude a settlement with Egypt.

Since the completion of the Egyptian-Israeli peace treaty, Peace Now's primary focus has been on the West Bank. The organization opposes ongoing Jewish settlements in these territories, and urges Israel to recognize Palestinian rights to a national existence.

Peace Now was in the forefront of the opposition to the Lebanese War (see next entry). On September 25, 1982, it organized the largest political demonstration in Israel's history. Approximately 400,000 Israelis, more than 10 percent of the country's Jewish population, assembled in Tel Aviv to demand a formal governmental investigation into the massacres that had occurred several days earlier at the Palestinian camps of Sabra and Shatilla in Beirut, Lebanon (see next entry). A few months later, in February 1983, a Peace Now activist, Emil Grunzweig, was murdered by a hand grenade thrown into a crowd of marchers. Although the murder was an act of an individual criminal, it profoundly shook Israelis of all political persuasions and drew temporary attention to the growing bitterness and violence in Israeli political life.

Despite its continuing insistence on Israel being open to exchanging land for peace, in 2006 Shalom Akhshav supported Israel's war against Hezbollah in Lebanon, noting that Israel was acting out of self-defense against an enemy who wished to destroy her.

SOURCES: Susan Hattis Rolef, ed., *State of Israel*, p. 249; William Frankel, *Israel Observed*, pp. 91–92.

175

LEBANESE WAR

"ALL WARS," AMERICAN HISTORIAN ARTHUR SCHLESINGER, JR., HAS said, "are popular in a democracy for the first thirty days." So indeed was the case with Israel's war in Lebanon, the longest war in Israel's history. At its outset, almost all Israelis identified with the war's goal: elimination of *PLO terrorists from southern Lebanon. Lebanon's south borders Israel's Galilee, an area that had often been subjected to PLO shelling and terrorist incursions. Indeed, the official Israeli name for the war was "Operation Peace in the Galilee." But within Israel, the war was commonly known as "Arik's war," after Israeli Defense Minister Ariel "Arik" Sharon, who hoped that a temporary Israeli conquest of Lebanon, accompanied by a destruction of the PLO forces there, would lead to a peace treaty between Israel and Lebanon.

Israel quickly learned that Lebanon was a singularly difficult country in which to try to impose her will. Lebanon is divided among a variety of hostile religious and ethnic groups: Maronite Christians, Sunni Muslims, Shiite Muslims, Druse, and Palestinians. "They hate each other more than they love their own children," is how one Lebanese official has explained the nonstop warfare these groups have long waged against each other.

In the late 1970s, Israel entered into an informal alliance with the Maronite Christians, who justifiably felt that they were being edged out of power by Muslim and Palestinian factions. At the time, Syria had recently sent troops into Lebanon; the Maronites also feared that the Syrians would take over the entire country. This, too, was not a baseless fear, for Syria always has maintained that Lebanon is part of her territory. Even before Menachem *Begin became prime minister, his predecessor, Yitzchak Rabin, sent weapons to the Phalangists (one of the Maronite forces) and also arranged for Israel's army to give them military advice.

At the same time, PLO bases in southern Lebanon frequently shelled Israeli settlements in northern Israel. On June 3, 1982, the Israeli ambassador to England, Shlomo Argov, was seriously wounded in a terrorist attack in London. The would-be assassins were sent by Abu Nidal, an Arab terrorist leader who was himself at war with Yasir Arafat and the PLO. Nonetheless, Israel responded by bombing PLO bases in Lebanon: The PLO in turn shelled Israeli settlements in the north, and Israel responded by invading Lebanon.

At the war's inception, the Israeli cabinet authorized a brief and limited strike. Israel's army was to go into Lebanon to a depth of only twenty-five miles, and to eliminate—presumably in a few days—the PLO bases there. But Israel found it easier to get into Lebanon than to get out and, under Sharon's guidance, the war escalated. Within several weeks, Israel occupied Beirut, the only time the Israeli Army has ever occupied an Arab capital. The army's sojourn there was an unhappy one. Thousands of PLO fighters in the city were dispersed among tens of thousands of Palestinian civilians living in the city's refugee camps. Thus, any Israeli attempt to bomb PLO fighters inevitably meant killing civilian Palestinians as well. Some days Israel did bomb PLO strongholds, and found herself roundly condemned throughout the world. Throughout this period, Yasir Arafat, the PLO leader, was holed up in a bunker inside Beirut. To Israeli Prime Minister Menachem Begin, Arafat's bunker recalled the bunker in which Adolf *Hitler isolated himself during the last months of World War II: He wanted to see Arafat and his forces destroyed forever.

Shortly after the Israeli takeover of Beirut, the PLO asked international diplomats to arrange their evacuation from Lebanon. Israel permitted the PLO to leave. At one point during the evacuation, an Israeli soldier had Arafat in his rifle sights. Nonetheless, he did not shoot him; Israel would have faced intolerable international censure if one of her soldiers had killed the PLO chief.

The PLO's departure from Lebanon was a significant victory for Israel. It was quickly followed by another piece of good news; the election of Bashir Gemayel, a Maronite Christian, as the country's new president. Gemayel promised that he would sign a peace treaty between Israel and Lebanon when he took office. Days before his inauguration, however, he was assassinated by pro-Syrian terrorists. The Phalangist forces that Gemayel headed were outraged by the loss of their leader. The following day, Israeli troops in West Beirut allowed Phalangist soldiers into the Palestinian refugee camps of Sabra and Shatilla, ostensibly to disarm the PLO terrorists remaining in the camps. Instead, the Phalangist soldiers carried out a massacre, killing about eight hundred people, very few of whom were PLO fighters. Around the world, Israel was held responsible for the massacres: To this day, most Arabs believe that it was not the Phalangists who carried out the massacres, but the

Israeli Army. An exasperated Prime Minister Begin said, "Non-Jews kill non-Jews and the Jews are blamed."

Inside Israel, there was horror at what the Phalangists had done in Sabra and Shatilla. Pressure built for Begin to appoint a special commission to assess whether Israel bore a moral responsibility for the attack by allowing the Phalangist troops into the camps, and whether Israeli army officials were passive even when they learned a pogrom was being carried out. Begin strenuously resisted appointing such a commission.

On Saturday night, September 25, 1982, at the largest political demonstration in Israel's history, 400,000 Israelis gathered to demand the appointment of a commission to investigate the events at Sabra and Shatilla. Begin finally acquiesced and announced the formation of a commission headed by Supreme Court Justice Yitzchak Kahan. The report concluded that "the Jewish public's stand has always been that the responsibility for such deeds falls not only on those who rioted and committed the atrocities, but also on those who were responsible for safety and public order." Several leading army figures were forced to resign, and Ariel Sharon was forced to relinquish his position as minister of defense.

More than 650 Israeli troops died in Lebanon, almost as many as had died in the *Six-Day War. In the case of Lebanon, however, when the war ended Israel had very little to show for it, and it was not until 2000 that Prime Minister Ehud Barak withdrew the final Israeli troops from southern Lebanon. Most significantly, in light of Israel's goal in starting the war, the PLO was not destroyed or driven out of existence. To this day, the Lebanese War remains the most controversial conflict in Israel's history.

SOURCE AND FURTHER READING: Ze'ev Schiff and Ehud Ya'ari, *Israel's Lebanon War.*

176

THE LAW OF RETURN

"Who Is a Jew?"

THE VERY FIRST LAW PASSED BY THE *KNESSET AFTER ISRAEL'S ESTAB-lishment was the Law of Return (*Khok ha-Sh'vut*), which guarantees all Jews the right to emigrate to Israel and claim immediate citizenship. The Law of Return is probably the most popular piece of legislation ever passed by the Knesset: It remains to this day a source of extraordinary psychological comfort to Jews throughout the world—even for those with no intention of ever moving to Israel.

Israel came into being only a few years after six million Jews were murdered in the Holocaust, and all Jews are aware that if the Law of Return had been in effect in 1939, these people would have been saved. Even today most Jews see Israel as their ultimate refuge in case their host countries turn anti-semitic.

Strangely enough, it is this very popular Law of Return that has led to extraordinarily acrimonious fights within the Jewish community. The law has one basic, simple component; it welcomes any Jew to come live in Israel. However, it does not answer a very basic question: "Who is a Jew?"

During the 1960s, a man named Daniel Rufeisen came to live in Israel and applied for immediate citizenship under the Law of Return. Although no one questioned that Rufeisen was born a Jew, his application was questioned because he now was a Catholic monk. Rufeisen argued that though he was a Christian by religion, he still considered himself Jewish. The case finally went before the Israeli Supreme Court, which ruled that under the Law of Return, Rufeisen could not be regarded as a Jew. In the court's opinion, the law was intended to provide a homeland for those who had not broken faith with the community of Israel; Rufeisen's conversion to another religion placed him outside this category. Instead, he was invited to remain in Israel and apply for citizenship under normal regulations—after three years' residence.

Most Jews had no problem with the Rufeisen ruling. The controversy surrounding the question of "Who is a Jew?" flared up years later, both in Israel and in the United States. Throughout Israel's history, the Orthodox rabbinate, which controls religious affairs in Israel, repeatedly ruled that people who were converted to Judaism by *Reform and *Conservative rabbis were not Jewish. In the 1970s and 1980s, Orthodox political parties attempted to have this policy formally written into Israeli law; a Jew would be defined as one who was either born to a Jewish mother, or who had converted to Judaism "according to halakha [Jewish law]." Since the Orthodox rabbinate in Israel also had sole responsibility for deciding which conversions had been carried out "according to halakha," the law's passage would have effectively guaranteed that non-Orthodox converts would be regarded as non-Jews in Israel.

In fact, the continuing controversy has greater emotional than practical significance; few Reform or Conservative converts to Judaism make *aliyah to Israel. The issue's emotional resonance, however, is great. Currently, an estimated 40 percent or more of American Jews intermarry. Most parents whose children intermarry hope that their son- or daughter-in-law will convert to Judaism. When conversions do occur—approximately five to ten thousand gentiles convert in the United States annually—they are overwhelmingly performed by Reform or Conservative rabbis. Tens of thousands of American Jews, therefore, understood that the "Who is a Jew?" bill being considered by the Knesset would be a formal denial of the Jewishness of their grandchildren, even when the child's mother had undergone a Reform or Conservative conversion. Hundreds of thousands of Reform and Conservative Jews were infuriated that the Knesset, composed largely of secular Jews, and non-Jews (as well as Orthodox Jews), was considering a law declaring non-Orthodox conversions to be invalid.

On several occasions, would-be Israeli prime ministers, hoping to entice the religious parties to join their coalition, promised to pass the "Who is a Jew?" law, with its fateful words, "according to halakha." Yet to date, no such law has passed. Government officials are well aware that the price Israel would pay for enacting such legislation would be a very serious, if not permanent, rupture with a large percentage of America's Jews. How ironic that the Law of Return—a law that symbolizes to all Jews their personal stake in Israel's existence—has led to bitter fighting and divisions within the Jewish community.

177

NETUREI KARTA

WHEN THE ZIONIST MOVEMENT WAS FOUNDED BY THEODOR *HERZL in the 1890s, most of organized Jewry opposed it. Reform Jews feared that Zionism's insistence that Jews should live in Palestine would call into question Jewish loyalties to their native lands. Most Jews on the left, socialists and Bundists (a Jewish socialist party founded in 1897, the same year as the *First Zionist Congress), saw Zionism as a parochial, chauvinistic movement. Orthodox leaders, by and large, rejected Zionism as a secular movement, and argued that God, in His own good time, would restore the Jews to Israel; any action to hasten such a restoration defied God's will.

After the Nazi rise to power, however, almost all committed Jews became Zionists; the price of not having a Jewish homeland was just too great. Nonetheless, one group of religious Jews, who styled themselves "The Guardians of the City [of Jerusalem]"—*Neturei Karta*, in the Aramaic words of the Talmud—continued to oppose Zionism. The Neturei Karta regarded *Ben-Gurion and the Zionist leadership as heretics, the moral equivalents of the ancient idolaters condemned by the Torah. In the years before Israeli statehood was declared, they repeatedly affirmed their preference for being ruled by either the British or the Arabs; what mattered most to them was that they not be ruled by Jews less religious than they.

Today, the Neturei Karta—who consist of several hundred families—are largely concentrated in the Jerusalem neighborhood of Mea Shearim, with some members living outside of Israel. This section of the city, which houses other ultra-Orthodox Jews as well, is generally remembered by tourists for its prominent signs ordering women to attire themselves in modest clothing. One routinely sees missives posted on Mea Shearim's walls denouncing the government, equating Zionism with Nazism, and condemning local residents by name for various "sins," such as installing televisions in their homes.

The Neturei Karta regard themselves as the only Jews who have not been corrupted by Zionism. They reserve great scorn for the ultra-Orthodox Agudat Yisrael party, which sits in the Israeli *Knesset and solicits government funding for its schools. The Neturei Karta, on the other hand, do not accept any money from the Israeli government, and do not vote in Israeli elections. Representatives of the movement would sometimes meet with Yasir Arafat, head of the *PLO, and publicly express their preference for Israel being turned into a Palestinian state.

Until his death in 1979, the movement regarded Rabbi Joel Teitelbaum, the *rebbe* of the Satmar *Hasidim in Williamsburg, Brooklyn, as its spiritual leader. The *Rebbe's* views were in line with the Neturei Karta's. For example, in discussing Israel's extraordinary victory in the *Six-Day War, Rabbi Teitelbaum acknowledged that miracles had taken place, but, in his opinion, they were performed by Satan, not God.

For many years, the head of the Neturei Karta in Jerusalem was a man named Amram Blau; in the last years of his life, he found himself ostracized by many of his former followers when he married a French convert to Judaism.

Anti-Zionists often point to the Neturei Karta as proof that one can oppose Israel's right to exist without being antisemitic. However, pointing to the Neturei Karta to prove anything about Jewish life is pointless. This tiny group is as unrepresentative of Jewish views as the snake-handling sects of West Virginia—which pass around poisonous snakes during church services—are of Christianity. Nor indeed do the Neturei Karta accept the anti-Zionist contention that the Jews are only a religion, and not a people. Furthermore, they do believe in the right of the Jews to the land of Israel and trust that someday God will send the *Messiah—dressed no doubt in the distinctive garb of the Neturei Karta—to restore all the Jews there.

SOURCES AND FURTHER READINGS: Yerachmiel Domb, "Neturei Karta," in Michael Selzer, ed., *Zionism Reconsidered*, pp. 23–47; Domb, ed., *Transformation: The Case of the Neturei Karta*; Emile Marmorstein, *Heaven at Bay: The Jewish Kultürkampf in the Holy Land*. In December 2006, there was great outrage throughout the Jewish world when photographs appeared of six Neturei Karta members in attendance at a Holocaust denier's conference in Iran (see page 427). Unlike other attendees at the conference, the Neturei Karta members did not deny that the Holocaust has occurred. Their presence presumably was to show identification with people who, like themselves, hated Zionism and the state of Israel. At the time, many members of the Neturei Karta sharply criticized the behavior of the "Teheran Six." (See *The Jewish Week*, December 22, 2006, pp. 1 and 14–15.)

178

ASHKENAZIM AND SEPHARDIM

THROUGHOUT ISRAEL'S HISTORY, HER GREATEST EXTERNAL PROBLEM
has been the refusal of her Arab neighbors to accept her existence (see, however, *Camp David*). Her greatest internal problem has been the relations
between Ashkenazim and Sephardim—Jewish citizens from different lands.
Although *Ashkenaz* in Hebrew means "Germany," the term *Ashkenazim* generally refers to Jews coming from Europe. While *Sefarad* in Hebrew means
"Spain," the term *Sephardim* refers to Jews coming from the Arab world.
Because the two communities have some differing religious traditions, they
are governed in religious matters by two Chief Rabbis, one Sephardic, the
other Ashkenazic.

It is estimated that worldwide, some 80 percent of all Jews are Ashkenazim, and only 20 percent Sephardim; in the United States Ashkenazim
outnumber Sephardim by an even greater percentage. In Israel, however,
about half of the Jewish population is Sephardic. This in itself is a relatively
recent development. When Israel was established in 1948, its population was
largely Ashkenazic. In Israel's early years, however, the only Jews who
migrated there in large numbers, aside from Holocaust survivors, came from
the Arab countries. At the time, many Israelis expressed fears that their society was being "overrun by primitive elements." On occasion, Israeli newspapers in the 1950s compared the Sephardic arrivals—particularly those from
Morocco—unfavorably with Palestinian Arabs.

Many Sephardim who arrived in Israel did have low levels of secular education and earned their living as manual laborers. Their lives were made
more difficult by the fact that Israel was a poor country at the time, and very
limited in what it could do to upgrade the newcomers' standard of living.
Tens of thousands of Sephardim were sent off to live in *ma'abarot* (primitive
transit camps). David Levy, a Moroccan Jew who was later to become Israel's
foreign minister, recalls that his father, who was a carpenter in Morocco, lost
his tools in transit to Israel and lacked the money to replace them. For the
Levy family the whole experience was traumatic. "I saw my father's terrible

tragedy . . . ," he told a reporter, "how in a few weeks he declined from a strong father respected by his family and community into a welfare case dependent on charity. . . ."

Yet, while tensions between religious and nonreligious Israelis and between Israel's Jewish and Arab citizens increase, the Ashkenazic-Sephardic rift is slowly but steadily diminishing. About one third of all Israeli marriages today are between Ashkenazim and Sephardim. Though Ashkenazim still outnumber Sephardim at Israeli universities, the gap is lessening there also. In 1978, Yitzchak Navon was elected Israel's first Sephardic president, and in 1983, the army appointed Moshe Levy as its first Sephardic chief of staff.

However, there remains a strong undercurrent of anger many Sephardim feel toward Ashkenazim, stemming largely from their bitter experiences during the 1950s. They recall how their parents were sprayed with disinfectants when they arrived in Israel, to ensure that they not bring in diseases, and how Sephardic family values and traditions were often denigrated as "primitive" by the largely secular Ashkenazic leadership.

At times, the depths of this bitterness are frightening. In the early 1970s, I was eating in a Jerusalem restaurant at a time when a high German official was visiting the country. A group of Sephardim were seated near me, discussing whether or not it was appropriate, in light of the Holocaust, to welcome a German official to Israel. One man said, "He is no enemy of ours. It was Ashkenazim the Germans killed, not Sephardim." The story of course is not characteristic, just illustrative.

In 1981, Libyan-born *Knesset member Ra'anan Na'im scored points with his backers by announcing that he couldn't stand gefilte fish. In turn, one periodically hears Ashkenazic tirades about how the Sephardim have ruined Israel. Israeli journalist Ze'ev Chafets reports that at the conclusion of a speech he gave in New York, an Israeli correspondent in the audience said: "My grandparents came to the land of Israel as pioneers," she said, "to build a just, beautiful place. My family fought for the country, sacrificed for it. And now [the Sephardim] . . . the kind of people who want [Prime Minister Menachem] *Begin, have ruined my country. These are brutal, vulgar people, people who have introduced violence and intolerance. I hate their values. . . . They've stolen my homeland. I feel like a stranger in my own country."

Despite the harsh and frightening rhetoric, it is fair to say that each succeeding generation of Israelis identifies more as Israelis than as Ashkenazim or Sephardim. However, Ashkenazic Jews remain on the average more affluent and educated than Sephardic Jews.

Sephardic Jews often incline to "hawkish" views on Arab-Israeli relations, perhaps because of the brutal discrimination they suffered under Arab rule. The Sephardim, therefore, are regarded as a backbone of support for Israel's right-wing *Likud party.

SOURCES AND FURTHER READINGS: Ze'ev Chafets, *Heroes and Hustlers, Hard Hats and Holy Men*, pp. 113–141; Susan Hattis Rolef, ed., *Political Dictionary of the State of Israel*, pp. 83–85; Daniel Elazar, *The Other Jews: The Sephardim Today*.

ETHIOPIAN JEWRY

THE BLACK JEWS OF ETHIOPIA WERE KNOWN FOR CENTURIES AS *Falashas* ("landless people" in Amharic), a word the community itself despises. Ethiopian Jews call themselves *Beta Yisrael* (House of Israel).

According to an old Jewish tradition, Ethiopian Jews are descended from the Israelite tribe of Dan. Whatever their antecedents, they clearly split from the rest of the Jewish people at a very early time. As a result, though conversant with the Bible, Ethiopian Jews were totally ignorant of the *Talmud, and their practice of Judaism differed greatly from the rest of Jewry. They were particularly scrupulous about the Torah laws concerning separation between couples during the woman's menstrual period, and built their villages in Ethiopia near small rivers that could serve as *mikva'ot* (singular, *mikveh), ritual baths.

The Ethiopian Jews' ignorance of talmudic Judaism caused many Orthodox rabbits to question their Jewishness. If the Ethiopians are to be considered age-old Jews, it challenges a basic tenet of Orthodoxy: that the *Oral Law of the Talmud dates back to the time of Moses. Why else would the Ethiopians be conversant with the Torah and not the Oral Law? Nonetheless, in 1973, Israel's Sephardic (see preceding entry) Chief Rabbi, Ovadia Yosef, ruled that the Ethiopians are to be regarded as Jews. That decision was opposed by many rabbis, primarily Ashkenazic.

That the Ethiopians had always been Jews seems very likely, since throughout their history the community had preserved seven words in

Hebrew, one of them *goy*. That in the remote villages of Ethiopia, this group divided the world into two camps, themselves and the *goyim* (the other nations) seems to be convincing proof of their Jewishness.

Uncertainty over their religious status, coupled with their relatively benign treatment under the administration of Ethiopia's emperor Haile Selassie, led the Israeli government and world Jewry to pay little attention to the Ethiopian Jews throughout the 1950s and 1960s. After the emperor was overthrown during the 1970s, Ethiopia turned Marxist, and the Jews' situation deteriorated rapidly. The country's leadership was strongly anti-Israel. In addition, Ethiopia was experiencing massive famines, and increasingly the Jews' neighbors blamed their economic problems on them.

Israel quietly started to smuggle out as many Jews as it could. The Ethiopian government officially did not permit or acknowledge this exodus—Ethiopia was too identified with the Arab cause to openly allow Jewish residents to emigrate to Israel—but it did tolerate it. Unfortunately, when journalists started reporting that thousands of black immigrants were arriving in Israel (the program was known as "Operation Moses"), the Ethiopian government immediately stopped the emigrations. A terrible situation ensued that was reminiscent of the Holocaust. Thousands of Ethiopians living in Israel were totally cut off from immediate family members they had left behind; they knew only that the situation in Ethiopia was very bad. Many of the Ethiopians who made it to Israel looked like Holocaust survivors themselves, famished and emaciated.

As time went on, an increasing number of Israeli rabbis acknowledged the Ethiopians as Jews. Nonetheless, to forestall any possible questions about their status, the Ethiopians were encouraged to undergo pro forma rituals of conversion to Judaism. Since the males had been circumcised at birth, all that was demanded was that a symbolic drop of blood be drawn from the male organ, and that men and women alike immerse themselves in a *mikveh*.

Early Ethiopian arrivals generally followed these procedures without protest. In his book, *Heroes and Hustlers, Hard Hats and Holy Men*, Israeli journalist Ze'ev Chafets relates a story told him by a senior Israeli political figure. In one town where many Ethiopian Jews migrated, the Ashkenazic and Sephardic rabbis competed as to who would convert them: "[A group of Ashkenazic rabbis] brought all the men together, pricked each one to draw a drop of blood, shook their hands and welcomed them to the Jewish people. The Ethiopians didn't really understand what it was all about, but they accepted it good-naturedly. After all, it was a small enough price to pay. But then, the next day, the Sephardic rabbis showed up. Once again they took out the equipment for drawing blood. Of course the rabbis didn't know that the Ashkenazic rabbis had been there first, but when they found out, they decided to go ahead with their ceremony anyway. The Ethiopians went along with it, too, but by this time they were getting a rather strange notion about Judaism. Every day," the Israeli official who told Chafets this story concluded, "another prominent rabbi wanting to take blood from their penis—that can be disconcerting, you know?"

In recent years, a growing number of Ethiopian Jews have refused to convert, arguing that to do so would imply that they were not Jewish until now; in addition, it would be a slur on the memory of their deceased ancestors.

SOURCES AND FURTHER READINGS: Wolf Leslau, *Falasha Anthology*; Louis Rapoport, *Redemption Song: The Story of Operation Moses*.

180

YORED/YERIDA

YORED (HEBREW FOR ONE WHO EMIGRATES FROM ISRAEL) IS A HIGHLY charged word. It literally means "one who descends." The term accurately describes the general contempt many Israelis have for a Jew who leaves the country to live elsewhere.

Nonetheless, despite the highly censorious attitude toward emigrants, an estimated 10 percent or more of Israel's population left the country during its first six decades. (Such a percentage applied to the United States would mean almost thirty million emigrants.) Most Israelis who leave have one destination in mind: the United States. There are an estimated 200,000 former Israelis living in the New York area, and an additional 80,000 in Los Angeles, though demographers note that such statistics are notoriously unreliable. There are also substantial numbers of former Israelis in South Africa, Australia, Great Britain, West Germany, and elsewhere throughout Western Europe.

American Jewry often has an ambivalent response to *yordim*. On the one hand, they are regarded as fellow Jews; on the other, they are seen as "deserters" from the Jewish homeland. The generally secular *yordim* usually shun involvement in Jewish communal life, and maintain social ties only with each other. A major reason for large-scale Israeli emigration to the United States is that it is a country of extraordinary economic opportunity, while Israel has a more bureaucratic economy. Not infrequently, in the past, Israeli taxi drivers would come to the States and become—taxi drivers. But, they maintained, they earned a better living driving a cab in New York than in Tel Aviv. Israeli Prime Minister Golda *Meir told of a waiter who once came over to her at a New York luncheon and whispered in Hebrew that there was ham in the dish she had been served. When she asked him how he knew Hebrew, he told her he was an Israeli. And what work had he done in Israel, she asked. He had been a waiter, he responded.

However, not all *yordim* come from Israel's lower classes. An increasing number of Israeli academics and professionals find it impossible to find job opportunities in their specialized disciplines in a country as small as Israel.

Another factor encouraging *yerida* is the perennial Israeli-Arab conflict. All Israeli men must serve in *Tzahal* (the Israeli Army) from the age of eighteen to twenty-one. Even after being discharged, they do extensive reserve duty until their forties. Although not often cited by *yordim* as a reason for leaving—perhaps they are embarrassed to acknowledge it—this, too, is a significant reason many Israelis leave.

During times of economic recession, the lines of Israelis applying for visas at the American embassy in Tel Aviv increase dramatically. In the 1960s, an Israeli cartoonist drew a mordant picture of a terminal at Ben-Gurion Airport. "Will the last Israeli to leave," the caption read, "please turn off the lights?"

A strange but very common feature among *yordim* is an unwillingness to acknowledge that they have permanently left Israel. Having themselves been raised to regard *yordim* as deserters, Israeli emigrants often insist that they will return to Israel in a few years, after they have made enough money. No one has yet figured out exactly how much money is enough, and as a result most *yordim* remain in the countries to which they have emigrated.

SOURCE AND FURTHER READING: Moshe Shokeid, *Children of Circumstances: Israeli Emigrants in New York.*

THE ASSASSINATION OF PRIME MINISTER
YITZCHAK RABIN, 1995

BEFORE 1995, THE LAST NOTED INSTANCE IN WHICH A JEWISH LEADER
was murdered by a fellow Jew happened more than 2,500 years ago. In the
aftermath of Judea's unsuccessful revolt against Babylon in 586 B.C.E. (see *Jeremiah*), the Babylonians appointed Gedaliah ben Akhikam governor of the Jewish province. A radical nationalist named Yishma'el, who despised the governor
as a lackey of Babylon, assassinated Gedaliah. Ever since, the day on which he
was killed (the third of *Tishrei*) has been observed as a fast day on the Jewish calendar (see *Minor Fast Days*).

On November 4, 1995, Yigal Amir, an Israeli law student and a political
and religious zealot, convinced that Israeli Prime Minister Yitzchak Rabin was
a traitor to the Jewish people, murdered Rabin at the conclusion of a pro-
peace rally in Tel Aviv. It had been Amir's intention also to kill Foreign Minister Shimon Peres, but when Peres departed the rally shortly before the prime
minister, Amir decided to content himself with the murder of Rabin alone.

The assassination came during a period of intense internal conflict within
Israel, following the Rabin-approved Oslo (Norway) Accords, in which Israel
recognized for the first time the right of Yasir Arafat and the *Palestine Liberation Organization to negotiate on behalf of the Palestinians. Rabin had
agreed to turn over Gaza and the city of Jericho and its environs to Palestinian self-rule. It was understood that, if the arrangement worked out, much
more of the West Bank would be entrusted to Palestinian rule. The accords
were signed by Rabin, Peres, and Arafat under the eye of American President
Bill Clinton at a widely attended and televised White House ceremony in
September 1993.

The Israeli right wing viewed Rabin's concessions to the PLO as catastrophic. Large parts of the historical land of Israel would be ceded to the very
people the Israeli right did not believe would ever accept a Jewish state. On
the far right, a campaign of delegitimization against Rabin was launched.

Signs were routinely held up at demonstrations denouncing the prime minister as a traitor, a particularly malevolent accusation given that Rabin, in his capacity at the time as military chief of staff, was widely credited as the architect of Israel's victory in the 1967 *Six-Day War, which, ironically, had brought the West Bank and Gaza under Israeli rule. Other marchers held up signs depicting Rabin in an SS uniform. On the day prior to the assassination, Leah Rabin, the prime minister's wife, claimed a picketer outside their residence had shouted, "Next year, we'll hang you like they hanged Mussolini and his mistress."

After Rabin's murder, a thorough police investigation revealed that Amir had acted alone, with some assistance from his brother and a friend. Amir was later sentenced to life imprisonment. During the months following the killing, rumors—which were neither fully substantiated nor proven false—circulated that some rabbis on the far right had given advance approval to Rabin's murder. They allegedly had done so on the grounds that Rabin's willingness to give Israeli land to enemies of the Jews branded him, according to Jewish law, a *rodef* (a pursuer), whom one is permitted to kill as an act of self-defense.

The assassination traumatized Israelis and Jews throughout the world, much like the 1963 killing of President John F. Kennedy shook and haunted Americans. In the murder's aftermath, one heard many calls in Israel for more restrained rhetoric, and for the nondemonization of one's political opponents. Whether these calls will have a long-lasting effect is not yet apparent.

SOURCES: Ehud Sprinzak, *Brother Against Brother: Violence and Extremism in Israeli Politics*; the picketer's threat against Leah Rabin is cited in Michael Karpin and Ina Friedman, *Murder in the Name of God*, p. 101.

182

CAMP DAVID, 2000
The Second Intifada

CAMP DAVID, THE PRESIDENTIAL RETREAT IN MARYLAND, WAS THE scene of the tense but ultimately triumphant negotiations between Israeli Prime Minister Menachem Begin and Egyptian President Anwar Sadat, with guiding and prodding by American President Jimmy Carter (see pages 352–353). Some twenty-three years later, the same site was the scene of a far less happy negotiation. During the final months of President Bill Clinton's administration, the president grew determined to try and bring about an enduring solution to the seemingly insoluble Israel/Palestinian conflict. Clinton hoped to effect a two-state solution, while forging an enduring peace between the two sides.

To Clinton, the goal seemed highly doable. Israeli Prime Minister Ehud Barak was eager to end Israel's permanent conflict with the Palestinians and most of the Arab world, while Chairman Yasser Arafat, head of the Palestinian Authority, had announced his recognition—at least in theory—of Israel's right to exist.

Toward this end, Clinton invited both Barak and Arafat, along with their negotiating teams, to Camp David. Unfortunately, the meeting was a fiasco, primarily, it seems, because Arafat was not prepared to make peace with Israel. At Camp David, he sometimes conveyed the impression that he had no desire to be there. Later, it was revealed that Arafat and most of the Palestinian leadership thought the time was not ripe to make peace with Israel. During the conference, Arafat made the startling, and false, claim that Jerusalem had never been the site of the Jewish temple. In addition to being untrue, the statement was itself a tip-off that the conference was going to fail: A leader anxious to make peace with his adversaries does not go to a conference to publicly deny his opponents' most basic historical claims and core beliefs. (Imagine, for example, that Barak had stated at the conference that prior to Israel's creation, there had never been an Arab entity known as the

Palestinian people; rather, the Palestinians had simply been regarded by others, and by themselves, as southern Syrians. Indeed, during the 1930s and 40s, the people referred to as "Palestinians" were the Jews living there. Even though such a statement would have been historically accurate, it would have been rightly perceived as provocative and animated by a desire to torpedo the conference.)

At Camp David, Barak made the most far-reaching offer ever proposed by an Israeli leader; it involved giving up Israel's control over Gaza and about 95 percent of the West Bank so that a Palestinian state could be established in that area. Barak made it clear that he also was willing to entertain the possibility of ceding control of parts of the Old City of Jerusalem (in effect, redividing the city) so that the Palestinians could establish their capital there. Barak's critics on the left claimed that although his offer was more generous than those made by any preceding Israeli prime minister, his obvious disdain for, and coldness toward, Arafat helped prevent the negotiations from succeeding.

Some Israelis were pleased with how far Barak was willing to go to make peace, others were horrified by how much he was willing to cede, and were particularly upset by his openness to dividing Jerusalem, the Jewish people's holiest city.

Israelis on both the right and the left were surprised, and many shocked, when Arafat denounced Barak's offers as inadequate and left the conference. Israelis were not the only ones taken aback by Arafat's rejection. Prince Bandar bin Sultan, Saudi Arabia's longtime ambassador to the United States, said at the time: "If Arafat does not accept what is available now, it won't be a tragedy, it will be a crime." (Two years later, in 2002, the Saudis announced—and the Arab League approved—an offer of peace and the establishment of normal relations with Israel in exchange for Israel withdrawing from all the land captured in the Six-Day War and for permitting Palestinian refugees "the right of return." Obviously, such a right if exercised by many Palestinians would lead to Israel becoming a binational, and eventually Arab, state, and no longer a Jewish homeland. In addition, the Saudi plan did not insist on Palestinian action against terrorism during the negotiations, a detail that mattered greatly to Israel given that as of 2006 Hamas was ruling in Gaza and Hezbollah in southern Lebanon and both groups denied Israel's right to exist, and supported terrorism against her. Nonetheless, both Prime Minister Olmert and Foreign Minister Livni declared that the plan had "positive elements.")

S. Daniel Abraham, a successful American businessman (he was the founder of Slim-Fast) and an energetic and tireless supporter of the Palestinian/Israeli peace process (see his *Peace Is Possible*), had ongoing ties with Arafat and many other Arab leaders, with much of the Israeli leadership (most notably former Prime Minister Shimon Peres and future Prime Minister Ariel Sharon), and with President Clinton. In the aftermath of the Camp David debacle, and while attending the United Nations Millennium Conference in New York, Barak called Abraham and told him that President Clinton had asked him to meet with Arafat. Olmert wanted the meeting to be low-keyed, and he asked Abraham to "do me a favor and arrange a dinner with Arafat and myself." After the Camp David debacle there had been much talk about the lack of personal chemistry between Barak (who, in general, does not seem to have an easy way with people) and Arafat. Abraham quickly contacted Arafat who agreed to the meeting. At the subsequent dinner and meeting, which occurred several weeks later in Israel, the two men seemed to achieve a more amicable relationship; attendees recall leaving the encounter hopeful that the negotiations between the Israelis and Palestinians could be renewed.

A few days later, however, Ariel Sharon, the former Israeli general and soon-to-be prime minister, and a man of a more hawkish disposition than Barak, visited the Temple Mount in Jerusalem, which was under the day-to-day administration of the Muslim religious leadership. While his visit proceeded uneventfully, within a day violent anti-Israel rioting erupted throughout Palestinian areas. It soon escalated into what became known as the Second Intifada, a years-long campaign punctuated by suicide bombings directed, mainly, against civilian targets in Israel. Characteristic of these attacks was the March 27, 2002, bombing of the Park Hotel in the Israeli city of Netanya. Hamas engineered the attack in which thirty Israelis, celebrating a Passover Seder, were killed. During the Second Intifada, well over a thousand Israelis were murdered. Israel responded by building a "security fence" around much of the country, the goal of which (and it was indeed largely successful) was to make it far harder for terrorists to infiltrate into Jewish areas.

At the Intifada's beginning, many people, both Arabs and Jews, attributed the uprising to Sharon's provocative visit to the Temple Mount. It subsequently became clear that the Palestinian leadership had been arranging for such rioting since the collapse of the Camp David talks, and had seized upon Sharon's visit as the right opportunity. Thus, on September 29, 2001, the first anniversary of the Intifada, Marwan Barghouti, the leader of the Tanzim, young militants loyal to Arafat, declared: "When Sharon visited the Al-Aqsa

Mosque, this was the most appropriate opportunity for the outbreak of the Intifada."

Oddly enough, when Sharon was elected in February 2001, as Barak's successor, he proved open to withdrawing from some of the areas controlled by Israel, believing that in some instances such withdrawal would benefit Israel's security. Indeed, Sharon was the architect of the 2005 Israeli disengagement from Gaza, an act which caused him to be denounced by the Israeli far right with the same sort of venom once reserved for Barak (see following entry).

In recent years, Israeli diplomat Dore Gold, author of *The Fight for Jerusalem*, and Israel's former permanent ambassador to the United Nations, has forcefully argued that no matter what settlement Israel reaches with the Palestinians, a division of Jerusalem will be a catastrophe for Israel, and will turn the city itself into the next great victim of global jihad. Gold argues that particularly now, with the flourishing of a highly intolerant anti-Western and fundamentalist Islam, only Israel can be trusted to treat fairly and equitably the religious sites of Christianity, Islam, and Judaism. In turn, Gold's critics from the "peace camp" maintain that without territorial concessions in Jerusalem—for example, giving up the Arab neighborhoods where Jews in any case don't venture—there is no chance of a peace agreement with the Palestinians.

SOURCES AND FURTHER READINGS: By 2007, Carter had turned sharply antagonistic toward Israel, as reflected in both the title and the content of his book *Palestine: Peace Not Apartheid*.

183

ISRAEL'S DISENGAGEMENT FROM
GAZA, 2005

IN AUGUST, 2005, ISRAEL CARRIED OUT THE EVACUATION—IN MANY cases, it was a forced removal—of almost 9,000 Jewish residents of Gaza. The area, which borders the Mediterranean Sea between Egypt and Israel, had originally come under Israeli rule during the 1967 Six-Day War; a few years later, Israeli Jews started to establish small, highly productive, settlements there. In 2004, Israeli Prime Minister Ariel Sharon, long regarded as a hawk, decided on a unilateral withdrawal from Gaza (there were no negotiations concerning the withdrawal with Palestinian officials). Sharon apparently hoped that this step would liberate Israel from ruling over more than 1.3 million angry and resentful Palestinians, and might ultimately help bring about an eventual settlement of the Israeli/Palestinian conflict. While a majority of Israelis supported the withdrawal, a significant minority on the right vociferously opposed it. They didn't wish to give up any territory under Israeli rule (particularly land on which thousands of Israelis lived), and feared that the withdrawal would serve as a precedent for Israel to cede—in later negotiations with Palestinians—large areas of the West Bank (Judea and Samaria). Notwithstanding the heartbreaking scenes of Israelis being forced out of beautiful towns they had built and developed, the withdrawal began in mid-August, 2005, and was finished before the end of the month.

Israel's move constituted its most dramatic territorial concession since its withdrawal from the Sinai almost thirty years earlier (see entry 166). The Sinai withdrawal was carried out within the context of a peace treaty with Egypt, one which guaranteed that country's recognition of Israel and which led to an exchange of ambassadors between Egypt and Israel. In contrast, the withdrawal from Gaza was undertaken unilaterally (in the face of a Palestinian leadership that was hostile to Israel) and no similar improvement in Palestinian-Israeli relations accompanied this initiative.

Indeed, it quickly became clear that the withdrawal was understood very differently by Israelis and Palestinians. For most Israelis, the intended message was that Israel was committed to resolving its dispute with the Palestinians, in part by ceding land that it did not deem vital to its security. What most Israelis hoped was that by leaving Gaza, Israel would set off a process that would result in a stable two-state solution, whereby the Palestinians would rule themselves, and prevent any terrorism against Israel from the territories that they would control.

The majority of Gaza residents understood the withdrawal very differently. To them, it proved that terrorism worked, and that the years of suicide bombings directed against Israeli civilians and soldiers demoralized Israelis and forced them to make the sort of territorial concessions that they would not otherwise have made.

Thus, while most Israelis hoped and assumed that the withdrawal would strengthen the hands of the more moderate figures within the Palestinian world by showing that moderation would gain concessions from Israel, the actual effect of the Israeli disengagement was precisely the opposite. Within months of Israel's evacuation, the Palestinians voted into power Hamas, a militant Islamic organization committed to terrorism and Israel's destruction. Israelis of a more liberal bent argued that Sharon had done nothing to strengthen Palestinian moderates. For example, rather than releasing Palestinian prisoners through negotiation with the more moderate Abu Mazen, president of the Palestinian Authority, Sharon ended up doing so as a response to Palestinian violence.

Did Israel then err in leaving Gaza? This subject continues to be hotly debated within the country. Those on the right generally view the withdrawal as a serious error. For one thing, they argue, it was a grave injustice to the almost 9,000 Israelis forced to give up their homes and villages in Gaza. For another, they believe that the withdrawal weakened Israel's security, gave an enormous impetus to the growth of Hamas, and set the stage for a serious escalation of Palestinian rocket attacks from nearby Gaza into Israel. The town of Sderot alone has been hit on an ongoing basis by well over a thousand rockets. And in July 2006, in an act that shocked Israel, Palestinians from Gaza stole into Israel, kidnapped Israeli soldier Gilad Shalit, and then brought him into Gaza where he has been held ever since, despite massive military and diplomatic efforts by Israel to have him freed.

More liberal Israelis generally believe that although the withdrawal has not yet brought about a reduction of tension, Israel is still better off without Gaza. Their argument is largely based on the conviction that it is not strategically or morally beneficial for Israel to rule over 1.3 million angry, resentful Palestinians. In this view, such a situation led to large numbers of Israeli troops permanently deployed to protect a small number of Jews who constituted only a little more than one-half of one percent of Gaza's population. In addition, Israeli liberals argue, Gaza has no significant strategic or religious significance to Israel. Thus, more "dovish" Israelis hope that in the long run the withdrawal from Gaza will lead to an increased separation between Israelis and Palestinians, and that this separation will ultimately lead to a decline in terrorism and hatred, and one day, perhaps, to peace.

And who is correct? As of early 2007, it is fair to say that the jury is still out.

HEZBOLLAH'S WAR AGAINST
ISRAEL, 2006
An Iranian Nuclear Bomb?

THE 2006 WAR BETWEEN HEZBOLLAH AND ISRAEL BEGAN ON JULY 12, when Hezbollah—a Shiite political and paramilitary organization, based in Lebanon and largely funded by Iran and also aided by Syria—started firing Katyusha rockets at towns along Israel's northern border. Then, with Israel distracted by this attack and its forces spread thin, Hezbollah infiltrated over a hundred fighters across the Israeli border who murdered three soldiers and kidnapped two others. Hezbollah had started out in the early 1980s as a pro-Iranian terrorist group; it attacked the U.S. Marine Corps barricades in Beirut in 1982, killing over 200 U.S. servicemen. Now it has reorganized itself into a regular army.

Prime Minister Ehud Olmert quickly denounced Hezbollah's attacks and the kidnapping of the soldiers as "an act of war." He also directed much of his ire at the Lebanese government for doing nothing to rein in Hezbollah (it would be as if the United States government permitted an anti-Canadian terrorist group to operate from American soil, and did nothing to stop it from murdering and kidnapping Canadian soldiers and firing missiles at Canadian cities). In fact, two members of Hezbollah served in the Lebanese cabinet; many others were members of the Lebanese parliament.

At first, some high Lebanese governmental officials did distance themselves from Hezbollah's actions, but within a week, Lebanese President Emil Lahoud promised to stand by Hassan Nasrallah, Hezbollah's leader, a man whose hatred for Israelis and Jews is Nazilike. On one noted occasion, Nasrallah had even encouraged Jews throughout the world to move to Israel on the grounds that "If [Jews] all gather in Israel, it will save us the trouble of going after them worldwide."

During the war's first days, Israel's air force attacked Hezbollah strongholds in southern Lebanon, along with some non-Hezbollah sites (such as

Beirut's international airport where the government allowed rockets and missiles intended for Hezbollah to be brought in; other Lebanese sites used to aid Hezbollah were bombed as well, and Lebanon, which Hezbollah had used as a training ground, suffered large-scale damage from the Israeli bombings). Hezbollah's dozens, and sometimes hundreds, of daily missile attacks resulted in at least 500,000 Israelis fleeing their homes in northern Israel to live in other parts of the country until the war ended; meanwhile, Israel's attacks on Lebanon, particularly in the south, resulted in the dislocation of an even greater number of Lebanese civilians.

More than forty Israeli civilians died in the Hezbollah attacks, and hundreds of others lost their homes. However, when Israel started to bomb the sites from which the missiles were fired, she ran into further difficulties—and into widespread condemnations. Hezbollah was firing many of its missiles not from its own camps (which it did not want targeted by Israel), but from Lebanese villages, which its soldiers entered, sometimes against the will of the residents, sometimes with their cooperation. Israel, needing to stop the attacks, had no choice but to bomb the missile sites, but inevitably doing so sometimes resulted in the unintended killing of some innocent Lebanese. In an attempt to minimize civilian casualties, Israel often dropped leaflets in the areas that were to be bombed warning people to evacuate.

Though the Arab world and much of Europe condemned Israel for these attacks, Alan Dershowitz, the well-known Harvard law professor and pro-Israel supporter, noted at the time that it was not Israel who was responsible for the deaths that ensued: "A bank robber who takes a teller hostage and fires at police from behind his human shield is guilty of murder if they [the police], in an effort to stop the robber from shooting, accidentally kill the hostage. The same should be true of terrorists who use civilians as shields from behind whom they fire their rockets. The terrorists must be held responsible for the deaths of the civilians, even if the direct physical cause of death was an Israeli rocket aimed at those targeting Israeli citizens" (see "The Arithmetic of Pain," *Wall Street Journal*, July 19, 2006).

The moral cogency of Dershowitz's argument was borne out by a rarely noted detail: When innocent Lebanese were killed, Israelis were deeply disturbed at the news, while Hezbollah members were happy, hoping that the deaths of the Lebanese would lead to more hatred against Israel in the Arab world (which indeed did happen).

Within days of the war's onset, when it became apparent that the Israeli air force could not bomb Hezbollah into submission, ground troops were sent into Lebanon. They frequently were forced to engage Hezbollah troops in hand-to-hand combat. 119 Israeli soldiers were killed during the conflict, including Roi Klein, an officer who became famous after jumping on a grenade in order to save the lives of the other soldiers under his command and standing alongside him. As Klein jumped, he shouted out *Sh'ma Yisra'el*, the Jewish credo, "Hear O Israel, the Lord is our God, the Lord is One," the final words a Jew is supposed to say prior to dying. Another soldier who died was Noam Mayerson, a twenty-three-year-old reservist (and the son of my dear friend and college roommate, Haim, and his wife, Gila), who was to be married just a month after his death. Mayerson's tank was hit by a Cornet missile used by Hezbollah and given to them by Syria. Syria in turn had acquired the missiles from Russia with the proviso that they were never to be supplied to terrorist groups, a condition Syria obviously, and often, ignored.

More than other wars fought between Israel and her neighbors, the summer 2006 conflict with Hezbollah prompted a new type of fear among Israelis. I was sitting in New York with two of my dearest friends, an Israeli couple who live in Jerusalem, when we learned that Haifa—Israel's third largest city, and the city in which their daughter was studying—had been bombed, with buildings destroyed. They reacted with the level of fright and shock with which an American would react if he learned that a foreign enemy had succeeded in bombing Seattle or Boston. Part of the shock for Israelis was that Hezbollah, a terrorist group and not a state, had been supplied by Iran and Syria with weapons normally found only among the army of a sovereign nation. During the month-long conflict, Hezbollah fired some 4,000 rockets into Israel, an estimated 23 percent (about 900) of which hit built-up areas, primarily civilian in nature.

On August 11, 2006, the U.N Security Council passed Resolution 1701, which was approved by both the Lebanese and Israeli governments. Among other provisions, it called for Hezbollah's disarmament, Israel's withdrawal from Lebanon, the return of the kidnapped Israeli soldiers, and the deployment of an enlarged U.N. Interim force in southern Lebanon (UNIFIL). With the resolution's passage, the fighting came to an end.

In the weeks following the war, it became clear that Israel had not achieved the goals it hoped to accomplish. Ehud Goldwasser and Uriel Regev remained in captivity (no information has been released about them), while Hezbollah, though badly damaged, was by no means destroyed. Even worse from Israel's perspective, Hezbollah gained increased political strength in Lebanon, precisely because it had taken on the strongest army in the Middle East and had not been destroyed. Further, shortly after agreeing to the terms of the U.N. resolution, and subsequent to Israel's departure from Lebanon, the Lebanese government and UNIFIL both stated that they would do nothing to disarm Hezbollah. In the months since the war ended, it is estimated that Hezbollah has been resupplied with the weapons it lost during the war; it now appears to be back to its pre-war strength of 13,000 or more missiles.

In April 2007, a government-appointed commission of inquiry, headed by retired judge Eliyahu Winograd, issued a report sharply criticizing Prime Minister Olmert, Defense Minister Amir Peretz, and then military chief-of-staff, Lt. General Dan Halutz, for entering the war unprepared and for conducting it in a reckless manner. The report reinforced the general consensus in Israel that that the war had neither been planned carefully nor fought wisely. Yet few Israelis could adequately answer the question: "What else can Israel do but fight when a terrorist group committed to its destruction sends troops to murder soldiers and successfully fires rockets at Israeli cities?"

A POSTSCRIPT ON IRAN AND ITS ATTEMPT TO
PRODUCE NUCLEAR WEAPONS

During the 2006 war, Iran, as noted, supplied Hezbollah with an almost unlimited supply of rockets to fire at Israeli cities and civilians. This behavior emanated out of the Iranian leadership's obsessive hatred for Israel. Indeed, Iranian President Mahmoud Ahmadinejad has long and publicly made it known that he wishes to "wipe Israel off the map."

Unfortunately, considerable evidence exists that the often-expressed desire of high Iranian government officials, starting with Ayatollah Khomeini, to destroy Israel is not mere rhetoric. In 1998, when my friend Dore Gold was appointed Israel's permanent ambassador to the United Nations, I asked him what he saw as the most important goal of his work. "To stop Iran from getting nuclear weapons," was his immediate response. I was shocked, for I had assumed that he would focus on winning diplomatic support for Israel in its ongoing conflict with the Palestinians. No one in the circles in which I turned was talking about Iran procuring nuclear weapons. Only later did I learn that among people in the know, fear about Iran's nuclear potential was deep and might already have affected the conduct of Israel's foreign policy. In an article published in *The New Republic* (February 5, 2007), Israeli historian

Michael Oren, and journalist Yossi Klein Halevi revealed that upon assuming office in 1992, the late Israeli Prime Minister Yitzhak Rabin had been deeply alarmed by the reports he received from military intelligence about the Iranian nuclear program. He concluded that a nuclear Iran would pose the one existential threat to which Israel would have no credible response.

Rabin experienced immense frustration when he tried to warn the Clinton administration of how catastrophic a nuclear Iran would be for Israel and the West, and found himself met with incredulity, as well as with naïve and foolish reassurances from the CIA that Iran's nuclear program was for civilian, not military, purposes. Oren and Halevi believe that Rabin's reversal of his long-stranding opposition to negotiations with the PLO (which subsequently led to the Oslo Accords) came about because of his conviction that Israel needed to neutralize what he defined as "its inner circle of threat" (the enemies on its borders), so that it could prepare for, and focus on, its eventual conflict with Iran, which he termed "the outer circle of threat." In other words, Rabin believed that the most significant threat to Israel's survival came from Iran and its development of nuclear weapons.

This threat now terrifies many Israelis. A recent poll revealed that some 27 percent of Israelis would consider leaving the country if Iran succeeds in developing nuclear weapons. In 2007, the Israeli historian Benny Morris wrote a frightening article entitled, "The Second Holocaust Will Not Be Like the First," in which he speculated on how an Israel-obsessed Iran will one day dispatch four or five nuclear weapons toward the Jewish state. Given Israel's small size, there will soon be "no more Israel," as a million or more Israelis will be killed and millions of others will be seriously irradiated.

The Israeli hope to forestall such a catastrophe is for the U.S. and the European Union to impose aggressive economic sanctions against Iran, which will force the country to choose between developing nuclear weapons and economic stability. If such sanctions don't work, the sole remaining option is a series of preemptive military strikes of the major sites (modeled on Israel's 1981 destruction of a nuclear reactor in Iraq that was being primed to produce an atom bomb)—dozens of such sites are spread throughout Iran—at which the Iranians are developing their bomb. Such an attack could set back the Iranian production of the bomb for many years, with the hope that in the interim a less evil government—and certainly a government less obsessed with destroying Israel—will come to power.

PART SEVEN

The Holocaust

185

ADOLF HITLER (1889–1945) AND NAZISM

Mein Kampf
Aryan Race
Nuremberg Laws

EVEN MORE THAN HE WAS A RACIST, WAS ADOLF HITLER AN ANTISEMITE. Although the Japanese were clearly of a different race from the Germans, he had no compunction about forging a military alliance with them and declaring Japan's yellow-skinned citizens to be "honorary Aryans." Yet Hitler would never have declared the Jews to be "honorary Aryans," even if it would have suited Germany's interests to do so. Well before he started murdering Jews, he harassed some of Germany's greatest scientists so much, only because they were Jewish, that they emigrated. Ironically, one of them, Albert *Einstein, came to the United States and played an important role in bringing about the creation of the atom bomb.

What was the source of Hitler's unbending hatred of the Jews? Though voluminous biographies of Hitler have been written, no one can be sure. There is no evidence, for example, that Hitler ever had bad personal experiences with Jews; indeed, a Jewish doctor worked heroically to save his mother's life. It is clear, however, that Hitler's hatred was directed as much against Judaism and its notion of God as against the Jews themselves. It was the Jews, he explained to onetime compatriot Hermann Rauschning, who brought their "tyrannical God," and His "life-denying *Ten Commandments" into the world; it was against these Ten Commandments, with their myriad prohibitions, that Hitler wished to wage war. Only if he murdered every Jew in the world, he concluded, could he hope to extirpate fully the Jewish idea of one God and one moral standard.

In Hitler's view, Jews maintained their "Jewish ideas" even when they converted to Christianity, or when they abandoned Judaism and became Communists. In this, Hitler differed therefore from almost all the antisemites who preceded him; he saw Christianity and Marxism as thinly disguised Jewish creations that were intended to subvert Germany's Aryan values.

But what were *Aryan* values? The only fully consistent value that scholars have been able to isolate is a hatred of Jews and Judaism. Aside from that, Aryanism seemed to consist of little more than an emphasis on healthy blond bodies, on the development of citizens who would unflinchingly obey one supreme leader—a *Führer*, as the Germans called Hitler, and a backward-looking ideology that glorified primordial man and his relationship with his land and culture. His ideology was less a systematic philosophic system than an emotional response to a world in which Germany had suffered.

Germany, of course, bore major responsibility for starting the First World War, and at the war's end, the victorious Allies punished her by making her pay high reparations to the countries against whom she had fought. The Allies also severely limited the size of Germany's army. These reparations, negotiated at Versailles, France, were unceasingly denounced by Hitler as "humiliating" to Germany.

Hitler started the Nazi party with a few dozen members, but the numbers increased rapidly, a testament to both his charisma and his ability to capitalize on the widespread economic dislocation and depression that spread throughout Germany in the 1920s and 1930s. Although the Depression was a worldwide phenomenon, its effects in Germany were particularly devastating, as millions were thrown out of work. Several years earlier (1923), millions more had had their life savings wiped out by a runaway inflation that reached astronomic proportions. In one infamous case, a man who had been making payments into a pension fund for twenty years was paid off; with the money he received he could only buy two loaves of bread. In so drastic an economic climate, Hitler's dual message, "I will give you jobs" and "It is the Jews who stabbed Germany in the back," found receptive ears.

By 1923, several hundred Germans followed Hitler in a violent revolt in Munich against the Bavarian government. Hitler led the attempted coup at a large beer hall where the state commissioner was speaking, and the insurrection became known as the Beer Hall Putsch. The revolt was quickly put down, and to Hitler's good fortune, Germany's leaders were of far milder temperament than he. He was sentenced to five years in prison, and paroled after only nine months. While incarcerated, he wrote his political testament, *Mein Kampf (My Battle)*. In later years, particularly after Hitler came to power, the book made him wealthy (by 1939, it had sold some 5.2 million copies). Every couple who married, for example, were expected to buy a copy.

A common myth has it that Hitler came to power in Germany by blaming all the country's ills on the Jews. Shortly after the war ended, however, political scientist Eva Reichmann documented that Hitler came to power largely on economic issues. Indeed, he somewhat downplayed his antisemitism during political campaigns—in any case, all Germans knew he hated the Jews—because he feared that the intensity of his Jew-hatred would alienate middle-class voters, who would dismiss him as a political crank. Hitler never won an absolute majority of the vote in a democratic election, but in July 1932, the Nazis received more votes than any other party in Germany. In January 1933, German President Paul von Hindenburg appointed Hitler chancellor. Within half a year, democracy had been outlawed in Germany.

Once in power, Hitler moved against the Jews almost immediately. He singled out certain professions in which Jews were heavily represented, such as the law, and excluded them from working in these fields. He declared a government-sponsored boycott of Jewish-owned stores, and had Nazi troops stand in front of the stores to warn away would-be customers. In retrospect, those German Jews who directly suffered from the Nazis' early antisemitic actions were often the lucky ones, since being singled out for discrimination caused many of them to leave Germany while it was still possible. A neighbor of my family in Brooklyn told us that in 1934, when he had been beaten up on a bus by a man in a Nazi uniform, not a single passenger intervened to help him. He left the country within days.

About half the Jews remained in Germany, however, hoping the situation would improve. Years later a bitter Jewish joke aptly summarized the situation: "The pessimists went into exile, and the optimists went to the gas chambers."

In 1935, after two years in power, Hitler escalated his anti-Jewish policies. The Nuremberg Laws deprived all Jews of German citizenship, and marriages and sexual relations between Jews and Germans were declared illegal. Subsequent Nazi legislation forbade non-Jews from working for Jews, and prohibited Jews from studying with non-Jews.

The most prominent German philosopher of the twentieth century, Martin Heidegger, endorsed Nazism and was appointed rector of the University of Freiburg. Heidegger apparently fell into the "some-of-my-best-friends-are-Jews" category of antisemite, since the only woman he apparently ever loved was the Jewish political scientist Hannah Arendt (see *Eichmann Trial*). (He even told his wife that Arendt was the love of his life.)

Between 1941 and 1945, murdering the Jews was as great a priority for

Hitler as winning World War II, if anything, greater. When the Nazis were forced to withdraw from Greece in 1944, almost all German trains were diverted to that country to bring back the troops; not a single train, however, was diverted from those that were taking Jews to death camps. When the Germans ordered a ban on all nonmilitary rail traffic, in order to free all trains for a summer offensive in southern Russia, the only trains exempted from this order were those transporting Jews to the death camps. Hitler's policy of murdering the Jews actually was destructive to the Nazi war effort, since it would have been more pragmatic to use them for slave labor. Yet, even those who were used for slave labor were so mistreated that many of them died within months. When a Nazi general, Kurt Freiherr von Grienanth, suggested in September 1942 that "the principle should be to eliminate the Jews as promptly as possible without impairing essential war work," he was demoted by the chief of the Gestapo, Heinrich Himmler, who denounced his proposal as a subtle effort to help the Jews.

In retrospect, it appears that antisemitism was the dominant passion of Hitler's life. In his final message to the German people, delivered the day before he committed suicide, he appealed to them to carry on a "merciless resistance against the world-poisoner of all nations, international Jewry."

SOURCES AND FURTHER READINGS: Hitler's statements to Hermann Rausch-ning are recorded in Armin Robinson, ed., *The Ten Commandments*, pp. IX–XIII. See also Alan Bullock, *Hitler: A Study in Tyranny*; John Toland, *Adolph Hitler*; Lucy Daw-idowicz, *The War Against the Jews*. Perhaps the finest reference work on the Holocaust is the four-volume *Encyclopedia of the Holocaust*, edited by Israel Gutman; it greatly helped me in the preparation of this section. Hitler's insistence on sending Jews to death camps, even when he desperately needed the trains transporting them for military purposes, is cited in Dawidowicz, *The War Against the Jews*, pp. 141–142. The story of Nazi General von Grienanth, who was demoted for suggesting that Jews be used for slave labor instead of being immediately murdered, is told in Dawidowicz, *A Holocaust Reader*, p. 85. See also Eva Reichmann, *Hostages of Civilisation: The Sources of National Socialist Anti-Semitism*.

As regards Hitler, American political commentator George Will has mordantly noted: "There is only one thing that can be said for Hitler's vicious life: It refutes the theory that only vast, impersonal forces, and not individuals, can shake the world."

186

YELLOW STAR

ON THE DAY (APRIL 1, 1933) THE NAZIS DECLARED A NATIONAL BOYCOTT of all Jewish-owned stores, they painted the word *Jude* (German for "Jew") inside large yellow Stars of David on the windows of Jewish stores. They did so to alert potential Aryan customers that the store they were about to enter was owned by a Jew. This infamous yellow star, which Jews were subsequently forced to sew in a prominent place on their garments, became the most visible symbol of Nazi antisemitism.

Few people know that it was not the Nazis who created the notion of special yellow badges for Jews; that distinction belongs to the ninth-century Abbassid caliph Haroun al-Raschid, who ordered Jews to wear a yellow belt at all times. Some four centuries later, at the Fourth Lateran Council in 1215, the Catholic Church regulated that Jews living under Catholic rule wear distinctive clothing as well. Fortunately, political authorities subsequently stopped enforcing this regulation.

The Nazis enforced the yellow badge with a vengeance: By 1941, all Jews six years old and up had to wear on their chests at all times a yellow six-pointed star with the word *Jude* inscribed on it. In Poland the Nazis issued a warning that Jews, including Jewish-born converts to Christianity, who did not wear the yellow badge on both the front and back of their clothing would be subject to execution.

In April 1933, in response to the Nazi boycott of Jewish stores, Robert Weltsch, a German Zionist leader, took advantage of the limited freedom of the press still existent in Germany to publish an editorial entitled, "Wear the Yellow Badge with Pride." Weltsch urged his fellow Jews not to allow their self-image to be debased by Nazi propaganda. To Weltsch the only offense of the Jews was their failure to heed Theodor *Herzl's Zionist message. "It is not true [as the Nazis say] that the Jews have betrayed Germany. If they have betrayed anything, they have betrayed themselves and Judaism." By all accounts, Weltsch's editorial, with its message of Jewish self-affirmation, greatly strengthened the morale of German Jewry.

After the war, however, Weltsch confided to friends that he regretted ever having written the piece. Instead of encouraging Jews to retain a sense of pride, he said, he should have urged them to flee Germany and save their lives. Of course, in 1933 when Weltsch wrote his editorial, no one could have guessed that the Nazis intended a murderous *Final Solution to their "Jewish problem."

In every European country the Nazis conquered, legislation was passed obligating Jews to wear a star sewed on to their clothes. In countries where antisemitism was prevalent, such as Poland, this badge enabled Poles to immediately identify Jews and push them off the long lines of people waiting to buy food.

SOURCES AND FURTHER READINGS: "Badge, Jewish," in Israel Gutman, ed., *Encyclopedia of the Holocaust*, vol. 1, pp. 138–143; Abraham Katsh, trans. and ed., *The Warsaw Diary of Chaim A. Kaplan*, p. 46.

MUNICH, 1938

Appeasement

THE MOST CHARITABLE THINGS THAT CAN BE SAID ABOUT BRITISH Prime Minister Neville Chamberlain are that he desperately wanted peace, and that he was a fool.

In 1938, Adolf *Hitler announced his intention to annex the Sudetenland, a part of Czechoslovakia in which about three million people of German ancestry lived. There was a tremendous outcry against Hitler, particularly, but not exclusively, by the Czechs themselves. Chamberlain, however, saw no reason for panic. On September 27, 1938, the day before he left for Munich, Germany, to negotiate with Hitler, he declared in a British radio broadcast: "How horrible, fantastic, incredible it is that we should be digging trenches and trying on gas masks here because of a quarrel in a faraway country between people of whom we know nothing." In light of Chamberlain's speech, no one was surprised when two days later he acceded to Hitler's demand for the Sudetenland.

Unfortunately, the loss of this strategically vital territory made Czechoslovakia indefensible: Five months later, Germany occupied the entire country. A bitter joke of the period claimed that after Chamberlain agreed to Hitler's demand for Czechoslovakia, the German dictator asked him for the umbrella which he always carried with him.

"*That* I can't give you," Chamberlain said.

"Why not?"

"You see, Herr Hitler, the umbrella is mine."

Chamberlain did tell Hitler that the Western world would not tolerate any further territorial demands by the Germans, and Hitler assured him that he would make no more such demands. Chamberlain then returned to England and announced that he had brought back "peace in our time."

At least one major figure in England was not reassured by Chamberlain's words. Winston Churchill, the man who was to succeed Chamberlain as prime minister, denounced him as a naive appeaser who believed that he could buy Hitler's goodwill by giving in to his immoral demands. "You were given the choice between war and dishonor," Churchill declared. "You chose dishonor, and you will have war." In the pacifist climate then prevailing in England, Churchill's rhetoric only convinced many Englishmen that he was a maniacal hater of Hitler, and that he could safely be ignored.

Within the year, Hitler confronted Chamberlain with a new demand. He now wanted Poland and, in August 1939, he signed a nonaggression pact with the Soviet Union according to which the two powers secretly agreed to divide up Poland between them. When the Nazis marched into Poland on September 1, 1939, Chamberlain, finally realizing that Hitler wanted nothing less than to take over Europe, declared war.

Chamberlain retired eight months later, and Churchill was appointed the new prime minister.

Chamberlain's desire to appease Hitler was apparently due to his great fear of Germany's military strength, a fear that might well have been reinforced by both the United States ambassador to England, Joseph Kennedy (father of President John F. Kennedy), and America's aviation hero, Charles Lindbergh. Kennedy and Lindbergh were convinced (erroneously) that Germany was far stronger than England, and that resisting Hitler would lead to catastrophic results. Apparently, the two men's fears were communicated to Chamberlain prior to his departure to Munich.

Had Chamberlain confronted Hitler at Munich, it is hard to imagine that the results would have been more catastrophic than the fifty-five million people subsequently killed during World War II. Indeed, Hitler might well have backed down and been forced to limit his murderous activities to his own country.

Since World War II, the term "appeaser" has been applied to any politician who advocates appeasing rather than confronting evil, and the city name "Munich" has come to symbolize giving in to evil.

SOURCE AND FUTHER READING: Hedva Ben-Israel, "Munich Conference," in Israel Gutman, ed., *Encyclopedia of the Holocaust*, vol. 3, pp. 1081–1086.

KRISTALLNACHT (NOVEMBER 9–10, 1938)

DURING HITLER'S FIRST FIVE YEARS IN POWER, THE NAZIS DID A great deal to make the lives of Jews miserable. They revoked their citizenship, ejected Jewish students from German schools, boycotted Jewish stores, and banned Jews from a large number of professions. On occasion, individual Jews were sent to *concentration camps; the Nazis, however, had not yet created death camps and, remarkably enough, people were sometimes released from concentration camps and allowed to go home.

On the night of November 9–10, 1938, the Nazis' discriminatory policy toward the Jews changed to wholesale violence as they carried out the largest *pogrom in the history of the world. The official pretext for this action was the killing in Paris of a low-level Nazi diplomat by a seventeen-year-old Jewish boy, Herschel Grynspan. The boy's Polish-born parents had been deported several weeks earlier from Germany back to Poland. The Poles, however, refused to accept Grynspan's parents, along with seventeen thousand other Polish-born Jews deported by the Nazis. These unfortunate Jewish refugees were left to rot, penniless, in the no-man's-land separating Germany and Poland. Cut off from contact with his parents, Grynspan shot the German official in retaliation. When the man died, the Nazis decided to punish all of German Jewry for Grynspan's deed.

The pogrom that ensued became known as Kristallnacht, the night of the broken glass. On that night, the glass windows in almost every German syna-gogue, and in most Jewish-owned businesses, were shattered. Shattered, too, were the lives of almost all German Jews. Ninety-one Jews were murdered during Kristallnacht; thirty thousand more were arrested and sent to concen-tration camps, where hundreds of them died.

World leaders denounced the Nazi pogrom, and American Jewry reacted by forming the *United Jewish Appeal, which soon became the greatest fund-raising organization in Jewish history. The Nazis scoffed at the protests. They announced that Kristallnacht had been carried out in honor of the birthday of Martin *Luther, the sixteenth-century antisemitic religious reformer whom Hitler greatly admired. The Nazis also announced the imposition of a one-billion-mark fine against the Jews; they would be forced to pay for the damage the Germans had inflicted on their synagogues and property.

German Jewry now knew that their situation was hopeless. While large numbers of them had left Germany during the first five years of Nazi rule, half of the community of 600,000 had remained, hoping that Nazi anti-semitism would moderate. After Kristallnacht, they recognized that such thinking was illusory; between that event and the outbreak of World War II, less than ten months later, virtually every Jew in Germany tried to emigrate. Few countries, however, were willing to accept them. The British imposed a *White Paper in Palestine to ensure that it not become a haven for Jews flee-ing Hitler. Some of the Jews who tried to emigrate to the United States suc-ceeded; most did not. In Canada a high government official was asked how many Jewish immigrants the country could accommodate. "None is too many," he answered.

It is no coincidence that Kristallnacht brought about the formation of the United Jewish Appeal, later to become a major financial supporter of Israel. More than any other event of the time, Kristallnacht converted large num-bers of Jews into Zionists; the price of not having a Jewish state, they realized, was too, too high.

SOURCES AND FURTHER READINGS: Anthony Read and David Fisher, *Kristallnacht, the Nazi Night of Terror*. Regarding Canada's attitudes toward the Jews of Europe, see Irving Abella and Harold Tropper, *None Is Too Many: Canada and the Jews of Europe, 1933–1948*.

189

WHILE SIX MILLION DIED

S.S. St. Louis

HITLER BELIEVED THAT THE ALLIES NEVER BOMBED *AUSCHWITZ, OR the railroad tracks leading to the death camp, because deep down they were very willing to accept his murder of the Jews. Unfortunately, this belief was not entirely baseless. We now know that the Allies *did* bomb Auschwitz twice during the summer of 1944. By then, they had such accurate maps of the camp that they were able to direct their bombs exclusively at Buna, the synthetic oil factory where camp inmates did forced labor for the Nazis. The Allied planes did not bomb the crematoria, where the Nazis burned Jewish bodies, or the gas chambers where the Nazis murdered the Jews, though they were less than five miles away from the oil factory. A Jewish woman who was at Auschwitz when the Allied planes flew overhead told me that she and the other Jewish inmates prayed that they bomb the gas chambers, "even if it meant we might be killed."

That the Allied leadership was relatively indifferent to the fate of Jews in Hitler's Europe cannot be denied. England responded to Hitler's anti-semitic persecutions by issuing the *White Paper, which severely limited Palestine as a place to which fleeing Jews could emigrate. In the United States, public opinion polls documented that most Americans wanted to bar substantial numbers of Jewish refugees from entering the country.

No instance better summarizes America's, and President Franklin Delano Roosevelt's, reaction to the Jewish situation than the fate of the S.S. *St. Louis,* whose seemingly endless trip from Germany to North America and back became known as the "voyage of the damned."

The *St. Louis* set sail from Germany in May 1939, some six months after the Kristallnacht pogrom (see preceding entry). Aboard were 937 Jews, almost all of whom held visas for Cuba. While en route, there was a change of government in Havana, and the new administration refused to honor the visas. For days the *St. Louis* remained docked in Havana's harbor, as representatives of international Jewish organizations tried moral suasion, and then bribery, to influence Cuba's leaders to admit the ship—to no avail.

American Jews likewise tried to influence their government to admit the refugees, and also had no success; the United States would not accept any of the Jews on the ship. Indeed, in 1989, I spoke to a survivor of the *St. Louis* who told me that when the ship neared the territorial waters of Florida, the Coast Guard fired a warning shot in its direction.

Hitler, meanwhile, was ecstatic. For all that world leaders publicly attacked Nazi antisemitism, they clearly did not want the Jews any more than he did.

The *St. Louis* finally started its tragic journey back to Germany. In the interim, several European countries, England, Belgium, Holland, and France, agreed to admit the passengers. Those fortunate enough to be admitted to England survived the war, but those who received visas for Belgium, Holland, and France lived securely only for a short time. By 1940, the Nazis had occupied all three countries: It can be surmised that most of the passengers on the "voyage of the damned" were murdered in Nazi *concentration camps.

The sheer pointlessness of these deaths was underscored by the survivor of the ship mentioned previously (she and her family had been admitted to England). "We were so close to Havana we could see the city clearly," she told me. That tantalizing and agonizing recollection undoubtedly accompanied many of the former *St. Louis* passengers on their trips to the death camps.

One of the few heroes in the whole episode was the German captain of the ship, Gustav Schroeder, who resisted leaving Cuban and American territorial waters for as long as possible. En route back to Europe, Schroeder planned, if no visas were forthcoming, to scuttle the ship off England in the hope that the passengers would be picked up and rescued.

In 1967, Arthur Morse published his pathbreaking book, *While Six Million Died*, the first systematic account of FDR's and other Allied leaders' basic indifference to the Jews' fate. Since then, other historical studies have corroborated the essential correctness of Morse's thesis. Prior to the publication of the book, Roosevelt was generally regarded as a great friend and hero of the Jews. At a synagogue symposium in the early 1970s, I was asked my reaction to Roosevelt's behavior during World War II. It reminded me, I said, of a young boy who was standing on a low roof, and who was told by his father to jump down; "I'll catch you," the father promised him. Still, the boy was afraid. "Don't worry. Just jump," the father said, "I'll catch you." The boy jumped, and the father let him fall to the ground. He hurt himself and started crying hard. "That will teach you," the father said, "never to trust anyone."

SOURCES AND FURTHER READINGS: David Wyman, *The Abandonment of the Jews: America and the Holocaust 1941–1945*; Martin Gilbert, *Auschwitz and the Allies.* American and British Jews did lobby their governments to bomb Auschwitz. In Britain the Air Ministry and Foreign Office opposed such action, on the grounds that "technical difficulties" made the mission dangerous and impossible. Wyman has documented that this was a lie; indeed, by the spring of 1944, the Allies controlled the skies of Europe. In the United States, the War Department offered a similar response, arguing that the bombing of Auschwitz would divert air support "essential" to other forces engaged in decisive operations. Wyman has documented that this, too, was a lie. Because of the synthetic oil factory located at Auschwitz, the camp itself was a military target. And in 1944 the Allies repeatedly bombed seven other synthetic oil factories located within forty-five miles of Auschwitz, repeatedly flying over railroad tracks leading to the death camp during those missions. For reasons never clarified, but which seem to indicate an indifference to Hitler's Final Solution or support for it, the British Air Ministry, the British Foreign Office, and the United States War Department all refused to bomb Auschwitz, even though they knew that they had the technical ability to do so, and that thousands of Jews were being murdered daily in the camp.

A more sympathetic explanation of FDR's behavior can be found in Henry Feingold, *The Politics of Rescue: The Roosevelt Administration and the Holocaust, 1938–1945.*

As regards the S.S. *St. Louis*, see Gordon Thomas and Max Morgan-Witts, *Voyage of the Damned.* Concerning the ship's fate, historian Arthur Hertzberg has written: "It was not noticed at the time that the voyage of the *St. Louis* was an eerie, but tragic, reenactment of the very first journey of a boatload of Jews to America. In 1654, the *Ste. Catherine*, carrying twenty-three refugees from Recife, Brazil, had stopped in Cuba and been turned away, like the S.S. *St. Louis* almost three centuries later. But when the *Ste. Catherine* arrived in New York, [Governor] Peter Stuyvesant did not send out the 'Coast Guard' to force the ship away. He eventually agreed to let them stay, on the assurances by the Jews of Amsterdam that they would not become a public charge. In 1939, a more 'enlightened' government in America was infinitely less decent" (*The Jews in America*, p. 293).

190

EINSATZGRUPPEN

Babi Yar, 1941

THE NAZI MASS MURDER OF THE JEWS DID NOT BEGIN WITH THE *concentration camps and gas chambers. It began earlier, with the Nazi invasion of Russia in June 1941. Special army forces, known as Einsatzgruppen, accompanied the German troops. They had one mission: to round up and murder every Russian Jew they could find.

Unfortunately, Russian Jews were particularly vulnerable to the Nazi threat. Unlike the rest of world Jewry, they did not know how deeply the Nazis hated them. During the 1939–1941 peace pact between Stalin and *Hitler, the Soviet dictator had censored all news reports of Nazi anti-semitism. As a result, when the Einsatzgruppen arrived in Russian cities and issued orders for Jews to present themselves, most of them complied. Once they arrived at the designated gathering place, they realized almost immedi-ately that the Germans intended to kill them. But it was too late, for they were surrounded by heavily armed troops. The Nazis forced the Jews to dig large pits, in front of which they were shot. Bodies fell upon bodies, as row after row of people were murdered. The very few Jews who survived the mas-sacres generally were those who were wounded and left for dead.

It was later revealed that the Einsatzgruppen leadership was disproportion-ately made up of highly educated men. Of the twenty-four leaders tried as war criminals after World War II, well over half held graduate degrees. Nine were lawyers, while other professionals included an architect, two econo-mists, a professor, a banker, a dentist, and a clergyman.

The Nazi troops were generally aided by the local Russian populace, particu-larly in the Ukraine. Ukrainian antisemitism had a long and bloody history, going back to the *Chmielnitzki pogroms of 1648. Jews have long been so con-scious of Ukrainian antisemitism that when the Jewish mayor of New York, Ed Koch, was invited to be the marshal of the Ukrainian Day Parade in New York City, he jokingly commented to the Ukrainian leader of the parade, "It's nice to be in New York, where I can be the marshal of this parade. In the old country, I'd be running down the street, and you'd be running after me with a knife."

The most infamous Einsatzgruppen massacre was carried out in the Ukrainian city of Babi Yar, during *Rosh ha-Shana (the Jewish New Year), 1941. More than 33,000 Jews were rounded up and murdered in two days. They were buried in enormous pits, and for years afterward, blood spurted up from the earth.

After World War II, Babi Yar came to symbolize Soviet, as well as Nazi and Ukrainian, Jew-hatred. Russia's Communist leaders refused to allow the Jews to erect a monument to the victims of Babi Yar. Every year on the anniversary of the murders, groups of Jews would come and offer a prayer service on behalf of the martyrs. On fortunate occasions, Communist officials only dis-persed the service; at less fortunate times, they arrested the Jews.

In 1961 the Russian poet Yevgeny Yevtushenko wrote a moving poem about the victims of Babi Yar:

No gravestone stands on Babi Yar [the poem begins]
Only coarse earth heaped roughly on the gash. . . .

A year later, Dimitri Shostakovich set the poem to music. In 1974, a memorial to the victims of Babi Yar was finally erected, but its inscription did not mention that Jews were the victims at this terrible place. It is estimated that of the six million Jews murdered by the Germans, between one million and one and a half million were murdered by the Einsatzgruppen.

A DESCRIPTION OF AN EINSATZGRUPPEN MASSACRE IN THE UKRAIN-IAN CITY OF DUBNO BY A GERMAN ENGINEER AND EYEWITNESS, HERMANN GRAEBE "Without screaming or weeping these people undressed, stood around in family groups, kissed each other, said farewells, and waited for the sign from the SS man who stood beside the pit with a whip in his hand. I watched a family of about eight persons, a man and a woman both of about fifty, with their children of about twenty to twenty-four, and two grown-up daughters about twenty-eight or twenty-nine. An old woman with snow-white hair was holding a one-year-old child in her arms and singing to it, tickling it. The child was cooing with delight. The couple were look-ing on with tears in their eyes. The father was holding the hand of a boy about ten years old, and speaking to him softly; the boy was fighting his tears. The father pointed to the sky, stroked his head and seemed to explain something to him.

"At that moment the SS man at the pit started shouting something to his comrade. The latter counted off about twenty persons and instructed them to go behind the earth mound. Among them was the family I have just mentioned. I well remember a girl, slim with black hair, who, as she passed me, pointed to herself and said, 'twenty-three.' I walked around the mound and stood in front of a tremendous grave. People were closely wedged together and lying on top of each other so that only their heads were vis-ible. Nearly all had blood running over their shoulders from their heads. Some of the people shot were still moving. Some were lifting their arms and turning their heads to show that they were still alive. The pit was nearly two-thirds full. I estimated that it already contained about a thousand people. I looked at the man who did the shooting. He was an SS man who sat at the narrow end of the pit, his feet dangling into the pit. He had a tommy-gun on his knees and was smoking a cigarette. The people, com-pletely naked, went down some steps which were cut in the clay wall of the pit and clambered over the heads of the people lying there, to the place to which the SS man directed them; some caressed those who were still alive and spoke to them in low voices" (cited in Robert Payne, *The Life and Death of Adolph Hitler*, pp. 472–473).

SOURCES AND FURTHER READINGS: A. Kuznetsov, *Babi Yar*; William Korey, "Babi Yar Remembered," *Midstream*, 15/3, 1969, pp. 24–39; Shmuel Spector, "Babi Yar," in Israel Gutman, ed., *Encyclopedia of the Holocaust*, vol. 2, pp. 433–439. The data on the educational attainments of Einsatzgruppen leaders are cited in Dr. Irving Greenberg, "Cloud of Smoke, Pillar of Fire: Judaism, Christianity, and Modernity After the Holocaust," in Eva Fleishner, ed., *Auschwitz: Beginning of a New Era*, p. 442, n. 16.

191

FINAL SOLUTION
GENOCIDE
HOLOCAUST

EVIL PEOPLE SELDOM SEE THEMSELVES AS EVIL. JOHN WILKES Booth, Abraham Lincoln's assassin and a man who arguably had a more malevolent impact on American history than any other single individual, regarded himself as a pure-minded saint. "I am here in despair," he wrote while hiding out a few days after murdering Lincoln. "And why? For doing what Brutus was honored for—what made Tell a hero. My action was purer than theirs. . . . I have too great a soul to die like a criminal." Hitler, too, saw himself as a great benefactor of mankind; this undoubtedly was one reason he chose so "idealistic" a name for his program to murder all the Jews: The Final Solution to the Jewish Problem. He knew that previous generations had suggested other solutions to the "Jewish problem." Christians, for example, long hoped to convert all Jews to their religion. In the Middle Ages, another "solution," expulsion of the Jews, was widely practiced, the most famous occurring in Spain in 1492 (see *The Spanish Expulsion, 1492*). In the nineteenth century, one of Russia's highest religious officials, and the architect of the czar's government policies, Konstantin Pobedonostsev, promulgated a three-pronged approach to the Jews; one third, he said, must convert to Christianity, one third must die, and one third must emigrate.

Hitler regarded all these previous efforts to deal with the Jews as ineffective. Despite fifteen hundred years of proselytizing, most Jews had not become Christians; those who had, he felt, "tainted" the religion with Jewish ideas. In any case, Hitler could hardly be impressed with Christianity, since its two founding figures, *Jesus and *Paul, were Jewish. In Hitler's view, the Jews were evil incarnate. It was therefore insufficient to expel them, for as long as they existed they would cause problems to non-Jews. In addition, there was always the risk that they would return one day to the countries that had expelled them.

Thus, the only effective solution to the "Jewish problem" was to annihilate every Jew in the world. To this day, no written record has been found in which Hitler specifically ordered the murder of the Jews. The order apparently was transmitted to his chief aides, who in turn transmitted it to their subordinates. Nonetheless, despite the secrecy, the Nazis saw murdering the Jews as their greatest act. Himmler declared in a secret talk to SS officers on October 4, 1943: "I shall speak to you here with all frankness of a very grave matter. Among ourselves it should be mentioned quite frankly, and yet we will never speak of it publicly. I mean the evacuation of the Jews, the extermination of the Jewish people. . . . Most of you know what it means to see a hundred corpses lie side by side, or five hundred, or a thousand. To have stuck this out and—excepting cases of human weakness—to have kept our integrity, this is what has made us hard. In our history, this is an unwritten and never-to-be-written page of glory."

Hitler's effort to wipe out an entire nation was unprecedented. There had been horrific, murderous attacks by the Turks against the Armenians during World War I, but even those murders were directed against Armenians in Armenia; Armenians living in Istanbul, the heart of the Ottoman Empire, were not targeted for death. To the Nazis, however, every Jew was a mortal enemy of the German people. That is why German troops had no compunctions about grabbing Jewish infants from their parents and throwing them against electrified fences, or tossing them up in the air and impaling them with their bayonets. Every Jew was equally targeted by the Nazis for murder. A new word was coined by Raphael Lemkin, a Polish-Jewish international lawyer, to describe this effort to wipe out a people: genocide.

The word "Holocaust" was not used during the war, and so far no one has tracked down when it first came into usage. By the late 1950s, however, "Holocaust" became the standard term used to describe the Nazi murder of the Jews. The word itself is religious, referring to one of the animal *sacrifices offered at the *Temple. In the case of most sacrifices, a part of the animal was offered to God, while the other part was eaten by the *priests. The "holocaust," however, was wholly burned and the entire animal was offered to God. Most of the six million Jewish victims of Hitler were, of course, wholly burned by the Nazis. Referring to their deaths as a "holocaust" therefore implies that these deaths should be regarded as offerings for God (see *Kiddush ha-Shem*).

SOURCES AND FURTHER READINGS: There is a vast body of literature on the Holocaust. Elie Wiesel's *Night* is an exceedingly powerful description of the fate of Jews who were sent to *concentration camps. Lucy Dawidowicz's *The War Against the Jews* is a one-volume overview of the Nazis' Final Solution. See also Yehuda Bauer, *A History of the Holocaust.* Himmler's secret talk to SS officers about the murder of the Jews is cited in Robert Wistrich, *Who's Who in Germany*, p. 141.

192

CONCENTRATION CAMPS

Auschwitz, Treblinka, Theresienstadt

THE MURDER OF THE JEWS WAS HITLER'S "FINAL," BUT NOT ONLY, GOAL in his war against the Jews; he wanted to torture and humiliate his victims first. Former inmate Dov Freiburg's sickening description of a typical day in a Nazi concentration camp offers, as much as any document, a profound insight into Hitler and the character of many of the Germans who supported him:

> I shall tell the story of one day, an ordinary day, much like any other. That day I worked cleaning out a shed. . . . An umbrella had gotten stuck in a roof beam, and the SS man Paul Groth ordered a boy to get it down. The boy climbed up, fell from the roof and was injured. Groth punished him with twenty-five lashes. He was pleased with what had happened and called over another German and told him he had found 'parachutists' among the Jews. We were ordered to climb up to the roof one after another. . . . The majority did not succeed; they fell down, broke legs, were whipped, bitten by [the German shepherd] Barry, and shot.
>
> This game was not enough for Groth.
>
> There were many mice around, and each of us was ordered to catch two mice. He selected five prisoners, ordered them to pull down their trousers, and we dropped the mice inside. The people were ordered to remain at attention, but they could not without moving. They were whipped.
>
> But this was not enough for Groth. He called over a Jew, forced him to drink alcohol until he fell dead. . . . We were ordered to lay the man on a board, pick him up and slowly march while singing a funeral march.
>
> This is a description of one ordinary day. And many of them were even worse.

The largest of the concentration camps to which Jews were sent was near the Polish city of Oswiecim (in English, Auschwitz). It is estimated that about 1.5 million Jews were gassed to death in that camp. As the inmates entered this hell, one of the first sights that greeted them was an enormous sign reading: ARBEIT MACHT FREI (WORK MAKES FREE), a cynical attempt to convince arriving prisoners that the Nazis had no evil intentions toward them.

In fact, the large majority of Jews who saw this sign were murdered within twenty-four hours. Almost immediately after the Jews entered the camp, the Nazis lined them up in front of German physicians, who rapidly dispatched each person to the right or left. (The most infamous of these doctors of death was Josef Mengele—see next entry.) Those sent to the left included the elderly, children, and anyone who appeared sickly or weak. Within hours, they were loaded into giant, closed rooms, known as gas chambers, into which the Germans released the poisonous Zyklon B gas. Within a manner of minutes everyone in the room choked to death, though the dreadful death agonies were prolonged because the Nazis used the minimum amount of gas necessary to kill. It is estimated that the gas cost the Nazis about two thirds of a penny for every Jew they murdered: As Rabbi Irving Greenberg has noted, "In the Nazi-dominated Europe of World War II, a Jewish life was worth less than one penny."

Those Jews "fortunate" enough to be sent to the right were put to work by the Germans. The conditions to which they were subjected, however, were torturous. Most workers became ill from their labors, and sick Jews were immediately sent to the gas chambers.

Those who survived the concentration camps were generally those who were sent there in the later stages of the war. Not all concentration camps were death camps like Auschwitz and Treblinka. Some of them were work camps, though the working conditions and treatment of the prisoners were so horrendous that being sent to one was often tantamount to a death sentence.

The Jews who died in the Nazi camps were not buried; instead, thousands were burned daily in giant crematoria. Indeed, the association of the burning of Jewish bodies with the Holocaust is one of the reasons many Jews still react with abhorrence to cremation of the dead (in addition, cremation is forbidden according to Jewish law). The Jewish workers who were forced to load the bodies into the crematoria and later unload their ashes were themselves killed after a few weeks or months of this gruesome work. The Nazis did not want living witnesses to their crimes.

In some camps, the destruction was almost total. It is estimated that some 870,000 Jews were murdered in Treblinka, and that only about 70 survived, less than 1 survivor for every 12,000 who were murdered.

One concentration camp, Theresienstadt, stood out. It was, relatively speaking, the most "livable" camp, because the Nazis made it a showplace. On one notable occasion (July 23, 1943), they even allowed the International Red Cross to examine the camp in order to prove that the Jews were not being mistreated there. In preparation for the visit, the Nazis deported many inmates to Auschwitz, so as to make the camp look less crowded. In addition, they erected dummy stores, a café, a bank, flower gardens, and a school. During the visit, needless to say, the prisoners were served much better food than usual. The inmates, of course, had no opportunity to speak privately with the Red Cross officials and relate to them the true nature of their treatment.

As a rule, the only time the Nazis served decent food to the concentration camp inmates was on the fast days of *Yom Kippur and *Tisha Be'Av. It was psychologically important to the Germans that they force the Jews to violate their most sacred traditions. Although Jewish law permitted inmates to eat on these days, because their lives were at risk if they fasted (see *Where Life Is at Stake/Pikuakh Nefesh*), a surprising number rejected the Nazi fare.

When the Allies liberated the camps, they were sickened by the condition of the starved, skeletonlike inmates. Overcome by pity, some soldiers gave inmates large quantities of food. This proved to be a tragic error. Many starved inmates gorged themselves on the first proper food they had been given in years, and their bellies burst. As a result, several thousand died.

Allied Commander in Chief Dwight Eisenhower forced German civilians living near the camps to dig graves into which the thousands of Jewish corpses could be buried. Invariably, the civilians claimed that they had no idea of what was going on inside the camps, a claim long since proven to be false.

The Jews were not the only people sent to the Nazi concentration camps. The Germans also murdered many Gypsies. However, the Nazi position vis-à-vis the Gypsies was inconsistent; some Gypsies, in fact, even served in the German Army.

Many homosexuals were sent to concentration camps, along with political opponents of the Nazis, among them some Christians and Communists. Many of these people were murdered by the Nazis as well. I do not use the usual expression "exterminated" to describe the Nazi murder of the inmates.

The Germans chose that word to imply that it was not human beings who were being killed, but rats who were being exterminated.

Though the Jewish community has long felt a grievance against the Vatican for doing little to protest the Nazi mistreatment of the Jews, it should be noted that the Vatican also did little to help Catholic priests who fell afoul of the Nazis. Ironically, in 1988, a group of Carmelite nuns established a convent at Auschwitz to pray for the souls of those who were murdered there. The nuns often note that one of the people killed at Auschwitz was a Catholic nun, Edith Stein, a Jew who had converted to Catholicism and joined the Carmelite order. Stein was murdered by the Nazis not because she was a Catholic or a nun, but because she had Jewish blood in her veins.

It is impossible today to estimate accurately how many non-Jews were murdered by the Nazis in concentration camps. The number is high, though we know now that the common figure of five million, first suggested by the famous Nazi-hunter Simon Wiesenthal, is an exaggeration. Wiesenthal has acknowledged that he put particular emphasis on the non-Jewish victims in an effort to influence non-Jews to become interested in the Holocaust. Nonetheless, as horrific as the Nazi murders were, the number of non-Jews systematically murdered by them was much fewer than five million.

The concentration camps remain today the most powerful symbols of the inhumanity people are capable of practicing against their fellow human beings.

SOURCES AND FURTHER READINGS: Dov Freiburg's testimony of a typical day in a concentration camp is cited in Yitzchak Arad, *Belzec, Sobibor, Treblinka: The Operation Reinhard Death Camps*, p. 200. The story of the Red Cross visit to Theresienstadt is described by Otto Dov Kulka, "Theresienstadt," in *Encyclopedia of the Holocaust*, vol. 4, p. 1463. As to what it was like to be in a concentration camp, see Elie Wiesel, *Night*; Viktor Frankl, *Man's Search for Meaning*; Terence Des Pres, *The Survivor: An Anatomy of Life in the Death Camps*; and Benjamin Ferencz, *Less Than Slaves: Jewish Forced Labor and the Quest for Compensation*.

193

DR. JOSEF MENGELE (1911–1978?)

AFTER *HITLER AND EICHMANN (SEE *EICHMANN TRIAL*), THE GERMAN name most associated with the Holocaust is that of Dr. Josef Mengele. The chief physician at Auschwitz, Mengele was one of several Nazi doctors who met the trains that daily delivered Jewish prisoners to the camp. He would quickly inspect each arrival as he or she marched in line in front of him. Those he deemed physically fit were sent to the right, where they were put to work as concentration camp slaves. Those he sent to the left were murdered within hours in Auschwitz's gas chambers. Unfortunately, even the prisoners who survived Mengele's first selection were not permanently safe from him. When he learned that one block at Auschwitz was infected with lice, he solved the problem by having all of its 750 women gassed.

Mengele also carried out so-called medical experiments. He had no compunctions about torturing Jewish and non-Jewish inmates. For a sadist such as Mengele, who also had some scientific interests, Auschwitz was utopia. Any experiment he wished to perform, no matter how cruel, was permitted. In one famous instance, he had two Gypsy children sewn together to create "Siamese twins." This "angel of death"—a nickname prisoners assigned him at Auschwitz—was particularly fascinated by twins and conducted barbarous experiments on them. Outside of Auschwitz, he initiated an experiment to breed a race of blond, blue-eyed Aryan giants. On occasion, he injected harmful substances into prisoners' veins and hearts to measure the suffering they caused, and to test how quickly they brought about death.

While the Nazi Germany leadership had no shortage of sadists, the long-standing Jewish and Western animus toward Mengele stems from his being a doctor. Quite simply, most people have higher expectations from educated people, particularly those who have taken the Hippocratic oath. It was, therefore, with a sense of extraordinary frustration that Jews the world over learned of Mengele's apparent drowning in Brazil in the late 1970s. That "the Auschwitz monster"—another nickname coined by the inmates of the camp—was able to avoid trial and punishment is just another horrendous injustice of the Holocaust.

SOURCES AND FURTHER READINGS: Robert Jay Lifton, *The Nazi Doctors: Medical Killing and the Psychology of Genocide*; Dr. Louis L. Snyder, *Encyclopedia of the Third Reich*, pp. 227–228.

194

JUDENRAT

KAPO

THROUGHOUT EUROPE, THE NAZIS APPOINTED GROUPS OF JEWISH LEADERS in the countries they conquered to serve as their liaisons to the local Jewish communities. These groups were known as Judenraete (singular Judenrat), Jewish councils: Unfortunately, instead of helping the Jews they often ended up facilitating the Nazis' work. When the Nazis decided, for example, to deport Jews, they often ordered the local Judenrat to bring a certain number of them to the train station on the following morning. Most Judenraete complied with such orders, and even sent out Jewish "police" to bring in whoever refused to obey the summons. Most Judenrat leaders rationalized such cooperation with the claim that it enabled them to save some Jewish lives.

Perhaps the most famous of the leaders who represented the Jews to the Nazis was Rudolph Kastner, who served as one of the heads of the Hungarian-Jewish community. Kastner dealt directly with Adolf *Eichmann, the architect of the *Final Solution. Though Kastner knew that Jews deported from Hungary were being shipped to death camps, he did not urge them to flee. In return for his silence, the Nazis enabled Kastner to save his own family and about 1,600 other, generally prominent, Hungarian Jews.

In the early 1950s, a Hungarian Jew living in Israel accused Kastner of being a Nazi collaborator, and Kastner—who was then an official in *Ben-Gurion's government—sued the man for libel. Kastner lost his suit, and was subsequently assassinated on a Tel Aviv street by enraged Holocaust survivors.

Jacob Gens, the Jewish police chief of the Vilna Ghetto, repeatedly justified his policy of choosing chronically ill and older Jews to be deported in lieu of women and children, on the grounds that the latter represented the future of the Jewish people. To the charge that he was helping murder many Jews, Gens reputedly answered that he was willing to be tried by a Jewish court at the war's end. No such trial ever took place; Gens himself was executed by the Nazis in the Vilna Ghetto in September 1943.

The head of the Warsaw Judenrat, Adam Czerniakow, cooperated with the Nazis in the running of the *Warsaw Ghetto. Thus, in the summer of 1942, when 300,000 Jews were rounded up, the ghetto police supervised this operation under his direction. Czerniakow's defense was that if he refused to cooperate by turning over many Jews, all Jews would be killed. In July 1942, he learned that the Nazis had denied his request to exempt children in the Jewish orphanage from deportations. On July 23 (the Jewish fast of *Tisha Be'Av, which commemorates the destruction of both Temples), he committed suicide by swallowing cyanide. The deportations continued, usually carried out by Jewish police. Each policeman was obliged to bring in at least five Jews a day; if this quota was not met, the policeman's own wife, children, and parents were deported instead.

It is reported of one Judenrat leader that when the Nazis ordered him to prepare a list of a hundred Jews for deportation, he handed in a sheet with his own name written one hundred times.

Clearly, most Judenrat leaders were not evil people; rather, they were tragic characters placed in impossible situations. In retrospect, however, it also seems that it would have been better if no Jews had cooperated with the Nazis. It would have made the Germans' work in ferreting them out more laborious, and hence would have slowed down the murders.

Inside the concentration camps, prisoners who cooperated with the Nazis in disciplining fellow inmates were known as Kapos. Most Kapos were non-Jewish, but some were Jews and, of course, despised by their fellow inmates. There are numerous reports of Kapos beating other Jews. To this day, to call a person a Kapo is about the most offensive thing one Jew can say to another. Because of their cooperation with the Nazis, a higher percentage of Kapos seems to have survived the war than other prisoners.

A woman I know who spent the war years in a *concentration camp was praying in her synagogue one Sabbath morning in New York City in the early 1980s. That day, there was an *aufruff—celebration of an upcoming wedding. The father of the groom was given the honor of blessing the Torah (see Aliyah), and the woman was shocked to recognize the man as a Kapo who had beaten her in a concentration camp almost forty years earlier. However, she still seemed somewhat terrified of him and said nothing except to members of her own family.

On occasion, some Kapos acted heroically. In *Hasidic Tales of the Holocaust*, Yaffa Eliach relates the story of a Jew named Schneeweiss. Despite his reputation for being antireligious, and cruel to the people who worked under him, one *Yom Kippur he decided to help his fellow Jews; he assigned them to the easiest possible work on that arduous fast day. When the Nazis came around in the middle of the day and offered them white bread, steaming hot vegetable soup, and huge portions of meat—food that Nazis offered Jews only on Jewish fast days—Schneeweiss told the Nazi officers: "We Jews do not eat today. Today is Yom Kippur, our most holy day."

"You don't understand, Jewish dog," the Nazi officer said to him. "I command you in the name of the Fuhrer and the Third Reich, *fress* [eat]."

Again, Schneeweiss refused, and the Nazi officer shot and killed him. The religious Jews who witnessed this scene were shocked: Schneeweiss, a man who had publicly and contemptuously violated the Jewish tradition in the past, had died a martyr's death (see *Kiddush ha-Shem*). As Rabbi Israel Spira, a *Hasidic *rebbe* who witnessed the murder, said: "Only then, on that Yom Kippur in Janowska did I understand the meaning of the statement in the Talmud, 'Even the transgressors in Israel are as full of good deeds as a pomegranate is filled with seeds' [*Eruvin* 19a]."

Elie *Wiesel has noted that in the camps there were Kapos "of German, Hungarian, Czech, Slovakian, Georgian, Ukrainian, French and Lithuanian extraction. They were Christians, Jews and atheists. Former professors, industrialists, artists, merchants, workers, militants from the right and left, philosophers and explorers of the soul, Marxists and staunch humanists. And, of course, a few common criminals. But not one Kapo had been a rabbi."

SOURCES AND FURTHER READINGS: Yaffa Eliach, *Hasidic Tales of the Holocaust*, pp. 155–159. The Wiesel quote is from *One Generation After*, p. 189. For a fictional account of a Jewish leader under the Nazis, see Robert St. John, *The Man Who Played God*. Regarding Judenraete, see Isaiah Trunk, *Judenrat: The Jewish Councils in Eastern Europe Under Nazi Occupation*; Yehuda Bauer and N. Rotenstreich, eds., *The Holocaust as Historical Experience: Essays and Discussion*. Having offered a rather unsympathetic portrayal of Rudolph Kastner, it should be noted that Yehuda Bauer, one of the leading historians of the Holocaust, feels that Kastner has been unfairly condemned, and that he acted as responsibly as could be expected in an impossible circumstance. Bauer believes, on the basis of how Jews reacted in other communities, that even had Kastner warned the Jews of the Nazis' plans, his warning would have been ignored. See Yehuda Bauer, *Jewish Reactions to the Holocaust*, pp. 182–190.

195

ANNE FRANK (1929–1945)

OF THE SIX MILLION JEWS WHO DIED IN THE HOLOCAUST THE MOST famous is Anne Frank, a Jewish teenager living in Amsterdam when the Nazis occupied Holland. In July 1942, as the Germans began to deport Jews, she went into hiding with her parents and sister in an annex of several back rooms of a warehouse that had been part of her father's business. Over the next two years, the Franks lived in the annex with four other Jews; they were supplied with food and necessities by heroic non-Jewish friends. The eight inmates of the annex never left the house for two years, until an unknown enemy betrayed their hiding place to the Nazis. On August 4, 1944, the apartment was invaded by the Germans, and all the inhabitants were deported to *concentration camps. Anne died in Bergen-Belsen in March 1945.

After the deportation, the Franks' gentile friends discovered Anne's diary: They later gave it to Anne's father, Otto Frank, the only member of the family to survive. The diary was published in Europe in 1947, but it was only after it was brought out in English in the United States that the book became an international bestseller. Eventually, the diary was translated into thirty-two languages. For many people—non-Jews in particular—the diary made the Holocaust real; it was no longer an aberration that had happened to six million nameless and faceless people.

The diary reveals Anne Frank to have been an uncommonly sensitive and profound girl. It is, therefore, unfortunate that the line in the diary for which she is most famous is actually banal: "In spite of everything I still believe that people are really good at heart." Of course, there is no way of knowing if Anne continued to hold to that belief after her deportation to the Bergen-Belsen concentration camp. Far more profound is her comment: "How wonderful it is that nobody need wait a single moment before starting to improve the world."

"Human worth does not lie in riches or power," she wrote on another occasion, "but in character or goodness. . . . If people would only begin to develop this goodness."

Though Anne Frank came from an assimilated family, her years in hiding led to an increased sense of pride in her Jewishness. She also made some deeply insightful observations about Nazi antisemitism: "Who has inflicted this upon us?" she inquired in her diary on April 11, 1944. "Who has made us Jews different from all other people? Who has allowed us to suffer so terribly up till now? It is God who has made us what we are, but it will be God, too, who will raise us up again. If we bear all this suffering, and if there are still Jews left when it is over, then Jews, instead of being doomed, will be held up as an example. Who knows, it might even be our religion from which the world and all peoples learn good, and for that reason and that reason only do we now suffer. We can never become just Netherlanders, or just English, or representatives of any country for that matter. We will always remain Jews, but we want to, too."

One of the first Americans to discover Anne Frank's diary was Meyer Levin, an American-Jewish novelist, who helped arrange for its English publication. Levin also procured from Otto Frank the right to adapt the diary as a play. Although the script Levin produced was extremely faithful to Anne Frank's original diaries, Lillian Hellman, one of the foremost playwrights of the period, told Otto Frank that Levin's script was unactable. Hellman, a pro-Stalinist, used her considerable influence to have *The Diary of Anne Frank* reassigned to friends, with whom she worked on the script. It was this version, and not Levin's, that was subsequently produced. In the final edition of the new script, Anne Frank's statement that Judaism and its ideals were the root cause of Nazi antisemitism was eliminated. Instead, words were put into the actress's mouth that Anne had never written but which reflected the world-view of the play's writers: "We are not the only people that have had to suffer . . . sometimes one race, sometimes another."

Today, the home where the Franks hid out in Amsterdam is known as the Anne Frank House, and draws several hundred thousand visitors each year.

For readers of her diary, Anne Frank remains forever fifteen and sixteen. If not for the Holocaust, she would now be almost eighty.

SOURCES AND FURTHER READINGS: Anne Frank, *The Diary of a Young Girl*; Dennis Prager and Joseph Telushkin, *Why the Jews? The Reason for Antisemitism*, pp. 57–58. In later years, Otto Frank described the scene the day the Nazis invaded the annex: "The SS man picked up a portfolio and asked me whether there were any jewels in it. I told him there were only papers. He threw the papers, and Anne's diary, on the floor, and put our silverware and a candlestick used to celebrate *Hannuka into his briefcase. If he had taken the diary with him, no one would ever have heard of my daughter" (Louis Snyder, *Encyclopedia of the Third Reich*, p. 97).

196

WARSAW GHETTO REVOLT

THE REVOLT OF THE INHABITANTS OF THE WARSAW GHETTO WAS THE largest Jewish uprising against the Nazis during the Second World War. In the end, it took Nazi troops longer to put down the ghetto revolt than it took them to conquer all of Poland.

Prior to its destruction, the ghetto had been the largest of those into which the Nazis had confined the Jews. At its peak, the ghetto's population reached some 500,000 people (30 percent of Warsaw's population) crowded into 2.4 percent of the city's area. Very rapidly, however, the Nazis reduced these numbers. In the first eighteen months of the ghetto's existence, some 15 percent to 20 percent of its residents were starved to death. The daily allocation of food to Jews in the Nazi ghettos averaged 184 calories, about one fourteenth of a normal adult's dietary requirement. By the winter of 1943, only sixty thousand Jews were left in the ghetto. More than 400,000 others had either died or been deported to *concentration camps, where the overwhelming majority were murdered within days.

Perhaps the most famous deportees from the Warsaw Ghetto were two hundred children living in an orphanage headed by the world-famous educator Janusz Korczak. The elderly Korczak turned down offers to save his life, and insisted on accompanying the children to the concentration camps. Emmanuel Ringelblum, a Jew living in the Warsaw Ghetto, recorded in his diary the scene as Korczak and the children were deported: "Korczak set the tone: everybody [all the instructors at the orphanage were] to go to the [concentration camps] together. Some of the boarding school principals knew what was in store for them, but they felt they could not abandon the children in this dark hour, and had to accompany them to their death." Korczak and the children marched to the train station in rows of four, he at the front, holding a child's hand on each side.

It was only after the population of the ghetto had been reduced to sixty thousand that many of the survivors decided to make a final stand against the Nazis. The Warsaw Ghetto revolt was mounted with no hope of victory, and little hope of survival. The Jews had almost no weapons with which to confront fully armed German troops, and the Polish underground—itself filled with antisemites—contributed almost no weapons to their Jewish compatriots. Nonetheless, groups of Jews, usually people living in the same building, prepared for the revolt by constructing underground bunkers.

The Nazis scheduled the final deportation of ghetto inhabitants for April 19, 1943, the first night of *Passover. (It was a traditional Nazi tactic to turn joyous Jewish holidays into days of mourning.) Nazi forces, under the direction of General Jürgen Stroop, invaded the ghetto at 3:00 A.M. They met with armed resistance, and retreated.

Over the next days, the Nazis started to burn down the ghetto, building by building. The Jews remained hidden in bunkers, which soon turned into infernos from the overhead fires. German troops lobbed hand grenades and tear gas into the bunkers, so that eventually almost all the Jews were forced to flee them. Remarkably, as many came out, they still managed to fire at least one shot at the first Nazi soldier they saw, although they were weak and in some cases only semiconscious.

On May 16, twenty-seven days after the revolt began, Stroop announced that he had completely liquidated the Warsaw Ghetto.

The revolt was a glorious failure. It had to fail, of course; a few hundred pistols, rifles, and Molotov cocktails could not overcome trained troops armed with tanks and machine guns. The revolt, however, immediately became known throughout Europe and the world, and has served as an inspiration to all Jews ever since. As Mordecai Anielewicz, the leader of the revolt, wrote in a letter smuggled out of the ghetto on the fourth day of the uprising: "The main thing is my life's dream has been realized; I have lived to see Jewish defense in the Ghetto in all its greatness and glory."

"The Warsaw Ghetto uprising," historian Israel Gutman has noted, "was the first instance in occupied Europe of an uprising [against the Nazis] by an urban population."

SOURCES AND FURTHER READINGS: Israel Gutman, "Warsaw Ghetto Uprising," in Israel Gutman, ed., *Encyclopedia of the Holocaust*, vol. 4, pp. 1624–1632; Y. (Israel) Gutman, *The Jews of Warsaw, 1939–1943*; Chaim Kaplan, *Scroll of Agony: The Warsaw Diary of Chaim Kaplan*, edited and translated by Abraham Katsh. There is an important work of fiction about the Warsaw Ghetto, *The Wall*, written by John Hersey. See also Janusz Korczak, *Ghetto Diary*. Some ten days before the children were deported, Korczak wrote in his diary: "Today . . . is the day on which I weigh the children, before they have their breakfast. This, I think, is the first time that I am not eager to know the figures for the past week." See also B. J. Lifton, *The King of Children: A Biography of Janusz Korczak*.

The antisemitism of the anti-Nazi Polish underground defies belief. Historian Yehuda Bauer notes the following: "General Bor-Komorowski, commander of the [Polish] underground Home Army . . . issued an order on Sept. 15, 1943, explicitly commanding the extermination of Jewish partisan groups fighting in Polish forests, because he accused them of banditry." When the Jews of the Warsaw Ghetto asked the Home Army for weapons with which to fight the Nazis, they received a total of 70 pistols, 1 hand machine gun, and 1 submachine gun, this from an army that claimed to possess, in 1941, 566 heavy machine guns, 1,097 light machine guns, 31,391 rifles, and 5 million units of ammunition—see Yehuda Bauer, *The Holocaust in Historical Perspective*, p. 58.

197

NUREMBERG TRIALS, 1946

IN NUREMBERG, GERMANY, TWENTY-ONE NAZI LEADERS WERE TRIED for the criminal acts committed by Germany during World War II. The international tribunal was composed of judges from the United States, England, France, and the Soviet Union. The most important of all the Nazis, Adolf *Hitler, was of course beyond the jurisdiction of the court; he had killed himself on April 30, 1945, a week before Germany's surrender.

Considerable testimony was taken at Nuremberg on the *concentration camps and the systematic murder of Jews and other prisoners. Most of the once arrogant Nazi leaders defended themselves by claiming either that they were ignorant of the Holocaust, or that they were only following orders. Only one of the defendants, the notorious Hans Frank, Nazi commandant of Poland, expressed unmitigated remorse over what Germany had done. "A thousand years will pass," Frank declared, "and the guilt of Germany will not be erased." Of course, this was Frank's view "after the fall." During his heyday, he supervised the deportation of almost all of Poland's 3.5 million Jews to concentration camps. In a speech on December 16, 1941, he declared: "I ask nothing of the Jews, except that they should disappear. . . . We must destroy the Jews wherever we meet them and whenever opportunity offers."

Julius Streicher, the newspaper publisher whose antisemitism rivaled

Hitler's, offered the novel defense that he had said nothing worse against the Jews than had been pronounced some four hundred years earlier by Martin *Luther. This was a grotesque exaggeration, though it did call attention to Luther's unbridled hatred of the Jews. Later, when Streicher was marched to the gallows, he called out *"Purimfest,"* a reference to the joyous Jewish holiday of *Purim. In the Purim story, too, ten antisemites, the sons of Haman—who like Hitler sought to murder all the Jews—were hanged in one day (Esther 9:7–10; see also 3:9 and the entry on *Esther*).

At the trials' end, eleven Nazis were sentenced to the gallows, though Hermann Göring eluded execution by biting down on a cyanide pill. The other ten Nazi leaders were put to death on October 16, 1946.

Throughout the world, there was no shortage of critics of the Nuremberg Trials. In the United States, the most notable opponent was Senator Robert Taft of Ohio. He opposed trying Nazi leaders on the grounds that they were being tried *ex post facto* (after the fact) for actions that had not been regarded as crimes in Nazi Germany. The speciousness of Taft's reasoning was obvious; the crimes of which most of the Nazi leadership stood accused, murdering innocent people, were recognized throughout the world as crimes, despite the Nazis' view that killing Jews was wonderful.

Senator Taft's opposition to the Nuremberg Trials provoked considerable wrath. Senator Alben Barkley of Kentucky, a future vice president, declared that the fiercely conservative Taft "never experienced a crescendo of heart about the soup kitchens of 1932, but his heart bled anguishedly for the criminals at Nuremberg."

Oddly enough, President John F. Kennedy saw Senator Taft's position as an act of political valor, and included it as one of the eight courageous political stances undertaken by American senators that he chronicled in his Pulitzer Prize–winning book, *Profiles in Courage.*

SOURCES AND FURTHER READINGS: R. E. Conot, *Justice at Nuremberg*; Streicher's comment that he had said nothing worse about the Jews than was said by Martin Luther is cited in A. Roy Eckhardt, *Your People, My People*, p. 24.

198

GERMAN REPARATIONS

THE NAZIS NOT ONLY MURDERED SIX MILLION JEWS DURING WORLD War II, they stole the property of all their Jewish victims as well. Even as the war was being fought, many Jews worldwide felt that provision must be made for Germany to make financial payments to those Jews who managed to survive the Nazi onslaught. In some cases, the payments would help compensate victims for property that had been stolen; in other cases, for slave labor that had been performed in Nazi *concentration camps. No one ever suggested, of course, that German reparations could compensate for the lives that had been extinguished, particularly since Jewish law holds human life to be of infinite value (see *Whoever Saves a Single Life It Is as If He Saved an Entire World*).

After the war, a vociferous minority of Jews opposed accepting money from Germany. I know one such Jew. The Nazis had murdered his entire family, and he himself had participated in the *Warsaw Ghetto revolt. "It's true," he said, "that the Germans stole my family's property before they killed them. But I want no money, for any reason, from the nation that murdered my parents."

In 1952, when the possibility was raised of Germany making formal reparation payments to the newly established State of Israel, ugly and violent fights broke out in the Jewish community. Israel was then only four years old, and in very difficult financial straits. The country's population had doubled from the time of its creation in 1948, and a large number of immigrants were concentration camp survivors. Israeli Prime Minister David *Ben-Gurion was desperately seeking sources of revenue, and it rankled him that Germany not only had murdered six million Jews but kept their property too.

At the same time, Konrad Adenauer, Germany's chancellor, wanted to make some restitution to the Jewish people. More than most of his countrymen, Adenauer recognized the enormity of the Nazi crimes against the Jews, and believed that Germany must make some gesture of reparation if it were to be reaccepted as a civilized state. In 1951, he announced West Germany's willingness to make payments to Israel, following negotiations with her and with representatives of Diaspora Judaism.

This was the background for a meeting in 1952 between Adenauer and Zionist leader Nahum Goldmann. Goldmann addressed Adenauer at length, emphasizing that Israel expected at least $1 billion from the Germans, a figure that represented part of the cost of absorbing hundreds of thousands of Holocaust survivors in Israel. He warned Adenauer that if Germany intended to haggle over the amount, it would be better not to start negotiations, since the dispute would further intensify Jewish bitterness toward Germany. Adenauer immediately responded that he recognized Goldmann's claim as just, and had every intention of paying the money.

Subsequent to the Goldmann-Adenauer meeting, Ben-Gurion requested the Israeli *Knesset to approve in principle such negotiations with Germany. Some of Ben-Gurion's own *Labor party members were not anxious to accept what they regarded as "blood money"; everyone understood that acceptance of reparations would help Germany win approval in the eyes of the world. The deepest opposition came from Ben-Gurion's longtime opponent, Menachem *Begin, head of the right-wing Herut party. To Begin, accepting money from Germany was equivalent to selling off the dead Jews at so much a body. Begin took to the streets, and urged people to riot against the Israeli government. When the police used tear gas to disperse the demonstrators, Begin charged—inaccurately—that the gas had been made in Germany. So provocative were Begin's attacks on Ben-Gurion that the Knesset temporarily expelled him from his seat. The Knesset finally approved the reparations agreement by the narrow margin of 61–50.

The massive aid extended to Israel by Germany led to an anomalous situation. Because of the Holocaust, many American Jews would not buy a Volkswagen. In Israel, however, since much of the German reparations came in the form of goods and not money, the Volkswagen became the most popular car.

Among American, European, and many Israeli Jews, the argument whether or not a Jew should buy a Volkswagen or any German product was carried on vigorously during the 1950s and 1960s. Significantly, the boycotting of German goods was, as a rule, the worst form of retaliation against Germany advocated within the Jewish community. It would seem that even though Jews are famous for having long memories, they are not by and large a vindictive people.

SOURCES AND FURTHER READINGS: Nahum Goldmann, *The Autobiography of Nahum Goldmann*. Nana Sagi, *German Reparations: A History of the Negotiations*.

EICHMANN TRIAL

THE MOST IMPORTANT TRIAL IN ISRAELI HISTORY WAS OF A NON-JEW, A nonresident, and a man whose crimes were committed before the State of Israel even existed. Yet few people, save antisemites, disputed Israel's right to try Adolf Eichmann, the chief administrator of the Nazi *Final Solution. Shortly before the Second World War ended, when it was apparent that the Nazis would lose the war, Eichmann is reputed to have gloated to confederates, "I will go to my grave happy that I murdered six million Jews."

At the war's end, Eichmann fled to Argentina, a haven for many escaped Nazis. For fifteen years, he lived inconspicuously in Buenos Aires. During this time, Simon Wiesenthal, the famous Vienna-based Nazi-hunter, constantly tried to amass data on Eichmann's whereabouts; he and Josef *Mengele (the most well known of the Nazi doctors at *Auschwitz) were the two most notorious war criminals still free (see *Nuremberg Trials*). Israel, too, was particularly anxious to catch Eichmann, in part because a mere fifteen years after the Holocaust, the memory of its atrocities was starting to recede.

When intelligence officials learned that Eichmann was in Buenos Aires, the Israeli government faced a quandary. They knew that Argentina would not cooperate in extraditing him. In May of 1960, it was arranged for Israeli cabinet member Abba Eban to be flown into Argentina on an El Al plane, and to fly out of Argentina on a commercial flight. Simultaneous with Eban's visit, Israeli agents kidnapped Eichmann off a Buenos Aires street, drugged him, and brought him through Argentinian customs in a wheelchair; they told the airport officials that he was a wealthy invalid who wished to die in the

Promised Land. A few hours later, Isser Harel, head of Israeli intelligence, brought the monumental news to Israeli Prime Minister David *Ben-Gurion, "Eichmann is in Israel."

More than any other event, Eichmann's lengthy trial made the details of the Holocaust known to the world. Every day throughout the trial, a half hour of highlights was televised in New York. In Israel the trial profoundly affected the populace. Many of the country's more than 200,000 survivors daily relived their nightmares.

Younger Israelis had a more complicated response. Many were ashamed to learn that most Jews had not fought back against the Nazis, and unfavorably contrasted their behavior with that of the Israeli Army. The expression "They went like sheep to the slaughter" (a reworking of Psalms 44:23) was applied to the six million derogatorily. Many such critics forgot, of course, that the State of Israel had survived because its army was trained and armed. The Jews rounded up by the Nazis had had no army and almost no armaments. When the *Warsaw Ghetto revolt erupted, bunkers jammed with forty Jews often had no more than one rifle per bunker. Jews who wished to escape death by fleeing from concentration camps were often stymied whether that was the morally right course; even if they succeeded, they knew that ten or a hundred other inmates might be tortured to death in retaliation. Furthermore, they could not count on support from local non-Jews living near the death camps. Polish peasants who found the fleeing Jews were more likely to alert the Nazis of their escape than to help them.

Hannah Arendt, the world-renowned political scientist, attended much of the trial as a correspondent for *The New Yorker*. She subsequently published her reflections on the trial in the book *Eichmann in Jerusalem: On the Banality of Evil*. Throughout the trial, Arendt had been struck by Eichmann's incredible ordinariness and "banality." Nothing in his appearance or demeanor betrayed that he was the greatest mass murderer in history; he looked rather like a clerk in a store.

Arendt also leveled charges against the European Jewish community, accusing the local *Judenraete (Jewish councils appointed by the Nazis to be their liaisons to the Jewish community) of having acquiesced to the Nazis' most terrible demands. When the Nazis ordered the Judenraete to supply Jews for deportation, they did so, fearing that if they didn't cooperate, the Germans would murder even more Jews. Although there is some justice to Arendt's critique, her exaggerated focus on the Judenraete's responsibility for the Final Solution made *Eichmann in Jerusalem* the most controversial Jewish book of the decade. Gershom Scholem, the great scholar of mysticism, accused Arendt of lacking an important and desirable trait in a Jewish scholar, *ahavat yisra'el*, a love of the Jewish people.

Throughout the trial, world Jewry was largely united in believing that Eichmann should be executed. The State of Israel normally had no provision for capital punishment, but several years before the trial, an exception had been made for Nazi war criminals. Nonetheless, the philosopher Martin *Buber opposed executing Eichmann, believing capital punishment to be wrong under all circumstances. As expected, despite the plea of Eichmann's lawyer that the death of the six million should be understood as the "will of God," the court convicted Eichmann and sentenced him to death. After Israeli President Yitzchak Ben-Zvi rejected his appeal for clemency, Eichmann was hanged on May 31, 1962. Among Eichmann's last words before he was executed was the statement "I am an idealist." His body was cremated, and the ashes scattered over the Mediterranean; Israel did not want his burial place to become a shrine for Nazis and other antisemites.

During the trial many Arab newspapers expressed support for Eichmann. One Lebanese daily newspaper, *Al-Anwar*, published a cartoon showing Ben-Gurion speaking to Eichmann. Ben-Gurion says, "You deserve the death penalty because you killed six million Jews." To which Eichmann responds, "There are many who say I deserve the death penalty because I didn't manage to kill the rest." On April 24, 1961, the Jordanian English-language daily, *Jerusalem Times*, published an "Open Letter to Eichmann," which concluded: "But be brave, Eichmann, find solace in the fact that this trial will one day culminate in the liquidation of the remaining six million to avenge your blood."

SOURCES AND FURTHER READINGS: Gideon Hausner, *Justice in Jerusalem*; Isser Harel, *The House on Garibaldi Street*. A corrective to Hannah Arendt's *Eichmann in Jerusalem* is found in Jacob Robinson, *And the Crooked Shall Be Made Straight: The Eichmann Trial, Jewish Catastrophe, and Hannah Arendt's Narrative*. The pro-Eichmann quotes from Arab newspapers are cited in Yehoshafat Harkabi, *Arab Attitudes to Israel*, p. 279. How Eichmann was smuggled through Argentinian customs is described in Jochen von Lang, ed., *Eichmann Interrogated*, p. 286.

200

YAD VASHEM

The United States Holocaust Memorial Museum

THERE ARE AS OF THIS WRITING WELL OVER 150 HOLOCAUST MUSEUMS and centers in the United States alone, a remarkable statistic given that in the 1950s there seemed a risk that the Holocaust itself might be forgotten. At that time, the new State of Israel established what has become the most important worldwide Holocaust center: Yad Vashem in Jerusalem. Yad Vashem was built next to Mount Herzl, where Theodor *Herzl, Zionism's founder, is buried. This prestigious location underscored the significance Israel attributed to Yad Vashem, much as if the United States constructed a specialized museum next to the Lincoln Memorial.

The name *Yad Vashem* (Hebrew for "a hand [or monument] and a name") comes from *Isaiah 56:5, where the prophet assures Jews who are childless that they will not be forgotten in future generations. "I will give them," the prophet says in the name of God, "in My house and in My walls, a monument and a name better than sons and daughters; I will give them an everlasting name that shall never be effaced."

Yad Vashem is as much a part of a first-time Jewish tourist's visit to Israel as is the *Western Wall. The museum contains numerous exhibits about the Holocaust, the most famous of which is a large map, superimposed on the floor, showing the location of the Nazi concentration camps. Yad Vashem's walls are filled with a photographic record of what the Nazis did to the Jews. It also houses an extensive library and research center, which serves as a major resource for historians and Holocaust researchers. A recently built Holocaust History Museum, a decade in the making, emphasizes for visitors the experiences of the individual victims through original artifacts, survivor testimonies, and personal possessions of victims recovered after the Holocaust. Outside the museum is a special grove, known as the "Avenue of the Righteous" (see next entry), in which non-Jews (or their relatives) who risked their lives to save Jews during World War II are invited to plant a tree. As an increasing number of cases of such gentile heroes have been uncovered, the grove has grown, reminding Jews that not all Europeans participated in, supported, or remained passive during the Holocaust.

The goal of the Hall of Names at Yad Vashem is to register as many of the six million names as possible: As of 2007, almost 3 million have been collected. Yad Vashem has also published under its imprint many books and studies on the Holocaust. A permanent exhibit has now been opened to commemorate the more than one million Jewish children murdered by the Nazis.

A visit to Yad Vashem is a mandated part of all foreign leaders' itineraries in Israel. The government wants to clearly impress upon such statesmen the fate that awaited Jews when they lived without a state. Oddly enough, however, when a gathering of Holocaust survivors met in Israel several years ago, they held their main ceremony at the Western Wall, not Yad Vashem. In their desire to find a place that symbolized Jewish survival, the Wall seemed more appropriate.

In the United States, the best known Holocaust center is the United States Holocaust Memorial Museum, which opened in Washington, D.C., in April 1993. As Elie Wiesel declared at the museum's widely broadcast opening ceremony, "Though the Holocaust was principally a Jewish tragedy, its implications are universal." As of 2006, thirteen years after its opening, more than 24 million people had visited the museum, including 7.8 million school children. The large majority of visitors are non-Jews.

One of the museum's most powerful exhibits is the one created by historian Yaffa Eliach, herself a survivor. Over several decades, she assembled the history of Eishishok, the Lithuanian town where she had been born and spent her early years. The floor-to-ceiling photographs Eliach gathered of the town, which are displayed in a tower, convey the vitality of a Jewish community that existed for nine hundred years and was destroyed by the Nazis and Lithuanian collaborators during two days of slaughter in September 1941. In other exhibits, visitors are confronted with personal items such as suitcases, toothbrushes, and prayer shawls that were confiscated from those who perished at Auschwitz.

Yad Vashem, the U.S. Holocaust Memorial Museum, and the many other museums and memorials devoted to the Holocaust play important roles in contemporary Jewish culture, for, as the founder of *Hasidism, Israel *Ba'al Shem Tov, taught—in a phrase that is printed over the entry door to Yad Vashem—"in remembrance lies the secret of redemption."

SOURCE AND FURTHER READING: Shmuel Spector, "Yad Vashem," in Israel Gutman, ed., *Encyclopedia of the Holocaust*, vol. 4, pp. 1681–1686.

201

RIGHTEOUS GENTILES
Raoul Wallenberg
Oskar Schindler

SINCE THE HOLOCAUST, AN ENORMOUS AMOUNT OF RESEARCH HAS been conducted aimed at finding out *why* people became antisemites and Nazis. The *American Jewish Committee sponsored the most elaborate of these studies, the lead volume of which was entitled *The Authoritarian Personality*. All such studies have generally reflected a distinctive bias: Human beings are born good, and any departure from the good must be viewed as aberrant behavior. For people with more sober views of human nature (see *Noah's Ark*), one of the most important aspects of the Holocaust to be studied is not the Nazis, but the people who risked their lives to save Jews and other victims of Nazism. Such people were indeed far rarer than Nazis and their fellow travelers, and humanity would profit greatly from learning how such moral giants were produced. Early studies of these heroes indicate that they were apt to come from religious (though not rigid) rather than secular homes, and to have a love of adventure and risk-taking. Significantly, the rescuers came from all economic classes, and more often than not had had some positive previous experiences with Jews.

One of the most dramatic instances of large numbers of non-Jews risking their lives to save Jews (see next entry for another such case) occurred in the small French town of Le Chambon, an overwhelmingly Protestant city led by a charismatic minister, Pastor André Trocmé. From 1941 to 1944, three to five thousand Jews were hidden throughout Le Chambon and in surrounding villages and farms. A cousin of the pastor's, Daniel Trocmé, was caught by the Nazis and murdered in Buchenwald.

The Hebrew term for people who risked their lives to save Jews from the Nazis is taken from the *Talmud—*Hasidei Ummot ha-Olam*, "Righteous Members of the Nations of the World" (condensed into "Righteous Gentiles"). Yad Vashem (see preceding entry) documents the stories of such rescuers and often brings them to Jerusalem, where they are invited to plant a tree in a special grove called the "Avenue of the Righteous." In recent years, several Jewish organizations, as well as the government of Israel, have undertaken the financial support of elderly and impoverished Righteous Gentiles.

The most famous individual to help the Jews during the Holocaust was Raoul Wallenberg, who is credited with saving the lives of 20,000 to 100,000 Jews.

Wallenberg came from one of Sweden's wealthiest families—"The Wallenbergs are the Rockefellers of Sweden," is how a tour guide in Stockholm described the family to me. In July 1944, Wallenberg was sent to Hungary as a diplomat; his mission was to help the 200,000 Jews remaining in Budapest; 437,000 of them had already been deported to Auschwitz. Because Sweden was neutral, Wallenberg was permitted to roam through much of the country. While Hungarian Jews who fled to the Swedish embassy in Budapest could be granted asylum, very few people could be accommodated there. Wallenberg therefore started acquiring buildings in Budapest, then he declared the buildings to be inviolable Swedish property, protected by international law. He quickly established thirty-one "safe" houses. Wallenberg then went around Budapest dispensing Swedish citizenship to thousands and thousands of Jews.

The Nazis and their Hungarian supporters did not know how to deal with him; they had no desire to antagonize Sweden, and at first they did not stop him. Wallenberg acted fearlessly, running after deportation trains, pulling off Jews, declaring them Swedish subjects and under his diplomatic protection.

"Overworked as he was," Wallenberg biographer John Bierman has written, "and concerned with the fate of thousands, Wallenberg nevertheless found time for individual acts of kindness. All hospitals were barred to Jews. . . . When Wallenberg heard that the wife of Tibor Vandor, a young Jew who was working . . . in a legation office in Tigris Street was about to have a baby, he swiftly rounded up a doctor, taking him and the young couple to his flat in Ostrom Street. There, he turned his own bed over to Agnes, the young mother-to-be, and went out into the corridor to sleep."

Increasingly, Wallenberg's life was in danger from infuriated Nazi troops and officials, but in the end it was the Communists who destroyed him. When the Soviets took control of Budapest from the Germans, the Communist leaders concluded that Wallenberg was an American spy (he had received some money for his efforts from the U.S. War Refugee Board; this was the one major American attempt, late in the war, to help save Jews from the Nazis). The Soviet leadership's Marxist worldview made them incapable of believing that a member of one of Sweden's richest families would risk his life to save Jews. It is questionable whether, in all of human history, any man ever suffered a greater injustice than Wallenberg did for his heroism. He was arrested and sent to a Siberian prison. The timid Swedish government, fearful of antagonizing its Soviet neighbor, did not aggressively pursue the issue of Wallenberg's fate with the Soviet government.

It has long been assumed that Wallenberg was murdered within a few years of his arrest in one of Stalin's camps. Well into the 1960s and 1970s, however, reports came from released Soviet political prisoners of an inmate who claimed to be Wallenberg. He told them that he was from a prominent Swedish family and had saved Jews in Hungary. The possibility that Wallenberg languished in a Siberian prison camp for over thirty years seems somehow more horrifying than the thought that he was killed quickly by Stalin's troops.

Wallenberg's most natural supporters, the Jews he saved, were shattered and penniless at the war's end, and without any political influence they could exert on his behalf. As time passed, more and more survivors achieved prominence and began agitating to learn if Wallenberg was alive, and if so, what could be done to help save him. Finally, Tom Lantos, one of the people Wallenberg rescued, was elected to the U.S. House of Representatives from a district in northern California. He sponsored a bill that made Raoul Wallenberg the only person aside from Winston Churchill to be awarded honorary American citizenship. Lantos hoped that this bill would give the American government added authority to push the investigation of Wallenberg's fate. Unfortunately, little hard knowledge has surfaced, though it now appears that Wallenberg was murdered by the Soviets in 1947.

Wallenberg is one of the great heroes of Jewish history, and his example is a forceful reminder that despite the long history of antisemitism, Jews have had some extraordinary friends in the non-Jewish world.

The other most widely known "righteous gentile" is Oskar Schindler, whose extraordinary activities were chronicled in Steven Spielberg's Academy Award–winning film *Schindler's List*. At the film's beginning—and in real life—Schindler was a disreputable figure, a Nazi party member, a womanizer, and a dishonest businessman and war profiteer. He was in charge of a factory that employed hundreds of Jews as slave laborers for the Third Reich, but when he came to understand that the Nazis intended to murder the Jews, Schindler became a man transformed. From that moment on until the war's end, he did everything within his power to protect all those who worked for him, and to bring into his employ other Jews so as to save their lives. Schindler repeatedly risked his own life to carry out this mission, and by war's end he had saved the lives of over 1,100 people.

A particularly powerful scene at the movie's conclusion shows many of the survivors and their children paying homage at Schindler's tomb in the Catholic graveyard on Mount Zion in Jerusalem. As of 1993, when the film was made, Schindler's survivors had produced many thousands of descendants, all of whom of course would never have been born if not for this remarkable man. The release of *Schindler's List* was an important factor in raising both Holocaust consciousness and interest in the righteous people who risked their lives to save Jews. It is estimated that twenty-five million Americans saw the movie in theaters and an additional sixty-five million people viewed it when it was first shown on television.

SOURCES AND FURTHER READINGS: Per Anger, *With Raoul Wallenberg in Budapest: Memories of the War Years in Hungary*; John Bierman, *Righteous Gentile: The Story of Raoul Wallenberg, Missing Hero of the Holocaust*—the story about Tibor Vandor's wife is told on p. 97. Historian Leni Yahil has written of a little-known episode just before the Nazi defeat in Hungary: "In the final days preceding Budapest's liberation, Wallenberg, with the help of Hungarians and the . . . Jewish Council was able to foil a joint SS and [Hungarian] Arrow Cross plan to blow up the [Jewish] ghettos before the city's impending liberation. Through this act—the only one of its kind in the Holocaust—some 100,000 Jews were saved in the two ghettos" (see Israel Gutman, ed. *Encyclopedia of the Holocaust*, vol. 4, p. 1591).

The story of the heroic village of Le Chambon is told in Philip Hallie, *Lest Innocent Blood Be Shed: The Story of the Village of Le Chambon and How Good Happened There*. Pierre Sauvage, who was born in Le Chambon to Jewish refugees hiding there, has produced a documentary film about the town's rescue effort, *Weapons of the Spirit*.

On the subject of Righteous Gentiles, see Nechama Tec, *When Light Pierced the Darkness*, and Katriel Katz, "Righteous of the Nations," in *Encyclopedia Judaica Year Book, 1986–1987*, pp. 123–131.

202

DENMARK

ONE OF THE FEW RAYS OF LIGHT IN THE DARK NIGHT OF THE HOLO-
caust was the behavior of the non-Jewish citizens of Denmark toward their
Jewish neighbors. Denmark was occupied by the Germans on April 9, 1940.
During the first years of the Nazi occupation, the small Jewish community of
eight thousand was allowed to go on living in its homes. In 1942, however,
Germany decided to incorporate Denmark into Germany, and in 1943 the
Nazis moved to deport Danish Jews to death camps. Word of this was leaked
to the Danish resistance, which decided, in concert with the rest of the coun-
try, to save the country's Jews.

The attitude of the Danes toward the Jews was in marked contrast to that of
almost all the rest of Europe, where most citizens either cooperated in the
roundup of Jewish citizens, or remained indifferent to their fate. In Denmark
the police refused to participate in rounding up the Jews: King Christian X
encouraged the pro-Jewish forces by announcing that all Danish citizens
were one, and that no one had the right to treat Danish Jews differently from
any other citizens. A popular, though not true, myth circulated that the king
himself put on the *yellow badge that the Jews were required to wear, and
instructed all Danes to do the same.

What the country did do, and this is no myth, was send virtually the entire
Jewish community by boat into Sweden. Sweden was neutral during the Second World War and had announced its readiness to accept all of Denmark's
Jews. The rescue was carried out over three weeks, and when the Nazis came
to deport the Jews on October 1–2, 1943, they found only about four hundred who had not yet escaped.

These four hundred Jews were sent to the *Theresienstadt concentration
camp, but the Danes continued to exert themselves on their behalf. The government repeatedly demanded permission to inspect the camp, and eventually the Danish Red Cross was allowed to visit Theresienstadt. Because of
their government's intercessions, the Danish Jews were not deported from
Theresienstadt to Auschwitz. Fifty-one of them died at the camp of "natural

causes" (of course, the horrible living conditions there hastened their deaths). Thus, only about 2 percent of Danish Jewry perished during the Holocaust, less than one fortieth of the percentage of Jews killed in much of Europe. At the war's end, when the Danish Jews came back from Sweden, most found their property intact.

After the war, Denmark became for Jews a symbol of hope and of love, a nation of Righteous Gentiles (see preceding entry). When I was twenty, and traveled to Europe, the first country I visited was Denmark. As a Jew who had read extensively about the Holocaust since my teenage years, it was the only country in Europe toward which I felt unambivalent affection. Many other Jews I know have expressed to me the same sentiment.

SOURCES AND FURTHER READINGS: Leni Yahil, *The Rescue of Danish Jewry*; L. Goldberger, *The Rescue of the Danish Jews: Moral Courage Under Stress*; *Encyclopedia Judaica*, vol. 5, pp. 1538–1540; Lucy Dawidowicz, *The War Against the Jews*, pp. 372–374.

203

HOLOCAUST REVISIONISTS

MORE THAN ANY OTHER EVENT IN HUMAN HISTORY, THE HOLOCAUST discredited antisemitism. Before 1945, few antisemites had any compunctions about publicly announcing their hatred for Jews. The revelations of the gas chambers, however, made antisemitism seem so odious that Jew-haters had one of two choices: either to call themselves anti-Zionists rather than anti-semites—a tactic generally adopted by enemies of the Jews in the Muslim and Communist worlds—or to simply deny that the Holocaust had occurred.

Amazingly, and despite very extensive pictorial and eyewitness evidence, the testimony of tens of thousands of survivors, and the confessions of thousands of perpetrators, a growing number of books, pamphlets, and articles have been published claiming that the Holocaust never happened. To make their case sound academically respectable, their authors refer to themselves as Holocaust revisionists.

Many of these "revisionists" do, indeed, come from the academic community. Arthur Butz, a professor of electrical engineering at Northwestern University near Chicago, wrote *The Hoax of the Twentieth Century*, a book that offered "proof" that the concentration camps were work camps where no Jews were killed. Given the indisputable evidence of a great decline in the number of Jews living in Europe after 1945, Butz claimed that millions of Jews were admitted secretly to America, or fled to the Soviet Union. Butz's thesis, of course, is as preposterous as arguing that blacks were never slaves in America, but migrated there willingly to take positions as paid servants and farm workers.

Yet shortly after publication of Butz's book, the Institute for Historical Review was founded in California, and issued a journal devoted to Holocaust revisionism. In 1980 and 1981, the institute offered a $50,000 "reward" to anyone who could prove that there had been Nazi death camps, and that Jews had been killed in them. A Holocaust survivor in Los Angeles claimed the money. When the journal refused to pay him, he sued and won.

During the early 1980s, Robert Faurisson, a neo-Nazi professor in France, published a book claiming that the Holocaust was a fiction made up by the Zionists. Although about 1.5 million Jews had been gassed at Auschwitz, Faurisson claimed that there were no gas chambers in the camp. His academic colleagues deemed his book sufficient reason for dismissing him from his university post. An international group of antisemites protested, on the grounds that Faurisson was being denied academic freedom. This was not the issue at all. To revert to the earlier analogy, an American university presumably would fire a professor who published a book claiming that blacks had never been slaves in the United States. As Bernard Baruch once said: "Every man has a right to his own opinion. But no man has a right to be wrong in his facts." Among the protestors on Faurisson's behalf was the well-known American-Jewish linguistics professor Noam Chomsky. While many thought Chomsky's involvement in a neo-Nazi cause peculiar, Jewish activists were not particularly surprised. Chomsky had long been known as an anti-Zionist and was widely regarded as a *self-hating Jew. Though Chomsky insisted that he was only concerned with defending the French professor's academic freedom, reporter Herbert Mitgang of *The New York Times* asked Chomsky to comment further on the professor's views. Chomsky responded that he had no views to state concerning the Holocaust. Martin Peretz, editor of *The New Republic*, noted that "on the question, that is, as to whether or not six million Jews were murdered, Noam Chomsky apparently is an agnostic."

In general, Holocaust revisionists are neo-Nazis. They know that much of the popular revulsion toward Nazism is a response to the Nazis' crimes against the Jews, and that "disproving" the Holocaust, therefore, could end much anti-Nazi feeling. Ironically, though revisionists claim that the Holocaust never happened, their writings leave one with the distinct impression that they think the Jews deserved it.

Some Arab spokesmen also have identified with the revisionists, particularly with their claim that the Zionists invented the story of the Holocaust to arouse worldwide support for a Jewish state.

In 1993, Professor Deborah Lipstadt of Emory University published *Denying the Holocaust*, the first comprehensive delineation of the worldwide campaign by neo-Nazis and their sympathizers to convince people that the Holocaust had not occurred. Among those who came in for sharp criticism in Lipstadt's book was David Irving, a British writer who had authored more than thirty books on World War II. Lipstadt wrote that Irving was "one of the most dangerous spokespersons for Holocaust denial," noting that "he is at his most facile at taking accurate information and shaping it to conform to his conclusions."

Irving responded with a suit against Lipstadt in England, alleging that her book had severely damaged his reputation as a historian. Although it is more difficult for defendants to prevail in libel cases in British courts (where defendants are required to prove the truth of their assertions) than in the United States, Lipstadt won a resounding victory against Irving. Judge Charles Gray of the British high court ruled that Irving could legitimately be described as a racist Holocaust denier, and one who distorted historical evidence so as to portray Adolf Hitler in a positive light.

Because of the extraordinary international attention accorded the 2000 trial (the verdict received page one treatment in *The New York Times*), the resounding nature of Lipstadt's win was regarded as particularly significant. As her lawyer, Anthony Julius, declared: "It's important to secure definitive rulings against Holocaust deniers, to send them back into the antisemitic ghetto from which they came."

It would be nice to report that Holocaust deniers are diminishing their efforts, but they aren't. In December 2006, Iranian president Mahmoud Ahmadinejad, along with the Iranian foreign ministry, convened an international conference in Teheran at which they brought together Holocaust deniers from throughout the world. Among those in attendance were David Duke, the former Ku Klux Klan leader in the United States who, in his speech, denied the existence of the gas chambers in which Jews died. Also in attendance was the previously mentioned Robert Faurisson, who claimed that the Holocaust was a myth propagated to justify the creation of Israel, a position that Ahmadinejad has often claimed (he has also repeatedly called for Israel to be wiped out). A year before the conference, the Iranian government sponsored a contest for cartoons denying the Holocaust; one of the cartoons published depicted *Anne Frank in bed with *Adolf Hitler.

The "revisionists' " attempts to convince the world that the Holocaust was a hoax seem to rely on a famous saying of Hitler: "The great masses of the people will fall more easily victim to a big lie than a small one." Unfortunately, despite Lipstadt's encouraging victory, there still is reason to fear that the revisionist cause will gain proponents in the coming decades. With each passing year, fewer Holocaust survivors remain alive, and by 2025, there will be almost none left. The Jewish community regards it as critical that the survivors' experiences be recorded now, so that future generations will possess full documentation of the greatest crime in the history of the world. It is with this end in mind that Steven Spielberg's Shoah Visual History Foundation has recorded tens of thousands of extensive interviews with Holocaust survivors.

SOURCES AND FURTHER READINGS: Martin Peretz's attack on Noam Chomsky is found in *The New Republic*, January 3–10, 1981, p. 38. See also Nadine Fresco, "The Denial of the Dead: The Faurisson Affair—and Noam Chomsky," *Dissent*, Fall 1981, pp. 467–483. See also Israel Gutman, "Holocaust, Denial of the," in Gutman, ed., *Encyclopedia of the Holocaust*, vol. 2, pp. 681–687; Wallace Greene, "The Holocaust Hoax: A Rejoinder," in *Jewish Social Studies*, Summer/Fall 1984, pp. 263–276; Deborah Lipstadt, *Denying the Holocaust: The Growing Assault on Truth and Memory*; a report on the verdict in the Lipstadt case is found in *The New York Times*, April 12, 2000, p. 1. Concerning the Iranian conference on the Holocaust, see *The New York Times*, December 6, 2006, A5.

204

"NEVER AGAIN"

WHEN JEWS SAY "NEVER AGAIN," THEY MEAN THAT NEVER AGAIN WILL they allow a holocaust to happen. Never again *Auschwitz, never again gas chambers, never again six million murdered Jews.

Unfortunately, it will not necessarily be within the Jews' power to stop a holocaust if another Hitler comes to power. Still, the phrase "Never again" is as good an explanation as any for much Jewish political behavior since the end of World War II.

For one thing, it explains why so many Jews became pro-Zionist after the Nazis' rise to power, and particularly after World War II. Jews realized that a state in which all persecuted Jews would be welcome would make another holocaust much more unlikely.

Similarly, "Never again" explains the enormous protest movement on behalf of Soviet Jewry that started in the United States during the 1960s. American Jewry had long felt a sense of guilt over its relative inactivity during the Holocaust: Now they were determined that "Never again" would Jews in the free world permit themselves to be quiet while Jews elsewhere were being persecuted (see *Soviet Jewry Movement*).

The sentiment of "Never again" also helps explain why Israeli Prime Minister Menachem *Begin, in 1981, bombed a nuclear reactor in Iraq that was being primed to produce an atom bomb. Begin explained that as long as the reactor remained standing, he saw the people of Israel facing a peril similar to that of Hitler. And though a good part of the world condemned Israel's action, almost no Jews were unhappy when the Iraqi reactor was destroyed; because of the Holocaust, they felt that "never again" could they allow enemies who had announced their intention to kill them gain access to weapons of mass death.

"Never again," more than any other phrase, explains world Jewry's commitment to maintain Israel's military strength. "Never again," as Rabbi Irving Greenberg has expressed it, must Jews be so powerless that their very powerlessness tempts their enemies to destroy them.

The origin of "Never again" is obscure, though in the early 1970s it became associated with the late Rabbi Meir Kahane of the Jewish Defense League, whose members used to shout the words repeatedly during demonstrations. In recent years, however, this short, powerful phrase has been used by Jews of far more moderate political affiliations.

Like the word "Holocaust," the expression "Never again" is one with which many non-Jews also are familiar. When an innocent black youth was murdered by a gang of white teenagers in New York in 1989, the Reverend Louis Farrakhan (see *Black-Jewish Relations*)—strangely enough himself an antisemite—announced that blacks must learn from the Jewish expression "Never again," and never permit such a thing to happen again.

205

ELIE WIESEL (B. 1928)

MORE THAN ANY OTHER PERSON, ELIE WIESEL IS RESPONSIBLE FOR THE widespread knowledge of the Holocaust among both Jews and non-Jews. His book *Night*, a re-creation of Wiesel's own Holocaust experiences, is the first account many people have read concerning the Nazi death camps. At age sixteen, he and his family were deported from their native Hungary to Auschwitz. There, Wiesel witnessed the death of his father, but managed to survive until the camp was liberated by the Allies. He entitled the book *Night* to underscore how unremittingly dark was the experience of the Holocaust.

The Hungarian-Jewish community, of which Wiesel was a part, was the last to be deported to the camps. It was only in 1944 that the Nazis actively assumed operation of the Hungarian government, and started to murder the country's 800,000 Jews. Although the Nazis had been killing Jews nonstop since 1941, Hungarian Jewry was unaware of what the Nazis intended to do to them. Wiesel himself says that he remembers *Passover 1943, a year before the Nazi occupation of Hungary. The Jews in Sighet, his hometown, had heard reports that Jews in the *Warsaw Ghetto had launched a revolt against the Germans, and Wiesel recalls his mother lamenting the act. To her, the Jews in Warsaw seemed to be acting foolishly. "Why didn't they just wait?" she said. "The war will be over soon, and they could have all survived."

One of Wiesel's early essays, "A Plea for the Dead," is a powerful response to those who have criticized the Holocaust's victims for not fighting back against the Germans (see *Eichmann Trial*). The Jews, as Wiesel notes, had no weapons. With what should they have confronted German machine guns and tanks—their fists? Should they have fled instead into a Polish countryside filled with peasants who were far more likely to turn them over to the Nazis than to shield them? "The Talmud teaches man," Wiesel concludes, "never to judge his friend until he has been in his place. But, for the world, the Jews are not friends. They have never been.

Because they had no friends they are dead. So [let the world] learn to be silent."

In addition to making the Holocaust widely known, Wiesel played a significant role in the 1960s in publicizing the oppression of Soviet Jewry. His *The Jews of Silence* remains one of the most moving books ever written on Soviet-Jewish life. Wiesel's title was intentionally ambivalent. Though one assumes at first that the title refers only to the forcibly silent Jews of the Soviet Union, it is clear by the end of the book that Wiesel is condemning "the Jews of silence" in the free world for their passivity in the face of Jewish suffering.

In 1986, Wiesel won a Nobel prize. Though primarily known as a writer, he was not awarded the prize for literature but for peace. The Nobel committee presumably saw his writings and actions on behalf of the Holocaust as having helped make another holocaust far less likely to occur to any group.

In 1985, Wiesel found himself on the front page of virtually every American newspaper. President Reagan had agreed to make a state visit to West Germany, during which he would go to the military cemetery at Bitburg, where forty-seven officers of the SS (the German division that carried out the Holocaust murders) were also buried. American Jews were deeply troubled by this presidential visit, as were, though it is almost never noted, groups representing American military veterans. During a White House ceremony at which President Reagan presented Wiesel with a Congressional Gold Medal, he firmly but respectfully urged the president to cancel his visit to Bitburg. "That place," he said to President Reagan, "is not your place. Your place is with the victims of the SS." The president was visibly moved by Wiesel's remarks, although he did not cancel his visit to the cemetery.

From the 1970s on, Wiesel became the most popular lecturer before Jewish audiences throughout the United States. In recent years, his talks have been less and less about the Holocaust; increasingly, he lectures on themes and personalities drawn from the Bible, the *Talmud, and the world of *Hasidism.

SOURCES AND FURTHER READINGS: Elie Wiesel, *Night, The Jews of Silence, Legends of Our Time.* Wiesel's eloquent speech before Reagan concerning Bitburg is reprinted in Ilya Levkov, ed., *Bitburg and Beyond,* pp. 42–44.

206

THE 614TH COMMANDMENT

Not to Grant Hitler Posthumous Victories

NO EVENT IN THE LAST TWO THOUSAND YEARS OF JEWISH HISTORY HAS shaken the faith of so many Jews as the Holocaust. Because of it, more than a few of them have concluded that the price Jews have paid for being Jewish—gas chambers—is too high. I know of Holocaust survivors who baptized their children as Christians, and tried to hide from them the knowledge of their Jewish background. Other Jews have concluded that a God who would allow a holocaust to happen either does not exist or is not worthy of being obeyed. They, too, feel that as a result of the Holocaust, it is not worth living as a Jew.

Such beliefs have an ironic consequence, as the late Jewish philosopher Emil Fackenheim noted: Jews who stop being Jewish as a result of the Holocaust are simply carrying on Hitler's mission. The Nazi dream was to rid the world of Jews and Judaism. If Jews, therefore, choose to assimilate, they will be posthumously fulfilling Hitler's dream. In response to the Holocaust, Fackenheim formulated what he called the 614th commandment—in addition to the *613 commandments of the Torah—not to grant Hitler posthumous victories.

On purely logical grounds, Fackenheim's 614th commandment makes little sense. Whether a Jew affirms or does not affirm Judaism should be based on his or her reaction to Judaism, and not on Hitler's reaction to Judaism. Another Jewish philosopher, Michael Wyschograd, has criticized Fackenheim. If Hitler had murdered stamp collectors, Wyschograd challenged, would we all be obligated to take up stamp collecting?

Emotionally, however, Fackenheim's 614th commandment has perfectly captured the mood of vast numbers of contemporary Jews. Hitler wanted to destroy the Jews, they reason, and even if one has doubts and uncertainties about Judaism, even if one feels angry at God, even if one fears that anti-semitism might someday triumph again, one *must* live as a Jew. To do otherwise would be to allow the antisemites to win. In other words, to complete Hitler's work.

SOURCES AND FURTHER READINGS: Emil Fackenheim, "The 614th Commandment," in *The Jewish Return into History*, pp. 19–24. See also Fackenheim, *God's Presence in History*.

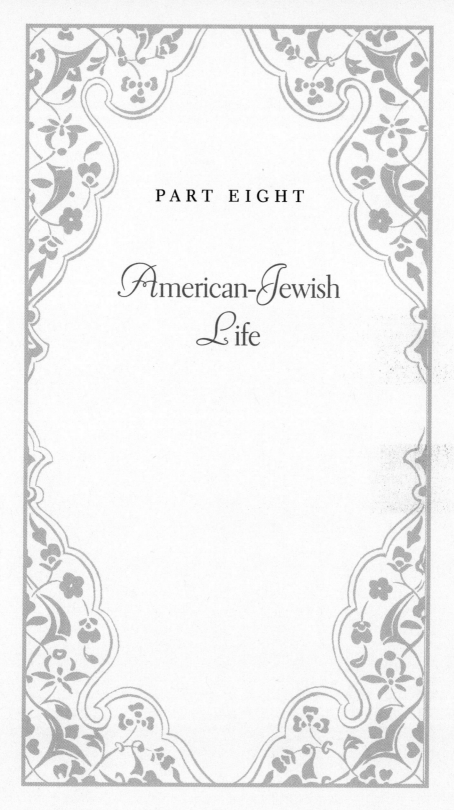

PART EIGHT

American-Jewish
Life

207

GEORGE WASHINGTON'S LETTER
TO THE JEWS OF NEWPORT,
RHODE ISLAND, 1790

THE UNITED STATES WAS THE FIRST COUNTRY IN WHICH THE JEWS received equal rights. Unlike in Europe, the Jews of America never had to fight for political and civic emancipation—it was offered to them from the country's outset. Not surprisingly, therefore, the two thousand Jews living in the United States at the time of the American Revolution (the majority of whom were descendants of the Jews who had been expelled from Spain in 1492; see *The Spanish Expulsion, 1492*) felt a deep gratitude to the founding fathers. When the newly elected president George Washington visited Newport, Rhode Island, in August 1790, he was presented with a warm and affectionate letter from the members of the Newport congregation: "Deprived as we heretofore have been of the individual rights of free citizens," the Jews wrote the president, "... we now behold a Government erected by the majesty of the people ... whose basis is philanthropy, mutual confidence, and public virtue."

Washington seems to have been deeply touched by the letter. He wrote a lengthy response, in which he went out of his way to assure the Jewish community that America would always be open to them: "May the children of the Stock of Abraham who dwell in this land," he wrote, "continue to merit and enjoy the good will of the other inhabitants, while everyone shall sit in safety under his own vine and fig-tree, and there shall be none to make him afraid." Washington went on to describe the sort of society he hoped would develop in the United States: "a government ... which gives bigotry no sanction ... persecution no assistance, [and] requires only that they who live under its protection should demean themselves as good citizens."

Washington's vision of the United States was, of course, exaggerated; the treatment of American blacks was hardly consistent with a society that gave "bigotry no sanction." Nonetheless, America's treatment of Jews was uniquely tolerant. Even in France, where the Jews were emancipated only a year later, no heads of state issued expressions of warmth for "the children of the Stock of Abraham" (see *Emancipation*). Only in America was Jewish equality taken for granted and Jews made to feel that they were more than tolerated strangers. The president's letter was widely distributed, and came to be regarded by American Jewry as a sort of Magna Carta.

SOURCE AND FURTHER READING: The complete text of Washington's letter to the Jews of Newport can be found in Abraham Karp, *Haven and Home: A History of the Jews in America*, pp. 22–23. A reproduction of the letter is available in Joseph Telushkin, *The Golden Land.*

REFORM JUDAISM

Isaac Mayer Wise
Hebrew Union College

IN ITS HEYDAY IN THE LATE NINETEENTH CENTURY, REFORM JUDAISM totally dominated American-Jewish religious life. Of the some two hundred major congregations in the United States in 1881, it is estimated that only a dozen were Orthodox, while almost all the rest were Reform (*Conservative Judaism did not yet exist). If not for the millions of Jews who came to the United States between 1881 and 1924, Reform Judaism might have become, for all practical purposes, the only Jewish denomination here. Indeed, Rabbi Isaac Mayer Wise, the leading figure of nineteenth-century Reform, was sure this would be the case and issued a prayerbook called *Minhag America (Religious Custom of America)*, which he intended to service all American Jews.

Though Reform Judaism in Europe had encompassed both those Jews who wished to effect moderate religious innovations as well as those whose aim was to make massive changes, the brand of Reform Judaism that triumphed in nineteenth-century America was of the more radical variety. As a rule, men were expected to remove any head covering during the Reform service (see *Kippah*), dietary and many other ritual laws were declared no longer binding (see *Kosher*), and some synagogues even shifted their main weekly service from Saturday to Sunday. At most Reform temples, the prayer service was predominantly recited in English rather than in Hebrew.

In lieu of rituals, Reform saw social activism as the central demand Judaism made of its adherents. In the words of the Pittsburgh Platform (see next entry), an 1885 document laying down the basic doctrines of the Reform movement, the mission of Judaism was to "solve on the basis of righteousness and justice the problems presented by . . . the present organization of society."

In 1875, Isaac Mayer Wise established the first American rabbinical seminary, the Hebrew Union College, in Cincinnati, Ohio. Prior to the college's establishment, every rabbi in the United States was imported from Europe, where the Reform movement had originated in the early part of the century (see *Reform Judaism* in the Modern Jewish History section). Wise realized, however, that the maturation of the American-Jewish community required homegrown, English-speaking rabbis who were intimately familiar with the lifestyles of the congregants they would be leading.

Hebrew Union College is today the broadest-based rabbinical school in the world, with four compuses. It still has its campus in Cincinnati, where Wise established the school, along with campuses in New York, Los Angeles, and Jerusalem. All Reform rabbinical students are currently required to spend their first year of study in Israel. This policy has resulted in a higher level of Hebrew knowledge among Reform rabbis, and increased involvement and commitment to Israel. During Reform's early years, the movement's opponents often charged that its rabbis were more familiar with biblical criticism than with the Bible itself, and had difficulty studying Jewish sources in the original. Indeed, a somewhat bitter professor at the Hebrew Union College in the 1930s coined the acid bon mot: "There are two kinds of Reform rabbis, those who believe that Judaism is social justice, and those who can read Hebrew."

The professor's comment, of course, cuts both ways. Too often, Judaic scholars have turned scholarship into an end in itself, and have ignored the fact that the great figures of the Bible and *Talmud whose lives they were studying saw ethics as Judaism's central demand. Indeed, the strength of Reform has been that so many of its clergy and lay people are involved in causes of social justice. When I lived in Los Angeles in the late 1970s, I was overwhelmed by the widespread involvement of Reform congregations in adopting Vietnamese refugees and Cambodian boat people. One of the chairpersons coordinating activities on behalf of the boat people was a Lutheran woman who was so impressed by the Reform community's activism that she subsequently converted to Judaism. While Reform's more traditional critics sometimes charge that the movement's values are more secular than religious, there is no question that much of the inspiration for these pro-refugee actions derived from the ethics of the biblical prophets, and the additional conviction that Jews should not abandon other people the way the Jews were abandoned during the Holocaust.

One issue that sets the Reform rabbinate apart from both the Conservative and Orthodox is its refusal to impose any religious standards on its rabbis. In many ways, this is a continuation of Reform's historical commitment to free inquiry. Today, quite literally, there is no religious action a Reform rabbi can take for which he or she would be thrown out of the Central Conference of American Rabbis, the official body of Reform rabbis. Such refusal to impose religious standards of behavior on its clergy helps account for the fact that although the Reform rabbinate has voted disapproval of its members performing intermarriages, about 50 percent or more of Reform rabbis do so, at least on occasion. Some rabbis co-officiate at intermarriages with priests and ministers.

The Reform movement has introduced many changes into Jewish life. It started confirmation classes for Jewish teenagers, and it was the first Jewish denomination to ordain women as rabbis (see *Women Rabbis*). Over a century ago, it dropped the requirement for a religious divorce (see *Get*), even though Jewish law regards a woman who remarries without such a divorce as violating the biblical commandment against adultery. In 1983, Reform altered the traditional definition of a Jew (a child born to a Jewish mother) to include anyone born of a Jewish father and a non-Jewish mother, as long as the child is raised with a Jewish identity (see *Patrilineal Descent*). This decision has proved particularly controversial, since it means that Reform Judaism recognizes people as Jews whom Conservative and Orthodox Jews do not. As regards conversion, Reform has dropped the requirement of *circumcision for males and immersion in a *mikveh for both female and male converts (see *Denominational Conflicts*), though an increasing number of Reform rabbis do insist on such procedures, and Temple Israel in Detroit, one of the largest Reform congregations in the United States, has built a *mikveh. In addition, Reform rabbis tend to be much more lenient regarding the rituals and Jewish laws they expect converts to observe subsequent to their conversion. In large measure, as a result of the more liberal standards of Reform Judaism, most conversions to Judaism in the United States are performed by Reform rabbis. The converts are most often non-Jews intending to marry Jews. Most converts are women.

In recent years, there has been a widespread openness to incorporating more ritual in the Reform movement. It is estimated that a substantial percentage of Reform rabbis ordained since 1970 keep *kosher, at least in their homes. This movement toward greater tradition has influenced many Reform lay people as well. Professor Michael Meyer, the foremost contemporary historian of Reform Judaism, has noted that twice as many Reform Jews today light Sabbath and *Hanukka candles and attend a *Passover *Seder as did a generation ago. The movement's prayerbook, *Gates of Prayer* (1975), reintroduced many prayers that had been excised from previous Reform prayerbooks. "The new prayerbook," Meyer has noted, "contain[s] nearly every classical theme except for the messianic hope of restoring the ancient sacrificial service" (see *Sacrifices*). Jews on the left wing of Reform were not ignored in the prayerbook either. Alternative services were included, largely in English, and with many traditional prayers eliminated or rewritten.

Despite recent openness to more ritual, for many Reform Jews the definition of Reform carries a negative connotation with respect to observance. If one asks them if they perform a certain ritual, one is apt to be told, "I don't have to do that. I'm Reform." When I worked as education director of the Brandeis Bardin Institute in southern California, we received hundreds of applications from college students wishing to participate in the institute's BCI (Brandeis Camp Institute) summer program. We quickly learned that whenever a student described himself as coming from a "very Reformed" background, this invariably was a euphemism for a home that had virtually no Jewish involvement at all. Leonard Fein aptly titled a study of Reform Judaism, "Reform is a Verb," the title underscoring that the movement needed to define itself by what it did, not by what it dropped.

Today, the Reform movement is the largest denomination in the American-Jewish community, claiming some one and a half million members in over 900 synagogues.

SOURCES AND FURTHER READINGS: The statistic that about half of all Reform rabbis perform intermarriages is cited in Jack Wertheimer, "Recent Trends in American Judaism," in David Singer, ed., *American Jewish Yearbook, 1989*, p. 105. Many of these rabbis do so only occasionally, and the percentage who routinely perform intermarriages is considerably smaller. A good overview of Reform Judaism's development in the United States can be found in W. Gunther Plaut, *The Growth of Reform Judaism*, and Michael Meyer, *Response to Modernity: A History of the Reform Movement in Judaism*; the statistics regarding contemporary Reform observance of rituals is found on pp. 374–375; see also Arthur Hertzberg, *The Jews in America*, pp. 144–150.

PITTSBURGH PLATFORM, 1885
COLUMBUS PLATFORM, 1937

IN 1885, A GROUP OF REFORM RABBIS MET IN PITTSBURGH AND REDE-fined the meaning of Judaism. Only the Torah's ethics and not its rituals, they ruled, would henceforth be binding: *"Love your neighbor" still applied, but not *kashrut or *Sabbath restrictions. The formulators of the document that quickly became known as the Pittsburgh Platform felt that rituals impeded the "mission of Israel" to bring about a universal morality. Rituals such as kashrut needlessly isolated the Jewish community from its neighbors by making it almost impossible to eat at non-Jews' homes.

In line with their desire to minimize barriers between Jews and non-Jews, the rabbis also voted that the Jews were no longer a nation, just a religion; there was no such thing as Jewish peoplehood. This last sentiment led most of Reform Judaism's leaders to oppose Zionism for many decades. In 1907, three faculty members of the Hebrew Union College were forced to resign because of their support for a Jewish national homeland. Later on, however, two of the leading figures of American Zionism were Reform rabbis, Abba Hillel Silver and Stephen Wise.

Some fifty years after the Pittsburgh Platform, at a rabbinical convention in Columbus, Ohio, in 1937, the Reform movement, under the leadership of Rabbi Felix Levy, acknowledged that the Jews were indeed a people and that many Reform Jews looked sympathetically at the Zionist efforts to rebuild a Jewish state in Palestine. This reassessment of both Jewish peoplehood and Zionism was in part a reaction to the rising menace of Hitler. With so many European Jews living in distress, Reform rabbis as well as lay people found that they related to their fellow Jews as members of an extended family, and it was false to claim that no ties of peoplehood bound them together.

A small but powerful minority of Reform rabbis were outraged at the Columbus Platform, seeing it as a betrayal of the Pittsburgh Platform. They went on to found the American Council for Judaism, virtually unknown today, although during the 1940s it exerted a fair amount of influence on Jewish life. Leaders of the organization testified against Zionism before congressional committees, and in 1943, the major Reform congregation in Houston, Texas, which identified with the American Council for Judaism, denied voting rights to any member who was pro-Zionist or believed in Jewish peoplehood. In the council's view, Judaism was a universal, ethical system in which ritual plays little part and Zionism none at all. The organization's longtime director, Rabbi Elmer Berger became perhaps the most disliked Jew—at least by other Jews—in United States history.

It is probably fair to say that for many, if not most, Reform Jews today, the peoplehood aspect of Judaism plays a more significant part in Jewish identity than does the religious aspect.

SOURCES AND FURTHER READINGS: The texts of both the Pittsburgh Platform and the Columbus Platform can be found in Michael Meyer, *Response to Modernity*, pp. 387–391. See also Walter Jacob, ed., *The Pittsburgh Platform in Retrospect*.

CONSERVATIVE JUDAISM

Jewish Theological Seminary
Solomon Schechter (1847–1915)

THE JEWISH THEOLOGICAL SEMINARY, THE RABBINICAL SCHOOL OF CONSERvative Judaism, was established in New York City in 1887. The school's founders were less intent on creating a new Jewish denomination than with offering a modern but traditional alternative to Reform Judaism. In the years immediately preceding the seminary's founding, Reform Judaism had radically broken with traditional Jewish theology and practice. In 1885, Reform's leading rabbis had declared the Torah's ritual laws to be no longer binding (see preceding entry). Two years earlier, Reform's rejection of Jewish law was concretely expressed at the celebration of the first graduating class of the *Hebrew Union College. At the time, this institution was the only rabbinical seminary in the United States, and a number of traditional Jews attended the lavish dinner honoring the new graduates. The first course served was shrimp, a food that typifies unkosher food as much as pork. Many people left the dinner in disgust. Hebrew Union College's leaders claimed that the unkosher food was served accidentally, but it seemed preposterous to imagine that the dinner's organizers had no idea what kind of food the caterer would be serving. The mere fact that they had not bothered to check was damning enough. The Jewish Theological Seminary's founders were intent on offering a more traditional approach to Judaism.

During its early years, the seminary languished, at one point almost going out of existence. In 1902, Rabbi Dr. Solomon Schechter was brought over from Cambridge University in England to head the school, and ever since, Conservative Judaism has been a major force on the American-Jewish scene.

When Schechter arrived in New York, he was already an internationally acclaimed Jewish scholar. It was he who made known to the world the Cairo *Geniza, an extraordinary archive of Jewish religious and historical documents from medieval Egypt. In addition to being a scholar of vast erudition, Schechter was a passionately committed religious Jew, one who could not, however, be pigeonholed into any of the denominations then existent. He was a traditionalist, yet he did not accept all the beliefs of Orthodoxy. Schechter popularized instead his concept of "Catholic Israel," by which he meant that the traditions and observances followed by Jews were important and sacred not just because they were Jewish laws but also because the majority of Jews throughout the world had hallowed them through centuries of observance.

To this day, Conservative Judaism strikes a middle road between Reform and Orthodox Judaism. Unlike Reform, it considers itself bound by almost all Torah rituals as well as Torah ethics; unlike Orthodoxy, it considers itself free to introduce innovations in Jewish law, particularly, but not only, in the laws formulated in the Talmud. For example, Orthodoxy insists that the full prayer service may be recited only in the presence of ten adult males, a *minyan, while Reform Judaism regulates that a minyan is not necessary. Conservative Judaism rules that a minyan is necessary, but that women can be counted in it as well as men. In its first decades, Conservative Judaism introduced almost no changes into the religion's legal system. Since 1950, however, the movement has become more aggressive in promoting legal innovations. Most notable are its decisions to permit driving to synagogue on the Sabbath, calling women to the Torah for aliyot (see *Aliyah), and permitting women to be invested as cantors and ordained as rabbis (see Women Rabbis). In 2006, a series of various and somewhat opposing rulings were passed, the effect of which was to permit the ordaining of gay rabbis.

The Jewish Theological Seminary of New York remains the center of the Conservative movement. Several of the leading figures in American-Jewish life have served on its faculty, most notably, Rabbi Mordecai *Kaplan and Rabbi Abraham Joshua *Heschel. Three longtime members of the faculty, the late professors Louis Ginzberg and Saul Lieberman, and Professor David Weiss-Halivni, who now resides in Israel, are widely acknowledged to be among the greatest Talmud scholars of the twentieth century.

In addition, the seminary houses one of the finest Jewish libraries in the world. It also serves as headquarters of the Rabbinical Assembly, the organization of Conservative rabbis, which was headed for over thirty-five years by the late Rabbi Wolfe Kelman, one of the wisest figures in the American-Jewish community.

The Conservative movement has a rabbinical school in Los Angeles (which was once, but is no longer, related to the Jewish Theological Seminary in New York; though officially non-denominational, Los Angeles's Ziegler School of Rabbinic Studies, part of the American Jewish University, is widely regarded as a Conservative institution), and in Israel, where all rabbinical students are required to spend at least one year in study. There is also a conservative seminary in Argentina.

The Conservative movement has also sponsored the creation of many Solomon Schechter schools, the largest federation of non-Orthodox *day schools in the United States. In addition, the movement has organized Ramah, a summer camp program with branches throughout the United States. Much of the current lay leadership of the Conservative movement received a good part of their Jewish education during the summer sessions of the camp.

Since the decision in the mid-1980s to admit women as rabbis, a small group on the right wing of Conservative Judaism has started a faction known as the Union for Traditional Conservative Judaism. The group has spoken of founding its own rabbinical school, and it is still possible, though not likely, that Conservative Judaism will eventually break up into separate traditional and liberal denominations. Since the early 2000s, there has been a widespread discussion of a malaise in the Conservative movement. Though Conservative Judaism had long been the largest denomination in the American-Jewish community, it was eclipsed in the 1990s by the Reform movement and, in recent years, has had a struggle to hold on to its numbers and to convey a sense of enduring vitality.

A recent study of American Jewry projected that about 1.3 million people identify themselves as Conservative Jews.

SOURCES AND FURTHER READINGS: Marshall Sklare, *Conservative Judaism: An American Religious Movement*; Nina Beth Cardin and David Wolf Silverman, ed., *The Seminary at 100: Reflections on the Jewish Theological Seminary and the Conservative Movement*; Solomon Schechter, *Aspects of Rabbinic Theology*, and *Studies in Judaism* (3 volumes). Nathan Glazer, *American Judaism*, contains an account of the famous unkosher graduation banquet (usually referred to as the *"trefa* banquet").

YESHIVA UNIVERSITY

AT THE TIME IT WAS ESTABLISHED, YESHIVA UNIVERSITY, TODAY THE best-known Orthodox rabbinical seminary in the United States, seemed to many a contradiction in terms; the word *"yeshiva" has long been applied to a religious seminary devoted solely to Jewish studies. At the traditional yeshivot in Europe, there were no secular studies at all.

In America, however, Orthodox Judaism tended to evolve in a more liberal spirit than in Eastern Europe. Though Yeshiva University traces its origins to a Jewish elementary school founded in 1886, the most dramatic growth in the university's history came in 1928, when the school inaugurated Yeshiva College. For the first time in Jewish history, it became possible for a student to pursue university studies and talmudic and rabbinical studies at the same institution.

In its early decades, Yeshiva University brought over many leading rabbinic scholars from Europe to teach at its Rabbi Isaac Elchanan Theological Seminary (RIETS). Foremost among them, perhaps, was Rabbi Moses Soloveitchik, scion of one of Orthodoxy's great intellectual dynasties. After his death in 1941, his son, Rabbi Joseph Baer *Soloveitchik, who had earned a doctorate in philosophy in Berlin during the 1930s, offered the highest Talmud *shiur* (class) to rabbinical students, and continued to do so until the early 1980s. During Rabbi Joseph Soloveitchik's tenure, he ordained well over a thousand rabbis, and came to be regarded as the leading representative of Modern Orthodoxy.

Yeshiva College's founding president was Rabbi Dr. Bernard Revel, whose educational achievements were honored in the 1980s with the issuance of an American postage stamp (it might well be the only postage stamp issued outside of Israel that features a Jew wearing a *yarmulka). After Revel's death in 1940, the presidency was assumed by Rabbi Dr. Samuel Belkin. It was Belkin who turned Yeshiva College into Yeshiva University. In the early 1950s, he established the Albert Einstein College of Medicine. At the time, many medical schools were known to maintain strict quotas limiting the number of Jewish students. In addition, the Einstein Medical School enabled Orthodox Jewish students to minimize religious conflicts (such as working on the Sabbath or on Jewish holidays) while learning their craft. Einstein quickly acquired a reputation as one of the leading medical schools in the United States. Belkin also established Stern College for Women as a counterpart to Yeshiva College. This was considered revolutionary: the first college in which a Jewish woman could simultaneously pursue religious and secular studies in an academic setting. During Belkin's tenure as well, an innovative Jewish Studies Program was established at Yeshiva College under the direction of Rabbi Morris Besdin. Its goal was to provide an intensive Jewish education for college students who had little, if any, previous Jewish education. The program was a massive success, and became one of the forerunners of the *ba'al teshuva movement—the return of Jews to Orthodoxy that has been widespread since the 1970s. Besdin's educational approach was innovative: Prior to the Jewish Studies Program, outreach to uneducated Jewish adults often consisted of little more than pep talks or inspirational classes. The program's strength lay in stressing the fundamentals, teaching people how to study Jewish texts on their own. "Some people like to teach about Judaism," Besdin used to say. "I just want to teach Judaism itself."

I entered Yeshiva University as a student in 1966, and earned my rabbinical ordination at its theological seminary in 1973. Class hours were long; in addition to a full set of college courses, Talmud was studied from 9:00 A.M. to 2:45 P.M., four or five days a week. Yet, the years I spent at Yeshiva were among the most exhilarating periods in my life. What made the atmosphere at the school particularly exciting was the attempt by many of the students and faculty to achieve spiritual wholeness in their lives. When the ethics of the war in Vietnam—the preeminent issue on American campuses in the late 1960s—were debated, rabbis participated in the discussion, as well as political scientists, and brought to bear on the issue the insights of Jewish law, philosophy, and ethics.

The school was also a natural recruiting ground for activists devoted to Jewish causes. During my years there, the university was a focal point for much of the protest activity on behalf of Soviet Jewry.

The tensions between the college and seminary faculties were sometimes exhilarating and sometimes depressing. When a professor of Jewish history, himself an Orthodox Jew, questioned the historicity of the *Hanukka miracle—that a small cruse of oil had burned for a full eight days—several rabbis in the seminary told their students that it was forbidden to attend the professor's classes unless he retracted his "heretical" views. The man was indeed forced to hedge somewhat in what he had said, and the crisis passed.

After Dr. Belkin's death in 1976, the presidency of Yeshiva University was assumed by Rabbi Dr. Norman Lamm, an alumnus of Yeshiva College and long acknowledged as one of Orthodoxy's most eloquent spokesmen in the United States. During Lamm's tenure, a law school was established, named for the second Jew appointed to the United States Supreme Court, Benjamin Cardozo, and Yeshiva University started to be consistently ranked in the annual *U.S. News & World Report* listings as among the fifty best universities in the United States. In 2003, Richard Joel, neither a rabbi nor an academic, succeeded Dr. Lamm. A man of charisma and extraordinary energy, Joel had long headed, and had revived, the Hillel movement (comprised of rabbis and other Jewish professionals serving students on college campuses). For the first time in its history, Yeshiva University is now headed by a president who has had extensive, and positive, professional involvement with non-Orthodox rabbis as well as Orthodox ones.

Yeshiva University in its insistence on synthesizing *Torah u-Mada* (Torah and secular studies) is still distinct from virtually every other yeshiva in the world; and in that regard remains as revolutionary today as it was when it was established in 1928.

SOURCES AND FURTHER READINGS: Jeffrey Gurock, *The Men and Women of Yeshiva: Higher Education, Orthodoxy and American Judaism.* In 1999, as Yeshiva University was widely perceived as drifting to the religious right, Rabbi Avi Weiss, a graduate of Yeshiva University, founded Yeshivat Chovevei Torah, the goal of which is to promote what he has termed "Open Orthodoxy," an ideology committed to Jewish law while maintaining an openness to modern culture. In its early years, the yeshiva has achieved considerable success.

ELLIS ISLAND

LOWER EAST SIDE

SOME TWO AND A HALF MILLION JEWS CAME TO THE UNITED STATES from Eastern Europe between 1881 and 1924. For most of those who arrived after 1892, their first stop was Ellis Island, a tiny islet between Manhattan and Staten Island. Though Ellis Island should logically have been remembered with great affection, it was the scene, unfortunately, of many horrendous tragedies. The health of the immigrants was examined there, and anyone who was found to have a certain eye disorder or a communicable disease was sent back to Europe. When a person was declared to be diseased, the other family members had to make an agonizing choice: to return to Europe or to send the sick person back alone. Immigrants were sometimes refused admittance for reasons other than health. In one noted case, Ellis Island officials deported an arriving Russian Jew on the grounds that he was a murderer. In actuality, the man had killed the person who had murdered members of his family during a *pogrom. The Ellis Island officials were not impressed with the explanation, and sent the man back to face czarist justice. A famous Yiddish poem memorialized the martyred man's estimate of American justice. "They have a statue of liberty, but people with hearts of stone."

Fortunately, the overwhelming majority of Jews—and other immigrants as well—made it through Ellis Island and were admitted to the United States. The first stopping place for most Jews was Manhattan's Lower East Side; at one time, this area became the most densely populated neighborhood in the country. Apartments were small, and families large; it was not uncommon for seven or eight people to live in a three-room apartment. In addition, before the rise of the unions, people often did "piecework" at home, particularly if they worked for clothing companies.

The East Side was the center of an active Jewish cultural and religious life, with a vibrant Yiddish theater and hundreds of tiny synagogues—known as *shtieblakh* (singular, *shtiebl*)—that were often named for the small *shtet-lach* in Russia or Poland from which most of the congregants came. Hundreds of organizations sprang up known as *Landsmannschaften*, consisting of people from the same town in Europe.

To this day, well over a half-century since Jews started moving out of the Lower East Side en masse, the neighborhood remains a center of kosher restaurants and stores selling Jewish books, foods, and ritual items. One can still go to the Lower East Side and buy pickles that are sold out of giant barrels. On the Sunday before the fall festival of *Sukkot, thousands of Jews stream to the area from all over metropolitan New York to buy *lulavim* and *etrogim* at outdoor markets. In recent years, some of the premier congregations of the Lower East Side, which had been barely used for decades, have undergone renovations, and Jews have again started to move into the neighborhood.

SOURCES AND FURTHER READINGS: Irving Howe, *World of Our Fathers*; Ronald Sanders, *The Downtown Jews: Portrait of an Immigrant Generation*; Moses Rischin, *The Promised City: New York's Jews 1870–1914*; Isaac Metzker, ed., *A Bintel Brief: Letters from the World of Our Fathers*.

THE GALVESTON PROGRAM

THE WAVES OF JEWISH IMMIGRANTS WHO POURED INTO AMERICA from Eastern Europe starting in the 1880s almost all opted to live in the large cities on the East Coast. The greatest concentration of Jewish immigrants was in New York City's Lower East Side (see preceding entry). As the number of these immigrants escalated sharply in the early 1900s, many of America's German-Jewish leaders, along with some Jews who had recently come from Eastern Europe, concluded that the newcomers should be encouraged to move to less populated parts of the United States. The New York job market was overcrowded, and these "native" Jews feared that the new immigrants would either become unemployed or would work for cheap wages and cause other workers to become unemployed. The latter concern in particular set off fears that the new Jewish migration might spawn antisemitism.

In 1907, Jacob Schiff, the greatest Jewish philanthropist of the time, formulated a plan to encourage Jews to migrate to the port city of Galveston, Texas, and go from there to the American Midwest and West. Schiff calculated that a fund of $500,000 (a very large sum at the time) would suffice to direct 20,000 to 25,000 Jews to Galveston. His plan took into account all relevant factors save one; few Russian Jews (Russia being the country from which most Jews were coming; see *Pogrom* and *Kishinev Pogrom*) had any desire to live in Galveston or its environs. For the Russian Jews, going to America meant going to New York or one of the other major cities on the East Coast; only there would they find a large and congenial Jewish population. Schiff hoped, however, to convince the Russian Jews that they would have far better economic opportunities and a better chance to become Americanized away from the East. During the eight years that he promoted the plan, some ten thousand Jews went to Galveston. In retrospect, Schiff's reasoning was largely correct; many rapidly acculturated and became affluent. Indeed, those Jews who migrated to Galveston, and from there to cities like Pine Bluff, Arkansas, became Americanized (and sometimes assimilated) much more rapidly than did their brothers and sisters on Hester Street and elsewhere on New York's Lower East Side.

SOURCE AND FURTHER READING: Abraham J. Karp, *Haven and Home.*

214

SWEATSHOPS

THOUGH TODAY AMERICAN JEWS ARE THE MOST AFFLUENT ETHNIC group in the United States—and a study some years ago revealed that their earnings exceeded the national average by about 70 percent—few Jews came to America rich. Of course, there were some very affluent Jews in Eastern Europe, but precisely because they were rich, they rarely emigrated. The 2.5

million Jews who did come to America between 1881 and 1924 generally arrived with little money and education and, as a result, most became physical laborers.

Tailoring was the most popular field in which to work, and the garment industry became as associated with Jews as was barbering with Italians and laundry shops with Chinese. Even now, Jews often speak of grandparents who worked in *shmattes*—Yiddish for "rags"—a term which Jews idiomatically apply to the whole clothing industry. One of the finest novels ever written about American-Jewish life, *The Rise of David Levinsky* by Abraham Cahan, tells of an immigrant who starts out as a tailor and becomes one of America's leading clothing manufacturers.

Most Jews, of course, did not achieve the success of the fictional David Levinsky. Instead, tens of thousands of poor Jews did "piecework," which meant that they were not even assured of a weekly or hourly wage, but paid according to the number of pieces they finished. Women, in even greater numbers than men, worked in dank, overcrowded factories known as sweatshops. The sweatshop workweek was oppressive, typically nine and a half hours a day, six days a week, for a salary that averaged about $115.40 a week (c. 1910).

The full horror of sweatshop conditions became public knowledge in 1911 when a fire broke out at the Triangle Shirtwaist Factory in Manhattan. One hundred and forty-six workers, most of them Jewish women, died, largely because the rear exit, a heavy iron door, had been locked by the factory owners; it was a company policy to ensure that all employees left by one front exit, where they could be checked to make sure they had not pilfered anything.

The fire, however, broke out in the front of the factory, and with the rear exit closed, the terrified employees had no escape route. Some thirty-four employees were later found pushed up against the barred exit door. The bodies of nineteen other women were discovered on top of an elevator cab; they had tried to slide down the elevator cables. Some women jumped from high floors, and went crashing through the sheets that were being held to catch them. Rose Freedman—whom I had the privilege of knowing—the last survivor of the fire (she died in 2001, at the age of 107) said, "The executives, with a couple of steps, could have opened the door."

A passing reporter described the macabre scene that could be viewed from the street as "a young man helped a girl to the window sill on the ninth floor. Then he held her out deliberately, away from the building, and let her drop. He held out a second girl the same way and let her drop. He held out a third girl who did not resist. They were all as unresisting as if he were help-

AMERICAN-JEWISH LIFE ⟡ 453

ing them into a streetcar instead of into eternity. He saw that a terrible death awaited them in the flames and his was only a terrible chivalry. He brought around another girl to the window. I saw her put her arms around him and kiss him. Then he held her into space—and dropped her. Quick as a flash, he was on the window sill himself. His coat fluttered upwards—the air filled his trouser legs as he came down. I could see he wore tan shoes."

The owners of the factories, like most of the victims, were Jews, as were the lawyers who arranged their acquittal. As a rule, the exploiters of the sweatshop workers were fellow Jews. Despite the owners' acquittal, however, the tragedy of the Triangle Shirtwaist Factory fire helped bring about stricter fire-prevention regulations, workmen's compensation, and factory-building legislation.

To a large extent, it was through the clothing business that the Jews made a considerable mark on the American labor scene. The International Ladies Garment Workers Union (ILGWU) was overwhelmingly Jewish in its early years. However, the Jews who worked in the sweatshops did not want their children working there—most of them, after all, did not want to be there themselves. It was common for Jewish laborers to pay children to read to them as they worked. A famous photograph, often displayed at exhibits on Jewish life in the *Lower East Side, shows a group of Jewish men and women working in a clothing factory, listening to a young boy who is reading to them from a *Yiddish newspaper.

The late Harry Golden, a writer and raconteur of the American-Jewish experience, worked for a few years in a company that made hats. The man next to him used to plunge the hats for several seconds into the vat in which the hats hardened. The amount of time the process required was the precise amount of time it took the man to sing one line of a Yiddish song: "There will come a time when there will be nothing to eat." Golden recalled hearing that mordant line hundreds of times a day. Fortunately, however, Golden and most American-born Jews escaped the sweatshops within a generation.

SOURCES AND FURTHER READINGS: Abraham Cahan, *The Rise of David Levinsky*; Harry Golden, *Only in America*, pp. 68–74; Irving Howe, *The World of Our Fathers*, pp. 304–306. The statistics on Jewish earnings in relation to the national average are cited in Thomas Sowell, *Ethnic America*, p. 5.

215

LEO FRANK CASE

ACCUSED IN 1913 OF MURDERING MARY PHAGAN, A THIRTEEN-YEAR-OLD employee in his Atlanta pencil factory, Leo Frank was convicted and sentenced to hang. A courageous Georgia governor, John Slaton, became convinced of Frank's innocence and commuted his sentence, but a Georgia mob kidnapped Frank from his prison and lynched him. Photographs of Frank's body swinging from a tree were sold for decades as picture postcards throughout the South.

Antisemitism in early twentieth-century Atlanta was sufficiently strong to allow Frank to be sentenced to death on the basis of the testimony of a black man, a unique occurrence in the segregationist South. Ironically, the black witness, Jim Conley, was himself the murderer, as he confessed to his attorney who originally withheld the information because of lawyer-client confidentiality. In 1982, *sixty-nine* years after the trial, an eighty-three-year-old white man, Alonzo Mann, confessed that he had seen Conley dragging the girl's body down the stairs into the factory's basement on the day of the murder, but he had been forbidden by his mother from getting involved. In 1986, after an extensive review of the evidence, Frank was awarded a posthumous pardon by the state of Georgia.

The Frank case was one of three major antisemitic trials in the late nineteenth and early twentieth centuries. The first two were held in Europe: that of Alfred *Dreyfus in France, and of Mendel Beilis in Russia. Although there was less antisemitism in the United States than in Europe, of the three cases, only Frank's resulted in the death of an innocent defendant. In France, after years of humiliation and imprisonment on a false charge of treason, Dreyfus was retried, reconvicted, but then finally exonerated. Beilis, the last major victim of a *blood libel, was accused in Russia in 1911 of murdering a Christian boy in a religious ritual. Although the full force of the czarist government stood behind the accusation, a jury of Russian peasants found him innocent. Strangely, it was only in the United States that justice was both delayed and denied. The conviction of the innocent man was the first injustice. The Supreme Court's refusal to hear his appeal, despite evidence of flagrant judicial misconduct at the original trial, was the second, and the murder of the hapless Frank was, of course, the third.

The Frank case brought about the development of two diametrically opposed organizations: the *Anti-Defamation League of *B'nai B'rith (Frank had been president of B'nai B'rith's Atlanta chapter), and the revived Ku Klux Klan.

SOURCES AND FURTHER READINGS: Harry Golden, A *Little Girl Is Dead*; Leonard Dinnerstein, *The Leo Frank Case*.

216

JEWISH ORGANIZATIONS

UJC — United Jewish Communities
Anti-Defamation League
AIPAC — American Israel Public Affairs Committee
Conference of Presidents of Major Jewish Organizations
CLAL — The National Jewish Center for
Learning and Leadership
Simon Wiesenthal Center
B'nai B'rith
American Jewish Committee

RELIGION IS GENERALLY A DIVISIVE RATHER THAN A UNIFYING FACTOR in American-Jewish life. To cite just one obvious example, Orthodox and non-Orthodox Jews normally cannot pray together. If women play a role in the service, Orthodox Jews will not participate; if women are excluded from public participation, non-Orthodox Jews will object. Furthermore, Orthodox and non-Orthodox Jews use different prayerbooks. As a result, the issues that unify American Jewry are peoplehood issues, most notably, support for Israel and opposition to antisemitism.

The largest of all Jewish charitable organizations was the United Jewish Appeal, known by its initials, UJA. The organization was founded in 1938—as a response to the *Kristallnacht *pogrom in Nazi Germany—to help Jews suffering from persecution. After the Second World War, the organization underwent tremendous expansion. Funds raised by the UJA were used to resettle the survivors of Hitler's *concentration camps.

After 1948, the UJA became the major fundraising organization on behalf of Israel. In recent years, it merged its annual campaign with that of the local Federation of Jewish Philanthropies, which had previously earmarked most of its funds for use on behalf of local Jewish causes. In virtually every Jewish community, the combined UJA-Federation campaign became the major charitable campaign conducted annually. In 1999, the two national organizations merged into the newly formed UJC, United Jewish Communities.

The UJC also sponsors educational activities that deal with religious, historical, and contemporary issues and are geared toward broadening the knowledge of future Jewish leaders. In recent decades, "young leadership" events have become a major part of UJC activities. Its programs are generally a mix of Jewish education and fundraising techniques.

Virtually every American city with more than a thousand Jews conducts its own UJC campaign. Most cities earmark a little under 30 percent of the monies they raise for Israel and other overseas communities in need; the rest is used to finance local and other international Jewish needs. Grants are dispensed to Jewish schools and family services, to help arriving Jewish immigrants—in recent years, particularly those from the former Soviet Union—and to meet the expenses of the federation itself. The annual campaign raises over $900,000,000 nationally. In 2006–2007, during and after *Hezbollah's war against Israel, a special campaign raised an additional $360,000,000 for Israel. This makes the UJC, which essentially limits its appeal for funds to about 2 percent of the American population, one of America's largest charities.

AIPAC, the American-Israel Public Affairs Committee, is one of the few Jewish organizations that does not have tax-exempt status, for it is a registered lobby on behalf of Israel. In existence since the late 1940s, AIPAC, headquartered in Washington, D.C., has become since the 1970s, one of the most powerful Jewish organizations in the United States. AIPAC's goal is to safeguard Israeli interests on all issues that come before the American Congress and the White House.

In 1981, President Ronald Reagan set himself on a collision course with

AIPAC when he insisted that the Senate approve American sale to Saudi Arabia of a highly sophisticated military airplane known as the AWAC. Because of Saudi Arabia's publicly declared support for Israel's destruction, AIPAC lobbied actively against the sale. After a bruising fight, and despite the president's immense popularity, Reagan won the vote by the surprisingly narrow margin of 52–48.

AIPAC's powerful influence in Congress has been greatly aided by the fact that Jews are among the largest donors to American political campaigns. Those senators and congressmen who have supported Israeli and Jewish interests have received generous contributions from Jewish donors and PACs (political action committees). The power ascribed to AIPAC has become legendary. This has made Jews both pleased and nervous; pleased because Jews are no longer as politically impotent as they were during World War II (see *While Six Million Died*), and nervous because the supposed strength of the "Jewish lobby" might be used to foment antisemitism.

There are several national organizations devoted to fighting antisemitism. The American Jewish Committee was established in 1906, in the wake of the more than six hundred pogroms sponsored by the czarist government against Jews in Russia. Today, the organization, headed by David Harris, continues to fight antisemitism, and in addition devotes its attentions to international Jewish affairs, and to significant issues in contemporary Jewish life (the last under the direction of Steven Bayme). The committee also publishes *Commentary* magazine, one of the leading journals of political thought in the United States.

The Anti-Defamation League, generally known as the ADL, is primarily devoted to combating antisemitism and was established by B'nai B'rith. The ADL came into being largely in response to the trial of Leo Frank in Georgia (see preceding entry). The conviction and subsequent lynching of Frank, a Georgia Jew wrongfully accused of murdering a young Christian girl, stimulated the revival of the Ku Klux Klan as well as creation of the ADL. Fortunately, the ADL has had considerably greater success. Today it is probably the leading Jewish group in the fight against antisemitism, and plays an ongoing, pivotal role in exposing racist and antisemitic hate groups throughout the United States.

B'nai B'rith itself was founded in 1843 by German Jews who had migrated to the United States. Its goal, in the words of its founders, was to create a "League of Brothers" who would support members and their families in times of illness and death, and provide both Jewish and general intellectual stimulation. As U.S. Jews have increasingly become integrated into the broader American society, B'nai B'rith has declined in size and its membership is aging. The organization has founded, however, other groups that have great influence in Jewish life. Besides the Anti-Defamation League, B'nai B'rith started Hillel, which is devoted to meeting the needs of Jewish college students. Most Hillels located at universities with large Jewish populations employ rabbis to minister to the needs of Jewish students on campus. B'nai B'rith also runs the B'nai B'rith Lecture Bureau, the largest supplier of speakers to Jewish organizations and synagogues.

A more recent organization is the Simon Wiesenthal Center of Los Angeles. It was founded at the headquarters of *Yeshiva University in Los Angeles in 1977, but the center has no theological agenda. Named for the prominent Nazi-hunter of Vienna, Simon Wiesenthal, the organization gained well over 250,000 supporters within the first decade of its founding. It has produced two Academy Award–winning films on the Holocaust, and has built a highly regarded Museum of Tolerance in Los Angeles. The Wiesenthal Center long concentrated particular efforts on the search for escaped Nazi murderers still living in the West (at this point, few are still alive), and on exposing the activities of antisemitic hate groups throughout the Western and Muslim worlds.

There is no one leader of American Jewry, no single figure who can negotiate on behalf of the Jewish people as the American president negotiates on behalf of the American people. The organization that comes closest to representing the Jewish community of the United States is the Conference of Presidents of Major Jewish Organizations. The presidents of more than fifty different Jewish groups serve as members of the conference, and its chairmanship circulates among the heads of the major Jewish religious and secular organizations. Whoever serves as the chairman generally finds himself the recipient of messages that the United States president and the political leadership wish to convey to the American-Jewish community.

CLAL, the National Jewish Center for Learning and Leadership, was founded with two agendas, one involving lay Jews, the other rabbis. It long coordinated extensive adult education classes and seminars on religious and historical subjects for leaders throughout the country. In addition, the particular passion of CLAL's founder and president, Rabbi Irving Greenberg, was to create a forum where rabbis of different denominations could engage in dialogue and formulate solutions to problems dividing American Jewry. During CLAL's early years, in the 1970s and early 1980s, it seemed as if Greenberg's dire warnings about the seriousness of Jewish disunity were a voice crying in the wilderness. But in recent years, with the growing uproar over the *"Who is a Jew?" issue, an increasing number of American Jews have come to believe that their survival is currently threatened more by deep internal divisions than by antisemitism. Greenberg's successor, Rabbi Irwin Kula, is devoted to developing a twenty-first-century Jewish theology, one that can articulate what Jewish insights can contribute to the Western experience while simultaneously acknowledging how modernity can and should impact Jews and Judaism. Also, the efforts CLAL once directed toward bridging gaps between different Jewish denominations (though CLAL still does inter-denominational work with rabbis) are now increasingly focused on establishing bridges with different religious groups, and in sharing Jewish wisdom with the wider culture. In 2006, Kula announced the appointment of Rabbi Brad Hirschfeld as CLAL's co-president, and Hirschfeld has focused particular efforts on outreach to the Muslim community in the United States.

Myriad religious organizations represent the rabbis and members of each denomination. This entry would grow to book length if every Jewish organization was described: Anyone wishing to learn more about the different groups in American-Jewish life should consult the *American Jewish Yearbook*, which is issued annually.

Membership in male Zionist organizations declined precipitously after Israel's creation in 1948. Their goal, to establish a Jewish state, made membership less appealing once a state existed. On the other hand, women's Zionist groups have remained large, perhaps because they have devoted attention less to ideological issues than to supporting health and educational ventures in Israel. Among the Orthodox women's groups, the two largest are Emunah Women and AMIT Women. Other major organizations are American ORT and the National Council of Jewish Women.

The largest Jewish organization in the United States, however, is Hadassah, a women's group that has approximately 350,000 members. The story of Hadassah's founder, Henrietta Szold, is so much a part of American-Jewish history that it is discussed separately in the next entry.

SOURCE AND FURTHER READING: The *American Jewish Year Book*, issued annually and published by the Jewish Publication Society.

217

HENRIETTA SZOLD (1860–1945)
HADASSAH

HAD HENRIETTA SZOLD BEEN BORN IN 1960 INSTEAD OF 1860, SHE probably would have become a rabbi. One of eight daughters of a Baltimore rabbi, Szold was a passionate and accomplished student of Judaism. She even won permission to study Jewish texts at the then male-only *Jewish Theological Seminary, on condition that she never agitate to be granted rabbinic ordination. Later, she translated Heinrich Graetz's monumental multivolume *History of the Jews* from German into English.

Szold was, in certain respects, a forerunner of Jewish women's liberation. When her mother died in 1916, a close male friend, Haym Peretz, volunteered to say the *Mourner's *Kaddish* for the dead woman. Szold graciously refused the offer. "I believe," she wrote him, "that the elimination of women from such duties was never intended by our law and custom—women were freed from positive duties when they could not perform them [because of family responsibilities] but not when they could. It was never intended that, if they could perform them, their performance of them should not be considered as valuable and valid as when one of the male sex performed them."

Szold's outstanding contribution to Jewish life was the creation of the largest Jewish organization in American history, Hadassah Women. Although Zionist, Hadassah particularly involved itself in meeting the health needs of both Jews and Arabs in Palestine. Today, the foremost hospital in Israel and the entire Middle East is the Hadassah Hospital in Jerusalem. Szold insisted that the most up-to-date medical treatment be extended to the Arabs of Palestine as well as to the Jews, and Hadassah played a major role in lowering Arab infant mortality. The Hadassah spirit of volunteerism and nondiscrimination was unfortunately rejected by the Arab leadership, which may have feared that its example would lessen hatred between Jews and Arabs. In early 1948, just before the State of Israel was declared, Arab troops ambushed and murdered seventy-seven Jewish doctors and nurses from Hadassah Hospital.

During the 1930s, Szold involved Hadassah in a program to rescue Jewish youth from Germany, and later from all of Europe. It is estimated that the program she created, "Youth Aliyah," saved some 22,000 Jewish children from Hitler's *concentration camps.

The personal tragedy of Szold's life was that she never married; this woman, whose life was devoted to saving the lives of children, never had children of her own. While in her forties, she did fall passionately in love with the great Talmud scholar Louis Ginzberg. He was fifteen years her junior, and returned her feelings only platonically. Shortly after their relationship ended, she wrote: "Today it is four weeks since my only real happiness was killed." Many years later, she confided to a friend: "I would exchange everything for one child of my own."

To this day Henrietta Szold is regarded as one of the genuine heroic figures of American-Jewish history, a scholarly woman, a passionately committed Jew, and a person who saved many thousands of lives.

The organization she founded, Hadassah, has about 350,000 members and is the largest Jewish organization in the United States.

SOURCES AND FURTHER READINGS: Szold's letter explaining why she would say the *Kaddish* for her mother is printed in *Response*, Summer 1973, p. 76. Szold's statement of loneliness is cited in Edward Wagenknecht, *Daughters of the Covenant: Portraits of Six Jewish Women*, p. 167. The standard biography of Szold is Joan Dash, *Summoned to Jerusalem: The Life of Henrietta Szold*.

218

LOUIS BRANDEIS (1856–1941)

WHEN THE LATE CHIEF RABBI OF PALESTINE, ABRAHAM ISAAC *KOOK, was on his deathbed, he asked his famous but irreligious Jewish doctor: "When will the day come when the Jews who are great will also be great Jews?"

Louis Brandeis, the first Jew appointed to the United States Supreme Court, was a great man who had a great Jewish heart. In 1917, he was a very successful lawyer, specializing in labor law, when President Woodrow Wilson offered his name in nomination for a Supreme Court vacancy. There was substantial congressional opposition, both because of Brandeis's liberal politics and because of his faith. After a hard-fought battle, however, his nomination was confirmed. In later years, American President Franklin Delano Roosevelt regarded Brandeis as a model of morality, and affectionately nicknamed him "Isaiah."

While on the Court, Brandeis was a tenacious defender of liberal values. In the face of a highly conservative Court, which routinely struck down new social legislation, Brandeis argued that the American Constitution did not embody any one particular social or economic approach. Among other issues, he wrote notable dissenting opinions on behalf of minimum wage laws, and in defense of the rights of labor unions. When he retired in 1939, the Court was rapidly moving toward accepting the views Brandeis had so long held in dissent.

Shortly before his appointment to the Supreme Court, Brandeis was converted into a passionate and highly involved Zionist. He served as president of the American Zionist Federation, and actively raised funds to further Jewish settlements and cultural life in Palestine. Subsequent to his appointment to the Supreme Court, he resigned from all extra-judicial affiliations except for his Zionist activities. In 1920, he even considered resigning from the Supreme Court to become head of the World Zionist Organization.

Brandeis aggressively criticized Jews who expressed fear that support for Zionism would call their loyalty to America into question. "Multiple loyalties," he cogently explained, do not necessarily imply "mutually exclusive loyalties. A man can be loyal to his family, his city, his state and his country, and need have no fear that these loyalties will conflict." Today, almost a century later, American Jews still cite Brandeis's formulation to counter accusations that those who work on behalf of Israel are guilty of having dual loyalties.

In the early 1920s, Brandeis had a falling-out with Chaim *Weizmann (the leading figure in world Zionism and, later, Israel's first president), and subsequently resigned from his leadership positions in the Zionist movement. He remained, however, an ardent supporter of Zionism, and upon his death, the largest bequest in his will was to the Zionist movement.

Until the end of his life, Brandeis remained ardently committed to the survival of American Jewry. He urged American Jews to deepen their own Jewish knowledge and involvement: "To be good Americans," he liked to preach, "we must be better Jews." For Brandeis, this statement was no mere rhetoric.

When Zionist educator Shlomo Bardin came to the United States from Israel in the 1930s, Bardin confided to him his unhappiness at the large number of Jewish college students who were alienated from their faith. Indifferent and alienated Jews, Brandeis believed, were bad both for the Jews and for America. He was particularly disheartened—as were many Jews and non-Jews—by the attraction of many secular Jews in the 1930s to communism and to Stalin. Brandeis urged Bardin to delay his return to Palestine and to work with the college youth. In the course of several conversations, Bardin and Brandeis developed the idea for what would become the Brandeis Institute, the first organization which Mrs. Brandeis permitted to be named for her husband after his death in 1941. At this institute, college students could immerse themselves in Jewish thinking and practice.

Today, the Brandeis-Bardin Institute is one of many Jewish institutions named after Judge Louis Brandeis (it is now part of the recently formed American Jewish University). The most famous is Brandeis University, a nondenominational university run under Jewish auspices, in Waltham, Massachusetts.

SOURCES AND FURTHER READINGS: Milton Konvitz, "Louis D. Brandeis," in Simon Noveck, ed., *Great Jewish Personalities in Modern Times*, pp. 295–316; *Brandeis on Zionism*, edited by Solomon Goldman; E. Rabinowitz, *Justice Louis D. Brandeis, the Zionist Chapter in His Life*. That Brandeis considered resigning his Supreme Court seat to become head of the World Zionist Organization is noted in Robert Burt, *Two Jewish Justices*, p. 8; see also pp. 6–36. Burt, himself a professor of law at Yale University, records the fascinating rationale offered by the seven past presidents of the American Bar Association who opposed Brandeis's appointment to the Supreme Court. Their spokesman declared before the Senate: "Mr. Brandeis does not act according to the canons of the Bar. The trouble with Mr. Brandeis is that he . . . always acts the part of a judge toward his clients, instead of being his client's lawyer, which is against the practices of the Bar." Professor Burt comments: "This may seem an extraordinary basis on which to find a person unfit for judicial office. But the charge was seriously meant: that Brandeis violated professional norms because he insisted on applying his own standards of right conduct to his clients and therefore was prepared to judge them before he would undertake advocacy on their behalf" (p. 9). In this regard, whether intentionally or not, Brandeis stood within the Jewish—if not the American—judicial tradition (see *Sanhedrin*).

219

ALBERT EINSTEIN (1879–1955)

ALBERT EINSTEIN MIGHT WELL BE THE MOST FAMOUS JEW OF THE twentieth century. In mankind's history, probably no person has ever been better known simply for being a genius. Einstein is primarily renowned for his theory of relativity. His importance in American history derives, in large measure, from a letter he wrote President Franklin Delano Roosevelt in 1939, alerting him to experiments in nuclear fission at Columbia University: "Some recent work by E. Fermi and L. Szilard leads me to expect that the element uranium may be turned into a new and important source of energy in the immediate future. . . . This new phenomenon could also lead to the construction of bombs, and it is conceivable—though much less certain—that extremely powerful bombs of a new type may thus be constructed."

Einstein's letter and international reputation were major factors in motivating Roosevelt shortly thereafter to assemble the Manhattan Project, which five years later produced the atom bomb that secured American victory over Japan and ended World War II. Einstein's response when he heard of the atomic attack on Hiroshima was a simple *"Oy vey."*

Unlike most twentieth-century Jews who achieved prominence in science and the arts, Einstein was fiercely loyal to his people. Even as his personal fame spread, he remained acutely conscious of their sufferings. When a journalist questioned him about international reactions to his scientific findings, the German-born Einstein responded: "If my theory of relativity is proved true, Germany will claim me as a German, and France will proclaim me a citizen of the world. If it is proved untrue, France will call me a German, and Germany will call me a Jew." Although not conventionally religious, Einstein maintained a strong conviction in a Supreme Being. "God does not play dice with the universe" was how he expressed his conviction that order, not anarchy, prevailed in the cosmos.

Einstein's life story has long been of solace to parents whose children have performed poorly in school. As a youngster, he was a mediocre student, preferring to pursue his own private interests (in recent years, it has been reported that his weakness as a student has been exaggerated). Later, when Einstein matured, he became the epitome of an absentminded professor, capable of showing up at a wedding reception in his trademark fisherman's cap, ill-fitting trousers, and sandals.

Ironically, though he is associated in the popular mind with the creation of the atom bomb, Einstein was a pacifist for much of his life. The rise of Nazism, however, caused him to reconsider his absolute opposition to warfare; to confront Nazism with pacifism, he believed, was to ensure its victory.

Shortly after the Nazis' rise to power in Germany, they made clear their contempt and hatred for Einstein. While he was lecturing in the United States in 1933, Nazi troops ransacked his residence. He never returned to Germany, accepting instead a professorship at Princeton University's Institute of Advanced Studies. He remained there until his death in 1955. It was during his years in Princeton that he received a disturbing report from Lise Meitner, a Jewish woman who had worked for the German scientist Otto Hahn at the Kaiser Wilhelm Institut in Berlin. She informed Einstein that Hahn was heading a team of German scientists charged with developing bombs, based on nuclear fission, of unprecedented destructive capability. He immediately perceived the implications of Hahn's work, understood the pressing need for the United States to pursue this field of inquiry, and thus wrote to Roosevelt. There is a certain delicious irony in the fact that Nazi antisemitism—responsible for chasing both Einstein, Meitner, and hundreds of thousands of other Jews out of Germany—also guaranteed that the Axis would lose the Second World War. If not for Nazi antisemitism, Germany would likely have been the first nation to develop the atom bomb, and the history of the world would have been radically different.

Throughout his life, Einstein identified with Zionism, and he was an early supporter of the Hebrew University in Jerusalem. Though he never took up residence in Palestine, when Chaim *Weizmann, Israel's first president, died in 1952, Prime Minister David *Ben-Gurion asked Einstein to become Israel's second president. While honored and heartened by the offer of the largely ceremonial office, Einstein refused, writing: "[I am] deeply touched by the offer, but [am] not suited for the post." Even in his last years, he clearly preferred working as a scientist than as a diplomat. Where his name alone could help, however, Einstein was always happy to make it available. Thus, he allowed *Yeshiva University to name its medical school the Albert Einstein College of Medicine. Einstein was generous to less prominent institutions as well. My late aunt, Nunya Bialik, was approached in the 1930s by the leaders of a small Jewish-sponsored hospital in New York who asked her to write a letter to Einstein requesting him to join its board of directors. My aunt composed the letter and sent it off. Quite quickly, Einstein responded; he would be honored to join the hospital's board, he wrote, only he hoped they would not be offended if his schedule precluded his attendance at board meetings. The hospital's directors, who were delighted that the name of the most famous scientist in the world would now adorn their masthead, gladly accepted this not unreasonable condition.

To this day, Einstein remains, for Jews and many non-Jews as well, the model of an intellectual and moral giant.

SOURCES AND FURTHER READINGS: Albert Einstein, *About Zionism*, and *Ideas and Opinions*; Ronald Wilson Clark, *Einstein: The Life and Times*.

RABBI JOSEPH SOLOVEITCHIK (1903 — 1993)

RABBI JOSEPH SOLOVEITCHIK WAS THE PREEMINENT FIGURE OF twentieth-century Modern Orthodox Judaism. During his more than three decades as professor of Talmud at *Yeshiva University, he ordained more than a thousand rabbis—probably more than had been ordained by any person in modern Jewish history—many of whom went on to occupy the leading Orthodox pulpits in the United States.

What was it about Rabbi Soloveitchik, Jews often ask, that marked him off as *modern* Orthodox, as opposed to Rabbi Moshe *Feinstein, who was regarded until his death in 1986 as the leader of *right-wing* Orthodoxy? For one thing, Rabbi Soloveitchik had a Ph.D. in philosophy from the University of Berlin. His high level of secular education immediately distinguished him from the world of East European Orthodoxy, in which a university education, in and of itself, was often regarded as proof of a man's irreligiosity.

Rabbi Soloveitchik's commitment to high-quality secular education helped induce him later to accept the position of *Rosh Yeshiva* (head of the yeshiva) at Yeshiva University. Unlike almost every other higher yeshiva in the world, Yeshiva University looks to achieve an integration between secular and religious studies.

Rabbi Soloveitchik also differed from the more right-wing yeshiva leaders in his commitment to Zionism. Most rabbis associated with the yeshiva world identify with the Agudat Yisrael, a *non-Zionist* Israeli political party which cooperates with the Israeli government but which refuses to attach any religious significance to a non-Orthodox Jewish state. Rabbi Soloveitchik long identified actively with Mizrachi, a religious pro-Zionist party. In the crucial months before the State of Israel was created, he declared that it is better to live in a Jewish state ruled by the most secular Jewish political parties than to remain in a religious Jewish neighborhood in Brooklyn.

Throughout his life, Rabbi Soloveitchik published few works, in line with a longstanding family tradition of issuing almost nothing during one's lifetime. His major, book-length essay *Ish ha-Halakha* (*Halakhic Man*) pictures an ideal Jew and rabbi in a manner markedly different from the depiction of the ideal rabbi in right-wing Orthodox circles. To the question "What is the primary function of a rabbi?" Rabbi Soloveitchik quoted approvingly the words of his grandfather, Rabbi Hayyim Brisker: "To redress the grievances of those who are abandoned and alone, to protect the dignity of the poor, and to save the oppressed from the hands of the oppressor." As Rabbi Soloveitchik himself concluded: "Neither ritual decisions nor political leadership constitute the main task of halakhic man."

In the yeshiva world, Rabbi Soloveitchik's grandfather, Reb Hayyim, was known for the exceedingly subtle form of analysis to which he subjected the Talmud. Because Reb Hayyim lived in the Russian city of Brisk (Brest-Litovsk), this analysis became known as the Brisker method of learning. In Rabbi Soloveitchik's life as well, the teaching of Torah was his dominating passion. During most of his more than five decades in the United States, he lived in Boston, commuting weekly to New York to give his Talmud classes at Yeshiva University. He delivered three weekly lectures at YU, each lasting between two and four hours. One evening each week, he also gave a public Talmud class in New York City. In addition, he delivered several more lectures every week in Boston, sometimes orating more than twenty hours in a week.

At Yeshiva University, Rabbi Soloveitchik was known simply as "The Rav." In his rabbinic capacities, both in New York and in Boston, he was frequently confronted with difficult questions on Jewish law. Although long reputed to be a liberal in responding to individual queries, he seldom allowed his liberal responses to be publicized. Those public pronouncements which he authorized generally were such that they would be accepted in the most Orthodox circles. For example, when a former student who lived near a Conservative synagogue asked if he could attend the congregation on Rosh ha-Shana in order to hear the *shofar (ram's horn) blown, Rabbi Soloveitchik ruled that it was better for the student to stay at home and not hear the *shofar* than to hear it blown in a Conservative synagogue. Rabbi Soloveitchik seems to have been particularly furious at the Conservative movement for its elimination of the *mekhitza (the partition in the synagogue that separates male and female worshipers). To the claim that changing times necessitate changes in Jewish traditions such as the *mekhitza*, Rabbi Soloveitchik responded with uncharacteristic intemperateness: "A transcendental tenet is binding regardless of its unpopularity with the multitude. Was the commandment against murder declared null and void while the Nazi hordes were practicing genocide?"

Nonetheless, Rabbi Soloveitchik became a prime symbol of an Orthodox Judaism that can achieve the highest levels of knowledge in both Jewish and secular studies.

SOURCES AND FURTHER READINGS: Rabbi Joseph Soloveitchik, *Halakhic Man*, translated by Lawrence Kaplan; Soloveitchik, "The Lonely Man of Faith," *Tradition* 7:2 (Summer 1965); Pinchas Peli, *On Repentance: A Collection of the Annual Discourses on Repentance Given by Rabbi Joseph B. Soloveitchik Before the High Holy Days*; Aharon Lichtenstein, "Rabbi Joseph Soloveitchik," in Simon Noveck, ed., *Great Jewish Thinkers of the Twentieth Century*, pp. 281–298. Soloveitchik's comment on the *mekhitza* is printed in Baruch Litvin, ed., *The Sanctity of the Synagogue*, p. 141.

221

RABBI ABRAHAM JOSHUA HESCHEL

(1907–1972)

RABBI ABRAHAM JOSHUA HESCHEL IS OFTEN THOUGHT OF AS THE JEWish equivalent of the Reverend Martin Luther King, Jr.—the quintessential Jewish leader and religious activist. Indeed, one of the most famous photographs of Heschel shows him marching arm in arm with King during the 1965 civil rights march in Selma, Alabama.

In fact, political involvements were only a small part of Heschel's life. His primary lifelong concern was to recapture Jewish scholarship from some-times esoteric, even obscurantist, academics. In the case of Bible studies, for example, Heschel was profoundly unhappy that so much scholarship focused on questions of philology (for example, comparing Ugaritic and ancient Hebrew), archaeology, or comparative jurisprudence. The power of the Bible, he believed, came from its ability to address every human being in every generation. Characteristic of Heschel's approach to Jewish studies was his statement in his biography of the firebrand *Hasidic *rebbe* Menachem Mendel of Kotzk: "A bridegroom," Rabbi Menachem Mendel had taught, "might under the bridal canopy repeat to the bride, 'You are betrothed' a hundred times. If however he does not add the [Hebrew word] *li*, '[you are betrothed] *to me*,' then it is as if he said nothing. The entire wedding with all its preparations are worthless. The crucial point is *li*—to me. All of scholar-ship . . . [is] worthless and all of worship is futile if they do not penetrate one's bones. Essential is *li* [emphasis added]."

In his pronouncements on Jewish law, Heschel's primary concern was to decipher the law's implications for modern Jews. "There are Jews," he noted, "who are more concerned with a blood-spot on an egg [which renders it unkosher], than with a blood-spot on a dollar bill." On occasion, Heschel ruefully noted the greater attention many Jews pay to ritual rather than ethi-cal laws. "The Jewish people," he declared, "are a messenger who have for-gotten their message."

Heschel grew up in Poland and received his secular education at the Uni-versity of Berlin. Just before World War II, he was rescued from Germany by *Hebrew Union College, the *Reform rabbinical seminary, which appointed him to the faculty of its Cincinnati campus. Heschel was scrupu-lously observant of Jewish rituals, while the Reform seminary had a much more lax attitude toward ritual observances. Several Reform rabbis who were HUC students during the early 1940s have reported that Heschel often was ridiculed for his religious piety. Most HUC students rarely had encountered another Jew who put on *tefillin* (phylacteries) and who observed *kashrut* (the college's own cafeteria was not kosher), and they tended to regard such observances as antiquated and pointless.

Nonetheless, Heschel always remained grateful to the Reform seminary for inviting him to America. However, in 1945, he accepted an appointment to the faculty of the *Conservative Jewish Theological Seminary. Here, too, he encountered considerable opposition, from two faculty members in particular, Mordecai Kaplan (see next entry) and Saul Lieberman. Kaplan, the founder of the *Reconstructionist movement, prided himself on being an absolute rationalist in his approach to religion. The most devastating critique he could direct at a student was to call him a mystic. Heschel was, however, deeply attracted to Jewish spirituality in general, and to mysticism in particular. Thus, Kaplan's attacks on mysticism were seen by many as attacks on Heschel as well.

Lieberman, the major scholar of Talmud at the seminary during Heschel's years there, was one of the twentieth century's great talmudic minds, and an *Orthodox Jew in practice. On religious issues, he shared little in common with Mordecai Kaplan. For him, however, the primary area of Jewish scholarship was Talmud study, and he regarded Heschel's focus on spiritual matters as a less worthy arena for Jewish scholars.

Nevertheless, Heschel's writings won him a wide following in the Jewish community as well as among Christian theologians. He produced a steady stream of books in an eloquent, poetic English, a remarkable feat for a man who did not learn the language until he was past thirty. Among his most important books are *Man's Quest for God* (on prayer), *God in Search of Man*, *The Sabbath*, and *The Earth Is the Lord's*.

In his later years, Heschel was invited to teach courses on Judaism at the Union Theological Seminary, which is one of the great Protestant seminaries in America and across the street from the Jewish Theological Seminary. He soon became renowned as a "prophet" of American Jewry, an image that went well with Heschel's long white beard and penetrating eyes. He represented American Jewry well in this new role, both through his involvement in the civil rights movement and through his early activities on behalf of Soviet Jewry.

Since his death, Heschel has become probably the greatest hero produced by the Conservative movement in the United States, and many Conservative day schools and other institutions have been named for him.

CHARACTERISTIC QUOTES OF HESCHEL

"It takes three things to attain a sense of significant being:
God
A Soul
And a Moment
And the three are always here" (*The Insecurity of Freedom*, p. 84).

"In biblical days prophets were astir while the world was asleep; today the world is astir while church and synagogue are busy with trivialities" (*The Insecurity of Freedom*, p. 174).

"God is of no importance unless He is of supreme importance" (*Man's Quest for God*, p. xiii).

"According to Albert Camus, 'There is only one really serious philosophical problem: and that is suicide.' May I differ and suggest that there is only one really serious problem: and that is martyrdom.

"Is there anything worth dying for?" (*Who Is Man?*, p. 92).

SOURCES AND FURTHER READINGS: Abraham Joshua Heschel, *Man's Quest for God; The Insecurity of Freedom; God in Search of Man*. The quotations are drawn from Samuel Dresner, ed., *I Asked for Wonder: A Spiritual Anthology [of] Abraham Joshua Heschel*. Edward Kaplan and Samuel Dresner, *Abraham Joshua Heschel: Prophetic Witness*.

RABBI MORDECAI KAPLAN (1881–1983)

RECONSTRUCTIONISM

Judaism as a Civilization

MORDECAI KAPLAN GREW UP AS AN *ORTHODOX JEW, LIVED MOST OF his life as a *Conservative Jew, and founded what is today a fourth denomination in Jewish life, Reconstructionism. Kaplan's break with his Orthodox upbringing was radical. In his adult years, he found himself rejecting two fundamental and traditional beliefs: that of a transcendent, personal God, and that of the Jews as God's *Chosen People.

For Kaplan, modern science rendered untenable the concept of a personal God Who intervenes in history and knows the mind of each individual. He believed rather in the doctrine of godliness, that inside each human being is a spirit that serves as the source of a person's moral values. Although such a doctrine logically should have led Kaplan to cease observing all Jewish rituals—there was, after all, no God who could have commanded them—he remained an observant Jew. He accepted the rituals not as divine commandments, but as "folkways" of the Jewish people.

Orthodox contemporaries of Kaplan were not impressed. When he issued a new prayerbook in 1945, critics joked that prayers in the book were not addressed to God but "To whom it may concern." Outraged by the changes Kaplan introduced into the prayerbook, a group of Orthodox rabbis excommunicated him and publicly burned his prayerbook.

Kaplan's rejection of a personal deity forced him to reject the Chosen People doctrine as well; without a personal God, the Jews obviously could not have been chosen. Kaplan also felt it was arrogant for Jews to assert that God had singled them out from all other nations and endowed them with a special mission. Dropping the idea of chosenness, he contended, would prove that Jews did not regard themselves as racially superior to their neighbors. One of the controversial changes he introduced into his prayerbook was an alteration in the blessing made by those called to the Torah for an *aliyah. In the traditional blessing, Jews thank God "who has chosen us from all the nations"; in Kaplan's prayerbook, "who has brought us nigh to Thy service," is said instead.

Even though he dropped belief in God as Jews had understood the term for three thousand years, Kaplan never considered dropping his Jewish affiliation. Basic to the Reconstructionist ideology that he developed was the conviction that Judaism is an "evolving religious civilization," one in which religious teachings, ritual observances, peoplehood, and culture all play a part. Kaplan entitled his first, and most important book, *Judaism as a Civilization*. Though he was fifty-three when it came out, he lived another forty-eight years, long enough to see his literary creation become the basis of a new Jewish denomination.

For decades after Kaplan began developing and teaching his philosophy of Reconstructionist Judaism, he resisted breaking with the Conservative movement; he taught at its *Jewish Theological Seminary for over half a century, from 1909 to 1963. This rationalist rejector of the traditional Jewish understanding of God exerted a powerful influence on many Conservative rabbis ordained from the 1920s to the 1950s and influenced many of them to stop believing in a personal God. It is probably no coincidence that the most popular professor at the seminary in the years following Kaplan's departure was Abraham Joshua Heschel (see preceding entry), in many ways his theological opposite. Heschel, an intensely spiritual Jew, was devoted in his writings and his life to finding ways for people to connect to God.

Yet Jewish life, outside of Orthodoxy, has been deeply affected by Kaplan. It was he who first developed the idea of *Jewish community centers as focal points where Jews could meet for reasons other than prayer. In 1922, Kaplan celebrated the *Bat Mitzvah of his daughter, Judith, the first such celebration for any Jewish girl in the United States. Since then, Bat Mitzvah ceremonies for women have become common. Kaplan also developed the idea of *havurot*, small Jewish groups that would band together for study and observe Jewish rituals and life-cycle events together. Kaplan's idea later evolved into the *havurah* movement, which enjoyed particular popularity in the 1970s and 1980s.

Upon Kaplan's departure from the Jewish Theological Seminary, his disciples felt free to go ahead and organize Reconstructionism as a separate movement with synagogues and a rabbinical association. In 1968, the Reconstructionist Rabbinical College (RRC) was founded in Philadelphia. Though Reconstructionism is based almost entirely on the writings and teachings of one man, the college has evolved very differently from the rationalist approach advocated by Kaplan. Indeed, some of Kaplan's fundamental teachings have been rejected by many Reconstructionists. Today, it is common for RRC students to accept the notion of a personal God, and to recite the blessings that speak of chosenness. However, in contrast to the Conservative movement's Jewish Theological Seminary, the college permits its rabbinical students much greater latitude in ritual observance and sets very few limits on the understandings of Judaism advocated by its students.

There are today over one hundred Reconstructionist synagogues throughout the United States. The movement's flagship synagogue, founded by Kaplan himself, is the Society for the Advancement of Judaism, which is located on New York's Upper West Side.

SOURCES AND FURTHER READINGS: Mordecai Kaplan, *Judaism as a Civilization*; Arthur Hertzberg, *The Jews in America*, pp. 260–263. Ira Eisenstein, "Mordecai Kaplan," in Simon Noveck, ed., *Great Jewish Thinkers of the Twentieth Century*, pp. 253–279. *Judaism* magazine, Winter 1981; most of the issue is taken up with fifteen assessments of Kaplan by many different Jewish scholars; it was published in honor of Kaplan's hundredth birthday. For a critique of Kaplan, see Eliezer Berkovits, *Major Themes in Modern Philosophies of Judaism*.

223

RABBI MOSHE FEINSTEIN/REB MOSHE
(1895–1986)

THE ONLY JEWS WHO CALLED MOSHE FEINSTEIN "RABBI FEINSTEIN" were those who didn't know him or appreciate his significance. Throughout Orthodoxy, he was known simply as Reb Moshe. He also was regarded as the outstanding scholar of Jewish law in the second half of the twentieth century. A popular joke among rabbis claimed that when yeshiva students were accorded rabbinical ordination, Reb Moshe's phone number was listed on the certificate, so that they could telephone him immediately when confronted with difficult questions of Jewish law and ritual. He was so widely and deeply loved that upon his death in 1986, some sixty thousand Jews accompanied his coffin in New York. His body was flown immediately to Israel, where 150,000 Israelis attended his funeral, an outstanding tribute to a man who had never lived in Israel.

Reb Moshe's popularity derived from a courageous willingness to answer by letter or on the telephone any and every question posed to him. He was renowned for considering all possible leniencies in instances where an individual's well-being and happiness were at stake. An Orthodox rabbi told me of a case in his congregation involving an irreligious young man who was a *Kohen (from a priestly family) and who became Orthodox. Shortly thereafter he fell in love with a young woman who was divorced. The Torah forbids a Kohen from marrying a divorcée (Leviticus 21:7). The young man approached the rabbi, who explained sadly that nothing could be done. Two months later, the rabbi received an invitation to the couple's wedding. He telephoned the young man and was told that he had received permission from Reb Moshe to marry the girl. Rabbi Feinstein had ruled that since the young man himself had not been raised as a religious Jew, indeed his family had been irreligious for several generations, it was inconceivable to rely on the testimony of his nonobservant father to affirm the young man's status as a Kohen. In effect, the several generations of irreligiosity in the family had invalidated the father's right to give testimony on religious matters, and so the son could not rely on his father's word that he was a *Kohen*. On the one hand, the ruling seemed a harsh attack on the reliability of nonreligious Jews. On the other hand, its effect was to permit a young couple in love to marry. Few other Orthodox rabbis would have had the courage to issue so far-reaching a judgment.

While known for being liberal when possible in private rulings, Reb Moshe was very illiberal in many of his public pronouncements. He regarded *Reform and *Conservative Judaism as heresies and granted them no religious status whatsoever. Even the harshness of this position, however, led to one lenient result. More than a century ago, Reform Judaism dropped the requirement that a divorced woman receive a Jewish divorce (see *Get*) from her husband. In the Reform movement a civil divorce decree is deemed sufficient. Orthodoxy rejects this ruling; a marriage that is entered into as a religious marriage can only be dissolved religiously. According to Jewish law, a woman who remarries without procuring a religious divorce is, Jewishly speaking, an adulteress, and any children resulting from the second union are *mamzerim* (bastards) and forbidden to marry all Jews except other *mamzerim*. The implications of this proscription for the contemporary Jewish community—in which many Jews divorce without procuring a *get*—is horrific (see *The Vanishing American Jew*). Reb Moshe ruled, however, that in almost all instances, marriages performed by Reform rabbis are not Jewishly valid, because neither the rabbis themselves nor the witnesses to the ceremony are fully observant of Jewish law. Thus, according to Reb Moshe, couples married by Reform (and, in Reb Moshe's opinion, almost all Conservative) rabbis are regarded as having lived together, and the dissolution of their relationship might well require no Jewish divorce. Reb Moshe's authority was such that this radical ruling has been accepted by many Orthodox rabbis, thereby solving in most instances what would otherwise be an insoluble problem for Orthodox Jews.

The ruling was certainly harsh in terms of the status Reb Moshe accorded non-Orthodox rabbis, and many other Orthodox rabbis have not agreed with Reb Moshe's position. But the ruling's practical result has been beneficial to tens of thousands of Jews who otherwise would be in danger of being marked off as *mamzerim*.

Should one regard Reb Moshe, therefore, as a conservative or a liberal on matters of Jewish law? This is not an easy question to answer. A more modern Orthodox rabbi might well have extended legitimacy to marriages performed by Reform rabbis. The result, however, would have been an enormous increase in the number of Jews regarded as adulterers and of children designated as bastards.

The thousands of questions posed to Reb Moshe covered all aspects of modern life. One asked if Jews were permitted to be shareholders in public companies that conduct business on the Sabbath or Jewish holidays. Shareholders are regarded as partners in a company, and it would seem forbidden for a Jew to profit from acts of Sabbath desecration. On the other hand, prohibiting Jews from owning stock would severely restrict the community from participating in a major part of the capitalist economy. After studying the issue of stock ownership, Reb Moshe ruled that while, technically speaking, shareowners are part owners of a company, in practice their participation in company affairs is so minimal (except if they own substantial blocks of the company) that they do not affect business policies, and so they cannot be held responsible for them. Instead of regarding shareholders as partners or part owners of the company, it is more realistic to see them as potential claimants to profits. Thus, Jews are permitted to own stocks in those companies.

Reb Moshe was highly esteemed throughout the Orthodox world, not only for his talmudic learning and knowledge of Jewish law, but also for his humility and friendliness. With his death, it was generally acknowledged that there was no one figure in Orthodox life as widely beloved and accepted as he.

SOURCES AND FURTHER READINGS: Shimon Finkelman, *Reb Moshe: The Life and Ideals of HaGaon Rabbi Moshe Feinstein* chronicles episodes reflecting the saintliness of Reb Moshe's character. Emanuel Rackman, "Halachic Progress: Rabbi Moshe Feinstein's *Igrot Moshe* on *Even ha-Ezer*," in his *One Man's Judaism*, pp. 238–252, examines important responsa of Reb Moshe on issues of marriage and divorce.

224

SUNDAY SCHOOL

HEBREW SCHOOL/*TALMUD TORAH*

DAY SCHOOL

YESHIVA

"IT WAS THE BEST OF TIMES, IT WAS THE WORST OF TIMES," CHARLES Dickens' oft-cited assessment of eighteenth-century Europe, remains a strikingly apt image of Jewish education in the United States. Never have so many young Jews received no Jewish education at all; never have so many young Jews received so intense a Jewish education.

The types of schools to which Jewish children are sent to study their religion, language, and history fall into several different categories.

Least intensive are the Sunday schools. These institutions are generally affiliated with synagogues, and students attend classes on Sunday mornings for one to three hours. Sunday schools suffer, however, from an inherently insoluble problem: The scope of material one must absorb to become Jewishly literate—the Bible, Talmud, Hebrew language, Jewish law, ethics, philosophy, and history—is so wide-ranging that one to three hours a week can never be enough. As a result, graduates of most Sunday schools come out knowing little more than a smattering of Bible stories, a few rituals and blessings, and the ability to haltingly read, but not understand, Hebrew.

Aligned with the Sunday school, though meeting for more hours per week, is the Hebrew school, often known as the *Talmud Torah*. Like the Sunday school, the *Talmud Torah* is generally affiliated with a synagogue, and students usually attend classes two or three times a week, for about four to six hours. *Talmud Torahs* meet in the late afternoon or early evening, after students have completed a regular school day. Unfortunately, this has proven to be a serious problem: Many students arrive at Hebrew school tired from a full day of secular studies, and with little desire to spend more hours in a classroom. In addition, the students perceive—correctly as a rule—that their performance in Hebrew school is much less important to their parents than their performance in secular school: They are attending Hebrew school, by and large, to prepare for their *Bar and Bat Mitzvahs. (Indeed, the only reason *Talmud Torahs* have as many students as they do is because most synagogues have regulations that bar any child who has not attended a *Talmud Torah* from celebrating a Bar or Bat Mitzvah in the congregation.) As a result, attendance at almost all Hebrew schools falls precipitously after the Bar and Bat Mitzvah celebrations.

Nonetheless, the *Talmud Torah*/Hebrew school has been the institution in which most American Jews have been religiously educated.

In recent years, the inadequacies of Sunday schools and *Talmud Torahs* have been widely recognized, and parents desiring a broader-based knowledge of Judaism for their children have been increasingly opting to send them to day schools—full-time elementary schools and high schools where students spend up to half of the day in Jewish studies and the rest in general subjects. In recent years, there has been an exponential growth in such schools; more than 93 percent of the Jewish day schools in the United States have been founded since 1940.

While day schools until recently were associated with the Orthodox community, there are now dozens of Conservative day schools, usually known as Solomon *Schechter schools (Schechter is regarded as the founding figure of Conservative Judaism in the United States). More recently, the Reform movement has shifted from an antagonistic attitude toward day schools (most early Reform rabbis feared that day schools would segregate American Jews from their gentile neighbors and retard their Americanization) to a more open, often positive attitude. There are now Reform day schools in the major cities of the United States: In Los Angeles, the schools affiliatated with Stephen S. Wise Synagogue, which run from nursery to twelfth grade, have about 1,600 students.

Nonetheless, the Jews most likely to send their children to day schools are still the Orthodox, and the growth of the day school movement in the United States has been largely due to the efforts of Orthodox parents and Orthodox educators. Currently, virtually every city in the United States with over five thousand Jewish residents has at least one day school.

A serious problem besetting day schools and their parents is that—as is the case with private schools in general—the tuition is very high. Middle-class parents in New York, for example, with three children in a Jewish day school may easily find tuition costs consuming twenty-five percent or more of their income.

While many day schools have the word "yeshiva" in their name (for example, the largest day school in the United States, the Yeshivah of Flatbush in Brooklyn, New York), the word itself has traditionally been applied to Jewish schools primarily devoted to the study of Talmud. Yeshivot have historically been Orthodox institutions, with all-male student bodies from Bar Mitzvah age up. The most liberal of the yeshivot in the United States is *Yeshiva University, where students are encouraged to pursue secular studies in addition to Jewish studies. At many of the more traditional Orthodox institutions, secular studies are frowned upon, if not banned. Perhaps the most famous of the religiously right-wing yeshivot is the Lakewood Yeshiva, located in Lakewood, New Jersey (its official name is *Beth Medrash Govoha*), where over 4,700 students are enrolled.

Some students stay at a yeshiva for a few years, then leave to start a career. Others "learn" at yeshivot for ten or fifteen years. The regimen of a traditional yeshiva is rigorous; students are expected to study ten or more hours a day. The primary subject studied at most yeshivot is the Talmud and its commentaries.

Today, there are advanced yeshivot throughout North America and Israel, and it is estimated that there is currently a larger student body at these institutions than there ever was at the advanced yeshivot of nineteenth- and early twentieth-century Eastern Europe.

SOURCES AND FURTHER READINGS: Alvin Schiff, *The Jewish Day School in America* and *Issachar American Style: Contemporary Jewish Education*; David Singer, "The Growth of the Day School Movement," *Commentary* 56:2 (August 1973), pp. 53–57; William Helmreich, *The World of the Yeshiva: An Intimate Portrait of Orthodox Jewry*; Oscar Fasman, "Trends in the American Yeshiva Today," *Tradition*, 9:3 (Fall 1967), pp. 48–64; a rejoinder to Fasman by Emanuel Feldman was published in *Tradition* 9:4 (Spring 1968), pp. 56–64; Eliezer Berkovits, "Jewish Education in a World Adrift," *Tradition* 11:3 (Fall 1970), pp. 5–12; Berkovits, "A Contemporary Rabbinical School for Orthodox Jewry," *Tradition* 13:1 (Fall 1971), pp. 5–20.

225

WOMEN RABBIS

FROM THE PERSPECTIVE OF JEWISH LAW, THE CONSERVATIVE MOVE-
ment's decisions to count women in a *minyan* (the quorum necessary to
conduct a public prayer service) and to permit Jews to drive to synagogue on
the Sabbath were far more radical innovations than allowing women to be
ordained as rabbis. Yet, the Jewish Theological Seminary's 1983 decision to
ordain women provoked fierce attacks, not only from the Orthodox but from
many traditional figures in the Conservative movement as well, particularly
among the seminary's Talmud faculty.

In fact, the decision seemed inevitable once the Reform movement started
ordaining women rabbis during the early 1970s. Within a decade of Rabbi
Sally Priesand's 1972 ordination by the Hebrew Union College, women
comprised more than one third of the students at the Reform seminary. The
*Reconstructionist Rabbinical College in Philadelphia likewise decided
early on to ordain women.

In his desire to avoid a schism, the Jewish Theological Seminary's chancellor, Dr. Gerson Cohen, deferred a vote on the issue for several years until a
strong majority was united behind the proposal. When the decision to ordain
women was finally made, it stimulated the formation of a new group within
the Conservative movement called the Union for Traditional Conservative
Judaism.

When women started to be ordained, some people expressed the fear that
the non-Orthodox rabbinate would become a women's profession, one from
which men would soon shy away. Indeed, the more or less simultaneous admis-
sion of women into the Reform movement's cantorial school has apparently led
to women becoming the large majority of those students. As regards rabbinical
students, the predictions did not come to pass, and rabbinic schools still attract
large numbers of male students. As a rule, women rabbis to date have not been
appointed to head many major congregations, although they have been
appointed to serve as associate rabbis in many, and senior rabbis in many small

and mid-size communities. A characteristic problem besetting many women rabbis, particularly in the Conservative movement, is one of acceptance, more commonly among older Jews whose association with rabbis is purely male. Among younger Jews, however, acceptance of women as rabbis in the non-Orthodox world has been achieved. Other problems, however, do beset female clergy. Thus, while all women professionals have to cope with the competing demands of motherhood, the problem is particularly acute in the rabbinate, where hours of work are undefined and, hence, often never-ending. Several leading women rabbis have left pulpit work after becoming mothers, and gone into chaplaincy and administrative positions. As of 2007, the Conservative movement had ordained about 200 women rabbis, and Hebrew Union College, the Reform seminary has ordained well over 450 women rabbis. Women serve in the Reconstructionist rabbinate as well.

Blu Greenberg, a prominent and scholarly Orthodox feminist, has predicted that Orthodoxy will eventually ordain women too. While few within the Orthodox world share her optimism, there has been a remarkable growth in the number of female Orthodox religious scholars, some of whom are studying the very talmudic and other texts that are required for those seeking Orthodox rabbinic ordination.

SOURCES AND FURTHER READINGS: Simon Greenberg, ed., *The Ordination of Women as Rabbis: Studies and Responsa*; Sylvia Barack Fishman, "The Impact of Feminism on American Jewish Life," in David Singer, ed., *American Jewish Year Book 1989*, pp. 50–54. An Orthodox attack on the ordination of women was published by Pinchas Stolper, "Women Rabbis as a Death Sign," *Sh'ma* 7/170, March 16, 1979, pp. 73–75.

226

PATRILINEAL DESCENT

ACCORDING TO JEWISH LAW, A JEW IS ONE WHO IS BORN TO A JEWISH mother or is converted to Judaism. Therefore, a child who is born to a Jewish father and a non-Jewish mother is not Jewish even if raised with a Jewish identity. Prior to the 1960s, when intermarriage in the United States was relatively uncommon, this law had few practical consequences. Today, however, more than one third of Jews intermarry and, more often than not, it is Jewish men who marry non-Jewish women. As a result, there are an estimated 220,000, and perhaps substantially more, children in the United States born to non-Jewish women who are married to Jewish men. In 1983, the *Reform movement broke with Orthodox and *Conservative Judaism, and with Jewish law, and declared that such children can be regarded as Jews if their parents raise them with an exclusively Jewish identity.

The Reform decision to regard a child as Jewish on the basis of patrilineal as well as matrilineal descent has prompted a bitter controversy. In the future, traditional Jews who wish to marry a Reform Jew will have to examine their prospective spouse's background to ensure that he or she is Jewish according to Jewish law. In truth, however, the Reform movement's change is not nearly as great as it first seemed. Had the Reform rabbis maintained the traditional definition of a Jew, and insisted on converting children of non-Jewish women married to Jewish men, Orthodox Jews would still have considered the conversions invalid, since they reject the validity of Reform conversions (see *Denominational Conflicts* and *Convert/Ger*).

Within the Reform movement, a significant number of rabbis initially opposed the ruling, and a few even agitated to have the decision rescinded. That might occur only if the Orthodox rabbinate agrees to accept the validity of Reform conversions. Since no such agreement seems to be forthcoming, the Reform decision—apparently passed in large measure to accommodate and reassure the tens of thousands of intermarried couples who belong to Reform synagogues—will undoubtedly remain in force.

Within the Conservative movement, a minority attempt to define Jewishness on the basis of paternity as well as maternity has so far been soundly rejected.

227

LUBAVITCH

Rabbi Menachem Mendel Schneersohn (1903–1994)

I HAVE SOMETIMES POLLED JEWISH COLLEGE STUDENTS AT PUBLIC lectures, and asked how many have had contact with Hillel, the national Jewish campus organization. Invariably, a substantial number have raised their hands. What has always amazed me, however, is that an almost equal number have also reported contact on their campuses with Lubavitcher *Hasidim.

Lubavitch is a Hasidic movement founded in Russia at the end of the eighteenth century. Today, it is headquartered in the Crown Heights section of Brooklyn, New York. Its *rebbe* (charismatic religious leader) from 1950 until his death in 1994 was Rabbi Menachem Mendel Schneersohn, the seventh leader to head the movement since its founding in the late 1700s. While most other Hasidic groups today are insular, Rabbi Schneersohn placed tremendous emphasis on outreach, particularly on influencing the nonobservant to accept Jewish ritual observances. The tactics used by the Lubavitcher *Rebbe's* followers are much more aggressive and direct than those used by other religious Jews. Lubavitch sometimes sends vans—known as *Mitzvah* Mobiles—into Jewish neighborhoods. Their representatives stop men in the street, asking, "Are you Jewish?" If the man answers affirmatively, he then is asked: "Have you put on *tefillin* [phylacteries] today?" If the answer is no, he is invited into the truck, where another Hasid wraps the *tefillin* on his head and either right or left arm (if you are right-handed you put the *tefillin* on your left arm, and vice versa), and teaches him the appropriate blessing to recite. Women too are stopped and asked if they light Sabbath candles on Friday night. If they reply that they don't, they are offered a pair of candlesticks and encouraged to start fulfilling this commandment. For many years, Lubavitch took out a small classified ad on the *front* page of each Friday's *New York Times*. "Jewish Women/Girls," it read. "Remember to light Shabbat candles 18 minutes before sunset. . . ." The advertisement then noted what time candles were to be lit that evening, and listed a phone number for those wishing further information.

The Lubavitcher *Rebbe*, it sometimes seemed, commanded the largest Jewish "army" outside of Israel. His followers regarded him as their commander in chief and obeyed all his orders. Hasidim routinely would uproot their families and move to whatever city the *Rebbe* directed them, in order to establish or strengthen a Lubavitch presence there. The loyalty to Lubavitch's mission continued even after the *Rebbe*'s death, so that there are now Lubavitcher representatives in over a thousand cities throughout the United States and the world. One of the great figures of Israeli Orthodoxy, Rabbi Joseph Kahaneman, is reputed to have said: "I have found two things in every city I have ever visited, Coca-Cola and Lubavitcher Hasidim."

Upon arriving in a new city, Lubavitch representatives immediately raise money to establish a Chabad House (Chabad is another name for Lubavitch), which serves as a synagogue and a center of Lubavitch activity. Fundraising is not low-key. In Los Angeles, Chabad of California conducts an annual telethon—modeled on Jerry Lewis's telethon for children with muscular dystrophy—which raises several million dollars. The movement has an uncanny ability to attract an unusual assortment of helpers. I once was amazed to hear actor Carroll O'Connor, famed for his TV role as Archie Bunker, making a radio pitch on behalf of the Los Angeles Chabad House.

The synagogue service that is conducted at Chabad Houses and at Chabad synagogues while being Orthodox, of course, places a greater emphasis on singing and joyous praying than do most Orthodox synagogues.

Another *mitzvah* associated with Lubavitch is *kashrut* (see *Kosher*). Lubavitch representatives have a standing offer to help people make their kitchens kosher, a process which includes blowtorching the stove. In many communities, Lubavitch offers to reimburse any Jew who needs to buy new sets of kosher dishes.

Lubavitch's interests are not restricted purely to ritual observances. Some Chabad Houses run drug-rehabilitation programs, and more than a few wealthy donors to Chabad are nonreligious Jews whose children were broken from drug habits by Lubavitcher rabbis. Non-Jews as well have been treated in these drug-rehabilitation programs.

Because of its outreach to even the most alienated Jews, Lubavitch has become the one Orthodox group to evoke great affection from large segments of American Jewry: Much of the money the movement raises comes from the non-Orthodox. As one such unaffiliated Jew explained to me: "Their dedication and commitment is so intense and sincere that Lubavitch is the one group of Jews I am absolutely sure will still be around in another century."

Nonetheless, the movement has on occasion provoked considerable antagonism from other Jewish groups. The late Reform Rabbi Arthur Lelyveld labeled
Lubavitch a cult that alienated children from their parents. While most non-
Orthodox Jews rejected Lelyveld's attack as extreme and unfair, Lubavitch came
under widespread attack in the late 1980s because of the Lubavitcher *Rebbe's*
forceful lobbying for a change in the *"Who is a Jew?" law in Israel. In effect,
the *Rebbe* wanted Israel to accept as Jewish only those people born to Jewish
mothers or converted to Judaism by Orthodox rabbis. The *Rebbe's* desire to
invalidate Reform and Conservative conversions horrified not only the rabbis of
those denominations, but all other Reform and Conservative Jews.

More surprisingly, Lubavitch has encountered some significant opposition within Orthodoxy. Much of this opposition focused on the charge that
many Lubavitcher Hasidim regard their *rebbe* as the Messiah. This charge
lies behind the great antagonism toward the movement expressed by the late
Eliezer Shach, one of Israel's leading ultra-Orthodox rabbis.

Nonetheless, despite the opposition, Lubavitch continues to maintain an
active presence in Jewish communities throughout the United States, Israel,
and the world, and continues to grow. In 2006, I attended the annual gathering of Lubavitch *Shluchim* (emissaries), at which almost 2,500 *Shluchim*
were in attendance, including representatives from Chabad Houses in the
Congo, Laos, and Ho Chi Minh City, Vietnam, along with emissaries from
the former Soviet Union (where there are almost 300 *Shluchim*), and many
hundreds more from throughout the United States (there are currently over
1,200 *Shluchim* in the United States). What is perhaps most remarkable is
that so much of this growth has occurred since the Rebbe's death in 1994.

SOURCES AND FURTHER READINGS: Herbert Weiner, "The Lubavitcher
Movement," in his *9½ Mystics*, ch. 6; Lis Harris, *Holy Days*; William Shaffir, *Life in a
Religious Community: The Lubavitcher Chassidim in Montreal*; Zalman Posner, *Think
Jewish: A Contemporary View of Judaism*. A sharp critique of those Lubavitcher Hasidim
who regard the Rebbe as the Messiah is found in David Berger, *The Rebbe, The Mes-
siah, and the Scandal of Orthodox Indifference*.

228

BA'AL TESHUVA MOVEMENT

ACCORDING TO A FAMOUS TEXT IN THE TALMUD, GOD HAS A HIGHER regard for non-religious Jews who become religious than for those Jews who have been observant their whole lives. The Talmud notes that "in the place where a penitent Jew—a *ba'al teshuva*—stands, a wholly righteous person cannot stand" (*Brakhot* 34b).

The apparent rationale of the rabbis for holding the *ba'al teshuva* in such high esteem was their belief that it is a much greater struggle for a nonreligious person to become religious and to give up formerly permitted practices, than it is for a religious person to remain religious. More than a few *ba'alei teshuva* (plural of *ba'al teshuva*) have told me that they desperately miss lobster or shrimp. As a Jew who was raised in a *kosher home, I confess that these foods have never tempted me.

During the last few decades tens of thousands of Jews throughout the world have become *ba'alei teshuva* and have accepted Orthodox observances. This phenomenon was totally unanticipated by Jewish scholars and lay people alike, most of whom assumed that Orthodoxy had no future in America. Indeed, most of the Eastern European Jews who emigrated to the United States in the late nineteenth and early twentieth centuries came from Orthodox families, but most of them gave up Orthodoxy. The first observance to be discarded was usually the Sabbath. At that time, the United States operated on a six-day workweek; if a person refused to work on Saturday, he was usually fired on Monday. The inability of most Jews to keep the Sabbath was a primary reason so many of the great rabbis of Europe agitated against Jews going to America. Though it was common in Europe for Jews to speak of America as a *goldene medina* (a golden land in which the streets were paved with gold), the rabbis were more apt to speak of it as a *treife medina* (an unkosher land). They feared, not unreasonably, that American Jews would assimilate.

The irreligiosity of American Jews was reinforced by the low level of Jewish education that long prevailed in the United States. In marked contrast with American Jewry's meager knowledge of Judaism, many second-generation Jews acquired a high level of secular education. The combination of a college education and a low level of Jewish knowledge proved deadly to Jewish religious commitment. In the whole history of the Jewish people, there probably never occurred as large-scale a defection from religious observance as during the Jews' first decades in America.

The *ba'al teshuva* movement, which started in the aftermath of World War II, was fueled by several factors, most notably perhaps a principle coined by historian Marcus Hansen, and known as Hansen's Law: "What the son wishes to forget, the grandson wishes to remember." The third generation of American Jews usually was more self-confident in its American identity than its parents, and thus less afraid of being perceived as different.

The Holocaust also contributed to the *ba'al teshuva* movement. For one thing, it disenchanted many Jews with the claims of secularism. For decades, large numbers of Jews associated religiosity with intellectual backwardness, while associating secularism with modernity and sophistication. After World War II, it was apparent that nothing taught at Germany's great universities had inhibited many German intellectuals from supporting the mass murder of the Jews.

The Holocaust stimulated the *ba'al teshuva* movement in yet another way. In the late 1940s and 1950s, large numbers of Holocaust survivors, including many Orthodox Jews, came to America. As a result, Orthodoxy quickly gained in numbers and was no longer as small a movement as it had been before the war. Jews now were more apt to meet Orthodox Jews than previously.

Israel's creation in 1948 prompted a resurgence of Jewish pride, which sometimes expressed itself in greater religious observance.

In addition, the growth of the American counterculture during the 1960s stimulated the return of many Jews to their roots. The counterculture generated a greater openness among many young Jews to ideologies that would have previously been rejected out of hand, and Orthodoxy gained some adherents as a result.

The Jewish Studies Program at *Yeshiva University, headed by the late Rabbi Moshe Besdin, was one of the first programs instituted to meet the needs of newly religious Jews, providing college students with four years of Jewish studies while they were earning their B.A.s. More than a few of the entering students had to prepare for the program by learning the Hebrew alphabet.

In Manhattan, Rabbi Shlomo Riskin attracted thousands to Jewish observance at his Lincoln Square Synagogue. Not a small part of his success was

due to Riskin himself being a *ba'al teshuva*. Having been raised as a nonobservant Jew, Riskin had an uncanny ability to identify with the needs of the
newly Orthodox. Much of Riskin's success was also due to his charismatic
and energetic education director, Rabbi Ephraim Buchwald, who started a
special Shabbat morning prayer service for Jews too unknowledgeable to
participate in the normal Orthodox service. Buchwald's goal was to gradually teach people the whole of the Orthodox service, and his "Beginner's
Minyan" has since been copied by congregations throughout the country.
Buchwald himself has gone on to form the widely successful National Jewish Outreach Program.

Many *ba'alei teshuva* have opted for an even more vigorous Orthodoxy
than the modern variety offered by Yeshiva University and Rabbi Riskin. To
meet their needs, a new type of *yeshiva was established, which quickly
became known in Orthodox circles as "a *ba'al teshuva* yeshiva." At these institutions, male students are encouraged to dress in black suits and hats, the style
among the most traditionally Orthodox, and to devote their intellectual activities solely to Jewish studies. Seminaries were established for female students
as well, where most branches of Jewish study, except for the *Talmud and
*Responsa literature, are taught. In the aftermath of the *Six-Day War in
1967, there was an explosive growth of such institutions in Israel. Many are in
Jerusalem, and most of their students come from the United States. The two
most famous are *Aish ha-Torah* (Fire of Torah), which now has branches
throughout North America, and *Ohr Sameach* (Happy Light). In addition, the
Lubavitch movement (see preceding entry) has been spreading the message of
Orthodox Judaism throughout the post–World War II world.

In theory, a *ba'al teshuva* can choose to identify as a Conservative or
Reform Jew, but in practice the term *ba'al teshuva* is so totally associated with
Orthodoxy that if a non-religious Jew, for example, becomes a Conservative
Jew, he will be referred to as a "Conservative *ba'al teshuva*." This, too, is a
phenomenon that has increased in recent years. Some years ago, *Esquire*
magazine ran a full-length story on Herman Gollob, the former editor in
chief of Doubleday, who in midlife learned to read Hebrew and celebrated
his *Bar Mitzvah when he was in his fifties. The most famous Conservative
ba'al teshuva is the late Paul Cowan, a staff writer for *The Village Voice* and a
political activist, who chronicled his return to Judaism in his powerful autobiography, *An Orphan in History*.

For Orthodox *ba'alei teshuva*, a common problem is a lack of full acceptance by the rest of the Orthodox community. Orthodoxy generally places

great stress on family background, particularly in choosing a spouse. A considerable number of Orthodox parents have expressed strong opposition to their children marrying a *ba'al teshuva*. Although the wish is not generally expressed publicly, it is often hoped that a *ba'al teshuva* man will marry a *ba'al teshuva* woman. There are even "personal" advertisements in some Jewish newspapers in which listing of marital assets include "F.F.B.," an acronym meaning *frum* (Orthodox) from birth. Indeed, the acronym "B.T." is often applied to *ba'alei teshuva* as in the question "Is he a B.T. or a F.F.B.?"

According to the Talmud, it is forbidden to remind a *ba'al teshuva* of his previous irreligiosity. This law, however, is frequently ignored. Most Orthodox Jews are fascinated to learn that another Jew has become religious, feeling gratified that others have become convinced of the truth they have been practicing. They frequently ask *ba'alei teshuva* to tell the story of how they became religious.

In any case, it can safely be said that the explosion of the *ba'al teshuva* movement has been one of the most exciting events in post-World War II Orthodox Jewish life.

SOURCES AND FURTHER READINGS: M. Herbert Danziger, *Returning to Tradition: The Contemporary Revival of Orthodox Judaism*; Janet Aviad, *Return to Judaism: Religious Renewal in Israel*; Ellen Willis, "Next Year in Jerusalem: A Personal Account," *Rolling Stone*, April 21, 1977, pp. 64–75; Mayer Schiller, *The Road Back: A Discovery of Judaism Without Embellishment*; Paul Cowan, *An Orphan in History*.

DENOMINATIONAL CONFLICTS

SEVERAL YEARS AGO, I CO-CHAIRED A SYMPOSIUM IN WHICH THREE prominent rabbis, one Orthodox, one Conservative, and one Reform, participated. Each was asked whether he perceived his own movement as the only authentic expression of Judaism, or as one of several legitimate models of Jewish living. The Orthodox representative responded that he saw Orthodoxy as the only authentic Jewish religious movement; Reform and Conservative

Judaism, though well-intentioned, had introduced illegitimate changes into the religion. The Conservative rabbi said that he regarded Conservative Judaism as coming closest to the religion God had revealed to Moses, but that he regarded the other two denominations as valid, though less authentic. The Reform spokesman said that he regarded all sincere expressions of Judaism as equally valid, and that he resented Orthodoxy's insistence that it alone was the true expression of Judaism.

The three responses adequately summarized the attitudes that the three main Jewish denominations have toward one another. The word "Orthodox," for example, literally means correct belief and, as a rule, Orthodox rabbis view rabbis and Jews who are non-Orthodox as having erroneous beliefs about Judaism. Thus, in 1956, eleven leading Orthodox rabbis in the United States issued a ruling banning Orthodox rabbis from belonging to any rabbinical organizations, such as the New York Board of Rabbis or any of the boards of rabbis that exist throughout the United States, in which non-Orthodox rabbis are members. The signatories contended that participation in these groups implied recognition of the rabbinic credentials of Reform and Conservative rabbis. Indeed, among right-wing Orthodox rabbis, Reform and Conservative rabbis are often not referred to as rabbis but as Reform and Conservative *clergymen*. In one noted ruling, the late Rabbi Moshe *Feinstein, the preeminent legal scholar of right-wing Orthodoxy, ruled that one should not answer "Amen" to a blessing recited by a non-Orthodox rabbi. Such men, Rabbi Feinstein reasoned, are heretics whose blessings should be ignored.

Significantly, the rabbinic leader of Modern Orthodoxy, Rabbi Joseph Baer *Soloveitchik, did not sign the 1956 ban. Consequently, most Orthodox rabbis ordained by Soloveitchik did not feel compelled to resign from their local boards of rabbis. On the other hand, Soloveitchik repeatedly affirmed his belief that non-Orthodox movements are invalid from the perspective of Jewish tradition. In one famous instance, Soloveitchik told a former student of his that it was better for him to pray at home alone on *Rosh ha-Shana than to hear the *shofar blown at a nearby Conservative synagogue. Soloveitchik probably did not mean that he preferred that Reform and Conservative Jews not attend synagogue. Still, some right-wing Orthodox rabbis have, on occasion, taken out newspaper advertisements before the *High Holy Days warning people that it is wrong to pray at a non-Orthodox service.

In recent years, the *"Who is a Jew?" issue has evoked the most bitter denominational conflicts. The overwhelming majority of Orthodox rabbis do not regard people converted to Judaism by non-Orthodox rabbis as Jewish. Jewish law requires that male converts to Judaism be circumcised, and that both male and female converts immerse themselves in a *mikveh*, ritual bath. In addition, converts are expected to undertake to observe Jewish law.

The Reform movement has long dispensed with the requirements of circumcision and immersion in a *mikveh*, and so Reform conversions are considered invalid by the Orthodox. Conservative conversions do include circumcision and *mikveh*, but because its standards of ritual observance are not those of the Orthodox, Conservative conversions are not generally accepted either (see *Convert/Ger*).

Some years ago, rabbis of different denominations in Denver, Colorado, tried to create a joint conversion board so that converts could be accepted universally. The effort fell apart after the Reform movement issued its *patrilineal descent ruling, affirming that children of Jewish fathers and non-Jewish mothers would no longer require conversion to Judaism if the child was raised with a Jewish identity. In the aftermath of the Denver experiment's failure, many Orthodox rabbis throughout the country denounced the traditional rabbis who had participated in it.

In Israel several Orthodox political parties have long agitated for the state to acknowledge as Jews only those born to Jewish mothers or converted to Judaism by Orthodox rabbis. This latter demand has incensed both non-Orthodox rabbis and lay leaders. In 1988, when it appeared that the Israeli *Knesset might pass the Orthodox definition of "Who is a Jew?," the Jewish federations in several American cities threatened to halt fundraising activities on behalf of the United Jewish Appeal if the legislation was enacted. For the first time in Israel's history, substantial segments of American Jewry confronted the Israeli government with a nonnegotiable demand, and the proposed legislation was dropped from the Knesset's agenda.

Unfortunately, the outlook for greater denominational cooperation seems fairly dim. In addition to the "Who is a Jew?" issue, there are serious disagreements among the Orthodox and non-Orthodox movements on the issue of divorce (see *Get*) and patrilineal descent.

One figure in contemporary Jewish life, Rabbi Irving Greenberg, has devoted much of his life to trying to bridge the denominational gap. Greenberg, himself Orthodox, believes that if American Jews do not find compromise solutions to the interdenominational disputes, the Jewish people will eventually cease being one people by or shortly after the year 2000 (see *The*

Vanishing American Jew). Orthodox Jews, Greenberg notes, will start keeping genealogical trees. In the mid-1970s, he created CLAL (see page 458), one of the few Jewish organizations that is both religious and nondenominational. As Greenberg has wittily put it: "I don't care what denomination in Judaism you belong to—as long as you are ashamed of it."

In 2007, a year-and-a-half after Hurricane Katrina, I was brought in to speak over Shabbat at four different synagogues in New Orleans, a Reform, Conservative, Orthodox, and Chabad, all situated within walking distance of each other. I witnessed an extraordinarily and profoundly moving level of cooperation between rabbis and members of the different congregations, and it left me with the hope that such friendship and cooperation—although unhappily precipitated in this instance by a devastating natural disaster— could be a model for Jews in many communities.

SOURCE AND FURTHER READING: Marc Lee Raphael, *Profiles in American Judaism,* is an overview of the different denominations in American-Jewish life.

230

THE VANISHING AMERICAN JEW
Low Birthrate, Assimilation, and Intermarriage

IN 1964, LOOK MAGAZINE RAN A COVER STORY ENTITLED, "THE VAN- ishing American Jew," which predicted that because of the low Jewish birth- rate and rising rates of assimilation, Jews would decline precipitously in numbers by the year 2000. But as my friend Michael Medved has noted: "It is now more than thirty-five years later. Look at the Jewish people, and look at *Look* magazine."

Not only *Look* magazine but many committed Jews as well have long pre- dicted the end of the Jewish people. Simon Rawidowicz, a Jewish philoso- pher at Brandeis University, wrote an essay on this pessimistic tendency entitled, "Israel: The Ever-dying People." He noted that fear of the Jewish people's demise is as old as Jewish history. The first Jew, *Abraham, was afraid that he would be the last; he was ninety-nine, his wife, *Sarah, was ten years younger, and they still had no offspring.

In the last two centuries, the fear that the Jewish people are coming to an end has often overwhelmed life in the Diaspora. Starting with the French *Emancipation in 1791, there have been high levels of intermarriage, assimilation, and conversion to Christianity in those societies that granted Jews equal rights. In the nineteenth century in Germany, predictions were commonly offered that within one or two generations, there would be almost no Jews left. As recently as 1967, just before the *Six-Day War in Israel, a Jewish sociologist in France published a book, *The End of the Jewish People?* At about the same time, it was commonly assumed that within twenty or thirty years almost all Soviet Jews would be permanently lost to the Jewish people. Instead, starting with the Six-Day War, Russia witnessed an extraordinary revival of Jewish life.

The size of the Jewish population in the United States is the source of debates among demographers, ranging from a low estimate of 5.2 million to estimates of 6.4 million and even higher. American Jewry is by far the largest concentration of Jews anywhere in the world, outside of Israel. However, American Jewry's population has remained relatively static for several decades. Three factors are generally understood to be responsible for this. One factor is that Jews are the most successful practitioners of birth control in the United States. The small size of Jewish families represents a relatively new trend in Jewish life. It is estimated that the Jewish population of Europe grew from two million to ten million between 1800 and 1900. In fact, Jews—at least in Eastern Europe—were the fastest-growing group in the population. That their American descendants, who are generally much more affluent, have so few children is particularly ironic. However, Orthodox Jews often have four or more children, and are thus rapidly growing as a percentage of the overall Jewish population. It appears that a significant number of committed but non-Orthodox Jews are also starting to have larger families.

A second factor threatening Jewish survival is intermarriage. Until the 1960s, sociologists estimated that fewer than 5 percent of American Jews married non-Jews. However, as more Jewish students started moving out of their parents' homes into university dormitories, and as Jews increasingly moved out of "Jewish ghettos" into mixed neighborhoods, intermarriage rates exploded. Today, it is estimated that about 47 percent of American Jews marry non-Jews. These intermarriage rates are not unique to American Jewry; a century ago, a similar percentage of French and German Jews intermarried. In those societies, however, intermarriage was almost always deadly for the Jewish community; a Jew who married a Christian either converted to Christianity or, at the very least, agreed to raise the children as Christians. In the United States, however, few Jews convert to Christianity, even when an intermarriage takes place. In most cases, neither party converts, and the couple usually resolve to expose their future children to both Judaism and Christianity. A large percentage of children of such marriages eventually identify as Christians, since that is the majority religion in the United States. However, in the United States, as opposed to Europe, a relatively high percentage of non-Jews who marry Jews convert to Judaism. Current figures suggest that from five to ten thousand non-Jews convert each year, with marriage to a Jew being the overwhelming impetus for these conversions. Unfortunately, in more than a few cases, the conversions are motivated overwhelmingly by the desire to pacify unhappy Jewish in-laws, and subsequent to the conversion, little Judaism is practiced in the newly married couple's home.

A third factor accounting for the static Jewish population is wide-spread assimilation. Assimilating Jews are not necessarily antagonistic to Judaism, just indifferent to the Jewish community, its religion and survival. A friend, who became more Jewishly committed in her late twenties, told me she had been so assimilated that when Israel's existence was threatened in 1967 (see Six-Day War), she was totally unconcerned with the country's fate. Assimilated Jews commonly move away from centers of Jewish population, often change Jewish-sounding last names, and eventually drop their Jewish identity entirely. Yet, as in the case of Soviet Jews, there has been a substantial return of formerly assimilated Jews to the community since the Six-Day War.

An additional, if seldom articulated, threat to American-Jewish survival is the possibility of a schism between Orthodox and non-Orthodox Jews. In an essay published in the 1980s, Rabbi Irving Greenberg argued that by the beginning of the twenty-first century, Orthodox Jews would challenge the Jewishness of perhaps 600,000 to 750,000 of the approximately six million Jews in this country. The overwhelming majority of "Jews by choice" in the United States are converted by Reform and Conservative rabbis, and the Orthodox do not regard such converts as Jews. By the early twenty-first century, Greenberg estimated, there would be about 250,000 to 350,000 such converts. In addition, because of the Reform movement's change in the definition of a Jew—from one having a Jewish mother to one having *either* a Jewish mother or father and raised with a Jewish identity—there would be an additional 220,000 or more children with Jewish fathers and non-Jewish mothers who will regard themselves as Jewish but who would not be considered so by Orthodox and many

Conservative Jews (see *Patrilineal Descent*). Finally, because the Reform movement insists that divorcing couples procure only a civil, and not a religious, divorce (see *Get*), many Reform Jews who divorce and remarry are, Jewishly speaking, committing adultery. The children of adulterous women, according to Jewish law, are regarded as *mamzerim* (bastards) and are forbidden to marry any but other *mamzerim*. Because of the growing rates of divorce and remarriage in the United States, there would likely be 100,000 to 200,000 *mamzerim* by the early twenty-first century.

None of these problems pose insurmountable threats to Jewish survival. In the case of people regarded as Jews by Reform and Conservative movements but not by the Orthodox, there is always the possibility that Orthodox rabbis will reconvert them. Realistically, however, most people who have already undergone one conversion will not react kindly to anyone questioning their Jewishness (with respect to the problem of *mamzerim*, see the entry on *Rabbi Moshe Feinstein*).

Along with possible explosions of antisemitism (though there does not seem to be any great danger of that at this time), the above factors represent the major threats to Jewish survival in the United States. When I outlined these dangers at a lecture on American Jewry's future, someone asked me: "Are you optimistic or pessimistic about Jewish survival?"

The question reminded me of a joke I had heard years earlier in Israel. A group of elderly, retired men used to gather every morning in a café to discuss the world situation. Because the news was so often grim, their conversations tended toward the gloomy. One day, a member of the group shocked his comrades by announcing that he was an optimist. The other men were all shocked, but then one of them noticed something incongruous. "If you are an optimist," he said to the man, "why do you look so worried?"

"You think it's easy to be an optimist?"

Regarding the future growth of American Jewry, most current Jewish leaders might be classified as optimists with worried looks on their faces.

SOURCES AND FURTHER READINGS: Thomas Morgan, "The Vanishing American Jew," *Look*, May 5, 1964; Simon Rawidowicz, "Israel: The Ever-dying People," in Nahum Glatzer, ed., *Studies in Jewish Thought: Simon Rawidowicz*, pp. 210–224; Irving Greenberg, "Will There Be One Jewish People in the Year 2000?" an article published by CLAL—the National Jewish Center for Learning and Leadership. Sociologist Steven Cohen, who believes that Greenberg paints an overly negative portrait of the Jewish future, has responded to Greenberg's article in *Moment*, March 1987; pp. 11–22. On the problem of *mamzerut*, see Louis Jacobs, "The Problem of the *Mamzer*," in his *A Tree of Life*, pp. 257–275, and a more stringent view in J. David Bleich,

"Mamzerut," in his *Contemporary Halakhic Problems*, pp. 159–176. As regards intermarriage, see Egon Mayer, *Love and Tradition: Marriage Between Jews and Christians.* For a discussion of current demographic estimates, see the front-page article in *Forward*, December 22, 2006. In contrast to American Jewry, Israeli Jewry has grown and is continuing to grow rapidly. In 1948, when Israel was established, its Jewish population was about one-ninth the size of American Jewry, 650,000 versus 6,000,000. By 2007, demographers estimated that the Jewish population of the two societies were drawing increasingly near to each otther in size. Yet, because Israelis have more children than American Jews, it is likely that within a few decades the number of Jews in Israel will far surpass the number in the United States.

231

SENATOR JOSEPH LIEBERMAN'S NOMINATION AS THE DEMOCRATIC VICE PRESIDENTIAL CANDIDATE, 2000

IN 1964, WHEN BARRY GOLDWATER WAS NAMED THE REPUBLICAN NOMinee for President, a Jewish wit quipped: "I always knew that the first Jew nominated for President would be an Episcopalian."

Indeed, had anyone predicted then that in 2000 a Jew would be named to the national ticket, most people would have assumed that the candidate would be an assimilated Jew, the kind commonly referred to in the Jewish community as a "three-day-a-year Jew," one who shows up in synagogue only on the High Holy Days and attends a Passover seder.

Instead, an unexpected event occurred. Senator Joseph Lieberman, perhaps the most religiously committed Jew ever to enter American political life, was named to a national ticket in August 2000 when Al Gore, the Democratic Party nominee, announced that he had selected Lieberman as his running mate.

The nomination electrified American Jewry. Even given the remarkable rise of Jews to positions of power, wealth, and influence in American society, many had felt that the country was not yet open to the possibility of a Jewish head of state. Indeed, many Jews and Jewish organizations claimed that there were far more antisemites in the United States than most people thought, and that they didn't exist only on the fringes of American life. I wondered at the time how leaders of such organizations would have responded if a high Democratic Party official called them and said, "Look, we want to nominate Lieberman, but the information put out by your organization makes us worry that enough Americans won't vote for him because he's a Jew to make him too much of a liability to put on the ticket. What do you think?"

After Lieberman's nomination, his widely commented-upon traditional observance of Jewish law ignited unusual national inquiries: For example, if a person doesn't use electricity for a day-long period each week, from Friday night to Saturday night, and is indeed committed to doing no work on that day, is it safe to entrust such a person with national office?

In truth, Lieberman's religiosity had not earlier hindered him politically and didn't do so now. Years earlier, when the Democratic convention in Connecticut, which had nominated him for the Senate, was held on a Saturday, he hadn't been present for his own nomination. Instead, Lieberman sent the convention a video in which he explained to the delegates that he did not work on his Sabbath (seeking a nomination definitely qualifies as work), but expressed his gratitude to them for nominating him. After such a well-publicized incident, his religious observance was well known to Connecticut voters, and it didn't seem to alienate many of them. In the Senate, his religiosity had not hurt him either. Lieberman likes to tell the story of how a crucial Senate vote came up on a Friday night, and so he resolved to remain in the Senate while the matter was debated and voted upon. Because he doesn't drive on the Sabbath, he arranged to sleep on a cot in his office, but Senator (and later Vice President) Al Gore arranged for him to stay at his parents' house across the street. On different occasions, other senators who live near the Capitol have offered to host him as well.

Regarding the argument that the traditional observance of Jewish law would make it impossible for one to function as president, in truth, Judaism is an eminently practical religion. Strict as the Sabbath laws are, Jewish tradition has always held that all these laws are suspended in cases of *pikuakh nefesh*, endangerment of life, and virtually any emergency matter that comes before the president can, and would, be classified in that category.

Although Gore and Lieberman, of course, lost the election to George Bush and Dick Cheney, for American Jews the breaking of what was regarded as the final professional taboo—a Jew being nominated to one of the two highest positions in American life—seemed a singularly auspicious way to inaugurate the new millennium.

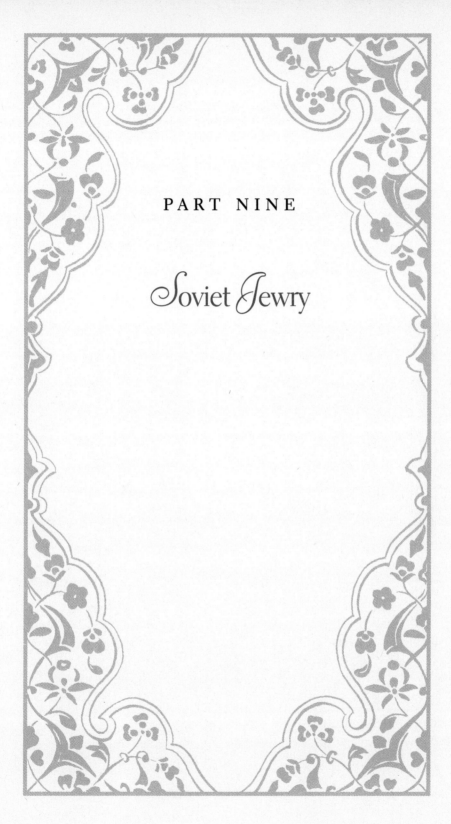

PART NINE

Soviet Jewry

232

BIROBIDZHAN

DURING THE 1920S, SOVIET DICTATOR JOSEF STALIN, ALARMED BY the attraction of many Russian Jews to Zionism, announced the creation of a Jewish homeland inside Russia in an area known as Birobidzhan (pronounced *Biro-bijan*). Unfortunately, it was located near Siberia, in an intemperate region close to the Chinese border. The Soviet press, nonetheless, gave extensive play to Comrade Stalin's offer to Russian Jews of their own "Autonomous Region," one in which Yiddish would be the official language and where Jews could work as farmers. Thousands of Russian Jews relocated to Birobidzhan. More remarkably, so too did some 1,400 Jewish Communists from the United States and other Western countries.

Birobidzhan never developed into a significant Jewish community. The area was too poor and isolated to attract large numbers of immigrants or to retain most of those who came. The early settlers had to build their own houses, with materials collected from local forests. It did not help matters that Birobidzhan was subjected to infestations of insects, heavy rains, and a disease that wiped out much of the horse population. Within a year of their arrival in 1928, more than 60 percent of the original settlers left. Though the Soviets had projected a Jewish population of 50,000 by 1933, the population reached only 8,200.

For decades, however, the Soviets maintained the fiction of Birobidzhan as an alternative Jewish homeland, and Yiddish continued to be taught in the cities' schools. When I visited the city of Khabarovsk in 1973, less than two hundred miles from Birobidzhan, there was a Yiddish newspaper, *Der Birobidzhaner Shtern (The Birobidzhan Star)*, in the waiting room at the airport. Though my Yiddish is weak, I quickly recognized that the paper was nothing more than a Yiddish version of *Pravda* or *Izvestia*, just as Birobidzhan itself was never meant to be anything more than a Yiddish-speaking version of the rest of the Soviet Union. It is hardly surprising that few Jews with Zionist inclinations were diverted from the dream of

Palestine by the offer of the would-be "Jewish Autonomous Region" of Biro-bidzhan.

SOURCE AND FURTHER READING: Zvi Gitelman, *A Century of Ambivalence: The Jews of Russia and the Soviet Union, 1881 to the Present*, pp. 157–163.

233

THE DOCTORS' PLOT (1953)

SHORTLY BEFORE HE DIED ON MARCH 5, 1953, SOVIET DICTATOR Josef Stalin accused nine doctors, six of them Jews, of plotting to poison and kill the Soviet leadership. The innocent men were arrested and, at Stalin's personal instruction, tortured in order to obtain confessions. "Beat, beat, and again beat," Stalin commanded the interrogators.

The unfortunate physicians can be described as lucky only in comparison with Stalin's tens of millions of other victims. The dictator died days before their trial was to begin. A month later, *Pravda* announced that the doctors were innocent and had been released from prison. It later became known that after their pro-forma trial and conviction, Stalin intended to organize *pogroms around the country, after which prominent members of the Jewish community would publicly beg him to protect the Jews by sending them all to Siberia. Indeed, when Stalin died, the supposedly spontaneous appeal by leading Jews had already been written and signed; the signatories had been coerced into signing.

In accusing the Jewish doctors of being poisoners, Stalin was, of course, reviving a libel that was common among medieval antisemites. The most notorious incarnation of the "Jews as poisoners" libel occurred in the fourteenth century when they were accused of having caused the devastating Black Plague by poisoning the wells of Europe. In addition to all the Jews who died from the plague, thousands more were murdered in pogroms prompted by these accusations. In 1610, the University of Vienna's medical faculty certified as its official position that Jewish law required doctors to kill one out of ten of their Christian patients. One wonders what it must have been like to be in a Jewish doctor's office—in back of nine other patients.

While one would think that all Jews would have breathed an enormous sigh of relief upon Stalin's death, there was no shortage of Russian Jews who shared in the country's paroxysm of grief. Even more peculiar, I. F. Stone, a well-known left-wing Jewish journalist in the United States, attacked President Eisenhower for not issuing a more effusive note of condolence on the mass murderer's death.

SOURCES AND FURTHER READINGS: Mikhail Heller and Aleksandr Nekrich, *Utopia in Power: The History of the Soviet Union from 1917 to the Present*, pp. 502–504; Yehoshua Gilboa, *The Black Years of Soviet Jewry*; Louis Rappaport, *Stalin's War Against the Jews: The Doctors' Plot and the Soviet Solution*. As regards the medieval accusations that Jews poison non-Jews, see Joshua Trachtenberg, *The Devil and the Jews: The Medieval Conception of the Jew and Its Relation to Modern Antisemitism*, and H. H. Ben-Sasson, *Trial and Achievement: Currents in Jewish History*, pp. 251–256.

234

RUSSIAN-JEWISH SIMKHAT TORAH

CELEBRATIONS

ASK JEWS WHAT IS THE MOST IMPORTANT JEWISH HOLIDAY, AND THE likely answer will be *"Passover" or *"Yom Kippur." During the 1960s and 1970s, however, many Soviet Jews would have answered *"Simkhat Torah," the festival that comes at the end of *Sukkot and celebrates the completion of the annual cycle of Torah reading. On any normal scale of Jewish religious priorities, Simkhat Torah is hardly the most significant Jewish festival; it is not even mentioned in the Bible. Yet, for many years on the night of Simkhat Torah, Russian Jews congregated in front of Soviet synagogues and danced and sang Hebrew and Russian-Jewish songs for hours. On this day alone, for reasons that are still not known, the Soviet authorities permitted the Jews to gather on Moscow's Archipeva Street, in front of the Great Synagogue. Thirty thousand or more Jews would come, at a time when any public display of Jewish commitment was often met by punishment.

The highlight of my own 1973 trip to the Jews of Russia was a visit to the Simkhat Torah celebration in Moscow. Many hours into the celebration, the

Soviets decided to break up the festive dancing, and loud-speakers ordered people to disperse and go home. The Russian Jews surrounding me had no intention of leaving, and continued dancing and singing. Finally, thuggish-looking young men, acting under police direction, linked arms across the width of the street and marched straight ahead, knocking down anyone in their path. I was thrown against a fence and the man next to me, Dmitri Ramm, was stomped by the marching invaders, and his leg was fractured. Year after year, however, the Soviet Jews came back to celebrate the festival.

Many people have commented on the irony of Jewishly illiterate Russian Jews choosing as their special day a festival celebrating the reading of the Torah. In all likelihood, what made Simkhat Torah so attractive to them was the very fact of its joyousness. For people who suffered so greatly for affirm-ing their Jewishness, it was perhaps more important to have this happy asso-ciation with Judaism than a somber one like Yom Kippur.

As reports of the Russian Jews' observance of Simkhat Torah spread, an increasing number of American and European Jews started going out into the streets of their cities on that day to sing and dance. Within a few years, the celebration initiated by the untutored Jews of Russia ended up stimulating a greater observance of Simkhat Torah by Jews around the world.

SOURCE AND FURTHER READING: Perhaps the most powerful description of the rise of Soviet-Jewish consciousness in the 1960s is found in Elie Wiesel, *The Jews of Silence*. Chapter 5 contains a description of a Simkhat Torah celebration Wiesel attended in Moscow. "He who has not witnessed [Simkhat Torah] in Moscow," Wiesel wrote of that experience, "has never in his life witnessed joy. Had I come to Russia for that alone, it would have been enough" (p. 45).

235

REFUSENIKS

THE FIRST JEWS I MET IN MOSCOW ON MY 1973 VISIT WERE VLADIMIR and Masha Slepak, who three years earlier had applied for permission to leave Russia for Israel. At the time, their three-year wait seemed intolerable. I returned to the United States, kept in touch with them for a while, and continued to read about their case, which was frequently cited in the news. Finally, in 1987, fourteen years after we had met and seventeen years after they had first applied, the Slepaks were allowed to leave for Israel.

A leading Jewish activist, Vladimir Slepak became the most famous of the refuseniks, Jews whom the Soviet Union refused to allow to leave. The Soviets often gave no explanation for the denial of an emigration visa, though they frequently attributed it to state security. Slepak was told that because he had worked as an engineer years earlier, it was feared that he would divulge Russian secrets to the West. The explanation was absurd, since any technological know-how that Slepak and the several thousand other refuseniks had, had long been superseded by the West's. One refusenik, Benjamin Bogomolny, actually entered the *Guinness Book of World Records* as "most patient"—he waited twenty and a half years to get permission to leave Russia (1966–1986—from the time he was twenty till he was forty).

The refuseniks' plight was horrendous. As soon as they applied to leave Russia, they were fired from their jobs; because the government is the only employer in Communist societies, it became impossible for them to find other work. Many Jews throughout the world sent the refuseniks money, a hefty percentage of which the government confiscated. Although many refuseniks were highly educated, they often had to accept whatever jobs were offered them (for example, cleaning streets at night) to avoid being arrested as "parasites" (a Soviet classification for any able-bodied person unemployed for two months). Yosef Begun, a Jewish mathematician who taught an underground Hebrew class, was fired from his job when he applied to live in Israel, then convicted for not working and exiled to Siberia.

In Novosibirsk the Poltinnikov family, Isaac, Irma, and their daughter Victoria, all three physicians, were refused permission to leave for Israel for nine years. Throughout this period, they were forbidden to work in their professions and were constantly harassed. The KGB periodically arrested them, subjected them to long interrogations, and on one occasion killed their dog. When the family was finally given permission to emigrate in 1979, Irma and Victoria concluded that it was a KGB trick, that they would all be arrested at the airport. Isaac Poltinnikov did leave and went to Israel. He immediately invited his wife and daughter to join him. The Soviets refused them permission. Irma died soon thereafter from malnutrition (she was afraid to leave her apartment), whereupon Victoria committed suicide.

Throughout the 1970s and 1980s, pro-Soviet Jewry organizations focused tremendous efforts on securing the refuseniks' emigration. It became common for Jewish communities and Jewish schools throughout the United States and Europe to "adopt" refusenik families, often writing and telephoning them. At many *Bar and *Bat Mitzvah celebrations, a young American Jew would "twin" himself or herself with a child reaching Bar or Bat Mitzvah age in Russia.

The refuseniks themselves served as the leadership of the Russian-Jewish revival that started after the 1967* Six-Day War. When my friend Dennis Prager visited Russia in 1969, a refusenik named Tina Brodetskaya asked him to smuggle out a document attacking Soviet antisemitism. When he asked her if she wasn't afraid of being sent to prison, Brodetskaya said: "Where do you think I am now?" Brodetskaya was subsequently permitted to leave for Israel.

With the rise of Gorbachev's policy of *glasnost* (greater openness and freedom), most of the longest-waiting refuseniks were permitted to leave, after having spent many of what should have been the most productive years of their lives unemployed, in fear of arrest, and under constant attack by their peers and neighbors.

SOURCES AND FURTHER READINGS: Mark Azbel, *Refusenik*; Joshua Rubenstein, *Soviet Dissidents: Their Struggle for Human Rights*; Cilly Brandstatter, ed., *Yosif Begun: The Struggle for Jewish Culture in the USSR, A Collection of Documents*; Louis Rapoport, "The Refuseniks," in the *Encyclopedia Judaica Year Book 1988/89*, pp. 76–83.

236

PRISONERS OF CONSCIENCE

Anatoly (Natan) Sharansky

FROM THE LATE 1960S THROUGH THE 1980S HUNDREDS OF RUSSIAN Jews were imprisoned in the Soviet Union on a variety of charges, but their real "crime" was invariably the same: wanting to live in Israel. Although the Soviets acknowledged the right of Jews to be reunited with family members in Israel, they desperately wanted to slow down the exodus of Jews applying to leave. Thus, they sponsored "show trials," at which Russian-Jewish activists were accused of anti-Soviet agitation and, in the most famous case, of Anatoly (Natan) Sharansky, of committing treason against the U.S.S.R.

Though the trials terrified many Russian Jews, they did not stop the spread of Jewish activism inside Russia, and they stimulated the growth of the international Soviet Jewry protest movement. The first large-scale show trial, in 1970, was directed against a group of Leningrad Jews who plotted to hijack an airplane to take them out of Russia. The attempted hijacking was motivated by despair, and was undertaken only after members of the group had spent years trying to leave the Soviet Union legally. Two leaders of the plot were sentenced to death, the rest to long prison terms. After an international public outcry, the death sentences were commuted.

The best known of the Leningrad prisoners of conscience was Yosef Mendelevich, who remained a religiously observant Jew under impossible conditions during more than ten years of incarceration.

In 1977, Sharansky was arrested. Because the charge was treason and carried a death sentence, his case triggered an unprecedented international reaction. *Time* and *Newsweek* carried cover stories on the Moscow dissident, and President Jimmy Carter publicly denied the Soviet charge that Sharansky had worked for the C.I.A. During the year and a half between his arrest and trial, Sharansky refused to kowtow to his Communist interrogators' demands for a confession, and became a symbol of Jewish heroism. His last speech before the Soviet court that sentenced him to thirteen years imprisonment became widely known throughout the Jewish world. Many people read it aloud at their *Passover *Seder:

"Five years ago I submitted my application for exit to Israel. Now I am further than ever from my dream. It would seem to be cause for regret. But it is absolutely otherwise. I am happy. I am happy that I lived honestly, in peace with my conscience. I never compromised my soul, even under the threat of death. . . . For more than 2000 years the Jewish people, my people, have been dispersed. But wherever they are, wherever Jews are found, each year they have repeated, 'Next year in Jerusalem.' Now, when I am further than ever from my people, from Avital [his wife], facing many arduous years of imprisonment, I say, turning to my people, my Avital: *Next year in Jerusalem!* And I turn to you, the court, who were required to confirm a predetermined sentence: to you I have nothing to say."

While in prison, Sharansky went on numerous hunger strikes, and refused to cooperate in any way with his jailers. His wife, Avital, who had been let out of Russia in 1974, was unremitting in her efforts to free him, and spent nine years traveling around the world, urging political leaders and Jews everywhere to keep up the pressure on the Soviets to release her husband. Under the impact of international pressure, the Soviets offered to release Sharansky on condition that he personally request them to do so for humanitarian reasons. He refused. Sharansky was finally released in February 1986. The Soviets had apparently tired of being pressured, and hoped that the release of their most famous political prisoner would divert attention from the other political prisoners they were still holding. Subsequent to his release, Sharansky has published a remarkable memoir, *Fear No Evil*, about his trial and prison experiences, and went on to become a prominent political figure in Israel.

By 1988, the *glasnost* (greater openness and freedom) pursued by Soviet leader Mikhail Gorbachev led to the release of all the other Jewish prisoners of conscience.

SOURCES AND FURTHER READINGS: Natan Sharansky, *Fear No Evil*; Martin Gilbert, *Shcharansky: Hero of Our Time*; Edward Kuznetsov, *Prison Diaries*; Student Struggle for Soviet Jewry, *Vladimir Prison: Joseph Mendelevich's Inside Story of Life in the Gulag*.

237

JACKSON-VANIK AMENDMENT

DÉTENTE

DURING THE 1970S, ONE OF THE FEW GENUINE LEADERS OF AMERICAN Jewry was the *non-Jewish* senator from the state of Washington, Henry Jackson. A domestic liberal and a staunch anti-Communist, Jackson adopted the Soviet Jewry cause as his own. Along with Congressman Charles Vanik of Ohio, he sponsored the Jackson-Vanik Amendment, which denied the Soviets favorable trading status until they allowed unimpeded emigration of Russian Jews from the Soviet Union: The benchmark figure that would show Soviet compliance with the amendment was sixty thousand Jews a year. Ironically, it was the *Jewish* secretary of state, Henry Kissinger, who most forcefully opposed the amendment's passage, out of the belief that it would be bad for America as well as for Russian Jews. Kissinger felt that since the Soviet Union would not allow its domestic policy to be determined by the American Congress, the amendment might well backfire and lead to a diminution in Jewish migration.

In the United States, all the Soviet Jewry organizations supported the amendment, as did the refuseniks (see preceding entry) inside Russia. In 1973, Jackson-Vanik passed and, whether for the reason suggested by Kissinger or otherwise, Russian-Jewish emigration did slow down at first, though it grew again in the late 1970s.

Until his death in 1983, Henry "Scoop" Jackson remained a hero among American Jews, many of whom actively supported his several unsuccessful efforts to secure the Democratic presidential nomination.

SOVIET JEWRY MOVEMENT
Student Struggle for Soviet Jewry

THE PROTEST MOVEMENT ON BEHALF OF SOVIET JEWRY, WHICH SPREAD throughout the United States and other Jewish communities during the 1960s and 1970s, was in large measure a response to the Holocaust. The revelations of what the Nazis had done to the Jews, coupled with the revelations of the general inactivity and indifference of much of the Western world's leadership to their fate (see *While Six Million Died*), left world Jewry (particularly that of America) with a deep sense of anger and guilt (the latter because of their own relative passivity during the years of the Holocaust). Thus, when news started to spread of the Soviet Union's attempts to destroy the Russian-Jewish community, many American Jews were outraged and determined to do something.

Of course, the Russian government was not seeking to annihilate the Jewish community (though in the early 1960s, well over one hundred Jews were executed on trumped-up charges of economic crimes). However, the govern-ment systematically closed down synagogues and published a large number of antisemitic books, some of which accused Judaism of being a Nazilike religion. Cartoons of Israeli General Moshe *Dayan routinely appeared in Soviet newspapers showing him wearing an armband with the Nazi swastika.

In 1964, the Student Struggle for Soviet Jewry (SSSJ) was founded in New York by Jacob Birnbaum, who headed it for decades along with Glenn Richter. From its inception, SSSJ was assertive in demanding the Jews' right to live as Jews within Russia, and to leave the country if they so wished. Other Soviet Jewry support groups were quickly founded around the country: Many of them eventually joined together to create the Union of Councils for Soviet Jewry. In 1971, the leading Jewish organizations in the United States founded the National Conference on Soviet Jewry. And in its early years, the Jewish Defense League, headed by Meir Kahane, used to follow and harass Soviet diplomats stationed in the United States.

The combined reach of the various Soviet Jewry protest organizations was extensive. To cite one example: When Soviet performers visited the United States, whether they were a small string quartet or the world-renowned Bol-shoi Ballet, they were greeted by Jewish pickets demanding rights for Soviet Jews.

At first, tangible results appeared to be small. The Soviet leadership made no concessions, presumably hoping that the Jewish community would grow discouraged and give up. After the *Six-Day War, however, the mood of Soviet Jewry changed markedly. Thousands, and then tens of thousands, of Russian Jews began to study Jewish history and texts, attend *Simkhat Torah celebrations, and apply for emigration visas to Israel. By the early 1970s, many were receiving such permission.

The Russian government, however, wanting to discourage large-scale Soviet-Jewish migration, often imprisoned leaders of the Jewish movement. These *prisoners of conscience became the new focus of the international Soviet-Jewish protest movement.

Simultaneous with public protests and marches, the Soviet Jewry groups lobbied actively in Washington. Their most prominent legislative victory was the congressionally sponsored Jackson-Vanik amendment (see preceding entry), which linked trade with Russia to freedom of emigration for Soviet Jews. The various Soviet Jewry organizations also encouraged thousands of American and Western Jews to visit Russia as tourists and to spend time with Jewish dissidents.

By the late 1980s, the Soviet-Jewish protest movement had achieved far more than its founders had expected. The large majority of Soviet Jews applying to emigrate were being permitted to do so, and inside the Soviet Union, for the first time since the Communist revolution of 1917, a *yeshiva was established. Nonetheless, the moves toward greater democratization introduced inside Russia by President Mikhail Gorbachev also guaranteed greater freedom for antisemitic groups. When groups such as the far right-wing, ultranationalist Parnyat started publicly propagating antisemitism, beginning around 1988, hundreds of thousands of Jews started clamoring to leave Russia. In early 1990, more than ten thousand were leaving Russia monthly, and by early in the twenty-first century, a million people had left the former Soviet Union for Israel, and over 300,000 for the United States.

SOURCE AND FURTHER READING: William Orbach, *The American Movement to Aid Soviet Jews.*

239

"LET MY PEOPLE GO!"
"AM YISRAEL CHAI"

"LET MY PEOPLE GO!" AND "AM YISRAEL CHAI" WERE RESPECTIVELY, the theme and theme song of the Soviet Jewry protest movement. The first, which repeated Moses' demand to Pharaoh (Exodus 7:16), became the most commonly displayed sentiment on posters at Soviet Jewry rallies. The image of Russia as Egypt, and of its leaders as Pharaoh, was also used by Soviet Jews. One of the early Soviet Union Jewish protest songs, brought to the West in 1969, declared:

> *To the Pharaoh, to the Pharaoh I say,*
> *Let my people go!*
> *Let the Jewish people go to its homeland . . .*

At one of the early demonstrations for Soviet Jewry in New York during the 1960s, the Jewish songwriter Rabbi Shlomo Carlebach introduced an inspirational song entitled, *"Am Yisrael Chai."* Though the song's words are few— *"Od avinu chai, am Yisrael chai*—Still our fathers [the Patriarchs] live, the Jewish people live on"—they are sung over and over, building to a crescendo, a testimony in both song and dance to the eternity of the Jewish people (see *Let My People Go!* in the Bible section).

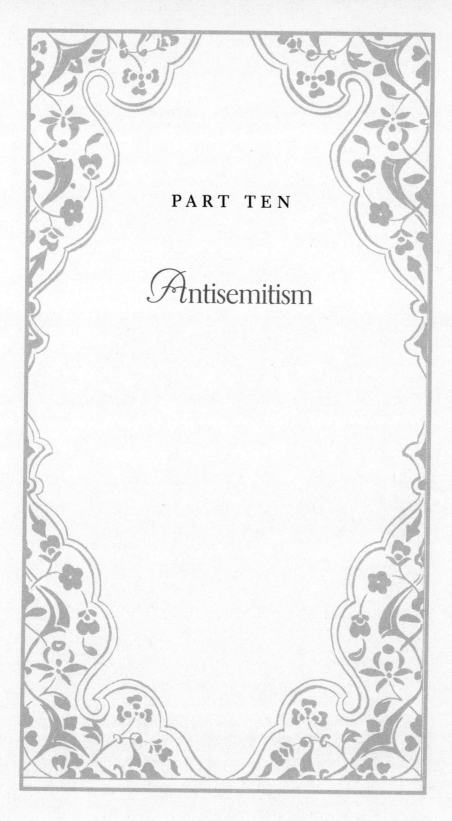

PART TEN

Antisemitism

240

"CHRIST-KILLER"

I DEBATED LONG AND HARD ABOUT WHETHER TO INCLUDE THIS TERM before deciding that leaving "Christ-killer" out of a book on Jewish literacy would make as little sense as leaving "nigger" out of a book on "black literacy." Certainly, it would be a better world if there was no need to know such words, and in the messianic age (see *Messiah*)—which Judaism believes lies in the future—such words, I am sure, will be totally forgotten. Until then, a few sobering reflections on this ancient and murderous epithet.

"Christ-killer" has been among the last words tens of thousands of Jews have heard before being murdered. So then, why is it still used in the present day? Can one imagine a contemporary visitor to Greece yelling "Socrates-killer" at the local Athenians? Furthermore, even if some Jews in the first century helped bring about Rome's execution of Jesus, the worst that might be said about Jews during the next nineteen centuries is that they are "descendants of Christ-killers." However, that expression has never been used. "Christ-killer" apparently means that by continuing to reject the claim that Jesus is the son of God and the Messiah, Jews in every generation are killing him again. This explains why Jews who convert to Christianity, along with Italians (descendants of the Roman executioners of Jesus), never have this epithet hurled at them.

The greatest oddity about the term is that it was the Romans, not the Jews, who killed Jesus. Outside of the New Testament, one of the earlist references to Jesus occurs in the writings of the Roman historian Tacitus, who notes Jesus' name and the fact of his crucifixion by the Roman authorities. Since Jesus' execution is the *one* fact attested to outside of the New Testament, the historically significant question is "For what offenses did Rome crucify prisoners?" We know of two: for rebelling slaves and for those who committed abominable crimes, particularly political rebels. Jesus fell into the second category, a fact evidenced by the sign that was hung over his head during the crucifixion: KING OF THE JEWS. It would appear that Jesus was one of many first-century Jewish political rebels against the Roman conquerors. An estimated

50,000 to 100,000 anti-Roman activists were crucified during the Roman rule over Judea. As historian Hyam Maccoby has written, "The cross became as much a symbol of Roman oppression as nowadays the gas chamber is a symbol of German Nazi oppression. . . . Associating the guilt of the cross with the Jews rather than the Romans is comparable to branding the Jewish victims . . . with the guilt of using gas chambers instead of suffering from them."

At Vatican II in 1962, the Catholic Church officially exonerated most of Jesus' Jewish contemporaries, and all subsequent Jews, of the charge of deicide (killing God). At that time, the Catholic writer Edward Keating suggested that instead of the antideicide resolution, "They should have come out with a very simple statement: We have been guilty of anti-semitism for two thousand years. Forgive us." To be fair to Pope John XXIII, who was the force behind the resolution, that sort of apology is precisely what he intended. Shortly before his death, the pontiff composed a prayer directed to Jesus, in which he asserted that Christian antisemitism constituted a second crucifixion of Christ (see the prayer cited in the entry on *Pope John XXIII*).

The belief that the Jews killed Jesus made the Jews seem not only hateful but also terrifying. After all, only a people with superhuman powers could "murder" God. One can only hope that the term continues to decline in usage, as it indeed has since the Holocaust. See also *Crusades, Blood Libel*, and the *Black Plague*.

SOURCE: One of the finest works of history on the subject of Jesus, his crucifixion, and the Jews, is Hyam Maccoby's *Revolution in Judaea: Jesus and the Jewish Resistance*. The selection from Maccoby's book is on p. 36.

241

JUDAS ISCARIOT

ALTHOUGH JESUS AND ALL HIS APOSTLES WERE JEWS, MOST JEWS AND Christians think of them as Christians. Names like Andrew and Peter, long common among Christians, were until recently rarely used by Jews.

The one apostle people naturally think of as Jewish is Judas, whose very name connotes Judah and Judaism. The New Testament's portrayal of Judas as having betrayed Jesus for thirty pieces of silver heightened considerably Christian enmity toward Jews, for not only does Judas betray Jesus, he does so in a particularly loathsome manner. He tells the Jewish priests who wish to arrest Jesus that they should follow him, and that the man whom he kisses will be Jesus (Matthew 26:47ff; Mark 14:43ff; and Luke 22:47–48). He literally betrays Jesus with a kiss. As theologian Richard Rubenstein has noted, the lesson Christians learned was that no matter how close you think you are to a Jew, at the very moment the Jew is kissing you, he may be betraying you.

All of this would be unfortunate enough were it based on a true episode. But as was indicated in the preceding entry on *Christ-killer* and in the entry on *Jesus*, there is little reason to think the Jews were responsible for Jesus' crucifixion, and many reasons to think they were not. Furthermore, the detail about the kiss of betrayal appears to have been added specifically to make Judas and his Jewish allies seem even more hateful. Would it not have been sufficient for Judas to inform the High Priest of Jesus' hiding place? Why kiss him? According to Jesus' testimony, the men who arrested him knew who he was and had no need of Judas' kiss of identification. "When I was with you day after day in the Temple," Jesus reminds those who arrest him, "you did not lay hands on me" (Luke 22:53).

According to a widespread historical account (dismissed by some as legendary), the story of Judas had horrible repercussions in 1492 for Spain's 300,000 Jews. In March of that year, acting under the influence of the head of the Spanish Inquisition, Father Tomás de Torquemada, King Ferdinand and Queen Isabella ordered the expulsion of all Jews from Spain. The Jewish finance minister, Don Isaac *Abravanel, tried to bribe King Ferdinand to do what was morally right and offered him thirty thousand dinars to cancel the decree. He seemed to be making some headway until Torquemada, who was listening in an adjacent room, burst into the king's chamber, threw his cross down on the floor, and cried out, "Will you betray our Lord Jesus for thirty thousand dinars as Judas did for thirty pieces of silver?" The discussion was ended, and the fate of Spanish Jewry sealed at that moment (see *The Spanish Expulsion, 1492*).

242

BLOOD LIBEL, ALSO KNOWN AS
RITUAL MURDER

ONCE THE CHRISTIAN WORLD BELIEVED THAT JESUS WAS GOD AND that the Jews had killed him (see *Christ-killer*), no crime seemed too bizarre or horrific to attribute to them. The blood libel, the accusation that Jews murder non-Jews in a religious ritual and then drink their blood, originated in twelfth-century England. Over the next seven hundred years, it led to the murder of tens of thousands of Jews.

The particular irony of the blood libel is that it was directed against the first nation in history to outlaw human sacrifice (see Genesis 22 and Deuteronomy 18:10), and the only people in the ancient Near East to prohibit the consumption of *any* blood (Leviticus 3:17; 7:26; 17:10–14; Deuteronomy 12:16; 12:23–25).

The first accusation was made in Norwich, England, in 1144, but since no victim was found, the case was dropped. Jews visiting Lincoln in 1255 to attend a wedding were not so fortunate. A day after the wedding, the body of a Christian boy named Hugh, who had been missing for three weeks, was found in a cesspool into which he had apparently fallen. The Christian townspeople believed otherwise. A contemporary chronicler, Matthew Paris, wrote: "The child was first fattened for ten days with white bread and milk, and then . . . almost all the Jews of England were invited to the crucifixion." Later, *under torture*, a Jew named Copin confessed "that the Jews had crucified the boy in the manner that the Jews had once crucified Jesus." Nineteen Jews were hanged without a trial.

Thereafter, the ritual murder accusation became unstoppable. A century later, in his *Canterbury Tales* Geoffrey Chaucer wrote of the Jews' supposed murder of Hugh in "The Prioress's Tale." *Six hundred years* after the fabricated incident, the English essayist Charles Lamb wrote: "I confess that I have not the nerve to enter their synagogues. Old prejudices cling about me. I cannot shake off the story of Hugh of Lincoln." Hugh's death also inspired dozens of ballads. Once, while taking a car trip through the Ozark Mountains of Arkansas, I purchased a book of Ozark Mountain folk songs, *printed in 1973,* which included a ballad inspired by the "murder" of Hugh. In this song, a Jewish woman invites a young Christian boy into her house, and then:

> *She pinned a napkin o'er his face*
> *And pinned it with a gold pin*
> *Then called for a vessel of blood*
> *To catch his heart blood in*
> *In, in*
> *To catch his heart blood in.*

By the fourteenth century, the ritual murder charge had become associated with *Passover; Jews were accused of mixing Christian blood into their *matzah and wine. The joyous holiday turned into a time of terror for Jews because of their fear that antisemites would frame them by murdering a Christian child and then dump his body in a Jewish house.

In 1840, Christian antisemites carried the blood libel into the Muslim world, and the hapless Jews of Damascus were charged with murdering a Capuchin monk (see *Damascus Blood Libel*). The "Damascus Affair" became a turning point in Jewish history; for the first time world Jewry, including communal leaders from England, France, Austria, Germany, and the United States, organized to protest antisemitism. Led by Sir Moses Montefiore, they succeeded in their efforts: Within months, the victims were released except for two who had died under torture.

The last major ritual murder trial was conducted in Kiev in 1913 under the impetus of the Czarist government. Remarkably, a peasant jury exonerated the accused, Mendel Beilis. The incident is the subject of Bernard Malamud's novel *The Fixer.*

During the 1930s, the Nazi newspaper *Der Stuermer* regularly carried illustrations of rabbis sucking the blood of German children. Although belief in the blood libel declined after the Holocaust, and is no longer accepted in the Christian world, in recent years, it has been resurrected with extraordinary ferocity in the world of radical and fundamentalist Islam (see page 244).

The fact that so many Christians believed and spread this lie for hundreds of years led the early Zionist thinker Ahad Ha-am to note one "consolation" in the blood libel: It enabled Jews to resist internalizing the world's negative portrayal of them. "Every Jew who has been brought up among Jews, knows as an indisputable fact that throughout the length and breadth of Jewry there is not a single individual who drinks human blood for religious purposes. . . . 'But,' you ask, 'is it possible that everybody can be wrong, and the Jews right?' Yes, it is possible: the blood accusation proves it possible."

SOURCES AND FURTHER READINGS: *Why the Jews? The Reason for Anti-semitism*, Dennis Prager and Joseph Telushkin, pp. 108–111. The Charles Lamb quote is taken from his essay "Imperfect Sympathies," in *Essays of Elia*, and the Ahad Ha'am quote is from his *Selected Essays*, pp. 203–204. The best overall treatment of the blood libel is found in Joshua Trachtenberg, *The Devil and the Jews: The Medieval Conception of the Jew and Its Relation to Modern Antisemitism*, pp. 97–155. See also H. H. Ben-Sasson, *Trial and Achievement: Currents in Jewish History*, pp. 243–251.

243

SHYLOCK

ONE OF THE UGLIEST CHARACTERS CREATED BY WILLIAM SHAKE-speare (1564–1616) is Shylock, a Jewish moneylender who insists that a non-Jew, Antonio, repay his overdue loan in a pound of flesh drawn from near his heart. The sadistic Shylock is ultimately thwarted by a legal trick, but the damage inflicted on the Jews by *The Merchant of Venice* has been far greater than a pound of flesh. The image of Jews as a nation of moneylending Shylocks has persisted throughout the Middle Ages into the modern world. To this day, the illegal industry of high-interest loans is known as "shylocking."

More remarkably, the odious Shylock was created out of thin air. Shake-speare had never met or seen a Jew in his life, since the Jews had been expelled from England in 1290 (see *Expulsion of Jews from England, 1290*), more than 350 years before his birth, and not readmitted until 1656, forty years after his death. This play is certainly not the only instance of Jews being vilified in a society in which they no longer lived. A century after their expulsion, Chaucer depicted Jews as ritual murderers of young Christian children in *The Canterbury Tales* (see preceding entry). Even after the Jews were readmitted to England, their image did not undergo a permanent improvement. In the nineteenth century, Charles Dickens fashioned yet another stereotypical Jewish villain, Fagin, who made his living training young boys to become pickpockets.

As befits a great playwright, Shakespeare did give Shylock a redeeming moment. In a powerful excoriation of those who denied the Jews' humanity, Shylock cries out: "I am a Jew. Hath not a Jew eyes? Hath not a Jew hands, organs, dimensions, senses, affections, passions. . . . If you prick us, do we not bleed?" Unfortunately, the point of this powerful rhetoric is to build up to Shylock's insistence on getting his pound of flesh: "And if you wrong us, shall we not avenge it?"

Many Jews and non-Jews alike believe erroneously that the involvement of medieval Jews in moneylending was a cause of antisemitism (see next entry). And, need it be added, there is no record of any Jewish moneylender ever asking for payment in flesh. That stunning literary device was left for Shakespeare to reveal to the world.

SOURCE AND FURTHER READING: Bernard Glassman, *Anti-Semitic Stereotypes Without Jews: Images of the Jews in England, 1290–1700.*

244

ANTISEMITISM

The Scapegoat Thesis

FEW PEOPLE KNOW THAT THE WORD "ANTISEMITISM" WAS CREATED BY an antisemite, Wilhelm Marr. Marr's intention was to replace the German word *Judenhass* (Jew-hatred) with a term that would make Jew-haters sound less vulgar and even somewhat scientific.

Unfortunately, the term Marr created is particularly misleading since it conveys the impression that antisemites oppose Semites. This misconception has enabled Jew-haters in the Arab world to deny that they are antisemites, on the eminently logical grounds that they themselves are Semites. But for Marr, and all subsequent enemies of the Jews, antisemitism has always been a code word used exclusively against Jews. The greatest antisemite of all, Adolf Hitler, had no compunctions about welcoming (Semitic) Arab leaders, including the Mufti of Jerusalem, to Berlin during World War II. For this reason, many writers today have adopted the practice initiated by several Jewish and Christian scholars, and write antisemite as one word; spelling it "anti-Semite" in the conventional manner only fosters the false impression that there is a wider ethnic entity against which "anti-Semitism" is leveled.

Throughout history, antisemitism has been directed against Judaism and its values. For that reason, Jews have long spoken of those who have been killed by antisemites as having died *al *kiddush ha-Shem*—to sanctify God's name. Until about 1800, the societies in which Jews lived were generally piously Christian or Muslim, and so antisemitism focused on Jewish concepts of God and law. In the last two centuries, during which nationalism became a dominant value in the Western and Arab worlds, antisemitism increasingly focused on the Jews' peoplehood and nationhood. In fact, many Jew-haters today even deny that they are antisemites, claiming only that they are anti-Zionists.

Since antisemitism has traditionally been directed against Judaism and its values, Jews who have been willing to disavow those values and convert to the majority religion have usually been able to evade antisemitism. Of course, this was not the case under the Nazis, since *Hitler believed that even Jews who abandoned Judaism carried Jewish ideas with them.

During the past century, as more and more Jews have become irreligious, it has no longer seemed logical to many academics, and lay people as well, that antisemitism had anything to do with Judaism or its values. Rather, they claim that antisemitism is caused by socioeconomic or cultural factors. For example, one theory is that Jews were hated in the medieval period because they were moneylenders. While it is true that a disproportionate number of medieval moneylenders were Jews, to assume that it is for that reason that Jews were hated, one must also assume that before becoming moneylenders Jews were active, well-integrated members of European society. Only on that momentous day when they collectively became moneylenders did antisemitism erupt. In actuality, Jews were first hated. Because they were hated, they were forbidden to practice other professions and forced to become moneylenders. Once they became moneylenders, it *exacerbated* an already existent antisemitism, but it did not cause it.

As regards economic explanations of modern antisemitism, which attribute the hatred of Jews to their wealth: Jews have never been as affluent as they are today in contemporary America—and never before have they encountered so little antisemitism. In fact, almost all American Jews whose families came from Eastern Europe have had grandparents and great-grandparents who were far poorer and suffered much more antisemitism.

Another popular explanation for antisemitism is the "scapegoat thesis": Jews are blamed for a society's ills by those who wish to mobilize the masses around a common hatred. Many people believe, for example, that Hitler blamed the Jews in order to win elections in Germany. The reality is that Hitler didn't blame the Jews to gain power; he gained power, in large measure, in order to act against the Jews. Hitler was sufficiently astute not to give full vent to his antisemitic passions during the German election campaigns—everybody knew he was an antisemite anyway—realizing that it needlessly alienated respectable middle-class voters.

The scapegoat thesis, in any case, does not explain why *Jews* are hated. What is it about this small group of people that can unite the far left and far right, rich and poor, religious and antireligious in opposition to them? Over sixty years ago, the Jewish writer Maurice Samuel pin-pointed the fallacy of the scapegoat thesis in his book *The Great Hatred*: "To say that a man has hallucinations when he is hungry makes sense; to say that he has hallucinations only about Jews when he is hungry does not."

It is one of history's intriguing ironies that when Wilhelm Marr created the term "antisemitism" in 1879, he intended to be known among all future antisemites as the leader of a powerful movement of Jew-haters. Today, however, his name is known only to Jewish scholars.

SOURCES AND FURTHER READINGS: Dennis Prager and Joseph Telushkin, *Why the Jews? The Reason for Antisemitism*; Maurice Samuel, *The Great Hatred*; Malcolm Hay, *Europe and the Jews*; Arthur Hertzberg, *The French Enlightenment and the Jews: The Origins of Modern Anti-Semitism*; Jacob Katz, *From Prejudice to Destruction: Anti-Semitism 1700–1933*; Jacques Maritain, *A Christian Looks at the Jewish Question*; Leon Poliakov, *The History of Anti-Semitism* (four volumes).

245

THE PROTOCOLS OF THE ELDERS OF ZION

THE MOST FAMOUS ANTISEMITIC DOCUMENT IN HISTORY, THE PROTO-
cols of the Elders of Zion, is a forgery. First circulated by Russian secret police
during the late 1800s, it purports to reveal the minutes of a secret meeting of
world Jewish leaders who are conspiring to take over the world.

The Protocols' original distributors claimed that it demonstrated that many
heads of state were under the domination of three hundred Jewish leaders
who were responsible for Europe's major problems. The Protocols, of course,
proved nothing of the kind. They were forgeries distributed by the czar's
secret police.

Thousands, perhaps even tens of thousands, of Jews have died because of
this infamous forgery. In Russia itself, the Protocols were used to provoke
hundreds of *pogroms during the Russian civil war of 1918–1920, when the
Jews were accused of having brought communism to Russia.

Unfortunately, the Protocols spread far beyond Russia. In the United
States, their most prominent proponent was Henry Ford, one of the most
admired men in the country. In addition to his automobile company, Ford
owned a weekly newspaper, The Dearborn [Michigan] Independent, which
he distributed through Ford car dealerships. For more than a year and a half
during the early 1920s, each issue of the paper carried reports on the worldwide Jewish conspiracy under the title The International Jew. In Germany
Hitler had these articles translated and widely disseminated. For several
years, American Jews were stymied; they did not know how to react to Ford's
calumnies. No legal mechanism was available to stop the libels, since American libel laws protect individuals but not groups from slander. (For example, were someone to charge Jews with killing non-Jews and drinking their
blood [see Blood Libel] the Jewish community could not sue the libel's perpetrator. Only if the "libeler" mentioned individual Jews as having performed the act would those people be able to sue.) When The Dearborn
Independent started accusing individual Jewish businessmen of economic
conspiracies and dishonesty, some of them fought back. The leading Jewish

lawyer in the United States, Louis Marshall—so prominent in American-Jewish life in the 1920s that American Jews were said to live under "Marshall Law"—sued on their behalf. Ford and his paper were convicted of libel, and the automobile magnate issued a statement repudiating *The International Jew* and requesting that all copies of it be withdrawn from distribution. This helped stop the *Protocols'* distribution in the United States, but Ford's *International Jew*, a reworking of the document, continued to lead a healthy life elsewhere.

Hitler continued to distribute the document in Germany. He apparently regarded Ford as an ally. The *Chicago Tribune* reported that "Hitler kept for many years a photograph of Ford on his desk. When he heard [in 1923] that Ford might run for president, he said: 'I wish that I could send some of my shock troops to Chicago and other big cities in America to help in the elections. . . . We look to Heinrich Ford as the leader of the growing Fascist movement in America. . . . We have just had his anti-Jewish articles translated and published. The book is being circulated in millions throughout Germany.'"

One might have thought that the Holocaust would have convinced anti-semites that world Jewry had very limited power; Jews could not, after all, stop the murder of one third of their people. After World War II, however, prominent leaders in the Arab world became the new disseminators of the *Protocols*. In an interview in the Indian magazine *Blitz*, in October 1958, Egyptian President Gamal Abdel Nasser commended the *Protocols* to its editor: "I wonder if you have read a book called *Protocols of the Learned Elders of Zion*. I will give you an English copy. It proves clearly, to quote from the *Protocols*, that 'three hundred Zionists, each of whom knows all the others, govern the fate of the European continents and they elect their successors from their entourage.'" The late King Faisal of Saudi Arabia used to give copies of the *Protocols*, and an anthology of other antisemitic writings, to guests of his regime. A group of journalists who accompanied French Foreign Minister Michel Joubert on a visit to Saudi Arabia in January 1974 were told by Saudi officials that "these were the king's favorite books." In the early 2000s, the *Protocols* was still a bestselling book throughout the Arab world, and the subject of a multi-episode series on Egyptian television.

Norman Cohn aptly entitled his definitive work on the *Protocols*, *Warrant for Genocide*. To the Nazis and their allies, the *Protocols* proved how deadly dangerous the Jews were and why they must all be murdered.

In the twentieth and twenty-first centuries, a charge every bit as false as the medieval blood libel or the accusation that the Jews caused the Black Plague by poisoning the wells of Europe has been believed by tens, if not hundreds, of millions of people.

SOURCES AND FURTHER READINGS: Norman Cohn, *Warrant for Genocide*; Hitler's statement about Henry "Heinrich" Ford is found on p. 162. The episodes concerning Nasser's and Faisal's espousals of the *Protocols* are cited in Dennis Prager and Joseph Telushkin, *Why the Jews? The Reason for Antisemitism*, pp. 109–112.

246

DEICIDE

POPE JOHN XXIII (1958–1963)

Vatican II

IF IT MAKES SENSE TO SPEAK OF THE JEWS HAVING A FAVORITE POPE, then John XXIII wins, with Pope John Paul II a close second. During his short tenure, he convened Vatican II, at which he helped bring about a resolution exonerating most Jews of Jesus' time, and all subsequent Jews, of the charge of deicide (the murder of God—see *Christ-killer*). In 1959, shortly after his elevation to the papacy, Pope John XXIII expunged the reference to "perfidious Jews" in the Good Friday prayer. The following year, he met with 130 Jewish members of a United Jewish Appeal delegation, and greeted them with the biblical verse, "I am Joseph your brother" (Genesis 45:4; the pope was born Joseph Roncalli). Shortly before he died, he composed the following prayer in atonement for the Church's history of antisemitism: "We realize now that many, many centuries of blindness have dimmed our eyes, so that we no longer see the beauty of Thy Chosen People and no longer recognize in their faces the features of our first-born brother. We realize that our brows are branded with the mark of Cain. Centuries long has Abel lain in blood and tears, because we had forgotten Thy love. Forgive us the curse which we unjustly laid on the name of the Jews. Forgive us that, with our curse, we crucified Thee a second time."

SOURCES AND FURTHER READINGS: Four particularly important books on Jewish life in the orbit of Christendom—all written by Christians, the first three by Catholics, the fourth by a Protestant—are Friedrich Heer, *God's First Love* (which contains the prayer of Pope John XXIII); Rosemary Reuther, *Faith and Fratricide*; Edward Flannery, *The Anguish of the Jews*; and A. Roy Eckhardt, *Your People, My People*. During the papacy of Pope John Paul II, the pope attended services at a synagogue in Rome, put a note into the Western Wall in Jerusalem asking forgiveness of Jews for earlier mistreatment by the church, and established diplomatic relations with Israel. A world-transforming figure, the Polish-born pope also played an important role in bringing down communism in Eastern Europe.

247

SELF-HATING JEWS

AN ANTISEMITE IS GENERALLY UNDERSTOOD TO BE SOMEONE WHO thinks Jews are worse than other people, and who wants to cause them harm. The above definition, strangely enough, applies to some Jews as well, and in the Jewish community they are known as self-hating Jews. Perhaps the most famous was Karl Marx, the founder of communism. A grandson of two Orthodox rabbis, Marx was converted to Christianity when he was only six years old. A Jew can convert to Christianity or assimilate without being self-hating; he simply might not find any spiritual or social sustenance in remaining Jewish. A self-hating Jew, however, is one who turns against the Jewish community. Although Marx clearly knew that both he and his parents had been born Jewish, his writings about Jews were so hateful and vituperative that Adolf Hitler claimed to have gained some of his "insights" into Jews by reading Marx. (For an example of Marx's antisemitic writings see entry on *Leon Trotsky*.)

Although Marx often protested on behalf of oppressed people, he never wrote a word on behalf of Jews murdered in the 1881 Russian *pogroms. One of his most prominent political opponents was the German-Jewish socialist leader Ferdinand Lasalle. Marx, a racist as well as a self-hating Jew, routinely referred to Lasalle as a "Jewish nigger":

One of the most famous American journalists of the twentieth century, Walter Lippmann, was another prominent self-hating Jew. Lippmann was not nearly as hostile to Jews as Marx; nonetheless, he was so indifferent—or antagonistic—to Jewish interests that when *Hitler came to power, he wrote of him sympathetically. A close friend, the Jewish lawyer and later Supreme Court justice Felix Frankfurter, was so upset by Lippmann's writings on Hitler that he broke off their friendship. Lippmann, in turn, was furious with Frankfurter for cutting him off over so provincial an issue.

Later, after the Jewish situation deteriorated markedly in Germany, Lippmann wrote that reports of atrocities against Jews were "exaggerated by those inclined toward hysteria." Indeed, in Lippmann's view, to judge Germany by its antisemitism would be like judging "the Catholic Church by the Inquisition, *Protestantism by the Ku Klux Klan, [and] the Jews by their *parvenus.*"

Although he often delivered public lectures, Lippmann made it a point never to accept speaking engagements before Jewish audiences. If Jewish interests were endangered, Lippmann tended to identify with antagonistic statements made by the Jews' enemies. When Harvard president A. Lawrence Lowell indicated his intention to limit the "excessive" number of Jewish students at the university in the early 1920s, Lippmann wrote, "I do not regard the Jews as innocent victims. They hand on unconsciously and uncritically from one generation to another many distressing personal and social habits."

In contemporary America, one of the most celebrated self-hating Jews is the world-renowned linguist Noam Chomsky. The son of a well-known Hebrew scholar, Chomsky has publicly argued for the elimination of Israel as a Jewish state. Chomsky also publicly attacked a French university for firing a professor who wrote that the Holocaust was a Jewish hoax, and he has, on at least one occasion, refused to answer whether or not he believes the Holocaust to have occurred (see *Holocaust Revisionists*). Because he advocates positions that are seen as antisemitic when advanced by non-Jews, most Jews regard Chomsky as a Jewish antisemite, or a self-hating Jew.

Jewish self-hatred can sometimes be practiced by Jews who are seemingly very religious. Some years ago in Borough Park, a largely Orthodox neighborhood in Brooklyn, a Conservative synagogue was defaced with a painted swastika. Although people assumed at first that some non-Jewish antisemites had invaded the neighborhood, it soon turned out that the desecration had been committed by a fringe group belonging to an organization called T.O.R.A.H., "Tough Orthodox Rabbis and Hasidim." Because they damaged the synagogue as neo-Nazis might, rather than by picketing or protesting specific synagogue policies, they can legitimately be called self-hating Jews. Indeed, the people who painted the swastika on the synagogue may have thought that Jews who prayed in a Conservative synagogue deserved the fate Hitler inflicted on all Jews.

In recent years, self-hating Jews have generally not caused the Jewish community much harm. They are, however, a perennial source of annoyance and emotional pain to other Jews. When some in the Jewish community identify with the Jews' enemies, the rest feel a deeper wound than when they are attacked by antisemites.

Yet, the term "self-hating Jew" is often used in Jewish life irresponsibly and unfairly. Jews also have to guard against the inclination to label any Jews with whom they disagree as "self-hating." For example, a Jew who actively supports Israel's right to exist and who advocates a Palestinian state on the *West Bank is not self-hating; a Jew who identifies with, and is happy when, Islamic terrorists murder Israelis and other Jews, is.

SOURCES AND FURTHER READINGS: Paul Marcus and Alan Rosenberg, "Another Look at Jewish Self-Hatred," *Journal of Reform Judaism*, Summer 1989, pp. 37–59; Karl Marx, "On the Jewish Question," in his *Early Writings*, translated by Rodney Livingstone and Gregor Benton; Julius Carlebach, *Karl Marx and the Radical Critique of Judaism*; Edmund Silberner, "Was Marx an antisemite?" *Historica Judaica*, April 1949; Marx's offensive comment about Ferdinand Lasalle is cited in Robert Wistrich, *Revolutionary Jews from Marx to Trotsky*, pp. 41–42; Ronald Steel, *Walter Lippmann and the American Century*.

PART ELEVEN

Jewish Texts

248

APOCRYPHA

IN MODERN ENGLISH, THE WORD "APOCRYPHAL" MEANS LEGENDARY or mythical; an apocryphal story is one that probably never happened. Many people, as a result, mistakenly believe that the post-biblical books known as the Apocrypha are mythical works. The original meaning of apocrypha, however, was "hidden away"; Jews regarded the books of the Apocrypha as hidden because they were not included in the Bible. When the rabbis designated the biblical canon, they excluded all works that they believed were written after the age of *Ezra, the great fifth-century B.C.E. sage. What unifies the books in the Apocrypha, therefore, is that they are all post-Ezra.

The Apocrypha's most famous volumes are the Books of *Maccabees, which tell the story of the Jewish revolt against King *Antiochus Epiphanes, the Syrian monarch who tried to wipe out Judaism. The *Hanukka story, and its heroes, Mattathias and Judah Maccabee, are known to us largely through these books. Strangely enough, though the Books of Maccabees were written shortly after the successful Jewish revolt against Antiochus, they do not mention the miracle most commonly associated with Hanukka, the one-day supply of oil that burned for eight days.

The Apocrypha's next most famous book is Ecclesiasticus, alternatively known as The Wisdom of Ben Sira. It contains hundreds of proverbs, as well as some poems, the best known of which (in the forty-fourth chapter) includes an opening verse used by James Agee as the title of *Let Us Now Praise Famous Men*. After exulting about the significance of important people, the author of Ecclesiasticus speaks out on behalf of the unknown: "And some there be, which have no memorial, who are perished, as though they have never been, and are become as though they had never been born. . . . But these were merciful men, whose righteousness has not been forgotten. . . . Their seed shall remain for ever, and their glory shall not be blotted out. Their bodies are buried in peace, but their names live forever more" (44:9–10;13–14).

Other books in the Apocrypha include the two Books of Esdras, attributed to Ezra; Tobit; Judith; some additions to the Book of Esther; a letter of *Jeremiah; and two short books about *Daniel.

Today, few Jews—aside from Bible scholars—read the Apocrypha, except perhaps for Maccabees. Ask a rabbi of any denomination what he knows about the Apocrypha, and it is unlikely that he or she will be able to talk about it for more than five minutes. Indeed, once the rabbis of the Talmud declared these books outside the biblical canon, they effectively guaranteed that they would become curiosities and of little religious significance to later generations of Jews.

249

ETHICS OF THE FATHERS/*PIRKEI AVOT*

SIXTY-TWO OF THE SIXTY-THREE SHORT BOOKS THAT MAKE UP THE *Mishna are legal texts. For example, *Brakhot (Blessings)*, the Mishna's opening tractate, delineates the appropriate blessings for various occasions. The tractate *Shabbat* specifies, as one would expect, the laws of the Sabbath. The only tractate of the sixty-three that does not deal with laws is called *Pirkei Avot* (usually translated as *Ethics of the Fathers*) and it is the "*Bartlett's*" of Judaism. *Pirkei Avot* transmits the favorite moral advice and insights of the leading rabbinic scholars of different generations.

The quotes found in *Pirkei Avot* generally are spiritual and edifying, but they can also be practical. Two thousand years ago, Ben Zoma rendered what remains, in my opinion, the best definition of happiness. "Who is rich? He who is happy with what he has" (4:1). *Hillel is frequently cited in *Pirkei Avot*. He is best known for "If I am not for myself who will be for me? But if I am only for myself, what am I?" (1:14). The last sentence should logically read *who* am I? But as Professor Louis Kaplan taught: "If you are only for yourself, you cease to be a real human being, and you become no longer a who, but a what." Hillel concludes the sentence with a thought that was borrowed two millennia later by President Ronald Reagan, who cited the sage's words while trying to push through urgently needed economic reforms: "And if not now, when?"

Jewish tradition encourages the study of one chapter of *Ethics of the Fathers* each Sabbath afternoon in the spring and summer months. As a result, religious Jews have been deeply influenced by the book, since they review it several times each year.

Because its reasoning is direct, and largely based on human experience, *Pirkei Avot* is the most accessible of the books making up the *Oral Law. It certainly is the handiest guide to Jewish ethics. In recent years, a three-volume English commentary on *Pirkei Avot*, Irving Bunim's *Ethics from Sinai*, has helped revive and deepen study of the book among traditional Jews. But Bunim's is only one of many commentaries that have been published on *Pirkei Avot*. In the past century alone, R. Travers Herford, a Christian religious scholar, published one that was intended in large measure to demonstrate to other Christians that the rabbis of the Talmud (see *Pharisees*) were deeply concerned with ethical questions. The late Chief Rabbi of England, Joseph Hertz, published another commentary in a prayerbook he translated. More recently, Reuven Bulka, a Canadian rabbi and a recognized scholar on psychology, has produced a commentary, *As a Tree by the Waters*, in which psychological insights are used to deepen the reader's understanding of the text.

The text of *Pirkei Avot* can be found in most prayerbooks, following the Sabbath afternoon service.

The following are some characteristic teachings of *Pirkei Avot*:

Shammai taught: "Say little and do much" (1:15).

Hillel taught: "Don't judge your fellowman until you are in his place . . . and don't say I will study when I have time, lest you never find the time" (2:4).

Hillel taught: "A person who is [too] shy [to ask questions] will never learn, and a teacher who is too strict cannot teach . . . and in a place where there are no men, strive to be a man" (2:5; for the meaning of the word "man" here, see *Mensch*).

Rabbi Tarfon taught: "It is not your responsibility to finish the work [of perfecting the world], but you are not free to desist from it either" (2:16).

Rabbi Chanina taught: "Pray for the welfare of the government, for without fear of governmental authorities people would swallow each other alive" (3:2).

Ben Zoma taught: "Who is wise? He who learns from every man. . . . Who is a hero? He who controls his passions" (4:1).

SOURCES AND FURTHER READINGS: Irving Bunim, *Ethics from Sinai* (three volumes); Reuven Bulka, *As a Tree by the Waters*; R. Travers Herford, *The Ethics of the Talmud: Sayings of the Fathers*. See also Judah Goldin, trans., *The Fathers According to Rabbi Nathan*, a rabbinic commentary on *Pirkei Avot*.

MISHNA/TALMUD/BABYLONIAN TALMUD/JERUSALEM TALMUD—*See Entry 83*

MIDRASH—*See Entry 84*

HAGGADA—*See Entry 309*

SIDDUR, MAKHZOR—*See Entry 342*

THE KUZARI—*See Entry 92*

250

GUIDE TO THE PERPLEXED/MOREH NEVUKHIM

THE GREATEST WORK OF MEDIEVAL JEWISH PHILOSOPHY IS *MAImonides's *Guide to the Perplexed (Moreh Nevukhim)*, his last major work of Jewish scholarship. Maimonides had been a lifelong student of philosophy and believed that almost all of Aristotle's truths were consistent with the Torah's. In one extraordinary passage in the *Guide*, he declared that if Aristotle's notion that matter is eternal (and thus either predated or was coexistent with God) was proven true, then the Torah would be void (Part 2, Chapter 25, in the *Guide*).

Maimonides's passionate attraction to rationalism, as suggested by the above statement, deeply alienated many traditional Jews: In the centuries following the writing of the *Guide*, more than a few rabbis banned it. Even among those religious Jews who didn't ban its study, the book was apt to be ignored.

Maimonides himself might not have been upset to learn that his book was attacked by many. Near its beginning, he wrote: "When I have a difficult subject before me . . . [and] can see no other way of teaching a well-established truth except by pleasing one intelligent man and displeasing ten thousand fools, I prefer to address myself to one man and take no notice whatsoever of the condemnation of the multitude."

The *Guide*'s early parts seek to prove God's existence, something few philosophers today believe is possible. In the Middle Ages, however, it was widely believed by the great Jewish and Christian figures (for example, Saint Thomas Aquinas) that God's existence *could* be proven. Not surprisingly, the sections of the *Guide* attempting to do so strike most modern readers as among the less interesting parts of the book.

Part 3 of the *Guide*, however, remains strikingly current, for here Maimonides offers a philosophical rationale for the Torah's laws. Over the centuries, this analysis has struck some of Maimonides's most traditional readers as impious. They believe that offering philosophical or historical reasons for God's laws suggests that the one offering the reasons sees himself as fully knowing God's mind. They also fear, perhaps, that people might accept the rationale as being the reason for the law, so that if someday the rationale no longer seems applicable, then people will stop observing the law. Maimonides quite vigorously asserts, however, that it is within human capability to discern the reasons for the laws of the Torah. His starting point is a verse in Deuteronomy (4:6), which declares that by observing the Torah's laws, the Jews will appear wise and discerning in the eyes of the nations. Unless the laws are part of a rational scheme, Maimonides argues, why would observing them make the Jews appear wise? Indeed, Maimonides is particularly scornful of those who deny the Torah's essential rationality:

> There is a group of human beings who consider it a grievous thing that causes should be given for any law; what would please them most is that the intellect would not find a meaning for the commandments and prohibitions. What compels them to feel thus is a sickness that they find in their souls, a sickness to which they are unable to give utterance and of which they cannot furnish a satisfactory account. For they think that if those laws were useful in this existence and had been given to us for this or that reason, it would be as if they derived from the reflection and understanding of some intelligent being. If, however,

there is a thing for which the intellect could not find any meaning at all and that does not lead to something useful, it indubitably derives from God: For the reflection of man would lead to no such thing (Part 3, Chapter 31).

Maimonides's treatment of Jewish laws as rational helped save Judaism from becoming either obscure or antirational. The early Church father Tertullian, tortured by the paradox of a messianic God/man who could be killed by his Roman jailers, was driven to exclaim, *"Credo quia impossible*—I believe because it is impossible." To Maimonides, such a statement is abhorrent (indeed, later Church teaching emphasized the rationality of belief in God). "I believe because it is true, and God has given me the intellect to prove it so" comes far closer to articulating Maimonides's theology.

SOURCE AND FURTHER READING: The best translation of *The Guide to the Perplexed* is that of Shlomo Pines; the excerpt cited is from pp. 523–524.

RASHI—See Entry 96

RESPONSA LITERATURE/SHE'ELOT
VE-TESHUVOT

WHILE JEWISH LAW IS BASED ON THE TORAH, AND THE INTERPRETA-tions of the Torah in the *Talmud, a Jew conversant only with the Torah and Talmud would still not find direct answers to many modern questions about Jewish law. For example, is it permitted to drive an automobile on the Sabbath? When the car was first invented, and that question was raised, Orthodox rabbis uniformly forbade its usage on the Sabbath. Although there is, of course, no reference to automobiles in the Torah, driving a car involves turning on the ignition, which in turn ignites sparks, an act that they understand as violating the Torah's law against making a fire on the Sabbath (Exodus 35:3).

The work that records legal questions Jews have posed to rabbis, and their answers, is known as responsa literature. In Hebrew, it is called *She'elot ve-Teshuvot*, which means simply "Questions and Answers."

Outside of Judaic scholars, few Jews are familiar with this extensive body of Jewish literature, which encompasses thousands of volumes. The Orthodox-sponsored Bar Ilan University in Israel has developed a computer-based responsa program, the goal of which is to index all major works in this genre, so a rabbi who is asked for a legal ruling will eventually be able to access all relevant previous rulings.

All three major Jewish denominations have scholars producing responsa to guide their adherents. The questions raised in the three movements, however, are often different and the answers even more so.

Because Orthodox Jews are likeliest to ask questions about Jewish law, most responsa are written by Orthodox rabbis. Several Orthodox periodicals publish newly written responsa. Some of the questions raised seem minor, almost trivial. For example, a prominent Orthodox rabbi wrote a responsum to a question concerning the playing of Scrabble on the Sabbath. Was it permitted to play this game, a correspondent wished to know, in light of the fact that it is forbidden to write on the Sabbath? The rabbi ruled that Scrabble is allowed; the words formed by moving the Scrabble blocks together cannot be classified as writing. At the conclusion, however, he reminded players not to write down their scores when playing on the Sabbath.

Many responsa, of course, deal with far more serious issues. Is a pregnant woman who runs a higher-than-average risk of conceiving a child with Down's syndrome permitted to have an amniocentesis? Most Orthodox rabbis answer no: Since Orthodoxy would not normally regard Down's syndrome as constituting permissible grounds for aborting a fetus, there is no reason for having an amniocentesis. Some Orthodox rabbis have even ruled that a woman who is pregnant as a result of rape cannot have an abortion, though I have always been more impressed by the ruling of the nineteenth-century Rabbi Yehuda Perilman, who wrote that women differ from "mother earth" in that they need not nurture seeds planted in them against their will.

Topics covered in responsa literature are as varied as the activities of the Jewish community. Here are some examples (I apologize in advance for not supplying quick yes or no answers):

May a Jew own stock in a company that sells unkosher food products or that conducts business on the Sabbath or holidays (see *Rabbi Moshe Feinstein*)?

May a Jewish woman who is married to an infertile man be artificially inseminated, or would such insemination constitute a violation of the law against adultery?

Should a non-Jew who converts to Judaism say the *Mourner's *Kaddish* for his dead non-Jewish father or mother?

Does a Jewish male have to wear a skullcap (see *Kippah or Yarmulka*) at his place of work?

May a non-Jew be accepted as a candidate for conversion if his or her sole reason for becoming Jewish is to marry a Jew?

Many of the questions discussed in the responsa literature deal with highly personal issues, such as relations between the sexes. A recent article in the *Journal of Halacha and Contemporary Society* opens with the following five questions:

"May a woman travel in a car on a deserted road with a man to whom she is not married? Is it *halakhically* [legally] permitted for a man and a woman to be alone together in an elevator? Is a man permitted to take his date to a drive-in movie theater, or to a secluded park? May a woman be alone with her [male] physician, counselor, or employer? May a foster parent be alone with an adopted child of the opposite sex?" The author of the article, Rabbi Azarya Berzon, notes, "These questions all hinge on an application of the laws of *yikhud* — the prohibition of a man and woman [who are not married to each other] being alone together."

Since Orthodox Judaism has no central authority, the rulings of one rabbi can be dismissed by other rabbis both in his or in other communities. In the United States, however, the late Rabbi Moshe *Feinstein was long acknowledged as the most famous decider of Jewish law: His rulings have generally been accepted by almost all Orthodox rabbis.

In the United States, Conservative rabbis are members of the Rabbinical Assembly, which has a permanent Committee on Jewish Law and Standards to decide questions of Jewish law. Many of the committee's decisions are acknowledged departures from traditional practice. Among its more noted innovative rulings is the responsum, issued in 1950, that permits Jews to drive to the synagogue on the Sabbath. Few Conservative Jews today are aware that the responsum limited such permission to one instance: driving to attend a synagogue service. Conservative Judaism does not permit a Jew to drive anywhere else on the Sabbath. The rationale for this ruling was largely sociological. As increasing numbers of Jews moved to the suburbs in the 1940s, many no longer lived within walking distance of a synagogue. If Conservative rabbis forbade their congregants to drive to the synagogue on the Sabbath, almost all would have either stayed home and not prayed, or gone golfing or shopping instead. Their Jewish identity, it was felt, would erode if they stopped attending synagogue, so driving was permitted as the lesser of two evils. The Orthodox rabbinate soundly condemned the Conservative decision, noting, among other things, that it would be better if Conservative rabbis encouraged their congregants to live within walking distance of their synagogues.

Many recent Conservative responsa have dealt with the status of women within Judaism, and have generally set out to equalize their role in religious life. A 1955 responsum authorized women to be called to the Torah for an *aliyah, a 1973 responsum authorized the counting of women in a *minyan, and a 1983 decision by the Jewish Theological Seminary's faculty entitled women to be ordained as rabbis (see Women Rabbis). In late 2006, a series of different responsa were offered, the effect of which was to clear the way for gay men and women to be ordained. In all these cases, a minority of Conservative rabbis registered their objection to this turning away from traditional Jewish practice.

The offices of the Rabbinical Assembly contain many volumes with hundreds of other questions addressed to the Committee on Jewish Law and Standards, and the accompanying answers. In one famous case, the committee ruled that synagogues should not sponsor Bingo games. Although sponsorship of such games was legal according to American law and brought in badly needed funds for the congregations involved, the committee ruled that the use of synagogue facilities for gambling events violated the sanctity of the synagogue.

In the Reform movement, responsa serve no legal function—only an advisory one. Some questions addressed to Reform legal scholars show a mind-set that is already vastly different from that of more traditional Jews. In 1973, for example, the journal of Reform's Central Conference of American Rabbis published several responsa on the question of whether a congregation that is predominantly homosexual in character should be acknowledged as a valid Reform congregation and admitted to the Union of American Hebrew Congregations. On the one hand, although the Reform movement does not consider itself bound by the Torah's ritual laws, it does consider itself obligated by its ethical laws. The Torah speaks of homosexuality as an "abomination," indicating that it sees it as an ethical, not a ritual, offense. The leading Reform expert on Jewish law, the late Rabbi Solomon Freehof, ruled therefore that a homosexual congregation should not be admitted to the Union of American Hebrew Congregations. Rather, its members should be encouraged to join existing congregations. The other rabbinic respondents opposed Freehof, however, and today the Reform movement not only accepts homosexual congregations, it ordains homosexuals as rabbis, and the majority of Reform rabbis support the legalization of homosexual marriages in the United States.

Many questions addressed to the Reform rabbinate are similar in character to questions posed by Orthodox and Conservative Jews. The difference, however, is that the answers regarding ritual questions are usually more permissive than those offered to Orthodox questioners.

The responsa literature is a particularly important resource for students of Jewish history. At the time of the *Crusades, for example, one finds numerous responsa on the status of Jews who saved their lives by converting to Christianity, but who subsequently wished to return to the Jewish community. Should the community accept them, questioners asked, and what punishments, if any, should be imposed on them? A reading of the responsa literature on this issue reveals how widespread the problem of forced apostasy was.

Contemporary responsa likewise reveal a great deal about the social conditions of modern Jews. As revealed in the questions concerning stock ownership, the wearing of a skullcap at one's place of employment, and amniocentesis, one senses an affluent American-Jewish community, one that simultaneously participates in the non-Jewish culture and society while trying to maintain a distinctive Jewish identity.

SOURCES AND FURTHER READINGS: I will cite just a few representative works of responsa being produced in the different movements. Orthodox: J. David Bleich, *Contemporary Halakhic Problems* (five volumes). The *Journal of Halacha and Contemporary Society*, edited by Alfred Cohen, prints articles on issues of current *halakhic* concern, though they are not formally phrased in response to questions. Conservative: Seymour Siegel, ed., *Conservative Judaism and Jewish Law*; Rabbinical Assembly, *Proceedings of the Committee on Jewish Law and Standards of the Conservative Movement, 1980–1985*. Also, Kassel Abelson and David J. Fine, eds., *Responsa 1991–2000*. Reform: Walter Jacob, *American Reform Responsa, 1889–1983*; Reform scholar Solomon Freehof published two works on the history of responsa, *The Responsa Literature* and *A Treasury of Responsa*; see also W. Gunther Plaut and Mark Washofsky, *Teshuvot for the Nineties: Reform Judaism's Answers for Today's Dilemmas*.

252

MISHNEH TORAH

THE TWELFTH-CENTURY RABBINIC SCHOLAR AND PHILOSOPHER MOSES *Maimonides compiled the first fully comprehensive code of Jewish law. He called his fourteen-volume work the *Mishneh Torah* ("a second Torah"). In his introduction, Maimonides expressed the hope that people would be able to consult the Torah and his code, and find the applicable Jewish law without having to consult any other text.

Maimonides wrote his code in the form of an expanded commentary on the Torah's *613 commandments. Before listing the laws of marital relations, for example, he noted that four of the 613 commandments explicitly deal with this issue. The laws against idolatry, on the other hand, were shown to be based on fifty-one laws in the Torah.

The first of the *Mishneh Torah's* fourteen volumes is called *Sefer ha-Mada (Book of Knowledge)*. In it Maimonides records, among other things, laws concerning the belief in God, idolatry, *repentance, and study of the Torah. His demands in regard to the latter sound rather utopian; a craftsman, Maimonides regulates, who can earn his living by working three hours a day at his job, should spend nine hours studying Torah ("Laws Concerning the Study of the Torah," 1:12; see also *Hebrew School/Talmud Torah*).

In more than a few cases, Maimonides's philosophical disposition shaped his religious rulings. He was particularly irked by Jews who believed that God has a physical form. In "Laws of Repentance" (3:6–7), he writes that Jews who interpret literally those verses in the Torah that attribute physical characteristics to God—for example, "the finger of God"—are heretics and will have no place in the world-to-come. Some of Maimonides's most noted contemporaries attacked him for excluding such religiously naive Jews from heaven.

The other thirteen volumes of the *Mishneh Torah* outline Jewish law in the ritual and civil spheres. Maimonides has separate sections detailing the laws of *blessings, *circumcision, the different holidays, male-female relations, the laws of *kashrut*, and business ethics.

Some contemporary scholars speculate that, in compiling the *Mishneh*

Torah, Maimonides was attempting nothing less than to draft the constitution and specific laws of a future Jewish state. He included very specific details, even listing the laws concerning animal *sacrifices at the *Temple, though in his philosophical writings he suggested that sacrifices were ordained in the Bible as a concession to the religious needs of a more primitive age, and implied that they would not be reinstituted. Nonetheless, since a Temple might someday be rebuilt, and his views on sacrifices rejected, he included these laws.

On almost all legal questions, Maimonides legislated in accordance with views expressed in the Talmud, although he sometimes formulated his teachings in new categories; for example, in delineating eight degrees of charity (see *Tzedaka*), Maimonides wrote that the highest degree of charity is to give a poor person a loan or establish him in business so that he would never again be in need of charity ("Gifts to the Poor," 10:7).

Although legal codes usually make very dry reading, the *Mishneh Torah* does not. Maimonides frequently infuses his legal rulings with the passions of the philosopher. In the laws concerning murder, he rules that it is forbidden for the family of a victim to accept any reparations from a murderer, for "the life of the murdered person is not the property of [the family] but the property of God, and Scripture says, 'Moreover, you shall take no ransom for the life of a murderer' [Numbers 35:31]. There is no offense about which the Law is so strict as it is about bloodshed, as it is said, 'So shall you not pollute the land wherein you are; for blood, it pollutes the land' [Numbers 35:33]. . . ." ("Murder and Preservation of Life," 1:4).

Maimonides concludes the *Mishneh Torah* with a speculative section about the time of the *Messiah. In it Maimonides details his utopian vision of a perfect world: "The sages and prophets," Maimonides writes, "did not long for the days of the Messiah that Israel might exercise dominion over the world, or rule over the heathens, or be exalted by the nations, or that it might eat and drink and rejoice. Their aspiration was that Israel be free to devote itself to the Law and its wisdom, with no one to oppress or disturb it, and thus be worthy of life in the world to come. In that [messianic] era, there will be neither famine nor war, neither jealousy nor strife. . . . The one preoccupation of the whole world will be to know the Lord . . . 'For the earth shall be full of the knowledge of the Lord, as the waters cover the sea' " (Isaiah 11:9; "Kings and Wars," 12:4–5).

Occasionally, one does find influences other than the Torah, Talmud, and philosophy affecting Maimonides's thinking. In one particularly unfortunate instance, he justifies beating a disobedient wife ("Laws Concerning Marriage," 21:10), a clear reflection, it would appear, of the Muslim society in which Maimonides lived in Egypt. While Islamic law forbade systematic physical abuse of women, the Koran (4:38) did advocate beating disobedient wives. Maimonides's contemporaries in Europe were shocked; "Wife beating is unheard of among the children of Israel," Rabbi *Tam of France wrote.

Although rabbis today, particularly Orthodox rabbis, usually base their legal judgments on the *Shulkhan Arukh (sixteenth-century code of Jewish law), they invariably check Maimonides's ruling on the issue under discussion. Indeed, the *Shulkhan Arukh* itself largely follows the order and format of the *Mishneh Torah.*

Nonreligious Jews and non-Jewish scholars primarily know Maimonides as a philosopher, and as the author of the medieval classic *The Guide to the Perplexed.* His importance among Orthodox Jews, however, derives far more from the *Mishneh Torah* than from any of his philosophical writings.

SOURCES AND FURTHER READINGS: The late Professor Isadore Twersky, perhaps the foremost modern scholar on Maimonides, has compiled a superb anthology of Maimonides's writings, *A Maimonides Reader,* primarily based on the *Mishneh Torah.* Most of the citations in this chapter come from this anthology. In addition, Twersky published a more scholarly work, *Introduction to the Code of Maimonides.* Yale University has published an almost complete translation of the fourteen volumes of the *Mishneh Torah.*

SHULKHAN ARUKH — See Entry 107

253

THE ZOHAR

THE TALMUD RECORDS A DISCUSSION AMONG THREE RABBIS OF THE SECond century concerning the Romans, who then occupied Israel. Rabbi Judah said the Romans were to be commended for the many beautiful things they had done. "They have fixed up the marketplaces, the bridges, and the bathhouses." Rabbi Yossi said nothing. Rabbi Shimon bar Yochai expressed annoyance at

Rabbi Judah's naiveté. "Whatever they have done has been done exclusively to benefit themselves. They have repaired the marketplaces to install whorehouses. The bathhouses they beautify for their own indulgence, and the bridges they repair so that they can collect tolls on them" (*Shabbat* 33b).

When Roman officials heard about Rabbi Shimon's incendiary comments, they sentenced him to death. He fled with his son to a cave, and hid there for twelve years. He did not even inform his wife where he and his son were hiding, fearing that she would reveal the information under torture. Throughout the twelve years, the Talmud records, Rabbi Shimon and his son were fed by a carob tree, and the two men spent their days together studying Torah.

More than a thousand years later, a Spanish rabbi named Moses De Leon electrified the Jewish world with the claim that he had unearthed a manuscript that Shimon bar Yochai had written during his years of hiding. The book was known as the *Zohar*, and since its revelation to the Jewish world in the thirteenth century, it has been regarded as the central work of the *kabbalah, Jewish mysticism.

While many Orthodox Jews today, particularly those who have a mystical bent, still believe in Rabbi Shimon's authorship of the *Zohar*, most Jewish scholars have long followed the lead of Gershom Scholem, the great scholar of Jewish mysticism, who believed that Rabbi De Leon was not the finder of the *Zohar*, but its author.

Scholem does not, however, regard De Leon's attribution of authorship to Shimon bar Yochai as an act of fraud. To De Leon, the mystical truths revealed in the *Zohar* were such obvious eternal truths that undoubtedly they were familiar to such a great scholar as Shimon bar Yochai. True, De Leon did not in fact possess a manuscript in which Rabbi Shimon wrote down these truths, but everything *could* have been written by him. Presumably, De Leon's attribution of authorship to the second-century sage was done to secure a wide readership for his book, which would have been denied him if people thought they were reading the work of a contemporary. In the world of traditional Judaism, the older the writing, the closer in time it is to the Revelation on Sinai, and hence the more likely it is to contain truth. To mystics, the *Zohar* is one of Judaism's greatest works.

The *Zohar* has provoked considerable, and frequently bitter, controversy. Jewish rationalists have often dismissed kabbalah and the *Zohar* as dangerous nonsense, feeling that they encourage Jews to act according to mystical impulses rather than reason.

The *Zohar* is written in the form of a commentary on the Torah, inter-twining mystical insights with revealing anecdotes about the great sages of Israel. Characteristic of the book's style is the following tale of a discussion between Rabbi Shimon and his colleagues:

> One day the friends were walking with Rabbi Shimon. He said: "I see all other nations raised and Israel humiliated. Why so? Because the King, God, has sent away the Queen, Israel, and has put the handmaid, the alien Crown, in her place." He wept and continued: "A king without a queen is no king; if the king is attached to the handmaid of the queen, where is his glory? The handmaid rules over Zion as the Queen once ruled over it. But one day the Holy One will restore the Queen to her rightful place; who shall then rejoice like the King and the Queen?"—the King because he has returned to her, and has separated from the handmaid, and the Queen because she is reunited to the King. Hence, it is written, "Rejoice exceedingly, O daughter of Zion" (Zechariah 9:9).

SOURCES AND FURTHER READINGS: The last selection is from Nahum Glatzer, ed., *The Judaic Tradition*, p. 463. See also two anthologies of the *Zohar*: Gershom Scholem, ed., *Zohar: The Book of Splendor*, and Daniel Matt, ed., *Zohar: The Book of Enlightenment*. On the issue of the *Zohar's* authorship, see Joseph Dan, *Gershom Scholem and the Mystical Dimension of Jewish History*, pp. 222–226. In recent years, Daniel Matt has started bringing out a major multivolume translation and commentary on the *Zohar*, called *The Zohar: Pritzker Edition*.

254

ROME AND JERUSALEM, 1862

AN EARLY ZIONIST CLASSIC, *ROME AND JERUSALEM*, WAS WRITTEN BY A man whom Karl Marx had once called "my Communist rabbi." As a young man, Moses Hess was an assimilated Jew with radical social and economic views. Hess's initial return to the Jewish people had less to do with Judaism than with his exposures to antisemitism (see also *Herzl* and *Jabotinsky*). He was galvanized by the 1840 *Damascus Blood Libel, an ugly incident in which a group of Syrian Jews were falsely charged with the ritual murder of a Catholic monk. Although his passion over Jewish issues soon abated, the subsequent rise of German racism reignited his Jewish feelings. The depth of his earlier alienation is made apparent on the opening page of *Rome and Jerusalem:*

> Here I stand once more, after twenty years of estrangement, in the midst of my people; I participate in its holy days of joy and mourning, its memories and hopes. . . . A thought which I had stifled forever within my heart is again vividly present with me; the thought of my nationality . . . the inheritance of my ancestors, the Holy Land and the eternal city, the birthplace of the belief in the divine unity of life and in the future brotherhood of all men. This thought . . . had for years throbbed in my sealed heart, demanding outlet. But I lacked the energy necessary for the transition from a path as apparently remote from Judaism as mine was to that new path which appeared before me in the hazy distance.

Hess argued that the Jews were as entitled as all other peoples to a homeland in which they could develop their culture and talents without suffering antisemitism. Consistent with his left-wing views, he hoped that the Jewish state would be humanely socialistic. Almost a century after his death, the Labor party of Israel arranged to have the remains of their socialist forebear brought from Germany and reinterred on an Israeli kibbutz, Kinneret.

Because Hess lived before the rise of political Zionism (1812–1875), his impact was more theoretical than practical. Nonetheless, there was a prophetic quality to his writings, and when Theodor Herzl read *Rome and Jerusalem* in 1901, he wrote in his diary: "Everything that we have tried is already in this book."

SOURCE AND FURTHER READINGS: Moses Hess, *Rome and Jerusalem;* Shlomo Avineri, *Moses Hess: Prophet of Communism and Zionism.*

THE JEWISH STATE—See Entry 136

I AND THOU AND TALES OF THE HASIDIM—
See Entry 125

255

THE STEINSALTZ TALMUD, THE ARTSCROLL TALMUD

MANY ENGLISH-SPEAKING JEWS BELIEVE THAT IF ONLY THEY KNEW Hebrew, they would be able to study the *Talmud on their own. Unfortunately, they are wrong. The Talmud is written in a mixture of Hebrew and Aramaic, and remains inaccessible to readers who know only Hebrew. In addition to the necessary linguistic skills, one must also be able to understand the shorthand style in which the Talmud's text is composed. It is rare that a thought is expressed in a complete sentence; rather, a few words are used to convey an argument. In addition, the pages of the Talmud are printed as one nonstop paragraph, with no punctuation. The reader, therefore, has to deduce for him- or herself where the discussion starts and where it ends. One positive repercussion of this is that people are forced to read the text much more slowly and carefully.

The Talmud was saved from obscurity in the eleventh century thanks to *Rashi's running commentary. He explained the meaning of those words that were no longer used, and he periodically summed up the debates conducted by the talmudic sages. Yet, as valuable as Rashi's nine-hundred-year-old commentary has been in elucidating the text, the Talmud remains for many twentieth-century Jews a closed book.

Adin Steinsaltz, an Israeli-born scholar and one of the genuine Jewish geniuses of the twentieth century, has devoted his life to making the Talmud accessible to all Jews. Steinsaltz himself was raised by irreligious parents, and discovered Judaism during his teenage years. He quickly became an expert on the Bible, the Talmud, and Jewish mysticism.

Steinsaltz has published his modern commentary on well over three-quarters of the entire Talmud, and hopes to complete it within the next few years. In his edition of the Talmud, the text is printed with punctuation. In the commentary, he first translates the Talmud word for word into modern Hebrew, then summarizes the discussion in the text. He offers extensive notes on the sides of the pages explaining, among other things, the Greek and Latin words that are used in the Talmud. He also notes rulings in Jewish law that are based on the talmudic discussion, and includes short biographies of the rabbis cited.

It is rare indeed that a work is regarded as a classic during the author's lifetime. But Steinsaltz's Talmud commentary is a classic, and it is no exaggeration to say that he has taught Talmud to more Jews than anyone since Rashi.

In 1989, Random House started publishing volumes of Steinsaltz's Talmud in English. Although a superbly accurate English rendering of the Talmud, published by the Soncino Press of London, has existed since 1935, it is hardly the kind of work that one can sit down and read through. The English used in the Soncino translation is quite formal, and people who have tried to read a volume have often reported that they became lost in the thicket of arguments, and it is hoped that the Steinsaltz edition will make the Talmud more accessible. In addition, an Orthodox publishing house, ArtScroll, has been bringing out the Talmud in a line-by-line translation into English, along with a running commentary. Both the translation and the commentary, which tens of thousands of people now use daily to study a page of Talmud, are on a very high level. In 2005, ArtScroll completed the translation of the entire Babylonian Talmud, one of the great achievements of modern Jewish scholarship, and has now started to bring out the shorter and less authoritative, but still very important, Jerusalem Talmud in English.

Another twentieth-century classic published in Israel is Pinchas Kehati's commentary on the *Mishna, the first compilation of the *Oral Law. Kehati translates the Mishna into modern Hebrew, and then summarizes the Talmud's discussion of the Mishnaic text. In recent years, this extraordinary work also has been published in an English translation, and is available in Jewish bookstores.

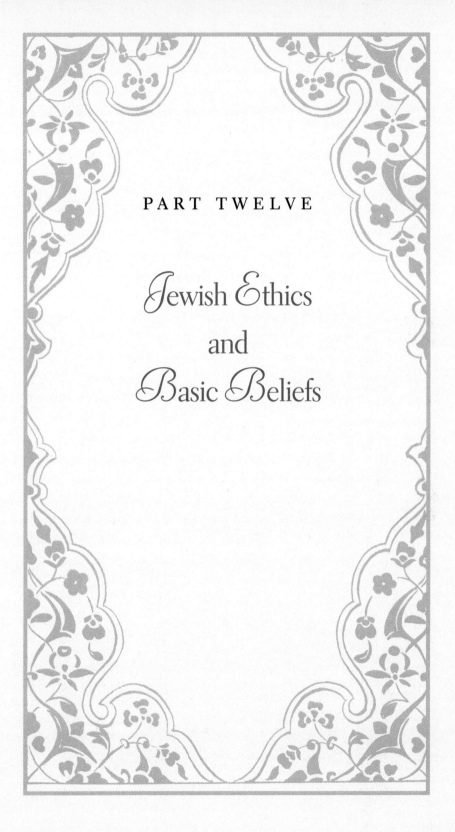

PART TWELVE

Jewish Ethics
and
Basic Beliefs

COMMANDMENT/MITZVAH

The 613 Mitzvot of the Torah

Mitzvot *Between People and Each Other and* Mitzvot *Between People and God/*Bein Adam le-Khavero, Bein Adam la-Makom

ASK EVEN KNOWLEDGEABLE JEWS WHAT THE WORD *MITZVAH* MEANS and you will often be told, "good deed." But in reality, *mitzvah* means "commandment." The difference between "good deed" and "commandment," though subtle, is significant. "Good deed" implies a voluntary act, "commandment" an obligatory one. In contemporary Western society, most people believe voluntary acts to be on a higher plane than obligatory ones; after all, they reason, isn't a person who does an act voluntarily nobler than one who does it because he feels obligated? Yet the Talmud takes precisely the opposite point of view: "Greater is he who is commanded and carries out an act, than he who is not commanded, and carries it out" (*Kiddushin* 31a). Apparently, the rabbis of the Talmud believed that obligatory acts will be carried out with greater consistency and staying power than voluntary ones. Two examples come to mind.

At one point or another almost all of us go on diets. The two standard motivations for dieting are very powerful: to be physically more attractive, and to be healthier. Yet almost all of us break our diets, usually quite quickly. Compare this unhappy reality with the experience of people who keep *kosher. Kashrut* does not guarantee health or greater physical attractiveness; yet, because its practitioners feel *obligated* to observe its laws, they can go a lifetime without eating pork or shellfish. In fact, I have often speculated that were the government to mandate putting pork into all chocolate products, I could finally take off the pounds I need to shed.

Similarly, people continue to pay taxes even during difficult financial periods, because the laws of the state obligate them to do so, and they will be punished if they don't. Charitable contributions, on the other hand, fall precipitously during rough financial times because they are perceived as voluntary.

Although the Torah itself never specifies a number, a talmudic tradition teaches that there are 613 *mitzvot* in the Torah. Many Jews erroneously believe that the biblical commandments are only concerned with rituals. After a synagogue lecture I once delivered, a woman told me, "I know all about the six hundred and thirteen commandments, but I'm not religious, so I don't keep any." I assured her that if she had not had sexual relations with her mother, father, or any of her siblings, she had already kept two Torah laws. She had forgotten that biblical commandments legislate ethical and social issues as well as ritual ones.

In today's world, no one observes all 613 commandments. Hundreds of the laws deal with purity and impurity, and with animal sacrifices. A great Eastern European rabbinic sage, the *Haffetz Hayyim* (1838–1933), computed that fewer than three hundred *mitzvot* are still practiced today.

Many, though not all, of the ethical concepts and laws described in the following pages come from the Torah, and are among its 613 commandments. Some of the other ethical laws discussed here are post-biblical and are legislated in the *Talmud. Even these laws, however, are usually connected by the rabbis of the Talmud to a verse in the Torah.

A common way of categorizing the commandments is into ethical and ritual spheres. Ethical or interpersonal commandments are known as *mitzvot* between a person and his fellow human being (in Hebrew, *bein adam le-khavero;*) ritual laws are called *mitzvot* between a person and God (*bein adam la-makom*). Some laws, however, that are predominantly ritualistic have strong ethical components. The laws of *kashrut,* for example, are generally regarded as the epitome of purely ritual legislation. Nonetheless, *kashrut* regulates that an animal that is to be eaten must be slaughtered with one stroke, so that it suffers the minimum pain possible. Prolonging death, such as often occurs when an animal is hunted, renders the animal unkosher. Clearly, then, the laws of kosher slaughter are concerned with the ethical treatment of animals as well as with ritual.

With regard to the laws of the *Sabbath, another set of regulations that people normally regard as purely ritual, the Torah commands that one's servants be freed from work on that day. Is that a ritual or an ethical ordinance? Clearly, the distinction between ritual and ethical laws is far from absolute.

SOURCES AND FURTHER READINGS: A full listing and explication of the 613 commandments in the Torah is found in Moses Maimonides, *The Commandments: Sefer Ha-Mitzvoth of Maimonides*, two volumes, translated by Charles Chavel.

IN GOD'S IMAGE

ALMOST THE FIRST THING THE BIBLE TELLS US ABOUT *ADAM IS THAT he was created in the "image of God" (Genesis 1:27). This description has confused more than a few people and been interpreted in widely disparate ways. A Mormon religious teacher once told me that it means that God has a body, and that the human form is created in the image of God's body. Jewish teachings hold, however, that God is incorporeal, without a body (see Deuteronomy 4:12,15).

In what sense then are human beings understood to be made "in God's image"? Unlike animals, they have the ability to reason and to know good from evil. People speak, for example, of a "good" dog, but all they mean is an obedient dog. A dog trained by anti-Nazi partisans to attack Nazis was no more a "good" dog than a dog trained by the Nazis to attack Jews in a concentration camp was "bad." Animals do not have the reasoning ability to make moral choices; human beings are the only creatures who do. It is in this regard that human beings are considered to be "in God's image."

SOURCES AND FURTHER READINGS: Samuel Belkin, *In His Image: The Jewish Philosophy of Man as Expressed in Rabbinic Tradition*; David Shapiro, "The Doctrine of the image of God and imitatio Dei," in Menachem Kellner, ed., *Contemporary Jewish Ethics*, pp. 127–151.

"DO NOT PUT A STUMBLING BLOCK IN FRONT OF A BLIND MAN"
(LEVITICUS 19:14)

UNLESS ONE IS A CONGENITAL SADIST, THE LAW IN LEVITICUS THAT forbids people from placing a stumbling block in front of a blind man would seem to be the easiest commandment in the Torah to observe. This *mitzvah* is so narrowly specific, however, that the rabbis of the *Talmud felt certain that the legislation had broader implications than mere protection of blind pedestrians. By the time they had finished explicating "Do not put a stumbling block in front of a blind man," they had given it so broad an interpretation — interpreting as "blind" "anyone who is blind in the matter at hand" — that today it is one of the hardest commandments never to violate.

From the rabbinic perspective, for example, people who make money in the stock market by trading on the basis of inside information violate, among other laws, "Do not put a stumbling block in front of a blind man." The people from whom they are purchasing stock are "blind" in the sense that they are unaware of the special information possessed by the inside trader and so are willing to sell the stock at a much lower price than its actual value.

I think there is wisdom in my friend Dennis Prager's suggestion that the law against placing a stumbling block before the blind might well be violated by a man who tells a woman that he loves her, when he doesn't, to influence her to sleep with him. In this case, he is taking advantage of a "blind passion," to influence the woman to do what she would not do if she knew his true feelings.

The rabbis apply the law of "Do not put a stumbling block" to seemingly obscure cases. For example, Torah law mandates that children show respect to parents, and severely punishes children who either curse or strike their parents (Exodus 21:15). The rabbis ruled, again on the basis of this law in Leviticus, that parents are forbidden to strike a grown child, lest they turn themselves into the stumbling block who causes the enraged child to become "blind" with fury and to strike or curse them, thereby violating a serious Torah law.

The most common application of the law is in the area of giving advice. When a person seeks advice, he has a right to expect that the guidance being offered is intended solely for his benefit. If, for some reason, a person feels incapable of offering neutral advice, he is obligated to explain why or to offer no advice at all. Most important, the rabbis forbid anyone from pretending to help someone by giving advice when the advice is actually intended to benefit the person offering it. That is once again considered to be taking advantage of another's blindness.

259

"JUSTICE, JUSTICE YOU SHALL PURSUE"

(DEUTERONOMY 16:20)

THE TORAH EXHORTS WITH EXTRAORDINARY PASSION: "JUSTICE, JUSTICE you shall pursue." The repetition of the word "justice" in this verse in Deuteronomy is interpreted by some as implying that means as well as ends must be just. Justice also is regarded as binding on God as well as human beings. When Abraham believes God is acting inappropriately, he confronts Him with a stark challenge: "Will the Judge of all the earth not act with justice?" (Genesis 18:25; see *Sodom and Gomorrah*). For the prophets, justice is what matters most to God. "Let justice well up as waters and righteousness as a mighty stream" declares *Amos in what is the most oft-quoted verse from his book (5:24).

The Torah's emphasis on justice has deeply affected subsequent Jewish legislation. For example, the English word "charity" comes from the Latin *caritas*, meaning "from the heart" and implying a voluntary act. The word for charity in Hebrew is *tzedaka*, which is simply the feminine form of the Hebrew word for justice, *tzedek*. In Jewish law, one who does not give charity is not just uncharitable, but unjust as well. Thus, Jewish courts had no compunctions about compelling people of means to give *tzedaka*.

Jews have frequently been accused of supporting revenge in the name of justice. In December 1989, while visiting Jerusalem, Nobel Peace Prize laureate Bishop Desmond Tutu told his Israeli hosts that the time had come for Jews to forgive the Nazis for the murder of six million Jews. Tutu advocated that forgiveness be extended as well to elderly Nazi war criminals who were living in freedom. Almost all Jews found Tutu's advice offensive. For one thing, Jewish tradition would consider it immoral for Jews to forgive murderers for acts committed against people other than themselves (see *Repentance/Teshuva*). Also, it would be unjust for murderers of men, women, and children to go on living unpunished. That Tutu believed that mass murderers should be left unpunished and unmolested struck most Jews as quintessentially unjust—and hence, un-Jewish.

SOURCES AND FURTHER READINGS: A. J. Heschel, *The Prophets*; George Foote Moore, *Judaism in the First Centuries of the Christian Era*, vol. 2, pp. 180–197.

260

"AN EYE FOR AN EYE" (EXODUS 21:24)

IF ONE COULD SPEAK OF BIBLICAL VERSES AS BEING VILIFIED, THEN "an eye for an eye" would be the most vilified verse in the Bible. It is commonly cited to "prove" the existence of an "Old Testament" ethic of vengefulness, and then contrasted with the New Testament's supposedly higher ethic of forgiveness. "An eye for an eye" is often associated with modern Jews as well, and invariably in a pejorative manner. Israel's critics, for example, commonly accuse her of practicing "eye for an eye" morality when she retaliates against Arab terrorist acts.

In actuality, the biblical standard of "an eye for an eye" stood in stark contrast to the legal standards prevailing in the societies that surrounded the ancient Hebrews. The Code of Hammurabi, a legal code hundreds of years older than the Torah, legislated retaliation even against innocent parties. Thus, if A constructed a building for B, and the building collapsed and killed B's daughter, then A's daughter was put to death (Law number 229). The biblical law of "an eye for an eye" restricted punishment solely to the perpetrator. Furthermore, unlike Hammurabi's code, one who caused another's death accidentally was never executed.

"An eye for an eye" also served to limit vengeance; it did not permit "a life for an eye" or even "two eyes for an eye." The operative biblical principle was that punishment must be commensurate with the deed, not exceed it. Blood feuds and vendettas were long practiced among the Israelites' neighbors—indeed, they have persisted in the Middle East until this century—and revenge was often carried out without restraint.

Christians often contend that Jesus went beyond the standard of "an eye for an eye," that he advocated forgiveness and saw retaliation as unworthy of man. Yet the New Testament records Jesus saying, "But the one who disowns me in the presence of men, I will disown in the presence of my Father in heaven" (Matthew 10:33). In other words, Jesus seems to advocate treating others as they have treated him; a standard of justice that is perfectly commensurate with the demand of "an eye for an eye."

In the time of the *Talmud, "an eye for an eye" was not carried out literally, and Orthodox Jewish scholars teach that it was never practiced. The Talmud's rabbis feared that the very process of removing the perpetrator's eye might kill him as well, and that, of course, would be forbidden (*Bava Kamma* 84a). "An eye for an eye" was therefore understood as requiring monetary compensation equivalent to the value of an eye. The same understanding was applied to almost all the other punishments enumerated in the same biblical verse, "a tooth for a tooth, a wound for a wound."

The only punishment in this set that was not converted to a monetary fine was capital punishment for murderers, "a life for a life." Because the Torah believed that premeditated murder deserved the death penalty, there was obviously no fear of punishing the killer excessively. Jewish law did dictate, however, that murderers be executed in the quickest manner possible. Hence, later Jewish law forbade the Roman punishment of crucifixion.

Torah law also forbade remitting a murderer's sentence with a monetary fine. Life and money, according to the biblical ethic, are incommensurate; one can never atone for murder by paying money. In this regard, too, Torah law differed from the laws of the ancient Jews' neighbors, which would sometimes fine those who had murdered people belonging to a lower social class and which made certain property crimes (for example, looting at a fire) capital offenses. In Jewish law, property crimes could never be punished with death, and murderers could never be let off with payment of money, even if the family of the victim were willing to accept it (see Numbers 35:31, and *Maimonides, *Mishneh Torah, "Laws Concerning Murder," 1:4).

Both in its insistence that evil must be punished and in its equal insistence on setting limits to that punishment, "an eye for an eye" is a basic principle of biblical justice.

SOURCE AND FURTHER READING: Moshe Greenberg, "Some Postulates of Biblical Criminal Law," in Judah Goldin, ed., *The Jewish Expression*, pp. 18–37.

261

"DO NOT STAND IDLY BY WHILE YOUR BROTHER'S BLOOD IS SHED" (LEVITICUS 19:16)

IN A DEPRESSING AND HIGHLY PUBLICIZED CASE THAT OCCURRED IN New York City in 1964, thirty-eight people peering out from their apartment windows watched as Kitty Genovese, a twenty-eight-year-old woman, was stabbed and murdered over a period of forty minutes—and did nothing. None of these witnesses even called the police, though doing so—especially in the early minutes of the attack—would have saved the woman's life. Only after it was too late was such a call made, and it was only while questioning the building's residents that the police learned about the numerous witnesses to the crime.

The revelation of these witnesses' behavior provoked widespread revulsion when it was revealed. But of course no witness was ever charged with a crime, since under American law, there is no obligation to help a person being attacked. For that matter, an individual who stands by and watches a toddler drown in a shallow pool of water similarly is not guilty of any crime under American law (unless the person has a special relationship or obligation to the child, such as a parent or a person hired to take care of the child).

From the perspective of Jewish law, however, the witnesses to Kitty Genovese's murder committed a most serious sin by violating the Torah law: "Do not stand idly by while your brother's blood is shed" (Leviticus 19:16).

In the rabbis' view, this law imposes a binding obligation on those who can help endangered people: "From where do we know that if one sees someone drowning in a river, or if one sees a wild beast attacking a person or bandits coming to attack him, that he is obligated to save the person? The Bible teaches, 'Do not stand idly by while your brother's blood is shed'" (*Sanhedrin* 73a).

This law has other ramifications. For example, if you hear people plotting to harm another, you are obligated to warn the would-be victim (*Shulchan Arukh, Choshen Mishpat* 426:1) or to inform the police. Similarly, if you know of evidence that will help exonerate a person unfairly accused, this law obligates you to step forward (*Sifra* on Leviticus 19:16), whether you have been subpoenaed or not.

In a shocking violation of this biblical law a century ago, *Leo Frank was falsely accused of murdering Mary Phagan, a fourteen-year-old girl who worked in his pencil factory in Atlanta. The chief prosecution witness against Frank was Jim Conley, another factory employee. On the basis of Conley's testimony, Frank was sentenced to death, and subsequently was lynched. Many decades later, it came out that a young man, Alonzo Mann, had witnessed Conley, who was in actuality the murderer, dragging the girl's body shortly after he had killed her. Conley threatened to kill Mann if he revealed what he saw. The climate of opinion in Atlanta, where the crime occurred, had been incredibly hostile to Frank, and Mann's mother ordered him not to make known to the police, and later to the prosecutor, what he knew.

I can think of few more flagrant violations of the biblical prohibition against standing by while your neighbor's blood is shed than that committed by Mann and his mother. Only when Mann was eighty-three years old, and facing death, did he finally confess to what he had witnessed sixty-nine years earlier.

This law also mandates that we actively oppose all acts of oppression that we might be able to eliminate or reduce. Thus, the American Jewish World Service, along with other Jewish and non-Jewish organizations, has played a major role in organizing protests to help stop the widespread murders being perpetrated in Sudan against the citizens of Darfur.

"FOR YOU WERE STRANGERS IN THE LAND OF EGYPT"
(EXODUS 22:20; LEVITICUS 19:34; DEUTERONOMY 10:19)

AS A RULE, BEING A VICTIM OF CRUELTY DOES NOT INCLINE ONE TO BE merciful. Children who are abused, for example, are far more likely to become abusive parents than children who were not abused. However, the Torah insists that human beings learn from their past sufferings how to be compassionate toward others who are presently suffering. Specifically because the Jews suffered as strangers and slaves in the land of Egypt, the Torah constantly reminds them to treat the strangers among them better than they were treated there: "The stranger who resides with you shall be to you as one of your citizens; you shall love him as yourself, for you were strangers in the land of Egypt" (Leviticus 19:34). Instead of using their own pain as a justification for inflicting pain on others, the Torah insists that the Jews become better people *because* of it.

The biblical rationale "for you were strangers in the land of Egypt" is repeated many times to remind Jews of their obligations to the non-Jews in their midst:

"You shall not wrong a stranger or oppress him, for you were strangers in the land of Egypt" (Exodus 22:20).

"You too must love the stranger, for you were strangers in the land of Egypt" (Deuteronomy 10:19).

"You shall not subvert the rights of the stranger or the fatherless. . . . Remember that you were a slave in Egypt and that the Lord your God redeemed you from there; therefore do I enjoin you to observe this commandment" (Deuteronomy 24:17–18).

It has often been noted that the long and historic Jewish involvement in human rights and civil rights movements—even in those societies where Jews already have had equal rights—is an outgrowth of this three-thousand-year-old reminder from the Torah, "for you were strangers in the land of Egypt."

"NOT TO OPPRESS THE STRANGER, THE ORPHAN, AND THE WIDOW" (DEUTERONOMY 24:17, 27:19; JEREMIAH 22:3)

IN THE BIBLE, THE STRANGER, THE ORPHAN, AND THE WIDOW ARE frequently offered as examples of the weakest, most unprotected people in society. Because of their vulnerability, the Torah repeatedly delineates the protection and help that must be afforded them. It regulates that there must be one standard of justice for both the strangers (non-Jews) and Jews (Numbers 15:15; see also Leviticus 19:34).

"The stranger, the orphan, and the widow" are linked together as naturally in the Torah as are the "Atcheson, Topeka and Santa Fe" in the famous American song. The moral measure of a society, the Torah constantly implies, can be gauged by how it treats its weakest members.

In the case of widows and orphans, later Jewish law stipulates that financial support is not enough; they must be given emotional support as well. In an uncharacteristically wordy ruling, *Maimonides writes: "A man ought to be especially heedful of his behavior toward widows and orphans, for their souls are exceedingly depressed and their spirits low. Even if they are wealthy, even if they are the widows and orphans of a king, we are specifically enjoined concerning them, as it is said: 'You shall not ill-treat any widow or orphan' [Exodus 22:21]. How are we to conduct ourselves toward them? One must not speak to them other than tenderly. One must . . . not hurt them physically with hard toil, or wound their feelings with harsh speech. One must take greater care of their property than of one's own. Whoever irritates them, provokes them to anger, pains them, tyrannizes over them, or causes them loss of money, is guilty of a transgression. . . . He who created the world by His word made a covenant with widows and orphans that when they will cry out because of violence, they will be answered, as it is said, 'If you do mistreat them, I will heed their cry as soon as they cry out to Me' [Exodus 22:22]."

Maimonides likewise enjoins teachers of orphans to "make a distinction in their favor. He should guide them gently, with the utmost tenderness and courtesy." An orphan is entitled to special treatment until he is no longer dependent on an adult, and can provide for his own needs.

The criss-crossing networks of charitable institutions that have long characterized Jewish life are a direct outgrowth of this biblical commandment concerning widows, orphans, and strangers (see *Tzedaka*).

SOURCE AND FURTHER READING: The two passages from Maimonides are found in his **Mishneh Torah*, "Laws of Moral Dispositions and Ethical Conduct," 6:10; I have cited the translation of Isadore Twersky, ed., *A Maimonides Reader*, pp. 62–63.

264

"FATHERS SHALL NOT BE PUT TO DEATH FOR THE SINS OF SONS, NOR SONS FOR THE SINS OF FATHERS" (DEUTERONOMY 24:16)

IN AN IDEAL WORLD, CHILDREN DO NOT SUFFER BECAUSE OF THE SINS or misdeeds of their parents; in the real world, they often do. Female drug users who contract AIDS, and then become pregnant, routinely transmit the fatal disease to their newborn children. Similarly, increasing evidence shows that children of alcoholics are much more likely to be alcoholic than are children of nonalcoholics.

Much of such suffering might be unavoidable, but the Torah was concerned that, at the very least, courts not punish children for their parents' offenses. While this might seem so obvious as to be banal, it is worth recalling that as recently as the first half of the twentieth century, the Bolshevik regime in the Soviet Union not only murdered the land-owning peasants known as Kulaks, but their children too.

Almost four thousand years ago, before the Torah was written, the propensity to punish children for their parents' misdeeds was formally written into the greatest legal work of the time, the Code of King Hammurabi of Babylon. In one famous case (law number 229; see *An Eye for an Eye*), it was legislated that if a man built a house for another man, and the house subsequently collapsed and killed the owner's son or daughter, the builder's son or daughter was put to death. Hammurabi reasoned that because children are their parents' property, when the parents sin, it is legitimate to take away some of their property.

Such reasoning was abhorrent to the Torah's thinking. Because it believes that each human being is created *in God's image, the Torah regards every person as possessing infinite, and individual, value (see *Whoever Saves a Single Life It Is as If He Saved an Entire World*). If a person is evil, that is no guarantee that his children also will be bad. This theme characterizes the narrative, as well as the legal, portions of the Torah. The very Pharaoh who ordered the drowning of every male baby of the Hebrews had a daughter who took pity on the infant *Moses and saved him.

Unfortunately, and perhaps somewhat inevitably, as Jewish life evolved, there *arose* a tendency to make children suffer for the sins of their parents, not judicially but societally. In the *shtetlakh* of Eastern Europe, if a parent did something disgraceful, his or her children would find it difficult, perhaps impossible, to find suitable marriage partners. Jews came to put great stress on *yikhus* (illustrious ancestry), and in cases of unimpressive ancestry, the children often paid the price. I am convinced that the Torah would have wanted to eradicate this sort of discrimination as well.

Oddly enough, in another well-known biblical verse, God arrogates to Himself the right to punish children for their parents' sins. In the *Ten Commandments, God declares that He remembers good for two thousand generations, and evil for only three or four (Exodus 20:5–6). Most Bible commentaries explain that God will punish the children of evil people only when they continue the evil perpetrated by their parents.

SOURCES AND FURTHER READINGS: A discussion of the legislation of the Torah and its differences with the Code of Hammurabi is found in Walter Kaufmann, *Religions in Four Dimensions*, pp. 29–41. As regards the murder of Kulaks and their children, see Mikhail Heller and Aleksandr Nekrich, *Utopia in Power: The History of the Soviet Union from 1917 to the Present*, p. 235, and Robert Conquest, *The Harvest of Sorrow: Soviet Collectivization and the Terror-Famine*, p. 284.

265

CHOSEN PEOPLE

THE JEWS' BELIEF THAT THEY ARE THE CHOSEN PEOPLE HAS OFTEN PRO-
voked antagonism from non-Jews. In the 1930s, as the Nazis were tightening the
noose around the necks of German Jews, George Bernard Shaw remarked that
if the Nazis would only realize how Jewish their notion of Aryan superiority was,
they would drop it immediately. In 1973, in the aftermath of the Yom Kippur
War, Yakov Malik, the Soviet ambassador to the United Nations, said: "The
Zionists have come forward with the theory of the Chosen People, an absurd
ideology. That is religious racism." Indeed, the most damaging antisemitic document in history, the forgery known as *The *Protocols of the Elders of Zion,* is
based on the idea of an international conspiracy to rule the world by the "Chosen People."

In light of these attacks, it is not surprising that some Jews have wanted to
do away with the belief in Jewish chosenness. The most noted effort to do
so was undertaken by Rabbi Mordecai *Kaplan, founder of the small but
influential Reconstructionist movement. Kaplan advocated dropping chosenness for two reasons: to undercut accusations of the sort made by Shaw
that the Chosen People idea was the model for racist ideologies, and
because it went against modern thinking to see the Jews as a divinely chosen people.

But does it? After all, how did the notion of one God become known to the
world? Through the Jews. And according to Jewish sources, that is the meaning of chosenness: to make God known to the world. As Rabbi Louis Jacobs
has written: "We are not discussing a dogma incapable of verification, but the
recognition of sober historical fact. The world owes to Israel the idea of the
one God of righteousness and holiness. This is how God became known to
mankind."

Does Judaism believe that chosenness endows Jews with special rights in
the way racist ideologies endow those born into the "right race"? Not at all.
The most famous verse in the Bible on the subject of chosenness says the
precise opposite: "You alone have I singled out of all the families of the earth.

That is why I call you to account for all your iniquities" (Amos 3:2). Chosenness is so unconnected to any notion of race that Jews believe that the Messiah himself will descend from *Ruth, a non-Jewish woman who converted to Judaism.

Why were the Jews chosen? Because they are descendants of *Abraham. And why were Abraham and his descendants given the task of making God known to the world? The Torah never tells us. What God does say in Deuteronomy, is that "it is not because you are numerous that God chose you, indeed you are the smallest of people" (7:7). Because of the Jews' small numbers, any success they would have in making God known to the world would presumably reflect upon the power of the idea of God. Had the Jews been a large nation with an outstanding army, their successes in making God known would have been attributed to their might and not to the truth of their ideas. After all, non-Muslims living in the Arab world were hardly impressed by the large numbers of people brought to Islam through the sword.

The Chosen People idea is so powerful that other groups have appropriated it. Both Catholicism and Protestantism believe that God chose the Jews, but that two thousand years ago a new covenant was made with Christianity. During most of Christian history, and among Evangelical Christians to the present day, Christian chosenness meant that only Christians go to heaven while the non-chosen are either placed in limbo or are damned.

*Mohammed, likewise, didn't deny Abraham's chosenness. He simply claimed that Abraham was a Muslim, and he traced Islam's descent through the Jewish *Patriarch.

Nations, as well as religions, see themselves as special. When I visited China, I learned that the Chinese word for China means "center of the universe." Nineteenth-century and early twentieth-century Americans had a belief in their "manifest destiny" to rule the North American continent.

Nonetheless, perhaps out of fear of sounding self-righteous or provoking antisemitism, Jews rarely speak about chosenness, and *Maimonides did not list it as one of the Thirteen Principles of the Jewish Faith.

SOURCES AND FURTHER READINGS: Dennis Prager and Joseph Telushkin, *Why the Jews? The Reason for Antisemitism*, pp. 25–29; Louis Jacobs, *A Jewish Theology*, pp. 269–275; the citation from his book is on p. 274; Hayim Greenberg, "The Universalism of the Chosen People," in Marie Syrkin, ed., *Hayim Greenberg Anthology*, pp. 22–83; Arnold Eisen, *The Chosen People in America*.

266

"WHO SAYS YOUR BLOOD IS REDDER?"

(PESACHIM 25B)

IN FOURTH-CENTURY BABYLON, A MAN CAME TO RABBI RAVA AND SAID: "The governor of my town has ordered me to murder someone [who is innocent], and has warned me that if I do not do so he will have me killed. [Can I murder the man to save my life?]" Rava refused him permission. "Let yourself be killed but do not kill him. Who says your blood is redder? Perhaps the blood of that man is redder." In other words, on what basis can a person argue that he is more worthy of living than his intended and innocent victim? Even if the questioner could posit some rationale to show that his life was more worthwhile, the mere fact that it could be saved only by shedding innocent blood would itself make it less worthy. Of course, Rava could have also told the man that he had every right to kill the governor who had ordered him to murder an innocent person. The governor, after all, was the one threatening his life, and Judaism affirms the principle of killing in self-defense. As the Talmud teaches, "He who comes to kill you, kill him first" (*Sanhedrin* 72a).

Once, when I taught this passage, a student challenged Rava's reasoning: "That's all very nice in theory," he said. "But in practice, no matter what the rabbi told him, he would kill the other guy. It's human nature to want to stay alive at any price."

Human nature or not, throughout history there have been pious Jews who abided by Rava's dictum, even at the cost of their lives, or their loved ones' lives. One of the most searing documents to come out of the Holocaust is a *responsum by Rabbi Tzvi Hirsch Meisels of Hungary, who was confronted by a question hauntingly similar to the one posed to Rava. The Nazis had ordered the murder of 1,400 Jewish teenagers in Auschwitz. The boys who were to be gassed that night were confined to a building that was kept under constant guard. One boy's father approached Rabbi Meisels. He had enough valuables, he told the rabbi, to bribe the guards to release his son. But if he did so, the guards would first kidnap another boy so that they could present the

Nazis with the precise number of expected victims. Did Jewish law, he asked, permit him to bribe the guards and save his son's life if it would lead to another boy's death? The rabbi hemmed and hawed; he had no texts with him to consult, and it was unclear if the case was precisely analogous to the case in the Talmud. In Rava's case, the man would personally have to carry out the murder: In the present situation, he would only be the cause of another person being murdered. Nonetheless, Rabbi Meisels did not feel he could approve the father's action. The man pressed the rabbi, but Rabbi Meisels told him he had no answer to give. According to Rabbi Meisels's account, the man finally said: "I did what I could . . . I asked a question of a rabbi, and there is no other rabbi here. Since you cannot answer me that I am allowed to ransom my child, this is a sign that according to the law you may not permit it. Were it permitted . . . you surely would have answered me that it is permitted. . . . This is enough for me. It is clear that my only child will be burned according to the Torah and the law, and I accept this. . . . I will do nothing to ransom him, for so the Torah has commanded." The rabbi reports that for the rest of the day, which was also the Jewish New Year, *Rosh ha-Shana, the father walked around praying that his sacrificial act be considered on a par with the binding of Isaac, which, according to Jewish tradition, also occurred on Rosh ha-Shana (see *The Binding of Isaac/Akedat Yitzchak* and *Whoever Saves a Single Life It Is as If He Saves an Entire World*).

The principle of "Who says your blood is redder?" can perhaps be applied to situations that are much more common and less dramatic than those of life and death. For example, we have no right to push ahead of other people waiting on a line because who says we are better than they and entitled to go first?

SOURCES AND FURTHER READINGS: The talmudic passage "Who says your blood is redder?" is translated and discussed in Louis Jacobs, *Jewish Law*, pp. 79–80. Rabbi Meisels's responsum has been translated and published in Robert Kirschner, *Rabbinic Responsa of the Holocaust Era*, pp. 111–119, and is also discussed in Irving Rosenbaum, *The Holocaust and Halakhah*, pp. 3–5.

267

THE SEVEN NOAHIDE LAWS

A FAMOUS YIDDISH PROVERB ASSERTS, "IT IS HARD TO BE A JEW." ONE reason, of course, is the ferocious antagonism Jews have often encountered. Another reason is the demanding nature of Jewish law, 613 commandments in the Torah alone and thousands more in the Talmud and legal codes.

Jewish tradition holds that non-Jews are bound by seven laws, presumed to date from the time of that most righteous of gentiles, Noah. There are six negative laws and one positive one:

1. Not to deny God (for example, idolatry)
2. Not to blaspheme God
3. Not to murder
4. Not to engage in incestuous, adulterous, homosexual, or bestial relations
5. Not to steal
6. Not to eat a limb torn from a living animal
7. To set up courts to ensure obedience to the other six laws (*Sanhedrin* 56a)

Since each law has extensions and interpretations (see number 4, for example) there are in fact far more than seven laws that gentiles are commanded to observe.

Judaism regards any non-Jew who keeps these laws as a righteous person who is guaranteed a place in the world-to-come (See *Righteous Non-Jews/Hasidei Ummot ha-Olam*). *Maimonides believed that a non-Jew was regarded as righteous only if he observed the laws because he believed that God ordained them (*Mishneh Torah*, "Laws of Kings," 8:11); however, this apparently was an innovative view of his, and not a talmudic demand.

The Seven Noahide Laws constitute the standard by which Jews assess the morality of a non-Jewish society: Are there laws against violence and cruelty?

Are there courts to combat anarchy? The main difference between Noahide and Torah legislation is that the latter commands hundreds of positive actions. For example, though non-Jews are forbidden to steal, they are not commanded to give charity to the poor, as are Jews (see *Tzedaka*).

Because Jewish law makes fewer demands on non-Jews, historically many rabbis have been hesitant to convert non-Jews to the more rigorous system of the Torah, believing that it is better that a person be a righteous non-Jew than a nonobservant Jew. In recent years, groups have been formed of non-Jews who regard themselves as bound by the Noahide laws.

SOURCES AND FURTHER READINGS: Aaron Lichtenstein, *The Seven Laws of Noah*; David Novak, *The Image of the Non-Jew in Judaism: An Historical and Constructive Study of the Noahide Laws*.

268

FEAR OF GOD

THE HEBREW BIBLE SPEAKS OF TWO EMOTIONS HUMAN BEINGS ARE to feel toward God: love and fear (Deuteronomy 6:5; 6:13; 10:20). Almost all people seem at least faintly uncomfortable with the latter emotion. A. S. Neill, the progressive educator and author of *Summerhill*, once wrote that though the Bible teaches that the fear of God is the beginning of wisdom, more often it is the beginning of neuroses. Yet in the Torah fear of God is seen as having two positive results:

1. It *liberates* people from fear of other human beings, and
2. It *defends* the weak and the disadvantaged from the powerful.

The first chapter of Exodus tells of Pharaoh's command to Shifra and Puah, two midwives, to drown all newborn Jewish male babies in the Nile. The women disobey the edict, and the Bible offers the reason for *this first recorded act of civil disobedience*: "They feared God." In other words, the "fear of God" *liberated* Shifra and Puah from the far more natural fear of Pharaoh.

At this point, the frustrated monarch enlisted the whole Egyptian popula-tion in carrying out the planned extermination, and we hear of no more refusals. Presumably, the fear of Pharaoh was sufficient to ensure obedience to his most immoral orders. In the past century, a disproportionate percent-age of resisters to the totalitarian and atheistic regimes of Nazi Germany and the Soviet Union were religious. As in the case of Shifra and Puah, it was not that these resisters did not fear Hitler, Stalin, or Brezhnev, it was just that they feared God more. As the Jews I danced with in Moscow on *Simkhat Torah, 1973, sang only a few minutes away from the Kremlin:

> Nye boyusa nikavo
> Krome boga odnavo.
> (*I fear no one*
> *Except God, the only One.*)

Furthermore, when the Bible appends the phrase "and you shall fear God" to a commandment, it clearly intends this fear to protect society's weak-est members, as in:

"You shall honor the old, *and you shall fear God*" (Leviticus 19:32).

"Take no interest [from him, who has become impoverished] *but you shall fear God*" (Leviticus 25:36).

"You shall not rule over [your servant] with rigor, *but you shall fear God*" (Leviticus 25:43; see also "*Do Not Put a Stumbling Block in Front of a Blind Man, but You Shall Fear God*" (Leviticus 19:14).

Normally, fear of other human beings is sufficient to restrain people from harming them. But in the cases legislated by the Torah, no such fear nor-mally applies. The maltreated servant usually has no one to whom to com-plain, and it is precisely in this instance that the Bible reminds people to fear God, who is on the side of the weak.

Finally, fear of God means being in awe of Him more than it means being afraid of Him. As the Muslim thinker Al-Qushayri taught: "He who truly fears a thing flees from it, but he who truly fears God, flees unto Him."

SOURCES AND FURTHER READINGS: Louis Jacobs, *Jewish Values*, pp. 31–49; Louis Jacobs, *A Jewish Theology*, pp. 174–182; Ephraim E. Urbach, *The Sages: Their Concepts and Beliefs*, translated by Israel Abrahams, vol. 1, pp. 400–419.

269

TZEDAKA

*Literally Justice or Righteousness,
It Is Usually Translated, Somewhat Inaccurately, as Charity*

LEGEND HAS IT THAT THE TACITURN CALVIN COOLIDGE ONCE returned from a church service.

"What did the minister speak about?" his wife asked him.

"Sin," Coolidge responded.

"And what did he say?"

"He was against it."

One might suppose that anyone writing about *tzedaka* would run into the same sort of difficulty as Coolidge's minister. After all, once one says that giving *tzedaka* is a good thing, what more remains to be said? Jewish sources reveal that there is a great deal more.

The word *tzedaka* derives from the Hebrew word *tzedek,* "justice." Performing deeds of justice is perhaps the most important obligation Judaism imposes on the Jew. *"Tzedek, tzedek* you shall pursue," the Torah instructs (Deuteronomy 16:20). Hundreds of years later, the Talmud taught: *"Tzedaka* is equal to all the other commandments combined" (*Bava Bathra* 9b). From Judaism's perspective, therefore, one who gives *tzedaka* is acting justly; one who doesn't, unjustly. And Jewish law views this lack of justice as not only mean-spirited but also illegal. Thus, throughout history, whenever Jewish communities were self-governing, Jews were assessed *tzedaka* just as everyone today is assessed taxes.

The Torah legislated that Jews give 10 percent of their earnings to the poor every third year (Deuteronomy 26:12), and an additional percentage of their income annually (Leviticus 19:9–10). Hundreds of years later, after the Temple was destroyed and the annual tithe levied upon each Jew for the support of the *priests and Levites was suspended, the Talmud ordered that Jews were to give at least 10 percent of their annual net earnings to *tzedaka* (*Maimonides, *Mishneh Torah,* "Laws Concerning Gifts for the Poor," 7:5).

Some years ago, my friend Dennis Prager suggested a hypothetical case, which has since been presented to several thousand Jewish and non-Jewish high school students:

Suppose two people who have the exact same earnings and expenses are approached by a poor man in desperate need of food and money for his family. The first person, after listening to the man's horrible experiences, cries and then out of the goodness of his heart gives him five dollars. The second person, although concerned, does not cry, and in fact has to rush away. But because his religion commands him to give 10 percent of his income to charity, he gives the poor person a hundred dollars. Who did the better thing—the person who gave five dollars from his heart, or the one who gave a hundred dollars because his religion commanded it? We discovered that 70 percent to 90 percent of the teenagers we questioned asserted that the person who gave the five dollars from his heart did the better deed.

This response suggests that in secular society, even charity is becoming a somewhat selfish act. Many people care less about the good their money is doing than about how they feel giving it. When we asked these same students who they would think had done the better deed if they were the ones who needed the money, many of them were brought up short. I think Dennis Prager has expressed the issue very well: "Judaism would love you to give 10 percent of your income each year from your heart. It suspects, however, that in a large majority of cases, were we to wait for people's hearts to prompt them to give a tenth of their income away, we would be waiting a very long time. Ergo, Judaism says, Give ten percent—and if your heart catches up, terrific. In the meantime, good has been done."

Because Judaism sees *tzedaka* as a form of self-taxation rather than as a voluntary donation, the Jewish community regards publicizing donors' gifts in the same spirit as the American practice of asking political candidates to release their tax returns. In both cases, public scrutiny causes people to act more justly.

SOME CHARACTERISTIC JEWISH TEACHINGS ABOUT *TZEDAKA*

A. On When It's Good to Be a Heretic

"Everything in God's creation has a purpose," a Hasidic *rebbe* once told his followers.

"In that case," asked a disciple, "what is the purpose of *apikorsus* [heresy], of denying that God exists?"

"*Apikorsus* is indeed purposeful," the *rebbe* replied. "For when you are confronted by another who is in need, you should imagine that there is no God to help, but that you alone can meet the man's needs."

B. The Highest Level of *Tzedaka*

"There are eight degrees of *tzedaka*, each one superior to the other. The highest degree . . . is one who upholds the hand of a Jew reduced to poverty by handing him a gift or a loan, or entering into a partnership with him, or finding work for him, in order to strengthen his hand, so that he will have no need to beg from other people" (Maimonides, *Mishneh Torah*, "Laws Concerning Gifts to the Poor," 7:7).

C. "*Tzedaka*"

"*Tzedaka* may not save us, but it makes us worth saving" (Professor Reuven Kimelman, "Tzedaka and Us," rephrasing the words of Abraham Joshua *Heschel, "Prayer may not save us, but it makes us worth saving").

D. The Omnipresence of *Tzedaka* in Traditional Jewish Life

"Life in the *shtetl* [the small villages of Eastern Europe] begins and ends with *tzedaka*. When a child is born, the father pledges a certain amount of money for distribution to the poor. At a funeral the mourners distribute coins to the beggars who swarm the cemetery, chanting, "*Tzedaka* saves from death.' At every turn during one's life, the reminder to give is present. . . . If something good or bad happens, one puts a coin into a box. Before lighting the Sabbath candles, the housewife drops a coin into one of the boxes. . . . Children are trained to the habit of giving. A father will have his son give alms to the beggar instead of handing them over directly. A child is very often put in charge of the weekly dole at home, when beggars make their customary rounds. The gesture of giving becomes almost a reflex" (Mark Zborowski and Elizabeth Herzog, *Life Is with People*).

SOURCES AND FURTHER READINGS: Jacob Neusner, *Tzedakah*; Cyril Domb, ed., *Maaser Kesafim: Giving a Tenth to Charity*.

MENSCH, MENSCHLIKHKEIT

IN ENGLISH THE EXPRESSION "HE'S A REAL MAN" GENERALLY SUG-
gests a "macho" male, one who has had numerous romantic and sexual
liaisons. The Jewish expression "He's a real *mensch*" (*mensch* is Yiddish for
"man") implies something altogether different. A *mensch* is a decent, honest
person, one who can be fully trusted. Furthermore, the term is not gender-
based: A woman can be as much of a *mensch* as a man.

The term is used in many contexts. "Be a *mensch*," might be the advice
given to someone who is not treating another person fairly. "He's not a *mensch*" would be a sufficient indictment for all to know that the person so
described should be avoided as a marriage partner or business associate.

A word based on *mensch, menschlikhkeit* refers to ethical behavior in general.
"The important thing," one might say, "is to always act with *menschlikhkeit*."

Because many observant individuals erroneously assume that Judaism
believes that God cares more about rituals than about how people treat one
another, Haskel Lookstein, a prominent Orthodox rabbi in New York, has written that Jews today need a new slogan: "*Menschlikhkeit* before Godliness."

TZADDIK

The Thirty-six Hidden Saints

TZADDIK LITERALLY MEANS A "RIGHTEOUS PERSON," BUT WHEN PEO-
ple use the term today—as in, "He's a real *tzaddik*"—they usually mean "saint."
Among the *Hasidim, *tzaddik* denotes the movement's rabbinic leader.

It is perhaps easiest to understand what *tzaddik* signifies in Jewish life by
examining the life of Rabbi Aryeh Levine, one of the great Jewish saints of the
past century. In an important book, *A Tzaddik in Our Time*, author Simcha
Raz records recollections about Reb Aryeh (as he was known) by hundreds of
people whose lives he touched.

Though Reb Aryeh was a religious scholar and teacher, he was known primarily for his goodness. Invariably, his main concern was to help people, not
to judge them. His son, Rabbi Raphael Binyamin Levine, recalls that his
father used to come early to the elementary school where he taught in order
to be present when the students arrived. He asked his father why he arrived so
early, and Reb Aryeh invited him to come and look. After the students had
gone into the school, his father asked Rabbi Levine what he had observed.
"It is quite interesting to watch them going in,' he replied. 'You can see
how eager they are to study the Torah. There I saw a boy pushing ahead of
another. He has a zest for learning. That one over there, though, is not at all
anxious to enter. His mind is still on the games he was playing.'

" 'Yet I look at different things altogether,' said Reb Aryeh. 'That child's
trousers are torn. This one's shoes are quite tattered and worn. That boy over
there is definitely hungry; how will he ever be able to study?'

" 'More than once,' his son later recounted, 'my father would take money
from his pocket and give it to children so that they could ride home on the
bus in the cold winter night and not have to trudge through the wet muddy
[unpaved] streets.' "

Reb Aryeh's desire to do good was so dominant a passion that he considered it a favor when people allowed him to help them. "As he saw it," his

friend Abraham Axelrod wrote, "life's main purpose is to help others. If a few days went by and he found no opportunity to help someone with a bit of advice, a kind word, or simply with a little chat to make a person feel better, he began to wonder if he was perhaps superfluous in the world, and the Almighty had no further use for him on earth."

Reb Aryeh was also an extraordinarily empathetic individual. When his wife suffered pain in her feet, he went with her to the doctor and told him, "My wife's feet are hurting us." Although he lived in a society that did not highly value romantic love, Reb Aryeh's love for his wife seems to have been deeply rooted in romance. A longtime friend who went to visit him one *Purim "noticed the picture of a beautiful young girl standing on his table. 'I thought it must be a portrait of his granddaughter,' " the man recalled. " 'Whose picture is that?' I asked. And he told me it was his dear departed wife. 'Well, why is her picture standing on the table today?' I wanted to know. 'Today is Purim,' [Reb Aryeh] answered. 'Everyone is happy and rejoicing. So I too, when I gaze at her portrait, I have pleasure and joy.' " The same friend once met him returning from the cemetery. " 'A grandson of mine just became engaged to be married,' Reb Aryeh explained, 'and I went to tell Hannah the good news.' "

Reb Aryeh's goal in life was not only to help people, but to do so in a way that would not cause them any embarrassment. A couple whose son had a life-threatening sickness, had been forced to stay up with the child night after night. The two were in a constant state of physical and emotional exhaustion. One evening, Reb Aryeh and his wife showed up at their house and insisted that the couple immediately go to sleep. "The two of us will stay with your child. You see, we have to talk something over, very important, and we cannot do so at home, where the children may eavesdrop."

On one occasion, Reb Aryeh was summoned to a meeting with the then president of Israel, Yitzchak Ben-Zvi. The president explained that he had been startled a few days earlier when an American Supreme Court justice, who was visiting Israel, asked him if he knew Reb Aryeh. The justice, it turned out, "had been present [as a guest] in the central prison in Jerusalem when the authorities were interviewing inmates who were due to be released early, with one third of their sentences removed as a reward for good behavior in the prison.

" 'Well [the American judge had told Ben-Zvi], in came a seasoned veteran thief whose behavior in prison had been exemplary . . . so that it was decided to reduce his term by a third. We asked him if he felt morally strong enough now to follow the straight and narrow path of honesty and do no more stealing. His reply was, 'In my heart there is no doubt whatever that I have returned to the proper way of life and I will never again go back to a life of crime.' He prepared to leave, but before he reached the door he turned around and said, 'Gentlemen, I will be honest with you. I feel that I will have to commit one more theft.' As the judges looked at him in wonder, he added, 'I just feel an inner need to steal a gold watch, in order to give it to Reb Aryeh Levine, because he brought me back to the good and decent path.'" Reb Aryeh indeed visited Jews in prison for over forty years. During the *British Mandate, he became particularly beloved by the Jews from the underground who had been incarcerated by the British. His effect on the prisoners' mood and morale was so profound that Israel's president, Chaim Herzog, recalled that British officials once asked his father, the late Chief Rabbi Isaac Herzog, to arrange to have Reb Aryeh meet with the Arab prisoners as well.

Reb Aryeh was an Orthodox Jew—actually what would commonly be regarded as ultra-Orthodox—and while he preached the importance of ritual observance his whole life, his major concern was helping people. His life became a permanent kiddush ha-Shem—sanctification of God's name (see next entry). If being religious can make someone become like Reb Aryeh, many Jews who had dealings with him concluded, then it was obviously worth becoming religious.

An old Jewish tradition, dating back to the Talmud, records that the world is sustained by the presence of at least thirty-six tzaddikim (Sanhedrin 97b; Sukkah 45b). These people do their good deeds quietly: Their neighbors do not know who they are. If, however, that minimum of truly saintly people does not exist, then the world itself will perish. A major novel about the Holocaust, André Schwartz-Bart's The Last of the Just, revolves around this theme, relating the story of a family of saints who have contributed martyr after martyr to history throughout the centuries. Most of the book focuses on the last of these just men, who dies in the Holocaust.

In Hebrew, the number thirty-six is formed by combining two letters, lamed (thirty), and vav (six). Even today, one might hear a truly wonderful human being described thus: "He's a real lamed-vavnik."

SOURCE AND FURTHER READING: Simcha Raz, A Tzaddik in Our Time.

272

KIDDUSH HA-SHEM, KHILLUL HA-SHEM

AS MONOTHEISM'S FIRST PROPONENTS, RELIGIOUS JEWS HAVE ALWAYS believed they are representing God on earth. How they conduct themselves, therefore, affects not only how others perceive them, but also how others react to God. If a religious Jew acts in a manner that evokes admiration, this is regarded as sanctifying God's name (in Hebrew, *kiddush ha-Shem*). A classic example of *kiddush ha-Shem* is recorded in the Palestinian Talmud:

"Rabbi Samuel . . . went to Rome. The Empress lost a bracelet and he happened to find it. A proclamation was issued throughout the land that if anyone returned it within thirty days, he would receive such-and-such a reward but if after thirty days he would lose his head. He did not return it within the thirty days but after the thirty days.

"She said to him: 'Were you not in the province?'

"He replied: 'Yes, I was here.'

"She said: 'But did you not hear the proclamation?'

" 'I heard it,' said he.

" 'What did it say?' she asked.

"He replied: 'If anyone returns it within thirty days he will receive such-and-such a reward but if he returns it after thirty days he will lose his head.'

"She said: 'In that case, why did you not return it within the thirty days?'

"He said: 'Because I did not want anyone to say that I returned it out of fear of you whereas, in fact, I returned it out of fear of the All-merciful.'

"She said to him: 'Blessed is the God of the Jews.' " (Palestinian Talmud, *Bava Mezia* 2:5).

Conversely, when a religious Jew acts dishonorably this is known as a *khillul ha-Shem* (desecration of God's name). His act alienates people not only from him but also from God. A *khillul ha-Shem* is one of the few sins that Judaism treats as unforgivable. Even if the guilty person repents of his bad behavior, he still cannot undo the damage. After all, he cannot guarantee that those who heard or read about his behavior and felt alienated from God as a result, will learn of his changed behavior.

Recognizing the extent to which people's attitudes toward God and Judaism are affected by the behavior of religious people, the Talmud comments: "If someone studies Bible and *Mishna [the *Oral Law] . . . but is dishonest in business and discourteous in relations with people, what do people say about it? 'Woe unto him who studies the Torah. . . . This man studies the Torah; look how corrupt are his deeds, how ugly his ways' " (*Yoma* 86a).

To this day, when a religious Jew acts nobly, other Jews say, "That's a real *kiddush ha-Shem*." And when a religious person acts badly, they say, "That's a real *khillul ha-Shem*."

Kiddush ha-Shem also has a far more tragic meaning: It refers to Jews who suffer martyrdom on account of their faith. The most famous Jewish martyr was the second-century rabbi *Akiva, who would not stop teaching Torah even when the Romans declared its study to be a capital offense.

One of the most poignant instances of *kiddush ha-Shem* occurred some 250 years ago in Vilna. A Polish-born aristocrat, Count Valentine Potocki, converted to Judaism at a time when becoming a Jew was a capital crime. When Potocki was captured by Polish authorities, he was sentenced to be burned at the stake. Old friends pleaded with him to recant his conversion; because of his family's prominence, he could still be spared. Potocki refused. "A poor man, in search of a lost bag of pennies," he answered them, "passed through a city where he found fame and fortune. Do you suppose he would resume his search for the missing pennies?" Just before his execution in front of a large crowd of Polish spectators, Potocki recited the blessing "Blessed are You, O Lord . . . who sanctifies Your name before multitudes."

SOURCES AND FURTHER READINGS: The story of the rabbi and the missing jewel is translated in Louis Jacobs, *Jewish Law*, p. 50. Count Valentine Potocki was executed on May 24, 1749. Arthur Cygielman reports in the *Encyclopedia Judaica* that after his execution, "a local Jew, Eliezer Ziskes, pretending to be a Christian, succeeded through bribery in collecting some of the ashes and a finger from the corpse, and these were eventually buried in the Jewish cemetery. From the soil over the grave of Potocki, who was called by them the *ger tzedek*—the righteous proselyte—there grew a big tree which drew vast pilgrimages of Jews. . . . The Jews of Vilna celebrated the anniversary of Potocki's death by reciting the Mourner's *Kaddish and by making pilgrimages to his purported grave on the *Ninth of Av and the *High Holy Days" (13:935). See also Jacob Katz, *Exclusiveness and Tolerance*, ch. 7, and H. H. Ben-Sasson, *Trial and Achievement*, pp. 209–216.

273

REDEEMING CAPTIVES/*PIDYON SHVUYIM*

WHILE MANY JEWS KNOW THAT IT IS A *MITZVAH* TO CONTRIBUTE money to build a synagogue, few are aware that it is sometimes a *mitzvah* to use that money for a totally different purpose. If funds are needed to ransom Jews who are being held hostage, Jewish law says that everything should be done to raise the necessary funds, even using money that was contributed to build a synagogue (*Maimonides, *Mishneh Torah*, "Laws Regarding Gifts to the Poor," 8:11). Unfortunately, the laws concerning the redeeming of captives (in Hebrew, *pidyon shvuyim*) have often been relevant in Jewish history.

In the Middle Ages, many non-Jewish criminals knew how seriously Jews took this law, and often kidnapped Jews and held them for high ransoms. The most famous such captive, Rabbi Meir of Rothenburg, refused to permit the Jewish community to pay the ransom demanded; he feared that this would set a dangerous precedent, and lead to other Jews being kidnapped.

At one point, the Jewish community offered to pay 23,000 pounds of silver to redeem him, but the offer was rejected. After years of being kept prisoner, Rabbi Meir died in captivity, whereupon his captors held his corpse for ransom. A Jew by the name of Alexander Wimpfen paid the ransom, and requested that when he died he be buried next to Rabbi Meir. His wish was carried out, and today one can still see the two tombstones next to each other in the ancient Jewish cemetery of Worms.

In line with Rabbi Meir's reasoning, the Jewish community was constrained to place a limit on the amount of ransom that would be paid: no more than a normal demand. Without such a limit, the rabbis feared, Jewish communities would feel obligated to bankrupt themselves.

When several people are held hostage, Jewish law rules that women are to be ransomed first, because it is assumed that they will suffer greater abuse in captivity (*Mishna Horayot* 3:7).

During the past hundred years, the *mitzvah* of *pidyon shvuyim* has often been applicable. Unfortunately, most efforts to redeem the captive Jews of

Europe during the Second World War failed. During the 1960s, when massive protests for Soviet Jewry began in the Western world, the movement was mainly led by religious Jews guided to a large extent by this commandment (see *Soviet Jewry Movement*). The more recent movement to save the Jews of Ethiopia (see *Ethiopian Jewry*) was yet a third instance in recent history when it has been necessary to redeem captives. Indeed, much of the money raised on behalf of Ethiopian Jewry was literally used to pay bribes and finance other means for getting them out of that country.

Pidyon shvuyim is one of the relatively few commandments that deal with matters of life and death (see next entry), which is why Jewish law regards it as more important than almost any other commandment in Judaism.

SOURCES AND FURTHER READINGS: The story of the most famous of all Jewish captives held for ransom is told in Irving Agus, *Rabbi Meir of Rothenburg*, two volumes. A discussion of *pidyon shvuyim* is found in Meir Tamari, *With All Your Possessions: Jewish Ethics and Economic Life*, pp. 265–269.

274

WHERE LIFE IS AT STAKE/*PIKUAKH NEFESH*

WITH THREE EXCEPTIONS, ALL JEWISH LAWS ARE SUSPENDED WHEN human life is at stake. For instance, although Jewish law traditionally forbids driving on the Sabbath, a Jew who refuses to drive a very sick person to the hospital on the Sabbath would be violating Jewish law. Even in a case where a non-Jew—not bound by Sabbath laws—is available to take the person, *Maimonides rules that it is preferable that a Jew do so, in order that people should know that the purpose of the laws of the Torah is to promote "compassion, loving-kindness and peace in the world" (see *Mishneh Torah*, "Laws of the Sabbath," 2:3).

The rationale for violating Jewish laws when life is at stake is based on *Leviticus* 18:5, which teaches: "You shall, therefore, keep My statutes and My ordinances, which if a man do he shall live by them." The rabbis understood this to mean " 'You shall live by them,' and not die by them" (*Yoma* 85b).

At one point, some Jews apparently rejected the principle that threats to life overrode other laws. The *Apocryphal Book of Maccabees records that a group of pious Jews in the second century B.C.E. refused to fight Syrian forces on the Sabbath and were all wiped out. *Mattathias, the leader of the Jewish revolt against *Antiochus, rejected the reasoning that led the martyrs to prefer death to fighting on the Sabbath: "If we all do as our brothers have done . . . then [the Syrians] will soon wipe us off the face of the earth." On that day, the Book of Maccabees records, the Jewish revolutionaries "decided that, if anyone came to fight against us on the Sabbath, we would fight back, rather than all die as our brothers . . . had done" (I Maccabees 2:40–41; see *Maccabees*).

The great scholar Rabbi Hayyim Soloveitchik was known for being lenient about allowing very sick people to eat on the fast of *Yom Kippur. When asked to explain why, Reb Hayyim answered: "I am not at all lenient about eating on Yom Kippur. I am just very strict in cases of *pikuakh nefesh* [where life is at stake]."

In three instances, as noted, Jewish law teaches that death is preferable to violating a traditional law. The most obvious case involves murder; if the only way one can remain alive is by murdering an innocent person, it is better to die (see *Who Says Your Blood Is Redder?*). Likewise, one must not save one's life by performing acts of *idolatry. It was for this reason that many medieval Jewish martyrs refused to be baptized and accepted execution (see *Crusades*). Even though Judaism has come not to regard Christianity as idolatrous, the martyrs felt that forsaking Judaism to save their lives would be a betrayal of God and tantamount to idolatry. Others who faced so unpalatable a choice, such as many Jews did in fifteenth-century Spain (see *The Spanish Inquisition/Marranos* and *The Spanish Expulsion, 1492*), did convert to Christianity or at least feigned conversion.

Finally, in cases of *gilui arayot* (forbidden sexual relations), death is preferred to violation of a law. It is hard to determine precisely those cases in which one is commanded to suffer death. A married woman, for example, is not required to resist a rapist unto death, although having sexual relations with a man other than her husband is normally a most serious offense. As a general rule, however, it would seem that talmudic law forbids men and women from engaging in incestuous or adulterous relationships even if doing so would somehow help keep them alive.

The laws regarding *pikuakh nefesh* reflect the very high value Judaism assigns to human life. The exceptions to the laws, in cases of murder, idolatry and perverse sexuality, show however that the highest value is not always placed on life.

275

LASHON HA-RA/GOSSIP

Literally Means "Bad Tongue"
(Similar to the English Expression "To Bad-mouth")

THE BIBLICAL COMMANDMENT FORBIDDING GOSSIP IS PROBABLY THE most widely disobeyed of the *613 laws of the Torah. Leviticus 19:16 teaches: "Do not go about as a talebearer among your people." This basic principle forbids saying anything negative about another person, *even if it is true*, unless the person to whom one is speaking or writing has a legitimate need for this information (for example, in submitting a reference for a job applicant).

In the Talmud, the rabbis greatly elaborated on this biblical verse, arguing that destroying another's name is akin to murder (*Arakhin* 15b), and like murder, the deed is irrevocable. The impossibility of undoing the damage done by harmful gossip is underscored in a *Hasidic tale about a man who went through his community slandering the rabbi. One day, feeling remorseful, he begged the rabbi for forgiveness, and indicated that he was willing to undergo any penance to make amends. The rabbi told him to take several feather pillows, cut them open, and scatter the feathers to the winds. The man did so, and returned to notify the rabbi that he had fulfilled his request. He was then told, "Now go and gather all the feathers."

The man protested. "But that's impossible."

"Of course it is. And though you may sincerely regret the evil you have done and truly desire to correct it, it is as impossible to repair the damage done by your words as it will be to recover the feathers."

Jewish law distinguishes three types of gossip:

Trivial, nondefamatory—This relatively innocuous form of gossip generally involves talking about the minutiae of other people's lives. While the damage done by such talk is minor, it almost inevitably leads to more damaging gossip. When people start talking about another person for more than a few minutes, for how long are most capable of confining themselves to positive or neutral observations? Unfortunately, juicy details tend to be more interesting than stories about a person's niceness.

Lashon ha-Ra—negative, though truthful, information about other people. While in American law, truth might be a defense against a libel charge, it constitutes no defense in Jewish law. Except in cases where people need to know, one has no right to spread negative information about others. The acceptance of this principle, however, does not provide definite guidelines for all situations. In 1972, the Democratic party nominated Thomas Eagleton as its vice-presidential candidate. The press soon revealed that Eagleton had been hospitalized three times for depression, and had twice been given shock treatments. Was the voting public entitled to know this? Many people argued that voters should be informed that a man who might become president had twice suffered nervous breakdowns. A significant minority contend, however, that people have an absolute right to have their medical and psychiatric history kept confidential (as a result of the Eagleton episode, they add, politicians who need to speak to a psychiatrist might now fear to do so).

In the Eagleton case, because of the extraordinary importance and pressures of the U.S. president's position, it seems to me that the public's right to know outweighed the senator's right to privacy. Nonetheless, this very example is the exception that proves the rule: It suggests that at almost all times when people speak *lashon ha-ra*, the information they are passing on is really nobody else's business.

Motzi Shem Ra—the spreading of malicious untruths. While most people probably feel confident that at least they haven't violated this law, anyone who has ever spread a rumor that turned out to be untrue is probably guilty of *motzi shem ra*. After all, most rumors are a little nastier than the "Hey, did you hear that so-and-so is really a wonderful person?" variety. On the other hand, if a rumor turns out to be true, then the person who spread it violated the laws of *lashon ha-ra*. A great impetus to the violation of *motzi shem ra* is, of course, the telephone, and more recently E-mail. Any rumors or scandals originating in New York can now be fully reported within minutes in California.

That the telephone, computers, and modern technology in general, have behavioral and ethical implications is reflected in a late nineteenth-century Hasidic story about a *rebbe* who declared one day to his Hasidim, "There is a lesson to be learned from everything on God's earth."

Thinking that the *rebbe* was speaking hyperbolically, a follower called out, "Oh, and what can we learn from the train?"

"That because of being one minute late," the *rebbe* answered, "you can lose everything."

"And from the telegraph?" another asked.

"That for every word you pay."

"And from the telephone?"

"That what we say *here,* is heard *there.*"

THREE CHARACTERISTIC JEWISH TEACHINGS ABOUT GOSSIP:

"The gossiper stands in Rome and kills in Syria" (*Jerusalem Talmud, Peah* 1:1).

"If you say of a rabbi that he does not have a good voice and of a cantor that he is not a scholar, you are a gossip. But if you say of a rabbi that he is no scholar, and of a cantor that he has no voice, you are a murderer" (Rabbi Israel *Salanter).

"Normally, we worry about our own material well-being and our neighbors' souls; let us rather worry about our neighbors' material well-being and our own souls" (Rabbi Israel Salanter).

SOURCE AND FURTHER READING: Zelig Pliskin, *Guard Your Tongue,* is an adaptation of the writings of Rabbi Israel Meir Kagan (the *Haffetz Hayyim*) on the subject of *lashon ha-ra*. See also Joseph Telushkin, *Words That Hurt, Words That Heal: How to Use Words Wisely and Well.*

276

PREVENTION OF CRUELTY TO
ANIMALS/TZA'AR BA'ALEI KHAYYIM

FEW PEOPLE REALIZE THAT KINDLY TREATMENT OF ANIMALS IS INDI-rectly legislated in the Ten Commandments. The fourth commandment rules: "The seventh day is a Sabbath of the Lord your God; you shall not do any work—you, your son or your daughter . . . your ox or your ass, or any of your cattle . . ." (Deuteronomy 5:14). If this weekly release from labor seems to be no great innovation, consider that 3,000 years later, in 1892, the great American philanthropist Andrew Carnegie was still requiring employees at his Homestead Steel Mine in Pennsylvania to work seven days a week.

Under the heading *tza'ar ba'alei khayyim* (prevention of cruelty to animals) other Torah laws regulated that an animal could not be muzzled while working in the field (Deuteronomy 25:4), so that it could eat all it wanted. Also: "You shall not plow with an ox and mule harnessed together" (Deuteronomy 22:10), since being of unequal size and strength both animals would suffer. A third example: When a man comes across a bird nest, he cannot slaughter the mother bird with the young, but must send her away (Deuteronomy 22:6) for, as *Maimonides has written, "the pain of the animals under such circumstances is very great (*The Guide to the Perplexed* 3:48). Hundreds of years later, the rabbis of the Talmud legislated that one is forbidden to eat before he has fed his animals (*Talmud Brakhot* 40a).

In addition, the laws of *kosher slaughtering regulate that an animal must be killed by a single continuous stroke: If the stroke is prolonged, the animal becomes unkosher. Thus, kosher slaughterers have an economic incentive to minimize the animal's suffering.

Because all kosher meat has to be ritually slaughtered, any animal killed through hunting, which Jewish sources denounce as cruel, is unkosher. Not surprisingly, Jews did not become hunters, and it has been my experience that even nonreligious Jews rarely hunt. The moral and psychological foundations of this widespread Jewish aversion were perhaps best articulated by the Jewish-born poet Heinrich Heine: "My ancestors did not belong to the hunters so much as to the hunted, and the idea of attacking the descendants of those who were our comrades in misery goes against my grain."

Logically then, in today's world, the laws of *tza'ar ba'alei khayyim* would prohibit wearing the skins of baby seals that have been clubbed to death, and eating veal from calves that have been kept caged from shortly after their birth until they are slaughtered.

SOURCES AND FURTHER READINGS: Natan Slifkin, *Man and Beast: Our Relationship with Animals in Jewish Law and Thought*. Aviva Cantor, "Kindness to Animals," in Sharon Strassfeld and Michael Strassfeld, eds., *The Third Jewish Catalog*, pp. 288–297; Sidney Hoenig, "The Sport of Hunting: A Humane Game?" *Tradition* 11:3, Fall 1970, pp. 13–21. Dennis Prager and Joseph Telushkin, *The Nine Questions People Ask About Judaism*, pp. 59–64.

277

HONORING PARENTS/*KIBUD AV VA'EM*
(*Literally, Honor For Father and Mother*)

"HONOR YOUR FATHER AND MOTHER" IS NOT ONLY ONE OF THE MOST famous of the *Ten Commandments, it is in many ways the most surprising. New religious or radical political groups usually try to distance children from parents. The Gospel of Luke, for example, quotes *Jesus as saying: "If any man comes to me without hating his father, mother, wife, children, brothers, sisters, yes and his own life too, he cannot be my disciple" (14:26).

As if to give legal expression to this sentiment, the Gospel of Matthew tells of a young man, a new disciple of Jesus, who asks to be excused to go home to bury his dead father. Jesus discourages him. "Follow me," he tells the man, "and let the dead bury the dead" (8:21–22). Clearly, no act would so permanently alienate a man from his family as not attending his father's funeral. Once Christianity became an established faith, however, it, too, emphasized close parent-child ties.

Today, one of the primary associations people have with cults is their hostility to the family. Instead of "Honor your father and mother," many cults come close to teaching "Have nothing to do with your father and mother." Although two major totalitarian movements in the twentieth century, Nazism and communism, have been pro-family in theory, in practice they made heroes of children who informed the authorities whenever their parents made critical remarks against the regime. Russian émigrés to the United States have told that when they joined the Soviet equivalent of the Boy Scouts, they took an oath to be like Pavlick Maroza, a young boy in the 1930s who informed officials that his father was hoarding a large bag of rice in the house. The authorities executed the boy's father, and the boy's uncle killed Pavlick in retaliation. Throughout the Soviet Union statues were built in honor of Pavlick Maroza.

The Hebrew Bible's unusual emphasis on parent-child closeness has affected Jewish life deeply. Throughout history, Jews have been stereotyped as people highly devoted to their families. So devoted that on occasion, the parent-child bond becomes a stock feature of Jewish humor. As one story has it, three elderly women are sitting on a bench in Miami Beach, each bragging how devoted her son is to her. The first one says, "My son is so devoted that for my birthday last year he gave me an all-expenses-paid cruise around the world." The second says, "That's nothing. My son is more devoted. For my birthday last year, he catered a large affair for me, and even gave me the money to fly down all my close friends from New York." The third woman says, "My son is the most devoted. Three times a week he goes to a psychiatrist. A hundred and eighty dollars an hour he pays him. And what does he speak about the whole time? Me."

There are two general injunctions in the Torah regulating how one is expected to feel and act toward one's parents: The fifth commandment, cited at the beginning of this entry, commands that one honor them, while a verse in Leviticus states: "Let each man be in awe of his mother and father, and keep My Sabbaths" (19:3). What is strangely lacking in the Torah is a commandment to love one's parents, even though the Torah has no compunctions about commanding love in other relationships; people are told to love their neighbor, the stranger, and God (Leviticus 19:18; 19:34; Deuteronomy 6:5). Perhaps it was believed that in a relationship as intimate as that between parents and children, love could not be commanded; either it is present or it isn't. What can be commanded, however, are honor and awe, acts and emotions that can be expressed and acted upon even during those painful periods when love might be lacking.

How are the words "awe" and "honor" defined in Jewish law? According to the rabbis, "awe" means deep, abiding respect, for example, as in not sitting in one's father's place at the table, or not siding with a parent's adversary during a dispute. When my mother was growing up on New York's *Lower East Side, some neighbors owned a nearby store. One day, the store's employees went on strike and the storeowner's twenty-year-old son led the pickets. Even if the boy's father had been in the wrong, the son's behavior, according to Jewish law, was also wrong. Where a child sees parents acting improperly, he should subtly and privately remind them that they are acting in violation of the Torah and Jewish ethics. "But, Father, does not the Torah teach . . . ?" is how Jewish law tells the child to express his criticism. Except in the most extreme cases, a child should not, however, attack his or her parents in public or identify with their opponents.

Honor in Jewish law is interpreted as undertaking basic obligations toward parents, including, if necessary, supplying them with food and clothing. Because of the enormous increase in recent decades in human longevity, a far larger percentage of people live now to their eighties and even nineties than in the past; often, however, with terrible mental and/or physical infirmities. Thus, the command to honor one's parents has in many ways become much more difficult to observe.

What a child does *not* owe the parents, according to Jewish law, is control over his or her conscience. The rabbis applied an unusual interpretation to the verse quoted earlier, "Let each man be in awe of his mother and father, and keep my Sabbaths." Why, they ask, is the commandment to keep the Sabbath cited immediately after the commandment to be in awe of one's parents? The *Talmud answers that the two are juxtaposed to teach that if parents order a child to violate the Sabbath, he should not listen to them (*Bava Mezia* 32a). True, a child should have awe for his parents, but they should be obeyed only when they tell him to do what is right. Parents, too, are commanded to follow God's laws, one of which is to observe the *Sabbath, so they are forbidden to command a child to break them.

Medieval rabbinic texts discuss how a child should react if his parents disapprove of his or her intended mate. Does the command "Honor your father and mother" mean that a child should break off the relationship? Rabbinic consensus says that one has the right to ignore a parent's opposition in such a case (as long as it is a marriage permitted by Jewish law). As one medieval rabbi reasoned, if a child breaks off a relationship with a person he loves, and instead marries a partner forced upon him by his parents, he will end up hating that spouse. By forcing the child to marry someone he or she will subsequently hate, it is tantamount to the parents demanding that the child violate the Torah law of *"Love your neighbor as yourself." And, as noted, parents have no right to compel a child to violate the Torah.

Even during times when marriages were arranged, and daughters, in particular, were seldom consulted, the Talmud ruled that "a father may not betroth his daughter while she is a minor. He must wait until she is grown up and says, 'I want so-and-so'" (*Kiddushin* 41a). The fact that many Jews violated this talmudic regulation, and arranged marriages for their children with persons unknown to them, would seem, therefore, to be a violation of Jewish law.

As regards parental responsibilities to children, the most important duty is to teach them Torah. A father also must teach his son a trade: "He who does not teach his son a profession," the Talmud rules, "it is as if he taught him to be a thief" (see *Kiddushin* 29a and 30b). The rabbis reasoned that if a man does not know an honest way to make a living, he will turn to dishonest activities. In the modern world, where women, too, are expected to be wage earners, parents have a similar obligation toward their daughters.

The Talmud also specifies that parents should teach their children how to swim. In the ancient world, where much travel occurred over water, swimming was a necessary survival skill. In modern parlance, this commandment means that parents are required to teach their children whatever self-defense skills are necessary for survival. In her book *How to Run a Traditional Jewish Household*, writer Blue Greenberg recalls an ugly incident in her neighborhood in which a number of antisemitic teenagers attacked and beat a group of Jewish teenagers. The local rabbi's response was a sensible one, and entirely consistent with the Talmud's ruling. "The time has come," he in effect told the parents, "to teach Jewish kids karate."

SOURCES AND FURTHER READINGS: The medieval Tosafot commentary on *Kiddushin* 41a notes the widespread violation of the talmudic regulation against marrying off minor children. The sole justification for this practice was that Jewish life had become so insecure that whenever a man procured sufficient money for a dowry he was tempted to arrange a marriage immediately. Much of the material in the Talmud regarding parent-child relations can be found in *Kiddushin* 29a–32b. Gerald Blidstein, *Filial Responsibility in Jewish Law*, provides a comprehensive overview of parent-child relationships in Jewish law. The last episode is mentioned in Blue Greenberg, *How to Run a Traditional Jewish Household*, pp. 172–173.

278

"WHOEVER SAVES A SINGLE LIFE IT IS AS IF HE SAVED AN ENTIRE WORLD"

ONE OF THE MOST ELOQUENT JEWISH STATEMENTS ABOUT THE VALUE of human life comes from a very odd source: the admonition administered by ancient Jewish courts to witnesses testifying in capital cases. In addition to the expected warnings against perjury, the judges offered a commentary on why God originally populated the world with only one person, Adam. "To teach you," the witnesses were warned, "that whoever destroys one life is considered by the Torah as if he destroyed an entire world, and whoever saves one life is considered by the Torah as if he saved an entire world" (*Mishna Sanhedrin* 4:5).

Having suggested at least one ethical lesson that can be learned from Adam's singular creation, the rabbis propose two others: "[God created all of mankind through Adam] for the sake of peace between people. So that no one can say to his neighbor, 'My father was greater than your father [since all human beings are descended from the same father].' " Furthermore, Adam's creation "proclaims the greatness of God, for when a man strikes many coins from one mold, they are all identical to each other, but the King of Kings, God, fashioned every human being with the stamp of Adam, and not one of them is identical to his fellow." Today, it sometimes seems as if knowledge of each person's uniqueness is sadly confined to criminologists, who are aware that all people, even identical twins, have distinctive fingerprints.

In many editions of the *Mishna, the rabbinic admonition has been altered to read: "Whoever destroys one *Jewish* life is considered by the Torah as if he had destroyed an entire world, and whoever saves one *Jewish* life is considered by the Torah as if he had saved an entire world." This change makes no sense since the proof of the infinite value of human life comes from Adam, and Adam was not a Jew.

The rabbinic belief that each human life is of infinite value has legal, not just sermonic, implications. It means, for example, that saving many lives at the expense of one *innocent* life is not permitted, since by definition many "infinities" cannot be worth more than one "infinity." During the Russian civil war, to cite one instance where this principle determined a legal ruling, a Jewish communist fled to his hometown of Dukor, where my grandfather, Nissen Telushkin, was the rabbi. All the local Jews knew where the man was hiding, but the government officials did not. One afternoon, the police chief swooped down on the synagogue and arrested my grandfather, along with nine men who were praying with him, and announced that they would all be shot the next morning if they did not reveal the fugitive's hiding place. My grandfather immediately ruled—based in part on this talmudic teaching—that since the man had not committed a capital crime but would be executed if he was caught, it was forbidden to inform on him, even though many lives might be thereby endangered. Fortunately, the police chief turned out to be corrupt, and could be bribed to release the condemned men. Unfortunately, the man whose life they saved turned out to be an idealist: When the Communists came to power, he tried to have my grandfather's synagogue closed down.

279

VISITING THE SICK/*BIKUR KHOLIM*

JEWISH LAWS ARE GENERALLY BINDING ON ALL JEWS; THERE ARE NO ordinances, for example, that are obligatory only for rabbis. In practice, however, the law mandating visits to sick people (in Hebrew, *bikur kholim*) today is reserved largely for rabbis; making hospital rounds to sick congregants is one of the major responsibilities of pulpit rabbis. Throughout most of Jewish history, however, this important commandment was considered binding on all Jews. Jewish communities even established *Bikur Kholim* societies to ensure visitations to all sick people.

In the past, this *mitzvah, today often neglected, was regarded to be of life-and-death significance. "Rabbi Helbo fell sick," the Talmud tells us, and no one visited him. Rabbi Kahana rebuked the sages: "Did it not once happen," he reminded them, "that one of Rabbi *Akiva's disciples fell sick and the sages did not visit him? So Rabbi Akiva himself visited him, and because [he arranged to have the floor] swept and washed, the sick man recovered. 'My master,' [the sick man] said [to Rabbi Akiva], 'you have revived me.' Rabbi Akiva went out and taught, 'He who does not visit the sick is like a shedder of blood' " (*Nedarim* 39b–40a).

Recognizing how psychologically important it is that the sick not feel abandoned, the rabbis declared that whoever visits a sick person removes one sixtieth of his illness (*Bava Mezia* 30b), while he who ignores a sick person hastens his death.

An extensive series of ordinances and suggestions were drawn up to guide people making sick calls. Most of the laws have little to do with ritual, being mainly concerned with interpersonal sensitivity. "Enter the room cheerfully," the medieval rabbi Eliezer ben Isaac of Worms taught, because an invalid carefully monitors the reactions of visitors, and any look of shock on a guest's face will be terribly demoralizing. Francine Klagsbrun, editor of *Voices of Wisdom,* cites a humorous story from a nineteenth-century Jewish anthology. "A visitor came to see a sick man and asked him what ailed him. After the sick man told him, the visitor said:

" 'Oh my father died of the same disease.'

"The sick man became extremely distressed, but the visitor said, 'Don't worry. I'll pray to God to heal you.'

"To which the sick man answered: 'And when you pray, add [a prayer] that I may be spared visits from any more stupid people.' "

Jewish law mandates withholding unhappy news from sick people, particularly news of the death of someone near to them. In the mid-1950s, Israeli Prime Minister David *Ben-Gurion was in the hospital when one of his closest aides and friends committed suicide. At first, it seemed impossible to keep such significant news from Ben-Gurion. However, his aides arranged to have radio stations not report the death, and persuaded the publishers of the newspapers that Ben-Gurion regularly read to print a few special copies, for "Ben-Gurion's eyes only," in which the suicide story was deleted.

If a close relative falls very seriously ill, Jewish law permits one to violate Sabbath restrictions against travel to visit the sick person. Given how loath the rabbis were to permit Sabbath travel, there is perhaps no better indication how crucial they regarded *bikur kholim* to a patient's recovery.

Jewish law expects whoever visits the sick, or hears about another's illness, to offer a prayer on behalf of the ailing person. The shortest prayer in the Bible is *Moses' prayer for his sick sister *Miriam: "O Lord, please heal her" (Numbers 12:13). In the synagogue, during the reading of the Torah, a prayer known as the *Mi Shebeirakh* is recited, petitioning God for the speedy recovery of an ill person (see *Aliyah*).

It is forbidden to leave a dying person alone and abandoned in his last minutes. According to Jewish law, even a corpse must be attended to until it is buried. Arrangements are made to have someone stand by the corpse (ideally, at least part of the time, it should be family members) and recite *Psalms.

Lest one need any further motivation to carry out the commandment of *bikur kholim* one should remember the following extraordinary promise from the Talmud: "He who visits the sick will be spared the punishments of the next world" (*Nedarim* 40a).

SOURCES AND FURTHER READINGS: Permission to travel on the Sabbath in order to visit a very sick person is cited in the legal text *Kol Bo Al Aveilut*, p. 22. See also Francine Klagsbrun, *Voices of Wisdom*, p. 222, citing a story taken from Zevi Hirsch Edelmann, ed., *Paths of Good Men*. See also Chana Shofnos and Bat Tova Zwebner, *Healing Visit: Insights Into the Mitzva of Bikkur Cholim*; Meyer Strassfeld, "Visiting the Sick," in Sharon Strassfeld and Michael Strassfeld, eds., *The Third Jewish Catalog*, pp. 140–145.

280

ACTS OF LOVING-KINDNESS/

GEMILUT KHESED

Free-Loan Societies/Gemilut Khesed Funds

GEMILUT KHESED, GENERALLY TRANSLATED AS AN "ACT OF LOVING-kindness," usually refers to a special type of *mitzvah*, one that is performed with no expectation of reward.

Often, a person who helps another is motivated, at least in part, by the hope that the other will someday reciprocate. But the acts that are classic definitions of *gemilut khesed* are done without such an expectation, for example, donating money to bury an indigent person. Giving charity anonymously is another example of loving-kindness. A friend of mine, who knew that her neighbor lacked money to buy food, filled several bags with groceries and left them in front of the woman's door.

Another way of fulfilling the commandment of *gemilut khesed* is to extend an interest-free loan to a person in need. Torah law forbids Jews from charging interest on loans to fellow Jews (Deuteronomy 23:20). During the biblical era, Jewish life was largely agrarian, and money was needed only in dire emergencies. As the economy developed, however, money came to be regarded as a commodity like any other, and people were loath to lend it if they did not receive some additional payment in return. So, a legal fiction was created that is still used by Orthodox Jews. A person who lends money is made a partner in the recipient's business, and the repayments the lender receives (which will be higher than the amount of the loan) are considered to come out of the business profits (all of this is written down in the form of a contract). Unlike a regular partner, however, the lender is expected to be paid even if the business does not make a profit.

This legal fiction—known in Jewish law as *heter iska*, "permission to do business"—is allowed only in cases of loans extended to businesses or to people of means. When lending money to the poor, Jewish law forbids any such legal fiction. In every Jewish community, *Gemilut Khesed* Societies (Free-Loan Societies) were set up so that poor people could procure interest-free loans. In Israel a professor at Hebrew University in Jerusalem told me that he is one of three directors of such a fund. People apply in person to one of the three directors for money to cover monthly rent, food for holidays, school tuition, and similar basic needs. Remarkably enough, the professor informed me, the society has almost never had a default on a loan, and as soon as a loan is repaid, the money is lent out to someone else. Such funds exist throughout the United States too; they are generally, but not exclusively, administered within the Orthodox community.

Acts of *gemilut khesed* are more wide-ranging than charity (see *Tzedaka*), since they often involve more than just donating money. Attending to the dead, as noted earlier, extending hospitality (see next entry), and visiting the sick (see preceding entry) are also considered as acts of loving-kindness.

Concerning *gemilut khesed*, the rabbis say that people will be rewarded by God "in this world" (during this life), and rewarded a second time in the "next world" (*Shabbat* 127a).

SOURCES AND FURTHER READINGS: C. G. Montefiore and H. Loewe, *A Rabbinic Anthology*, pp. 412–439; David Shapiro, "The Concept of *Chesed* in Judaism," in his *Studies in Jewish Thought*, vol. 1, pp. 98–121. Warren Zev Harvey, "Grace or Loving-Kindness," in Arthur A. Cohen and Paul Mendes-Flohr, eds., *Contemporary Jewish Religious Thought*, pp. 299–303. Danny Siegel, "The Tale of the *Shaliah*/Messenger," in Sharon Strassfeld and Michael Strassfeld, eds., *The Third Jewish Catalog*, pp. 19–28, cites dozens of examples of individuals carrying out acts of loving-kindness in contemporary Israel, ranging from people who lend out wheelchairs and hospital beds to those who can't afford them, to people who specialize in training hearing-impaired children, to others who run Life-Line for the Old, an organization that sets up workshops in which old people can do creative work.

281

HOSPITALITY/HAKHNASAT ORKHIM

IN JEWISH LAW, HOSPITALITY (IN HEBREW, HAKHNASAT ORKHIM) IS NOT JUST A pleasant social nicety but a serious legal obligation. Inhospitality, on the other hand, is viewed not simply as ungracious behavior but as vile and forbidden. A particularly grotesque form of inhospitality characterized the citizens of the biblical cities of *Sodom and Gomorrah. When the Sodomites heard that Lot, *Abraham's nephew, had invited two guests to his house, they crowded around his doorway and demanded that the guests be presented to them so they could rape them. Fortunately, Lot's guests were angels who afflicted the inhospitable and lustful Sodomites with blindness (Genesis 19).

More than fifteen hundred years later, the Talmud attributed the *destruction of the Second Temple—one of the greatest catastrophes in Jewish history—to causeless hatred, which the rabbis believed was epitomized by an act of inhospitality. A certain man had a friend named Kamtza and an enemy named Bar Kamtza. The man held a large banquet, and instructed his servant to invite Kamtza along with many leading rabbinic sages. The servant erred, and invited Bar Kamtza instead. At the dinner, the host was so incensed when he saw his adversary that he demanded that the guest leave. Bar Kamtza pleaded with the host not to throw him out, and even offered to pay for the cost of his dinner. The host refused. Bar Kamtza offered to pay half of the expenses of the entire affair. Still, the host refused. Bar Kamtza finally offered to pay for the entire dinner, at which point the host ordered his servants to forcibly eject Bar Kamtza.

Immediately thereafter, Bar Kamtza sought revenge not only against his host, but against the entire city of Jerusalem. Many of the city's leading rabbis had been present, he reasoned, and none had prevented his disgrace. Bar Kamtza sought out the Roman emperor and convinced him that the Jews of Jerusalem were conspiring against him. According to the Talmud, Jerusalem's destruction, which followed shortly thereafter, came about because of the nameless host's act of inhospitality (*Gittin* 55b–56a).

Hakhnasat orkhim is, in actuality, one of the most pleasant commandments to perform. Any Jew who travels extensively, and has made contact with Jews in other countries, can testify how pleasant it is to enjoy hospitality when far away from home. However, my favorite experience of *hakhnasat orkhim* occurred in the United States. I and a friend had gone on a three-week car tour of the South. One Friday morning in central Louisiana, we realized that we wanted to spend the *Sabbath with fellow Jews. We had brought the *Jewish Travel Guide* with us, and upon looking up the nearest city, Alexandria, saw a listing that read: "Anyone wishing *kosher food should contact Dr. So-and-So." We called the man, the late Dr. Bernard Kaplan, and ended up spending the Sabbath with him, his wife Jean, and their seven children. We have remained close friends ever since.

In the past, the commandment of hospitality was largely an extension of the commandment of charity (see *Tzedaka*): Many poor Jews, particularly travelers, needed food and lodging. The Talmud records, for example, that before beginning a meal, Rabbi Huna would stand outside his door and announce: "Let all who are hungry come in and eat" (*Ta'anit* 20b). Rabbi Huna's invitation is still echoed by Jews during the *Passover *Seder, though today most people's doors are closed and bolted when the invitation is extended. A paragraph in the Passover *Haggada* reads: "Let all who are hungry come in and eat, let all who are needy come and make Passover."

Nobel laureate Shmuel Yosef Agnon wrote a beautiful story, "The Passover Celebrants," about the difference between the "hungry" and the "needy." In a small town in Eastern Europe there lived a poor *shamash* (synagogue sexton). When Passover arrived, he did not even have enough money to purchase the necessary foods for the holiday. As Passover began, he was hungry and alone.

In the same town lived a wealthy widow, who was experiencing her first Passover since her husband's death. As was her habit, she set a beautiful Seder table, but she was in despair, for she was all alone.

The widow came across the hungry sexton and invited him to make the Seder with her. During the course of the meal, they draw close to each other, and by the Seder's end, it appears that there will soon be a better future for each of them, in which the sexton will no longer be "hungry," and the widow no longer "needy."

In the contemporary Jewish world, there are not many (although there are some) starving or homeless Jews. *Hakhnasat orkhim* has, therefore, become more of a social *mitzvah*. If, indeed, the Jewish community has relatively few members who are hungry, then one must seek out those who are needy, for example, new people in the community. Many synagogues and Jewish organizations run programs matching Jews in need of hospitality with local families for the Passover Seder.

Just as Jewish law insists that a host be hospitable and generous, so it demands that a guest be grateful. Two thousand years ago or so, the Talmud criticized ungrateful guests in terms that remain remarkably relevant. When a guest departs a home, the Talmud suggests that he think to himself: "How much trouble my host has gone to for me. How much meat he has set before me. How much wine he has given me. How many cakes he has served me. And all this trouble he has gone to for my sake!" The Talmud contrasts this with a bad guest who thinks rather: "What kind of effort did the host make for me? I have eaten only one slice of bread. I have eaten only one piece of meat, and I have drunk only one cup of wine! Whatever trouble the host went to was done only for the sake of his wife and children" (*Brakhot* 58a).

In the recitation of the *Birkat ha-Mazon* (Grace After Meals), the guest inserts a special blessing on behalf of his host's family.

Graciousness, however, is expressed by more than just saying thank you. A nineteenth-century story tells of two great rabbis who ate a meal at an inn owned by a widow. Throughout the dinner, one rabbi sat and conversed with the rather talkative woman; the other rabbi sat quietly and, when not eating, studied from a book. At the meal's end, the widow refused to let the rabbis pay. Later, the rabbi who had talked with the woman said to his friend: "It seems to me that the meal you ate at the widow's table was stolen."

"What do you mean?" the other rabbi protested. "She said she didn't want us to pay."

"She didn't want us to pay money," the first rabbi answered. "But the payment she wanted was that we listen to her and speak with her. This, you did not do."

One instance in which Jewish law permits holding back on the truth is when a person is asked if he enjoyed being a guest at someone's house. If he enjoyed the experience, he should say so, but he should hold back from fulsome praise, lest his gracious host be swamped with unwanted guests.

According to Jewish folklore, guests who stay for more than three days are probably overstaying their welcome. A rabbinic *Midrash* says: "On the day a guest arrives, a calf is slaughtered in his honor; the next day, a sheep, the third day, a fowl, and on the fourth day, he is served just beans" (*Midrash Tehillim* 23:3).

SOURCES AND FURTHER READINGS: The translation of the passage on hospitality from *Brakhot* is from Francine Klagsbrun, *Voices of Wisdom*, p. 60. The Agnon story, "The Passover Celebrants," is found in Philip Goodman, *The Passover Anthology*, pp. 229–236. See also C. G. Montefiore and H. Loewe, *A Rabbinic Anthology*, pp. 451–459.

282

RIGHTEOUS NON-JEWS/*HASIDEI UMMOT HA-OLAM*

JUDAISM HAS NEVER TAUGHT THAT ONE HAS TO BE JEWISH IN ORDER to be saved. In contrast to medieval Christianity, which held that there was no salvation outside the Church, the rabbis believed that "the righteous of the nations of the world have a portion in the world-to-come" (*Tosefta Sanhedrin* 13:2).

The rabbis of the Talmud had a high regard for righteous non-Jews, and even held them up on occasion as moral examplars. A certain man, Dama ben Netina, was known for being particularly scrupulous in honoring his parents: "Our rabbis say that some of our wise men came to him to buy a precious stone in place of one which had fallen out, and been lost, from the breastplate of the High Priest. . . . They agreed with him to give a thousand gold pieces for the stone. He went in, and found his father asleep with his leg stretched out on the box which contained the jewel. He would not disturb him, and came back without it. When the wise men perceived this, they thought that he wanted more money, and they offered him ten thousand gold pieces. When his father woke up, he went in, and brought out the jewel. The wise men offered him the ten thousand pieces, but he replied: 'Far be it from me to make a profit from honoring my father; I will take only the thousand which we had agreed on' " (*Deuteronomy Rabbah* 1:15).

Whereas Jews are considered bound by the 613 laws of the Torah, Judaism demands from non-Jews fulfillment only of the Seven Noahide Laws, modeled on the quintessentially ethical non-Jew Noah (see *Noah* and *Seven Noahide Laws*).

In recent years, the term *hasidei ummot ha-olam* has become associated with European non-Jews who risked their lives during World War II to save Jews from the Nazis. At *Yad Vashem, the Jerusalem museum set up to commemorate the Holocaust, a grove of trees has been planted to honor these heroes (see *Righteous Gentiles*).

To this day, it is not uncommon to hear traditional Jews refer to a non-Jewish friend of the Jews as "one of the *hasidei ummot ha-olam*"—literally, "one of the righteous of the nations of the world." The *Zohar*, the major work of Jewish mysticism, states that all non-Jews who do not hate Jews and treat them justly are *hasidei ummot ha-olam* (Exodus 268a).

While many Jews are knowledgeable about the history of antisemitism, fewer are aware of the smaller, but vital, tradition of philosemitism, whose adherents are the *hasidei ummot ha-olam* who have worked on behalf of Jews and ethical causes.

SOURCES AND FURTHER READINGS: In the tale cited from *Deuteronomy Rabbah*, I have followed the translation of C. G. Montefiore and H. Loewe, A *Rabbinic Anthology*, p. 504. See also Aaron Lichtenstein, *The Seven Laws of Noah*, and David Novak, *The Image of the Non-Jew in Judaism: An Historical and Constructive Study of the Noahide Laws*.

283

FAMILY HARMONY/SHALOM BAYIT

"IF YOUR WIFE IS SHORT," A TALMUDIC PASSAGE TEACHES, "BEND over to hear her whisper" (*Bava Mezia* 59a).

While there is no shortage of misogynistic statements in Jewish literature, a longstanding tradition in Judaism enunciates and legislates the kind and generous treatment of wives. The rabbis commend a man who loves his wife as much as himself, and honors her more than himself (*Yevamot* 62b). The law in the Torah that enjoins Jews to rejoice on the holidays is interpreted in the Talmud as obligating husbands to buy pretty clothes for their wives before the Jewish holidays (*Pesachim* 109a). The Talmud similarly teaches that a good husband is willing to go without new clothes for himself, as long as he can buy attractive clothing for his wife (Palestinian Talmud, *Ketubot* 6:5).

While the rabbis of the Talmud were not characteristically romantic, they waxed exceedingly sentimental on the subject of first marriages: "If a man divorces his first wife, even the altar sheds tears" (*Gittin* 90b). Elsewhere, they taught, "All things can be replaced except the wife of one's youth" (*Sanhedrin* 22a).

While Jewish law did disadvantage women in certain areas—most notably in the laws of divorce (see *Get*)—the Jewish tradition enjoined men to treat their wives with such respect that Jewish husbands acquired the reputation of being committed family men.

The rabbis designated the whole area of husband-wife relations under the rubric *shalom bayit* (family harmony). Professor Reuven Kimelman has suggested that the reason the Talmud applies the law of *"Love your neighbor as yourself" specifically to one's wife is because people are often less sensitive to their spouses than to their neighbors. Not infrequently, at social occasions, a man will say things about his wife that he would not say about his business partner if he intended to stay in business with him. Yet if you challenge him as to why he speaks so harshly, he will answer, "I can say it. I love her." From the Jewish perspective, whether one has fulfilled the law of love of neighbor is proved not by saying, "I love her [or him]," but by whether one's spouse feels that he or she has been treated with love.

The principle of *shalom bayit* requires in particular that members restrain their tempers, as in family settings it is common to hear raised, angry voices. Though people often claim that they can't control their temper, Israeli Rabbi Zelig Pliskin has noted that this defense is usually false. Indeed, in the middle of an outburst, "if someone they want to impress knocks on the door . . . they will be able to answer the door and immediately talk calmly and pleasantly."

Because of Judaism's belief in the importance of family harmony, Jewish law permits divorce in cases where such harmony does not exist. According to Jewish tradition, all that is required for a couple to divorce is mutual consent; if a house is no longer a center of *shalom bayit*, it is probably better that the unhappy couple live apart. See also *Ketuba*.

SOURCES AND FURTHER READINGS: C. G. Montefiore and H. Loewe, *A Rabbinic Anthology*, pp. 500–522; Reuven Bulka, *Jewish Marriage: A Halakhic Ethic*; David Kraemer, ed., *Jewish Family: Metaphor and Memory*. The comment about "Love your neighbor," I heard from Rabbi Reuven Kimelman, though the version quoted here is based on my recollection and are not his words. See also Zelig Pliskin, *Gateway to Happiness*.

284

YOU CAN'T SAY "I WAS JUST FOLLOWING ORDERS"/*AIN SHALIAKH LE-DVAR AVEIRAH* (*KIDDUSHIN* 42B)

SINCE EVERY HUMAN BEING IS ENDOWED WITH FREE WILL, EVEN IF A superior orders you to perform an evil act, Jewish law forbids your following the order. If you do carry out the order, you cannot then blame the person who issued it, for you should not have listened to it. From the Jewish perspective—indeed, from any religious perspective—God is on a higher plane than the person who gives the illegal order: One must follow God's commandment and not an immoral one.

At the trials of the Nazi war criminals held after World War II (see *Nuremberg Trials*), most Nazis offered the defense that they were only "following orders." From the perspective of Jewish law, this was no defense.

On October 29, 1956, the eve of Israel's Sinai campaign against Egypt, the Israeli government feared a "fifth column," and issued an order to Arabs living in Israel to remain inside their villages under curfew. At one Arab village, Kfar Kassem, some people went to work, apparently unaware that a curfew had been imposed. Israeli troops, encountering them, opened fire and killed forty-nine villagers. At their court-martial, the soldiers defended themselves with the claim that they were following military orders. The court rejected this defense and eight of the soldiers were convicted of murder. They should have known, the judges ruled, that it was immoral and forbidden to open fire on unarmed civilians. No "order" from a superior officer could justify what they had done.

The most famous defendant at an Israeli trial to offer the "I-was-just-following-orders" defense was, Adolf *Eichmann, one of the main architects of the Nazi *Final Solution. Here, too, the court rejected Eichmann's defense and sentenced him to death.

Quite simply, according to Jewish law, if one is given an immoral order, one is obligated *not* to carry it out. If one *does* implement it, he or she is no less blameworthy than the person who ordered it. In the Talmud, this principle is known as *Ain shaliakh le-dvar aveirah.* This expression means literally, "There is no messenger in a case of sin." A messenger normally cannot be blamed for the contents of the message he delivers, no matter how ugly or infuriating it is. All blame should be directed at the one who sent the message. But if a messenger is sent to perform evil, he cannot defend himself by saying that he was acting only as someone else's agent. Because "there is no messenger in a case of sin," he bears full and personal responsibility for any evil he does (see *Who Says Your Blood Is Redder?*).

SOURCE AND FURTHER READING: For further details about the incident at Kfar Kassem, see Susan Hattis Rolef, ed., *Political Dictionary of the State of Israel,* pp. 174–175.

285

REPENTANCE/TESHUVA

I REMEMBER ONCE SEEING A CARTOON THAT SHOWED A FATHER EXAMining his young son's report card, which was filled with Ds and Fs. As the father scowled, the boy asked: "What do you think it is, Dad, heredity or environment?" Over and above heredity and environment, Judaism insists on a third factor that influences human behavior: the soul. The notion of a soul, possessed of free will, explains why two brothers can be born to the same parents, and raised in the same environment, yet one ends up a criminal and the other a fully responsible individual, sometimes even a saint. It is also the soul that makes possible a person's ability to repent.

Most Jews associate repentance with the *High Holy Days. The ten-day period from the start of *Rosh ha-Shana to the end of *Yom Kippur is known as *Aseret Y'mai Teshuva,* the Ten Days of Repentance. However, attendance at synagogue on these days, even when accompanied by sincere repentance, only wins forgiveness for offenses committed against God. As the Talmud teaches: "The Day of Atonement atones for sins against God, not for sins against man, unless the injured party has been appeased" (*Mishna Yoma* 8:9).

That last clause, "unless the injured party has been appeased," suggests that for at least one crime, murder, there can be no complete repentance, since there is no way to appease the injured party. This distinctively Jewish belief separates most Jewish thinkers from their Christian counterparts.

In Simon Wiesenthal's *The Sunflower*, written in 1976, there is an autobiographical account of an incident involving an acute ethical dilemma from the Viennese Nazi-hunter's own life. Late in the war, when Wiesenthal was a prisoner in a Nazi *concentration camp, he was plucked one morning from his work detail by a nurse and taken to the bedside of a dying Nazi soldier. The soldier proceeded to tell Wiesenthal much of his life story; most significantly, that though he had been raised as a Catholic altar boy, he had later joined the SS. During the invasion of Poland, he had rounded up Jews: In one town, he had herded the local Jewish community into a building, which was then set on fire.

Now that he had spent days lying in bed waiting to die, he realized the awful thing he had done and needed to know that a Jew forgave him. Wiesenthal remained silent and left the room. Thirty years later, he sent his account of the incident to leading Jewish and Christian figures, and asked them: "Was I right in not forgiving this repentant Nazi?" With few exceptions, the Christian respondents said that he should have done so. As Gustave Heinemann, the former German minister of justice, put it: "Justice and Law, however essential they are, cannot exist without forgiveness. That is the quality that Jesus Christ added to justice." Likewise, almost without exception, the Jewish respondents argued that he could not forgive the Nazi. The only ones empowered to grant forgiveness were the victims, which is why in this case forgiveness was literally a "dead issue."

In the case of almost all other sins, fortunately there is room for repentance. However, there are at least two common offenses, defrauding the public and damaging another person's good name, in which the damage inflicted comes dangerously close to being irrevocable. In the first instance, it is nearly impossible to locate and compensate every individual who has been defrauded; in the second, it is equally difficult to find every person who has heard and accepted an ugly rumor (see *Lashon ha-Ra*). The point is not to demoralize would-be penitents, but to underscore how cautious people must be before committing acts that have irrevocable consequences. As American humorist Josh Billings wrote: "It is much easier to repent of sins that we have committed than to repent of those we intend to commit."

Jewish tradition holds that *teshuva* should consist of several stages: The sinner must recognize his sin, feel sincere remorse, undo any damage that he can, pacify the victim of his offense, and resolve never to commit the sin again.

Jewish law also offers some guidelines to the victim of the sin. In the normal order of events, if the offender *sincerely* requests forgiveness, the victim is required to grant it—certainly by the third request. Withholding forgiveness is considered cruel and is itself a sin.

Concerning offenses committed against God, a characteristic Jewish teaching is that of Rabbi Bunam of Pzsyha, who once asked his disciples: "How can you tell when a sin you have committed has been pardoned? His disciples gave various answers but none of them pleased the rabbi. "We can tell," he said, "by the fact that we no longer commit that sin."

SOME JEWISH TEACHINGS ON REPENTANCE

When to repent

Rabbi Eliezer said: "Repent one day before your death."

His disciples asked him, "Does then one know on what day he will die?"

"All the more reason he should repent today, lest he die tomorrow" (*Shabbat* 153a).

Two Guides to Repenting

"The repentant sinner should strive to do good with the same faculties with which he sinned. . . . With whatever part of the body he sinned, he should now engage in good deeds. If his feet had run to sin, let them now run to the performance of the good. If his mouth had spoken falsehood, let it now be opened in wisdom. Violent hands should now open in charity. . . . The trouble-maker should now become a peacemaker" (Rabbi Jonah Gerondi, thirteenth century).

"It is told that once there was a wicked man who committed all kinds of sins. One day he asked a wise man to teach him an easy way to repent, and the latter said to him: 'Refrain from telling lies.' He went forth happily, thinking that he could follow the wise man's advice, and still go on as before. When he decided to steal, as had been his custom, he reflected: 'What will I do in case somebody asks me, "Where are you going?" If I tell the truth, "To steal," I shall be arrested. If I tell a lie, I shall be violating the command of this wise man.' In the same manner he reflected on all other sins, until he repented with a perfect repentance" (Rabbi Judah ben Asher, fourteenth century).

Maimonides on Repentance

"What constitutes complete repentance? He who is confronted by the identical situation wherein he previously sinned and it lies within his power to commit the sin again, but he nevertheless does not succumb because he wishes to repent, and not because he is too fearful or weak [to repeat the sin]. How so? If he had relations with a woman forbidden to him and he is subsequently alone with her, still in the throes of his passion for her, and his virility is unabated, and [they are] in the same place where they previously sinned; if he abstains and does not sin, this is a true penitent" (*Mishneh Torah*, "Laws of *Teshuva*," 2:1).

SOURCES AND FURTHER READINGS: The quote from Rabbi Bunam of Pzsyha is in Martin Buber, *Tales of the Hasidim—Later Masters*, p. 253. See also Pinchas Peli, *On Repentance: A Collection of the Annual Discourses on Repentance Given by Rabbi Joseph B. Soloveichik Before the High Holy Days*; Abraham Isaac Kook, *Philosophy of Repentance*, translated by Alter Metzger. Joseph Telushkin, *A Code of Jewish Ethics, Volume 1: You Shall Be Holy*, pp. 150–193.

286

FORGIVENESS

THE POPULAR UNDERSTANDING OF CONTEMPORARY CHRISTIANITY'S attitude concerning forgiveness is that Christians are instructed to always forgive the sins of another, whether or not the sinner has requested forgiveness and whether or not the sin was committed against oneself or against others. Characteristic of this attitude was the prayer offered by Pope John Paul II on September 11, 2002, the first anniversary of the terrorist attacks on New York and Washington, D.C.: "We pray for the victims today, may they rest in peace. And may God show mercy and forgiveness for the authors of this terrible attack." (Technically, of course, the Pope wasn't offering forgiveness to the terrorists but was only praying that God do so. However, the thrust of such a prayer suggests that the Pope was forgiving them as well.)

The Jewish attitude on forgiveness is quite different and, indeed, as we shall see, forbids forgiveness in a case such as the above. Rather, there are three approaches toward forgiveness within Judaism: instances when it is obligatory, when it is optional, and when it is forbidden.

What is perhaps most important to note is that in the overwhelming majority of cases Jewish law regards forgiveness as obligatory for offenses committed against oneself. Thus, if someone has inflicted *non-irrevocable* harm upon you, and sincerely seeks forgiveness, Jewish law insists that you pardon the offender. To refuse to do so, Maimonides writes, is to act as an *achzari*, a cruel person.

Jewish law also mandates that the offender, if not forgiven after the first request, must make up to two additional requests (on separate occasions). If after three requests, the hurt party has still not granted forgiveness, the offender is regarded as having repented appropriately, and need make no further requests to be forgiven.

In some circumstances, however, the granting of forgiveness is optional. Thus, Jewish law does not require one to forgive a person who does not ask for forgiveness. Although forgiveness in such situations is optional, sometimes it is wise to grant it, if only because holding onto one's anger can sometimes have a detrimental effect on the injured party. Rabbi Harold Kushner recalls an instance of a woman he knew who, ten years earlier, had been badly mistreated by her husband, who had also divorced her. Kushner was in no way surprised at the woman's deep rage against her ex-husband. But a full decade later, when her anger had still not abated, he said to her: "For ten years you have been walking around with a hot poker in your hand ready to throw it at your ex-husband. But all you've done is burn a hole in your hand."

Recognizing the value in letting go of rage, Jewish liturgy offers a prayer that Jews are encouraged to recite before going to sleep: "Master of the Universe, I hereby forgive anyone who angered or antagonized me, or who sinned against me—whether against my body, my property, my honor, or against anything of mine; whether he did so accidentally, willfully, carelessly, or purposely."

We also have the option to not forgive one who has inflicted upon us irrevocable damage, for example, a person who has besmirched our good name. Because it is generally impossible to fully undo the effects of such damage, we are not required to forgive the offender, even if he or she offers a sincere—even three sincere—apologies. However, for the reasons cited earlier, it might still be the wise and gracious thing to do, particularly if the offender is truly remorseful.

Finally, we come to Judaism's most innovative teaching about forgiveness: its insistence that there are times when forgiveness is forbidden. This prohibition applies to instances such as the one cited earlier concerning Pope John Paul II. Jewish tradition prohibits forgiving a crime committed against another, since forgiveness can be granted only by the victim (Mishnah *Yoma* 8:9). That is why murder constitutes an unforgivable offense, since the only party which can grant forgiveness in such a case is dead. Thus, from Judaism's perspective, if parents choose to forgive their child's murderer, all that they can really forgive is the suffering they themselves have endured, but they cannot forgive the murder itself.

But, again, in the large majority of cases when forgiveness is requested, Judaism deems it obligatory to forgive.

287

HOW AND WHEN TO CRITICIZE

ONLY ONE VERSE BEFORE ORDAINING ITS MOST FAMOUS LAW, "LOVE your neighbor as yourself," the Torah commands, "You shall rebuke, yes rebuke, your fellow, and not bear sin because of him" (Leviticus 19:17). The verse's implication is that if you see someone acting wrongly and make no effort to challenge or change the person's behavior, you share in the responsibility for his or her sin.

The Talmud teaches that this law has far-reaching implications: "Whoever can stop the members of his household from committing a sin but does not, is held responsible for the sins of his household. If he can stop the people of his city from sinning, but does not, he is held responsible for the sins of the people of his city. If he can stop the whole world from sinning, and does not, he is held responsible for the sins of the whole world" (*Shabbat* 54b).

This talmudic teaching implies that only if you have reason to believe that you can influence another's behavior are you obliged to speak up, but if you have no reason to believe that your words will make an impact, then you are not obligated to do so. Thus, if the person you are trying to influence is of such a violent or disagreeable nature that you have reason to fear that criticizing the person will endanger you, you are freed from the obligation to offer rebuke. Then again, unless you really feel threatened you should not too readily conclude that you cannot influence the other. The best thing is to try and fulfill the words of the Torah and to offer rebuke when appropriate.

Nathan, a contemporary of King David, is the biblical model for how to express criticism effectively. When the king committed an egregious sin with the married Bathsheba, and arranged for her husband Uriah to die in battle, Nathan did not confront David with the kind of direct accusation that would likely have been met with defensiveness or denial. Rather, he approached David as if to solicit his advice on a case of injustice that had been brought to Nathan's attention: "There were two men in the same city, one rich and one poor. The rich man had very large flocks and herds, but the poor man had only one little ewe lamb that he had bought. He tended it and it grew up together with him and his children: it used to share his morsel of bread, drink from his cup, and nestle in his bosom; it was like a daughter to him. One day, a traveler came to the rich man, but he was loath to take anything from his own flocks or herds to prepare a meal for the guest who had come to him, so he took the poor man's lamb and prepared it for the man who had come to him." David flew into a rage against the man, and said to Nathan, "'As the Lord lives, the man who did this deserves to die!'" Nathan responded to David, "'That man is you!'" (II Samuel 12:1–7).

By offering a story, instead of confronting the king directly, Nathan enabled David to view the issue in its moral simplicity. David had taken another man's wife, just as the rich man had stolen the lamb that the poor man loved. Once David declared his verdict—"The man who did this deserves to die" and Nathan responded, "That man is you!"—David had no choice but to acknowledge that he merited condemnation. Because Nathan knew how to offer criticism, David learned how to repent.

Maimonides offers three important guidelines to follow when reproving another. First, offer the rebuke in a loving and gentle manner. If your goal is to influence another to recognize the wrong he or she has committed, such recognition is most likely to happen when you make it clear that you speak out of love, and even use terms of endearment. In contrast, when expressed harshly, criticism is apt to provoke a defensive response, and not bring about change. Second, Maimonides teaches that you must speak in a patient and non-peremptory manner: Since few of us can acknowledge all our flaws and transform ourselves immediately, it is unfair to get angry at others when they don't do so. Finally, you should deliver your rebuke in private. Rashi offers a twist on the words in the Torah, "and not bear sin because of him": "Though rebuking him, you should not publicly embarrass him, in which case you will bear sin on account of him." In like manner, the Talmud, in responding to the question "Should you rebuke one to the point that his face changes color" [from embarrassment], answers unequivocally, "No" (*Arakhin* 16b).

Jewish teachings offer guidance not only on how to offer criticism, but also on how to respond when you are being criticized. Unless you have reason to believe that your critic's intentions are malicious, you should remain quiet while the criticism is offered, and to try and consider whether there is some truth in the other's words. Rabbi Simcha Zissel Ziv (nineteenth century) suggested that we react to a critic as we do to a physician. Just as we don't get angry at a doctor who diagnoses an illness from which we are suffering; so should we understand that only by learning what is wrong with us is there a chance that we can be healed. We should react similarly, when one informs us of a wrong we have done or of a fault in our character. Only when we are made aware of such behavior is there hope for improvement. And just as we are grateful to a doctor who has accurately diagnosed us, so should we be grateful to one who offers us the sort of criticism that can help us improve our character.

288

YETZER HA-TOV, YETZER HA-RA

SIGMUND *FREUD'S NOTION OF THE ID, THE REPOSITORY OF AGGRESsive instincts, energy, and amoral desires, is strikingly similar to the ancient rabbinic notion of the *yetzer ha-ra*, the aggressive instinct that encompasses also the human predilection for evil. According to the rabbis, all people are born with the *yetzer ha-ra*, and only acquire a predilection for good—*yetzer ha-tov*—as they mature.

The rabbinic observation seems to accord with reality. Infants might be blessed with cuteness but seldom with altruism. If they want something at four in the morning, they howl, even if Mommy and Daddy haven't had a full night's sleep in two months. The infant is not at fault, but then again the rabbis did not see the self-centered *yetzer ha-ra* as entirely evil. "The *yetzer ha-ra* is very good," one rabbi counseled his colleagues. "How so? Without it, a man wouldn't build a house, marry a woman, have children and conduct a business. As *Solomon taught [Ecclesiastes 4:4]: 'I have also noted that all labor and skillful enterprise come from men's envy of each other' " (*Genesis Rabbah* 9:7).

Pure and beautiful things, the rabbi seems to be teaching, can be prompted by motives that are not totally pure. From sexual intercourse a child may be created, although a couple's motives for mating may be much more complicated than simply a "pure" desire to have a child.

Other Jewish teachings emphasize that people should examine themselves to learn in what direction their *yetzer ha-ra* inclines them; in that way, they can marshal a potentially bad tendency and use it for good. A rich person, for example, might have an overwhelming desire to be famous. Let him fulfill that potentially ignoble desire through *tzedaka (charity); that way his name will be known because it is engraved on the wing of a hospital, or a college library, or a Jewish day school. These sorts of activities would clearly fulfill another rabbinic teaching, that people should worship God with both their *yetzer ha-tov* and *yetzer ha-ra*.

The terms *yetzer ha-tov* and *yetzer ha-ra* are part of the active vocabulary of religious Jews. *Yetzer ha-ra* is often used as a synonym for lust, and not sexual lust alone. "I have a real *yetzer ha-ra* for chocolate," someone might say. The phrase is also used to describe more serious peccadillos. "I have to control my *yetzer ha-ra* for money," a person might confess: "It's really tempting me to cheat in business."

The *yetzer ha-tov* is less frequently discussed. Perhaps good always seems more boring than evil, or lust, or temptation. Of a very fine person, people might say, "He seems to have no *yetzer ha-ra*."

SOURCE AND FURTHER READING: Solomon Schechter, *Aspects of Rabbinic Theology*, chapter XV.

289

MESSIAH / MA-SHI-AKH

Messianism

MANY JEWS HAVE LONG BEEN SKEPTICAL OF PREDICTIONS ANNOUNCING the imminent arrival of the Messiah (*Ma-shi-akh*). The first-century sage Rabban *Yochanan ben Zakkai once said: "If you should happen to be holding a sapling in your hand when they tell you that the Messiah has arrived, first plant the sapling and then go out and greet the Messiah." An old Jewish story tells of a Russian Jew who was paid a ruble a month by the community council to stand at the outskirts of town so that he could be the first person to greet the Messiah upon his arrival. When a friend said to him, "But the pay is so low," the man replied: "True, but the work is steady."

Yet, the belief in a messiah and a messianic age is so deeply rooted in Jewish tradition that a statement concerning the Messiah became the most famous of *Maimonides's Thirteen Principles of Faith: "*Ani Ma'amin*, I believe with a full heart in the coming of the Messiah, and even though he may tarry, I will wait for him on any day that he may come." It is reported that there were Jews who sang the *Ani Ma'amin* while walking to the gas chambers in the *concentration camps.

On the one hand, ironic jokes and skepticism; on the other, passionate faith: What then is the Jewish position on the Messiah?

Most significantly, Jewish tradition affirms at least five things about the Messiah. He will: be a descendant of King David, gain sovereignty over the land of Israel, gather the Jews there from the four corners of the earth, restore them to full observance of Torah law, and, as a grand finale, bring peace to the whole world. Concerning the more difficult tasks some prophets assign him, such as *Isaiah's vision of a messianic age in which the wolf shall dwell with the lamb and the calf with the young lion (Isaiah 11:6), Maimonides believes that Isaiah's language is metaphorical (for example, only that enemies of the Jews, likened to the wolf, will no longer oppress them). A century later, Nachmanides rejected Maimonides's rationalism and asserted that Isaiah meant precisely what he said: that in the messianic age even wild animals will become domesticated and sweet-tempered. A more recent Jewish "commentator," Woody Allen, has cautioned: "And the lamb and the wolf shall lie down together, but the lamb won't get any sleep."

The Jewish belief that the Messiah's reign lies in the future has long distinguished Jews from their Christian neighbors who believe, of course, that the Messiah came two thousand years ago in the person of *Jesus. The most basic reason for the Jewish denial of the messianic claims made on Jesus' behalf is that he did not usher in world peace, as Isaiah had prophesied: "And nation shall not lift up sword against nation, neither shall they learn war anymore" (Isaiah 2:4). In addition, Jesus did not help bring about Jewish political sovereignty for the Jews or protection from their enemies.

A century after Jesus, large numbers of Palestinian Jews followed the would-be Messiah, Simon Bar-Kokhba, in a revolt against the Romans. The results were catastrophic, and the Jews suffered a devastating defeat (see *Bar-Kokhba Rebellion*). In 1665–1666, large segments of world Jewry believed that *Shabbetai Zevi, a Turkish Jew, was the Messiah, and confidently waited for Turkey's sultan to deliver Palestine to him. Instead, the sultan threatened Shabbetai with execution and the "Messiah" saved his life by converting to Islam.

In the modern world, *Reform Judaism has long denied that there will be an individual messiah who will carry out the task of perfecting the world. Instead, the movement speaks of a future world in which human efforts, not a divinely sent messenger, will bring about a utopian age. The Reform idea has influenced many non-Orthodox Jews: The oft-noted attraction of Jews to liberal and left-wing political causes probably represents a secular attempt to usher in a messianic age.

Among traditional Jews, the belief in a personal messiah seems to have grown more central in recent years. When I was growing up, the subject of the Messiah was rarely, if ever, mentioned at the Jewish school I attended, the Yeshiva of Flatbush. Today, however, one large movement within Orthodoxy, *Lubavitch, has placed increasing emphasis on the imminence of the Messiah's arrival.

At the same time, the subject of the Messiah has become more significant to many religious Zionists in Israel, particularly to many disciples of the late Rabbi Abraham Isaac *Kook. The event that helped set the stage for a revived interest in the *Messiah was the *Six-Day War of 1967, in which Israel captured the Old City of Jerusalem and, for the first time in over two thousand years, achieved Jewish rule over the biblically ordained borders of Israel.

A sober reading of Jewish history, however, indicates that while the messianic *idea* has long elevated Jewish life, and prompted Jews to work for *tikkun olam (perfection of the world), whenever Jews have thought the Messiah's arrival to be imminent, the results have been catastrophic. In 1984, a Jewish religious underground was arrested in Israel. Among its other activities, the group had plotted to blow up the Muslim Dome of the Rock in Jerusalem, so that the Temple Mount could be cleared and the *Temple rebuilt. Though such an action might well have provoked an international Islamic *jihad* (holy war) against Israel, some members of this underground group apparently welcomed such a possibility, feeling that a worldwide invasion of Israel would force God to bring the Messiah immediately. It is precisely when the belief in the Messiah's coming starts to shape political decisions that the messianic idea ceases to be inspiring and becomes dangerous.

SOURCES AND FURTHER READINGS: Rabbi Yochanan's observation that if one is planting a sapling and hears that the Messiah has arrived is found in *Avot d'Rabbi Nathan*, version B, ch. 31, Schechter edition. See also Joseph Klausner, *The Messianic Idea in Israel*; Gershom Scholem, *The Messianic Idea in Judaism*; R. J. Zvi Werblowsky, "Messianism in Jewish History," in H. H. Ben-Sasson and S. Ettinger, *Jewish Society Through the Ages*; Abba Hillel Silver, *A History of Messianic Speculation in Israel*.

290

AFTERLIFE/*OLAM HA-BA*

OLAM HA-BA (AFTERLIFE) IS RARELY DISCUSSED IN JEWISH LIFE, BE IT among Reform, Conservative, or Orthodox Jews. This is in marked contrast to the religious traditions of the people among whom the Jews have lived. Afterlife has always played a critical role in Islamic teachings, for example. To this day, Muslim terrorists who are dispatched on suicide missions are reminded that anyone who dies in a *jihad* (holy war) immediately ascends to the highest place in heaven. In Christianity, afterlife plays a critical role; the vigorous missionizing efforts of many Protestant sects are rooted in the belief that converting nonbelievers will save them from hell.

Jewish teachings on the subject of afterlife are sparse: The Torah, the most important Jewish text, has no clear reference to afterlife at all.

Since Judaism does believe in the "next world," how does one account for the Torah's silence? I suspect that there is a correlation between its nondiscussion of afterlife and the fact that the Torah was revealed just after the long Jewish sojourn in Egypt. The Egyptian society from which the Hebrew slaves emerged was obsessed with death and afterlife. The holiest Egyptian literary work was called *The Book of the Dead*, while the major achievement of many Pharaohs was the erection of the giant tombs called pyramids. In contrast, the Torah is obsessed with this world, so much so that it even forbids its priests (see *Kohain*) from coming into contact with dead bodies (Leviticus 21:2).

The Torah, therefore, might have been silent about afterlife out of a desire to ensure that Judaism not evolve in the direction of the death-obsessed Egyptian religion. Throughout history, those religions that have assigned a significant role to afterlife have often permitted other religious values to become distorted. For example, belief in the afterlife motivated the men of the *Spanish Inquisition to torture innocent human beings; they believed it was morally desirable to torture people for a few days in this world until they accepted Christ, and thereby save them from the eternal torments of hell.

In Judaism the belief in afterlife is less a leap of faith than a logical outgrowth of other Jewish beliefs. If one believes in a God who is all-powerful and all-just, one cannot believe that this world, in which evil far too often triumphs, is the only arena in which human life exists. For if this existence is the final word, and God permits evil to win, then it cannot be that God is good. Thus, when someone says he or she believes in God but not in afterlife, it would seem that either they have not thought the issue through, or that the divine being in whom they believe is amoral or immoral.

According to Judaism, what happens in the next world? As noted, on this subject there is little material. Some of the suggestions about afterlife in Jewish writings and folklore are even humorous. In heaven, one story teaches, *Moses sits and teaches Torah all day long. For the righteous people (the *tzaddikim*), this is heaven; for the evil people, it is hell. Another folktale teaches that in both heaven and hell, human beings cannot bend their elbows. In hell people are perpetually starved; in heaven each person feeds his neighbor.

All attempts to describe heaven and hell are, of course, speculative. Because Judaism believes that God is good, it believes that God rewards good people; it does not believe that Adolf *Hitler and his victims share the same fate. Beyond that, it is hard to assume much more. We are asked to leave afterlife in God's hands.

SOURCE AND FURTHER READING: C. G. Montefiore and H. Loewe, *A Rabbinic Anthology*, pp. 580–608.

291

ETHICAL MONOTHEISM

Perfection of the World/Tikkun Olam

JUDAISM BELIEVES THAT THE GOAL OF JEWISH EXISTENCE IS NOTHING less than "to perfect the world under the rule of God" (from the *Aleinu* prayer).

In Jewish teachings, both clauses—the world's ethical perfection and the rule of God—are equally important. Human beings are obligated to bring mankind to a knowledge of God, whose primary demand of human beings is moral behavior. All people who hold this belief are ethical monotheists, and thus natural allies of religiously committed Jews.

Unfortunately, although ethical monotheism is the goal of Judaism (see *Micah/To Do Justice, and to Love Goodness, and to Walk Modestly with Your God*) and the purpose of the Jewish mission in the world, more than a few Jews have lost sight of this goal. As the late Rabbi Abraham Joshua *Heschel lamented: "The Jewish people are a messenger who have forgotten their message." Among religious Jews today, disproportionate emphasis often is placed on rituals, as if Judaism's ethical laws were offered merely as an extracurricular activity and are not as binding or important as the rituals. The Israeli Bible scholar Professor Uriel Simon has noted the paradox that Jews who most passionately believe that the Jews are God's *Chosen People are the ones most likely to justify any acts of the Israeli government on the grounds that "we have a right to act like any other nation."

Strangely enough, however, secular Jews are as likely as religious Jews to believe that the Jews have a special mission. As Simon goes on to note:

"And those Jews who don't believe in chosenness are the ones who are most likely to hold Israel to a higher standard than they hold any other nation."

The principle of ethical monotheism, the obligation to try to "perfect the world under the rule of God," is reiterated three times a day in the *Aleinu* prayer, which closes the morning, afternoon, and evening prayer services. The term "ethical monotheism" itself is generally credited to nineteenth-century *Reform Judaism, and remains, in my view, nineteenth-century Reform's most enduring contribution to Jewish thought.

292

DIVINE PROVIDENCE/*HASHGAKHA PRATIT*
Bashert

MANY RELIGIOUS PEOPLE USE THE EXPRESSION "GOD WILLING" WHEN they describe their future plans. But do they all believe that everything that happens is really God's will? This is, indeed, a hotly debated subject among religious Jews. The generally ascendant view in *Orthodox Judaism is that everything that happens in this world has been divinely ordained: "Not a grain of sand moves from its place on the beach except by divine fiat," as a popular proverb has it. God's will is presumed to be apparent in minor events as well as in major ones. Years ago, I recall seeing a young Orthodox woman I know searching for lost keys. "I wonder what *Ha-Shem* [God] is punishing me for," she told me.

Divine providence (in Hebrew, *hashgakha pratit*) is related to the Yiddish word *bashert* (fated). Both terms suggest that no accidents happen in the world. Forty days before a male baby is born, the Talmud teaches, a heavenly decree is issued: "So-and-so shall be married to the daughter of so-and-so" (*Sotah* 2a). Among Orthodox Jews, it is common to speak of one's spouse as his or her *bashert*. I recently came across a "personals" ad in a Jewish newspaper in which a single Orthodox woman asked: "Contact me and let's find out if we are each other's *bashert*." When a couple are divorced, it is assumed that their marriage was an error; they weren't each other's *bashert*.

In popular parlance, the term *bashert* is generally used to refer only to happy events. Yet logic dictates that *bashert* also governs tragedies. If a man is run over, *bashert* means that he was fated to spend a precise amount of time brushing his teeth that morning to guarantee that he would be crossing the street at precisely the time a driver would be losing control of his car. On a broader level, the doctrine of *hashgakha pratit* means that the Holocaust was not just the will of Hitler, but also the will of God.

There are, however, traditional Jewish thinkers—most prominent among them the fourteenth-century Gersonides—who reject the notion that everything that happens on this planet is God's will. For one thing, because God endowed people with free will, He had to allow for the possibility that they would use it to do things of which He would not approve (see *Theodicy*).

Thus, on the issue of divine providence there is no one unequivocal Jewish teaching. All that the Bible teaches definitively is that God sometimes acts in this world. God chose *Abraham, God led the Jews out of Egypt, God gave the Jews the Torah at Sinai. However, God's overt actions in these particular cases do not necessarily mean that everything else that happens in this world similarly occurs at His command.

I find my own response on this issue to be paradoxical. Intellectually, it does not make sense that *everything* that happens in this world is God's will. Yet when people dear to me become sick, I pray to God. Because God is God, anything, including a miracle, is possible. Yet because God has given man free will, the history of the world is not just the history of what God has done, but of what man has done too.

SOURCES AND FURTHER READINGS: Yaakov Elman, "When Permission is Given: *Aspects of Divine Providence*," *Tradition, Summer 1989*, pp. 24–45; Alexander Altmann, "The Religion of the Thinkers: Free Will and Predestination in *Saadia, Bahya and *Maimonides," in S. D. Goitein, ed., *Religion in a Religious Age.*

293

IDOLATRY/*AVODAH ZARA*

AMONG THE TORAH'S 613 LAWS, NONE PROHIBITS ATHEISM. THE Torah possibly did not believe that there truly are atheists. People who reject God invariably find something else to worship, and any time people worship something other than God they are committing idolatry (*avodah zara*).

The idolaters against whom the Torah warred worshiped a pantheon of gods, most of them modeled on the universe's natural forces. They worshiped rain gods, fertility gods, gods of nature, and many others. Unlike the Jews, the idolaters were not commanded to love their gods; that command is apparently distinctive to the Torah. Rather, ancient idolaters feared their gods so much that they constantly tried to propitiate them, on occasion sacrificing to them their most precious possessions, their sons, ideally their firstborn sons. The Book of II Kings records, for example, that the king of Moab, desperate to forestall an Israelite victory, "took his first-born son, who was to succeed him as king, and offered him up on the wall as a burnt offering" (3:27).

The Torah was more horrified and angered by the ritual of child sacrifice than by any other aspect of *avodah zara*. Among the Hebrews, child sacrifice had been outlawed from their very beginnings (see *The Binding of Isaac/Akedat Yitzchak*). British scholar Louis Jacobs has argued persuasively that the prophetic attacks against idolatry are not intellectual (that is, idolaters err in substituting polytheism for monotheism) but moral: "Nowhere in the prophetic writings are the [non-Jewish] nations condemned for worshipping their gods, only for the ethical abominations such as child sacrifice associated with the worship." In addition to child sacrifice, the Jews' idolatrous neighbors practiced bestiality (see Leviticus 18:21–30), and the Torah warns the Jews that if they carry out the same sort of depravities in Canaan, the land will "vomit them out" as it did the previous inhabitants (Leviticus 18:28).

From the Jewish perspective, is Christianity, with its attribution of divinity to a human being, idolatry? Throughout Jewish history, the question of whether or not Christianity was idolatry was not an academic one. The Talmud had long proscribed Jews from having any commercial dealings with idolaters for three days before their holidays. Since Christians celebrate Sunday as a holiday, Jews would have been prohibited from dealing with Christians every week from Thursday through Sunday.

Throughout the centuries, more than a few Jewish thinkers have argued that the idea of the trinity (the Father, the Son, and the Holy Ghost) seemed idolatrous. Ultimately, however, the majority of Jewish scholars concluded that although Christianity speaks of a trinity, it does not conceive of the three forces as separate with different and conflicting wills. Rather, the trinity represents three aspects of one God. While Jews are forbidden to hold such a belief, it is not *avodah zara*.

According to the rabbis, whoever rejects idolatry is regarded as if he kept the entire Torah. Indeed, the struggle against *avodah zara* is so central to the Torah that more than 50 of its 613 laws are directed against idolatry.

SOURCE: Louis Jacobs, "The Relationship Between Religion and Ethics in Jewish Thought," in Gene Outka and John Reeder, Jr., eds, *Religion and Morality*, p. 159.

294

THEODICY

SOME THIRTY YEARS AGO, RABBI HAROLD KUSHNER PUBLISHED *WHEN Bad Things Happen to Good People*, which quickly became a runaway best seller. I have long been struck, however, by how often I hear people erroneously refer to the book as "*Why* Bad Things Happen to Good People." Obviously, neither Kushner, nor anyone else for that matter, would have been able to answer *that* question. As a medieval Jewish proverb declared: "If I knew God, I would be God." But the fact that so many people remember Kushner's title in the same incorrect way reflects how desperately people want to know if there is any reason or ultimate meaning to human suffering.

Theodicy means the attempt to vindicate God's goodness in the face of the existence of so much evil in the world. One biblical book in particular, Job, is obsessed with the problem of theodicy (see *The Trial of Job*). In short order,

Job, a singularly good man, loses his children and his wealth and is then afflicted with horrendously painful boils. Throughout the book, Job asks God the same question, in one form or another: Why? God never tells him why. At the end of the book, He appears to Job out of the whirlwind and affirms that He is the Lord who created heaven and earth. If Job understands nothing of how God accomplished such a miracle, God asks him, then how can he expect to understand everything that has happened to him?

God's answer, of course, does not address Job's question. Job asks, "Why?" and God answers, "Because." Yet the mere fact that God personally addresses him is very reassuring to Job.

Generally, theodicy tries to understand two forms of suffering, man-made and natural. Since the Holocaust, most questions of theodicy raised by Jews deal with God's seeming passivity during the Holocaust. Why did God allow the Nazis to triumph for so long?

While it would be presumptuous to try to answer this question, it is important to note that man-made evil is not, in and of itself, an overwhelming challenge to the idea of God's goodness. It is a basic tenet of Judaism that God gave man free will, and that as a result human beings can choose to do evil. If God stopped people every time they tried to do evil, there would be no more free will, which is the essence of what makes human beings human (see *In God's Image*). Of course, this does not entirely resolve the problem of evil in the world. Why, for example, did God create in human beings—or at least in some human beings—the desire to torture other people? There could have been free will without endowing some people with a propensity for sadism.

The problem of God's apparent passivity in the face of many evil acts is exacerbated by Judaism's belief that God sometimes *does* intervene to stop evil. "According to the Torah," one frequently hears post-Holocaust Jews say, "God intervened in Egypt and took the Jews out of slavery. Why did He not destroy the death camps?"

The question is poignant, but naive. The account in Exodus makes it clear that God did not intervene when Pharaoh enslaved the Jews. Generations suffered under Egyptian cruelty, and untold numbers of male Jewish babies were drowned in the Nile before God sent *Moses to confront Pharaoh. From that perspective, it has been noted, one could say that God intervened in the Holocaust as well: Indeed, He stopped it, but only after six million Jews had been murdered. I do not claim that this answer is satisfactory; in all likelihood, there probably is no satisfactory answer.

One of the dangers of theodicy, in fact, is that in its attempts to justify God's ways to man, it frequently blames man for his sufferings. For example, one sometimes hears ultra-Orthodox Jews speak of the Holocaust as God's punishment for Jewish irreligiosity. Aside from the fact that suffocating a small child in a gas chamber seems an excessive response to the Sabbath violations of that child's parents, such a view makes no sense on other grounds. However irreligious European Jewry was in the 1930s and 1940s, the percentage of Jews in the United States who were religiously nonobservant was much higher. Yet American Jewry was spared the Holocaust and has had a very prosperous history.

Some anti-Zionist ultra-Orthodox thinkers explain the Holocaust as God's punishment for Jews turning to the secular, Zionist movement. This explanation seems even more far-fetched, since among the few European Jews who escaped the Holocaust were the Zionists who left Europe before 1939 and emigrated to Palestine. Indeed, some religious Zionist thinkers understand the Holocaust as God's punishment of those Jews who did not become Zionists and chose instead to stay in Europe. This argument is morally offensive, too. Putting children into gas chambers as punishment for their parents' refusal to respond to Theodor *Herzl's challenge seems equally grotesque.

What is offensive about most attempts to explain the Holocaust is that, in one form or another, they convert Hitler into God's ally, or at least into His lieutenant. Somehow, Hitler is seen as carrying out God's will (see *Divine Providence/Hashgakha Pratit*). Invariably, the people who offer such explanations accuse Jews other than themselves of having provoked God's wrath. Such theologians undoubtedly hope that if they can isolate what it is precisely that so angers God, then they will be in a better position to pacify Him. Rather than trying to decipher why God would have "wanted" six million Jews to be murdered by order of the most wicked human being who ever lived, the proposition that the Holocaust, murders, and many other daily cruelties are the result of human free will seems to make more sense.

There is no comparably easy answer to explain natural suffering. Why are there earthquakes, floods, cancer? Clearly, there is no discernible relationship between human goodness and human suffering. When a truly evil person becomes ill, many people feel a certain satisfaction that someone who has caused so much suffering is now experiencing it. Indeed, if illness or tragedy befell only bad people, we would undoubtedly witness massive movements of repentance. However, suffering seems to be quite evenly distributed among the good and the bad, and remains the single greatest challenge to religious belief.

Without suffering, there would probably be few nonbelievers in the universe. But, as Rabbi Milton Steinberg has written, "if the believer has his troubles with evil, the atheist has more and graver difficulties to contend with. Reality stumps him altogether, leaving him baffled not by one consideration but by many, from the existence of natural law through the instinctual cunning of the insect to the brain of the genius and the heart of the prophet. This then is the intellectual reason for believing in God: That, though this belief is not free from difficulties, it stands out, head and shoulders, as the best answer to the riddle of the universe."

SOURCES AND FURTHER READINGS: The concluding quote is from Milton Steinberg, *Anatomy of Faith*. See also Eliezer Berkovits, *Faith After the Holocaust*; Solomon Schechter, "The Doctrine of Divine Retribution in Rabbinical Literature," in his *Studies in Judaism*, vol. 1, ch. 8; John Hick, *Evil and the God of Love*.

295

TORAH STUDY/*TALMUD TORAH*

"AN IGNORAMUS CANNOT BE A RIGHTEOUS PERSON," *HILLEL TAUGHT some two thousand years ago (*Pirkei Avot* 2:5). Hillel presumably did not mean that ignorant people necessarily lack the desire to do good; their deficiency, rather, is intellectual. Right actions require knowledge, and people lacking that knowledge will not know the proper way to behave.

Because the Torah is considered to be the source of correct knowledge, studying it is ranked in Jewish law as the highest commandment. The *mitzvah* of study is commanded in the Torah in a paragraph that forms part of the *Sh'ma* prayer. Parents are instructed: "And you shall teach [the Torah] to your children, and you shall speak of it, when you sit in your house, when you walk on the road, when you lie down and when you rise up" (Deuteronomy 6:7).

Largely in consequence of this biblical injunction, Jewish law ruled two thousand years ago that parents are forbidden to live in a city without schools. Talmudic law even said that no teacher was to be assigned more than twenty-five pupils; if the class was larger, a second teacher had to be hired. The poor, it also ruled, must be taught free of charge.

The penchant for education among Jews was well-known. In medieval Europe, when nearly all Christian and Muslim men, and certainly women, were illiterate, nearly all Jews could read and write, and many achieved high levels of knowledge. A twelfth-century monk, a student of the great Catholic theologian Peter Abelard, reported that "a Jew, however poor, if he has ten sons, would put them all to letters, not for gain, as the Christians do, but for the understanding of God's Law, and not only his sons but his daughters."

At about the same time, we find a Jewish woman on her deathbed in Egypt writing to her sister: "If the Lord on High should decree my death, my greatest wish is that you should take care of my little daughter and make an effort for her to study. Indeed, I know that I am imposing a heavy burden on you. For we do not have the wherewithal for her upkeep, let alone the cost of tuition. But we have an example from our mother and teacher, the servant of the Lord." As historian Haim Hillel Ben-Sasson has noted: "Here is an instance of a Jewish family that was certainly not well-to-do in which the women of two generations were educated and saw to the education of their daughters."

Jewish education, however, was by no means restricted to the young. Adult Jews, as well, met in regular study. The importance of such study was underscored by *Maimonides in his code of Jewish law, the *Mishneh Torah*, written in the twelfth century: "If a parent wishes to study Torah, and he has a child who must also learn, the parent takes precedence. However, if the child is more insightful or quicker to grasp what there is to be learned, the child takes precedence. Even though the child gains priority thereby, the parent must not ignore his own study, for just as it is a *mitzvah* to educate the child, so, too, is the parent commanded to teach himself" ("Laws of Torah Study," 1:4). A few paragraphs later, Maimonides concludes: "Until what period in life ought one to study Torah? Until the day of one's death" (1:10).

Study of Jewish texts was clearly widespread in the Jewish community. At the YIVO Institute in New York, an organization which commemorates Jewish life in pre–World War II Eastern Europe, there is a volume of the *Mishna saved from the Nazis and brought to the United States. On the front page the book is stamped "The Society of Woodchoppers for the Study of Mishna in Berditchev." That the men who chopped wood in Berditchev, a job that had no status and required no education, met regularly to study Mishna shows the pervasiveness of study in the Jewish community. It also helps explain the avidity for education among the grandsons and granddaughters of these woodchoppers in the United States.

Unfortunately, with notable exceptions, the Jewish community did neglect the educational needs of Jewish women. However, in recent years there has been a greatly increased emphasis on Jewish education for women within all branches of Judaism.

Among Orthodox Jews, study of the Talmud in particular is regarded as the most elevated activity in which one can engage, and people known as scholars of Talmud (*talmidei khakhamim*) have high status in the community.

An unfortunate tendency toward elitism among the Torah-educated has long been present in Jewish life, and the Talmud records a rather painful anecdote about *Rabbi Judah the Prince, the leading scholar of his generation and the editor of the Mishna. The conclusion of the story suggests, however, the Talmud's disapproval of Rabbi Judah's original attitude:

"Once, when there was a drought [in Israel], Rabbi Judah the Prince opened the food warehouses and announced, 'Let all those who have studied Bible, Mishna, Gemara . . . come in, but those who are ignorant of Torah should not enter.'

"Rabbi Yonatan ben Amram forced himself in [presumably, as shall soon be apparent, in disguise] and said to him, 'My teacher, feed me!'

"He said to him, 'My son, have you studied the Bible?'

"He answered, 'No.'

" 'Did you study the Mishna?'

"He answered, 'No.'

" 'If that is the case, how can I feed you?'

He answered, 'Feed me as you would feed a dog or a raven.'

"He fed him.

"When [Rabbi Yonatan] left, Rabbi Judah the Prince remained troubled, saying, 'Woe is me! I have given food to one who is ignorant of Torah.'

"His son, Rabbi Shimon, said, 'Maybe that was your student, Rabbi Yonatan ben Amram, who has never wanted to gain any advantage because he has studied Torah?'

"They checked and discovered that that was, indeed, the case. Rabbi Judah the Prince then said, 'Let everyone enter' " (*Bava Batra* 8a).

For many nonreligious Jews, study of the Talmud, the highest branch of Jewish learning, seems irrelevant. The Talmud, they feel, is filled with arcane disputes on remote subjects.

However, discussions of topics that might at first seem obscure can often clarify more immediate issues. The rabbis of the Talmud, for example, raise the following hypothetical question: Two men are in the desert, and only one of them has water. If he shares the water with his companion, he and his companion will both die; if he keeps the water for himself, he will live and only his companion will die. What should he do?

One rabbi, Bar Petura, rules that the man should split the water, even if he dies as a result. Rabbi *Akiva teaches, however, that the man with the water has the right to drink it (*Siphra* on Leviticus 25:36).

The debate had long struck me as interesting but remote, until I heard Elie *Wiesel, the noted writer and Holocaust survivor, refer to it in a lecture he delivered on Rabbi Akiva. "Rabbi Akiva," Wiesel said in reference to Akiva's statement that the man with the water had the right to drink it, "was very hard, very hard on the survivor."

Wiesel's comment made me understand why almost every Jew who survived the concentration camps had feelings of guilt after the Holocaust. Almost all camp survivors had survived in part by making the choice of Rabbi Akiva, and not splitting their meager provisions; as morally justifiable as this choice was, life forever after was filled with a sense of guilt.

In a world that glorified power, Jewish tradition glorified study. As the Talmud ruled: "A scholar takes precedence over a king of Israel, for if a scholar dies no one can replace him, while if a king dies, all Israel is eligible for kingship" (*Horayot* 13a).

SOURCES AND FURTHER READINGS: In the talmudic story regarding Rabbi Judah the Prince, I have largely followed the translation of Danny Siegel, *Family Reunion: Making Peace in the Jewish Community*, pp. 42–43; the translation of the talmudic passage cited in the final paragraph is taken from Francine Klagsbrun, *Voices of Wisdom*, p. 252. See also Louis Jacobs, "The Study of the Torah," in his *Jewish Values*, ch. 1; Louis Ginzberg, "The Rabbinical Student," in his *Students, Scholars and Saints*; Aharon Lichtenstein, "Study," in Arthur A. Cohen and Paul Mendes-Flohr, eds., *Contemporary Jewish Religious Thought*, pp. 931–937. For a general overview of the laws concerning study of Torah, see Joseph Telushkin, *A Code of Jewish Ethics, Volume 1: You Shall Be Holy*, pp. 496–520.

PART THIRTEEN

The Hebrew Calendar and Jewish Holidays

296

LISTING OF JEWISH HOLIDAYS IN CONTEXT OF SOLAR/LUNAR CALENDAR

THE JEWISH CALENDAR IS A LUNAR ONE, LASTING 354 DAYS; IT IS, however, closely tied to the 365-day solar calendar. The calendar has a nineteen-year cycle; during seven years out of the nineteen, an extra month is added to ensure that holidays occur in their appropriate seasons. For example, the Torah speaks of Passover as being the holiday of spring. Yet if the lunar calendar were allowed to proceed unadjusted, Passover would fall eleven days earlier each year; within a span of only five years, the holiday would occur during the winter and, some years later, in the fall.

In a nonleap year, the Jewish calendar has twelve months, lasting either twenty-nine or thirty days.

Tishrei is the Jewish month that is the most heavily weighted with holidays. It begins with the High Holy Days, which commence the Jewish year and generally occur in the early fall. Rosh ha-Shana, the first two days of *Tishrei*, celebrates the creation of the world. According to the Jewish calendar's reckoning, *Adam and Eve, the first human beings created *in God's image, lived about 5,770 years ago.

Adar, the month in which the holiday of Purim falls, is regarded as a time of happiness. "From the beginning of *Adar*," the rabbis teach, "we increase our happiness" (*Ta'anit* 29a). Conversely, the month of *Av*, which occurs in July or August, is the unhappiest month. "From the beginning of *Av*," the rabbis teach, "we diminish happiness" (*Mishna Ta'anit* 4:6). *Av* contains the saddest of Jewish holidays, Tisha Be'Av, which commemorates the destruction of both Temples as well as many other tragic events in Jewish history.

The *kosher catering business is deeply affected by the Jewish calendar. Marriages are not performed on the Sabbath: They also are not performed during the *three weeks preceding Tisha Be'Av, or during most of the time between Passover and *Shavuot—generally between mid-April and early June. Certain days during this last period are exceptions, and if you have your heart set on a May wedding, there is a good chance your wish can be accommodated. However, plan a year ahead of time, before the date is taken.

Most of the holidays listed are discussed in separate entries under the holiday's name in this section.

ENGLISH MONTHS	HEBREW MONTH	HOLIDAY
September–October	*Tishrei*	New Year/*Rosh ha-Shana*, *Tishrei* 1–2
		Fast of Gedaliah/*Tzom Gedaliah, Tishrei* 3
		Day of Atonement/*Yom Kippur, Tishrei* 10
		Tabernacles/*Sukkot*, *Tishrei* 15–22— Eighth Day of Assembly/*Shmini Atzeret*, *Tishrei* 22 (in Israel, the holiday is celebrated together with *Simkhat Torah*—see next holiday)
		Rejoicing at the Completion of the Torah Reading/*Simkhat Torah*, *Tishrei* 23
October–November	*Kheshvan*	
November–December	*Kislev*	*Hanukka, Kislev* 25 (8 days)
December–January	*Tevet*	The Fast of the Tenth of *Tevet/Asara B'Tevet*
January–February	*Shvat*	The Fifteenth of *Shvat/*Tu B'Shvat*
February–March	*Adar*—in leap years, seven years out of nineteen (the third, sixth, eighth, eleventh, fourteenth, seventeenth	The Fast of Esther/*Ta'anit Esther, Adar* 13
		Purim, *Adar* 14

ENGLISH MONTHS	HEBREW MONTH	HOLIDAY
	and nineteenth), there is a second month of *Adar*	
March–April	*Nissan*	*Passover/*Pesach, Nissan* 15–22 (in Israel, one day less)
		Holocaust Memorial Day/ * *Yom ha-Shoa, Nissan* 27
April–May	*Iyyar*	Israeli Independence Day/*Yom ha-Atzma'ut, Iyyar* 5
		*Lag Ba-Omer, *Iyyar* 18
		Jerusalem Day/*Yom Yerushalayim, Iyyar* 28
May–June	*Sivan*	*Shavuot, *Sivan* 6–7 (in Israel, only one day)
June–July	*Tammuz*	*Fast of the Seventeenth of *Tammuz/Shiva Asar Be' Tammuz*
July–August	*Av*	*Tisha Be'Av, *Av* 9
August–September	*Elul*	The month is traditionally devoted to spiritual stock-taking in preparation for Rosh ha-Shana

SOURCES AND FURTHER READINGS: There are a number of fine books on the Jewish holidays. One of the best is Irving Greenberg, *The Jewish Way: Living the Holidays*; Greenberg does a superb job in explicating the meaning of each Jewish holiday for modern Jews. Blu Greenberg, his wife, has written *How to Run a Traditional Jewish Household*, which has extensive material on how to celebrate the holidays, as does Richard Siegel, Michael Strassfeld, and Sharon Strassfeld, eds., *The Jewish Catalog*; see also Michael Strassfeld, *The Jewish Holidays*. Eliyahu Kitov, *The Book of Our Heritage* is an important three-volume study of the Jewish calendar and holidays. Three good guides to the laws of the holidays are Hayim Donin, *To Be a Jew* (Orthodox), Isaac Klein, *A Guide to Jewish Religious Practice* (Conservative), and Peter Knobel, ed., *Gates of the Seasons: A Guide to the Jewish Year* (Reform). Philip Goodman has edited a series of anthologies on many of the holidays for the Jewish Publication Society: *The Passover Anthology*, *The Shavuot Anthology*, *The Sukkot Anthology*, *The Rosh Ha-Shanah Anthology*, *The Yom Kippur Anthology*, and *The Purim Anthology*.

297

NEW YEAR/ROSH HA-SHANA

High Holy Days
Days of Awe/Yamim Nora'im
Shofar
Makhzor
Apples and Honey

PERHAPS THE STRANGEST FACT ABOUT THE JEWISH NEW YEAR, ROSH ha-Shana, is that it falls in *Tishrei*, the seventh month of the Hebrew calendar; it is as if the Western world's secular New Year were to be celebrated on July 1 instead of January 1. Indeed, Jews date as the first month, *Nissan*, the month of the Exodus from Egypt, when the Jewish people began to be forged into a nation. On the other hand, *Tishrei* commemorates the month in which God created the world.

Most Jewish holidays celebrate national events in Jewish history. *Passover, for example, commemorates the Exodus; *Shavuot, the giving of the Torah; and *Purim, the deliverance from Haman. Rosh ha-Shana and *Yom Kippur are much more personal in nature. In Hebrew they are known as *Yamim Nora'im* (Days of Awe); in English they are commonly referred to as the High Holy Days. On these two holidays, and during the weeks preceding them, Jews are instructed to scrupulously examine their deeds and, more significantly, their misdeeds during the preceding year. Rosh ha-Shana and Yom Kippur's goal is nothing less than an ethical and religious reassessment of one's life. Of equal concern, however, is the year that is about to begin. On these Days of Awe, Jewish tradition teaches, God decides who shall live and who shall die during the coming year. The liturgy prayers attempt to influence God's decisions.

One powerful instrument used to motivate repentance during Rosh ha-Shana is the *shofar* (ram's horn), which is blown in the synagogue one hundred times on each of the two days of Rosh ha-Shana. When one of the two days falls on the Sabbath, the *shofar* is not blown.

*Maimonides describes the goal of the piercing cry of the *shofar* as "an allusion, as if to say, 'Awake, O you sleepers, awake from your sleep! O you slumberers, awake from your slumber! Search your deeds and turn in *teshuva [repentance].' "

Blowing the *shofar* is not as simple as blowing a horn. It requires a compression of the lips that is difficult to perform, and even experienced *shofar* blowers often have to make several attempts before achieving the right sound. Three specific notes are blown on Rosh ha-Shana: an unbroken sound, called *teki'ah*; a wailing sound broken into three parts, known as *shva'rim*; and a sobbing sound broken into nine parts, called *tru'ah*.

The Rosh ha-Shana prayer service is long—the only one longer is the service on *Yom Kippur—and usually runs from the early morning until one-thirty or two in the afternoon. Even small congregations that cannot afford a full-time cantor try to hire someone with a commanding voice to lead the High Holy Day services. Because there are so many special prayers that are distinctive to Rosh ha-Shana and Yom Kippur, a special prayerbook known as the *Makhzor is used on these holidays.

One of the most famous prayers in the Rosh ha-Shana liturgy, the *U-ne-ta-neh Toh-kef*, addresses a fundamental theme of the holiday: life and death. "On Rosh ha-Shana," the prayer reads, "it is written, and on Yom Kippur it is sealed, how many shall leave this world, and how many shall be born into it, who shall live and who shall die, who shall live out the limit of his days and who shall not, who shall perish by fire and who by water . . . who shall be at peace and who shall be tormented. . . . But penitence, prayer, and good deeds can annul the severity of the decree." Famous also is the *Avinu Malkeinu* (Our Father, Our King) prayer. Traditionally, the entire congregation sings the last verse in unison: "*Avinu Malkeinu, khaneinu va-aneinu, kee ein banu ma'asim. Asei eemanu *tzedaka va-khesed vehoshee-einu*—Our Father, our King, answer us as though we have no deeds to plead our cause; save us with mercy and loving-kindness."

The theme of life and death could easily have turned Rosh ha-Shana into two days of morbidity. To prevent this, the rabbis encouraged Jews to observe Rosh ha-Shana in a spirit of optimism, confident that God will accept their repentance and extend their lives. For example, they ordained that honey be served at all Rosh ha-Shana meals, and that slices of apple be dipped into it. A special prayer is then recited: "May it be Thy will, O Lord, Our God, to grant us a year that is good and is sweet."

SOURCES AND FURTHER READINGS: The Maimonides quote is from his *Mishneh Torah*, "Laws of Repentance," 3:4; I have followed the translation in S. Y. Agnon, *Days of Awe*, pp. 72–73. The translation from the prayerbook is that of Jules Harlow, ed., *Mahzor*, pp. 241, 243, 753. See also Agnon, *Days of Awe*, and the books mentioned in the note to entry 296.

298

TASHLIKH

THE PROPHETIC BOOKS OF THE BIBLE SELDOM SERVE AS A SOURCE FOR Jewish laws or customs. Yet the Jewish practice known as *Tashlikh* (Hebrew for "throw") is derived from a verse from the prophet *Micah, "And You [God] shall throw their sins into the depths of the sea" (7:19). Based on the prophet's words, a Jewish custom arose during the Middle Ages. On the first day of Rosh ha-Shana (see preceding entry) Jews go to a river and symbolically cast their sins into the water. In many communities, people pull out their pockets and shake them, emptying them of the sins they contained. (If the first day of Rosh ha-Shana falls on the Sabbath, the ceremony is deferred until the second day.) If no nearby river is available, one may observe *Tashlikh* at a reservoir or at any body of water.

I once spent Rosh ha-Shana as a guest of the Jewish community in Tokyo. The Jews there carried out the *Tashlikh* ceremony at a reservoir. The rabbi, Marvin Tokayer, told me that several years earlier he had led a group of men to the reservoir, they had shaken out their pockets over the water and recited the appropriate verses. Suddenly, a group of policemen descended; they had been summoned by a Japanese woman who had seen a procession of well-dressed Western men throwing something into the Tokyo water system.

"What did you put in the water?" a policeman asked the rabbi.

"Nothing."

"Are you saying that the woman lied? We must know what you put in, so that we can put in an antidote."

Rabbi Tokayer explained that they had cast their sins into the water.

One policeman checked the English-Japanese dictionary he had brought along, but because there is no concept precisely analogous to "sin" in Japanese, the word did not appear.

Rabbi Tokayer finally succeeded in conveying to the officers that nothing tangible had been put into the reservoir, and the group was allowed to leave. Many Jews, feeling they should throw something tangible into the water, cast in bread crumbs or small pieces of bread to symbolize the sins they are discarding.

In recent years, for reasons that have nothing to do with the ceremony itself, *Tashlikh* has become a very social *mitzvah. People often descend on the same body of water from different neighborhoods, where they encounter friends and acquaintances they may not have seen since the preceding *Tashlikh*. Partially for that reason—even though the ceremony itself is solemn—*Tashlikh* has become more widely observed.

299

"TEN DAYS OF REPENTANCE"/*ASERET Y'MEI TESHUVA*

"May You Be Inscribed for a Good Year"/Le-Shana Tova Teekataivu

DURING THE WEEKS BEFORE ROSH HA-SHANA, AND CONTINUING through Yom Kippur, Jews traditionally greet each other with *"Le-shana tova teekataivu*—May you be inscribed for a good year." The "inscription" referred to is based on a verse in *Psalms (69:29) which speaks of a "book of life" into which God inscribes the names of the righteous. Jewish folklore teaches that God writes down the names of all who will live through the coming year into this Book of Life.

Of course, Judaism does not believe in a literal Book of Life. God's memory presumably suffices to recall each person's fate; He does not need to write down names. Nonetheless, folk imagination has long endowed the Books of Life and Death with a tangible existence, and during prayers many Jews imagine the two books open in front of God. The *Talmud itself speaks of three books: Those who are clearly righteous are immediately inscribed in the Book of Life, those who are clearly wicked in the Book of Death, and all others are classified as *beinonim* (in the middle), and their fate is decided between Rosh ha-Shana and Yom Kippur. In Jewish tradition today, all Jews are advised to consider themselves *beinonim*.

For that reason, the days between Rosh ha-Shana and Yom Kippur assume tremendous significance; how one acts during these days may well influence God's decree. This ten-day period is known as the "Ten Days of Repentance" (*Aseret Y'mei Teshuva*), and during this time, religious Jews take special care to give to charity, to avoid gossiping (see *Tzedaka* and *Lashon ha-Ra*), and to be helpful to others. If one has a big favor to ask of a religious Jew, it is not a bad idea to wait until the *Aseret Y'mei Teshuva* to do so.

SOURCES AND FURTHER READINGS: S. Y. Agnon, *Days of Awe*, and the books mentioned in the note to entry 296.

300

YOM KIPPUR

Kol Nidrei
Ne'ilah

THE ERRONEOUS PERCEPTION OF YOM KIPPUR AS A DAY OF SADNESS IS due in large measure to it being a fast day. The holiday's goal, however, is to bring about reconciliation between people, and between individuals and God. Concerning the character of the holiday, the rabbis of the Talmud wrote: "There were no days as happy for the Jewish people as the fifteenth of [the Hebrew month of] Av [a day on which marriages were arranged] and Yom Kippur" (*Mishna Ta'anit* 4:8).

Another popular myth about Yom Kippur is that all-day attendance at synagogue, accompanied by earnest praying, wins forgiveness from God for all sins. In fact, the only sins forgiven on Yom Kippur are those committed against God.

As for offenses committed against other people, the Mishna writes, "Yom Kippur does not atone until [one] appeases his neighbors" (*Mishna Yoma* 8:9).

Therefore, Jewish tradition encourages people to begin the process of repenting (see *Teshuva*) well in advance of the holiday. If one has injured or offended another person, one is obliged to request forgiveness sincerely. Even if the request is refused initially, at least two more attempts at reconciliation should be made. The victim of the offense likewise is required to be forgiving, provided the request for forgiveness is made sincerely. The rabbis regard a person as cruel who withholds forgiveness even after three requests. Obviously, this designation would not necessarily apply if the offense committed was extreme or if it inflicted irrevocable damage.

Yom Kippur is the only fast day mandated in the Torah (Leviticus 23:27; the verse specifically speaks of "afflicting your souls"). The fast commences an hour before the holiday begins, and concludes twenty-five hours later. On Yom Kippur, Jews are also forbidden to drink any liquid, bathe, engage in sexual relations, or wear leather shoes. The latter prohibition was intended to somewhat diminish comfort on this holiday of introspection. A popular modern explanation for the ban on leather shoes suggests that it would be presumptuous to appear before God asking for mercy while wearing shoes made from the skin of a slaughtered animal. As a result of this ban, traditional Jews dress incongruously on Yom Kippur—attired in their most formal suits and dresses, but with running or tennis shoes on their feet.

The last meal before the holiday is known as the *se'uda mafseket* (closing meal). It is usually a fairly light early dinner; traditionally, boiled chicken is served. Many Jews serve only one course. Salty and spicy foods are avoided so as not to make the fasters thirsty.

Children under age nine are forbidden to fast and are served regular meals. Children older than nine are encouraged to eat less than usual during the holiday, but not to fast the whole twenty-five hours. Females, twelve years and older, and males, thirteen years and older, are obligated to fast the whole day (see *Bar and Bat Mitzvah*). Anyone suffering from a potentially life-threatening illness, and women who have given birth in the preceding three days, are freed from the requirement of fasting. Pregnant women who feel tremendous hunger pangs are given the option of eating something until their hunger abates. A general operative principle in Jewish law is that endangerment of life takes precedence over observance of the law (for the few exceptions to this principle, see *Where Life Is at Stake/Pikuakh Nefesh*).

Yom Kippur has the longest synagogue service of any day in the Jewish year.

On the first night, the service is inaugurated with a haunting prayer called the *Kol Nidrei* (All Vows). In this prayer, one asks to be released in advance from any vows made and not kept. In the nineteenth century, Samson Raphael *Hirsch, the leading figure of German Orthodox Judaism, suspended recitation of the *Kol Nidrei* for several years, fearing that it would cause non-Jews to think that Jews do not feel obligated to fulfill their oaths. In actuality, the release requested in the *Kol Nidrei* does not apply to vows made to other people.

The service on the day of Yom Kippur generally lasts from morning till nightfall; in many synagogues, there is a break for a few hours during the mid-afternoon. A characteristic, recurring prayer is the *Al Khet* (For Sins [that we have committed]), an acrostic in which one confesses to a multitude of sins committed during the previous year. While reciting the prayer, people beat their fists lightly against their chests as they enumerate each of the sins. The overwhelming majority of offenses designated in the *Al Khet* prayer are moral: wronging others, deriding parents and teachers, using foul speech, being dishonest in business, swearing falsely, and gossiping.

The strangest *Al Khet* confession reads, "For sins that we have committed under duress." Generations of Jews have pondered how an act committed under duress could be regarded as a sin. The late Jewish scholar Ernst Simon suggested, however, that although people sometimes claim they were forced to do something, very often it is not true. As Supreme Court Justice Louis *Brandeis once wrote, "The irresistible is often only that which is not resisted."

The sins enumerated in the *Al Khet* prayer are confessed to in the plural. Even if one has not committed the particular offense mentioned, Jewish tradition teaches that each Jew bears a certain measure of responsibility for sins committed by other Jews.

During the afternoon *minkha* service, the Book of Jonah is read. Its predominant theme is God's willingness to grant forgiveness to those who sincerely repent (see *Jonah and the Whale*).

The final Yom Kippur service is called *Ne'ilah* (Shutting) because of the prayer imagery, which refers to the "shutting of the gates." Jewish tradition regards Yom Kippur as the day on which God decides the fate of each human being. As the holiday comes to an end, the liturgy vividly depicts gates beginning to close. During the *Ne'ilah* service, people pray with special intensity, hoping to be admitted to God's loving presence before the gates leading to Him are closed. At the very end of Yom Kippur, a single long note is sounded on the *shofar*.

Given the life-and-death issues dominating the day of Yom Kippur, why *does* the Talmud regard it as a happy day? Because by its end, people experience a great catharsis. If they have observed the holiday properly, they have made peace with everyone they know, and with God. By the time the fast ends, many people therefore feel a deep sense of serenity.

SOURCES AND FURTHER READINGS: See the list of books mentioned in the note to entry 296.

301

SUKKOT, SUKKA,
LULAV AND ETROG
SHMINI ATZERET

TISHREI IS THE JEWISH MONTH MOST FILLED WITH HOLIDAYS. IT starts with Rosh ha-Shana, followed just over a week later by Yom Kippur. Then, only four days after Yom Kippur, comes the longest Jewish festival, in which three distinct holidays are combined into one continuous celebration: Sukkot, Shmini Atzeret, and Simkhat Torah.

Prior to the start of Sukkot, Jews are instructed to erect a *sukka*, a temporary dwelling large enough for a family to eat and live in. While many Jews build *sukkot*, very few people today live in the *sukka* during the holiday. The *sukka* symbolizes the booths or tents in which the Jewish people lived during their forty years wandering in the desert (Leviticus 23:42–43). The walls are normally made of wood or canvas, and the whole structure is covered by *sekhakh*, a covering that must be made of material that grows in the ground and has been detached from it. Usually, cut branches, plants, or bamboo sticks are used. The *sekhakh* should loosely cover the roof, so that people inside the *sukka* still can see the sky and stars.

Children characteristically decorate the *sukka* with beautiful fruits and with signs quoting verses from the Bible or depicting beautiful scenes from Israel. In Jerusalem the municipality annually conducts a contest to find the most beautiful *sukka* in the city.

According to Jewish law, all food eaten during Sukkot should be eaten in the *sukka*. At the meal's beginning, a special blessing is made to God "who has commanded us to dwell in the *sukka*." If there is heavy rain, the requirement to eat in the *sukka* is suspended, although on the first night of the holiday, Jews wait until midnight before giving up on having a meal in the *sukka*.

Sukkot also is an agricultural holiday (Leviticus 23:39), celebrating the harvest in the land of Israel. Special prayers are recited during which one holds four varities of plants in one's hands (Leviticus 23:40). The largest of these plants is the *lulav* (palm branch), which is bound together with two willow twigs and three myrtle twigs. The fourth plant is the *etrog* (citron), which looks like a large, somewhat elongated lemon. Jews try to acquire an *etrog* with no blotches, spots, or other discoloration on the skin. To be ritually valid, the *pitom*, the stem at the tip of the *etrog*, must be unbroken.

Non-Jews and irreligious Jews are often shocked to learn that pious Jews routinely spend fifty, even one hundred dollars or more for a perfect *etrog*. On the Sunday before Sukkot, one can find an active outdoor market where *lulavim* and *etrogim* are being sold, on Manhattan's Lower East Side. On occasion, I have seen people inspecting *etrogim* with magnifying glasses to ensure that the skin is unblemished. In all of Israel's major cities, there are also active markets where one can purchase the four plants.

During certain prayers on Sukkot, congregants wave the *lulav* and *etrog* together, up and down, left and right. The Talmud teaches that we wave toward the four points of the world in honor of God, to whom the four corners of the world—upward and downward, heaven and earth—belong (*Sukkot* 37b).

On each morning of Sukkot, near the end of the prayer service, men carry the *lulav* and *etrog* around the synagogue while reciting a penitential prayer. On the holiday's seventh day, Hoshana Rabba, all the Torah scrolls are withdrawn from the Ark, and the congregants march around the synagogue seven times carrying the *lulav* and *etrog*.

The eighth day of the holiday is known as Shmini Atzeret. Its major feature is the recitation of the prayer for rain; the holiday falls at the beginning of Israel's rainy season. Rabbi Irving Greenberg has called Shmini Atzeret the "Zionist holiday" because it kept alive a strong identification between world Jewry and the land of Israel. Reciting the prayer for rain when it was needed in Israel, and not in their native lands, "was the Jews' way of maintaining an unbroken tie, a statement that as Jews they were living on

Jerusalem Standard Time, not Greenwich Meridian or Central Mountain Time."

ON SUKKOT AND THE JEWISH HISTORICAL CONDITION

The sukka provides a corrective to the natural tendency of becoming excessively attached to turf. It instructs Jews not to become overly rooted, particularly not in the exile. For thousands of years Jews built homes in the Diaspora, and civilization of extraordinary richness . . . were created. But, outside of Israel, all such Jewish homes and civilizations have proven thus far to be temporary ones, blown away when a turn of the wheel brought new forces to power. Often, self-deception and the desire to claim permanent roots led Jews to deny what was happening until it was too late to escape (Irving Greenberg, *The Jewish Way: Living the Holidays*, p. 101).

SOURCES AND FURTHER READINGS: Irving Greenberg's comment on Sukkot as a "Zionist holiday" is found in his *The Jewish Way: Living the Holidays*, p. 109. See also Isaac Klein, *A Guide to Jewish Religious Practice*, pp. 155–173, and the books mentioned in the note to entry 296. In 2004, *Ushpizin*, a beautiful Israeli film dealing with Sukkot and a poor newly religious family's attempt to celebrate it properly, was released internationally.

302

KHOL HA-MOED

KHOL HA-MOED IS THE ONLY HEBREW OXYMORON WITH WHICH I AM familiar; *khol* means "secular" and *moed* means "holiday." The "secular holidays" referred to are the days that fall in the middle of *Passover and *Sukkot. Both these holidays start and finish with two days of *Yom Tov* (literally "good day," it is observed for only one day in Israel), during which work is forbidden and there are extended prayer services. Between the two sets of *Yom Tov* come four days of Khol ha-Moed on Passover and five on Sukkot. During these days, the prohibitions of work are greatly relaxed. Aside from that, the distinctive features of each holiday remain in force; on Passover one must not eat bread or any leavened products, and on Sukkot one must eat all meals in a *sukka*. At the conclusion of Khol ha-Moed come the final days of *Yom Tov*, during which the restrictions on work again apply.

In line with its unusual name, Khol ha-Moed days have both a weekday and holiday quality. Although the rabbis of the *Talmud wanted the holiday quality to dominate, even most religious Jews regard Khol ha-Moed as more akin to weekdays than holy days. Indeed, one reason the Khol ha-Moed period might have been mandated was to extend the sense of holiday without compelling people to refrain from working for more than a week. In Israel Khol ha-Moed is a special time for children; schools are closed and joyous outings are arranged.

If a death occurs on Khol ha-Moed, the funeral takes place immediately, unlike on the *Sabbath or *Yom Tov*, when funerals are forbidden. Aside from funerals and burials, all other mourning observances (see *Shiva*) are suspended until after the holiday.

An entire tractate of the Talmud deals with the special laws of Khol ha-Moed. The tractate's name, *Moed Kattan* (*Little Holiday*), reflects the rabbis' ambiguity about these days.

SOURCES AND FURTHER READINGS: See the list of books mentioned in the note to entry 296.

303

SIMKHAT TORAH

Hakafot

ALMOST FIFTEEN HUNDRED YEARS AGO, *MOHAMMED LABELED THE Jews "the people of the Book." The book to which Islam's founder was referring was, of course, the Bible. Nothing better conveys the Jewish attachment to the Torah than Simkhat Torah (literally, "Rejoicing in the Law"), one of the most joyous of Jewish holidays.

Simkhat Torah marks the completion of the annual cycle of Torah read-ings. Each week throughout the year, a portion of the Torah is read (see *Torah Portion of the Week/Parshat ha-Shavua*): On Simkhat Torah, Jews fin-ish reading the last verses of Deuteronomy, then immediately start the cycle anew by reciting the first verses of Genesis. While the equally happy holidays of *Purim and *Hanukka celebrate Jewish victories over enemies trying to wipe them out, Simkhat Torah has only positive associations: delight at hav-ing completed the study of God's word, and joy at the opportunity to start studying His words again.

The holiday is celebrated on the twenty-third of *Tishrei* (in Israel, it is observed on the twenty-second), right after the end of *Sukkot and *Shmini Atzeret. During the morning service of Simkhat Torah, traditional congre-gations divide into small prayer groups, each using one of the synagogue's Torah scrolls. This multiplicity of *minyanim* (prayer groups) enables every member of the synagogue to be called up to bless the Torah (see *Aliyah*).

Although Jewish law forbids boys under the age of thirteen from having an *aliyah* (see *Bar Mitzvah*), they too are summoned to the Torah on this day, accompanying a parent or other adult who has been called up to bless the Torah. In most non-Orthodox congregations, women and girls are also given an *aliyah*.

Although the atmosphere in most traditional synagogues is normally quite informal, the lack of decorum during the Simkhat Torah morning service can become extreme. Congregants sometime drink liquor even as the service is taking place, and people think nothing of intentionally drown-ing out the cantor's voice with lyrics of their own. I have powerful memories of Simkhat Torah at the congregation where my grandfather was the rabbi. One of our favorite activities as children was to tie together shoelaces of two different men, and watch when one of them tried to walk away.

For all the hilarity at the morning service, however, the highlight takes place the preceding evening, at the beginning of the holiday. The Torah scrolls are removed from the Ark and handed to the congregation's most prominent members. They march around the circumference of the syna-gogue, and everyone kisses the Torah scrolls as they pass. This ceremony is known as a *hakafah* (plural, *hakafot*), which means "to march around" or "to encompass." When the marchers arrive back in front of the Ark, other con-gregants circle around and dance with them. The whole time, the marchers continue to carry the Torah scrolls, which is no small feat; a full-sized Torah can weigh twenty to thirty pounds.

After the singing and dancing has gone on for ten or twenty minutes, a new group is entrusted with the Torah scrolls: A second *hakafah* is begun and the joyous ritual continues through seven *hakafot* in all.

While Simkhat Torah has long been one of Judaism's happiest days, the holiday's observance received a tremendous inspiration in recent years from the Jews of Russia. During the 1960s, Soviet Jews adopted Simkhat Torah as their special day of celebration; among many Russian Jews, it became more widely observed than *Passover or *Yom Kippur (see *Russian-Jewish Simkhat Torah Celebrations*). Although from the perspective of Jewish law, Simkhat Torah is less significant than either Passover or Yom Kippur, Soviet Jews were so limited in the Jewish rituals they could practice (or were knowledgeable about) that they instinctively chose to identify with a holiday that is totally joyous.

SOURCES AND FURTHER READINGS: See the list of books mentioned in the note to entry 296.

304

HANUKKA

Menorah
Dreidl

A JEWISH PROVERB CLAIMS THAT EVERYTHING DEPENDS ON LUCK, even the fate of a Torah scroll in the Ark (if a particular scroll is lucky, it will be the one chosen to be read publicly; if it is unlucky, it will be left in the Ark and another scroll will be chosen).

Hanukka's good fortune in the Western world results from a singularly un-Jewish circumstance, its close proximity to Christmas. The holiday begins on the twenty-fifth of *Kislev*: Because of the vagaries of the Jewish lunar calendar, this can occur any time between late November and late December. In the United States, Hanukka is the most widely observed Jewish holiday after *Passover and *Yom Kippur, although in Jewish law it is less significant than the *Sabbath, or *Rosh ha-Shana, *Sukkot, and *Shavuot.

Because Western Jews live in a predominantly Christian society, and because of Hanukka's proximity to Christmas, many parents have converted it into a Jewish form of this major Christian holiday. Jewish children are given daily gifts throughout the holiday. By making it into a fun-filled occasion, many parents hope that their children will not feel they are missing out on Christmas trees and gifts brought by Santa Claus. For many years, my father was the accountant for a Jewish company that produced Hanukka candles, toys, and decorations. The closer Hanukka fell to Christmas, the more business the company did.

Hanukka is, indeed, one of the happiest of Jewish holidays. In 167 B.C.E., the Syrian emperor *Antiochus set out to destroy Judaism by making its observance a capital offense. In one horrible instance, two Jewish mothers who had secretly circumcised their sons were paraded through the streets of Jerusalem and then executed along with the infants. A Jew named *Mattathias, along with his five sons, initiated a revolt against the Syrian monarch. Three years later, the rebels ousted Antiochus's troops from Palestine.

The Jewish revolutionaries, known as *Maccabees or *Hasmoneans, regained control of the *Temple in Jerusalem, which during the years of Syrian control had been spiritually raped. Antiochus had even arranged for swine to be sacrificed in the Temple. The Jewish troops wept when they saw the Temple's degradation, and immediately resolved to restore it to a state of ritual purity. According to Jewish tradition, they could find only one cruse of uncontaminated olive oil; unfortunately, it contained oil sufficient for only one day. The Jews were very upset because it would take eight days to prepare ritually permitted oil. However, a miracle happened and the small quantity of oil continued to burn the full eight days.

In commemoration of this happy event, Hanukka is celebrated for eight days. On the first night, one candle is lighted, on the second, two candles, and so on, until the last night, when eight candles are lighted. The candles are placed in a *menorah*, a candelabrum that has eight openings, and a ninth, elevated opening known as a *shamash*. The *shamash* candle, which is lit first, is used to light the others.

Jewish law dictates that the candles be placed near a window, so that passersby can see them from the street. This is in fulfillment of the rabbinic dictum "to publicize the miracle." Indeed, this is the sole function of the Hanukka candles; it is forbidden to use them for any other purpose; one cannot, for example, read by the Hanukka lights (it is fully permissible, however, to use the Sabbath lights for illumination). During the time the candles are burning, it is also customary that women relax and not work.

A popular Hanukka children's game is spinning the *dreidl*, a four-sided cylindrical figure that spins like a top. On each side, a Hebrew letter is printed: *Nun, Gimmel, Hay, Shin*, which make the acronym "*Nes Gadol Haya Sham*—A Great Miracle Happened There [in Israel]." Bets are taken on what letter will be showing when the *dreidl* stops spinning. If it stops on the *nun*, no one wins; on the *gimmel*, the spinner takes the pot; on the *hay*, half the pot; and on the *shin*, he or she puts money into the pot.

Among American Jews, the *latke*, a pancake made of potatoes and onions fried in oil, is the food most associated with Hanukka. And because the Hanukka miracle concerned oil, all the preferred holiday foods are fried in oil; in Israel the most popular Hanukka delicacy is the *sufganiyah*, a fried jelly roll.

SOURCES AND FURTHER READINGS: See the list of books mentioned in the note to entry 296.

TU B'SHVAT

JUST AS JEWISH TRADITION REGARDS THE FIRST DAY OF *TISHREI* AS THE New Year (*Rosh ha-Shana) for mankind, so it regards the fifteenth day of *Shvat* as the New Year for trees. Tu B'Shvat—*tu* expresses the number fifteen in Hebrew—generally falls between mid-January and mid-February, and is celebrated in Israel by planting trees. Many American and European Jews observe the holiday by making contributions to the Jewish National Fund, which uses the funds to develop forests in Israel. The holiday, however, is an old one, predating the State of Israel by thousands of years.

Throughout the world, religious Jews strive to eat foods on Tu B'Shvat that are distinctive to, or characteristic of, the land of Israel, specifically the seven types of fruits and grains mentioned in Deuteronomy 8:8. When I was a child, my father used to bring home an Israeli-grown carob, a fruit with the decidedly un-Jewish name of St. John's Bread. In Yiddish it was known as *buxer*. Carob is incredibly hard and has little taste, though I have been told that if it is eaten right after falling from the tree, it is deliciously sweet.

Some Jews, basing themselves on a tradition initiated by Jewish mystics (see *Kabbalah*) in the sixteenth century, make a special *Seder on Tu B'Sh-vat, largely modeled on the structure of the *Passover Seder: Four cups of wine, for example, are served during the meal. Thirteen biblical verses that speak of the vegetation of Israel are read, and many different foods are blessed and eaten. Among the foods served at such a Seder are olives, dates, grapes, figs, pomegranates, apples, walnuts, carob fruit, pears, cherries, sunflower seeds, and peanuts. Currently, the Tu B'Shvat Seder is not widely observed; in recent years, however, it has become increasingly popular among mystically and ecologically oriented Jews.

SOURCES AND FURTHER READINGS: See the list of books mentioned in the note to entry 296, particularly Irving Greenberg, *The Jewish Way*, pp. 418–420.

306

PURIM

PERHAPS THE ODDEST COMMANDMENT IN JEWISH LAW IS THE ONE ASSO-ciated with Purim in which Jews are instructed to get drunk until they can no longer differentiate between "Blessed is *Mordechai," and "Cursed is *Haman."

Although recovering alcoholics, people with health problems, those planning to drive, and pretty much anyone who doesn't want to do it are freed from observing this commandment, a fair number of Jews do get drunk on Purim. After all, how often can one do something normally regarded as wrong, and be credited with fulfilling a commandment?

The obligation to drink stems largely from Purim's being one of the happiest holidays in the Jewish calendar. Haman, an ancient Persian forerunner of *Hitler, plotted to kill all the Jews. They foiled his plan, however, and then avenged themselves on this would-be mass murderer and his supporters (see *Esther*).

The rabbis were so enamored of Purim that they declared in a maxim, "From the beginning of *Adar* [the month in which Purim falls], we increase our happiness" (*Ta'anit* 29a). In fact, they predicted that Purim would be observed even in the messianic days, when almost all other Jewish holidays would be abolished (*Midrash Mishlei* 9).

Purim is observed on the fourteenth of *Adar*, just a month and a day before *Passover; in Jerusalem, Hebron, and the Old City of Safed, the holiday is observed one day later. This odd scheduling is because a statement in the Book of Esther (9:18–19) ordains that Purim be observed one day later in walled cities (Jerusalem was still a walled city at the time Esther was written). Thus, in Israel anyone so inclined can observe Purim twice, on the fourteenth of *Adar* throughout most of the country, and on the fifteenth in Jerusalem, Hebron, and the Old City of Safed.

Women as well as men are commanded to hear the public reading of the biblical scroll of *Esther. The reading is conducted in the synagogue amid much revelry. Almost all children, and some adults, come to the service with *groggers* (noisemakers), which they sound whenever Haman's name is read. Since Haman is mentioned more than fifty times in Esther, the reading is constantly interrupted by shouts, screams, boos, and the rattling of *groggers*. Because Jewish law requires people to hear every word of the scroll of Esther, the person chanting the book is forbidden to resume until the noise abates.

While Jews normally come to synagogue in suits and dresses, their attire on the playful holiday of Purim is more likely to be costumes and masks. Although many women model themselves on Queen *Esther and many men on Mordechai, I have seen people come to services dressed as robots or as members of the Women's Liberation Army of Shushan (the Persian city where the Purim story takes place).

The synagogue service is usually followed by a party where the command to get drunk is carried out. Very often, members of the congregation perform skits based on the Purim story (see *Esther*). At many *yeshivot, *Purimshpiels* are performed, and fun is poked—through plays and skits—at the school, its teachers and rabbis, as well as at traditional texts that are usually treated with reverence.

Another Purim commandment is to send *mishloakh manot* (gifts of food and drink) to other Jews. The minimum gift one must give is two portions of different foods; they must require no preparation but be ready to eat. In recent years, as the Jewish community has become more affluent, *mishloakh manot* have grown more elaborate, and many people send them to large numbers of friends.

On Purim one is commanded to be charitable to everyone, even to beggars whose requests for charity one has reason to believe are bogus. On this day of unbridled joy, no questions are to be asked. When I was a student at *Yeshiva University, there were two women who used to accost students every morning and afternoon, asking for money. A rabbi I knew there—a generous man—never contributed to them; he told me he knew for a fact that they had independent and substantial means. Nonetheless, on Purim he made sure to give them a donation.

Throughout Jewish history, many communities and families established their own special Purim holidays to commemorate annually the anniversaries of events in which Jewish communities or individuals were saved from death at the hands of antisemites. In the 1970s, a prominent American rabbi was among those kidnapped and held hostage by Muslim terrorists at the *B'nai B'rith headquarters in Washington, D.C. All the hostages survived, and subsequently, the rabbi conducted an annual special Purim celebration with his family on the Hebrew date on which he was released.

Another commandment associated with the holiday is to enjoy a large, festive repast known as the Purim *se'udah* (meal). The dessert normally served at this meal, and eaten throughout the whole holiday, is *hamantashen*, small cakes of baked dough filled with prunes, apricot, poppy seed, or other filling. During the *Birkat ha-Mazon (Grace After Meals), a special prayer is recited, thanking God for the miracles that occurred during the days of Mordechai.

The observance of Purim was apparently well known to the Nazi leadership. Julius Streicher, perhaps the most vicious antisemite among the defendants at the *Nuremberg Trials, shouted out as he was marched to the gallows, *"Purimfest."*

SOURCES AND FURTHER READINGS: See the list of books mentioned in the note to entry 296.

307

MA'OT CHITTIM

PASSOVER (SEE NEXT ENTRY) IS THE MOST EXPENSIVE OF JEWISH HOLI-days. One needs to have a special set of both milk and meat dishes that cannot be used the rest of the year; also, almost all regular food supplies must either be discarded or locked away during the holiday's eight days. Finally, one must purchase large quantities of *matzah and other foods.

Concerned over the economic strain Passover imposed on poor Jews, the rabbis established an annual fundraising campaign, known as *Ma'ot Chittim*, whose sole purpose is to enable all Jews to observe Passover. This charity has been taken very seriously throughout Jewish history and in Jewish communities throughout the world. My grandfather, who was the rabbi in a small *shtetl* in Russia, would go to every single house in the village before Passover: "There was only one rule. Every Jewish family had to either give or receive help." Because he and one other man visited every house in the village, no one else knew the identity of the people who needed help.

A famous story is told of the nineteenth-century rabbi Yosef Dov Soloveitchik. A man once came to him with a legal question. "Can I use milk rather than wine," he asked, "to satisfy the requirement of four cups [of wine] at the *Seder?" Instead of answering the question, the rabbi simply gave him twenty-five rubles to buy the necessary provisions.

After the poor man left, a bystander asked the rabbi, "A few rubles would have been sufficient to buy the wine he needed. Why did you give him so much money?"

"If he was intending to use milk at the Seder," the rabbi answered, "it meant he had no money for meat either [Jewish law forbids the consumption of meat and milk at the same meal—see *Kosher*], and I wanted to ensure that he could observe the holiday properly."

In recent years, as many American Jews have become more affluent,

Ma'ot Chittim funds are sometimes used to airlift Seder provisions to poor Jews living in other countries, including the former Soviet Union. It must be remembered, however, that there are poor Jews in the United States, particularly elderly ones and the unemployed, who are in need of help.

PASSOVER/*PESACH*

Searching for Leaven/Bedikat Khametz

PASSOVER (PESACH) IS THE MOST WIDELY OBSERVED JEWISH HOLIDAY. It celebrates not only God's freeing the Jewish slaves from Egyptian slavery, but the beginning of Jewish nationhood as well.

The story of the first Passover dominates Exodus, the second book of the Torah. Pharaoh enslaved *Jacob's descendants, who were living in Egypt, and attempted to murder all male infants born to them. One of the Hebrew babies, *Moses, was saved by Pharaoh's daughter, who adopted him.

When Moses grew up, he saw an Egyptian overseer mercilessly whipping a Hebrew slave. He killed the overseer. Pharaoh, hearing what Moses had done, sought to kill him, and Moses was forced to flee Egypt.

Many years later, God summoned Moses from his exile in Midian to liberate the Egyptian Jews from slavery. When Pharaoh resisted Moses' entreaties to free the Hebrews, God afflicted Egypt with *Ten Plagues, the last of which was by far the most devastating: The firstborn son in every Egyptian family died, perhaps in retaliation for the earlier murder of the Hebrew infants.

The day before the killing of the firstborn, Moses instructed the Israelites to slaughter a lamb (an animal that was also an Egyptian deity), and to sprinkle some of its blood on their doorposts. Thus, when the Angel of Death saw the blood, he would know that the house was occupied by an Israelite and would *pass over* (in Hebrew, *pesach*) it when he came to slay the firstborn.

After the tenth plague began, Pharaoh became terrified and announced that the Hebrews were free to leave. They fled Egypt so quickly that the dough they had started to prepare for bread did not have sufficient time to rise. As a result, the slaves departed from Egypt with the flat bread that became known as matzah. Since that first Passover, Jews commemorate the holiday by eating matzah, which symbolizes, among other things, that it is better to live in freedom and eat poor food than to remain in slavery even if one eats well.

For most of the twelve hundred years after the Exodus, the major ritual of Passover was to bring a lamb to the *Temple in Jerusalem as a sacrifice, in commemoration of the sacrifice made by every Hebrew family that last day in Egypt. At the Temple, the lamb was first slaughtered by a priest, with part of the animal offered as a sacrifice, then the family who had brought it gathered together to eat the rest of the lamb. During the celebratory meal, parents and children engaged in a lengthy discussion of the Exodus, fulfilling the Torah's command that fathers tell their children the story of how God freed the Jews (Exodus 13:8, 14–15). This meal is the origin of the Passover Seder (see next entry).

Since the *destruction of the Second Temple in 70 c.e., Jews no longer offer animal sacrifices. Rather, the Seder now serves as the ritual commemoration of "the going forth from Egypt."

Bread products are forbidden during all eight days of the holiday (seven days in Israel). During the weeks preceding Passover, the house is systematically cleaned, and all bread and other *khametz* (leavened products) are removed. *Khametz* is any foodstuff containing flour that has fermented (such as breads, cakes, and pasta), and dough made from wheat, barley, rye, spelt, and oats. Whiskey and other alcoholic beverages made from fermented grain are also forbidden.

On the last night before the holiday, a ceremony called *bedikat khametz* (searching for the *khametz*), intended to arouse the curiosity of children, takes place. Even in modern, electrically equipped dwellings, every family member is given a lighted candle to carry around the house (to avoid any danger, some people use flashlights). Before the search begins, the parents strategically place ten small pieces of bread in different rooms. The searchers then find them and put them into bags. The following morning, these pieces of bread, along with all other *khametz* not previously discarded, are burned. *Khametz* that is too valuable to be destroyed can be sealed up and sold to a non-Jew for the duration of the holiday. It is sold because Jews are forbidden to own *khametz* during the holiday. Such sales are generally arranged through one's rabbi.

Of all the holidays, none falls harder on the Jewish housewife than Passover. The thorough cleaning of the house, coupled with the need to use different plates and silverware, cause much onerous work. Throughout Jewish history, some wealthy Jews would build an extra kitchen into their homes, which they would use only during the eight days of Passover. In recent years, it has become increasingly common for more affluent Jews to go away to *kosher hotels for the holiday.

SOURCES AND FURTHER READINGS: See the list of books mentioned in the note to entry 296.

309

HAGGADA

ASK JEWS WHO IS THE FIGURE THEY MOST ASSOCIATE WITH *PASSOVER and the *Exodus from Egypt, and the most likely answer will be *Moses. How surprising then that in the *Haggada*, the text that is read at the Passover Seder (see next entry), Moses' name is mentioned only once, and that in passing. The rabbis almost left him out to ensure that God remains the hero of the Passover story.

To commemorate the Exodus, the rabbis composed the *Haggada*, a small book that is read aloud at the Seder, the festive meal celebrated on Passover's first two nights (in Israel the Seder is celebrated only on the first night). Some parts of the *Haggada* quote the Torah, other parts were written some two thousand years ago, and still other parts date from the Middle Ages. Reading the *Haggada* aloud fulfills the Torah's command to all fathers to tell their children the story of the liberation from Egyptian slavery (Exodus 13:8, 14–15). Indeed, few other *mitzvot* have been as widely observed in Jewish history. For that reason, the *Haggada* is probably familiar to more Jews than is the Torah.

Perhaps the most famous passage in the *Haggada* is the Ma Nish-tana, which begins, "Why is this night different from all other nights?" The paragraph is recited by the youngest person at the Seder; for most Jewish children, this reading constitutes their first experience of public speaking. In the Ma Nish-tana, the child asks the reason behind some of the holiday's unusual rituals, for example, "On all other nights, we eat bread and matzah, why tonight do we only eat matzah?" The remainder of the *Haggada* is designed to answer the child's questions.

Another well-known passage speaks of four sons: one wise, one wicked, one simple, and one too young even to ask questions. The reading describes the different responses the father should give each child to inspire his or her observance of the holiday.

The spirit of Passover is summarized in one characteristic teaching of the *Haggada:* "In every generation, a man is obligated to regard himself as if he personally was liberated from Egypt." To reenact the experience of becoming free, some *Sephardic Jews have the custom of throwing a bag over their shoulders and walking around the table.

One of the familiar songs in the *Haggada* is a recurring refrain called "Dayeinu," which means "It would have been sufficient." The song recounts every miracle and kindness God performed for the Jews when He took them out of Egypt, and it insists that each one alone would have been sufficient. More than a few Jews have been puzzled by the line that reads: "If He had taken us out of Egypt but had not split the Red Sea, it would have been sufficient" (see *The Splitting of the Red Sea*). Had God not split the Red Sea, the Egyptians would have killed all the Hebrews and there would be no Jews today. The statement might be understood, rather, as an ecstatic declaration of faith, similar to the unrealistic verse at the end of the *Birkat ha-Mazon* (Grace After Meals), "I was a young man and now I am old, and never have I seen a righteous man deserted and his children lacking for bread."

One of the *Haggada*'s most famous songs is the one that concludes the Seder: "Had Gadya." The verses tell of a man who buys a goat for the very small sum of two *zuzim*. Unfortunately, a cat eats the goat, following which a dog bites the cat, a stick beats the dog, a fire burns the stick, water quenches the fire, an ox drinks the water, a slaughterer kills the ox, and the Angel of Death takes the slaughterer. Finally, God Himself comes and slays the Angel of Death. Jewish commentaries generally regard the goat as symbolizing the Jewish people, and the animals, objects, and elements that attack it and each other as standing for the nations that have subjugated Israel. Those who harass the Jews will ultimately be destroyed by others: In the end, God will vanquish the Angel of Death, and redeem the whole world.

After "Had Gadya," the Seder is concluded by singing, *"Le-Shana ha-Ba'ah Be-Yerushalayim* — Next Year in Jerusalem."

The *Haggada* is the most widely reprinted book in Jewish history; well over two thousand editions have been published since the first *Haggada* was printed in Spain about 1482. In the United States, each Jewish denomination has produced its own *Haggada*, and new editions of the *Haggada* are published every year.

SOURCES AND FURTHER READINGS: Among the more recent *Haggadot*, I have found Shlomo Riskin, *The Passover Haggadah*, to be particularly helpful to those leading a Seder. See also Daniel Goldschmidt, *The Passover Haggadah*, translated and edited by Nahum Glatzer. A fine book about the *Haggada* is Chaim Raphael, *A Feast of History*. A contemporary Jewish artist, David Moss, has produced a *Haggada* entitled, *A Song of David*, of stunning beauty and depth. Irving Greenberg has called it "a magnificent work of art, possibly the most beautiful *Haggada* of all time."

310

SEDER

MATZAH

MAROR

FOUR CUPS OF WINE

ELIJAH'S CUP

AFIKOMAN

THE PASSOVER SEDER COMBINES BOTH THE RELIGIOUS AND NATIONAL aspects of Jewish identity. Even the most secular, antireligious *kibbutzim in Israel conduct a Seder. Indeed, because the Seder celebrates the liberation of the Jewish slaves from Egypt, and commemorates the beginnings of the Jewish people, it appeals to identifying nonreligious and antireligious Jews.

The traditional Seder has more rituals than any other Jewish ceremonial meal. Most important, participants are expected to read through the *Haggada* (see preceding entry), a short book detailing the story of the Jewish Exodus from Egypt. At the Seder, participants are supposed to lean on pillows and recline in their chairs, in the style of free men of leisure.

The food that most typifies the Seder meal is matzah, a form of flat and unleavened bread (see *Passover*). Many observant Jews eat a special matzah during Passover, particularly during the two *Sedarim* (plural of Seder). This unleavened bread is called *shmurah matzah* (guarded matzah). From the time the wheat used in *shmurah matzah* is harvested, it is kept under guard to ensure that no water or leavening agents have contact with it.

Another Seder ritual involves eating *maror*, a bitter herb that represents the bitterness of Jewish servitude in Egypt. Oddly, one herb commonly used at Seders is romaine lettuce, which is not particularly bitter. Other Jews prefer horseradish, which would seem to represent more closely the bitterness of *maror*. Another food item, *kharoset*, is made of nuts and apples crushed together into a mortarlike substance; it symbolizes the mortar the slaves were required to produce for their Egyptian masters.

Despite the *maror* and *kharoset*, the Seder is basically a joyous meal. Its spirit of good cheer is most obviously represented by the four cups of wine drunk at various points during the recitation of the *Haggada*. Unless a Jew has a health problem that would be exacerbated by consuming liquor—alcoholism would be such a problem—he or she is expected to drink wine at the Seder. Jews who cannot or should not drink wine drink grape juice. The ancient rabbis disputed whether four or five cups should be drunk. Jewish law ultimately ruled that four cups were sufficient, but in deference to the minority view, a fifth cup of wine—Elijah's Cup—is filled and put on the table. According to Jewish legend, Elijah visits every Seder, and drinks a few drops from his cup. Jewish children invariably watch Elijah's cup during the "*She-fokh Kha-Matkha*—Pour Out Thy Wrath" prayer to see if there is any diminution in the contents. According to Jewish tradition, Elijah is the prophet who will announce the arrival of the Messiah. Presumably, he will also reveal at that time whether four or five cups are needed.

Some of the Seder's ceremonies are performed by children, such as the reading of the *Ma Nish-tana* ("Why is this night different from all other nights?"—see preceding entry). Since the Seder's goal is to teach children that the Jews once were slaves in Egypt, and that God led them out with "a strong hand and an outstretched arm," the rabbis introduced other rituals to ensure their active participation. For example, at the beginning of the Seder, three matzot are placed under a large cover. Early in the Seder, half of one matzah, known as the *afikoman*, is broken off and hidden away. At the end of the Seder meal, the *afikoman* is distributed to all participants. It is the last food Jews are commanded to eat at the Seder, and without it the traditional meal cannot be concluded. Children are encouraged to take advantage of this law, steal the *afikoman* from its hiding place, and hide it themselves. They then demand a ransom to reveal its whereabouts. All this is obviously done in good fun. It provides an opportunity for children to bargain for a toy or some other desired treat while ensuring their involvement in the Seder until the very end.

A friend of mine once volunteered to conduct a Seder inside an Israeli prison. Everything was done according to traditional Jewish law, he later told me, but the warden did announce that the stealing of the *afikoman* would not be permitted.

The Seder meal is interspersed with much singing and readings from the *Haggada*. At many Sedarim, the *Haggada* is read in both Hebrew and English to ensure that its contents are understood by all participants.

SOURCES AND FURTHER READINGS: See the list of books mentioned in the note to entry 296.

HOLOCAUST MEMORIAL DAY/YOM HA-SHOA

HOLOCAUST MEMORIAL DAY (YOM HA-SHOA) IS SO RECENT AN OBSERVANCE that it still has no set rituals. Only in Israel is there a uniformly observed practice: the sounding of sirens for two minutes throughout the country at eleven A.M. All people stop whatever they are doing and stand at attention. Highway traffic pulls over to the side of the road as the sirens begin; drivers park and exit their cars. As deeply moving as this observance is, no doubt other, more spiritual, practices will develop in the future to commemorate Yom ha-Shoa.

One problem with establishing rituals for Yom ha-Shoa is that the Holocaust's horror overwhelms the religious imagination. What ritual can adequately convey Auschwitz, and what the Nazis did there?

Another problem is that Jewish holidays generally express gratitude toward, and love of, God. For most Jews, those are hardly the emotions Yom ha-Shoa evokes. A number of years ago, I heard a prominent Orthodox rabbi suggest that Jews congregate in synagogues on Yom ha-Shoa—and say nothing. "They should sit there quietly," the rabbi said. "They should not say the *Kaddish* [the memorial prayer for the dead] because the prayer is really an exaltation of

God's greatness, and that is not what needs to be expressed on Yom ha-Shoa."

At a Jewish conference I attended, another rabbi suggested that the Holocaust be commemorated every Sabbath. Instead of serving the usual, rather luxurious, Sabbath lunch, he suggested that people eat a replica of the "meals" Jews ate at Auschwitz, such as rotting potatoes and stale poor bread. Such a ritual, it occurred to me, might ensure that Jews perpetually remember the Holocaust, but more likely it would lead to a diminution of Sabbath observance.

Yom ha-Shoa is observed on the twenty-seventh day of *Nissan*, which usually falls between mid-April and early May. This date was officially designated by the Israeli *Knesset, although the Israeli rabbinate had lobbied for the tenth of *Tevet*, one of the four minor fast days in the Jewish calendar (see *Minor Fast Days*). The tenth of *Tevet* commemorates the beginning of the siege of Jerusalem in 586 B.C.E., and the rabbinate felt it should commemorate the Holocaust as well. Many survivors and other Jews opposed this date, feeling strongly that the Holocaust was so momentous that it deserved its own commemoration.

Some secular Israelis also opposed the twenty-seventh of *Nissan*. In their opinion, only one day could adequately commemorate the Holocaust: April 19, 1943, which is when the Jews of the *Warsaw Ghetto launched their remarkable revolt against the Nazis. The suggestion was a sensible one, and it accorded with the official name the holiday was given in Israel, *Yom ha-Shoa ve-ha-Gevurah* (The [Memorial] Day for the Holocaust and for Acts of Courage). However, April 19, 1943, was also the fifteenth of *Nissan*, the first day of *Passover. This was no coincidence: The Nazis wanted to destroy the Warsaw Ghetto on one of the most joyous of Jewish holidays.

Had the Knesset agreed to make the fifteenth of *Nissan* Yom ha-Shoa, Jews observing the day would have gone about in a state of mourning, while the rest of Jewry would have observed the Passover *Seder in a state of joy.

As a compromise, the twenty-seventh of *Nissan* was chosen, a date that commemorates no particular Holocaust event. However, it does fall within the time span during which the Warsaw Ghetto uprising was fought, and occurs precisely one week before Israeli Independence Day (see next entry). The government wanted to underscore the connection between the murder of the six million and the creation, three years after the end of the war, of the Jewish state.

Unfortunately, some religious Jews resent the fact that this date was chosen, because of the long-standing tradition that *Nissan* (the month when the Jews were liberated from Egyptian slavery) is one of the happiest months in the Jewish calendar and must not be marred with sadness. (In fact, when a funeral occurs during *Nissan*, Jewish law states that no eulogies should be delivered. An exception is made for an important person; however, many rabbis will declare almost every person to be important, so that he or she can be honored with a eulogy.)

Another rarely articulated reason why some religiously right-wing Orthodox Jews do not observe Yom ha-Shoa is probably because they are afraid that observing the day will stimulate doubts about God, or anger at Him, rather than faith. Aside from these groups, however, Yom ha-Shoa is widely commemorated in the Orthodox world.

From year to year, observance of Yom ha-Shoa is becoming more prevalent in Jewish life. In the United States, an increasing number of synagogues hold special services during the evening, often bringing in lecturers to discuss the themes of the day. Many times, the speakers themselves are Holocaust survivors. For young Jews, hearing the story of the Nazis from a survivor is the only direct way they will learn about the Holocaust. By the year 2025, there will be very few *concentration camp survivors still alive.

That Yom ha-Shoa will become a permanent part of the Jewish calendar now seems certain. That it will be widely observed will largely be a function of developing rituals and liturgy that succeed in symbolically expressing some of the horrors and pain of the Holocaust.

SOURCE AND FURTHER READING: Irving Greenberg, *The Jewish Way*, pp. 314–372.

312

ISRAELI INDEPENDENCE DAY/YOM HA-ATZMA'UT

REMEMBRANCE DAY/YOM HA-ZIKARON

ISRAELI INDEPENDENCE DAY (YOM HA-ATZMA'UT) IS OBSERVED NOT only by Israelis but also by many Diaspora Jews. The day commemorates the declaration of Israeli statehood on May 14, 1948, the fifth of *Iyyar* in the Jewish calendar (see *Declaration of Israeli Independence*—1948). Yom ha-Atzma'ut is always celebrated on its Hebrew date.

In Israel the holiday is sometimes commemorated with a military parade, and always with partying. Among religious Jews, special prayers are recited, most notably *Hallel*, which is otherwise recited only on religiously mandated holidays. Some Orthodox Jews, whose feelings about Zionism are neutral or negative, have condemned the practice of treating Yom ha-Atzma'ut as a religious holiday. It is said that the noted Israeli rabbi Joseph Kahaneman was once asked if he said *Hallel* on Israeli Independence Day. The sharp-witted rabbi responded: "I act the same way as the [nonreligious] prime minister, David *Ben-Gurion. He doesn't say *Hallel*, and I don't say *Hallel*."

In New York, Los Angeles, and many other centers of Jewish life in the United States, large celebrations and marches are arranged on a Sunday that falls close to Yom ha-Atzma'ut.

The day before Yom ha-Atzma'ut is as somber as Yom ha-Atzma'ut is happy. It is called *Yom ha-Zikaron*, a day of remembrance for the approximately 24,000 Israelis killed in the Israeli-Arab wars. At eleven A.M. on Yom ha-Zikaron, all of Israel comes to a stop—all traffic, business, and conversation cease for two minutes of silence.

SOURCE AND FURTHER READING: Irving Greenberg, *The Jewish Way*, pp. 373–404.

LAG BA'OMER

THE ORIGINS OF THE HAPPY HOLIDAY OF LAG BA'OMER ARE SHROUDED in mystery. To this day, no Jewish scholar can state with certainty exactly what Lag Ba'Omer celebrates. The ancient rabbis speak, somewhat obscurely, of the cessation of a terrible plague that raged among Rabbi *Akiva's students on Lag Ba'Omer. But what sort of plague? If it was a physical illness, why did it apparently strike only talmudic scholars, and not the populace at large?

Most modern scholars assume that the plague referred to was not an illness. The second-century rabbi Akiva was a fervent supporter of Simon *Bar-Kokhba's rebellion against Rome. Moreover, he declared Bar-Kokhba the Messiah who would liberate the Jews from Roman domination. Although Bar-Kokhba did achieve some early military successes, eventually the Romans suppressed his revolt with incredible brutality. Among Bar-Kokhba's leading soldiers were, not surprisingly, thousands of Rabbi Akiva's students. Thus, it is likely that Lag Ba'Omer was a day on which the Jews either achieved a victory over the Romans or gained some respite from the slaughter.

The traditional observance of the holiday suggests some military origin: Children are taken to the park or countryside, where they often play games with bows and arrows.

The first word of the holiday's name, *Lag,* is simply a combination of two Hebrew letters, *lamed* (which stands for the number thirty) and *gimmel* (which stands for the number three). Lag Ba'Omer is so named because it falls on the thirty-third day of the counting of the *Omer* (see *The Omer*).

For many adult Jews, the primary association with Lag Ba'Omer is romantic. The seven weeks between *Passover and *Shavuot, the period in which Jews count the *Omer,* are regarded in Jewish law as a period of semimourning during which no marriages are to be performed. But because of Lag Ba'Omer's happy associations, the rabbis made an exception for this day.

Nowadays, most religious Jews who are Zionists also celebrate weddings on two other new Jewish holidays that fall during the period of the *Omer:* Israeli Independence Day/*Yom ha-Atzma'ut* (see preceding entry) and Jerusalem Day/*Yom Yerushalayim* (see next entry). Marriages also are permitted on the last days before Shavuot.

SOURCES AND FURTHER READINGS: See the list of books mentioned in the note to entry 296.

JERUSALEM DAY/YOM YERUSHALAYIM

JERUSALEM DAY (YOM YERUSHALAYIM), THE NEWEST JEWISH HOLIDAY, was declared in the aftermath of the 1967 *Six-Day War, during which Israel captured the Old City of Jerusalem, which contains the Temple's still-standing *Western Wall. When Israel's *War of Independence concluded in 1948, the Jewish state controlled the new city of Jerusalem, while Jordan held the Old City. In the subsequent armistice agreement, Jordan agreed to permit Jews to visit and pray at the Western Wall. This clause, however, was never honored, and for the nineteen years before the Six-Day War, the Jordanians forbade Jews from entering the Old City.

This was a particularly painful deprivation, since for Jews Jerusalem has been the holiest city since the reign of King *David, about 1000 B.C.E. Its liberation in 1967 was not only the high point of the Six-Day War, but one of the highlights of Israel's existence. Even today, although many Israelis would willingly trade land to the Arab world in return for peace, few would support returning the Jewish holy sites of Jerusalem to non-Jewish rule. As General Moshe *Dayan declared the day the Old City was captured, "Jerusalem is united, never again to be divided." For the first time in almost two thousand years the holiest spot in Jewish life was under Jewish control.

When Israel gained control of the entire city in 1967, frustrated and infuriated Muslim leaders claimed that Jerusalem was Islam's third holiest city, after Mecca and Medina. (For Muslims, Jerusalem's sanctity derives from the belief that *Mohammed ascended to heaven from there; Muslims today have full access to their religious sites in the city.) Yet it seems clear that the Arab furor about Jerusalem has less to do with the city's sacredness than with its being under Jewish control. Between 1948 and 1967, when Jerusalem was under Jordanian rule, only one Arab leader, King Hassan of Morocco, bothered to visit the city. Today, Yom Yerushalayim is celebrated by many Jews with special prayers, most notably *Hallel, a collection of joyous *Psalms.

COUNTING THE OMER

SHAVUOT

TIKKUN

HOW MANY DAYS ARE THERE BETWEEN NEW YEAR'S DAY AND JULY 4? Or between *Sukkot and *Hanukka? It is unlikely that almost anyone knows the answers to these questions off the top of his or her head. But all religious Jews know that there are precisely fifty days between the second day of *Passover and *Shavuot. During the first forty-nine days of this period, known as the *Omer*, each day is counted aloud during the evening service. After reciting a special blessing—"Blessed are You, Lord our God . . . who has commanded us to count the *Omer*"—congregants say, "Today is the third day [or the twentieth or the fortieth] in the *Omer*." On the fiftieth day, Shavuot is celebrated.

In Hebrew, *omer* means sheaves of a harvested crop. When the *Temple stood, priests would offer there, on behalf of all Israel, newly harvested barley (an *omer*) on the second day of Passover. Their doing so signaled the beginning of Israel's harvest season, a period that lasted seven weeks.

In the Torah, Shavuot is thus referred to as *Hag ha-Katzir*—the Holiday of Harvest (or, more precisely, the holiday celebrating the harvest's end).

Although one would think of the harvest period as joyous, in Jewish life the *Omer* is considered a time of semimourning. To this day, no scholar is sure why this is so. The Talmud speaks obscurely of a plague occurring on one *Omer* that killed 24,000 students of the second-century rabbi *Akiva. Given Akiva's role in supporting Simon *Bar-Kokhba's rebellion against Rome, it is possible that the students were slaughtered in battle. Whatever the origins of the custom of semimourning, traditional Jews do not get haircuts or celebrate weddings during this period (for the exceptions, see *Lag Ba'Omer*).

The *Omer* period is often called by another name in Hebrew, *Sefirah*, the word for "counting."

Shavuot is not as widely observed by contemporary Jews as Passover or
*Yom Kippur, yet it celebrates the most important event in Jewish history:
the giving of the *Torah. The *Talmud teaches that God gave the Jews the
*Ten Commandments on the sixth of *Sivan*, the first night of Shavuot. In
commemoration, many religious Jews convene the whole night at the synagogue, or in a home, to study Torah, other biblical books, sections of the
Talmud, and additional sacred writings. This annual all-night gathering is
known as a *tikkun*, and in recent years, there seems to have been a growth in
the number of Jews observing this tradition. At daybreak, the participants
break from study and recite *shakharit*, the morning prayer service. By about
7:30 A.M., well before others have arrived in the synagogue, the service is over.

In Jerusalem tens of thousands of Jews who have studied Torah the whole
night walk down to the *Kotel* (Western Wall) at the break of dawn to recite
the morning service. This custom received a particular impetus in the aftermath of the 1967 *Six-Day War. Israel captured Jerusalem in early June of
that year, but, for security reasons, the civilian populace was initially not
allowed to visit the Old City. On Shavuot the Western Wall was first opened
to civilian visitors, and an estimated 200,000 Israelis flocked to the *Kotel* on
that day.

An interesting Shavuot custom, whose origins are unknown, mandates
that only dairy foods be eaten on the holiday's first day. A popular folk tradition explains that, in the aftermath of the Exodus, the Jews had killed many
animals, but after receiving the Torah, they learned that this meat was
unkosher, so they ate dairy instead. In imitation of them, we likewise refrain
from eating meat. Somehow this explanation hardly seems definitive, but it
will have to do until someone comes up with a more convincing one.

By the way, there are 185 days between New Year's Day and July 4—186
days in a leap year—and, depending on the year, either 69 or 70 days
between Sukkot and Hanukka.

SOURCES AND FURTHER READINGS: See the list of books mentioned in the
note to entry 296.

THE THREE WEEKS/THE NINE DAYS

THERE ARE PRECISELY THREE WEEKS BETWEEN THE FAST DAY OF THE seventeenth of *Tammuz* (see *Minor Fast Days*) and the fast of Tisha Be'Av (see next entry). It was on the seventeenth of *Tammuz* in 70 C.E. that the Romans breached the walls of Jerusalem. For three weeks, Roman troops ransacked and destroyed the city until, on the ninth of *Av*, they burned down the *Temple. Ever since, Jews have observed this three-week period, which falls between mid-July and mid-August, as a time of mourning. During "the three weeks," weddings are prohibited.

The spirit of mourning intensifies during the final nine days of "the three weeks"—from the first until the ninth of *Av*. The Talmud teaches: "From the beginning of *Av*, we diminish happiness" (*Mishna Ta'anit* 4:6). During "the nine days," Jews are not supposed to cut their hair or shave—in ancient times, to let one's hair grow long was a sign of mourning—and are not permitted to drink wine and eat meat except on the Sabbath. For people who are particularly "carnivorous," there is a legally mandated way around the restriction on eating meat. One can attend a *siyyum*, a public reading and explanation of the concluding passage of a talmudic tractate. Anyone who participates in a *siyyum* is entitled to join in a festive meal afterward (known in Hebrew as a *se'udat mitzvah*, a "commanded meal"), at which eating meat is permitted.

During "the nine days," many religious Jews do not engage in any activity whose sole purpose is pleasure, for example, swimming. The Talmud also proscribes washing clothes during "the nine days," except for those needed for immediate wear. Because wearing freshly cleaned clothes is pleasurable, laundering and dry cleaning is delayed until after the fast of Tisha Be'Av.

The escalating effect of "the three weeks," and then "the nine days," ensures that when Tisha Be'Av arrives, people really feel like mourners.

THE NINTH OF AV/TISHA BE'AV

THE SADDEST DAY IN JEWISH HISTORY IS THE NINTH OF AV, WHICH falls some time between late July and mid-August. On this day, the Babylonians destroyed the First Temple in 586 B.C.E., and the Romans burned down the Second Temple in 70 C.E. The events commemorated by Tisha Be'Av are so tragic that, two millennia ago, the rabbis ordained that Jews should refrain from most pleasurable activities from the beginning of the month during which Tisha Be'Av falls (see preceding entry). This date marks as well the day on which the Jews of England were expelled from that country in 1290. The greatest catastrophe of medieval Jewish history, the expulsion of the Jews from Spain, occurred on the ninth of Av in 1492; it is possible that King Ferdinand and Queen Isabella sadistically chose the date to intensify the Jews' misery and horror. During the Holocaust, the Nazis took pleasure in organizing murderous actions against the Jewish community on the ninth of Av (see *Jeremiah, Destruction of the Second Temple, Expulsion of Jews from England, 1290, The Spanish Expulsion*).

To commemorate the destructions of the two Temples, the rabbis designated Tisha Be'Av as a full fast day, lasting from one evening to the next. In addition to not eating, it is forbidden to drink any liquid, bathe, wear leather shoes, put on makeup or perfume, or have sexual relations. As on *Yom Kippur, pregnant women, nursing mothers, and severely ill individuals are freed from the obligation of fasting if their health will be endangered. They are expected to eat, however, only what is necessary, no more. Unlike on Yom Kippur, one is permitted to work on Tisha Be'Av, although one should not work if it distracts him or her from mourning.

On the evening of Tisha Be'Av, Jews gather in the synagogue to read the biblical book of *Eicha* (Lamentations), an ancient dirge attributed to the prophet *Jeremiah and written after the destruction of the First Temple. This short book is unrelentingly horrifying, as it recounts not only the destruction of Judea, but also of much of the Jewish moral fiber. Jeremiah describes Jewish mothers cannibalizing their dead children to survive during the Babylonian siege of Jerusalem.

The public reading of Lamentations is often punctuated by sobs from members of the congregation. A story told by English Jews, perhaps apocryphal, tells of a prominent nineteenth-century British politician who was walking near a synagogue on Tisha Be'Av and heard wailing coming from inside. He looked in and was informed that the Jews were mourning the loss of their ancient Temple. Deeply impressed, the politician remarked, "A people who mourn with such intensity the loss of their homeland, even after two thousand years, will someday regain that homeland."

During the synagogue service, it is customary to sit on the floor, not in seats, in the style of mourners. As is the case with mourners, Jews are not supposed to greet each other on Tisha Be'Av.

During the morning service, men do not put on *tefillin; it is considered too joyous an act for so sad a day. The donning of tefillin is postponed to the afternoon *minkha service.

There is only one happy association with the holiday of Tisha Be'Av. According to an ancient Jewish tradition, the *Messiah will be born on this day.

SOURCES AND FURTHER READINGS: See the list of books mentioned in the note to entry 296.

318

MINOR FAST DAYS

THE MINOR FAST DAYS DO NOT COMMEMORATE "MINOR" EVENTS IN Jewish history. They are called minor because they are only halfday fasts; food is forbidden only from dawn till evening. On the "major" fast days, *Yom Kippur and Tisha Be'Av (see preceding entry), food is forbidden from the eve of the fast day to the following evening. On the minor fast days, it also is permissible to bathe and work.

Three of the minor fasts are observed in memory of the destruction of the two *Temples. The tenth of *Tevet* (Asarah Be'Tevet), which usually falls in

January, commemorates the beginning of the Babylonian siege of Jerusalem in 586 B.C.E.

During the summer, Jews observe the seventeenth of *Tammuz* (Shiva Asar Be'Tammuz), the day Roman troops breached the walls of Jerusalem in 70 C.E. That act led, three weeks later, to the *destruction of the Second Temple. The fast of the seventeenth of *Tammuz* is more widely observed than the tenth of *Tevet*, because it inaugurates a *three-week period of mourning. This period culminates with the observance of Tisha Be'Av, the "major" fast commemorating the destruction of both Jewish Temples.

The third minor fast connected to the loss of Jewish sovereignty commemorates an unhappy event that befell Israel shortly after Jerusalem was sacked in 586 B.C.E. The Babylonian conquerors installed a Jewish governor, Gedaliah ben Akhikam, to rule over Judea. Although Gedaliah's powers were limited, most Jews were happy to have a committed Jew, rather than a Babylonian official, rule over them. Some more radical Jews, however, regarded Gedaliah as a puppet. They invited him to a meeting and, although he was warned by advisers not to go alone, he went, naively certain that Jews would not kill another Jew. He was wrong. Yishma'el, son of Netanya, and his cohorts murdered Gedaliah (Jeremiah 40:7–41:3; II Kings 25:25), after which the Babylonians decided to administer Judea's affairs directly.

Gedaliah's assassination was a terrible blow to the prophet Jeremiah, who had long warned the Jews that to revolt against Babylon was a mistake (see *Jeremiah*). Jeremiah's sole solace after the Temple's destruction had been that Gedaliah ruled in Judea. The prophet hoped that the Babylonians would allow Gedaliah to rebuild the Temple someday. For Jeremiah the murder of the Jewish governor was the final tragedy of the Babylonian revolt (Jeremiah 40:7–41:3; II Kings 25:22–26). Ever since, Jewish law has ordained a fast day to be observed on the third of *Tishrei*, the anniversary of Gedaliah's murder. This day is known in Hebrew as *Tzom Gedaliah* (The Fast of Gedaliah), and it is observed the day after *Rosh ha-Shana. (According to some traditions, Gedaliah was killed on Rosh ha-Shana, and so the fast was moved to the day after Rosh ha-Shana.)

As a rule, the three minor fasts associated with the Temple's destruction are kept only by highly observant Jews. An old Jewish joke tells of a man who asked his friend if he fasted on Tzom Gedaliah.

"No," the man said.

"Why not?"

"I have three reasons. First, if Gedaliah hadn't been assassinated, he would be long dead by now anyway. Second, if I had died, would Gedaliah have fasted for me? And third, if I don't fast on Yom Kippur, why should I fast on Tzom Gedaliah?"

If any of these fasts falls on the Sabbath, it is observed on Sunday instead, for it is considered a violation of Sabbath joy to fast on that day. (The only fast day that supersedes the Sabbath is Yom Kippur, which the Torah calls "the Sabbath of Sabbaths" [Leviticus 23:32].)

Another minor fast falls on the day preceding *Purim. This one commemorates a three-day fast, which the rabbis fortunately restrict to one day. When Haman influenced King Ahasuerus to issue an edict to murder all the Jews in his kingdom, Mordechai implored his cousin, Queen Esther, to intervene with the king to annul the decree. Esther hesitated to do so. She was permitted to see the king only at his direct invitation: To enter his presence uninvited was a capital offense. Mordechai dismissed her fears with the memorable words:

"Do not imagine that you, of all the Jews, will escape with your life by being in the king's palace. On the contrary, if you keep silent in this crisis, relief and deliverance will come to the Jews from another quarter, while you and your father's house will perish. And who knows, perhaps you have attained to royal position for just such a crisis" (Esther 4:13–14).

Esther finally agreed to see Ahasuerus, but only after fasting and praying to God for three days. She requested that Mordechai and the Jews of Shushan fast and pray on these three days as well. Today, the day before Purim is observed as the Fast of Esther (Ta'anit Esther).

A final fast is obligatory for only a small percentage of Jews, firstborn children who are males (if the firstborn child is a girl, the parents' first son is not obligated to fast). This day is called, logically enough, the Fast of the First-born, and it is observed the day before *Passover. It commemorates the tenth plague that God inflicted on the Egyptians, the killing of firstborn sons (see The Ten Plagues). In gratitude for their having been saved, all firstborn Jewish males fast and thank God.

The joy of Passover influenced the rabbis to be lenient about excusing men from observing this fast. To be exempt, it is sufficient for a firstborn male to participate in the joyful *mitzvah of hearing and celebrating another Jew's completing the study of a tractate of *Talmud. The person completing the tractate is, of course, also exempt from the fast. Most Orthodox and many Conservative synagogues schedule such a public celebration on the morning before Passover.

SOURCES AND FURTHER READINGS: See the list of books mentioned in the note to entry 296.

NEW MONTH/*ROSH KHODESH*

IN THE HEBREW CALENDAR, ALL MONTHS HAVE EITHER TWENTY-NINE or thirty days; some vary between twenty-nine and thirty from year to year. The first day of each month is called Rosh Khodesh (the Head of the Month) just as the first day of the Jewish New Year is called *Rosh ha-Shana (the Head of the Year). In cases of thirty-day months, Rosh Khodesh is celebrated for two days, on the thirtieth day of the old month and on the first day of the new one.

Early in Jewish history, for unknown reasons, Rosh Khodesh became associated with women, who were exempt from working on Rosh Khodesh. The holiday became a day of leisure for them. Unfortunately, at least for women, this custom is no longer observed. Today Rosh Khodesh is like any other day, except for some additions to the prayer service. In recent years, many women have developed Rosh Khodesh groups which commemorate and celebrate the new month together.

The joyous *Hallel* is added to the morning prayers, as are several other prayers and there is a special reading from the Torah. Additions are also made to the afternoon and evening services as well as to the *Birkat ha-Mazon (Grace After Meals). The Sabbath before Rosh Khodesh is called *Shabbat Mevarkhim* (the Sabbath on Which a Blessing Is Made), and special prayers for the new month are recited in the synagogue. This part of the service is particularly beautiful, and synagogue attendance often increases markedly on *Shabbat Mevarkhim*.

Since the fourth century, the Jewish calendar has been regulated according to a set formula; as a result one can look up when Rosh Khodesh will be celebrated even a thousand years from now. Until the early centuries of the Common Era, however, the day on which it fell was declared each month by the Jewish high court only after it had received eyewitness testimony that a new moon had been sighted.

SOURCES AND FURTHER READINGS: See the list of books mentioned in the note to entry 296.

SABBATH/SHABBAT

Thirty-nine Melakhot
Muk-tze
Eruv

THAT BIBLICAL LAW FORBIDS WORKING ON THE SABBATH (SHABBAT) IS widely known; less familiar is the rabbinic definition of "work." For example, Jewish law forbids turning on a switch that ignites a fire in a stove. While few people would regard such an activity as work, Jewish law does. On the other hand, the law does not forbid moving a heavy piece of furniture *inside* one's home on the Sabbath, although most people would regard such a strenuous act as labor.

Rabbi Abraham Chill has defined the work (*melakha*) prohibited on the Sabbath as follows: "The biblical concept of *melakha* applies to work involving the production, creation, or transformation of an object. One may spend the entire Sabbath opening and closing books until one drops with exhaustion and yet not violate the Sabbath. On the other hand, the mere striking of a match, just once, is a desecration of the Sabbath because it involves creation."

The Torah itself does not define which labors are forbidden on the Sabbath. In the *Mishna, the rabbis designate thirty-nine forbidden labors, including: plowing, reaping, baking, dyeing wool, weaving, tying a permanent knot, sewing, slaughtering an animal, building, and pulling down a structure. The thirty-eighth forbidden labor is "striking with a hammer," which means putting the finishing touches on a job, while the thirty-ninth is carrying an object from one's private domain (in which it is permitted to carry) into another.

There is a general principle in Jewish jurisprudence that mandates not only observing the law, but also "putting a fence around the law." This odd expression implies that not only should one avoid forbidden acts, one must also avoid doing anything that might lead to performing a forbidden act. For example,

Jewish law forbids spending money on the Sabbath; thus, the rabbis elaborated that one should not even handle money on Shabbat. As a rule, anything that is forbidden to be used on the Sabbath is also forbidden to be handled. Such objects are known as *muk-tze*. Among Orthodox Jews, you might hear a parent say to a child on the Sabbath, "Don't play with coins. They're *muk-tze*."

As noted, it is forbidden to carry any object outside a private domain. Inside private residences or a synagogue, however, carrying is permitted. This law can lead to considerable hardships, since carrying even a handkerchief or housekey is forbidden. One way to circumvent this restriction is to convert a carried object into one that is worn. For example, Orthodox Jews will "transform" a housekey into a fancy tieclip and wear it. However, the prohibition against carrying falls very hard on mothers of infants or young children. They are confined to their homes on Shabbat, since it is forbidden to carry a child outside the house.

To circumvent such restrictions, the rabbis permitted, under certain circumstances, the establishment of an *eruv*. The *eruv* takes advantage of the legally mandated permission to carry inside a private domain, by converting a large public area into a huge "private domain." A common way of making an *eruv* is to surround an area with a partition made up of posts, which are linked by wire that goes over the top of the posts. Doing so makes the area into a single domain, in which it is permitted to carry.

In Israel the office of the chief rabbi has arranged for *eruvim* (plural of *eruv*) to be constructed in all cities. Until several decades ago, there were very few *eruvim* in the United States. In the past years, however, in most cities that have substantial Jewish populations, Orthodox Jews, acting in conjunction with municipal officials, have established *eruvim*.

SOURCES AND FURTHER READINGS: The definition of *melakha* is found in Abraham Chill, *The Mitzvot*, p. 37. On the Sabbath and its significance, see Abraham Joshua *Heschel, *The Sabbath*; Isidor Grunfeld, *The Sabbath: A Guide to Its Understanding and Observance*; Emanuel Rackman, "Sabbath and Festivals in the Modern Age," in Leon Stitskin, ed., *Studies in Torah Judaism*; and Samuel Dresner, *The Sabbath*. See also the books mentioned in the note to entry 296.

321

SABBATH RITUALS IN THE HOUSE

Candle Lighting
Blessing the Children
A *Woman of Valor*/Aishet Khayyil
Two Challot
Kiddush
Netilat Yadayim
Ha-Motzi
Zmirot
Grace after Meals/Birkat ha-Mazon
Shabbat Shalom! Gut Shabbes!

THE SABBATH BEGINS WITH THE LIGHTING OF CANDLES. ALTHOUGH this ritual is traditionally performed by women, Jewish law obligates males to light candles if no women are available. A minimum of two candles are lighted (in many families, an additional candle is kindled for each child). Then a blessing is said: "Blessed are You, Lord our God, King of the Universe . . . who has commanded us to light the Sabbath candles." It has become customary in many Jewish households for all females, including children, to light and bless the Sabbath candles.

After the candle lighting, the father customarily blesses the children (mothers can do so as well). He puts his hands over each child's head, saying to the boys: "May God make you like Ephraim and Menashe" (the two sons of *Joseph). When blessing girls, he says, "May God make you like Sarah, Rebecca, Rachel, and Leah" (the *Matriarchs).

For many years, blessing the children became largely unobserved outside the Orthodox community. Herbert Wiener, an American Reform rabbi who witnessed an elderly Jew dispensing Sabbath blessings in Safed, Israel, was moved to write: "I could not help but think of successful suburban fathers who had made comfortable provisions for their children, yet would never receive the honor and respect that had fallen to the lot of the old North African Jew who could offer only blessings." In recent years, however, there has been a significant increase in the number of parents outside of the Orthodox world who bless their children.

Before the Sabbath meal, the husband customarily reads aloud a biblical poem expressing admiration for his wife. The poem is generally referred to by its opening words, *Aishet Khayyil* (A Woman of Valor—see Proverbs 31:10–31). Such a woman's worth, the poem declares, "is far beyond that of rubies. . . . She gives generously to the poor, her hands are stretched out to the needy. . . . Her mouth is full of wisdom, her tongue with kindly teaching. . . . Grace is deceptive, beauty is illusory, a woman who fears the Lord is to be praised." The expression *aishet khayyil* is traditionally applied to any admirable Jewish woman (see, for example, this book's dedication).

The family then sings "Shalom Aleichem," a hymn about the special angels that Jewish tradition teaches accompany every Jew on the Sabbath.

Following this, the *kiddush* prayer is recited over the wine. Wine is served at all festive Jewish meals. Consequently, Jews are accustomed to drinking liquor from very young ages. Indeed, it is a common practice to give eight-day-old baby boys a drop of wine right after they are circumcised. More than a few sociologists have speculated that the low level of alcoholism among traditional Jews is partially attributable to the early training in moderate drinking acquired by observant Jews at the Sabbath table. At the several thousand Sabbath meals in which I have participated, wine has always been served, yet I have never seen anyone become inebriated.

The *kiddush* prayer, recited immediately before drinking the wine, emphasizes two themes: first, God's creation of the world. On the Sabbath, humans are to refrain from creating, in imitation of God who refrained from creating on the seventh day (Genesis 2:2–3). The second theme of the prayer is the *Exodus from Egypt. Slaves cannot rest when they wish; they can only do so when their masters permit it. We Jews, however, who are free—because God led us out of Egypt—can choose to rest on the Sabbath.

At the conclusion of the *kiddush*'s final blessing, the participants respond "Amen," and wine is distributed to everyone at the table.

The participants then wash their hands in a ceremony known as *netilat yadayim*. According to Jewish law, washing one's hands is mandated prior to any meal at which bread is eaten. This is because bread in Jewish tradition represents a complete meal, as opposed to a snack. The purpose of the ritual washing of hands is religious, not hygienic—indeed, one's hands must be clean before the *netilat yadayim*—and is intended to endow the meal with spirituality. In the ceremony, one fills a pitcher or cup with water, pours a small quantity of water two or three times over each hand, then recites a blessing to God, "Who has commanded us to wash the hands."

Washing the hands is followed immediately by blessing and then eating a large fluffy braided bread called *challah*: It is customary to refrain from speaking between the two acts; several minutes might pass until everyone finishes the hand washing. Nonetheless, the head of the household is expected to wait before reciting the blessing over the bread.

It is traditional to have two challot (plural of challah) at the Shabbat table, in memory of the double portion of manna the Israelites received in the Sinai Desert every Friday (Exodus 16:11–30; on other days they received only one portion). The additional portion of manna freed the Israelites from having to collect the manna on Saturday morning. The two challot symbolize that, like the Israelites in the desert, we have sufficient food so as not to have to work on the holy day of Shabbat. *Hamotzi*, the blessing recited over the bread, is one of the best-known Hebrew blessings and concludes with the words, "*Hamotzi lekhem min ha-aretz*—Who brings forth bread from the earth." The challah is then cut or torn by hand, and distributed to all present.

Later during the meal, it is customary to sing special Shabbat table songs known as *zmirot*, most of which deal, in one way or another, with the themes of the Sabbath. Many families also discuss the *weekly Torah portion during the meal.

The meal concludes with the *Birkat ha-Mazon* (Grace After Meals), an extended series of blessings to God for the food He has provided. Among traditional and knowledgeable Jews, the *Birkat ha-Mazon* is often sung in its entirety; this lasts about ten minutes. While Jewish law obliges one to recite the *Birkat ha-Mazon* after every meal in which bread is eaten, it is normally sung aloud only on the Sabbath, Jewish holidays, and other festive occasions (such as weddings).

The traditional greeting between Jews on the Sabbath is the Hebrew *Shabbat Shalom!* (A Peaceful Sabbath!) or the Yiddish *Gut Shabbes!* (A Good Sabbath!).

SOURCES AND FURTHER READINGS: Dennis Prager and Joseph Telushkin, *The Nine Questions People Ask About Judaism*, pp. 162–169 and pp. 53–57. Herbert Wiener, 9½ *Mystics*, p. 257. See also the books mentioned in the note to entry 296.

322

THE THIRD MEAL/*SHALOSH SE'UDOT*

IN TALMUDIC TIMES, THE AVERAGE PERSON ATE TWO MEALS A DAY, IN the morning and at night. Because Shabbat was a joyous day, the rabbis mandated that people eat three meals: on Friday evening, on Saturday after the morning prayers, and again in the late afternoon. Because the third meal was the unusual one, it acquired a special name, *shalosh se'udot,* which simply is Hebrew for "three meals." People commonly slur the pronunciation of these words; they usually wind up sounding something like *shalla shudess.*

In most synagogues, this third meal, served on the premises between the Saturday afternoon and evening services, is usually quite simple, consisting of little more than bread, herring, and gefilte fish. The meal, however, is not to be rushed: Often the rabbi or another learned member of the congregation teaches a lesson in Torah or *Talmud during the meal.

Among *Hasidic Jews, the *shalosh se'udot* frequently lasts for several hours, until well after the Sabbath itself has ended. The room in which the meal is served often has little lighting, and in the growing darkness, the Hasidim sing a *niggun* (wordless melody), which can be repeated for ten minutes or more. Interspersed with the singing and eating are "words of Torah" from their *rebbe*. The length of the *shalosh se'udot* itself symbolizes the Hasidim's reluctance to let go of Shabbat and return to the weekday world.

HAVDALA

THE SABBATH STARTS WITH THE LIGHTING OF CANDLES AND IT CON-
cludes the same way. The meaning of the two ceremonies, however, is very
different. While candles lighted on Friday evening symbolize the joy and
"lightness" of the day that is just beginning, the candle that is lit on Saturday
night symbolizes a return to the workday world in which lighting a fire and
performing work are again permitted. Accompanying the Saturday night candle lighting are several other symbolic rituals, accompanied by a prayer. The
ceremony is known as *havdala*, or "separation," the separation being that
between the Sabbath and the weekdays. Rabbi Irving Greenberg has called
havdala the **kiddush* (the prayer over wine recited at the two main Sabbath
meals) for the week.

The candle for the *havdala* is generally about a foot long and has several
wicks. It is usually held by a girl or young woman, and custom dictates that
she hold it high, to the height that she would like her future husband to be.

Also used in the *havdala* ceremony is a wine cup filled to the point of
overflowing. It is customary to hold the cup over a bowl and to let the over-
flow spill into it. The slight wasting of wine is intended to symbolize prosperity: People should feel so materially at ease that they can dispense wine
generously without worrying about being economical. Many Jews are
unaware that Jewish law permits beverages other than wine to be used for
havdala; in fact, any popular drink, except for water, is permitted. When I
was growing up, my father used to make *havdala* over orange juice.

The third item used in *havdala* is a box filled with a fragrant spice. Jewish
law does not dictate any special spice though tradition prefers one that gives
off a sweet smell. An old Jewish folk tale teaches that each Jew is given a second soul on the Sabbath, which departs at the end of the holiday. The fragrance of the spice is intended to give a "lift" to the body which has just been
deprived of that extra soul.

During the *havdala* ceremony, the wine, the spices, and the fire (of the candle) are each blessed individually. When the blessing over the fire is recited, it is customary to raise one's fingernails opposite the flame and look at them. An Iranian-Jewish friend recalled an interpretation of this ceremony that he had heard as a child in Teheran: "Holding up your fingernails to the fire, and showing them to be clean, indicates that one did not do any work during the Sabbath."

While the lighting of candles at the Sabbath's beginning is practiced by many Jewish women, the *havdala* ceremony is observed largely by Orthodox Jews. Among non-Orthodox Jews, it is often associated with Jewish summer camps. As the Sabbath draws to a close, hundreds of youngsters are brought together in concentric circles: They sway and chant the *havdala* prayer together.

Among Jews of all persuasions, the song generally sung just before or after the *havdala* tells of *Elijah the Prophet, who will someday return to announce the coming of the Messiah. *"Eliyahu ha-Navi,"* the words run, *"Eliyahu ha-Tishbi*—Elijah the Prophet, Elijah from Tishbi . . . Let him come quickly to us in our day, with the Messiah, Son of David."

SOURCES AND FURTHER READINGS: See the books mentioned in the note to entry 296.

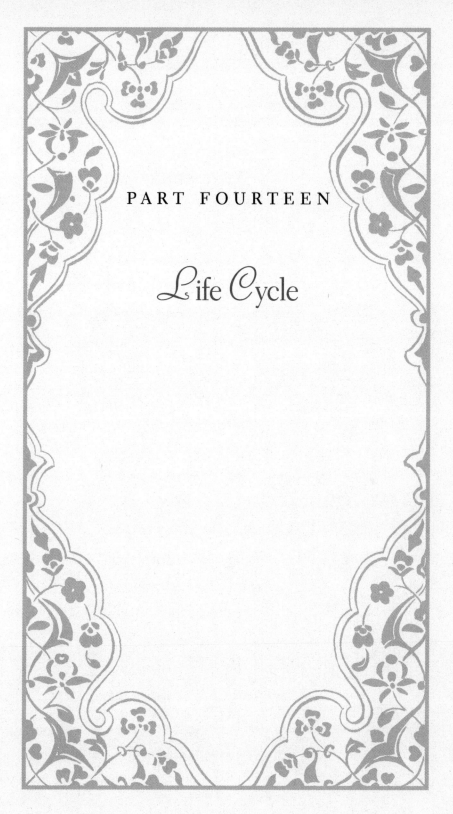

PART FOURTEEN

Life Cycle

324

CIRCUMCISION/*BRIT MILAH*
REDEMPTION OF THE FIRSTBORN/
PIDYON HA-BEN
NAMING CEREMONY FOR GIRLS

CIRCUMCISION (*BRIT MILAH*) IS THE OLDEST RITUAL IN JUDAISM, going back to Abraham. The *Patriarch was instructed to have himself circumcised at the age of ninety-nine, to circumcise his thirteen-year-old son Ishmael (Genesis 17:9–14 and 24–25), and, later, to circumcise Isaac when he was eight days old (Genesis 21:4).

The ceremony, which involves removing the foreskin of the penis continues to be performed on Jewish male infants at the age of eight days (Leviticus 12:3).

Throughout history, circumcision has been the physical mark that distinguished Jewish males from their non-Jewish neighbors. Three centuries ago, Benedict Spinoza said that as long as Jews practice circumcision, they will survive as a separate people. Spinoza's statement was particularly applicable in Europe, where few non-Jews were circumcised. During the Second World War, the Nazis often forced men to drop their pants, to check if they were circumcised. Although circumcision was not generally practiced in England, it was common among the royal family, which, it has long been rumored, trusted a Jewish *mohel* (circumciser), not a doctor, to carry out the procedure. In the United States, however, circumcision is widely practiced among non-Jews and no longer necessarily distinguishes Jews from their neighbors.

In the nineteenth century, some leading figures in Reform Judaism wished to see circumcision abolished. Rabbi Abraham *Geiger referred to it in a letter as a "barbaric bloody rite." Among contemporary Reform Jews, however, one rarely hears attacks against circumcision.

Nowhere in the Torah is a rationale given for this unusual commandment. Perhaps circumcision represents a symbolic subjugation to God of man's supposedly uncontrollable sexual urges.

Aside from newborn boys, the only other people requiring circumcision are male converts to Judaism. In the United States, where most non-Jews are already circumcised, this requirement is fulfilled by taking a symbolic drop of blood from the penis.

Undoubtedly, the requirement of circumcision helped account for the far greater number of female than male converts to Judaism in the ancient world. By dropping the demands for circumcision and observance of Jewish law, Christianity made conversion a much easier procedure than did Judaism.

Jewish lore abounds in jokes about the person who performs the *brit milah*, the *mohel*, most—though not all—in bad taste. In one story, a man is walking down a street and sees an enormous watch hanging over a store window. He brings in his watch to be repaired, but the proprietor tells him he doesn't repair watches, he is a *mohel*.

"Why then are you hanging a watch in the window?" the man asks.

"What do you suggest, mister, I put in the window?" the *mohel* answers.

Another ritual associated with the birth of a male is the *pidyon haben*, literally, "redemption of the [firstborn] son." In Jewish life, a firstborn son (one who is both male and the first child born to his mother) is supposed to be dedicated to God (Exodus 13:1–2), and to perform religious services for the priests (see *Kohanim*). On the thirty-first day after the child's birth, however, the father can pay a priest five silver shekels (see Numbers 18:16; today five dollars in silver coins is generally used) to have the child released from this obligation. The ceremony of redeeming the firstborn is still practiced among observant Jews.

According to Jewish tradition, a baby girl is named in the synagogue during the first Torah reading following her birth (the Torah is read every Monday, Thursday, and Saturday). Many parents wait for the Sabbath morning Torah reading to perform the ceremony. In *Orthodox congregations, the father is given an *aliyah* to the Torah, while in non-Orthodox synagogues, the mother is likely to be called up as well (that is, if she is well enough to be at the service). After the Torah portion is completed, a special prayer is recited for the newborn during which the child's name is announced. There is much less ritual and drama than at a circumcision—when male babies are named—and the lack of ceremony has unfortunately made the birth of a girl seem less significant than that of a boy. One often hears close relatives of a pregnant woman say, "If she has a boy, we will fly in for the *brit*, but if it's a girl, we'll wait for a better time to visit."

In recent years, with the rise of feminism, new ceremonies have been created to celebrate a girl's birth. Reform Judaism has developed a ritual for naming a girl called *brit ha-hayim* (covenant of life), and it is found in the Reform movement's home prayerbook, *Gates of the House*. Naming ceremonies for girls are performed by some Conservative and Modern Orthodox Jews as well. As of yet, there is no formal liturgy for this ritual, and copies of many different ceremonies are currently circulating.

The name given a child at circumcision, or in the synagogue or baby-naming ceremony, is a Hebrew name. In the United States, the child is often known, however, by his or her English name, which is generally the one that appears on the birth certificate. Often the names are similar. My Hebrew name, for example, is *Yosef*, the biblical name for Joseph (I was also given the Hebrew name Yisra'el [Israel] to honor the fact that I was born in the same year [1948] in which the modern state of Israel was created). In many instances, however, the connection between the Hebrew and English names is very tenuous. A friend told me he heard a rabbi announce in synagogue, "And the boy is named Sean, in honor of his late grandfather, *Shmuel* [Hebrew for Samuel]."

Traditionally, one does not refer to a child by name until he or she is officially named at the circumcision or in the synagogue. This can cause considerable confusion in the case of male babies whose circumcisions are delayed for health reasons. Parents who are strict about observing this tradition sometimes tell people what the child's English name will be. But this is of little help if, as is increasingly common, the English and Hebrew names are the same (for example, Tzvi).

SOURCES AND FURTHER READINGS: Isaac Klein, *A Guide to Jewish Religious Practice*, pp. 420–432. For an example of a naming ceremony for a baby girl, see Blu Greenberg, *How to Run a Traditional Jewish Household*, pp. 248–250. Whether or not circumcision confers a health benefit on circumcised males has long been debated, but it is interesting to note that a front-page article in *The New York Times* (12/14/06) reported that U.S. government health officials announced that circumcision appears to reduce a man's risk of contracting AIDS from heterosexual intercourse by half. Earlier studies carried out in South Africa reached the same conclusion.

325

BAR MITZVAH AND BAT MITZVAH

As a quick test of your Jewish knowledge, fill in the blank. The one religious ceremony that a boy must perform at thirteen in order to become Bar Mitzvah is _____.

The correct answer is: None. A boy becomes Bar Mitzvah whether he spends his thirteenth birthday in synagogue or in bed. The words "Bar Mitzvah" mean literally "son of the commandments," one who is bound by the commandments. In Judaism boys become obligated to fulfill Jewish laws at thirteen, girls—who generally mature earlier—at twelve.

Two commandments that have become particularly associated with Bar Mitzvah are the daily donning of *tefillin* and being called to the Torah for an *aliyah* on the Shabbat following one's thirteenth birthday. The relevant date for determining when a child is Bar Mitzvah is the Hebrew birthdate.

In America the Bar Mitzvah has turned into a large industry. The child's parents are expected to host a lavish party to celebrate the occasion. Some years ago, a Bar Mitzvah party held in Miami became a media event; the parents rented out the Orange Bowl for the evening and even had cheerleaders perform. As one wag put it: "A lot of Bar Mitzvahs are more bar than *mitzvah.*"

In recent years, to underscore the religious significance of the occasion, an increasing number of American Jews have chosen to celebrate a Bar Mitzvah in Israel, with the prayer service itself held at the *Western Wall.

Among religious Jews, the Bar Mitzvah marks a significant turning point in a boy's life as he starts to experience growth toward adulthood. He is now counted in a *minyan* (prayer quorum), which according to traditional Jewish law must be composed of ten adult men. I remember the pride I felt in being counted in a *minyan* subsequent to my Bar Mitzvah. In Orthodox schools, boys of Bar Mitzvah age generally study longer hours and spend more time learning the *Talmud, which is considered one of the most difficult branches of Jewish study.

In America today, of course, nobody takes the idea of thirteen-year-olds being adults very seriously. As my son Benjamin said at the time of his Bar Mitzvah, "If people really meant that becoming Bar Mitzvah means becoming a man, why do they always refer to the person having the Bar Mitzvah as the Bar Mitzvah boy?" During the era of the Talmud, however, boys could be married off within a few years of their Bar Mitzvah, and girls in even closer proximity to their reaching the age of Bat Mitzvah.

In the synagogue, on the Shabbat of his Bar Mitzvah, an Orthodox boy usually reads the whole Torah portion, or at least the *Haftorah, and perhaps leads another section of the service. In more traditionally Orthodox congregations, he will also give a short discourse on a topic in Jewish law, or speak about the Torah portion and its significance.

Among Conservative and Reform Jews, the portion of the service led by the Bar Mitzvah boy varies. At some synagogues, he will read the entire Torah portion; at many he will read the *Haftorah*. At minimum, the Bar Mitzvah boy will be honored with an *aliyah* to the Torah. The Bar Mitzvah will also usually expound on the Torah portion.

While the Bar Mitzvah is intended to mark the beginning of a Jewish boy's adulthood, for many less religious Jews it frequently signifies the end of his Jewish education. Many parents insist that a child attend afternoon Hebrew school at least until his Bar Mitzvah, if only because most synagogues otherwise will not allow him to celebrate his Bar Mitzvah there. An American-Jewish journalist, the late Trude Weiss Rosmarin, proposed that the Bar Mitzvah age be raised in the United States to sixteen or eighteen, so that children would have to attend classes in Judaism for several more years.

Other people have suggested that a Bar Mitzvah be celebrated every thirteen years, so that a person recommits himself to Judaism and the Jewish people at ages twenty-six, thirty-nine, etc. Because the Bible speaks of seventy years as a normal life span, some people celebrate a second Bar Mitzvah at the age of eighty-three. Indeed, a few years ago, the renowned actor Kirk Douglas, who started to study Judaism late in life with great intensity celebrated a second Bar Mitzvah upon reaching this birthday.

In recent years, it has become increasingly common for Jews who never celebrated a Bar or Bat Mitzvah in their youth to do so as adults. Several years ago in San Francisco I supervised such a ceremony, and commented that not only was it the first time I ever saw a "Bar Mitzvah boy" come to the service with his wife, but with two children as well. For those who come to Jewish commitment later in life, marking it with a synagogue service can be a powerful experience.

The Bat Mitzvah ceremony is of much more recent vintage. The first woman to celebrate a Bat Mitzvah was Judith Kaplan, daughter of Rabbi Mordecai *Kaplan, the founder of the *Reconstructionist movement, who had her Bat Mitzvah in the early 1920s. Bat Mitzvahs today are routinely celebrated by Reform, Reconstructionist, and Conservative Jews, and the girls perform the same synagogue rituals as the boys. In most instances, the Bat Mitzvah is celebrated at thirteen, although according to Jewish law, women become Bat Mitzvah at twelve. There has been less acceptance of the Bat Mitzvah ceremony among the Orthodox, since most Orthodox congregations do not permit women to participate publicly in the synagogue service. Nonetheless, such celebrations are gradually becoming more popular among Orthodox Jews as well. The family will often arrange a dinner in honor of the Bat Mitzvah, at which the girl presents a *dvar Torah (usually an explication of some issue in the week's Torah portion), which the girl links with her Jewish coming-of-age. In some Orthodox synagogues, there are women's services, at which the Bat Mitzvah girl reads from the Torah, and leads the service.

SOURCE AND FURTHER READING: Blu Greenberg, *How to Run a Traditional Jewish Household*, pp. 264–282.

326

AUFRUFF

MARRIAGE CEREMONY/*KIDDUSHIN*

SHEVA BRAKHOT

BREAKING THE GLASS

GROOM AND BRIDE/*KHATTAN VE-KALLA*

THOUGH THE TORAH ASSUMES THAT MEN AND WOMEN WILL MARRY—"Therefore shall a man leave his father and mother and cling to his wife and they shall be one flesh" (Genesis 2:24)—nowhere does it specify a marriage ceremony. The ceremony's details are codified, rather, in the *Talmud.

In the talmudic era, a man and woman formally signified their intention to marry a full year before the wedding, in a ceremony known as *erusin*. During the twelve months following the *erusin*, the woman was expected to assemble her trousseau and prepare for marriage, while the man readied himself financially. If either party wished to terminate the *erusin*, which was a legally binding engagement, a full ceremony of divorce had to be carried out (see *Get*). Today, both *erusin* and marriage (*nisu'in*) take place at the wedding.

On the Sabbath preceding the wedding, the groom (*khattan*) is honored by being called up to the Torah for an *aliyah*. (Some *Sephardic Jews honor the groom at the first Sabbath service *after* the wedding.) In many congregations, when he finishes blessing the Torah, members of the congregation throw candy at him, symbolically expressing their wishes that he and his fiancée have a sweet future. This special Sabbath celebration is known by the Yiddish word *aufruff*. Among Orthodox Jews, the bride (*kalla*) is usually not present at the *aufruff*. Jewish custom, not law, dictates that the bride and groom not see each other the week before the wedding.

The wedding day is regarded in Jewish law as sacred, a sort of mini-*Yom Kippur. The bride and groom are encouraged to fast, and even to recite certain penitential prayers that are also said on the Day of Atonement.

The wedding ceremony itself is brief and simple. There is an ancient custom—it is not mandatory, and its origin is uncertain—that under the canopy, the bride walks around the groom seven times. Afterward, the couple stands in front of the officiating rabbi, who recites the first two blessings, which are those that were recited at the ancient ceremony of *erusin*. The groom then places a ring on the forefinger of the bride's right hand and recites nine words in Hebrew: "*Ha-rei aht me-ku-deshet li be-ta-ba'aht zoh, ke-daht Moshe ve-Yisra'el*—You are hereby sanctified unto me with this ring according to the laws of Moses and Israel."

The rabbi then reads aloud the Aramaic marriage contract known as the *ketuba* (see next entry), which lists the groom's obligations to the bride. He then recites the seven marriage blessings (*sheva brakhot*), which consecrate a Jewish wedding.

The ritual that concludes the public part of the ceremony is the smashing of a glass under the groom's foot. The glass is first wrapped in a cloth napkin so that no one is injured by flying fragments. The tradition of breaking a glass dates back to the Talmud. Rav Ashi was celebrating his son's wedding when the atmosphere among the guests, many of whom were rabbis, grew raucous. The rabbi lifted up an exceedingly valuable white glass and smashed it in front of them. The Talmud reports that the shocked guests sobered up quickly (*Brakhot* 31a). Breaking a glass soon became incorporated into all wedding ceremonies, though with a different rationale. The smashing of something valuable slightly diminishes the great joy of the occasion, and serves as a poignant reminder that the *Temple is still in ruins. I once introduced the ceremony at the wedding of close friends as follows: "The smashing of the glass reminds us as well that we still live in an unredeemed world. May the children of your union help to bring about the world's redemption."

Given the sadness that the breaking of the glass is intended to evoke, it is almost comical that at all Jewish weddings today, the act produces joyous shouts of "*Mazal Tov!*" (Congratulations! or literally, "Good luck!"). In consequence, Rabbi Maurice Lamm has suggested that rather than wait till the end of the wedding to perform this ritual, the glass be broken in the middle of the ceremony.

After breaking the glass, and before the bride and groom join the wedding reception, they are taken to a locked room where they stay alone for about ten minutes. This is known as *yikhud* (separation), and is a symbolic ceremony of great significance. In Jewish law, a man and woman who are not married or closely related are forbidden to be alone in an inaccessible room. *Yikhud*, then, is the final act in the wedding ceremony, indicating that the couple is now married and sexually permitted only to one another.

For the week after the wedding, it is traditional for relatives and friends of the newly married couple to make a party for them each day. At least one of the guests at each party should be someone who was not at the wedding itself, and who will therefore bring a new and spontaneous reaction of joy to the occasion. At each party's conclusion, when the *Birkat ha-Mazon* (Grace After Meals) is said, the same seven blessings that were recited under the canopy are repeated. Because these seven blessings are known in Hebrew as *sheva brakhot*, these wedding parties have become known as *sheva brakhot*, and among traditional Jews, it is common for someone to say, "I am going to a *sheva brakhot* tonight for so-and-so."

SOURCE: Maurice Lamm, *The Jewish Way in Love and Marriage*.

327

THE MARRIAGE CONTRACT/*KETUBA*

THE *KETUBA* IS THE MARRIAGE CONTRACT THAT ALL GROOMS ARE required to give their brides at a Jewish wedding. It spells out the husband's obligations to the wife, and is considered so binding that a couple whose *ketuba* has been lost is forbidden to live together until a new one is written. In the *ketuba* the man undertakes to provide his wife with "food, clothing, and necessities, and live with you as a husband according to universal custom."

The phrase "live with you" is a euphemism for sexual relations. The rabbis spelled out this obligation contractually because they believed that most women would be too shy or modest to initiate relations, and needed protection from a husband's possible sexual indifference. During times when polygamy was still permitted in Jewish law (see *Ban on Polygamy—The Decrees of Rabbi Gershom*), the guarantee of sexual relations also protected older and less attractive wives from being ignored. The minimal frequency of marital relations legislated in the Talmud was based on a man's profession and the amount of time he spent at home: "Every day for those who have no occupation, twice a week for laborers, once a week for ass-drivers; once every thirty days for camel drivers; and once every six months for sailors" (*Mishna Ketubot* 5:6; *Ketubot* 62b–62b). As Rabbi Louis Jacobs has noted: "A husband cannot change his occupation without his wife's consent if this will affect her conjugal rights—from an ass-driver to a camel-driver, for instance—since it can be assumed that a wife will prefer to have her needs satisfied even if, as a result, her husband's earnings will be less." For married couples, part of the Sabbath joy is to have relations on Friday night.

The clause obligating a man to supply his wife's financial needs entitles him to her earnings; however, the wife has the option of releasing him from this responsibility, and keeping all her income.

Consistent with Judaism's legal, and generally nonromantic, character, the *ketuba* also spells out the husband's financial obligations in the event of divorce or death. In recent years, the Conservative movement has added a clause to the *ketuba* that effectively compels the husband to give his wife a Jewish divorce, a *get*, in the event of a civil divorce (see *Get* and *Agunah*). A growing number of Orthodox rabbis are asking grooms to sign a civilly binding prenuptial agreement to this effect.

The *ketuba* currently used was written in the second century B.C.E. Just before the wedding ceremony, two witnesses sign the document, certifying that they have witnessed the groom agreeing to abide by all of its provisions. During the ceremony, the document is read aloud in the original Aramaic, summarized in English, and then entrusted to the wife.

Throughout Jewish history, scribes and artists have created elaborate and illuminated *ketubot* (plural of *ketuba*), which often are displayed in the couple's house. Recently, there has been a resurgence of interest in beautiful *ketubot*, and an increasing number of couples, instead of using a standard printed *ketuba*, are commissioning artists to design the document.

SOURCES: Louis Jacobs, *What Does Judaism Say About?*, pp. 281–288, discusses Judaism's attitudes toward sex. On the *ketuba* itself, see Louis M. Epstein, *The Jewish Marriage Contract*.

328

MIKVEH

LAWS OF FAMILY PURITY/
TAHARAT HA-MISHPAKHA

THE TORAH CATEGORICALLY PROHIBITS SEXUAL RELATIONS BETWEEN husband and wife during the woman's menstrual period (Leviticus 18:19 and 20:18), as well as during other times of uterine bleeding. The rabbis, concerned that women would not be able to distinguish the sources of the bleeding, collapsed all distinctions (see Leviticus 15:25–33) and decreed that sexual relations be prohibited for a full seven days after the woman has experienced the last flow of blood.

The laws concerning sexual separation are known as *taharat ha-mishpakha* (the laws of family purity). Along with the *Sabbath and *kashrut*, these laws constitute one of three ritual areas whose strict observance generally differentiates Orthodox from non-Orthodox Jews.

While the law in the Torah only forbids intercourse during a woman's menstrual period, subsequent Jewish laws also forbid any heterosexual contact that might stimulate sexual excitement and lead to relations. Those Jews who strictly observe *taharat ha-mishpakha* do not kiss, hug, or otherwise touch their spouse during the forbidden days. At night, husband and wife sleep in separate beds. Some Orthodox males will not hand something directly to their wives during this time; they set the desired object down on a table for the wife to pick up.

Unlike the Sabbath and *kashrut*, the laws of family purity are virtually unknown to non-Orthodox Jews. In the Orthodox world, however, new books on the subject are constantly being published, often directed toward engaged couples. In one recent work, the author advised couples not to go for pleasure rides in automobiles during the forbidden days. If it was absolutely necessary for them to drive together, he advised the nondriving partner to sit in the backseat.

Throughout the woman's period, and for seven days after, she is called *tahmay*. Unfortunately, the only translation for *tahmay* is "impure," a word that carries an infinitely worse connotation in English than in Hebrew. *Tahmay* is simply an ancient term applied to anyone who is forbidden to have contact with sacred food, or to enter the Temple precincts in Jerusalem (see *The Temple/Beit ha-Mikdash*). For example, if a man or woman comes in direct contact with a corpse, then the Torah legislates that they are *tahmay* for seven days. Certainly, no stigma of impurity is attached to them for having touched a dead body; nonetheless, because they are *tahmay*, certain ritual acts are forbidden to them.

Many modern Jews have nonetheless expressed discomfort with the laws of family purity, feeling that they might cause a menstruating woman to feel like a pariah. On the other hand, Dr. Norman Lamm, the former president of *Yeshiva University, has written a brilliant overview of the laws of sexual separation, entitled *A Hedge of Roses*, in which he argues that these laws have enhanced Jewish marital and sexual happiness. An Orthodox Jewish educator told me she believes that *taharat ha-mishpakha* is responsible for maintaining a frequent level of sexual activity among Orthodox couples. Studies of the American population, she noted, indicate that newly married couples have sexual relations very frequently. After several years, however, the frequency declines dramatically, and continues to decline throughout the marriage. Among

Orthodox Jews, however, the prohibition of sexual relations for twelve successive days each month leaves a couple hungering for each other, even after many years of marriage. Even if the couple's biological clocks are not normally in sync, they will certainly be so at the end of the twelve days. The Talmud specifically recognized the rejuvenating effect the laws of separation can have on a marriage: "The husband becomes over-familiar with his wife and tires of her. Thus, the Torah prohibited her to him [for certain days each month] so that she may remain as beloved to him as she was on her wedding day" (*Niddah* 31b).

Before sexual relations resume, however, one more ritual must be carried out: The wife must go to a *mikveh* (ritual bath). Most *mikva'ot* (plural) are located in buildings, although a lake, river, or ocean—in fact, any body of natural water—can serve as a valid *mikveh*.

Women go to the *mikveh* on the first evening on which they are permitted to resume relations. During evening hours the *mikveh* is run by women, and no men are present when women use it. The woman undresses and immerses herself in the waters of the *mikveh* while totally unclothed. She then recites a blessing to God "who has sanctified us with His commandments, and commanded concerning immersion." Only after thoroughly immersing herself is a woman permitted to resume sexual relations with her husband.

Unmarried women do not go to the *mikveh*; if they did, they would presumably be permitted to have relations, and Orthodoxy in no way wishes to encourage premarital sex. An Orthodox rabbi told me that the most unusual query ever posed to him came from a young Orthodox woman who had decided to live with her boyfriend. "No matter what you say, rabbi," she told him, "I plan to move in with my boyfriend. When I do so, is it better that I put a ring on my finger and go to a *mikveh* each month and immerse myself, or not go to a *mikveh* at all?" The rabbi ruled that attending a *mikveh* was preferable. Other rabbis have ruled the opposite, that it is preferable that she not go to the *mikveh* in such a case, since permitting her to do so would lead to increased promiscuity. Indeed, although it will come as a surprise to most non-Orthodox Jews, an unmarried woman who goes to the *mikveh* and sleeps with her boyfriend is committing a lesser offense, according to Jewish law, than a married Jewish couple that has sexual relations without the woman going to the *mikveh*.

The only unmarried woman who is expected to go to the *mikveh* is a bride just before her wedding. For that reason, among traditional Jews it is always the woman who sets the wedding date, so as to ensure that it not fall within her forbidden days.

Many women whose weddings I have performed—most of whom were non-Orthodox—have told me that the trip to the *mikveh* was one of the spiritual high points of their lives and significantly deepened the sense of sanctity surrounding their marriage.

Although the *mikveh* is generally associated with menstruating women, it is also indispensable in the conversion of non-Jews to Judaism. The one ritual act required of female converts is immersion in a *mikveh*, while men who convert are required to immerse themselves, and undergo *circumcision.

The Christian ritual of baptism is based on the *mikveh* immersion. The institution itself is so ancient that remnants of a *mikveh* have been found in the remains of the destroyed Jewish fortress at *Masada.

In contemporary American-Jewish life, interdenominational conflicts have unfortunately sometimes erupted around the use of the *mikveh*. In most cities, the *mikva'ot* are under the control of Orthodox Jews; in general, the Orthodox are almost the only ones who use them. Many Orthodox rabbis will not permit Reform and Conservative rabbis to use the *mikveh* to perform conversions. (Since the Orthodox do not regard non-Orthodox conversions as valid, they do not wish such ceremonies to gain a patina of legitimacy through the use of a *mikveh*.) The Conservative Jewish community of Los Angeles has, as a result, built its own *mikveh*. Significantly, the Conservative movement has never officially ruled that monthly immersion in a *mikveh* is optional for its female adherents; in practice, however, few Conservative Jews practice the laws of family purity. Thus, the Conservative *mikveh* was built largely for use by converts. In recent years, Temple Israel in Detroit, one of the largest congregations in the Reform movement, has built its own *mikveh*. In addition to its use by converts, members are encouraged to immerse themselves at other times, such as before Rosh Hashana and Yom Kippur, to aid in their spiritual preparation for the holidays.

Some Jewish men, particularly among the *Hasidim or those with mystical inclinations, periodically immerse themselves in the *mikveh*, especially before Jewish holidays, the High Holidays in particular. A few do so daily or just on Fridays, in preparation for the Sabbath.

SOURCES AND FURTHER READINGS: Norman Lamm, *A Hedge of Roses*; Blu Greenberg, *How to Run a Traditional Jewish Household*, pp. 120–136; Moses Tendler, *Pardes Rimonim: A Marriage Manual for the Jewish Family*; Richard Siegel, Michael Strassfeld, and Sharon Strassfeld, eds., *The Jewish Catalog*, pp. 167–171. One of the standard works on the laws of *mikveh* was written in Hebrew by my late grandfather, Rabbi Nissen Telushkin, and is entitled *Taharat Mayim*.

BEIT DIN

THROUGHOUT MOST OF JEWISH HISTORY, THE COMMUNITY VEHEMENTLY opposed its members' summoning each other before gentile courts. Jews who had legal disputes with other Jews were expected to summon their opponents before a *beit din* (Jewish court) composed of three rabbis. Each side was entitled to choose one rabbi, and then the two rabbis would choose a third rabbi. The *beit din* would hear the testimony and arguments of each side. Litigants would generally represent themselves, and were questioned by the judges—who would then issue a ruling.

There are still American Jews, almost all of them Orthodox, who bring business disputes before rabbinic courts. In one instance several years ago, both sides in the case agreed to abide by the rabbinic court ruling, but after the decision was announced, one of the litigants sued again in civil court. He argued that the rabbis had been prejudiced against him. One of the three rabbis was subpoenaed, and the judge asked him to respond to the litigant's allegation. "Before I heard the case," the rabbi told the judge, "I was not prejudiced against the man. After I heard it, I did become prejudiced against him." The judge dismissed the suit.

On one occasion, my grandfather sat on a *beit din* with the late Rabbi Moshe *Feinstein, perhaps the preeminent scholar of Jewish law in the twentieth century. In this particular instance, there was no question of conflict or litigation; the three rabbis were simply trying to decide a complicated question that had been posed to them. The rabbis were not happy with the result, because the law's application seemed to impose an injustice against the man who had raised the question. The rabbis could not find a way to resolve the problem. Finally, Reb Moshe said, "I am not leaving this room until I find a basis [in Jewish law] for ruling differently." It took him till the following morning, but he did so.

Two popular books contain descriptions of how Jewish law functions in adjudicating modern problems. In the first chapter of *Friday the Rabbi Slept Late*—the first of Harry Kemelman's highly readable series of murder mysteries starring a rabbinic sleuth—Rabbi David Small resolves a conflict between two members of his congregation. One has borrowed the other's car and seems to have caused massive damage to the vehicle while it was in his possession. In Isaac Bashevis Singer's haunting memoir of his childhood, *In My Father's Court,* he recalls his father's experiences as a Hasidic rabbi in Warsaw, and chronicles several cases that came before him for judgment. The strangest case had nothing to do with business or civil law. A man asked if he could sleep in one bed with his dead wife; his wife had died a few hours earlier. The couple was very poor, and lived in a cellar. If he rested her body on the ground, rats would gnaw at it. Singer's father did not answer the man's query. He gave him money, and raised more money from other Jews. Very quickly, someone procured a cot for the man. In another case, a man summoned his fiancée before Singer's father and announced that he wished to break off their engagement. The woman refused to accept this breach of the engagement contract; she insisted that she still loved him. After a lengthy talk with the parties involved, Singer's father ruled that such a contract could not be enforced against a party's will, but the woman was entitled to keep all the gifts the man had given her.

Today, the *beit din* is most often used to issue Jewish divorces and to supervise conversions to Judaism (see the next two entries).

SOURCES AND FURTHER READINGS: Joseph Stern, "Bet Din," in Sharon Strassfeld and Michael Strassfeld, eds., *The Third Jewish Catalog,* pp. 151–163. See also James Yaffe, *So Sue Me: The Story of a Community Court,* which presents actual cases brought before the Jewish Conciliation Board.

330

JEWISH DIVORCE/GET

AGUNAH

THE TORAH HAS ONLY ONE VERSE ON THE SUBJECT OF DIVORCE: "When a man takes a woman, and marries her, then it shall come to pass, if she find no favor in his eyes, because he has found something unseemly in her, that he shall write her a bill of divorcement, and give it into her hand" (Deuteronomy 24:1).

The *Mishna records a debate on the meaning of the word "unseemly" that took place in the first century C.E. between the two foremost rabbinical academies in Israel. Beit Shammai believed that this word meant adultery, and that the sole grounds for divorce, therefore, was sexual impropriety. Beit Hillel ruled that "unseemly" might refer to any act that made a husband unhappy, even something as minor as his wife's cooking (*Gittin* 9:10). Jewish law ultimately ruled according to Hillel's dictate, though the rabbis did create an important safeguard, the *ketuba*, to protect women from being treated unfairly. The *ketuba* is a prenuptial contract witnessed just before the wedding ceremony that guarantees that any man who divorces his wife has to pay her considerable alimony. Nonetheless, in early times Jewish men could still compel their wives to accept a divorce. It was only in the tenth century C.E. that *Rabbenu Gershom legislated that a woman could not be divorced against her will. Today, therefore, a Jewish divorce is granted only if both parties agree to it. Mutual consent, however, is all that is required; in Jewish law, incompatibility is sufficient grounds for a divorce.

The Torah's wording, "and he shall write her a bill of divorcement," is interpreted literally in Jewish law. The divorce document is known as a *get*, and must be written either by the husband or by a representative appointed by him. The laws concerning the writing of divorce decrees are so complicated that only rabbinic experts are empowered to issue a *get*.

Every *get* follows a standard format: twelve lines, written by hand, in which the city where the divorce occurs is invariably identified by reference to the nearest river. The husband first commissions a scribe to write the document in the presence of witnesses. The *get* is then given to the husband, who walks over to his wife and drops it into her hands. The woman walks around the room by herself, symbolically indicating her new independent status. The rabbi then informs her that she cannot remarry for a minimum of ninety days (lest she become pregnant immediately and questions arise as to the paternity of the child).

Several people who have been religiously divorced have told me that the ceremony conferred a greater sense of finality than the civil divorce. One divorced woman told me, "The whole experience of divorce lawyers and divorce courts was very cold. For me, the *get* was a poetic release."

According to Jewish law, a man or woman who has been married in a Jewish ceremony, and then has a civil but not a religious divorce, is still married. A woman who remarries without first receiving a *get* is regarded as an adulteress, and any children of her second union are considered *mamzerim* (bastards) and are permitted to marry only other *mamzerim* (because Torah law permits polygamy, the implications of a male remarrying without giving his first wife a *get* are less serious). This is the sole instance in which the Torah punishes an innocent party (the *mamzer*) for the sin of another (his or her parents). The strictures of Jewish law concerning adultery are so severe that religious Jews are very conscientious about securing a *get*.

Unfortunately, more than a few religious men have taken advantage of their estranged wives' need for the *get*, and have refused to grant it. There are usually two motives for such a refusal: a simple desire to hurt the woman, or, more commonly, as a form of blackmail. Particularly when the wife comes from a wealthy family, some men will set a price tag before issuing the *get*.

The threat to the woman is a serious one. Some years ago, in a case widely discussed in religious circles in New York, a man told his estranged wife that he would not issue her a *get* until she was past childbearing age. In recent years, Jewish women's groups have picketed in front of the offices and stores of men who refuse to issue their wives a *get*. These groups have often been successful in pressuring recalcitrant husbands to issue a *get*. In Israel, religious courts are empowered to imprison a man until he issues the religious divorce, although women's groups complain the courts rarely use this power.

The problem of a man refusing to issue a *get* is a long-standing one in Jewish life. Eight centuries ago, *Maimonides ruled that the recalcitrant husband should be whipped until he says "I want to give the *get*" (**Mishneh Torah*, "Laws of Divorce," 2:20). If the husband refuses, Maimonides advocates whipping him until he dies; the woman would then be permitted to remarry as a widow. Although Maimonides's ruling is harsh, men who refuse to grant their wives a *get* are generally regarded by other Jews with the same affection American society extends toward child molesters.

The Reform movement in Judaism has circumvented the issue by nulifying the need for a *get*. Reform Judaism believes that the biblical demand that a husband write a bill of divorcement is fulfilled by the issuance of a civil divorce. This position is rejected by the Conservative and Orthodox movements. Rabbis of both denominations will not remarry either a man or a woman who has not obtained a religious divorce.

Conservative Judaism has largely overcome the problem of a husband who refuses to grant a *get* by inserting into the *ketuba* (marriage contract) a clause that effectively empowers the rabbis to force the issuance of a *get*.

An increasing number of Orthodox rabbis encourage couples to sign a prenuptial agreement in which the husband consents that, in the event of a civil divorce, he will also issue a *get*. Such contracts are civilly binding in

New York State, where secular courts can compel the issuance of the *get* as a condition of the civil divorce. Although some people have expressed concern about an American court intruding itself into a purely religious issue, the concern is specious. If a caterer, for example, signs a contract to provide a *kosher banquet and then serves a suckling pig as the main course, he can be sued in civil court for violating the contract. So, too, can a husband be sued for violating a contractually valid prenuptial agreement.

However, some religious Jews question whether a *get* issued under duress is valid. Even if the prenuptial agreement is civilly binding, is a *get* that is issued as a result of it religiously binding if the husband claims that he subsequently changed his mind and is issuing the *get* under coercion?

A woman who has not received a *get* is known colloquially as an *agunah*—a chained woman; her status is indeed as pitiable as that of a woman in chains.

SOURCES AND FURTHER READINGS: David Amram, *The Jewish Law of Divorce*; Jacob Fried, ed., *Jews and Divorce*. A more detailed description of the procedure of giving a *get* is found in Blu Greenberg, *How to Run a Traditional Jewish Household*, pp. 284–286, and Sharon Strassfeld and Michael Strassfeld, eds., *The Second Jewish Catalog*, pp. 113–116. See also Blu Greenberg, "Jewish Attitudes Toward Divorce," in her *On Women and Judaism: A View from Tradition*, pp. 125–145; Irwin Haut, *Divorce in Jewish Law and Life*; J. David Bleich, "The Aguna Problem," in his *Contemporary Halakhic Problems*, pp. 150–159.

331

CONVERT/*GER*

THERE IS A WIDESPREAD MYTH THAT JUDAISM HAS NO INTEREST IN SEEK-ing converts. In actuality, ancient Jews actively sought converts. One of the great rabbis of the talmudic era, the third-century Eleazar ben Pedat, declared that God sent the Jews into exile to bring people to Judaism (*Pesakhim* 87a). The large number of conversions to Judaism was noted in the first century by the Jewish historian *Josephus. From his writings, it appears that women were more apt than men to become Jews, probably because they were spared the painful necessity of undergoing *circumcision. At about the same time as Josephus, the New Testament speaks of *Pharisees who would "sail the seas and cross whole countries to win one convert" (Matthew 23:15).

The defeats the Romans inflicted on the Jews in the first and second centuries (see *The Great Revolt* and *Bar-Kokhba Rebellion*), along with the spread of Christianity throughout the Roman Empire, greatly slowed the pace of conversions. Still, shortly after the Roman Empire became Christian in the fourth century, converting to Judaism was decreed a capital crime, an indication that such conversions were still taking place. Indeed, the fact that the Catholic Church repeatedly reconfirmed the death sentence for converts suggests that Jews must have continued to seek them. In the Arab world, too, Muslim religious leaders made conversion to Judaism a capital crime.

Despite intense persecutions, the Jewish commitment to making the religion of their forefathers known to the world persisted. In the thirteenth century, a French rabbi, Moshe of Coucy, author of a Jewish legal code, *Sefer Mitzvot Ha-Gadol* (The Great Book of the Commandments), wrote that a Jew must be particularly scrupulous in business dealings with non-Jews, for if a Jew cheats a gentile, the latter might resolve never to convert to Judaism.

Nonetheless, by the late Middle Ages, the Jewish community was actively discouraging converts; the dangers both to the converts and to the communities facilitating the conversions were too great. In the sixteenth century, Rabbi Solomon Luria, perhaps the leading Talmud scholar of his age, wrote: "Under the present conditions, when we live in a country that is not ours, like slaves under the rod of a master, if a Jew encourages someone to become a proselyte he becomes a rebel against the government, subject to the death penalty. . . . Therefore, I caution anyone against being party to such activity when the law of the state forbids it, for he thereby forfeits his life." As late as the mid-eighteenth century, Count Valentine Potocki, a convert to Judaism, was burned at the stake in Vilna (see *Kiddush ha-Shem*).

Today, most conversions to Judaism occur because of a romantic involvement between a Jew and non-Jew. Although this is not the ideal motive for conversion, it is permitted if the rabbi supervising the conversion believes that the convert will live as a sincerely committed Jew (see *Tzitzit*).

At the time of conversion, both male and female converts immerse themselves in a ritual bath, the *mikveh.* Male converts also must be circumcised. In the United States, where most males are circumcised at birth, all that is required is a symbolic drop of blood taken from the male organ. Converts also are expected to declare their readiness to observe Judaism's laws.

This last requirement has become a bone of contention between Orthodox and non-Orthodox Jews. Most Orthodox rabbis insist that only those who are prepared to become fully observant Orthodox Jews should be converted. To convert anyone else, the Orthodox argue, is to do the would-be convert a disservice. Better that he or she remain a righteous non-Jew than become a nonobservant, sinning Jew.

Conservative and Reform rabbis, and some Orthodox rabbis, will convert non-Jews without demanding that they commit themselves to observe Jewish law fully. The Conservative movement does require, however, that male converts be circumcised, and that all converts immerse themselves in a *mikveh*, while the Reform movement in general makes no formal ritual requirements. (Some Reform rabbis do insist on the observances of *mikveh* and circumcision.) As a rule, rabbis of all denominations insist that would-be converts undertake a course of study of Judaism prior to conversion.

The word for convert in Hebrew is *ger* (plural, *gerim*). It is estimated that five thousand to ten thousand non-Jews convert to Judaism annually in the United States.

QUOTATIONS ABOUT CONVERTS

"If a man wishes to convert to Judaism, but says, 'I am too old to convert,' let him learn from *Abraham, who when he was ninety-nine years old, entered God's covenant" (*Tanhuma B, Lekh Lekha* 24).

"Said Resh Lakish: The convert is dearer than the Jews who stood before Mount Sinai. Why? Because had they [the Jews] not seen the thunder, and the mountains quaking and the sounds of the horn, they would not have accepted the Torah. But this one, who saw none of these things, came, surrendered himself to the Holy One and accepted upon himself the kingdom of heaven. Could any be dearer than he?" (*Tanhuma B, Lekh Lekha* 6).

SOURCES AND FURTHER READINGS: The statement of Rabbi Moshe of Coucy is found in his book *Semag*, p. 152b, and is cited in Jacob Katz, *Exclusiveness and Tolerance: Jewish-Gentile Relations in Medieval Times*, p. 80. Regarding the Jewish commitment to seeking converts in the ancient world, see George Foote Moore, *Judaism in the First Centuries of the Common Era*, vol. 1, pp. 323–353. See also Bernard Bamberger, *Proselytism in the Talmudic Period*; Joseph Rosenbloom, *Conversion to Judaism: From the Biblical Period to the Present*. The admonition of Rabbi Solomon Luria is found in his commentary to the Talmudic tractate *Yevamot* 49a, cited in Ben-Zion Bokser, *Jews, Judaism and the State of Israel*, p. 134.

BURIAL SOCIETY/*CHEVRA KADISHA*

AFTER A JEW DIES, A BURIAL SOCIETY, KNOWN IN ARAMAIC AS THE *Chevra Kadisha* (literally, "Holy Society"), prepares the body for interment. This process, called *tahara* (purification), involves the ritual cleaning of the corpse, by men for males and by women for females. Jewish tradition regards it as exceptionally meritorious to join a *Chevra Kadisha*, particularly because so many people are reluctant to do so. Although relatively few Jews, particularly outside the Orthodox community, are even aware of *Chevra Kadisha* societies, they exist in virtually every Jewish community and have recently been growing in numbers in the non-Orthodox world as well. It is traditional for members of a *Chevra Kadisha* to fast on the seventh of *Adar*, the anniversary of Moses' death, to atone for any disrespect they may have shown to the dead. The night after the fast, they hold a joyous banquet, celebrating their honored position in Jewish life.

A moving description of the work of a *Chevra Kadisha* was given by Professor Jacob Neusner concerning the death of his father-in-law, who died while on a trip to Jerusalem: "Those beautiful Jews," Neusner wrote of Jerusalem's *Chevra Kadisha*, "showed me more of what it means to be a Jew, of what Torah stands for, than all the books I ever read. They tended the corpse gently and reverently, yet did not pretend it was other than a corpse." At the conclusion of the burial, the head of the *Chevra Kadisha* said, "in a loud voice, that the dead should hear, and the living; 'Mordecai ben Menahem, all that we have done is for your honor. And if we have not done our task properly, we beg your forgiveness.' "

SOURCES AND FURTHER READINGS: Jacob Neusner, "Death in Jerusalem," in Jack Riemer, ed., *Jewish Reflections on Death*, pp. 158–159. The general activities of the *Chevra Kadisha* are described in Maurice Lamm, *The Jewish Way in Death and Mourning*, pp. 239–248. See also Jonathan Chipman, "Hevra Kadisha," in Sharon Strassfeld and Michael Strassfeld, eds., *The Third Jewish Catalog*, pp. 136–139; and Louis Jacobs, "The Religious Year," in Robert Seltzer, ed., *Judaism: A People and Its History*, p. 239.

KRI'A

SHIVA

SHIVA VISIT

AVEILUT

AMERICANS OFTEN DELAY OR AVOID CONFRONTATIONS WITH DEATH. That is one reason corpses are often made to look as lifelike as possible. In conversation, people search for euphemisms to avoid using the word "dead," as, for example, "He is no longer with us."

Jewish tradition actively discourages any denial of the reality of death. Almost immediately after a person dies, the body is covered with a sheet. At the funeral, the casket is closed. Later, when the casket is lowered into the ground, the immediate mourners are expected to pour the first shovelfuls of earth over it. The terrible patter of the earth hitting the casket effectively forces the mourners to accept the totality of their loss.

This realization, however, can be oddly therapeutic. Most important, it frees Jewish mourners from the constraints that Western society often imposes on the bereaved. In America mourners are commonly encouraged to "keep a stiff upper lip" and not weep in public. At Jewish funerals, on the other hand, it is considered proper to display intense emotions, and the codes of Jewish law state that the goal of the funeral oration, the *hesped*, is to make everyone present feel the depth and pain of the loss.

At the funeral, Jewish law mandates that a tear—in Hebrew, a *kri'a*—be made in the mourner's garment, on the left side of the garment for a parent, on the right side for other relatives. Representing the sundering that the death has caused in the mourner's life, the *kri'a* is started with a small knife and then is extended a few inches. Ideally, it should be performed on a jacket, shirt, or blouse. At many funeral parlors, mourners are supplied with an inexpensive ribbon to be cut at the appropriate time. It is highly questionable if such a ribbon fulfills the letter of the law; it certainly does not fulfill its spirit.

After the burial, mourners return home (or, ideally, to the home of the deceased) to sit *shiva* for seven days. *Shiva* is simply the Hebrew word for seven. During the *shiva* week, mourners are expected to remain at home and sit on low stools. This last requirement is intended to reinforce the mourners' inner emotions. In English we speak of "feeling low," as a synonym for depression; in Jewish law, the depression is acted out literally.

There are seven relatives for whom a Jew is required to observe *shiva*: father or mother, sister or brother, son or daughter, and spouse. During the *shiva* week, three prayer services are conducted daily at the mourners' house. The synagogue to which the mourning family belongs usually undertakes to ensure that a **minyan* (at least ten adult Jews) be present at each service. Among Orthodox Jews, a male mourner leads the service and recites the *Kaddish* prayer (see next entry) for the dead. Some Orthodox, and virtually all non-Orthodox, Jews encourage women to recite the *Kaddish* as well.

According to Jewish law, there is a specific etiquette for paying a *shiva* visit. Visitors are to enter quietly, take a seat near the mourner, and say nothing until the mourner addresses them first. This has less to do with ritual than with common sense: The visitor cannot know what the mourner most needs at that moment. For example, the visitor might feel that he or she must speak about the deceased, but the mourner might feel too emotionally overwrought to do so. Conversely, the visitor might try to cheer the mourner by speaking of a sports event or some other irrelevancy at just the moment when the mourner's deepest need is to speak of the dead. And, of course, the mourner might just wish to sit quietly and say nothing at all. Unfortunately, people frequently violate this Jewishly mandated procedure. Particularly if the deceased was very old, the atmosphere at a *shiva* house often becomes inappropriately light-hearted, as Jews also try to avoid confronting the fact of death.

Mourners must not shave, take a luxurious bath, wear leather shoes (which Jewish tradition regards as particularly comfortable), have sex, or launder their clothes during the week of *shiva*. If the family of the deceased is in desperate economic circumstances, its members are permitted to return to work after three days of mourning. In the past, when the Jewish community was less affluent, this leniency was utilized more frequently. Solomon Luria, a great Polish rabbinical scholar of the sixteenth century, was asked by a *melamed* (a teacher who tutored young boys in Hebrew) if he might return to work before *shiva* was complete; otherwise he feared the parents would hire another teacher for their children. Rabbi Luria gave him permission on the grounds that his livelihood was at stake and on the further, rather pathetically humorous, grounds that since a Hebrew teacher's life is quite miserable, everyone would know he was not returning to work out of pleasure.

On the Sabbath that falls during the *shiva*, the public laws of mourning are suspended. Mourners are permitted to leave the house in order to attend synagogue services.

Upon entering the house after returning from the cemetery, the first thing the mourners do is sit down and eat. Jewish tradition dictates that neighbors come to the mourners' house to prepare food for them before they return from the cemetery. The rabbis realized that if food were not prepared, the mourners might not eat at all.

The seven days of mourning officially begin when the mourners return home from the cemetery. On the seventh day, the mourners are required to sit *shiva* for only a small part of the day. After a half hour or so in the morning of the seventh day, *shiva* ends. Often the rabbi or a synagogue representative comes to the house on the last morning and escorts the mourners on a short walk around the block, symbolizing the mourners' return to the regular world.

Shiva is followed by progressively longer and less intense stages of mourning. First comes *shloshim* (thirty), a thirty-day period during which male mourners are not supposed to shave or cut their hair—in ancient times, letting one's hair grow long was a sign of mourning—although they are permitted to do so if it will be injurious to their livelihood, or if they appear terribly unkempt. Following this comes the year of *aveilut* (mourning). Jewish law mandates a full year of mourning only for one's parents; the mourning period for other close relatives, including spouses, terminates at the end of *shloshim*.

During the period of mourning, whether it is thirty days or a year, mourners are not to participate in public celebrations, such as weddings. These restrictions are suspended for those whose livelihood depends on attending such events, for example, photographers, musicians, and caterers. The laws are also suspended for an occasion in which the mourner himself or herself is the celebrant. The obligation to rejoice at one's own wedding, and to celebrate with one's bride or groom during the first week of married life, takes precedence over the laws of mourning. Even during that week, however, the mourner must still say the Mourner's *Kaddish*.

In Jewish tradition, acts performed for the dead are called acts of loving-kindness—in Hebrew, *gemilut khesed*. When one does something for the dead—for instance, helping pay for a funeral—it is done, of course, without any expectation of the recipient repaying the kindness. Such acts of gratuitous kindness are regarded as being on the highest moral plane.

SOURCES AND FURTHER READINGS: A general overview of the laws of mourning is found in Maurice Lamm, *The Jewish Way in Death and Mourning*. Rabbi Solomon Luria's permission to the Hebrew teacher to resume giving lessons during *shiva* is found in his book of responsa, number 66, and is translated into English in Simon Hurwitz, *The Responsa of Solomon Luria*, pp. 138–139.

334

MOURNER'S KADDISH

YAHRZEIT

YIZKOR

Peace Be Upon Him/Alav Ha-Shalom
Peace Be Upon Her/Aleha Ha-Shalom

THROUGHOUT THIS BOOK, I HAVE GENERALLY TRIED TO BE DESCRIPtive rather than prescriptive. However, when it comes to reciting the Mourner's *Kaddish*, I feel compelled to urge my readers, "Do it."

The *Kaddish*, an Aramaic prayer that is more than two thousand years old, is recited in slightly different variations at every prayer service. Although one form of the *Kaddish* is recited in memory of the dead, the prayer itself says nothing about death; its theme is the greatness of God, reflected in its opening words: "*Yitgadal ve-yitkadash, Shmei rabbah*—May His name be magnified and made holy. . . ." The prayer's conclusion speaks of a future age in which God will redeem the world.

Why then was this prayer designated by Jewish law to memorialize the dead? There is no definite answer; the tradition dates only from the Middle Ages. Most likely, people believed that the finest way to honor the dead was to recite the *Kaddish*, thereby testifying that the deceased person left behind worthy descendants, people who attend prayer services daily and proclaim their ongoing loyalty to God.

Reciting the *Kaddish* also forces mourners to go out in public. After the death of a loved one, a person might well wish to stay home alone, or with a few family members, and brood. But saying *Kaddish* forces a mourner to join with others. According to Jewish law, the *Kaddish* cannot be recited unless a minimum of ten adult Jews are gathered in a *minyan*.

Because of the *Kaddish*'s therapeutic value, I believe it is important that it be recited by women as well as men. Throughout Jewish history, only men had the obligation to say the *Kaddish*. So associated was this prayer with men that Eastern European parents sometimes referred to a son as their *Kaddishel*—the one who would recite *Kaddish* for them. Among traditional Jews, it was considered disadvantageous to have only daughters, because there would be no child to say *Kaddish* after the parents' deaths.

However, even before the rise of feminism, there were Jewish women who said *Kaddish*. A gem of modern Jewish literature is a letter written by Henrietta *Szold, one of eight daughters of a Baltimore rabbi and a great figure in American-Jewish history. When Szold's mother died, a close male friend of the family, Haym Peretz, offered to say *Kaddish* on her behalf. An excerpt from the letter in which Szold refused his offer, insisting that she would say the *Kaddish* herself, is found in the entry on her life in this book.

Kaddish is recited every day during the morning, afternoon, and evening services. Ideally, one should attend every service, but if one cannot do so, it is desirable to attend at least one of the three daily services. In the observance of *Kaddish*, as in most areas of Jewish life, something is better than nothing. If one chooses not to attend a daily service, then one should at least say the *Kaddish* on the Sabbath.

In the case of the death of a sibling, a child, or a spouse, *Kaddish* is recited for one month; when a parent dies, it is recited for eleven months, even though the full mourning period lasts for twelve. According to a statement in the Talmud, when the most wicked people die, they are consigned to hell for a maximum of twelve months. Since recitation of the *Kaddish* is believed to help elevate the soul of the dead (see *Sanhedrin* 104a), reciting it for a full year would imply that one's parent is one of those wicked people sentenced to a full year in hell; hence, the *Kaddish* is recited for only eleven months.

When the year of mourning is over, mourners are expected to return to a fully normal life. "One should not grieve too much for the dead," the *Shulkhan Arukh*, the sixteenth-century code of Jewish law, notes, "and whoever grieves excessively is really grieving for someone else." But there are several occasions each year when the dead are memorialized. The most significant of these is *yahrzeit*, the anniversary of the death, which is observed according to the Hebrew calendar. Most synagogues keep registries of the

Hebrew dates of members' deaths and send out notices reminding family members of the *yahrzeit* date. As is the case in all Jewish holidays, *yahrzeit* observance begins at night. A twenty-four-hour candle is lit and, as one woman I know says: "The spirit of the dead person fills the room again for twenty-four hours." One attends synagogue for the evening, morning, and afternoon services and again recites the *Kaddish*. One should not go to a celebration or party on the day of *yahrzeit*, and some people fast on that day.

Four times a year—on *Yom Kippur, and the final day of *Sukkot, *Passover, and *Shavuot—a special memorial prayer called *yizkor* (remember) is recited in the synagogue for one's deceased relatives. In many Orthodox, and some non-Orthodox, congregations, children whose parents are still living are asked to exit the sanctuary during the *yizkor* recitation. The rationale is largely superstitious; it is regarded as unlucky for the parents to have their children present while this prayer is being recited. Other congregations have dropped the practice, for some good reasons: For one thing, young children who have lost a parent remain in the synagogue to recite *yizkor*, and the mass exodus of their friends can only deepen their sense of aloneness. For another, many congregations today add a special *yizkor* for the six million Jews murdered in the Holocaust, many of whom left no one behind to recite either *Kaddish* or *yizkor*. Since the entire congregation is expected to recite this special *yizkor*, there is no reason for anyone to step outside. It is, however, notoriously difficult to break people from superstitions associated with death.

The phrase Jews most usually append when mentioning the name of a dead person is *alav ha-shalom* or *aleha ha-shalom*—"peace be upon him or her." Many Jews who are otherwise Jewishly illiterate use this Hebrew expression, often swallowing the words. I once heard of a Jew who claimed that his last religious relative was his great-grandfather "Oliver Shalom"; he had never heard the man referred to in any other way. When speaking of an exceptionally righteous person, the expression used is *"Zai-kher tzaddik livrakha*—May the memory of the righteous be for a blessing."

SOURCES AND FURTHER READINGS: The quote from the *Shulkhan Arukh* is found in *Yoreh Deah* 394:1, and is translated by Chaim Denburg in Jack Riemer, ed., *Jewish Reflections on Death*, p. 23. Riemer's entire book is a very fine collection of essays on the Jewish confrontation with death. See also Maurice Lamm, *The Jewish Way in Death and Mourning*.

335

MEZUZAH

THE MOST FAMOUS PRAYER IN JUDAISM IS THE *SH'MA, WHOSE OPENING paragraph reads: "And you shall speak of them [the Torah's laws] when you sit in your house, when you walk by the way, when you lie down, and when you rise up. . . . And you shall write them upon the doorposts of your house and upon your gates" (Deuteronomy 6:7,9). The Hebrew word for doorpost is *mezuzah*, and for thousands of years Jews have posted small boxes, also known as *mezuzot*, on their doorposts. Inside each box is a small scroll, which must be written by a scribe. It contains the first and second paragraphs of the *Sh'ma*, including the commandment concerning the *mezuzah*. When a Jew enters his house, he sees the *mezuzah* and is thereby reminded how he should act in his home. Likewise, when a Jew leaves the house, the *mezuzah* reminds him of the high level of behavior he is expected to maintain wherever he goes.

To ensure that the *mezuzah* is always visible, it is attached to the upper third of the doorpost, at a slant. Every room in the house, except for the bathroom, should have a *mezuzah* on its doorpost. When a Jew moves into a new home, he or she is expected to put up a *mezuzah* immediately, or at least within the first thirty days. A special blessing is recited when the *mezuzah* is installed: "Blessed are you, Lord our God, King of the Universe, who has sanctified us with His commandments, and who has instructed us to put up a *mezuzah*."

Many Jews kiss the *mezuzah* when they pass it, generally by touching it with a fingertip and then kissing the finger.

In recent years, an unfortunate superstition has developed around the *mezuzah*, a belief that Jews who have suffered tragedy are being punished for having unkosher *mezuzot* on their doorposts. An unkosher *mezuzah* is one that was not written properly by a scribe, or one in which a word or a letter has become erased. To avoid having unkosher *mezuzot*, many Jews have their scrolls periodically checked by a scribe.

While ritual scrupulousness may be quite commendable, the stories spread by some Orthodox Jews that associate human tragedies with unkosher *mezuzot* are very disturbing. In the most widely circulated such story, it is claimed that after twenty-five Jewish children in Ma'alot, Israel, were murdered in their school by Arab terrorists in 1974, it was discovered that there were twenty-five unkosher *mezuzot* in the building. Not infrequently, such stories embitter people against a Deity who would visit cruel suffering upon individuals for inadvertently tacking up a *mezuzah* with an error in the scroll.

SOURCES AND FURTHER READINGS: Hayim Donin, *To Be a Jew*, pp. 152–155, describes the procedure for putting up a *mezuzah*. Orthodox rabbi Martin Gordon, "*Mezuzah*: Protective Amulet or Religious Symbol?," *Tradition* 16:4 (Summer 1977), pp. 7–40, discusses and documents the tendency to see the *mezuzah* as a protective amulet. He notes (p. 8) one Orthodox publication that declared in the aftermath of the rescue of the Jewish hostages at *Entebbe, Uganda, in 1976: "Due to the fact that most of the *mezuzot* in the homes of the hostages, upon examination were found to be defective, improperly placed, or not in every doorpost, *all* Jews should check their *mezuzot* immediately."

336

KOSHER, *KASHRUT*

MILCHIG, FLEISHIG, PAREVE

RITUAL SLAUGHTER/*SHEKHITA*

MASHGIAKH

AMONG JEWS THERE ARE COMMON MISCONCEPTIONS ABOUT KOSHER food, ranging from the notion that kosher food means that it has been blessed by a rabbi to the belief that the kosher laws are part of an ancient Jewish health code. "Pig was forbidden to Jews," one hears many Jews explain, "so that Jews would not get trichinosis."

However, the system known as *kashrut* is given a rationale in the Torah that has nothing to do with rabbinic blessings or with health. The Torah associates *kashrut* with holiness (see, for example, Leviticus 11:44–45, and Deuteronomy 14:21).

Kashrut's laws regulate that Jews are not permitted to eat whatever they may want, and that even permitted foods must be prepared in a special way. For example, the only animals designated by the Torah as kosher are those that have cloven hooves and that regurgitate their food. The most commonly eaten kosher animals are the cow and the lamb. But even these animals must be ritually killed by a *shokhet* (slaughterer). Jewish law obligates the *shokhet* to kill the animal with one quickly drawn stroke against its throat. If he delays the stroke, thus needlessly prolonging death, the animal is rendered unkosher and Jews are forbidden to eat it.

Because of the laws of kosher slaughter, Jews are forbidden to kill animals through hunting: This method of slaughter automatically renders an animal unkosher. The prohibition against hunting, already several thousand years old, has generally become incorporated into the Jewish psyche; even among nonreligious Jews one finds relatively few hunters.

A Torah law, addressed to all mankind, and not just Jews, forbids consuming an animal's blood (Genesis 9:4; see also Leviticus 17:10–14). "The blood is the life," the Torah rules and therefore the blood of a dead animal must be treated with respect. In the case of some animals, the blood is drained from the slaughtered creature and covered with earth. Later, the meat must be salted until all traces of blood are removed.

It is likely that Judaism's abhorrence at the possibility of consuming even a drop of blood is related to the general abhorrence of bloodshed in the Jewish community. Wherever they have lived, Jews have committed fewer crimes of violence and bloodshed than their non-Jewish neighbors. Unless one assumes that Jews are genetically different, this must be because of some different values they practice. *Kashrut*, it would seem, has helped civilize the Jewish spirit.

Among fish, only those with fins and scales are designated kosher (Leviticus 11:9–12; Deuteronomy 14:9–10); no reason is given for this law. All shellfish are forbidden, so many popular fish, such as shrimp and lobster, are unkosher. Two fish have been the subject of long-standing controversy between Conservative and Orthodox Judaism: sturgeon and swordfish. The argument hinges on whether their scales qualify according to Jewish law; the Orthodox say no, the Conservative say yes.

Among birds, only those specifically enumerated in Jewish tradition are permitted; they include chicken, turkey, and duck.

Permitted animals are herbivorous. All meat-eating animals and birds that prey on other birds are all forbidden. The Talmud notes that one of the signs of a forbidden bird is that it has a talon to kill.

In three separate places, the Torah legislates: "You shall not seethe a kid in its mother's milk" (Exodus 23:19, 34:26; Deuteronomy 14:21). In the ancient Near East, a young kid boiled in its mother's milk was apparently regarded as a great delicacy. The rabbis deduced from the law's threefold repetition that it is also forbidden to prepare meat and milk products together as well as eat them during the same meal. Because of this law, kosher homes have two sets of dishes and cutlery, one for meat meals, one for dairy. In Jewish life, meat products, including fowl, are called by a Yiddish word, *fleishig*—an easy word to remember since it incorporates the word "flesh." Milk products are known as *milchig*, incorporating the word "milk." Foods such as fish, fruits, and vegetables, which are neither meat nor milk, are called *pareve*, and may be eaten with either milk or meat meals. Among knowledgeable Jews, the word *pareve* is also used to designate people who have wishy-washy personalities, as in, "He has a *pareve* personality." The expression presumably originated because *pareve* food has no positive identity, being neither meat nor milk.

Because meat takes a long time to digest, Jewish law rules that one must wait a designated period after eating a meat meal before ingesting milk products. Jews fortunate enough to come from Holland, or to trace their ancestry to Dutch Jews, generally wait only one hour, while German Jews wait three hours. In most of Europe, however, the rabbis insisted upon a six-hour wait. The waiting time between milk and meat is much shorter. One is generally permitted to eat meat a half hour or so after a milk meal, or after thoroughly rinsing one's mouth.

Restaurants that are designated as kosher employ a *mashgiakh*, whose responsibility is to guarantee that the laws of *kashrut* are observed scrupulously in the kitchen. Many American food companies also hire *mashgikhim* (plural) to certify their products as kosher. Today, there are tens of thousands of products under rabbinical supervision in the United States. All carry a *heksher*, a certification affirming that they are kosher. The most common symbol confirming *kashrut* is the letter U surrounded by a large O, the trademark of the Orthodox Union, the country's largest dispenser of *hekhsherim* (plural). However, numerous other rabbis and rabbinical organizations supervise the *kashrut* of various products. All companies that desire to have rabbinical supervision must issue the *mashgiakh* a key, so that he can enter the food establishment at will to make sure no unkosher products are being secretly or inadvertently introduced into the food being prepared.

Within the Jewish community, one finds extraordinary variations in the way Jews observe the dietary laws. The most observant will eat only in their own homes, in the homes of people they know to be scrupulously kosher, or in restaurants under rabbinical supervision. If they attend a meeting at a nonkosher home or restaurant, they usually restrict themselves to water, coffee, and fresh fruit. They will not eat any hot food because although the food itself might be kosher, it most probably has been prepared in pots and pans used for unkosher foods.

Some Jews keep kosher at home; "outside," they will eat in nonkosher homes and in restaurants those foods that are kosher, even when they have been prepared in pots and pans that also are used to prepare unkosher foods. These people believe that the use of such utensils does not render kosher items unkosher.

There are many American Jews who keep kosher at home but eat unkosher foods outside the home. Other Jews, both more and less observant, often ridicule such behavior as hypocritical. Yet, from the perspective of Jewish law, it is clearly preferable to keep kosher at home than not to keep it at all.

Still other Jews do not keep kosher in the home but refrain nonetheless from serving foods that are symbolically regarded as the "most" unkosher—pig and shellfish. Still others serve pig and shellfish in their homes, but maintain a semblance of *kashrut* during the eight days of *Passover, when they refrain from having any bread products in the home (see *Khametz*).

In Hebrew the word "kosher" literally means "fit," which is why one can ask about a business venture of questionable legality: "Is it kosher?" Similarly, one might say of a very fine Jew, "He is a kosher Jew."

The opposite of kosher is *treif.* One distinction children growing up in kosher homes learn is that certain things in life are kosher, and others are *treif.*

SOURCES AND FURTHER READINGS: The biblical laws of *kashrut* are found in Leviticus 11 and Deuteronomy 14:4–21. See also Dayan Dr. Isadore Grunfeld, *The Jewish Dietary Laws* (two volumes). On variations in *kashrut* regulations between the Orthodox and Conservative movements, see Hayim Donin, *To Be a Jew,* and Blu Greenberg, *How to Run a Traditional Jewish Household,* pp. 95–119 (both Orthodox), and Isaac Klein, *A Guide to Jewish Religious Practice,* and Samuel Dresner, *The Dietary Laws* (both Conservative).

PART FIFTEEN

Synagogue and
Prayers

337

TEMPLE/SYNAGOGUE/SHUL/SHTIEBL

Jewish Community Centers

REFORM JEWS ATTEND SERVICES AT A TEMPLE, CONSERVATIVE JEWS pray at a synagogue, Orthodox Jews *daven* (Yiddish for "pray") at a *shul*. While the distinctions are not hard-and-fast—Conservative Jews sometimes speak of "going to *shul*," Orthodox Jews of "attending synagogue"—these are the terms generally used by members of each denomination to describe the places where they pray.

Temple, synagogue, and *shul* all mean the same thing: a house of worship. *Shul*, a Yiddish word that means school as well as synagogue, reflects the fact that Orthodox synagogues long tended to be centers of learning as well as of prayer.

To make the nomenclature even more complicated, in recent years many Orthodox Jews have chosen to pray at *shtieblakh*. *Shtieblakh* (singular, *shtiebl*) are smaller in size than synagogues, and more often than not are private houses that have been converted into synagogues. Many *shtieblakh* are under the spiritual direction of Hasidic *rebbes* (see *Hasidism*). Congregants who pray at *shtieblakh* generally claim that the atmosphere is more intimate, friendly, and spiritual than at conventional synagogues. *Shtieblakh* are more apt to be attended by the most traditional Orthodox Jews; at many, men wear black suits and black hats.

An Orthodox synagogue's sanctuary physically differs from Reform and Conservative ones in two significant ways: First, there is a **mekhitza* (separation) between the men's and women's sections; in the most Orthodox synagogues, men cannot see women during the service. Women, in fact, play no public role during the prayers at an Orthodox service. At Reform and Conservative synagogues, men and women sit together.

In addition, in Orthodox congregations the Torah is read from the *bimah* (a platform), which is located in the middle of the congregation. When the Torah is read in an Orthodox synagogue, the reader therefore faces in the same direction as the rest of the congregation, toward the Ark. In Reform and Conservative congregations, the Torah service is usually conducted from the front of the sanctuary, and the reader faces the congregation. In addition, many Reform and some Conservative synagogues use an organ to accompany the cantor. At Orthodox synagogues, neither an organ nor any other musical instrument is played on the Sabbath or on most Jewish holidays.

For much of American-Jewish history, the wealthiest Jews tended to be Reform. To this day, many of America's most beautiful temples are affiliated with this movement. Perhaps the best-known Reform congregation is the very large and very beautiful Temple Emanu-El in New York City. In its early years, Emanu-El dropped so many of the traditional Jewish trappings—it even held its major weekly service on Sunday mornings—that in 1910, Rabbi Judah Magnes made the disconcerting announcement that the previous Sunday a Christian visitor to New York had come to the service and realized that he was not in a church only because of a chance remark by the rabbi. In recent decades, however, Reform Judaism has started to reincorporate many traditional rituals and Hebrew into the service. Another famous Reform synagogue is the Wilshire Boulevard Temple in Los Angeles. It was headed for more than six decades by Rabbi Edgar Magnin, known in Hollywood as "rabbi to the stars." Magnin numbered among his close friends and parishioners the Jewish producers who created Hollywood: Louis Mayer even offered to establish the multitalented Magnin as a movie director. Magnin preferred to remain in the rabbinate, but the Judaism he preached represented the most liberal wing of Reform Judaism; he did not regard the rituals of Jewish law (for example, *kashrut* and Sabbath restrictions) as binding (see *Pittsburgh Platform*). Since Magnin's death, in the early 1980s, Wilshire Boulevard Temple too has shifted toward a more traditional Jewish approach.

The Conservative synagogue movement expanded exponentially in the years after World War II, attracting large numbers of Jews who had moved to the suburbs.

An institution that has proved especially attractive to suburban Jews is the Jewish community center. In certain ways, these centers are Jewish versions of YMCAs, in which an active program of sports and health club facilities is supplemented with Jewish cultural programming. The goal of the centers is to create an environment in which Jews can socialize together. In recent years, as American society has become more open and socially mobile, an increasing number of non-Jews have joined the JCCs, often because they are the health club facility nearest their homes. As a result, many centers have been grappling recently with the issue "What should be Jewish about *Jewish* community centers?" The centers play a pivotal role in many Jewish communities, particularly the smaller ones. Their memberships are often far larger than those of any one synagogue and represent for many people their only formal connection to organized Jewish life. The Jewish community centers host an ever-growing number of Jewish book fairs each November, and are increasingly becoming centers of adult Jewish study.

SOURCES AND FURTHER READINGS: A discussion of the different denominations and synagogue movements in American-Jewish life is found in Jack Wertheimer, ed., *The American Synagogue: A Sanctuary Transformed.* Rabbi Edgar Magnin and his involvement with the Jewish Hollywood directors are discussed in Neal Gabler, *An Empire of Their Own: How the Jews Invented Hollywood,* pp. 266–310.

MINYAN

JEWISH LAW PREFERS THAT JEWS PRAY COMMUNALLY RATHER THAN privately. For one thing, the rabbis apparently felt that public prayers are more apt to be offered for that which benefits the entire community, whereas individuals often pray for that which benefits only themselves, even if it be at the expense of someone else. For example, a person who has applied for a job may pray to God that he or she gets it, although others have applied for the same position and presumably want it just as much. Because communal prayers are said by, and on behalf of, large numbers of people, they tend to be more concerned with the public good.

In traditional Jewish law, the minimum number necessary to form a community is ten adult males, a group known as a *minyan.* If ten men are not present, many of the important prayers in the service—the **Kaddish,* the reading of the Torah (see *Torah Portion of the Week/Parshat ha-Shavua*), and the **Barkhu*—cannot be recited. During the eleven months I was reciting the **Mourner's Kaddish* for my late father, I sometimes attended services at a small synagogue a block away from my apartment. I finally had to stop going there because it was a constant struggle to procure a *minyan*. As soon as seven or eight men arrived, the sexton would start telephoning every male member in a ten-block vicinity, telling whomever he reached to rush over. For people like myself, who were saying *Kaddish*, the wait until the *minyan* was complete was agonizing. Fortunately, we never missed saying it.

In religious neighborhoods, where many small congregations known as *shtieblakh* abound (see preceding entry), one often sees men sticking their heads out of a window and shouting at passersby, "We need a tenth for a *minyan*." Guilt-ridden, I have often entered such synagogues only to find that they also needed a fifth, sixth, seventh, eighth, and ninth for a *minyan*. They probably assumed that no one would come in if they called out, "We need six more for a *minyan*."

A famous American play on a Jewish theme is Paddy Chayefsky's *The Tenth Man*, which tells the story of a young, rather assimilated Jew whose life is permanently affected when he is drafted to be "the tenth" to form a *minyan*.

In 1973, the *Conservative movement ruled that women could be counted in a *minyan*: The movement regarded the exclusion of women from the prayer quorum as discriminatory. The Orthodox leadership denounced this ruling as a violation of Jewish law. A *minyan*, according to the Orthodox interpretation, can be composed only of people who are obligated by Jewish law to participate in communal prayer. Jewish law had always excused women from the obligation of communal prayers because of their responsibilities at home. Even within Orthodox law, however, women were specifically obligated to be present for the public reading of the Book of *Esther on *Purim, and because they are obligated to do so, they can be counted as part of the *minyan* at that reading. Conversely, a man who has lost an immediate family member, but has not yet buried the dead person, is exempt from the obligation to pray until after the funeral. At a service before the funeral, he is, therefore, not counted in a *minyan*.

When the Conservative decision was first announced, some of the more traditional congregations rejected it. Today, however, almost all Conservative congregations count women in a *minyan*.

Since Reform Judaism does not consider itself bound by the category of *minyan*, a full prayer service is conducted even in the absence of ten adult Jews.

An Orthodox congregation in Cambridge, Massachusetts, tried to redefine a *minyan* some years ago, so as not to discriminate in any way against women. They decided that they would not begin services until at least ten men and ten women were present. Unfortunately, because women have traditionally not been counted in a *minyan*, Orthodox women usually feel no compunction about arriving in synagogue quite late; after all, their absence does not delay the service. As a result, the Cambridge congregation found that its services were starting very late each week, and quickly returned to the traditional male-only definition of *minyan*.

In Jewish life, the word *minyan* is often used as a synonym for synagogue. A religious Jew might ask another, "What *minyan* do you *daven* [pray] at?" in the same way another person would say, "Which synagogue do you go to?"

MEKHITZA

THE MOST OBVIOUS PHYSICAL DIFFERENCE BETWEEN ORTHODOX AND non-Orthodox synagogues is the *mekhitza* (separation) that divides the men's and women's sections of the synagogue. Orthodox synagogues separate men and women during prayer services; non-Orthodox synagogues do not. The separate section for women is an old tradition in Judaism, and we know that there were separate women's sections as long ago as the beginning of the Common Era, at the time of the *Temple in Jerusalem.

Today, many non-Orthodox Jews feel that a separate women's section is offensive, that it consigns women to an inferior status. While there are Orthodox laws that clearly disadvantage women—most notably, the laws of divorce (see *Get*)—it is by no means clear that the *mekhitza* is, or was, intended to be discriminatory. It seems, rather, to have been a response to human nature. God is abstract, and it is an effort for people to focus on an abstract Deity while praying. For many, perhaps most men, it is a natural reaction to look around when a group of women is present and let one's gaze rest on a pretty woman. Indeed, people usually dress up before going to synagogue, in an effort to look attractive. In the "battle" between an intangible God and a tangible member of the opposite sex, Jewish law assumed that the tangible is more likely to win. Hence, physical separation can help bring about spiritual concentration for both sexes.

It must also be acknowledged, however, that the *mekhitza* is sometimes used to discriminate against women. I have been to Orthodox synagogues where the *mekhitza* was so remote that women were effectively cut off from participating in the service. Not surprisingly, women in such congregations often spend the service talking and gossiping, and then are condemned by the men for not praying. In many modern Orthodox synagogues, the *mekhitza* is drawn down the center of the synagogue, so that men and women can equally observe the cantor and the service.

In recent years, a number of Orthodox women have founded separate women's prayer groups in which they can lead the service. Some Orthodox rabbis have condemned such prayer groups, arguing that they are only a concession to feminism. The response has been that something is not *ipso facto* un-Jewish because it is feminist; if feminism has prompted people to see an injustice in the Jewish community, then it becomes a Jewish issue as well.

The issue of the *mekhitza* provokes powerful emotions in Jewish life. Jewish feminists have on occasion demanded that all Jews committed to women's rights refuse to attend any service in which women are segregated and denied public participation. Orthodox Jews, on the other hand—men and women alike—will not participate in a service at which men and women sit together. When national Jewish organizations meet, separate services must therefore be arranged for Orthodox and non-Orthodox participants.

340

RABBINIC ORDINATION/*SEMIKHA*

THOUGH *SEMIKHA* CONNOTES RABBINIC ORDINATION, IN HEBREW THE word literally means to "lean on." Until the early centuries of the Common Era, the ordaining rabbi would place his hands over the head of the man being ordained, in other words, lean on his head.

According to Jewish tradition, *Moses appointed Joshua his successor in this manner (see Numbers 27:18–23), and Joshua appointed the leader of the next generation—who did the same for the following generation—by the laying on of hands. The rabbis of the ancient world must have had an extraordinary sense of empowerment knowing that those who ordained them had themselves been ordained by rabbis of the previous generation, in an unbroken line going back to Moses.

In an effort to extinguish Judaism in the aftermath of the *Bar-Kokhba revolt, the Romans made the ceremony of *semikha* a capital offense, both for the ordaining rabbi and the man being ordained. Yet the ritual of *semikha* apparently continued underground, although around 425 C.E. it seemingly came to an end.

Although the term *semikha* is still applied to rabbinic ordination, new candidates no longer are ordained by the laying on of hands. Because modern rabbis cannot trace their ordination back to Moses, Orthodox Judaism believes that they have less power than the rabbis of old to make changes in Jewish law. Nonetheless, those who are ordained are deemed qualified to answer questions of Jewish law, and serve as religious leaders of the Jewish community.

In modern Jewish life, most of the people who are ordained are Orthodox. It is a long-standing Orthodox tradition to encourage young men to study for ordination, even if they do not intend to work as rabbis. Ordination is seen less as a professional degree than as tangible evidence that one has studied Jewish law in depth. My father, for example, was an ordained rabbi, although he worked professionally as an accountant. Among the rabbis who graduated *Yeshiva University in my class, about half went into fields other than the rabbinate or Jewish education.

In the *Reform, *Conservative, and Reconstructionist movements, almost all those who study for ordination subsequently work as rabbis or Jewish educators.

While ordination normally is granted by rabbinical seminaries, there is no law in the United States preventing anyone who wishes to do so from calling him or herself rabbi. Because the telephone company used to give discounts to clergy, some lay people listed themselves as rabbis. To the question "Who ordained them?" the answer given was, "The telephone company." In the 1890s, on New York's Lower East Side, a rabbi from Eastern Europe had a large painted sign placed over his dwelling designating him as THE CHIEF RABBI OF THE UNITED STATES. When people asked, "Who made him chief rabbi?" they were told, "The sign painter."

The most dramatic change in rabbinic ordination in recent years has been the decision of the *Reform, *Reconstructionist, and *Conservative movements to ordain women (see *Women Rabbis*). Orthodoxy opposes this tendency: Although one female Orthodox scholar, Blu Greenberg, has predicted that Orthodoxy will eventually ordain women, few others share her optimism. Nonetheless, in recent years a number of schools for women have opened in the Orthodox world in which women study many of the same texts studied by male students in advanced *yeshivot*.

A person who is ordained is called in Hebrew a *mus-makh*, as in "he is a *mus-makh* from Yeshiva University."

SOURCES AND FURTHER READINGS: On the life of rabbis in the United States, see Murray Polner, *Rabbi: The American Experience*; Jacob Neusner, *American Judaism: Adventure in Modernity*; "The Making of American Rabbis," *Encyclopedia Judaica Year Book 1983–1985*, pp. 84–105.

COMMON TERMS USED IN THE SYNAGOGUE
Bimah
Mizrakh
Aron Kodesh
Hagba *and* Glila
Chazzan
Gabbai
Ba'al Koh-Rey
Trope

BIMAH (HEBREW FOR "PLATFORM") IS THE PLACE WHERE THE CANTOR stands when leading the service, and where the Torah scroll is read. A person honored by being called up to bless the Torah might be told, "Go up to the *bimah* now. You have an *aliyah to the Torah."

Mizrakh is the Hebrew word for "east." Since ancient times, Jews have faced in the direction of Jerusalem and the *Temple when praying. For almost all Jews, except those living in certain Arab countries, this meant facing east. Even when praying alone, a Jew is supposed to face east, particularly when reciting the *Amidah prayer. As a rule, synagogues are built facing east, and the seats up front by the eastern wall are generally the most coveted. The rabbi's seat, for example, is invariably there. In the musical *Fiddler on the Roof*, Tevye fantasizes how wonderful life would be "if I were a rich man." One benefit would be "a seat by the eastern wall." In many Jewish homes, a work of art containing the word *mizrakh* is hung on an eastern wall, so that visitors will know immediately which direction to face when praying.

Aron Kodesh, meaning "Holy Ark," refers to the Ark in which are kept the Torah scrolls, the holiest objects in Jewish life. Taking out the Torah is a highlight of the Shabbat morning service. When the Torah is removed, the congregation sings "*Kee mi'Tzion tey-tzey Torah*—For from Zion shall go forth the Torah, and the word of God from Jerusalem" (Isaiah 2:3).

It is considered a great honor to perform any synagogue ritual connected with the Torah, starting with *petikha*, drawing apart the curtain in front of the *Aron Kodesh* just before the Torah is taken out. When the Torah reading is concluded, two members of the congregation are summoned for *hagba* and *glila*. *Hagba* means "to lift," and the person assigned this honor lifts the Torah, with its text showing, and raises it above his head for all to see. Since a Torah can weigh twenty to thirty pounds, this is an arduous job; it is considered "macho" in religious circles to open the Torah wide enough to allow many columns of text to be seen. People stand when the Torah is lifted, and recite in Hebrew, "This is the Torah that Moses placed before the children of Israel according to the word of God, through Moses' hand." The person assigned *glila* dresses the Torah. The Torah scroll is first tied up with a simple cloth wrapper, then a covering, usually quite ornate, is put over it.

In addition to the rabbi (see preceding entry), several other people play important roles in the service. The cantor (in Hebrew, *chazzan*) leads the chanting of the service. The *gabbai* is responsible for almost everything else that occurs during services. It is he, for example, who informs the people who are to receive an *aliyah*, and who maintains decorum throughout the service. The *gabbai* also pronounces a special blessing for all who have received an *aliyah*, and he says a blessing on behalf of those who are ill. The person who reads the Torah is known as the *ba'al koh-rey*, literally, "master of reading." The job is a difficult one because the Torah is not read in a monotone, but is chanted according to specific musical notes known as the *trope*. The notes are not marked in the Torah scroll but must be memorized in advance.

SOURCE AND FURTHER READING: Hayim Donin, *To Pray as a Jew*.

342

SIDDUR

MAKHZOR

MORNING SERVICE/SHAKHARIT

AFTERNOON SERVICE/MINKHA

EVENING SERVICE/MA'ARIV

ADDITIONAL SERVICE ON SHABBAT AND

HOLIDAYS/MUSSAF

THE WORD *SIDDUR* IS USUALLY TRANSLATED AS "PRAYERBOOK," THOUGH "arranged in order" probably comes closer to expressing what the Hebrew term means. What is arranged in order is a large collection of disparate Jewish writings written over more than two thousand years. Many of the oldest prayers come from the *Psalms, some from the rabbinic period of the *Talmud (about two thousand years ago), while others were composed during the Middle Ages. As a rule, Orthodox *siddurim* (plural of *siddur*) contain almost no new prayers, although the Modern Orthodox have included a special prayer for the State of Israel in *siddurim* published since the State's creation in 1948. The *siddurim* of the Reform, Reconstructionist, and Conservative movements often include some newly composed prayers.

The traditional Orthodox *siddur* contains no prayers that are not in Hebrew. Jewish law permits Jews to pray in any language they wish; presumably, God is a polyglot. Nonetheless, the prayers recited by the congregation in unison are restricted to Hebrew. This has resulted in a peculiar situation in which many Jews do not understand the prayers they are reciting. On the other hand, precisely because the *siddur* is in Hebrew, it has played a more important role than any other book in ensuring that Jews have a basic knowledge of Hebrew. Had Jews, in each of the lands of their dispersion, prayed only in their native countries' languages, it is very doubtful that Hebrew could have been revived in the twentieth century and become the language of Israel (see *Eliezer Ben-Yehuda and the Revival of Hebrew*). The *siddur* thus also played an important role in maintaining the unity of the Jewish people.

Although many nontraditional Jews have pressured their denominations to lessen the number of prayers in Hebrew, all denominations have maintained some. Most Jews acknowledge that they feel a deeper emotion in chanting, *"Sh'ma Yisra'el Adonai Eloheinu, Adonai Ekhad,"* than in reciting, "Hear, O Israel, the Lord is Our God, the Lord is One."

The daily *siddur* consists of three services: The morning service is called *shakharit* (Hebrew for "morning"), the afternoon service *minkha,* and the evening service *ma'ariv* (evening). While it is permissible for a Jew to pray by him- or herself, Jewish tradition expresses a strong preference that prayers be recited together with other Jews, in a **minyan.* Most Orthodox and many Conservative synagogues have two daily *minyanim,* one in the morning for *shakharit,* and one that carries through from the late afternoon till the early evening, at which *minkha* and *ma'ariv* are recited. Jews saying the **Mourner's Kaddish* recite it at these services.

Shakharit is quite lengthy, running from thirty-five to fifty minutes. On Mondays and Thursdays a small section of the **Torah portion of the week is chanted aloud during the service; the rabbis wished to ensure that Jews not go three days without hearing a section from the Torah. The afternoon *minkha* and evening *ma'ariv* services are shorter; each lasts ten to fifteen minutes.

On the Sabbath and holidays, the services, particularly in the morning, are considerably different from, and much longer, than the weekday services. Though *shakharit, minkha,* and *ma'ariv* are recited on all holidays, extra prayers are inserted in honor of the special days, including a service added to the morning prayers, called *mussaf. Mussaf* (Hebrew for additional) originally referred to the additional sacrifice that used to be offered at the **Temple on the Sabbath and holidays. In addition, the Torah reading on the Sabbath and holidays is considerably longer than the small selection read on Monday and Thursday mornings.

Because the service for the High Holy Days includes so many special prayers, it was necessary to compile a separate *siddur* for these holidays. This *siddur,* known as a *makhzor,* is used during the **Rosh ha-Shana and **Yom Kippur services.

SOURCE AND FURTHER READING: Hayim Donin, *To Pray as a Jew.*

343

TORAH SCROLL/*SEFER TORAH*

WHILE MANY JEWS KNOW THAT THE TORAH CONTAINS *613 COMMAND-
ments, few know that the very last commandment obliges every Jew to write a
Torah scroll, a *sefer Torah*, during his lifetime. Today, almost no one carries
out this commandment literally, but many Jews observe it through an agent,
i.e., by contributing money to hire a scribe to write a *sefer Torah*. A number
of years ago, the *Lubavitch movement initiated a program encouraging Jewish children to contribute nickels, dimes, and quarters so that they could participate in fulfilling the 613th commandment.

Because the Torah is the only document that Jewish tradition regards as containing God's words and only God's words, it is considered the holiest object
in Jewish life. Jewish law ordains that those Torah scrolls that are read publicly during the synagogue service—every Monday, Thursday, and Shabbat
morning, on Shabbat afternoons, and on Jewish holidays—must be written
by hand.

The scribe who writes a *sefer Torah* is known as a *sofer*. He is required to be
a religious Jew who can be trusted to carry out the numerous regulations
regarding this holy task. There are exceedingly complex laws regulating the
precise shape of the letters; the sheets on which the text is written must be
parchment from a ritually clean animal (generally, sheepskin), and the writing must be done in black ink, in straight lines, with a quill. It is customary
for scribes to immerse themselves in a *mikveh (ritual bath) before they write
the name of God. It usually takes an experienced scribe about one year to
complete the writing of a Torah.

An error in the spelling of a word invalidates the Torah for communal use
until such time as it is corrected. Indeed, because of the extraordinary care
with which Torah scrolls are written, few errors or discrepancies have crept
into this ancient and sacred text. Compared with the Torah text, there are far
more discrepancies in ancient manuscripts of Plato and Aristotle. Even

printed Bibles have had their fair share of errors. In 1631, two English print-ers brought out a version of the Bible in which the seventh of the *Ten Com-mandments was accidentally altered to read: "Thou shall commit adultery." Not surprisingly, the edition became known as the "Adulterer's Bible," and the printers were fined three hundred pounds. Nor was this error in a printed Bible a singular instance. In comparison, few handwritten Torahs have been discovered to contain errors of any significance.

The enormous amount of labor that goes into the writing of a Torah has caused the price to rise tremendously in recent years. It is common for a newly commissioned Torah to cost between twenty-five and fifty thousand dollars. Starting in the 1970s, there was a disturbing increase in Torah scrolls being stolen from synagogues by thieves who hoped to sell them to other synagogues. To guard against this, most Torah scrolls have been registered. If a synagogue is approached by someone wishing to sell it a Torah, the congregational leaders can quickly check its registration number to see if it is "hot."

Any time a *sefer Torah* is visible and being carried in the synagogue, peo-ple are expected to stand. When the Torah is taken out of the Ark during the service, whoever leads the service carries it very carefully against his chest as he walks around the synagogue. Torah scrolls can weigh twenty or more pounds, and if a scroll is dropped, all who witness it are expected to fast for a whole day. In Sephardic synagogues, the Torah is generally carried inside a large wooden cylinder that stands erect when open; the Torah parchment is therefore in a standing position inside the cylinder when it is read.

As the person carrying the Torah wends his way through the synagogue, con-gregants kiss the scroll, though usually not directly. Either they touch the cov-ering around the scroll with their fingers or, in the case of men, with the fringes of their *tallit*, and then they kiss their fingers or the fringes; alternatively, they kiss their fingers and touch it to the Torah cover. A friend of mine once brought a recently arrived Russian Jew to a Sabbath service in New York. It was the first time the man had been inside a synagogue. As he saw the Torah being kissed, my friend asked him if he knew what the people were kissing.

"Some sort of an icon?" the Soviet Jew guessed.

"No," my friend told him. "It is a book containing the laws of how to be a good human being, and a good Jew. And we kiss it because it is the most valu-able possession we have."

SOURCES AND FURTHER READINGS: Alfred Kolatch, *This Is the Torah*; Jeffrey Cohen, *Horizons of Jewish Prayer*, pp. 203–220.

344

TORAH PORTION OF THE WEEK/

PARSHAT HA-SHAVUA

HAFTORAH

DVAR TORAH

THE *TORAH, THE SINGLE MOST IMPORTANT DOCUMENT IN JEWISH LIFE, is in effect the constitution of the Jewish people. In order to ensure that all Jews are familiar with its contents, Jewish law regulates that it be read through in its entirety in synagogue each year.

The rabbis divided the Torah into 54 portions of unequal lengths—they range from 30 to more than 150 verses. There was a need to have more than 52 portions, because in 7 out of 19 years, the 354-day lunar calendar is lengthened by adding on several weeks to the calendar. In nonleap years, since there are more Torah portions than there are weeks, some portions are combined and read together.

The weekly Torah reading is divided into seven sections, and a member of the congregation is called up to bless the Torah before each section is read (see next entry). At the end of the reading, the last few verses are repeated, and are called *maftir*.

The Torah reading is the centerpiece of the Shabbat morning service, coming after the morning *shakharit* service and followed by the concluding *mussaf* service. The Torah's removal from the Ark just prior to its being read is in many ways the service's highlight. As the Torah is taken out, the congregation sings, *"Kee miTzion tey'tzey Torah*—For from Zion shall go forth the Torah, and the word of God from Jerusalem." The person leading the service carries the Torah around the synagogue, and the congregants kiss it (see preceding entry).

Strangely, despite the importance of the Torah reading, congregants often talk to each other while it is being read. In the Orthodox *shul* where I grew up, the Torah reader would periodically stop chanting while the *gabbai angrily scolded people for talking. Perhaps because the Torah is read through in its entirety every year, people assume they are so familiar with its contents that they don't have to listen carefully.

A convention of synagogue life is that the rabbi's weekly sermon is based on a verse or topic in the weekly Torah reading. For example, on the Sabbath when the portion called *Kedoshim* is read (Leviticus 19:1–20:27)—the portions are named after their first significant Hebrew word—in which appears the command "Do not go about as a talebearer among your people" (19:16), the rabbi might speak about the laws against gossiping (see *Lashon ha-Ra*). When *Va-Yera* (Genesis 18–22) is read, wherein occurs the story of the *binding of Isaac (22), the rabbi might speak about the sacrifices people must be willing to make on behalf of religion. Most rabbis, however, occupy the same pulpit for many years and, since they cannot give the same sermon year after year, become adept at linking any subject on which they wish to speak with the Torah reading.

Though the Hebrew term *parshat ha-shavua* means "[Torah] portion of the week," religious Jews often just condense the expression into one word, *parsha*, as in "What *parsha* are we reading this week?" In invitations sent out by traditional Jews to *Bar and Bat Mitzvahs and weddings, it is common to cite the Torah portion for the week in which the celebration will occur. "The wedding will be held," an invitation might read, "during the week of *Brei'sheet* [Genesis 1:1–6:8], wherein occurs the verse 'Therefore shall a man leave his father and mother and cleave to his wife, and they shall be one flesh' " (2:24).

The Hebrew term *dvar Torah*, which literally means "a thing of Torah," refers to any talk one gives on Torah or Judaism. Any Jew, of course, can give a *dvar Torah*, and one need not be ordained to do so.

The *Haftorah*, a selection from the prophetic books of the Bible, is chanted in the synagogue immediately after the reading of the weekly Torah portion. It almost always bears some relationship to the reading that has just been concluded. The *Haftorah* for the first chapters of Genesis, for example, begins with *Isaiah 42:5, which speaks of "He that creates the heavens," thus recalling the story of creation with which Genesis begins. The following week's *Haftorah* is also from Isaiah, and it includes chapter 54, verse 9, which refers to "the waters of Noah," a clear reminder of the Noah story that dominates that week's Torah portion.

When the Sabbath falls on the last day of a Hebrew month (see *Rosh Khodesh*), the *Haftorah* reading is from 1 Samuel 20. In verse eighteen, with which the *Haftorah* begins, *Jonathan, the son of King *Saul, reminds his best friend, *David, that "tomorrow is the new moon," and goes on to warn him how he should hide himself from Saul's wrath.

To be assigned the public reading of the *Haftorah* is a great honor. It also signifies a significant degree of Jewish learning, since the *Haftorah* reader must be able to read the Hebrew text fluently, and to chant each word according to its prescribed musical note (see *Trope*). As a rule, boys chant the *Haftorah* on their Bar Mitzvah, and the preparation for this can take several months. In Reform, Conservative, and Reconstructionist synagogues, girls also are invited to chant the *Haftorah*, and some modern Orthodox congregations have women's *minyanim* at which the Bat Mitzvah girls do so as well. On the Sabbath before a wedding, it is customary to invite the groom to chant the *Haftorah* (see *Aufruff*). For many people, the months of preparation before a Bar or Bat Mitzvah are sufficient to enable them to sight-sing any *Haftorah* for the rest of their lives.

SOURCES AND FURTHER READINGS: Four of the basic one-volume commentaries on the Torah (divided into its weekly portions) are: Joseph Hertz, *The Pentateuch and Haftorahs* (Orthodox), Nosson Scherman, *The Chumash: The Stone Edition* (Orthodox), David Lieber, ed., *Etz Hayim: Torah and Commentary* (Conservative), and W. Gunther Plaut, ed., *The Torah: A Modern Commentary* (Reform). Nehama Leibowitz, a Torah scholar in Israel, published six volumes of incisive commentaries covering all five books of the Torah, entitled *Studies in . . .* At the end of each section, Leibowitz suggests questions for further discussion.

ALIYAH

PRIEST, LEVITE, ISRAELITE/*KOHAIN*, *LEVI*, *YISRA'EL*

THE WEEKLY TORAH PORTION (SEE PREVIOUS ENTRY) IS DIVIDED INTO seven sections on the Sabbath. Before each section is read, a member of the congregation is summoned to bless the Torah. To be called up to the Torah is to receive an *aliyah* (which literally means "going up," as in making *aliyah to Israel) and it is one of the greatest honors a Jew can receive in the synagogue.

There are four life-cycle events at which it is virtually mandatory to have an *aliyah*—at one's *Bar Mitzvah (in non-Orthodox synagogues, at a *Bat Mitzvah, too), on the Sabbath before one's wedding (see *Marriage Ceremony—Aufruff*), after the birth of a baby girl (a girl child is officially named in the synagogue after her father's *aliyah*; boys are named at the *circumcision), and on the Sabbath before observing *yahrzeit*, the anniversary of an immediate family member's death.

There is a set order governing how the *aliyot* (plural) are disbursed. The first is always assigned to a *Kohain*, a Jew of priestly descent. The *Kohanim* are regarded as Judaism's spiritual aristocracy, and have been honored with the first *aliyah* for at least two thousand years. Although Jewish religious identity is transmitted through the mother (see *Who Is a Jew?*), "tribal" identity is transmitted through the father. Therefore, one whose father is a *Kohain* is a *Kohain* as well. Most Jews with the name Cohen are *Kohanim*, as are most Jews with the names Kaplan, Rappaport, and Katz (the name Katz is a contraction of two Hebrew words, *Kohain tzedek*, "a righteous priest"). Last names, however, are not determinative; family history is.

The second *aliyah* is reserved for a Levite, a member of the tribe that assisted the *Kohanim* in the *Temple services. Today, when *Kohanim* are called up during holiday services to bless the congregation (see next entry), the Levites first pour water over their hands. Most Jews with the names Levy, Levine, or variations thereof (Levinsky) are Levites.

Aside from the *Kohanim* and *Levi'im*, all other Jewish tribal identities have long been lost. No Jews today can trace their identity to the tribe of Reuben, or Gad, or Asher, and consequently, all other Jews are labeled Israelites (in Hebrew, *Yisra'el*). With the exception of the first two, the rest of the *aliyot* are reserved for Israelites, who make up the overwhelming majority of the Jewish population. Since the third *aliyah* (known in Hebrew as *shlishi*, "third") is the first *aliyah* to be offered to any member of the congregation, it is considered a great honor. For obscure reasons, in parts of Eastern Europe the sixth *aliyah* was not considered an honor. An old Jewish joke has it that a stranger in town goes to the local synagogue on the Sabbath, and is called up sixth.

"Where I come from," he protests to a synagogue officer, "*shishi* [the sixth *aliyah*] is given only to horse thieves."

"Here too," the synagogue officer tells him.

On the other hand, it became a custom among *Hasidim to give the sixth *aliyah* to their *rebbe*.

The person honored with an *aliyah* is summoned by his Hebrew name and by the Hebrew name of his father. For example, my Hebrew name is *Yisra'el Yosef* (Israel Joseph) and my father's name was *Shlomo* (Solomon), so I am called up as *Yisra'el Yosef ben* (son of) *Shlomo*. A person may ask to be called up by both his parents' names. A person given an *aliyah* generally kisses the Torah (at the place where the reading of the Torah begins or continues) with the fringe of his *tallit, and recites a blessing that begins "Barkhu et Adonai hamevorakh — Blessed is the God who is blessed."

In Orthodox congregations, only men receive *aliyot*; in Reform congregations, men and women alike are called. In the 1950s, the Conservative movement ruled that each Conservative synagogue had the option of calling up women for *aliyot*. Throughout the 1950s and 1960s, very few Conservative congregations took advantage of this ruling, but with the spread of feminism in the 1970s, almost all of them began granting *aliyot* to women. In recent years, it has also become more common for women in non-Orthodox congregations to wear *tallitot*.

The person who is honored with an *aliyah* stands next to the table where the Torah is read while the one who reads it, the *ba'al koh-rey*, chants a section of the Torah. When that portion is completed, the person with the *aliyah* recites an additional blessing, and is then blessed by the *gabbai with a Mi Shebeirakh, a prayer that calls forth God's blessing on him. If a member of the congregation, or a relative or friend of a member, is sick, a special Mi Shebeirakh is also recited between *aliyot*. The sick person's name is given in Hebrew followed by the Hebrew name of the person's mother. At the conclusion of the Mi Shebeirakh, the individual who has received the *aliyah* remains at the table where the Torah is read, and stays there throughout the reading of the next section. He then returns to his seat.

At that point, members of the congregation call out to him the Hebrew equivalent of "Congratulations," *Yasher koach*, which literally means "May your strength increase." The correct response to such a greeting is "Barukh ti-hiyeh — May you be blessed." Jews who come from the Sephardic world generally call out *Chazak Barukh* ("May you be strong and blessed").

Only on the Sabbath are seven people given *aliyot* to the Torah. During the Monday and Thursday readings, only three people are called up. The rabbis had no desire to prolong the service on a weekday, when people had to rush off to work. On the festive first day of each month—*Rosh Khodesh—there are four *aliyot*; on holidays, five; and on *Yom Kippur, six.

SOURCES AND FURTHER READINGS: Hayim Donin, *To Pray as a Jew*, pp. 49–54; Jeffrey Cohen, *Horizons of Jewish Prayer*, pp. 221–242.

346

PRIESTLY BLESSING/DUKHANING

THERE MIGHT WELL BE NO GROUP IN THE WORLD THAT CAN TRACE ITS ancestry as far back as can Jewish priests/*Kohanim* (see preceding entry). According to tradition, the first priest was *Moses' brother, *Aaron, and the Torah designated that Aaron's descendants forever minister as the priests of Israel (Numbers 3:10). In the time of the *Temple, the priests supervised and performed all rituals and *sacrifices. On *Yom Kippur, the High Priest prayed on behalf of all Jewry at the Temple's Holy of Holies, a room that was entered only on that day.

After the *destruction of the Temple, the priests lost their primary function in Jewish life. Nonetheless, from generation to generation parents continued to transmit to children the knowledge that they came from this special class. While it is considered a great honor to be a *Kohain*—in the future, when the *Messiah comes, *Kohanim* will conduct the affairs of the *Temple—there are also some serious disadvantages. For one thing, the Torah forbids *Kohanim* to marry divorced women (Leviticus 21:7). A forty-year-old bachelor I know told me that the older he became, the fewer single women he came across who had never been divorced. Reform Judaism has long renounced observance of this biblical ordinance; the Conservative movement is generally willing to ignore this prohibition if the *Kohain* who marries a divorcée renounces his priestly status both for himself and his descendants. Even among the Orthodox, permission can occasionally be obtained for a *Kohain* to marry a divorcée, specifically in cases where the *Kohain*'s parents were not religiously observant. In such instances, a rabbi can *sometimes* invalidate someone's priestly status if the only person who asserts that he is a *Kohain* is his father, since Jewish law generally does not accept testimony on religious matters from Jews who are nonobservant. Another biblical law forbids *Kohanim* from having contact with dead bodies (Leviticus 21:1–4); as a result, strictly Orthodox Jews who are *Kohanim* cannot generally attend medical school or go to a cemetery (except in the case of the burial of an immediate family member).

In Jewish life today, there are three rituals primarily associated with priests: the redemption of a firstborn male infant on the thirty-first day after birth—*pidyon ha-ben*; the honor of receiving the first *aliyah* to the Torah (see preceding entry); and the blessing of the rest of the Jewish community on holidays. This blessing is known in Hebrew as *birkat kohanim* (the priests' blessing), but many Jews refer to the ceremony by its Yiddish name, *dukhaning*. Outside of Israel, the *dukhaning* is performed about fifteen minutes before the end of the service on *Passover, *Shavuot, and *Sukkot mornings (in Israel it is performed daily), as well as on *Yom Kippur. The *Levites in the congregation (see preceding entry) wash the hands of the priests. The priests remove their shoes and go up to the front of the congregation, where they recite the priestly blessing:

> May the Lord bless and protect you.
> May the Lord make His face shine upon you and be gracious to you.
> May the Lord lift up His countenance upon you and grant you peace.

While pronouncing the blessing, the priests hold their hands in an unusual fashion, the ring and middle fingers held together and the two small fingers together. *Star Trek* fans who have seen the Vulcan Mr. Spock performing the same gesture should be aware that this is no coincidence. The actor playing Spock, Leonard Nimoy, is himself a Jew and he decided to utilize this synagogue ritual in his portrayal of the character.

In Orthodox synagogues, the males commonly draw their *tallit* (prayer shawls—see following entry) over their heads during the *dukhaning*. I have vivid childhood memories of being with my father under his *tallit* while the priests were reciting the blessing. The reason for the custom is that God's presence is assumed to become manifest at the spot where the priests are standing, and—in accordance with the biblical claim that man cannot see God and live (Exodus 33:20)—it is forbidden to gaze in the direction of the priests. Almost every child who has grown up in an Orthodox synagogue has heard it said that anyone who looks directly at the priests during the *dukhaning* will go blind. An even more mordant claim was made in some congregations that the first time one looks, one becomes blind; the second time, one dies. A great rabbinic scholar established his reputation for brilliance at the age of three by pointing out the absurdity of this belief. "If you go blind the first time you look," he asked, "how can you look a second time?"

In any case, I am happy to note that children today are less frequently threatened with this frightening punishment.

Several years ago, I interviewed the playwright Arthur Miller, who told me that his earliest Jewish memory was of being in a synagogue with his grandfather, while up in the front of the congregation, a group of men in stocking feet seemed to be dancing and chanting, all the while with their hands uplifted. The experience had remained with Miller more than sixty years later. "It seemed so glorious," he told me.

347

TZITZIT

Tallit

TZITZIT ARE RITUAL FRINGES THAT ARE TO BE ATTACHED TO ANY four-cornered garment worn by a male. During prayer services, the fringes are affixed to a large prayer shawl which is known as a *tallit*. The law concerning the ritual fringes known as *tzitzit* is one of relatively few biblical laws for which the Torah offers a reason: "And you shall see [the fringes at the corner of the garment] and remember all the commandments of the Lord, and observe them" (Numbers 15:39). The biblical notion that seeing will lead to remembering is familiar to many people from childhood. When given an errand to perform, children are sometimes told to tie a string around a finger as a reminder. *Tzitzit* are an *ethical* string-around-the-finger to remind Jews of God's commandments.

The fringes themselves are attached to two different kinds of garments. During the day, they are worn by males under the shirt in a garment called an *arba kanfot* (four corners). This garment is placed over the head like a poncho. Since the biblical verse instructs that the fringes be seen, some

Orthodox Jews make sure that the fringes of their *arba kanfot* hang out. Others, who are self-conscious about looking noticeably different, wear the *arba kanfot*, fringes included, under their shirt.

During morning services, a *tallit*, a garment with fringes at the four corners, is worn over the shoulders like a cape. While the *tallit* is usually quite large, the only part of it that is religiously mandated are the four fringes.

One of the few truly romantic tales in the *Talmud concerns the ritual fringes. A young student, the Talmud reports, was particularly scrupulous in observing the laws of *tzitzit*. Nonetheless, when he heard of a stunningly beautiful harlot in a far-off land, his passion overcame him. He sent the woman her fee of four hundred golden *dinarim*, the equivalent of thousands of dollars, and set off to see her. When he arrived at her house, the harlot's maid informed her that the man who had sent the four hundred golden *dinarim* had arrived, and he was invited in. He entered the woman's room and saw her, beautiful and naked, lying on her bed. He began to undress but, in the poetic description of the Talmud, when he started to remove his *tzitzit*, the fringes flew up and slapped him in the face. At that point, he turned from the prostitute and sat down upon the floor. The woman came down from the bed and asked him if he found fault with her. No, he said, she was indeed the most beautiful woman he had ever seen but . . . and he proceeded to tell her about *tzitzit*. The woman said to him: "I shall not let you go until you tell me your name, the name of your city, the name of your rabbi, and the name of the school where you study Torah." When the young man left, she sold her possesions, gave a third of her money to charity, and went to Jerusalem. She went to the man's teacher, Rabbi Hiyya, and said, "Convert me."

Rabbi Hiyya, seeing this great beauty of the Roman world seeking his assistance, must surely have been puzzled. "Perhaps you have fallen in love with one of my students?" he asked.

The woman gave no response, just handed over the note the man had given her.

Rabbi Hiyya read the note and recognized his student's handwriting. He converted the woman and arranged for her marriage to the young man (*Menakhot* 44a).

Among other things, the tale is meant to convey, of course, that *tzitzit* can give a person the strength to overcome illicit passion. This student, in fact, might well have been so scrupulous about this particular commandment precisely because he needed a corrective for his strong passions. The story's moral, however, is not obvious to everyone. At a class where I taught the story, one pupil's reaction was: "The lesson is, if you go to a prostitute, leave your *tzitzit* at home."

A QUOTE ABOUT *TZITZIT*

"How does the mere act of looking upon *tzitzit* serve to remind one of God's commandments? I suggest that it's like a uniform worn by soldiers in the army. When wearing a uniform, one is especially mindful to whom one owes one's allegiance" (Rabbi Hayim Donin, *To Pray as a Jew*, p. 155).

SOURCES AND FURTHER READINGS: Hayim Donin, *To Pray as a Jew*, pp. 155–159; Isaac Klein, *A Guide to Jewish Religious Practice*, pp. 3–6. There is an illuminating discussion of the story of the student and the harlot in Eliezer Berkovits, *Crisis and Faith*, pp. 64–73.

348

TEFILLIN

TEFILLIN ARE TWO SMALL BLACK BOXES WITH BLACK STRAPS ATTACHED to them; Jewish men are required to place one box on their head and tie the other one on their arm each weekday morning. *Tefillin* are biblical in origin, and are commanded within the context of several laws outlining a Jew's relationship to God. "And you shall love the Lord your God with all your heart, with all your soul, and with all your might. Take to heart these instructions with which I charge you this day. Impress them upon your children. Recite them when you stay at home and when you are away, when you lie down and when you get up. Bind them as a sign on your hand and let them serve as a frontlet between your eyes" (Deuteronomy 6:5–8).

Certain Jewish groups—including probably the *Sadducees, and definitely the medieval *Karaites—understood the last verse to be figurative; it means only that one should always be preoccupied with words of Torah, as if they were in front of one's eyes. The *Pharisees, however, took the text literally; the words of the Torah are to be inscribed on a scroll and placed directly between one's eyes and on one's arm. *Tefillin* are wrapped around the arm seven times, and the straps on the head are adjusted so they fit snugly.

The text that is inserted inside the two boxes of *tefillin* is hand-written by a scribe (see *Sefer Torah*), and consists of the four sets of biblical verses in which *tefillin* are commanded (Exodus 13:1–10, 11–16; Deuteronomy 6:4–9, 11:13–21). Because each pair of *tefillin* is hand-written and hand-crafted, it is relatively expensive, and a well-made pair costs several hundred dollars, and often even more.

The word *tefillin* is commonly translated as "phylacteries," though the Hebrew term is more often used. I have never met a Jew who puts on *tefillin* who calls them "phylacteries."

Putting on *tefillin* is the first *mitzvah* assumed by a Jewish male upon his *Bar Mitzvah. Usually, boys are trained to start wearing them one to two months before their thirteenth Hebrew birthday. During the training period, boys don *tefillin*, but do not recite a blessing. Subsequent to the Bar Mitzvah, a specific blessing, "Blessed are You, Lord our God, King of the universe, who has sanctified us with His commandments and commanded us to put on *tefillin*," is recited whenever they are worn. Many Jews say an additional blessing and prayer upon putting on *tefillin*.

Tefillin are worn each weekday morning, but not on the Sabbath or on most Jewish holidays. On the fast day of *Tisha Be'Av, and on that day only, they are put on during the afternoon instead of the morning service.

Among observant Jews, *tefillin* is a *mitzvah* of the greatest significance. Recently, an eighty-nine-year-old rabbi told me that, in the seventy-six years since his Bar Mitzvah, he had not missed putting on *tefillin* even once. Since the Holocaust, stories have circulated of Jews who managed to smuggle *tefillin* into Nazi *concentration camps and put them on each morning.

One Jewish group, the *Lubavitcher Hasidim, have made a particular effort to promote the *mitzvah* of *tefillin* among Jewish males. They often set up vans, known as Mitzvah Mobiles, in neighborhoods frequented by Jews, and ask men who pass by: "Are you Jewish?" If the answer is yes, they continue: "Did you put on *tefillin* today?" If the person says, "No," they invite him inside the van. First they put on the box that goes on his arm (for right-handed people, the *tefillin* go on the left arm; left-handed people wear them on the right arm) and wrap the strap around the arm seven times. Then the other box is put on his head. They lead him in the recitation of the blessing over the *tefillin*, and in certain other major prayers, such as the *Sh'ma.

In Jerusalem Lubavitcher Hasidim also are present every day, except the Sabbath, at the *Western Wall (*Kotel*), encouraging people to fulfill the *mitzvah* of *tefillin*.

Many years ago, the Lubavitcher *Rebbe* advised the world-famous sculptor Jacques Lipchitz to start wearing *tefillin* and to pray every morning. Lipchitz subsequently described the effect of these two acts on his life: "I *daven* [pray] every morning. It is of great help to me. First of all, it puts me together with all my people. I am with them. And I am near to the Lord, the Almighty. I speak with Him. I cannot make my prayers individual, but I speak to Him. He gives me strength for the day. . . . I could not live anymore without it."

SOURCES AND FURTHER READINGS: Hayim Donin, *To Be a Jew*, pp. 144–152; Isaac Klein, *A Guide to Jewish Religious Practice*, pp. 6–9. The quote from Jacques Lipchitz is found in *The Reconstructionist*, February 1974, p. 20.

349

KIPPAH OR YARMULKA

IN THE WESTERN WORLD, A MAN SHOWS RESPECT BY TAKING OFF HIS hat; in Jewish life, he shows respect by putting it on. In Jewish tradition, covering the head conveys the wearer's sense that there is a force in the universe above him.

The head covering generally worn today is much smaller than a hat. Known in Hebrew as a *kippah*, it is usually made of cloth and is several inches in diameter. A *kippah* is worn by Orthodox males at almost all times, and by Conservative males in the synagogue and sometimes when eating. Some very observant Conservative women also wear a *kippah*. In Orthodox circles, women would never wear a *kippah*, though the more traditional Orthodox married women cover their hair either with a handkerchief or a wig. Once a woman is married, her husband is the only male who is supposed to see her hair. The Reform movement is agnostic on the issue of male head covering. In the past, some Reform synagogues actually forbade Jewish men from wearing a *kippah*. In recent years, there has been something of a return to tradition in Reform, and one now sees many males wearing a *kippah* at services.

Many American Jews know the word *kippah* by its Yiddish name, *yarmulka*. The Yiddish word is of uncertain origin, though it has been conjectured that it is a shortened form of two Aramaic words, *yarei me-elokha* (one who fears God).

The *kippah* is a well-known symbol of Jewish religiosity. I once performed a wedding ceremony at which a member of the American cabinet, Jack Kemp (some years later, the Republican vice-presidential candidate), was present. He asked me whether he was required to put on a head covering. I told him he could if he wished, but Jewish law does not insist that a non-Jew attending a religious ceremony follow the Jewish rituals. He then asked with a smile: "But are we *goyim* allowed to wear *yarmulkas?*" I assured him that there was no objection to a non-Jew doing so. Indeed, during every election year, one finds non-Jewish candidates putting on a *kippah* when speaking in Orthodox or Conservative synagogues.

Although the *kippah* might symbolize to many non-Jews a high level of Jewish religiosity, wearing one is a custom, not a law. Nowhere does either the Torah or *Talmud mandate that a Jewish male wear a head covering. In the sixteenth century, Rabbi Solomon Luria, one of the leaders of Polish Jewry, was asked by a man who suffered from headaches whether he was permitted to eat bareheaded. Rabbi Luria responded that, in theory, there is no requirement to wear a head covering even during prayers; one can say the *Sh'ma* without covering one's head. But since the custom of Jewish males covering their heads has become so widely accepted, people will think that anyone who goes about bareheaded is impious. He therefore suggested that the man wear a soft *kippah* made of fine linen or silk.

Among Orthodox Jews, various types of male head covering reflect the different movements within Orthodoxy. Among the most Orthodox, hats, which cover the entire head, are preferred to *yarmulkas*. The *Hasidim wear fur hats on Jewish holidays. Other, somewhat more liberal Orthodox Jews wear black *yarmulkas*. The Modern Orthodox are more apt to wear smaller, knitted *kippot* (plural of *kippah*; suede *kippot* are also popular). The very expression *kippah seruga*, which literally means, "knitted *kippah*," signifies the Modern Orthodox community. One might even hear it said of someone, "He's a *kippah seruga*," which simply means that the person being described is Modern Orthodox. The more Orthodox groups have long opposed the knitted *kippah* phenomenon, because the *kippot* are often knitted by girls for boyfriends, and the most Orthodox are presumably fearful where this premarital *yarmulka* knitting might lead.

A funny caption to a photograph is reputed to have appeared in *The Jerusalem Post* in 1964—I have not seen the original—when Pope Paul VI visited Israel. He was met by the Israeli president, and the caption under the photograph read: "The Pope is the one wearing the *yarmulka.*"

SOURCE AND FURTHER READING: Rabbi Luria's reply, number 72 in his collected responsa, is translated in Simon Hurwitz, *The Responsa of Solomon Luria,* pp. 109–111.

350

SOME FAMOUS PRAYERS

Barkhu

Amidah, *Alternatively* Shmoneh Esray; *and* Kedusha

Ashrei

Adon Olam

Ein Kayloheinu

Aleinu

Hallel

CERTAIN PRAYERS, SUCH AS THE *BARKHU*, ARE RECITED AT EVERY MORNing and evening service. This prayer introduces the main part of the service, during which the *Sh'ma* (see next entry) and *Amidah* also are recited.

The word *barkhu* comes from the Hebrew word *berekh*, meaning "knee." When the prayer leader starts, "*Barkhu et Adonai ha-mevorakh*—Bless the Lord who is blessed," the entire congregation bends its knees, bows the head, and responds: "Blessed is the Lord who is blessed for eternity."

For seven years, I worked as education director at the Brandeis-Bardin Institute, near Los Angeles. Its founder and director, Dr. Shlomo Bardin, was a brilliant educator of fiery temperament. On one occasion, a man who was attending a weekend institute publicly announced his refusal to bend down at the *Barkhu*. "I bow to no one," he told Bardin.

"We bow down at the *Barkhu*," Bardin answered, "because we are acknowledging that there is a God in the world who is higher than us. If you don't believe in God, then bow down to the idea that you are not the highest thing in the world; there is something higher than you, perhaps the eternity of the Jewish people. But bow down, damn you," Bardin concluded, "bow down."

The *Amidah*, also known as the *Shmoneh Esray* (Eighteen Blessings) is the central prayer in the Jewish service; it is recited three times a day, during the morning, afternoon, and evening services, and during all Sabbath and holiday services.

Despite its name, the prayer actually has nineteen blessings; the last, calling forth God's condemnation of slanderers and informers, was composed in the first century of the Common Era, during the time when Judea was ruled by the Romans and some Jews collaborated with them. The other blessings beseech God, among other things, for wisdom, the ingathering to Israel of the Jewish exiles, forgiveness of sins, the end of tyranny, and healing of any diseases or sickness. The version of the *Shmoneh Esray* that is recited on holidays has only seven blessings; nonetheless, it is still referred to as the *Shmoneh Esray*.

The *Shmoneh Esray* is actually recited twice during the morning and afternoon services. The first time, it is said silently and individually by members of the congregation. Jewish law dictates that it be recited standing with one's feet together, in the manner that talmudic tradition assumes angels stand (*Brakhot* 10b; that is why it also is known as the *Amidah*, from the Hebrew word for "standing"). The silent version of the *Shmoneh Esray* concludes with a meditation: "My God, guard my tongue from evil, and my lips from speaking falsehood. . . . May the words of my mouth and the meditation of my heart be acceptable in Your presence, O Lord." The *Shmoneh Esray* is then repeated aloud by the cantor (public recitation of this prayer originally was instituted on behalf of Jews who were illiterate and could not recite it on their own), but only when a *minyan of ten adult worshipers is present. The cantor does not repeat the *Shmoneh Esray* during the evening service.

When the prayer leader reaches the *Kedusha* prayer, the whole congregation rises again and reads certain verses (among them *Isaiah 6:3, *Ezekiel 3:12, and *Psalms 146:10) in response to the words being read by the cantor. The *Kedusha* praises God with the kind of language Jewish tradition assumes is used by the angels when praising God: "Holy, holy, holy is the Lord of hosts; the whole earth is full of His glory."

Because the recitation of the *Shmoneh Esray* is a particularly solemn part of the service, it is strictly forbidden to speak during the silent reading of this prayer.

The *Ashrei* prayer, recited twice during the morning service and again at the beginning of the afternoon service, is mainly drawn from Psalm 145, although it opens with verses from Psalms 84:5 and 144:15. The prayer is in the form of an acrostic: Each verse begins with a succeeding letter of the Hebrew alphabet. The unifying theme of Psalm 145 is the happiness of those who dwell in the house of God; it also emphasizes God's caring concern for humankind. Because the *Ashrei* is recited so frequently, most observant Jews know it by heart. The Talmud makes an extraordinary promise: Any Jew who recites this prayer three times a day is assured of a place in the world to come (*Brakhot* 4b; see *Afterlife*).

The *Adon Olam* (Master of Eternity) is recited by some Jews every morning, and at the conclusion of the Sabbath service on Saturday mornings. It is a paean of praise to God "who ruled before everything," and who will exist after the world has ceased. There are hundreds of different melodies for the prayer, which partly accounts for the *Adon Olam*'s long-lasting popularity. In Jewish terms, it is a relatively new prayer, having been composed during the Middle Ages, and incorporated into the liturgy about the fifteenth century.

The prayer *Ein Keyloheinu* (There Is None Like Our God) is recited near the conclusion of the Saturday morning service. *Sephardic Jews recite it every day (as do certain Ashkenazic Jews who follow the Sephardic prayer rite). The prayer has a recurring theme that is repeated with slightly different words in each stanza:

> *There is none like our God*
> *There is none like our Master*
> *There is none like our King*
> *There is none like our Savior.*

The same melody is used for the *Ein Keyloheinu* prayer in most congregations, which has made it one of the best-known of all synagogue prayers.

The *Aleinu* prayer is recited three times every day. In the middle of the first paragraph of the prayer, congregants bend their knees and incline their heads before God, accepting Him as their ruler. In the Middle Ages, many Jewish martyrs went to their deaths singing the *Aleinu*. In an important segment in the second paragraph, Jews entreat God's help "to perfect the world under the rule of God" (see *Ethical Monotheism—Tikkun Olam*).

The *Hallel* prayer is a collection of joyous psalms (113–118). On Rosh

Khodesh (the beginning of each Jewish month) and during the last six days of *Passover, a slightly abbreviated version of the *Hallel* is recited. The full version is recited in the synagogue on the first two days of Passover, on *Shavuot, *Sukkot, *Hanukka, and in the home during the reading of the *Haggada* at the Passover *Seder.

Because the *Hallel's* theme is gratitude to God, religious Zionists have argued that it should be recited on *Israeli Independence Day and on *Jerusalem Day, the anniversary of the day on which Israel regained control of the Old City in the *Six-Day War of 1967. This seemingly innocuous expression of piety has been roundly condemned by many religiously right-wing Orthodox Jews, who argue that Zionism is a secular phenomenon and thus its holidays should not be honored with any religious rituals.

SOURCES AND FURTHER READINGS: Philip Birnbaum, *Encyclopedia of Jewish Concepts*, see separate entries for each prayer; Hayim Donin, *To Pray as a Jew*; B. S. Jacobson, *Meditations of the Siddur*; Raphael Posner, Uri Kaploun, and Shalom Cohen, *Jewish Liturgy: Prayer and Synagogue Service Through the Ages*.

"SH'MA YISRA'EL — HEAR, O ISRAEL"

ALTHOUGH JUDAISM HAS NO CATECHISM, THE BIBLICAL VERSE "SH'MA *Yisra'el, Adonai Eloheinu, Adonai Ekhad*—Hear, O Israel, the Lord Is Our God, the Lord Is One" (Deuteronomy 6:4), comes closest to being Judaism's credo. In just six Hebrew words, it sums up Judaism's belief in monotheism, and its rejection of all idols. For two thousand years, the *Sh'ma* has been the verse with which many Jewish martyrs have gone to their deaths, while those fortunate enough to meet more peaceful endings try to die with the *Sh'ma* on their lips. To this day, Jews are supposed to recite the *Sh'ma* four times a day, twice during morning prayers, once during the evening service, and, finally, at home before going to sleep.

In addition to the first six words, the *Sh'ma* usually is recited with three additional paragraphs, all from the Torah (Deuteronomy 6:4–9; Deuteronomy 11:13–21; and Numbers 15:37–41). The range of Jewish concepts and laws enumerated in these paragraphs is so significant that most of them have separate entries in this book. They include the commandments of:

1. Monotheism (see *Ethical Monotheism*)
2. Loving God, "and you shall love the Lord your God, with all your heart, with all your soul, and with all your means"
3. Teaching Judaism to one's children (see *Torah Study/Talmud Torah*)
4. *Tefillin*
5. *Mezuzah*
6. Reward and punishment
7. *Tzitzit*

Rabbi *Akiva, the second-century sage tortured to death by the Romans for his support of the *Bar-Kokhba rebellion, was the most famous martyr to die with the *Sh'ma* on his lips. The Talmud records: "When Akiva was being tortured, the hour for saying the [morning] *Sh'ma* arrived. He said it and smiled. The Roman officer called out, 'Old man, are you a sorcerer [because Akiva seemed oblivious to the torture] . . . that you smile in the middle of your pains?' 'No,' replied Akiva, 'but all my life, when I said the words, "You shall love the Lord your God with all your heart, with all your soul, and with all your means," I was saddened, for I thought, when shall I be able to fulfill this command? I have loved God with all my heart, and with all my means [possessions], but to love him with all my soul [life itself] I did not know if I could carry out. Now that I am giving my life, and the hour for reciting the *Sh'ma* has come, and my resolution remains firm, should I not smile?' As he spoke, his soul departed" (Palestinian Talmud, *Brakhot*, 9:5; see also *Brakhot* 61b).

A friend of mine in Israel, Rabbi Levi Weiman-Kelman, advises people to meditate for a moment before reciting the *Sh'ma*, in order to create the mind-set they wish to express. They can recite the *Sh'ma* as they imagine Rabbi Akiva recited it, "with all your soul." Similarly, they can recall, and try to simulate, the passion with which a Jewish legend says these words were recited by Jacob's sons when they reassured their father on his deathbed that they never had, and never would, stray from their belief in one God.

Another friend, who learned Hebrew as an adult, told me he underwent a bit of frustration until he learned the twenty-two letters of the Hebrew alphabet, and was even more frustrated until he understood how to pronounce the vowels placed under each letter. But the hours of tedium were all worth it when he could pick up a prayerbook and recite the words of the *Sh'ma* in the original, as Jews have recited it for three thousand years. He felt then, he told me, that he was finally part of the eternal Jewish choir.

SOURCE AND FURTHER READING: Hayim Donin, *To Pray as a Jew*, pp. 144–156.

BLESSING/*BRAKHA* (PLURAL, *BRAKHOT*)
HA-MOTZI
GRACE AFTER MEALS/*BIRKAT HA-MAZON*
SHE-HE-KHI-YANU

A LARGE NUMBER OF JEWISH BLESSINGS REVOLVE AROUND FOOD; indeed, the rabbis believed that eating food without first blessing God was a form of stealing (*Brakhot* 35a–b), since the blessing is the only "payment" God demands for the food He provides man. The most well-known of the blessings over food is the *Ha-Motzi*: "Blessed are You, Lord our God, King of the Universe, who brings forth bread from the earth."

Blessings, whether said over food or anything else, generally start with the same formula, "Blessed are You, Lord our God, King of the Universe," before becoming specific. The blessing over wine says: "who creates the fruit of the vine"; cakes and pastries, "who creates various kinds of foods"; vegetables and fruits that grow on trees, "who creates the fruit of the trees"; fruits and vegetables that grow on the ground, "who creates the fruits of the earth"; and other foods, "by whose word all things come into being."

Many blessings currently recited were formulated some two thousand years ago, during the time when Judea was under Roman rule. The blessings' emphasis on God's responsibility for all creation may well have helped inspire ancient Jews not to be overawed by Rome's technological and military might; after all, everything in the world was due to God. In addition, at a time when many Jews might have felt abandoned by God, the blessings reminded them, several times each day, that God was still with them.

In the modern world, blessings play a similar function, reminding us throughout the day that God cares and provides for us. As Abraham Joshua *Heschel wrote: "[When we drink a glass of water] we remind ourselves of the eternal mystery of creation, 'Blessed are You . . . by whose word all things came into being.' A trivial act and a reference to the supreme miracle. Wishing to eat bread or fruit, to enjoy a pleasant fragrance or a cup of wine . . . on noticing trees when they blossom; on meeting a sage in Torah or in secular learning . . . we are taught to invoke His great name and our awareness of Him. . . . This is one of the goals of the Jewish way of living: to feel the hidden love and wisdom in all things."

In Jewish life, there are blessings to be recited on seeing the wonders of nature, such as lightning ("Blessed are You . . . who has made the works of creation"); on seeing beautiful trees and animals ("Blessed are You . . . who has such as these in His world"); on meeting a person of profound secular learning ("Blessed are You . . . who has imparted of your wisdom to flesh and blood"); on meeting a great Torah scholar ("Blessed are You . . . who has given of His wisdom to those who revere Him"); on hearing bad news ("Blessed are You . . . the true Judge"), and on hearing good news ("Blessed are You . . . who are good and beneficent").

At the conclusion of a meal at which bread has been eaten, Jewish law ordains the *Birkat ha-Mazon*, a long series of paragraphs and blessings thanking God for giving mankind food. The first blessing is characteristic of the whole: "Blessed are You, God, who feeds all living things."

At all Orthodox, and many non-Orthodox, weddings, the *Birkat ha-Mazon* is printed in a small book, which guests are invited to take home as a memento of the celebration; the name of the couple and the date of the wedding are usually printed on the book's cover.

A Jew who recites the three daily services, and recites the other appropriate blessings throughout the day, offers to God a total of at least one hundred blessings every day.

The word for blessing in Hebrew is *brakha*, which comes from the word *berekh*, meaning "knee"; thus, the word suggests a bended knee, the proper posture for one who is approaching God.

One of the best-known Jewish blessings is the *She-he-khi-yanu*: "Blessed are You, Lord our God, King of the Universe, who grants us life and sustenance and has permitted us to reach this [festive] occasion." The *She-he-khi-yanu* is recited when tasting a fruit for the first time in the season, when moving into a new house, putting on new clothes, at the beginning of Jewish holidays, and on many other happy occasions. It is omitted at the *circumcision ceremony because of the infant's pain upon being circumcised.

As I finish this work, which has occupied me emotionally and intellectually for much of my life, I slightly adapt this traditional blessing, and say: "Blessed are You, Lord our God, King of the Universe, who has granted me life and sustenance and has permitted me to reach this occasion."

SOURCES AND FURTHER READINGS: An overview of many of the blessings is found in Hayim Donin, *To Pray as a Jew*, pp. 284–318. The Heschel quote is from Abraham Joshua Heschel, *God in Search of Man*, p. 65.

Index